Paris

Steve Fallon
Daniel Robinson
Tony Wheeler

W9-BEL-068

LONELY PLANET PUBLICATIONS
Melbourne • Oakland • London • Paris

Paris
3rd edition – January 2001
First published – November 1996

Published by
Lonely Planet Publications Pty Ltd A.C.N. 005 607 983
90 Maribyrnong St, Footscray, Victoria 3011, Australia

Lonely Planet Offices
Australia Locked Bag 1, Footscray, Victoria 3011
USA 150 Linden St, Oakland, CA 94607
UK 10a Spring Place, London NW5 3BH
France 1 rue du Dahomey, 75011 Paris

Photographs
All of the images in this guide are available for licensing from
Lonely Planet Images.
email: lpi@lonelyplanet.com.au

Front cover photograph
The Moulin Rouge, long a symbol of Parisian nightlife (Martine
Mouchy, Tony Stone Images)

ISBN 1 86450 125 1

Contents

2 Contents

The Authors

Steve Fallon

A native of Boston, Massachusetts, Steve graduated from Georgetown University with a Bachelor of Science in modern languages and then taught English at the University of Silesia near Katowice in Poland. After he had worked for several years for a Gannett newspaper, his interest in Asia led him to Hong Kong, where he lived and worked for 13 years for a variety of publications and owned a travel bookshop. Steve lived in Budapest for 2½ years from where he wrote Lonely Planet's *Hungary* and *Slovenia* guides before moving to London in 1994. He has written or contributed to a number of other Lonely Planet titles.

Daniel Robinson

Daniel was raised in the USA (the San Francisco Bay area and Glen Ellyn, Illinois) and Israel. His passion for shoestring travel was kindled at the age of 17 with a trip to Cyprus, and since then he has spent several years on the road exploring some of the more remote parts of Asia, the Middle East and Europe. His work for Lonely Planet has included the 1st editions of the award-winning *Vietnam* and (with Tony Wheeler) *Cambodia*, and contributing to all four editions of *France*. Daniel has a BA in Near Eastern Studies from Princeton University and is currently finishing an MA in Israeli history at Tel Aviv University.

Tony Wheeler

Tony was born in England but grew up in Pakistan, the Bahamas and the USA. He returned to England to do a degree in engineering at Warwick University, worked as an automotive design engineer, returned to London Business School to complete an MBA, then set out on an Asian overland trip with his wife, Maureen. That trip led to Tony and Maureen founding Lonely Planet Publications in Australia in 1973, and they've been travelling, writing and publishing guidebooks ever since. In 1996 they spent a year in Paris, with their children Tashi and Kieran.

From Steve Fallon

Once again, my share of this guidebook is dedicated to Michael Rothschild (Cupid draw back our Bow).

A number of people helped in the updating of *Paris*. Resident Brenda Turnnidge provided invaluable support; her efficiency is unequalled, her enthusiasm for the City of Light palpable. Emma Bland, marketeer *par excellence*, was kind enough to cover Paris' markets for me, and matchless trainspotter Daniel Robinson got me on the right track with one of the transport chapters. Thanks too to Christine Coste, Rob Flynn, Zahia Hafs, Chew Terrière and Frank Viviano for assistance, ideas, hospitality and/or more than a few laughs along the way. It was a great pleasure once again working with ace editor Tim Ryder; unflappable cartographer Angie Watts was a Rock of Gibraltar fiddling with all those map keys that will get you where you want to go. And, finally, to all you wonderful *and* infuriating Parisians I met along the way – elegant and stylish, cultured and entertaining, bitchy and attitudinous *à l'extrême* – *merci encore une fois*. You're just what the world needs more of.

This Book

The 1st edition of *Paris* was written by Daniel Robinson and Tony Wheeler. The 2nd edition was updated and expanded by Steve Fallon, who went back to Paris to revise and update this 3rd edition.

From the Publisher

This book was produced in Lonely Planet's London office. Tim Ryder coordinated the editing, and was assisted by Joyce Connolly. The book was proofread by Joyce, with help from Tim, Paul Bloomfield and Michala Green. Angie Watts was responsible for mapping, design and layout. Ed Pickard and Sara Yorke assisted with the mapping, Adam McCrow designed the cover and Jim Miller drew the back-cover map. Tim produced the index, with help from Paul. Asa Andersson supplied the illustrations. Special thanks to Paul for his rundown on the latest Parisian grooves.

The quotations on pages 10 and 128 are from *A Moveable Feast* by Ernest Hemingway. Copyright © 1964 by Mary Hemingway. Copyright renewed © 1992 by John H Hemingway, Patrick Hemingway and Gregory Hemingway. Reprinted by permission of Scribner, a division of Simon & Schuster, publisher for the USA and Canada, and Jonathan Cape, publisher for the rest of the world.

Thanks

Many thanks to the following travellers who wrote to us with helpful hints, useful advice and interesting anecdotes:

J Adams, K Ahmann, M Aird, R Allenby, E Azri Mat Jamial, C Bailey, J Bain, P Barker, E Berg, A Blichfeldt, S Brennan, T Bridgewater, Brooke, J Buruma, R Busch, E Caney, N Carin, E Carlson, J Carty, M Chafong, M Coburn, PJ Colbourn, Dr Y Copperman, J Cross, C Davidson, J Davidson, A Debeest, K Douglas, Douglas and Clarice, B Earls, J Eicher, E Ellsworth, J Engmann, A Faafeng, M Fischer, D Fisher, SM Foley, P Fonquernie, C Gervais, T Gorfine, FC Grijpink, M Gruzen, L Hammerschlag, D Harris, R Hartwell, A & T Hodgson, M Holloway, G Holt, Thng Hui Hong, M Horta e Costa, B Jacobs, P Johnson, A Johnston, M Johnstone, S Kemp, T Kirby, M & S Koomen, L Laplante, CH Lee, I Lege, RL Leonard, S Li, T Lim, J Littell, I Macfarlaine, Dr Malvena, C Mariani, LD Matthews, R McCallum, R McDonald, AP Melgrave, E Miali, R Miotto, D Monahan, D Morgan, Nick, J Oats Sargent, C Orriss, M Owen, J Phillips, JD Phillips, K Phua, M Poletti, Y Pollett, F Radcliff, L Rademacher, G Roberts, J Roider, K Schlottmann, E Schoenfeld, J Scholin, E Schulze, J Sears, S Sincock, J Shortt, J Smith, H Stambaugh, J Suiser, L Tait, G Taylor, R Taylor, S Taylor, K Terauds, F Trafford Walker, M Truelove, B Turner, L Valtonen, R Valtonen, A van Oort, R Vaughan, D Virginie, UE Wasse, D Wicksman, JE Wilson, M Wise, P Wood, C Xuereb, M Yubas.

Foreword

ABOUT LONELY PLANET GUIDEBOOKS

The story begins with a classic travel adventure: Tony and Maureen Wheeler's 1972 journey across Europe and Asia to Australia. Useful information about the overland trail did not exist at that time, so Tony and Maureen published the first Lonely Planet guidebook to meet a growing need.

From a kitchen table, then from a tiny office in Melbourne (Australia), Lonely Planet has become the largest independent travel publisher in the world, an international company with offices in Melbourne, Oakland (USA), London (UK) and Paris (France).

Today Lonely Planet guidebooks cover the globe. There is an ever-growing list of books and there's information in a variety of forms and media. Some things haven't changed. The main aim is still to help make it possible for adventurous travellers to get out there – to explore and better understand the world.

At Lonely Planet we believe travellers can make a positive contribution to the countries they visit – if they respect their host communities and spend their money wisely. Since 1986 a percentage of the income from each book has been donated to aid projects and human rights campaigns.

Updates Lonely Planet thoroughly updates each guidebook as often as possible. This usually means there are around two years between editions, although for more unusual or more stable destinations the gap can be longer. Check the imprint page (following the colour map at the beginning of the book) for publication dates.

Between editions up-to-date information is available in two free newsletters – the paper *Planet Talk* and email *Comet* (to subscribe, contact any Lonely Planet office) – and on our Web site at www.lonelyplanet.com. The *Upgrades* section of the Web site covers a number of important and volatile destinations and is regularly updated by Lonely Planet authors. *Scoop* covers news and current affairs relevant to travellers. And, lastly, the *Thorn Tree* bulletin board and *Postcards* section of the site carry unverified, but fascinating, reports from travellers.

Correspondence The process of creating new editions begins with the letters, postcards and emails received from travellers. This correspondence often includes suggestions, criticisms and comments about the current editions. Interesting excerpts are immediately passed on via newsletters and the Web site, and everything goes to our authors to be verified when they're researching on the road. We're keen to get more feedback from organisations or individuals who represent communities visited by travellers.

Lonely Planet gathers information for everyone who's curious about the planet – and especially for those who explore it first-hand. Through guidebooks, phrasebooks, activity guides, maps, literature, newsletters, image library, TV series and Web site we act as an information exchange for a worldwide community of travellers.

Research Authors aim to gather sufficient practical information to enable travellers to make informed choices and to make the mechanics of a journey run smoothly. They also research historical and cultural background to help enrich the travel experience and allow travellers to understand and respond appropriately to cultural and environmental issues.

Authors don't stay in every hotel because that would mean spending a couple of months in each medium-sized city and, no, they don't eat at every restaurant because that would mean stretching belts beyond capacity. They do visit hotels and restaurants to check standards and prices, but feedback based on readers' direct experiences can be very helpful.

Many of our authors work undercover, others aren't so secretive. None of them accept freebies in exchange for positive write-ups. And none of our guidebooks contain any advertising.

Production Authors submit their raw manuscripts and maps to offices in Australia, USA, UK or France. Editors and cartographers – all experienced travellers themselves – then begin the process of assembling the pieces. When the book finally hits the shops, some things are already out of date, we start getting feedback from readers and the process begins again …

WARNING & REQUEST

Things change – prices go up, schedules change, good places go bad and bad places go bankrupt – nothing stays the same. So, if you find things better or worse, recently opened or long since closed, please tell us and help make the next edition even more accurate and useful. We genuinely value all the feedback we receive. Julie Young coordinates a well travelled team that reads and acknowledges every letter, postcard and email and ensures that every morsel of information finds its way to the appropriate authors, editors and cartographers for verification.

Everyone who writes to us will find their name in the next edition of the appropriate guidebook. They will also receive the latest issue of *Planet Talk*, our quarterly printed newsletter, or *Comet*, our monthly email newsletter. Subscriptions to both newsletters are free. The very best contributions will be rewarded with a free guidebook.

Excerpts from your correspondence may appear in new editions of Lonely Planet guidebooks, the Lonely Planet Web site, *Planet Talk* or *Comet*, so please let us know if you *don't* want your letter published or your name acknowledged.

Send all correspondence to the Lonely Planet office closest to you:

Australia: Locked Bag 1, Footscray, Victoria 3011
USA: 150 Linden St, Oakland, CA 94607
UK: 10A Spring Place, London NW5 3BH
France: 1 rue du Dahomey, 75011 Paris

Or email us at: talk2us@lonelyplanet.com.au

For news, views and updates see our Web site: www.lonelyplanet.com

HOW TO USE A LONELY PLANET GUIDEBOOK

The best way to use a Lonely Planet guidebook is any way you choose. At Lonely Planet we believe the most memorable travel experiences are often those that are unexpected, and the finest discoveries are those you make yourself. Guidebooks are not intended to be used as if they provide a detailed set of infallible instructions!

Contents All Lonely Planet guidebooks follow roughly the same format. The Facts about the Destination chapters or sections give background information ranging from history to weather. Facts for the Visitor gives practical information on issues like visas and health. Getting There & Away gives a brief starting point for researching travel to and from the destination. Getting Around gives an overview of the transport options when you arrive.

There peculiar demands of each destination determine how subsequent chapters are broken up, but some things remain constant. We always start with background, then proceed to sights, places to stay, places to eat, entertainment, getting there and away, and getting around information – in that order.

Heading Hierarchy Lonely Planet headings are used in a strict hierarchical structure that can be visualised as a set of Russian dolls. Each heading (and its following text) is encompassed by any preceding heading that is higher on the hierarchical ladder.

Entry Points We do not assume guidebooks will be read from beginning to end, but that people will dip into them. The traditional entry points are the list of contents and the index. In addition, however, some books have a complete list of maps and an index map illustrating map coverage.

There may also be a colour map that shows highlights. These highlights are dealt with in greater detail in the Facts for the Visitor chapter, along with planning questions and suggested itineraries. Each chapter covering a geographical region usually begins with a locator map and another list of highlights. Once you find something of interest in a list of highlights, turn to the index.

Maps Maps play a crucial role in Lonely Planet guidebooks and include a huge amount of information. A legend is printed on the back page. We seek to have complete consistency between maps and text, and to have every important place in the text captured on a map. Map key numbers usually start in the top left corner.

Although inclusion in a guidebook usually implies a recommendation we cannot list every good place. Exclusion does not necessarily imply criticism. In fact there are a number of reasons why we might exclude a place – sometimes it is simply inappropriate to encourage an influx of travellers.

Introduction

It is not hyperbole to say that Paris is the most beautiful city in the world. The architecture, the tidy green spaces, the timeless Seine, the café life and its citizens' *joie de vivre* all combine to make it a monumental, handsome and fun place in which to live, work, study and visit.

But everybody who's been here before – from Julius Caesar to Cole Porter – has recognised that and has said so. Indeed, Paris has just about exhausted the superlatives that can be reasonably applied to any world-class city. Notre Dame, the Eiffel Tower, ave des Champs-Élysées – at sunrise, at sunset, at night, under a blanket of snow – have all been described innumerable times, as have the Seine and the subtle (and not-so-subtle) differences between the Left and Right Banks. What most writers have struggled to capture, though, is the sheer magic of strolling under the plane trees, along the broad avenues that lead from impressive public buildings and exceptional museums to parks, gardens and esplanades.

Paris has more familiar landmarks and aspects than any other city in the world. As a result, first-time visitors often arrive in the French capital with all sorts of expectations: of grand vistas, of intellectuals discussing weighty matters in cafés, of romance along the Seine, of naughty cabaret revues, of rude people who won't speak English but will rip you off. To be sure, if you look around, you'll find all those things. But another approach is to set aside your preconceptions of Paris and explore the city's avenues and backstreets forgetting that the tip of the Eiffel Tower or the spire of Notre Dame is about to pop into view at any moment.

Paris is no longer the living museum or Gallic theme park it may have seemed a generation ago. The city has changed, and it's a welcoming, fun and increasingly cosmopolitan city to visit. By all means do the sights and visit the museums – they're part of the Paris package. But then jump on the metro or a bus and get off at a place you've never heard of, wander through a *quartier*

RICHARD I'ANSON

The heart of the city: looking across the Seine towards Pont Neuf and the Île de la Cité

(neighbourhood) where French mixes easily with Arabic or Vietnamese, poke your head into little shops, invite yourself to play *boules* or basketball in a park or just perch on a café terrace with a *grand crème* or a glass of wine in front of you and watch Paris pass by.

Parisians believe (and as far as we're concerned, the notion is an accurate one) that they have *savoir-faire* – the inherent knowledge of how to live well – and indeed you'll find that Paris is a feast for the senses. It's a city to look at, with wide boulevards, impressive monuments, great works of art and magic lights. It's a city to taste – cheese, chocolate, wine, *charcuterie*, bread. It's a city to hear, whether you're partial to opera, jazz or rap. It's a city to smell – the perfume boutiques, the cafés with their fresh coffee and croissants, and chestnuts roasting on charcoal in winter. It's a city to feel: the wind in your face as you cycle along the Seine, the *frisson* of fear and pleasure as you peer out from the top of the Eiffel Tower or

the Grande Arche de la Défense. Above all, it's a city to discover. This book is designed to whet your appetite and to guide you when you arrive, but remember that it's a guidebook not a handbook. Leave it in your hotel from time to time, and wander outside to find your own Paris.

Do so and you'll soon discover, as so many others have before you, that Paris is enchanting almost everywhere, at any time, even when it drizzles, even when it sizzles. And, like a good meal, it excites, it satisfies, the memory lingers. In *A Moveable Feast*, his book of recollections of Paris in the 1920s, Ernest Hemingway wrote: 'If you are lucky enough to have lived in Paris as a young man, then wherever you go for the rest of your life, it stays with you, for Paris is a moveable feast.'

Those of us who were able to take Hemingway's advice in our salad days couldn't agree more. We're still dining out on the memories.

And so will you.

Facts about Paris

HISTORY
The Romans & the Gauls

The Celtic Gauls moved into what is now France between 1500 and 500 BC. Some time during the 3rd century BC, members of a Celtic tribe called the Parisii – believed to mean 'boat men' – lured by the city's remarkable river system, set up a few huts made of wattle and daub on what is now the Île de la Cité and engaged in fishing and trading.

Centuries of conflict between the Gauls and Rome ended in 52 BC, when Julius Caesar's legions led by Labienus took control of the territory, and the settlement on the Seine prospered as the Roman town of Lutetia (from the Latin for 'Midwater Dwelling'), counting some 10,000 inhabitants by the 3rd century AD. A temple to Jupiter was established where Notre Dame now stands, and the Roman town spread to the south bank, with rue Saint Jacques as the main north-south axis and a forum at the corner of today's rue Soufflot, near the Panthéon and the Jardin du Luxembourg.

The Great Migrations, beginning around AD 253 with raids by the Franks and then the Alemanii from the east, left the settlement on the south bank scorched and pillaged, and its inhabitants fled to the Île de la Cité, which was subsequently fortified with stone walls. Christianity had been introduced early in the 2nd century AD, and the first church, probably made of wood, was built in the western part of the island.

The Merovingians & Carolingians

Roman occupation of what had by then become known as Paris (after its first settlers) ended in the late 5th century when a second wave of Franks and other Germanic groups under Merovius overran the territory. Merovius' grandson, Clovis I, converted to Christianity and made Paris his seat in 508. Childeric II, Clovis' son and successor, founded the Abbey of Saint Germain des Prés in 558, and the dynasty's most productive ruler, Dagobert, established an abbey at Saint Denis, which would soon become the richest and most important monastery in France and for a time the final resting place of its kings.

The militaristic rulers of the Carolingian dynasty, beginning with Charles Martel (688-741), were almost permanently away fighting wars in the east, and Paris languished, controlled for the most part by the counts of Paris. When Charles Martel's grandson, Charlemagne (768-814), moved his capital to Aix-la-Chapelle (today's Aachen in Germany), Paris' fate was sealed. Basically a group of separate villages with its centre on the island, Paris was badly defended throughout the second half of the 9th century and suffered a succession of raids by the 'Norsemen', or Normans.

The Middle Ages

The counts of Paris, whose powers had increased as the Carolingians feuded among themselves, elected one of their own, Hugh Capet, as king at Senlis (see the Excursions chapter) in 987. He then made Paris the royal seat. Under Capetian rule, which would last for the next 800 years, Paris prospered as a centre of politics, commerce, trade, religion and culture.

By the time Hugh Capet had assumed the throne, the Normans were in control of northern and western French territory. In 1066 they mounted a successful invasion of England – the so-called Norman Conquest – from their base in today's Normandy. This would lead to almost 300 years of conflict between the Normans and the Capetians.

Paris' strategic riverside position ensured its importance throughout the Middle Ages, although settlement remained centred on the Île de la Cité at first, with the *rive gauche* (left bank) turned into fields and vineyards. The Marais area, north of the Seine on the *rive droite* (right bank), was exactly what its French name suggests, a waterlogged 'marsh'. The first guilds were established in the 11th century and rapidly grew in importance; in the middle of the 12th century the ship merchants' guild bought the principal river port, by today's Hôtel de Ville, from the crown.

This was a time of frenetic building activity in Paris. Abbot Suger, both confessor and minister to several Capetian kings, was one of the powerhouses of this period, and in 1135 he commissioned the basilica at Saint Denis (see the Excursions chapter). Less than three decades later, work started on the cathedral of Notre Dame, the greatest creation of medieval Paris. At the same time Philippe-Auguste (ruled 1180-1223) decided to have a city wall built, interrupted by 39 towers.

The marshes of the Marais were drained and settlement finally moved to the north (or right) bank of the Seine, which would become the mercantile centre, especially around place de Grève (today's place de l'Hôtel de Ville). The food markets at Les Halles first came into existence around 1110, the beautiful Sainte Chapelle on the Île de la Cité was consecrated in 1248 and the Louvre began its existence as a riverside fortress in the 13th century. In a bid to do something about the city's horrible traffic congestion and stinking excrement (the population numbered about 200,000 by this time), Philippe-August paved some of Paris' streets for the first time since the Romans.

Meanwhile, the area south of the Seine – today's Left Bank – was developing as a centre of learning and erudition, particularly in the area known as the Latin Quarter, where students and their teachers communicated in that language. The ill-fated lovers Abélard and Héloïse (see the boxed text 'Star-Crossed Lovers') wrote their treatises on philosophy and the finest poetry at this time, Thomas Aquinas taught at the new University of Paris (founded under papal protection in about 1215), and some 30 other colleges were established, including the Sorbonne, founded in 1257 by Robert de Sorbon, confessor to Louis IX.

In 1337, some three centuries of hostility between the Capetians and the Normans degenerated into the Hundred Years' War, which would be fought on and off until 1453. The Black Death (1348-9) killed about a third of Paris' population (an estimated 80,000 souls) but only briefly interrupted the fighting. Paris would not see its population reach 200,000 again until the beginning of the 15th century.

The Hundred Years' War and the plague, along with the development of free, independent cities elsewhere in Europe, brought political tension and open insurrection to

Star-Crossed Lovers

He was a brilliant 39-year-old philosopher and logician who had gained a reputation for his controversial ideas. She was the beautiful niece of a canon at Notre Dame. And like Bogart and Bergman in Casablanca and Romeo and Juliet in Verona, they had to fall in love – in medieval Paris, of all damned places.

In 1118, the wandering scholar Pierre Abélard (1079-1142) went to Paris, having clashed with yet another theologian in the provinces. There he was employed by Canon Fulbert of Notre Dame to tutor his niece Héloïse (1098-1164). One thing led to another and a son, Astrolabe, was born. Abélard did the gentlemanly thing and married his sweetheart. But they wed in secret and when Fulbert learned of it he was outraged. The canon had Abélard castrated and sent Héloïse packing to a nunnery. Abélard took monastic vows at the abbey in Saint Denis and continued his studies and controversial writings. Héloïse, meanwhile, was made abbess of a convent.

All the while, however, the star-crossed lovers continued to correspond: he sending tender advice on how to run the convent and she writing passionate, poetic letters to her lost lover. The two were reunited only in death; in 1817 their remains were disinterred and brought to Cimetière du Père Lachaise, where they lie today beneath a neo-Gothic tombstone.

Paris. In 1356, the provost of the merchants, a wealthy draper named Étienne Marcel, allied himself with peasants revolting against the dauphin (the future Charles V) and seized Paris in a bid to limit the power of the throne and secure a city charter. But the dauphin's supporters recaptured the city within two years, and Marcel and his followers were executed. Charles then had a new city wall built on the right bank.

After the French forces were defeated by the English at Agincourt in 1415, Paris was once again embroiled in revolt. The dukes of Burgundy, allied with the English, occupied the capital in 1420. Two years later John Plantagenet, duke of Bedford, was installed as regent of France for England's Henry VI, then an infant. Henry was crowned king of France at Notre Dame less than 10 years later, but Paris remained under siege from the French almost continuously for much of that time.

In 1429, a 17-year-old peasant girl known to history as Jeanne d'Arc (Joan of Arc) persuaded the French pretender Charles VII that she had received a divine mission from God to expel the English from France and bring about Charles' coronation. She rallied the French troops and defeated the English at Patay, north of Orléans, and Charles was crowned at Reims. Charles made his triumphal entrance into Paris in 1437, but the English were not entirely driven from French territory until 1453 (and even then they held on to Calais).

The occupation had left Paris a disaster zone. While the restored monarchy moved to consolidate its power, conditions improved under Louis XI (1461-81), during whose reign the city's first printing press was installed at the Sorbonne. Churches were rehabilitated or built in the Flamboyant Gothic style and a number of *hôtels particuliers* (private mansions) – such as the Hôtel de Cluny and the Hôtel de Sens, now the Bibliothèque Forney at 1 rue du Figuier, 4e – were erected.

The Renaissance

The culture of the Italian Renaissance (French for 'rebirth') arrived in full swing in

ROB FLYNN

Maid of Orléans: Joan of Arc rides again in place des Pyramides.

France in the early 16th century, during the reign of François I (1515-47), partly because of a series of indecisive French military operations in Italy. For the first time, the French aristocracy was exposed to Renaissance ideas of scientific and geographical scholarship and discovery, and the value of secular over religious life. It also took a fancy to Italian food (see the boxed text 'Italian Takeaway') and made it its own.

Writers such as Rabelais, Marot and Ronsard were influential at this time, as were the architectural disciples of Michelangelo and Raphael. Around Paris evidence of this architectural influence can be seen in François I's chateau at Fontainebleau and the Petit Château at Chantilly (for both see the Excursions chapter). In the city itself, a prime example of the period is the Pont Neuf (literally 'new bridge'), the oldest bridge in Paris. The Marais remains the best area for spotting reminders of Renaissance

Italian Takeaway

The 16th century was also something of a watershed for French cuisine. When Catherine de Médecis, future consort to François' son, Henri II, arrived in Paris in 1533, she brought with her a team of Florentine *maître queux* (master chefs) and pastry cooks adept in the subtleties of Italian Renaissance cooking. They introduced such delicacies as aspics, truffles, *quenelles* (dumplings), artichokes, macaroons and puddings to the French court. Catherine's cousin, Marie de Médecis, imported even more chefs into France when she married Henry IV in 1600.

The French cooks, increasingly aware of their rising social status, took the Italians' recipes and sophisticated cooking styles on board, and the rest – to the eternal gratitude of epicures everywhere – is history.

Paris; see the Marais walking tour in the Things to See & Do chapter.

This new architecture was meant to reflect the splendour of the monarchy, which was fast moving toward absolutism, and of Paris as the capital of a powerful centralised state. But all this grandeur and show of strength was not enough to stem the tide of Protestantism that was flowing into France.

The Reformation

By the 1530s the position of the Protestant Reformation sweeping across Europe had been strengthened in France by the ideas of John Calvin, a Frenchman exiled to Geneva. The Edict of January (1562), which afforded the Protestants certain rights, was met by violent opposition from ultra-Catholic nobles whose fidelity to their religion was mixed with a desire to strengthen their power bases in the provinces. Paris remained very much a Catholic stronghold, and trials and executions by burning at the stake in place de Grève continued apace up to the religious civil war.

The Wars of Religion (1562-98) involved three groups: the Huguenots (French Protestants supported by the English), the Catholic League and the Catholic king. The fighting severely weakened the position of the monarchy and brought the kingdom close to disintegration. The most deplorable massacre took place in Paris on 23-24 August 1572, when some 3000 Huguenots who had come to Paris to celebrate the wedding of the Protestant Henri of Navarre (the future Henri IV) were slaughtered in what is now called the St Bartholomew's Day Massacre. In 1588, on the so-called Day of the Barricades, the Catholic League rose up against Henri III and forced him to flee the Louvre; he was assassinated the following year.

Henri III was succeeded by Henri IV, who inaugurated the Bourbon dynasty. In 1598 he promulgated the Edict of Nantes, which guaranteed the Huguenots religious freedom and many civil and political rights as well, but this was not universally accepted. Catholic Paris refused to allow its new Protestant king entry into the city, and a siege of the capital continued for almost five years. Only when Henri embraced Catholicism at Saint Denis – '*Paris vaut bien une messe*' (Paris is well worth a Mass), he is reputed to have said upon taking Communion there – did the capital submit to him.

Henri consolidated the monarchy's power and began to rebuild Paris (the population of which was by now about 400,000) after more than three decades of fighting. The magnificent place Royale (today's place des Vosges in the Marais) and place Dauphine at the western end of Île de la Cité are prime examples of the new era of town planning. But Henri's rule ended as abruptly and violently as that of his predecessor. In 1610 he was assassinated by a Catholic fanatic named François Ravaillac when his coach got stuck in traffic along rue de la Ferronnerie in the Marais.

Henri IV's son, the future Louis XIII (1601-43), was too young to assume the throne at the time of his father's death so his mother, Marie de Médecis, was named regent. She set about building the magnificent Palais du Luxembourg and its enormous gardens for herself, just outside the city wall.

Louis XIII ascended the throne in 1617 but remained under the control of his ruthless chief minister, Cardinal Richelieu, for most of his undistinguished reign. Richelieu is best known for his untiring efforts to establish an all-powerful monarchy in France, opening the door to the absolutism of Louis XIV, and French supremacy in Europe. Under Louis XIII's reign, two uninhabited islets in the Seine – Île Notre Dame and Île aux Vaches – were joined to form the Île Saint Louis, and Richelieu commissioned a number of palaces and churches, including the Palais Royal and the Église Notre Dame du Val-de-Grâce.

Louis XIV & the Ancien Régime
Le Roi Soleil (literally 'the Sun King') ascended the throne in 1643 at the tender age of five. His mother, Anne of Austria, was appointed regent and Cardinal Mazarin, a protégé of Richelieu, was named chief minister. When Mazarin died in 1661, Louis XIV assumed absolute power until his own death in 1715. Throughout his long reign, he sought to project the power of the French monarchy – bolstered by claims of divine right – both at home and abroad. He involved France in a long series of costly, almost continuous wars with Holland, Austria and England, which gained it territory but terrified its neighbours and nearly bankrupted the treasury. State taxation to fill the coffers caused widespread poverty and vagrancy in Paris, by then a city of 600,000 people.

But Louis – whose widely quoted line '*L'État, c'est moi*' (I am the State) is often taken out of historical context – was able to quash the ambitious, feuding aristocracy and create the first truly centralised French state, elements of which can still be seen in France today. He did pour huge sums of money into building his extravagant palace at Versailles, 23km to the south-west of Paris, but by doing so he was able to sidestep the endless intrigues of the capital. And by turning his nobles into courtiers, Louis forced them to compete with one another for royal favour, reducing them to ineffectual sycophants. Although Louis detested Paris, he commissioned the fine place Vendôme, place des Victoires, the Hôtel des Invalides and the colonnaded Cour Carrée at the Louvre.

Louis mercilessly persecuted his Protestant subjects, who he considered a threat to the unity of the State and thus his power. In 1685 he revoked the Edict of Nantes, which had guaranteed the Huguenots freedom of conscience.

It was Louis XIV who said '*Après moi, le déluge*' (After me, the flood); in hindsight his words were more than prophetic. His grandson and successor, Louis XV (1710-74), turned out to be an oafish, incompetent buffoon, and grew to be universally despised. Louis XIV's regent, however, the Duke of Orléans, did move the court from Versailles back to Paris; in the Age of Enlightenment, the French capital had become, in effect, the centre of Europe.

As the 18th century progressed, new economic and social circumstances rendered the *ancien régime* (old order) dangerously out of step with the needs of the country and its capital. The regime was further weakened by the anti-establishment and anticlerical ideas of the Enlightenment, whose leading lights included Voltaire, Rousseau and Montesquieu. But entrenched vested interests, a cumbersome power structure and royal lassitude prevented change from starting until the 1770s, by which time the monarchy's moment had passed.

The Seven Years' War (1756-63) was only one of a series of ruinous military engagements pursued by Louis XV, and it led to the loss of France's flourishing colonies in Canada, the West Indies and India. It was in part to avenge these losses that Louis XVI sided with the colonists in the American War of Independence (1775-83). But the Seven Years' War cost France a fortune and, even more disastrously for the monarchy, it helped to disseminate at home the radical democratic ideas that were thrust upon the world stage by the American Revolution.

The French Revolution & the First Republic
By the late 1780s, the indecisive Louis XVI (1754-93) and his dominating queen, Marie-Antoinette, had managed to alienate virtually every segment of society – from enlightened groups to conservatives – and

he became increasingly isolated as unrest and dissatisfaction reached boiling point. When the king tried to neutralise the power of the more reform-minded delegates at a meeting of the États-Généraux (States General) at the Jeu de Paume at Versailles from May to June 1789 (see the boxed text 'The Tennis Court Oath' in the Excursions chapter), the masses took to the streets of Paris. On 14 July, a mob raided the armoury at the Hôtel des Invalides for rifles and then stormed the prison at Bastille – the ultimate symbol of the despotic ancien régime. The French Revolution had begun.

At first, the Revolution was in the hands of the moderate republicans called the Girondins. France was declared a constitutional monarchy and various reforms were carried out, including the adoption of the *Déclaration des Droits de l'Homme and du Citoyen* (Declaration of the Rights of Man), the document setting forth the principles of the Revolution. But as the masses armed themselves against the external threat to the new government posed by Austria, Prussia and the many exiled French nobles, patriotism and nationalism mixed with revolutionary fervour, popularising and radicalising the Revolution. It was not long before the Girondins lost out to the radical Jacobins, led by Robespierre, Danton and Marat, who abolished the monarchy and declared the First Republic in September 1792 after Louis XVI proved unreliable as a constitutional monarch. The National Assembly was replaced by a Revolutionary Convention.

In January 1793, Louis XVI, who had tried to flee the country with his family but only got as far as Varennes just outside the city, was convicted of 'conspiring against the liberty of the nation' and guillotined at place de la Révolution, today's place de la Concorde. His queen was executed in October of the same year. In March 1793 the Jacobins set up the notorious Committee of Public Safety to deal with national defence and to apprehend and try 'traitors'. This body virtually had dictatorial control over the city and the country during the so-called Reign of Terror (September 1793 to July 1794), which saw religious freedoms revoked, churches desecrated and closed, and cathedrals turned into 'Temples of Reason'. (Thankfully the magnificent cathedral at Chartres was spared the same fate; see the boxed text 'Saved by Red Tape' in the Excursions chapter.)

Marat was assassinated in his bathtub by the Girondin Charlotte Corday in July and by autumn, the Reign of Terror was in full swing; by mid-1794 some 2500 people had been beheaded in Paris and more than 14,500 elsewhere in France. In the end, the Revolution turned on itself, 'devouring its own children' in the words of the Jacobin Louis

Republican Calendar

During the Revolution, the Convention adopted a new, more 'rational' calendar from which all 'superstitious' associations (eg, saints' days) were removed. Year I began on 22 September 1792, the day the Republic had been proclaimed. The 12 months – renamed Vendémaire, Brumaire, Frimaire, Nivôse, Pluviôse, Ventôse, Germinal, Floréal, Prairial, Messidor, Thermidor and Fructidor – were each divided into three 10-day weeks called *décades*. Based on the cult of nature, the poetically inspired names of the months were chosen according to the seasons: the autumn months, for instance, were Vendémaire, derived from *vendange* (grape harvest or vintage); Brumaire, derived from *brume* (mist or fog); and Frimaire, derived from *frimas* (frost). The last day of each décade was a rest day, and the five or six remaining days of the year were used to celebrate Virtue, Genius, Labour, Opinion and Rewards. These festivals were initially called *sans-culottides* in honour of the *sans-culottes*, the extreme Revolutionaries who wore pantaloons rather than the short breeches favoured by the upper classes. While the Republican calendar worked well in theory, it caused no end of confusion for France in its communication and trade abroad as the months and days kept on changing in relation to those of the Gregorian calendar, which Napoleon eventually re-introduced to France in 1806.

Antoine Léon de Saint-Just, an intimate of Robespierre. Robespierre sent Danton to the guillotine; Saint-Just and even Robespierre himself eventually met the same fate.

After the Reign of Terror, a five-man delegation of moderate republicans led by Paul Barras, who had ordered the arrests of Robespierre and Saint-Just (among others), set itself up to rule the Republic as the Directory. On 5 October 1795 (or 13 Vendémiaire in the year 6; see the boxed text 'Republican Calendar'), a group of royalists bent on overthrowing the Directory was intercepted on the rue Saint Honoré by loyalist forces led by a dashing (though short) young Corsican general named Napoleon Bonaparte. For his efforts, Napoleon was put in command of French forces in Italy, where he was particularly successful in the campaign against Austria. His victories soon turned him into an independent political force.

Napoleon & the First Empire

The post-revolutionary government was far from stable, and when Napoleon returned to Paris in 1799 he found a chaotic republic in which few citizens had any faith. In November, when it appeared that the Jacobins were again on the ascendancy in the legislature, Napoleon tricked the delegates into leaving Paris for Saint Cloud to the southwest 'for their own protection', overthrew the discredited Directory and assumed power himself.

At first, Napoleon took the title of First Consul. In 1802, a referendum declared him 'Consul for Life' and his birthday became a national holiday. By 1804, when he had himself crowned 'Emperor of the French' by Pope Pius VII at Notre Dame, the scope and nature of Napoleon's ambitions were obvious to all. But to consolidate and legitimise his authority, Napoleon needed more victories on the battlefield. So began a seemingly endless series of wars and victories by which France came to control most of Europe.

In 1812, in an attempt to do away with his last major rival on the Continent, the tsar, Napoleon invaded Russia. Although his Grande Armée captured Moscow, it was wiped out by the brutal Russian winter. Prussia and Napoleon's other adversaries quickly recovered from their earlier defeats, and less than two years after the fiasco in Russia the allied armies entered Paris. Napoleon abdicated and left France for the tiny Mediterranean island-kingdom of Elba.

At the Congress of Vienna (1814-15), the Allies restored the House of Bourbon to the French throne, installing Louis XVI's brother as Louis XVIII (the second son of Louis XVI had been declared Louis XVII by monarchist exiles and died in 1795). But in March 1815, Napoleon escaped from Elba, landed in southern France and gathered a large army as he marched northwards towards Paris. His so-called Hundred Days back in power ended, however, when his forces were defeated by the British under the Duke of Wellington at Waterloo in Belgium. Napoleon was exiled to the remote South Atlantic island of Saint Helena, where he died in 1821.

Although reactionary in some ways – he re-established slavery in France's colonies, for example – Napoleon instituted a number of important reforms, including a reorganisation of the judicial system; the promulgation of a new legal code, the Code Napoléon (or civil code), which forms the basis of the French legal system to this day; and a new educational order. More importantly, he preserved the essence of the changes brought about by the Revolution. Napoleon is therefore remembered by many French as a great hero.

Gone but not forgotten: Napoleon's tomb in the Église du Dôme, Invalides

Few of Napoleon's grand architectural plans for Paris were completed, but the Arc de Triomphe, the Arc de Triomphe du Carrousel, La Madeleine, the Pont des Arts, rue de Rivoli and the Canal Saint Martin all date from this period.

The Restoration & the Second Republic

The reign of Louis XVIII from 1814 to 1824 was dominated by the struggle among extreme monarchists who wanted to return to the ancien régime, liberals who saw the changes wrought by the Revolution as irreversible and the radicals of the working-class neighbourhoods of Paris. Charles X (1824-30) handled this struggle with great ineptitude and was overthrown in the so-called July Revolution of 1830 when a motley group of revolutionaries seized the Hôtel de Ville. The Colonne de Juillet in the centre of place de la Bastille honours those

ROB FLYNN

A revolutionary roundabout: the Colonne de Juillet in place de la Bastille

killed in the street battles that accompanied the uprising; they are buried in vaults under the column.

Louis-Philippe (1773-1850), an ostensibly constitutional monarch of bourgeois sympathies and tastes, was then chosen by Parliament to head what became known as the July Monarchy. He was in turn overthrown in the February Revolution of 1848, and the Second Republic was established.

The Second Empire

In presidential elections held in 1848, Napoleon's useless nephew Louis Napoleon Bonaparte was overwhelmingly elected. Legislative deadlock caused Louis Napoleon to lead a coup d'etat in 1851, after which he was proclaimed Emperor Napoleon III (Bonaparte had conferred the title Napoleon II on his son upon his abdication in 1814 but he never ruled) and moved into the Palais des Tuileries, which would be destroyed during the Paris Commune two decades later.

The Second Empire lasted from 1852 until 1870. During this period, France enjoyed significant economic growth, and Paris was transformed under Baron Haussmann (see the boxed text 'Baron Haussmann' in the Things to See & Do chapter). In just 17 years this visionary oversaw the construction of a new city – though displacing hundreds of thousands of poor people in the process – of wide boulevards, fine public buildings and beautiful parks, serviced – not insignificantly – by a modern sewerage system. The 12 avenues leading out from the Arc de Triomphe, for example, were his work. The city's first department stores were also built at this time (eg, Au Bon Marché in 1852), as were the *passages*, Paris' delightful covered shopping arcades (see the Passages walking tour in the Things to See & Do chapter).

Unfortunately, Napoleon III – like his uncle before him – embroiled France in a number of costly conflicts, including the disastrous Crimean War (1853-6). In 1870, Otto von Bismarck goaded Napoleon III into declaring war on Prussia. Within months the thoroughly unprepared French army was defeated and the emperor taken prisoner. When news of the debacle reached Paris, the masses took to the streets and demanded that a republic be declared.

The Third Republic & the Belle Époque
The Third Republic began as a provisional government of national defence in September 1870. The Prussians were, at the time, advancing on Paris and would subsequently lay siege to the capital, forcing starving Parisians to bake bread laced with sawdust and consume most of the animals in the menagerie at the Jardin des Plantes. In January 1871 the government negotiated an armistice with the Prussians, who demanded that Assemblée Nationale (National Assembly) elections be held immediately. The republicans, who had called on the nation to continue to resist the Prussians and were overwhelmingly supported by Parisians, lost to the monarchists, who had campaigned on a peace platform.

As expected, the monarchist-controlled assembly ratified the Treaty of Frankfurt (1871). However, when ordinary Parisians heard of its harsh terms – a 5 billion FF war indemnity and surrender of the provinces of Alsace and Lorraine – they revolted against the government.

Following the withdrawal of Prussian troops on 18 March 1871, an insurrectionary government, known to history as the Paris Commune, was established and its supporters, the Communards, seized control of the capital while the legitimate government fled to Versailles. In late May, the government launched a week-long offensive, now known as La Semaine Sanglante (Bloody Week), on the Commune in which several thousand rebels were killed. After a mop-up of the Parc des Buttes-Chaumont, the last of the Communard insurgents, cornered by government forces in the Cimetière Père Lachaise, fought a hopeless, all-night battle among the tombstones. In the morning, the 147 survivors were lined up against the Mur des Fédérés (Wall of the Federalists), shot and buried where they fell in a mass grave. A further 20,000 or so Communards, mostly working-class, were rounded up throughout the city and summarily executed.

Despite this disastrous start, the Third Republic ushered in the glittering *belle époque* (literally 'beautiful age'), with Art Nouveau architecture, a whole field of artistic 'isms' from impressionism onwards and advances in science and engineering, including the construction of the first metro line, which opened in 1900. *Expositions universelles* (world exhibitions) were held in Paris in 1889 (showcasing the Eiffel Tower, which was much maligned at the time) and again in 1901 in the purpose-built Petit Palais. The Paris of nightclubs and artistic cafés made its first appearance around this time.

France was obsessed with a desire for revenge after its defeat by Germany, and jingoistic nationalism, scandals and accusations were the order of the day. But the greatest moral and political crisis of the Third Republic was the infamous 'Dreyfus Affair', which began in 1894 when a Jewish army captain named Alfred Dreyfus was accused of betraying military secrets to Germany, courtmartialled and sentenced to life imprisonment on Devil's Island, a penal colony off the northern coast of South America. Despite bitter opposition from the army command, right-wing politicians and many Catholic groups, leftists and liberals in Paris, including the novelist Émile Zola, succeeded in having the case reopened and Dreyfus was vindicated in 1900. The Dreyfus affair discredited both the army and the Catholic Church in France. The result was more rigorous civilian control of the military and, in 1905, the legal separation of Church and State.

WWI & the Interwar Period
Central to France's entry into WWI was the desire to regain Alsace and Lorraine, lost to Germany in 1871. Indeed, Raymond Poincaré, president of the Third Republic from 1913 to 1920 and prime minister throughout most of the 1920s, was a native of Lorraine and a firm supporter of war with Germany. But when the heir to the Austrian throne, Archduke Franz Ferdinand, was assassinated by Serbian nationalists in Sarajevo on

28 June 1914, Germany jumped the gun. Within a month, it had declared war on Russia and France.

By early September German troops had reached the River Marne, just 15km east of Paris, and the government was moved to Bordeaux. But Marshal Joffre's troops, transported to the front by Parisian taxis, brought about the 'Miracle of the Marne', and Paris was safe within a month. In November 1918 the armistice was signed.

The defeat of Austria-Hungary and Germany in WWI, which regained Alsace and Lorraine for France, was achieved at unimaginable human cost. Of the eight million French men who were called to arms, 1.3 million were killed and almost one million crippled. In other words, two out of every 10 Frenchmen aged between 20 and 45 years of age were killed in WWI. At the Battle of Verdun (1916) alone, the French, led by General Philippe Pétain, and the Germans each lost about 400,000 men.

The 1920s and 1930s saw Paris as a centre of the avant-garde, with artists pushing into the new fields of cubism and surrealism, Le Corbusier rewriting the architectural text book, foreign writers such as Ernest Hemingway and James Joyce attracted by the city's liberal atmosphere, and nightlife establishing a cutting-edge reputation for everything from jazz clubs to the cancan.

France's efforts to promote a separatist movement in the Rhineland and its occupation of the Ruhr in 1923 to enforce German reparations payments proved disastrous. But it did lead to almost a decade of accommodation and compromise with Germany over border guarantees and Germany's admission to the League of Nations. The naming of Adolf Hitler as German chancellor in 1933, however, would put an end to all that.

WWII

During most of the 1930s, the French, like the British, had done their best to appease Hitler but, two days after the German invasion of Poland on 1 September 1939, Britain and France declared war on Germany. By June 1940 France had capitulated and Paris was occupied; almost half the population of five million fled the city by car, on bicycle or on foot. The British expeditionary force sent to help the French barely managed to avoid capture by retreating to Dunkirk and crossing the English Channel in small boats. The expensive Maginot Line, a supposedly impregnable wall of fortifications along the Franco-German border, had proved useless – the German armoured divisions simply outflanked it by going through Belgium.

The Germans divided France into a zone under direct German rule (along the west coast and in the north, including Paris) and a puppet state based in the spa town of Vichy, led by Pétain, the ageing WWI hero of the Battle of Verdun. Both Pétain's collaborationist government, whose leaders and supporters assumed that the Nazis were Europe's new masters and had to be accommodated if not welcomed with open arms, and French police forces in German-occupied areas including Paris helped the Nazis round up French Jews and others for deportation to concentration and extermination camps.

After the fall of Paris, General Charles de Gaulle, France's under-secretary of war, fled to London and, in a famous radio broadcast on 18 June 1940, appealed to French patriots to continue resisting the Germans. He also set up a French government-in-exile and established the Forces Françaises Libres (Free French Forces), a military force dedicated to continuing the fight against the Germans.

The underground movement known as the Resistance, whose active members never amounted to more than about 5% of the population (the other 95% were either collaborators – such as the film stars Maurice Chevalier and Arletty, and the designer Coco Chanel – or did nothing at all), engaged in such activities as sabotaging the railways, collecting intelligence for the Allies, helping Allied airmen who had been shot down and publishing anti-German leaflets. Paris was the centre for the activities of the Resistance movement.

The liberation of France began with the Allied landings in Normandy on D-day (Jour-J in French): 6 June 1944. On 15

August, Allied forces also landed in southern France. After a brief insurrection by the Resistance, Paris was liberated on 25 August by an Allied force spearheaded by Free French units led by General Leclerc, who were sent in ahead of the Americans so that the French would have the honour of liberating the capital. Hitler, who visited Paris in June 1940 and loved it, ordered that the city be torched towards the end of the war. It was an order that, thankfully, was ignored.

The Fourth Republic

Charles de Gaulle returned to Paris and set up a provisional government, but in January 1946 he resigned as president, wrongly believing that such a move would provoke a popular outcry for his return. A few months later, a new constitution was approved by referendum.

The Fourth Republic was a period that saw unstable coalition cabinets follow one another with bewildering speed (on average, one every six months), and economic recovery, helped immeasurably by massive American aid. The war to reassert French colonial control over Indochina ended with the disastrous French defeat at Dien Bien Phu in 1954. France also tried to suppress an uprising by Arab nationalists in Algeria, where over one million French settlers lived.

The Fifth Republic

The Fourth Republic came to an end in 1958, when extreme right-wingers, furious at what they saw as defeatism rather than tough action in dealing with the uprising in Algeria, began conspiring to overthrow the government. De Gaulle was brought back to power to prevent a military coup and possible civil war. He soon drafted a new constitution that gave considerable powers to the president at the expense of the National Assembly.

The Fifth Republic, which continues to this day, was rocked in 1961 by an attempted coup staged in Algiers by a group of right-wing military officers. When it failed, the Organisation de l'Armée Secrète (OAS; a group of French settlers and sympathisers opposed to Algerian independence) turned to terrorism, trying several times to assassinate de Gaulle. The book and film *The Day of the Jackal* portrayed a fictional OAS attempt on de Gaulle's life.

In 1962, de Gaulle negotiated an end to the war in Algeria. Some 750,000 *pieds noirs* (literally 'black feet'), as Algerian-born French are known, flooded into France and the capital. In the meantime, almost all of the other French colonies and protectorates in Africa had demanded and achieved independence.

Paris maintained its position as an artistic and creative centre, and the 1960s saw large parts of the Marais beautifully restored. But the loss of the colonies, the surge in immigration and economic difficulties, including an increase in unemployment, weakened de Gaulle's government.

In March 1968, a large anti-Vietnam war demonstration in Paris led by a German student named Daniel Cohn-Bendit ('Danny the Red') gave impetus to the student movement and protests were staged throughout the spring. A seemingly insignificant incident in May, in which police broke up yet another in a long series of demonstrations by students of the University of Paris, sparked a violent reaction on the streets of the capital; students occupied the Sorbonne and barricades were erected in the Latin Quarter. Workers joined in the protests and some six million people nationwide participated in a general strike that virtually paralysed both France and its capital.

The alliance between workers and students couldn't last long. While the former wanted to reap greater benefit from the consumer market, the latter wanted to destroy it. De Gaulle took advantage of this division and appealed to people's fear of anarchy. Just as Paris and the rest of France seemed on the brink of revolution and an overthrow of the Fifth Republic imminent, stability was restored. The government made a number of immediate changes, including the decentralisation of the higher education system, and reforms (eg, lowering the voting age to 18, an abortion law and workers' self-management) continued through the 1970s.

FACTS ABOUT PARIS

1969 to the Present

In 1969 de Gaulle was succeeded as president by the Gaullist leader Georges Pompidou, who was in turn replaced by Valéry Giscard d'Estaing in 1974. François Mitterrand, long-time head of the Partie Socialiste (PS), was elected president in 1981 and, as the business community had feared, immediately set out to nationalise 36 privately owned banks, large industrial groups and various other parts of the economy, increasing the state-owned share of industrial production from 15% to over 30%. During the mid-1980s, however, Mitterrand followed a generally moderate economic policy and in 1988, at the age of 69, he was re-elected for a second seven-year term. In the 1986 parliamentary elections, the right-wing opposition led by Jacques Chirac, mayor of Paris since 1977, received a majority in the National Assembly, and for the next two years Mitterrand was forced to work with a prime minister and cabinet from the opposition, an unprecedented arrangement known as *cohabitation*.

In the May 1995 presidential elections Chirac – the ailing Mitterrand, who would die in January 1996, decided not to run again – walked away with a comfortable victory. In his first few months in office, Chirac received high marks for his direct words and actions in matters relating to the European Union (EU) and the war raging in Bosnia. His cabinet choices, including the selection of 'whiz kid' foreign minister Alain Juppé as prime minister, were well received. But Chirac's decision to resume nuclear testing on the Polynesian island of Mururoa and a nearby atoll was met with outrage both in France and abroad.

On the home front, Chirac's moves to restrict welfare payments (a move designed to bring France closer to meeting the criteria for European Monetary Union) led to the largest protests since 1968. For three weeks in late 1995 Paris was crippled by public-sector strikes, leaving the economy battered.

In 1997 Chirac took a big gamble and called an early parliamentary election for June. The move backfired. Chirac remained president but his party, the Rassemblement

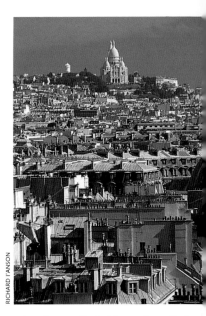

Looming over the Parisian rooftops: Montmartre's exquisite Basilique du Sacré Cœur

pour la République (RPR; Rally for the Republic) lost support and a coalition of Socialists, Communists and Greens came to power. Lionel Jospin, a former minister of education in the Mitterrand government (who, most notably, promised the French people a shorter working week for the same pay), became prime minister. France had once again entered into a period of *cohabitation* – with Chirac on the other side this time around.

For the most part, Jospin and his government continue to enjoy the electorate's approval, thanks largely to a recovery in economic growth and the introduction of a 35-hour working week, which has created hundreds of thousands of (primarily parttime) jobs. The prime minister remains the frontrunner to succeed Chirac as president at the next national election (due in 2002 at the latest), especially if the right remains the factional shambles that it is today, but his probable residency at the Palais de

RICHARD l'ANSON

l'Élysée will be foreshortened. In September 2000 the French electorate was expected to vote to reduce the president's term of office from seven to five years in a national referendum.

GEOGRAPHY
The city of Paris – the capital of both France and the historic Île de France region – measures approximately 9.5km (north to south) by 11km (west to east), not including the Bois de Boulogne and the Bois de Vincennes; its total area is 105 sq km. Within central Paris – which the French call *intra-muros* (Latin for 'within the walls') – the Rive Droite (Right Bank) is north of the Seine, while the Rive Gauche (Left Bank) is south of the river.

Paris is a relatively easy city to negotiate. The ring road known as the Périphérique makes a neat oval containing the whole central area. The Seine cuts an arc across the oval, and the terrain is so flat that the 126m-high Butte de Montmartre (Montmartre Hill) to the north really stands out.

CLIMATE
The Paris basin lies midway between Brittany and Alsace, and is affected by the climates of both. The Île de France region records the nation's lowest annual precipitation (about 575mm), but rainfall patterns are erratic; you're just as likely to be caught in a heavy spring or autumn downpour as in a sudden summer cloudburst. Paris' average yearly temperature is 12°C (3°C in January, 19°C in July), but the mercury sometimes drops below zero in winter and can climb to the mid-30s or higher in the middle of summer.

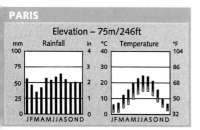

ECOLOGY & ENVIRONMENT
For a densely populated urban centre inhabited for more than two millennia, Paris is a surprisingly clean and healthy city. Thanks are due mainly to Baron Haussmann (see the boxed text 'Baron Haussmann' in the Things to See & Do chapter), who radically reshaped the city in the second half of the 19th century, and a city ordinance requiring residents to have the façades of their buildings cleaned every 10 years.

These days, despite the city's excellent public-transport system, Haussmann's wide boulevards are usually choked with traffic, and air pollution is undoubtedly the city's major environmental hazard. Second on the list is probably the noise generated by the same traffic, especially motorbikes and trucks (a pair of earplugs is a worthwhile investment if you value your sleep).

Fortunately, Parisians are rediscovering the joys of the *vélo* (bicycle), and a network of some 130km of city cycle lanes has been created over the past few years. Car owners are encouraged to leave their vehicles at home on specially earmarked days.

Be prepared to inhale second-hand cigarette (and even cigar) smoke pretty much everywhere – including restaurants and no-smoking areas. Drinking water is of high quality (though tasting strongly of chlorine), and steady efforts have been made to clean up the Seine – these days it's muddy rather than dirty.

FLORA & FAUNA
At first glance Paris does not appear to have much parkland. There are no great inner-city green spaces like London's Hyde Park or Central Park in Manhattan, although there are the two 'lungs of Paris': the Bois de Boulogne on the western edge of the city and the Bois de Vincennes to the south-east. Other parks tend to be small or, like the famous Jardin du Luxembourg and Jardin des Tuileries, formal affairs, often with more statuary, fountains and paths than grass. Nevertheless, there are splashes of green, many of them the work of Baron

Haussmann's urban planning, which produced interesting parks like the Parc des Buttes-Chaumont and the Parc de Monceau. In virtually every park in Paris, regardless of the size, you'll see a signboard illustrating and explaining the trees, flowers and other plants of the city.

The parks of Paris are particularly rich in birdlife, including magpies, jays, blue and great tits, and even woodpeckers. In winter, seagulls are sometimes seen on the Seine, and a few hardy ducks also brave the river's often swift-flowing waters. Year round, kestrels nest in the towers of Notre Dame (see the boxed text 'Notre Dame's Kestrels' in the Things to See & Do chapter), but in built-up areas the only birds you're likely to encounter are those ubiquitous winged rats called pigeons. Believe it or not, there are actually crayfish in the city's canals.

GOVERNMENT & POLITICS
National Government
France is a republic with a written constitution. As the capital city, Paris is home to almost all the national offices of state, including the National Assembly and the Senate.

The 577 members of the Assemblée Nationale (National Assembly) are directly elected in single-member constituencies for five-year terms. The 321 members of the rather powerless Sénat (Senate), who serve for nine years, are indirectly elected. The president of France is directly elected for a term currently lasting seven years, although the French electorate was expected to vote to reduce this to five in a national referendum in September 2000.

Executive power is shared by the president and the Council of Ministers, whose members (including the prime minister) are appointed by the president but are responsible to parliament. The president serves as commander-in-chief of the armed forces and theoretically makes all major policy decisions.

Local Government
The city is run by the *maire* (mayor), who is elected by the 163 members of the Con-

The elegant Hôtel de Ville was the traditional venue for lavish state banquets.

seil de Paris (Council of Paris), who are elected for six-year terms. The mayor has 18 *adjoints* (deputy mayors), whose offices are in the Hôtel de Ville (city hall).

The first mayor of Paris to be elected with real powers was Jacques Chirac in 1977. From 1871 until 1977, the mayor was nominated by the government as Paris was considered a dangerous and revolutionary city. Following the 1995 election of Chirac as president, the Council of Paris elected Jean Tiberi as mayor, a man who is very close to the president and is also from the RPR. The next election is scheduled for May 2001.

The mayor has many powers, but they do not include control of the police, which is handled by the Préfet de Police (Chief of Police), part of the Ministère de l'Intérieur (Ministry of the Interior).

Ever since Chirac became mayor in 1977, the Council of Paris has been run by right-wing parties, either the Union for French Democracy (UDF) or, more frequently, the RPR.

Paris is a *département* (department or, loosely, county) as well as a city and the mayor is the head of both. The city is divided into 20 arrondissements and each has its own *maire d'arrondissement* (mayor of the arrondissement) and *conseil d'arrondissement* (council of the arrondissement), who are also elected for six-year terms. They have very limited powers, principally administering local cultural, sporting and social activities.

ECONOMY

France's economy may not be the power-house of Europe – Germany lays claim to that distinction – but French financial leaders have enough clout to have a major influence on the course of European Monetary Union (EMU). Although Frankfurt – and not Paris – was chosen as the headquarters of the European Central Bank, the French won a victory in 1998 that surprised many European observers: the bank's chief, a Dutchman, would have a much shorter term in office than originally envisaged, and its second head would be a French official.

For the traveller in France the most important consequence of EMU will be the disappearance of the franc in 2002, when the euro becomes the currency of 11 EU countries (see the boxed text 'Bonjour Euro, Adieu Franc' in the Facts for the Visitor chapter).

To the surprise of many outsiders, the French *dirigiste* (interventionist) model of state ownership is still alive and well. More than 50% of GDP is spent by the government, which employs one in every four French workers despite a series of heavyweight privatisations during the 1990s. The 'family silver' – including Air France, France Telecom and Aerospatiale – has been partly sold off, but many other mammoth concerns, such as the car-maker Renault, remain government-controlled.

Pragmatism had something to do with the Socialist-dominated coalition of Lionel Jospin going back on its word and opting for privatisation, as it helped to top up the state coffers. After the overtaxed, free-spending 1980s, the next decade brought sluggish growth and high unemployment as France curbed its deficit spending to qualify for EMU. The effort has paid off: the French economy is turning over nicely (with growth of around 3% predicted for 2001) and unemployment is expected to fall to below 9%, the lowest level in over a decade. Inflation is negligible.

France is one of the world's most industrialised nations, with some 40% of the workforce employed in the industrial sector. About half of the economy's earnings come from industrial production. However, there is poor coordination between academic research and the companies that might turn good ideas into products, and the country has fewer large corporations – an important source of private capital and investment in research and development – than other industrialised nations of similar size.

France can also lay claim to being the largest agricultural producer and exporter in the EU. Its production of wheat, barley, maize (corn) and cheese is particularly significant. The country is to a great extent self-sufficient in food except for certain tropical products such as bananas and coffee.

About 20% of all economic activity in France takes place in the Paris region. Because of the centralised bureaucracy, the capital accounts for 40% of the nation's white-collar jobs.

POPULATION & PEOPLE

The population of Paris is 2.2 million, while the Île de France, the greater metropolitan area of Paris, has nearly 9.4 million inhabitants, or just over 16% of France's total population of 58 million people. Paris today is a very cosmopolitan city with many residents from other EU nations and a large English-speaking constituency.

France has had waves of immigration, particularly from its former colonies – see the special section 'Paris Mondial' after this chapter. The number of immigrants in central Paris is 341,000, or 15.5% of the city's population.

In recent years there has been a racist backlash against the country's nonwhite immigrant communities, especially Muslims from North Africa. In 1993, the French government changed its immigration laws to make it harder for immigrants to get French citizenship or bring their families into the country.

Estimates number the homeless on the streets of Paris at upwards of 50,000.

EDUCATION

France's education system has long been highly centralised; teachers are in fact civil servants. Its high standards have produced great intellectuals and almost universal literacy, but equal opportunities are still not available to people of all classes. Most children attend a primary school and then the *lycée* (secondary school), with some 73% of students sitting the matriculation exam called the *baccalauréat* (or *bac*). Education is obligatory until 16 years of age. The largest university, of which there are 77 in France, is the University of Paris system, with 13 divisions. One of these is the prestigious Sorbonne, which has for centuries attracted many of France's most talented and energetic people to Paris, creating a serious provincial brain drain. About one-third of all tertiary students in France study in Paris.

PHILOSOPHY

France has produced many luminary thinkers, particularly in the late 19th and early 20th centuries, including Henri Louis Bergson, Jean-Paul Sartre, Gabriel Honoré Marcel, Maurice Merleau-Ponty, Michel Foucault, Jacques Derrida and the French feminists headed by Simone de Beauvoir. Sartre was the foremost proponent of French existentialism, a philosophical movement stressing the importance of personal responsibility in a seemingly meaningless universe.

ARTS
Dance

The first *ballet comique de la reine* (dramatic ballet) in France was performed at an aristocratic wedding at the French court in

Together again: Jean-Paul and Simone commemorated in the 6e

BRENDA TURNNIDGE

1581. In 1661 Louis XIV founded the Académie Royale de Danse (Royal Dance Academy), from which ballet around the world developed.

By the end of the 18th century choreographers like Jean-Georges Noverre had become more important than the musicians, poets and dancers themselves. In the early 19th century, romantic ballets such as *Giselle* and *Les Sylphides* were more popular than opera in Paris.

Between 1945 and 1955, Roland Petit created such innovative ballets as *Turangalila*. Maurice Béjart shocked the public with his *Symphonie pour un Homme Seul*, which was danced in black in 1955, *Le Sacre du Printemps*, and *Le Marteau sans Maître*, with music by Pierre Boulez.

Today French dance seems to be moving in a new, more personal direction with performers such as Caroline Marcadé and Maguy Martin and choreographers such as Odile Duboc, Jean-Claude Gallotta and Jean-François Duroure.

Music

In the 17th and 18th centuries, French Baroque music influenced and informed much of Europe's musical output. Composers François Couperin and Jean Philippe Rameau were two major players in this field.

France produced and cultivated a number of musical luminaries in the 19th century. Among these were Hector Berlioz, Charles Gounod, César Franck, Camille Saint-Saëns and Georges Bizet. Berlioz was the founder of modern orchestration, while Franck's organ compositions sparked a musical renaissance in France that would produce such greats as Gabriel Fauré and the impressionists Claude Debussy and Maurice Ravel. Contemporary composers include Olivier Messiaen, who combines modern, almost mystical music with natural sounds such as birdsong, and his student, the radical Pierre Boulez, who includes computer-generated sound in his compositions.

Jazz hit Paris in the 1920s with a bang and has remained popular ever since. France's contribution to the world of jazz has been great, including the violinist

Francophonic Underground

Taking new ideas in electronica and adding a very French twist, Parisian hip-hop, house and techno have burst onto the international club scene over the past decade. Following on from the success of Afro-French rappers such as MC Solaar in the late 1980s and early 1990s, the mellow hip-hop of DJ Cam (alias Laurent Daumail) has explored darker territories and created a distinctly urban-Parisian sound. The prominence of Daft Punk, the hard-and-fast disco-house duo who made waves in international clubbing circles with their breakthrough track 'Da Funk' and the 1997 album *Homework*, paved the way for the current darlings of the music scene, Air. Mixing loungecore with dance sensibilities, Air's songs are equally at home in pumping clubs or art-house cinemas – a fact not lost on director Sophia Coppola, whose film *The Virgin Suicides* (2000) boasts a soundtrack by the band. Other leftfield Parisian exports include up-and-coming jazzy hip-hop outfit Cassius, house-disco twosome Motorbass and hotly tipped deckmeister Dimitri from Paris, already a regular favourite at London's hipper clubs.

Paul Bloomfield

Stéphane Grappelli and the legendary three-fingered Roma guitarist Django Reinhardt.

The most appreciated form of indigenous music is the *chanson française*, with a tradition going back to the troubadours of the Middle Ages. French songs have always favoured lyrics over music and rhythm, which partly explains the enormous popularity of rap in France today. The chanson tradition was revived from the 1930s onwards by such singers as Edith Piaf (see the boxed text 'The Urchin Sparrow' in the Entertainment chapter) and Charles Trenet. In the 1950s singers such as Georges Brassens, Léo Ferré, Claude Nougaro, Jacques Brel and Barbara became national stars.

Today's popular music has come a long way since the *yéyé* (imitative rock) of the 1960s sung by Johnny Halliday – though you might not think so listening to middle-of-the-roaders Vanessa Paradis and Patrick

Bruel. Listen out for rappers MC Solaar, Doc Gynéco and I Am from Marseilles. Evergreen balladeers/folk singers include Francis Cabrel, Julien Clerc, Jean-Jacques Goldman and Jacques Higelin, while the late Serge Gainsbourg remains enormously popular. Some people like the New Age space music of Jean-Michel Jarre; others say his name fits his sound.

But France's main claim to fame over the past decade has been *sono mondiale* (world music) – from Algerian *raï* and other North African music (Cheb Khaled, Natache Atlas, Jamel, Cheb Mami, Racid Taha) to Senegalese *mbalax* (Youssou N'Dour), West Indian *zouk* (Kassav, Zouk Machine) and Cuban salsa. Les Négresses Vertes and Mano Negra were two bands in the late 1980s that combined many of these elements – often with brilliant results.

Etienne Daho continues to top the charts with his trance numbers, and another recent and pretty bizarre development is Astérix rock, a home-grown folk-country sound based on accordions.

Literature

The great landmarks of French Renaissance literature are the works of Rabelais, La Pléaide and Montaigne. François Rabelais' exuberant narrative blends coarse humour with encyclopaedic erudition in a vast oeuvre that seems to include every kind of person, occupation and jargon to be found in mid-16th-century France.

During the 17th century, François de Malherbe brought a new rigour to the treatment of rhythm in literature. Transported by the perfection of Malherbe's verses, Jean de La Fontaine recognised his vocation and went on to write his charming *Fables* in the manner of Aesop. The mood of classical tragedy permeates *La Princesse de Clèves* by Marie de La Fayette, which is widely regarded as the first major French novel.

The literature of the 18th century is dominated by philosophers, among them Voltaire and Jean-Jacques Rousseau. Voltaire's political writings, in which it is argued that society is fundamentally opposed to nature, were to have a profound

Strangers in Paris

Foreigners (*ètrangers*, or strangers, to the French) have found inspiration in Paris since Charles Dickens used it alongside London as the backdrop to his novel on the French Revolution, *A Tale of Two Cities* (1859). The glory days of Paris as a literary setting, however, were without doubt the interwar years (see the Latin Quarter walking tour in the Things to See & Do chapter).

Ernest Hemingway's *The Sun Also Rises* and *A Moveable Feast* both portray bohemian life in Paris between the wars; many of the vignettes in the latter – dishing Ford Maddox Ford in a café, 'sizing up' F Scott Fitzgerald in a toilet in the Latin Quarter, and overhearing Gertrude Stein and her lover, Alice B Toklas, bitching at one another from the sitting room of their salon near the Jardin du Luxembourg – are classic and very Parisian.

Language guru Stein, who could be so tiresome with her word plays and endless repetitions ('A rose is a rose is a rose') in books like *The Making of Americans*, was able to let her hair down by assuming her lover's identity in *The Autobiography of Alice B Toklas*. It's a fascinating account of the author's many years in Paris, her salon on rue de Fleurus and her friendships with Matisse, Picasso, Braque, Hemingway and others. It's also where you'll find the classic recipe for hashish brownies. Stein's *Wars I Have Seen* is a personal account of life in German-occupied Paris.

Down and Out in Paris and London is George Orwell's account of the time he spent working as a *plongeur* (dishwasher) in Paris and living with tramps in both cities in the early 1930s. Both *Tropic of Cancer* and *Quiet Days in Clichy* by Henry Miller are steamy novels set in the French capital; his *Max and the White Phagocytes* and *Black Spring* are among some of his less raunchy Parisian writings. Mention should also be made of Anaïs Nin's voluminous diaries and fiction, and especially her published correspondence with Miller, which is highly evocative of 1930s Paris.

---

and lasting influence. Rousseau's sensitivity to landscape and its moods anticipates romanticism, and the insistence on his own singularity in *Les Confessions* makes it the first modern autobiography.

The 19th century brought Victor Hugo, widely acclaimed for his poetry as well as for his novels. *Les Misérables* (1862) describes life among the poor and marginalised of Paris during the first half of the 19th century. The flight of the central character, Jean Valjean, through the sewers of the capital is memorable as are Hugo's descriptions (all 20 pages of them). *Notre Dame de Paris* (The Hunchback of Notre Dame; see the boxed text in the Things to See & Do chapter), published three decades earlier, had made Hugo the key figure of French romanticism.

Other outstanding 19th-century novelists include Stendhal, Honoré de Balzac, Aurore Dupain (better known as George Sand) and, of course, Alexandre Dumas, who wrote the swashbuckling adventures *The Count of Monte Cristo* and *The Three Musketeers*. The much loved latter tells the story of

d'Artagnan (based on the historical personage Charles de Baatz d'Artagnan, 1623-73), who arrives in Paris determined to become one of Louis XIII's guardsmen.

In 1857 two landmarks of French literature appeared: *Madame Bovary* by Gustave Flaubert and *Les Fleurs du Mal* by Charles Baudelaire. Both writers were tried for the supposed immorality of their works. Flaubert won his case, and his novel was distributed without cuts. Baudelaire, who moonlighted as a translator in Paris (he introduced the works of the American writer Edgar Allan Poe to Europe in translations that have since become French classics), was obliged to cut several poems from *Les Fleurs du Mal*, and he died an early and painful death, practically unknown. Flaubert's second-most popular novel, *L'Éducation Sentimentale*, presents a vivid picture of life among Parisian dilettantes, intellectuals and revolutionaries during the decline and fall of Louis-Philippe's monarchy and the February Revolution of 1848.

The aim of Émile Zola, who came to Paris in 1858 with his close friend Paul

Cézanne, was to convert novel-writing from an art to a science by the application of experimentation. His theory may seem naive, but his work influenced all the significant French writers of the late 19th century and is reflected in much 20th-century fiction as well. *Nana* tells the decadent tale of a young woman who resorts to prostitution to survive in the Paris of the Second Empire.

Paul Verlaine and Stéphane Mallarmé created the symbolist movement, which strove to express states of mind rather than simply detail daily reality. Arthur Rimbaud, apart from crowding an extraordinary amount of rugged, exotic travel into his 37 years and having a tempestuous homosexual relationship with Verlaine, produced two enduring pieces of work: *Illuminations* and *Une Saison en Enfer* (A Season in Hell).

Marcel Proust dominated the early 20th century with his giant seven-volume novel, *À la Recherche du Temps Perdu* (Remembrance of Things Past); it is largely autobiographical and explores in evocative detail the true meaning of past experience recovered from the unconscious by 'involuntary memory'. In 1907, Proust moved from the family home near ave des Champs-Élysées to the apartment on blvd Haussmann famous for the cork-lined bedroom from which he almost never stirred. The original room is now on display in the Musée Carnavalet. André Gide found his voice in the celebration of homosexual sensuality and, later, left-wing politics. *Les Faux-Monnayeurs* (The Counterfeiters) exposes the hypocrisy and self-deception with which people try to avoid sincerity – a common theme with Gide.

André Breton ruled the surrealist group and wrote its three manifestos, although the first use of the word 'surrealist' is attributed to the writer Guillaume Apollinaire, a fellow traveller. As a poet, Breton was overshadowed by Paul Éluard and Louis Aragon, whose most famous surrealist novel was *Le Paysan de Paris*.

Colette enjoyed tweaking the nose of conventionally moral readers with titillating novels that detailed the amorous exploits of such heroines as the schoolgirl Claudine.

One of her most interesting works concerned the German occupation of Paris, *Paris de Ma Fenêtre* (Paris from My Window). Her view, by the way, was from 9 rue de Beaujolais, 1er, overlooking the Jardin du Palais Royal.

After WWII, existentialism developed as a significant literary movement around Jean-Paul Sartre, Simone de Beauvoir and Albert Camus, who worked and conversed in the cafés around the Église Saint Germain des Prés. All three stressed the importance of the writer's political engagement. *L'Age de Raison* (The Age of Reason; 1945), the first volume of Sartre's trilogy *Les Chemins de la Liberté* (The Roads to Freedom), is a superb Parisian novel; the subsequent volumes recall Paris immediately before and during WWII. De Beauvoir, author of the ground-breaking study *The Second Sex*, had a profound influence on feminist thinking.

In the late 1950s, some younger novelists began to look for new ways of organising the narrative. The so-called *nouveau roman* (new novel) refers to the works of Nathalie Sarraute, Alain Robbe-Grillet, Boris Vian, Julien Gracq and Michel Butor, among others. However, these writers never formed a close-knit group, and their experiments have taken them in divergent directions. Today the nouveau roman is very much out of favour in France.

Mention should also be made of *Histoire d'O*, the highly erotic sadomasochistic novel written (under a pseudonym) in 1954 by Dominique Aury (1907-98). It has sold more copies than any other contemporary French novel outside France.

In 1980 Marguerite Yourcenar, best known for her memorable historical novels such as *Mémoires d'Hadrien*, became the first woman to be elected to the Académie Française (French Academy).

Marguerite Duras came to the notice of a larger public when she won the prestigious Prix Goncourt for her novel *L'Amant* (The Lover) in 1984. She was also noted for the screenplays of *India Song* and *Hiroshima Mon Amour*, described by one critic as part nouveau roman, part Mills & Boon.

Philippe Sollers was one of the editors of *Tel Quel*, a highbrow, then left-wing, Paris-based review that was very influential in the 1960s and early 1970s. His 1960s novels were highly experimental, but with *Femmes* (Women) he returned to a conventional narrative style.

Another editor of *Tel Quel* was Julia Kristeva, best known for her theoretical writings on literature and psychoanalysis. In recent years she has turned her hand to fiction, and *Les Samuraï*, a fictionalised account of the heady days of *Tel Quel*, is an interesting document on the life of the Paris intelligentsia. Roland Barthes and Michel Foucault are other authors and philosophers associated with this period.

More accessible authors who enjoy a wide following include Françoise Sagan, Patrick Modiano, Yann Queffélec, Pascal Quignard and Denis Tillinac. The *roman policier* (detective novel) has always been a great favourite with the French and among its greatest exponents has been the Belgian-born Georges Simenon, author of the Inspector Maigret novels (*Maigret at the Crossroads* portrays Montmartre at its sleazy and seedy best).

Architecture

Gallo-Roman Traces of Roman Paris can be seen in the residential foundations and dwellings in the Crypte Archéologique (Map 6) under the square in front of Notre Dame, in the partially reconstructed Arènes de Lutèce (Map 5), and in the *frigidarium* (cooling room) and other remains of Roman baths dating from around 200 AD at the Musée National du Moyen Age (Map 6).

Merovingian & Carolingian Although quite a few churches were built during the Merovingian and Carolingian periods (5th to 10th century), very little remains of them in Paris. Archaeological excavations in the crypt of the 12th-century Basilique Saint Denis have uncovered extensive tombs from both the Merovingian and Carolingian periods. The oldest of these dates from around 570 AD.

Romanesque A religious revival in the 11th century led to the construction of a large number of *roman* (Romanesque) churches, so called because their architects adopted many architectural elements (eg vaulting) from Gallo-Roman buildings still standing at the time. Romanesque buildings typically have round arches, heavy walls whose few windows let in very little light and a lack of ornamentation that borders on the austere.

No churches in Paris are entirely Romanesque in style, but a few have important representative elements, including the Église Saint Germain des Prés (Map 6), the Église Saint Nicholas des Champs (Map 6) and the Église Saint Germain L'Auxerrois (Map 6), which was built in a mixture of Gothic and Renaissance styles. The Tour Clovis, a Romanesque tower within the grounds of the prestigious Lycée Henri IV (Map 5), just east of the Panthéon, is all that remains of an abbey founded by the eponymous Merovingian ruler.

Gothic The Gothic style originated in the mid-12th century in northern France, where great wealth attracted the finest architects, engineers and artisans. Gothic structures are characterised by ribbed vaults carved with great precision, pointed arches, slender verticals, chapels (often built by rich people or guilds), galleries and arcades along the nave and chancel, refined decoration and large stained-glass windows.

The first Gothic building to combine various late Romanesque elements to create a new kind of structural support in which each arch counteracted and complemented the next was the basilica at Saint Denis, which served as a model for many other 12th-century French cathedrals, including Notre Dame and the one at Chartres.

In the 14th century, the Rayonnant (Radiant) Gothic style – named after the radiating tracery of the rose windows – developed, with interiors becoming even lighter thanks to broader windows and more translucent stained glass. One of the most influential Rayonnant buildings was the Sainte Chapelle, whose stained glass forms a sheer

Holy light: the exquisite Sainte Chapelle was built in just under three years.

MARTIN MOOS

curtain of glazing. The two transept façades of Notre Dame and the Conciergerie's vaulted Salle des Gens d'Armes (Cavalry-men's Hall), the largest surviving medieval hall in Europe, are other fine examples of the Rayonnant Gothic style.

By the 15th century, decorative extrava-gance led to Flamboyant Gothic, so named because its wavy stone carving was said to resemble flames. Beautifully lacy examples of Flamboyant architecture include the Clocher Neuf at Chartres, the Église Saint Séverin (Map 6) and the Tour Saint Jacques (Map 6). Inside the Église Saint Eustache (Map 6) there's some exceptional Flamboy-ant Gothic archwork holding up the ceiling of the chancel.

Renaissance The Renaissance, which began in Italy in the early 15th century, set out to realise a 'rebirth' of classical Greek and Roman culture. It had its first impact on France at the end of the 15th century, when Charles VIII began a series of invasions of Italy. The French Renaissance introduced a variety of classical components and decora-tive motifs, which were blended with the rich decoration of Flamboyant Gothic.

The Early Renaissance style of architec-ture is best exemplified in Paris by the churches of Saint Eustache on the Right Bank and Saint Étienne du Mont on the Left Bank.

Mannerism, a later version of Renaissance architecture, is reflected in the Louvre's Cour Carrée (Map 6), the Petit Château at Chantilly and many of the Marais' fine hôtels particuliers, including the Hôtel Car-navalet (now part of the Musée Carnavalet; Map 7) and Hôtel Lamoignan.

Baroque During the Baroque period, which lasted from the tail end of the 16th century to the late 18th century, painting, sculpture and classical architecture were in-tegrated to create structures and interiors of great subtlety, refinement and elegance. Among some of the best examples in Paris are the Palais du Luxembourg (Map 5), the Église Notre Dame du Val-de-Grâce (Map

The Église du Dôme – a Baroque masterpiece

The graceful Musée d'Orsay on the Left Bank

5), the chateau at Vaux-le-Vicomte, the Église du Dôme (Map 4) at Invalides and the Chapelle de la Sorbonne (Map 5).

Neoclassicism Neoclassical architecture, which emerged in about 1740 and remained popular in Paris until well into the 19th century, had its roots in the renewed interest in classical forms. Although it was in part a reaction against Baroque and rococo, with their emphasis on decoration and illusion, neoclassicism was more profoundly a search for order, reason and serenity through the adoption of the forms and conventions of Graeco-Roman antiquity: columns, simple geometric forms and traditional ornamentation. Among the earliest examples of this style in Paris are the Église Saint Sulpice (Map 6), the Arc de Triomphe (Map 2), the Arc de Triomphe du Carrousel (Map 6), the Église de la Madeleine (Map 2), the Pont des Arts (Map 6), the Bourse (Map 3) and the Assemblée Nationale (Map 4). The climax of 19th-century classicism in Paris is considered to be the Palais Garnier (Map 2).

Art Nouveau Art Nouveau, which emerged in Europe and the USA in the second half of the 19th century under various names (Jugendstil, Sezessionstil, Stile Liberty), caught on in Paris, although it was regarded as outdated by around 1910. There are some fine Art Nouveau interiors in the Musée d'Orsay, an Art Nouveau glass roof over the Grand Palais and, on rue Pavée in the Marais, a synagogue (Map 7). Several department stores, including Au Bon Marché (Map 4), Galeries Lafayette (Map 2) and La Samaritaine (Map 6), also have elements of this style throughout.

Modern Architecture Until 1968 French architects were still being trained almost exclusively at the conformist École des Beaux-Arts, which certainly shows in most of the early structures erected in the sky-scraper district of La Défense (eg, the CNIT building). Among some of the more forgettable buildings around are the UNESCO building (1958; Map 4) and the Tour Montparnasse (1974; Map 4).

For centuries France's leaders have sought to immortalise themselves by erecting huge, public edifices – known as *grands projets* – in Paris. The recent past has been no different; the late Georges Pompidou commissioned the once reviled but now much loved Centre Beaubourg (1977) – later renamed the Centre Pompidou (Map 7) – while president, and his successor, Giscard d'Estaing, was instrumental in transforming a derelict train station into the glorious Musée d'Orsay, which opened in 1986. But François Mitterrand surpassed them both with his dozen or so monumental commissions in Paris alone.

Since the early 1980s, Paris has seen the construction of such projects as IM Pei's glass pyramid at the Louvre (Map 6), an architectural *cause célèbre* in the late 1980s; the city's second opera house, Opéra Bastille (Map 6); the Grande Arche at La Défense (see the La Défense map in the Things to See & Do chapter); the huge science museum and park at La Villette (Map 1); Parc André Citroën (Map 1) in the western corner of the 15e arrondissement; the Ministry of Finance offices in Bercy (Map 5); and the controversial Bibliothèque Nationale de France François Mitterrand (Map 9).

One of the most beautiful modern buildings in Paris is Jean Nouvel's Institut du Monde Arabe (Map 5), a highly praised structure (opened in 1987) that successfully mixes modern and traditional Arab and Western elements.

Painting

Voltaire wrote that French painting began with Nicolas Poussin (1594-1665), a Baroque painter who frequently set scenes from classical mythology and the Bible in ordered landscapes bathed in golden light.

In the 18th century, Jean-Baptiste Chardin brought the humbler domesticity of the Dutch masters to French art. In 1785 the public reacted with enthusiasm to two large paintings with clear republican messages: *The Oath of the Horatii* and *Brutus Condemning His Son* by Jacques Louis David. David became one of the leaders of the Revolution, and a virtual dictator in matters of art, where he advocated a precise, severe classicism. He was made official state painter by Napoleon. He is perhaps best remembered for the famous painting of Marat lying dead in his bath.

Jean Auguste Dominique Ingres, David's most gifted pupil, continued in the neoclassical tradition. The historical pictures to which he devoted most of his life are now generally regarded as inferior to his portraits.

The gripping *Raft of the Medusa* by Théodore Géricault is on the threshold of romanticism; if Géricault had not died young, he would probably have become a leader of the movement, along with his friend Eugène Delacroix. Delacroix's most famous picture, perhaps, is *La Liberté Conduisant le Peuple* (Freedom Leading the People), which commemorates the July Revolution of 1830.

The members of the Barbizon School brought about a parallel transformation of

East meets West at the Institut du Monde Arabe, a triumph of modern architecture.

Art Nouveau elegance at Bastille metro station

SIMON BRACKEN

NEIL SETCHFIELD

A cubist cornucopia at the excellent Musée Picasso

landscape painting. The school derived its name from the village of Barbizon near the Forêt de Fontainebleau (see the Excursions chapter), where Camille Corot and Jean-François Millet, among others, gathered to paint in the open air. Corot is best known for his landscapes, while Millet took many of his subjects from peasant life and had a strong influence on Van Gogh.

Millet anticipated the realist program of Gustave Courbet, a prominent member of the Paris Commune, whose paintings show the misery of manual labour and the cramped lives of the working class.

Édouard Manet used realism to depict the life of the Parisian middle classes, yet he included in his pictures numerous references to the old masters. His *Déjeuner sur l'Herbe* and *Olympia* were considered scandalous, largely because they broke with the traditional treatment of their subject matter.

Impressionism, initially a term of derision, was taken from the title of an 1874 experimental painting by Claude Monet, *Impression: Soleil Levant* (Impression: Sunrise). Monet was the leading figure of the school, which counted among its members Alfred Sisley, Camille Pissarro, Berthe Morisot and Pierre-Auguste Renoir. The impressionists' main aim was to capture

fleeting light effects, and light came to dominate the content of their painting.

Edgar Degas was a fellow traveller, but he preferred his studio to open-air painting. He found his favourite subjects at the racecourse and the ballet. Henri de Toulouse-Lautrec was a great admirer of Degas and chose similar subjects: people in the bars, brothels and music halls of Montmartre. He is best known for his posters and lithographs, in which the distortion of the figures is both satirical and decorative.

Paul Cézanne is celebrated for his still lifes and landscapes depicting the south of France, while the name of Paul Gauguin immediately conjures up his studies of Tahitian women. Both he and Cézanne are usually referred to as postimpressionists, something of a catch-all term for the diverse styles that flowed from impressionism.

Henri Rousseau was a contemporary of the postimpressionists but his 'naive' art was totally unaffected by them. His dreamlike pictures of the Paris suburbs and of jungle and desert scenes have had a lasting influence on 20th-century art.

Gustave Moreau was a member of the symbolist school. His eerie treatment of mythological subjects can be seen in his old studio (now the Musée Gustave Moreau) in Paris.

Fauvism took its name from the slur of a critic who compared the exhibitors at the annual Salon d'Automne (Autumn Salon) in 1905 with *fauves* (beasts) because of their radical use of intensely bright colours. Among these 'beastly' painters were Henri Matisse, André Derain and Maurice de Vlaminck.

Cubism was effectively launched in 1907 by the Spanish prodigy Pablo Picasso with his *Les Demoiselles d'Avignon*. Cubism, as developed by Picasso, Georges Braque and Juan Gris, deconstructed the subject into a system of intersecting planes and presented various aspects simultaneously.

After WWI, the School of Paris was formed by a group of expressionists, mostly foreign-born, including Amedeo Modigliani from Italy and the Russian Marc Chagall. Chagall's pictures combine fantasy and folklore.

Dada, a literary and artistic movement of revolt, started in Germany and Switzerland during WWI. In France, one of the key Dadaists was Marcel Duchamp, whose *Mona Lisa* adorned with moustache and goatee epitomises the spirit of the movement.

Surrealism, an offshoot of Dada, flourished between the wars. Drawing on the theories of Freud, it attempted to reunite the conscious and unconscious realms, to permeate everyday life with fantasies and dreams.

WWII ended Paris' role as the world's artistic capital. Many artists left France, and though some returned after the war, the city never regained its old magnetism. Bernard Buffet, who died in 2000, was probably France's leading postwar painter; his portraits are both sad and moving.

Sculpture

By the 14th century, sculpture was increasingly commissioned for the tombs of the nobility. In Renaissance France, Pierre Bontemps decorated the beautiful tomb of François I at the Basilique Saint Denis (see Saint Denis in the Excursions chapter) and Jean Goujon created the Fontaine des Innocents in central Paris. The Baroque style is exemplified by Guillaume Cous-

tou's *Horses of Marly* at the entrance to ave des Champs-Élysées.

In the 19th century, memorial statues in public places came to replace sculpted tombs. One of the best artists in the new mode was François Rude, who sculpted the statue of Marshall Ney outside the Closerie des Lilas and the relief on the Arc de Triomphe. Another sculptor was Jean-Baptiste Carpeaux, who began as a romantic, but whose work – such as *The Dance* on the Palais Garnier and his fountain in the Jardin du Luxembourg – look back to the warmth and gaiety of the Baroque era.

At the end of the 19th century, Auguste Rodin's work overcame the conflict between neoclassicism and romanticism. His sumptuous bronze and marble figures of men and women did much to revitalise sculpture as an expressive medium. One of Rodin's most gifted pupils was Camille Claudel, whose work can be seen along with that of Rodin in the Musée Rodin.

Braque and Picasso experimented with sculpture and, in the spirit of Dada, Marcel Duchamp exhibited 'found objects' – for example, a urinal that he entitled *Fountain* and signed.

One of the most influential sculptors to emerge after WWII was César Baldaccini, who used iron and scrap metal to create his imaginary insects and animals, later graduating to pliable plastics.

Cinema

France's place in the film history books was firmly ensured when the Lumière brothers invented 'moving pictures' and organised the world's first paying (1FF) public film-screening – a series of two-minute reels – in Paris' Grand Café on blvd des Capucines on 28 December 1895.

In the 1920s and 1930s avant-garde directors such as René Clair, Marcel Carné and the intensely productive Jean Renoir, son of the famous artist, searched for new forms and subjects.

In the late 1950s a large group of new-generation directors burst onto the scene with a new genre, the *nouvelle vague* (new wave). This group included Jean-Luc

Godard, François Truffaut, Claude Chabrol, Eric Rohmer, Jacques Rivette, Louis Malle and Alain Resnais. This disparate group of directors believed in the primacy of the film-maker, giving rise to the term *film d'auteur* (loosely 'arthouse film').

Many films followed, among them Alain Resnais' *Hiroshima Mon Amour* and *L'Année Dernière à Marienbad* (Last Year at Marienbad). François Truffaut's *Les Quatre Cents Coups* (The 400 Blows) was partly based on his own rebellious adolescence. Jean-Luc Godard made such films as *À Bout de Souffle* (Breathless), *Alphaville* and *Pierrot le Fou*, which showed even less concern for sequence and narrative. The new wave continued until the 1970s, by which stage it had lost its experimental edge.

Of the directors of the 1950s and 1960s not part of this school, one of the most notable was Jacques Tati, who made many comic films based around the charming, bumbling figure of Monsieur Hulot and his struggles to adapt to the modern age.

The most successful directors of the 1980s and 1990s included Jean-Jacques Beineix, who made *Diva* and *Betty Blue*, and Jean-Luc Besson, who made *Subway*, *The Big Blue* and *The Fifth Element*. Léos Carax, in his *Boy Meets Girl*, created a kind of Parisian purgatory of souls lost in the eternal night.

Light social comedies such as *Trois Hommes et un Couffin* (Three Men and a Cradle), *Romuald et Juliette* by Coline Serreau and *La Vie Est un Long Fleuve Tranquille* (Life Is a Long Quiet River) by Étienne Chatiliez have been among the biggest hits in France in recent years.

Other well-regarded directors today include Bertrand Blier *(Trop Belle pour Toi)*, Eric Klapisch *(Un Air de Famille)*, Claude Sautet and André Téchiné. Matthieu Kassovitz's award-winning *La Haine* examined the prejudice and violence of the world of the *beurs*, young French-born Algerians. Alain Renais' *On Connaît la Chanson*, based on the life of the late British television playwright Dennis Potter, received international acclaim and six Césars (the French film awards) in 1997. Bruno Dumont's *Humanité*, probably the slowest murder investigation ever filmed, picked up several major awards in 1999.

Other film-makers to look out for include German-born Dominik Moll, whose delightful black comedy *Harry, un Ami Qui Vous Veut du Bien* (Harry, a Friend You Wish Well) was selected at Cannes in 2000. Don't miss a showing of *Saint Cyr* (called The King's Daughters in English), a visually stunning historical drama directed by Patricia Mazuy.

Theatre

Molière, an actor, became the most popular comic playwright of the 17th century. Plays such as *Tartuffe* are staples of the classical repertoire. The playwrights Pierre Corneille and Jean Racine, in contrast, drew their subjects from history and classical mythology. Racine's *Phèdre*, for instance, taken from Euripides, is a story of incest and suicide among the descendants of the Greek gods.

SOCIETY & CONDUCT

The French are generally more relaxed about relations between men and women – and about sex – than many English-speaking visitors might be accustomed to. Most are genuinely bemused by the American 'political correctness' of the past two decades and the fuss made over sex scandals involving politicians. Touching, kissing and flirting are a generally accepted part of daily relationships, even at work.

On the other hand, French public life and business is still dominated by men. At street level, visitors are often surprised to find hoardings featuring half-naked women still being used to sell cars and watches.

A polite way of getting rid of guests – essentially telling them that the party's over – is to serve them all a glass of orange juice, a sign recognised by most that it's time to say *bonne nuit* (good night). The idea is that the vitamin C will dilute the alcohol for those driving – or staggering – home.

Dos & Don'ts

While the stereotype of the haughty, arrogant and unhelpful Parisian may have been

ASA ANDERSON

accurate 20 years ago, it's certainly not true today. Parisians tend to be shy with strangers, but will readily help if approached in a friendly manner and with a word or two of imperfect French. As in other cities around the world, however, the more tourists a particular area or district attracts, the less patience the locals tend to have for them.

A few dos:

• The easiest way to improve the quality of your relations with Parisian merchants is always to say *'Bonjour, monsieur/madame/mademoiselle'* when you walk into a shop, and *'Merci, monsieur/madame/mademoiselle – au revoir'* when you leave. *Monsieur* means 'sir' and can be used with any male person who isn't a child. *Madame* is used where 'Mrs' or 'ma'am' would apply in English, whereas *mademoiselle* (Miss) is used when talking to unmarried women. When in doubt, use madame. Similarly, if you want help or to interrupt someone, begin with *'Excusez-moi, monsieur/madame/ mademoiselle'*.

• When greeting one another it is customary for people who know each other to exchange *bises* (kisses). Close male friends and relations always did this in the south of France, but it is becoming increasingly common nowadays among younger and educated 21st-century Parisian men who don't give a hoot that older males consider it *pédérastique* (queer or 'poofy'). The usual ritual is one glancing peck on each cheek, but some people go for three or even four kisses. People who don't kiss each other will almost always shake hands when meeting up.

• If you are invited to someone's home for a meal, always bring some sort of gift, such as good wine (not a cheap *vin de table* or table wine). Flowers are another good idea, but *chrysanthèmes* (chrysanthemums) are only brought to cemeteries and *œillets* (carnations) bring bad luck – avoid both types.

A few don'ts:

• When buying fruit, vegetables or flowers anywhere except at supermarkets, do not touch the produce or blossoms unless invited to do so. Show the shopkeeper what you want and they will choose for you.

• If you arrive at a restaurant without a reservation do not ask for a table but state the number of covers *(couverts)* you require (eg, *'Avez-vous deux couverts?'*). Never, ever, summon the waiter by shouting *'Garçon!'*, which they always seem to do in old films. Garçon means 'boy' and saying *'S'il vous plaît'* ('Please') is the way it's done now.

• In general, Parisian lawns are meant to be looked at and praised for their greenness, not sat upon; watch out for *pelouse interdite* (keep off the grass) signs. This has, however, been changing in recent years, with such signs being removed and replaced with *pelouse autorisée*, meaning you're permitted to sit, eat, play and walk on the grass of certain parks (those where you're still not allowed include the Jardin des Tuileries and Jardin du Luxembourg).

RELIGION
Roman Catholics
Some 80% of French people identify themselves as Roman Catholic but, although most have been baptised, very few ever attend church. The Catholic Church in France is generally very progressive and ecumenically minded. Cardinal Jean-Marie Lustiger, archbishop of Paris since 1981, was born in Paris to Jewish immigrants from Poland in 1926. He converted to Catholicism at the age of 14.

Muslims
France has between four and five million nominally Muslim residents, and they now make up the country's second-largest religious group. The vast majority are immigrants (or their offspring) who arrived from North Africa during the 1950s and

1960s. In recent years, France's Muslim community has been the object of racist agitation by right-wing parties and extremist groups. Many North Africans complain of discrimination by the police and employers.

Protestants

France's Protestants, who were severely persecuted during much of the 16th and 17th centuries, now number about one million. They are concentrated in Alsace, the Jura, the south-eastern part of the Massif Central and along the Atlantic coast.

John Calvin (1509-64), born in Noyon in northern France, was educated in Paris, Orléans and Bourges but spent much of his life in Geneva.

Jews

There has been a Jewish community in France for most of the time since the Roman period. During the Middle Ages, the community suffered persecution and there were a number of mass expulsions. French Jews, the first in Europe to achieve emancipation, were granted full citizenship in 1790-1. Since 1808, the Jewish community has had an umbrella organisation known as the Consistoire, based in Paris.

The Jewish community, which now numbers some 650,000 (the largest in Europe), grew substantially during the 1960s as a result of immigration from Algeria, Tunisia and Morocco. France generally enjoys a good relationship with its Jewish community, and there have been relatively few incidents of anti-Semitism reported in recent years.

LANGUAGE

Around 200 million people around the globe speak French regularly as their first or second language. France has a special government ministry (the Ministère de la Francophonie) to deal with the country's relations with the French-speaking world.

French was *the* international language of culture and diplomacy until WWI, and the French are somewhat sensitive to its decline in importance since then. Your best bet is always to approach people politely in French, even if the only words you know are *Pardon, parlez-vous anglais?* (Excuse me, do you speak English?)

For more on what to say and how to say it *en français* (in French), see the Language chapter at the back of the book. Lonely Planet also publishes the comprehensive *French phrasebook*.

Paris Mondial

And you thought it was all berets, baguettes and bistros. To be sure, Paris is and always will be French. But it's a much more international world nowadays and Paris vibrates to its rhythms. Paris is a magnet attracting musicians and performers from around the globe. Once pretty much satisfied with French cuisine, the city now regularly dines out on dishes from Vietnam, Mauritius, Senegal and Brazil. And in some of its colourful ethnic markets you could be forgiven for thinking you were in Africa or Asia. This is Paris Mondial (literally 'World Paris'), a diverse, dynamic, multicultural city.

The People of Paris Mondial

France ruled a considerable part of the world until as recently as the middle of the 20th century, and today its population includes a large number of immigrants and their descendants from its former colonies and protectorates in Africa, Indochina, the Middle East, India, the Caribbean and the South Pacific. At the same time France has continued to accept significant numbers of exiles and refugees.

Immigrants make up some 15.5% of the 2.2 million people living in central Paris. According to the latest figures (1998), the most significant group is the Algerians, with a population of just under 47,000. Their Moroccan and Tunisian neighbours number about 28,000 and 24,000 respectively. Another significant, though perhaps less visible, group is the Portuguese (41,000). The largest Asian assembly is made up of ethnic Chinese with a population of around 13,500, followed by Sri Lankans (8650), Japanese (6750) and Cambodians (4550). The largest groups from sub-Saharan Africa are those from Mali (8655), Senegal (6950) and the Côte d'Ivoire (4235).

Title Page: Facing the future: Chinese New Year in the 3e (photograph: Brenda Turnnidge)

Top: Young Africans in the 18e

Bottom Left & Right: Getting ready for the procession: Chinese youngsters show off their make-up.

Algerians, Moroccans and Tunisians have been settling and working in France since the beginning of the 20th century, especially in the districts of Belleville in the 19e and 20e and La Goutte d'Or in the 18e. Morocco and Tunisia were French colonies until 1956; Algeria fought a bloody war with France before gaining independence in 1962. French-born North Africans are often called *beurs*: the term is not pejorative and is often used by the media, anti-racist groups and, importantly, second-generation North Africans themselves, who frequently feel torn between two cultures and are struggling to integrate yet trying to maintain links with their family and ethnic roots.

The majority of black Africans in Paris hail from Mali, Senegal, the Côte d'Ivoire, Togo, Benin, Cameroon and the Congo. Among the first immigrants were Senegalese soldiers who had fought for the French during WWI. They moved into the 18e, which remains the heart of African Paris. African students and intellectuals arrived in the 1940s and 1950s, some returning to their homelands to become leaders during the postcolonial period. Immigration was actively promoted during the 1950s and 1960s to boost France's workforce, but recent history has been more tumultuous, with the expulsion of *les sans-papiers* (those 'without papers') following tough anti-immigration policies in the 1990s.

Many of the ethnic Chinese in Paris hail from the former French colonies of Indochina. Large waves of Asian immigrants arrived in France at the end of the Indochinese war in 1954, to escape the Pol Pot régime in Cambodia in the 1970s, and as a result of the exodus of the Vietnamese boat people that continued well into the 1980s. The events in Tiananmen Square in 1989 prompted the flight of many Chinese. But Chinese immigration is nothing new; Chinese from Zhejiang Province have been settling in Paris since the 1920s, mainly in the 3e, 13e, 19e and 20e arrondissements.

BRENDA TURNNIDGE

Right: Immigrant song: *sans-papiers* demonstration on 1 May

Immigrants from India, Pakistan, Bangladesh and Sri Lanka, as well as from the former colonies of Madagascar and Mauritius and the overseas *département* of Réunion, often appear to share a common culture, but each group is quite distinct and has its own network in Paris. The gaining of independence of the French colonial trading-post of Pondicherry in India in 1954 sparked the first wave of emigration from the region; more recent arrivals include Sri Lankan refugees. Many immigrants from the region tend to work in and around the 10e, often commuting from the suburbs.

Jews have come to live and work in Paris since the Middle Ages, and today Ashkenazi Jews live in the 4e while Sephardic Jews live in Belleville. In fact, in the latter the so-called *Tunes* have managed to recreate something of the Tunisia they left behind in the 1950s. Other Jews work around rue du Sentier, 2e, the heart of Paris' rag trade and fast becoming the centre of a fledgling dot.com industry.

The Portuguese presence in Paris dates back to the late 19th century. Political refugees were fleeing Portugal up until 1974, but the majority of Portuguese living in greater Paris are workers who helped build the new suburbs.

Turks started arriving in the late 1960s. Of an estimated 45,000 in the greater Paris region, a third are in fact Kurds. They, too, commonly live in the suburbs and commute into Paris.

The city has always been a haven for intellectuals in search of freedom of expression and democracy. Many of the Paris-based Greeks arrived during the colonels' dictatorship (1967-74); exiles from South America settled in the city for similar reasons. Many of the 4500 Lebanese immigrants fled the civil war that began in 1975.

BRENDA TURNNIDGE

Russians have emigrated to Paris throughout the 20th century. Immigration from Poland and other Eastern and Central European countries has also figured largely. In inner Paris there are now some 10,500 immigrants from the former Yugoslavia.

But there's a down side to Paris Mondial. What may appear exotic to the outsider is often tough for those struggling for survival. The truth is that racism exists, especially in Paris' crowded suburbs. In the workplace, young people of non-French origin often face discrimination.

Left: Into the light: leaving church at Greek Orthodox Easter

Belleville (Map 3)

One destination you shouldn't miss is Belleville,
20e (metro Belleville), where Jewish kosher and
Muslim halal butchers share the streets with
cavernous Chinese eating establishments. On
market day the atmosphere is reminiscent of
the Mediterranean, Africa or even Asia – see the
special section 'The Markets of Paris' after the
Places to Eat chapter. Watch the elegant, tur-

baned African women in technicolour boubous brush past frenzied,
upwardly mobile Chinese with mobile phones glued to their ears, and
more relaxed Orthodox Jews wearing yarmulkes alongside North
Africans in jellabas on their way to the mosque.

From Belleville metro station head south on blvd de Belleville. Stay
on the Tunisian (eastern) side of the street, with its many terraced
eateries. Stop at a *pâtisserie cachère* for a piece of kosher pastry or
peek into the synagogue that looks like it has taken over a former
cinema. The Tunisian flower-sellers will be happy to put a bunch of
jasmine behind your ear.

The overstocked shops along the way offer everything from hair prepa-
rations to narghiles (hookahs). Travel agents offer cheap fares to Mecca
and Shanghai. A restaurant sign reminds you to place your Sabbath
orders. A fabric shop displays photographs of beaming, satisfied brides.

You can leave blvd de Belleville by heading east along rue Ram-
poneau or rue Bisson. In the former you'll encounter a Jewish bookshop and a tiny Spanish restaurant specialising in paella and religious
icons, where free meals are offered to the needy, regardless of race or
creed. Go north along rue de Tourtille, which debouches into rue de
Belleville. To the east is a string of Asian restaurants whose names
evoke Thailand and Laos, as well as an Egyptian grocer's called Le
Caire. Heading west will take you back to Belleville metro station.

Top: Echoes of the East:
the Mosquée de Paris in
the 5e

Right: People from all
corners of the globe
meet in Paris Mondial.

If you're hungry for some more, take a detour. At the President, a landmark Chinese restaurant on the other side of the street, turn south again on the blvd de Belleville and turn west at Couronnes metro station into rue Jean-Pierre Timbaud. In the surrounding neighbourhood, you'll discover a mosque, several Islamic bookshops, an Egyptian-style tea and narghile establishment scenting the air with honey-tobacco, an Oriental patisserie and a sprinkling of trendy bars where you can sip on *caipinhas* (a cocktail of Brazilian *cachaça* and lime juice) or Cuban rum-based *mojitos*.

Château Rouge (Map 8)

Jambo Africa! (Welcome to Africa!) The name of a shop in the heart of this district in the 18e says it all. From Château Rouge metro station, turn right past a florist and right again into Marché Dejean, an open market held Tuesday to Sunday at noon where fishmongers offer fresh Senegalese fish alongside stalls selling Caribbean chillies, plantains and dasheen (taro). The numerous exotic food shops evoke places in Africa and the West Indies but are often run by Vietnamese Chinese. In nearby rue des Poissonniers, the 'Fishermen Street' that is anything but, you'll find halal butchers offering special deals on 5kg packets of chicken and the odd sheep's head surveying you as you gingerly scurry past.

The sounds of Africa No 1 radio station (107.5MHz FM) fill the air. Visit the African music shops and listen to the latest in Cameroonian *bikutsi* (a fusion of ancestral rhythms and speedy electric guitars) or Senegalese *mbalax* (popularised by Youssou N'Dour). Look out for posters advertising upcoming concerts; African stars fill Paris' biggest concert halls, such as the Palais Omnisports de Paris-Bercy in the 12e and Le Zénith in the 19e (see Rock in the Entertainment chapter).

The fabric shops of Château Rouge offer the finest Java batik in cuttings of six yards (the British imperial measure being *de rigueur* in African shops to this day). Look at the street names as you wander, recalling the canals that facilitated international commerce a hundred years ago: rue de Panama and rue de Suez.

Left: Exotic delights: Afro-Caribbean food shop in Château Rouge

Night-time is the best time to sample African cuisine here; try Senegalese *tiéboudienne* (smoked fish and rice with vegetables) or *maffé*, a dish of lamb or beef sauteed in peanut sauce.

La Goutte d'Or (Map 8)

You can visit the North African area of 'The Golden Drop' (the name is derived from a vineyard that produced white wine here in the 19th century) in the 18e at the same time as you visit Château Rouge by walking south from rue Myrha, or you can access it from Barbès Rochechouart metro station. At the station, you'll most likely be presented with the calling cards of various mediums or fortune-tellers.

From the station walk north up blvd Barbès, past numerous goldsmiths and fast-food shops, and turn east into rue de la Goutte d'Or. Building in the 1990s took away much of the soul of the area, but some local colour remains. If you're nostalgic for the souk or wish to hone your haggling skills, this is the place to come. You may leave with a set of gaudy tea glasses, a pair of pointy-toed leather *babouches* (slippers) or a belly-dancer's costume.

The sounds of *raï* (a fusion of Algerian folk music and rock) and the king of the genre, Cheb Khaled, fill the air. Radios are tuned to Beur FM (106.7 MHz FM) and Radio Orient (94.3 MHz FM). If you're hungry, this is where you'll find the cheapest couscous (25FF to 30FF) in all of Paris, and there's plenty of choice on rue Myrha. You can snack on Oriental pastries such as baklava or have a bowl of *chorba*, a hearty soup of mutton, chickpeas and vegetables. It is advisable to show a little decorum; many of the smaller restaurants here are the domain of men exiled from their families who like to while away the hours after work sipping mint tea and watching satellite TV direct from Algeria. And don't bother asking for a glass of wine at a couscous or grill restaurant in La Goutte d'Or; these places follow Islamic guidelines and won't serve it. The Mosquée Al-Fath, 55-57 rue Polonceau, 18e, is close to travel agents advertising pilgrimages to Mecca.

Right: World rhythms: the Afro-Cuban All Stars hit their stride in La Villette.

BRENDA TURNNIDGE

If you're in La Goutte d'Or around Ramadan, you'll find a huge selection of Oriental sweets, often sold from makeshift stalls in front of grocer's shops or restaurants. They are used to break the day-long fast at sundown. And try to be here for La Goutte d'Or en Fête at the beginning of July (see Public Holidays & Special Events in the Facts for the Visitor chapter).

Rue du Faubourg Saint Denis (Map 3)

This 2km street in the 10e links Turkey with India. For those wishing to take an Afro-Caribbean beauty detour, there's the possibility of straying off the road to rue du Château d'Eau and blvd de Strasbourg to check out the Afro hairdressers.

From Strasbourg St Denis metro station and the Porte Saint Denis arch walk north along rue du Faubourg Saint Denis, where you'll be offered kebabs, *pide* (Turkish pizza, for want of a better term) and *lahmacun*, thin pitta bread topped with minced meat, tomatoes, onions and fresh parsley – everything 100% halal, of course.

Passage du Prado runs between 12 rue du Faubourg Saint Denis and 18-20 blvd Saint Denis and holds a few surprises. The cheapest haircut in town (40FF) is available here, and there are a couple of Mauritian eateries, Turkish teahouses straight out of the Bosphorus and shops selling Ramadan cards year-round. Peek into doors left ajar and you may wish you hadn't – these are the hidden sweatshops that employ immigrant workers to sew 'designer' labels into the clothes they labour over.

Continue up rue du Faubourg Saint Denis, past Julien, an Art Nouveau extravaganza of a brasserie, to No 46 and the entrance to passage Brady (you can also enter from 58 blvd de Strasbourg, 10e), the heart of Indian Paris. Somewhat decrepit now and eagerly awaiting a face-lift, passage Brady was built in 1828 and housed some 100 tiny boutiques in its heyday in the middle of the 19th century. It's now

Bottom Left & Right: Smash it up: symbolic breaking of coconuts at the annual Fête de Ganesh

the place to buy your curry mixes, *poppams* (poppadoms), ginger root, brinjals (miniature aubergines) and mangoes in season. Back on the street, wall space is shared by posters of Kurdish freedom fighters and African singers.

A few blocks up past an excellent Polish delicatessen and another whose owners speak Slovene, you leave Turkey behind you. Suddenly the grocers betray their British colonial past: traditional British brandnames rub shoulders with naan and *dosai* mixes in the well stacked shopfronts. The names of nearby streets and passages – rue de Paradis, rue de la Fidélité, passage du Désir – suggest that this was once a redlight district.

Rue du Faubourg Saint Denis cuts across blvd Magenta; the first blocks are not very interesting but keep heading north in the direction of La Chapelle metro station. Visit the splendid sari palaces, some of which also stock groceries round the back. Stop for the local speciality, *masala dosas* (stuffed pancakes), or a *vindaloo*. Some of the shops boast the most unusual window displays in the capital: Krishna and Shiva share space with Jesus and Mahatma Gandhi while Eiffel Towers flirt with Taj Mahals.

No trip to Indian Paris would be complete without a visit to the Sri Manikar Vinayakar Alayam, a Hindu temple founded in 1985 and dedicated to the elephant god Ganesh. It's beyond La Chapelle metro station at 72 rue Philippe de Girard and the best time to visit is at the end of August or the beginning of September for the annual Fête de Ganesh.

Asian Paris (Maps 1, 6 & 9)

Apart from the community in Belleville described earlier, there are two major Chinatowns in Paris: rue au Maire (Map 6) and the surrounding narrow lanes south of Arts et Métiers metro station in the 3e, and the

Right: Waving the flag: celebrating the Year of the Rabbit in rue du Temple

BRENDA TURNNIDGE

southern 13e (Map 1) with its Hong Kong-style tower blocks.

Just how many Chinese live in the 3e no-one knows. They have a tight network, speak their own dialect and excel in business (some have even managed to buy out the Jewish wholesale jewellers in nearby rue du Temple). This is where you'll find the cheapest Chinese cuisine in Paris, although the Vietnamese *pho* place in one of Paris' oldest buildings in rue Volta beats the lot. In late January or early February, Paris' most authentic Chinese New Year celebrations are held to the sound of exploding firecrackers (see Public Holidays & Special Events in the Facts for the Visitor chapter). The best place to watch or join in morning *tai chi* or *qi gong* practice is square du Temple (Map 6), just off rue du Temple to the north-east.

In the 13e ethnic Chinese live in tower blocks with Italian names. To visit this area, concentrated around blvd Masséna, ave d'Ivry and ave de Choisy, get off at Tolbiac metro station and walk east along rue de Tolbiac between a pharmacy and a branch of BNP, passing gift shops selling a multitude of smiling Buddhas. At the crossroads (note the excellent Sinorama restaurant in front and the Vietnamese *pho* shop on your left) turn into ave d'Ivry. Suddenly you're in the leafy Saigon of the 1930s: clusters of Asian restaurants beckon and the aromas of lemon grass, fresh limes, spicy coconut-based curries and fragrant rice fill the air.

The Buddhist temples in this area pop up in the most unusual places. Enter the labyrinthine car park beneath the Olympiades shopping centre (Map 9) at 37 rue du Disque, 13e, and continue past the dustbins to a red banner welcoming you to a 'Buddhist altar' deep in the bowels of high-rise Parisian Chinatown.

As in Asia, the shopping centres are crammed with CD shops, ladies' boutiques, bookshops and open-front snack and noodle shops. Try

Bottom Left & Right:
Cambodian New Year is celebrated every April in the Centre Bouddique in the Bois de Vincennes.

BRENDA TURNNIDGE

Vietnamese *bo bun* (salad with spring rolls), *banh xio* (Vietnamese crepes) or *bun rieu* (soup with vermicelli, pork and crab). Even the brasseries are Asian-run and the music played in them is strictly Indo-chinese.

Before leaving, make sure you visit Tang Frères, an enormous Laotian-Chinese food shop. You can find anything here from durian fruit to Chinese wines.

If you wish to visit other Buddhist spiritual centres, head for the Bois de Vincennes, 12e, where you'll find the Centre Bouddique (Buddhist Centre), with temples for both Tibetan and South-East Asian Buddhists. It is housed in the Cameroon building erected for a colonial exhibition held here in 1931, just south of Lac Daumesnil. The Cambodians celebrate New Year – like a Cambodian village festival, with food stalls, delicious home-cooking and live performances – on the second weekend in April.

The Japanese have never been economic immigrants in Paris, but the city continues to attract Japanese students, businesspeople and travellers. Hyper-trendy, peroxide-headed young Japanese who look like serious art students can be seen in Paris' trendiest spots. The authentic restaurants and noodle shops, where the Japanese go, are in and around rue Sainte Anne off ave de l'Opéra, 1er.

Paris des Îles

Top: Out with the old: Buddhist New Year celebrations in the Centre Bouddique

France has five overseas *départements*, including Martinique and Guadeloupe in the Caribbean Antilles and Réunion in the Indian Ocean, as well as three overseas territories in the South Pacific. Very active in the capital's music scene, West Indian musicians know how to add spice to the capital's nights out with their zouk, Haitian *compas*, or their more traditional *biguines* (a cousin of the polka) and roots-style *gwoka*. No particular arrondissement is favoured by *les Antillais* and families often prefer the greener suburbs. There are several good restaurants dotted around the city; head for the 9e or 14e.

Latino Paris

South Americans and people from the Spanish-speaking Caribbean islands are numerous in Paris, but again dispersed throughout the city. Music, dance and national holidays bring them together. If it's tango you're into, head for quai Saint Bernard (Map 5), opposite the Institut du Monde Arabe, 5e, on a hot summer's night at the weekend and tango the moonlit night away. The yearly Fête de la Musique on 21 June often features Latino bands (see Public Holidays & Special Events in the Facts for the Visitor chapter).

Jewish Paris (Map 7)

The Jewish community is concentrated mainly around the Marais in the 4e, specifically in rue des Rosiers, as well as in Belleville and in the area

north of the Grands Boulevards. In the Marais, you can visit a synagogue in rue des Tournelles, galleries exhibiting Jewish artists, bookshops, and Eastern European *traiteurs* and patisseries – not to mention the new Musée d'Art et d'Histoire du Judaïsme (Art and History of Judaism Museum; see Marais in the Things to See & Do chapter). Stop for a quick falafel sandwich or perhaps something more elaborate while in the area but remember that much is closed on Saturday for the Sabbath.

Brenda Turnnidge

Left: A Jewish bakery in the Marais, one of dozens of places for a tasty snack

NEIL SETCHFIELD

Facts for the Visitor

WHEN TO GO
As the old song tells us, Paris is at its best in springtime – though winter-like relapses and heavy rains are not unknown in the otherwise beautiful month of April. Autumn is also pleasant, but of course the days are fairly short. In winter Paris has all sorts of cultural events going on, while in summer the weather is warm – even hot. In August, when Parisians flee for the beaches to the west and south, many restaurateurs lock up and leave town too, but this is changing rapidly and you'll find considerably more places open in summer than even a decade ago.

If you understand French you can find out the weather forecast for the Paris area by calling ☎ 0 836 68 02 75. The national forecast can be heard on ☎ 0 836 70 12 34. Each call costs five *télécarte* (phonecard)

units or 2.23FF per minute. On Minitel, key in 3615 MET or 3617 METPLUS.

To ensure that your trip does (or does not) coincide with a holiday or festival, refer to the Public Holidays & Special Events section later in this chapter.

ORIENTATION
This book gives you three ways to find the addresses mentioned: by map reference, by arrondissement and by metro station.

Arrondissements
Paris is divided into 20 *arrondissements* (districts), which spiral out clockwise from the centre like a conch shell. Paris addresses always include the number of the arrondissement as streets with the same name exist in different districts.

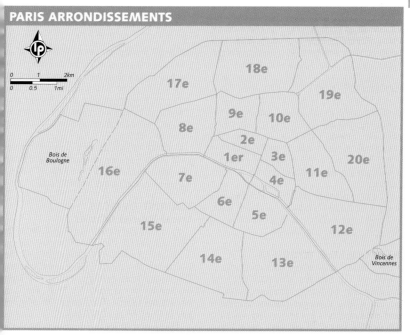

PARIS ARRONDISSEMENTS

In this book, arrondissement numbers are given after the street address using the usual French notation: 1er for *premier* (1st), 2e for *deuxième* (2nd), 3e for *troisième* (3rd) and so on. On some signs or commercial maps, you will see the variations 2ème, 3ème etc.

Metro Stations

There is almost always a metro station within 500m of wherever you want to go in Paris, so all offices, museums, hotels, restaurants and so on included in this book have the nearest metro station given immediately after the contact numbers. Metro stations usually have a useful *plan du quartier* (map of the neighbourhood) on the wall near the exits.

MAPS

The most useful map of Paris you can buy is the 1:10,000 scale *Paris Plan* published by Michelin. It comes in booklet form (No 11 or 14) or as a fold-out sheet (No 10 or 12) for 35FF or, under the name *Atlas Paris 15*, in large format (75FF). The Lonely Planet *Paris City Map* is a handy, laminated product, with a street index, that covers the more popular parts of town in detail.

Many Parisians swear by *Paris par Arrondissement* (57FF), a pocket-sized book that has a double-page hand-drawn street plan of each arrondissement. Others find it confusing, though it does list the appropriate metro station with each street name in the index. A more user-friendly choice is *Paris Practique par Arrondissement* (36FF), a slimmer pocket-sized atlas with a larger format.

The best place to find a full selection of Institut Géographique National (IGN) maps is at the Espace IGN; see Bookshops in the Shopping chapter for details.

RESPONSIBLE TOURISM

Paris already has enough cars clogging its highways and byways. Not only does the ensuing air pollution damage people's health, it also damages historic buildings and monuments – sometimes irrevocably. Do us all a favour: leave your car at home

MARTIN MOOS

Many Parisians use Sunday's traffic-free *quais* to get in some exhaust-free exercise.

and resist the temptation to rent one unless you're touring around the Île de France (see the Excursions chapter). Instead, bring or rent a bike (see Bicycle in the Getting Around chapter), enjoy the city on foot (Paris is an eminently walkable city) and/or use the public transport system – it's cheap and very efficient.

For further tips on how you can reduce your impact on the environment, contact Les Amis de la Nature (☎ 01 46 27 53 56), 197 rue Championnet, 75018 Paris.

TOURIST OFFICES
Local Tourist Offices

Paris' main tourist office (Map 2, ☎ 0 836 68 31 12, fax 01 49 52 53 00, metro George V) is at 127 ave des Champs-Élysées, 8e. It's open daily, except 1 May and Christmas Day, from 9 am to 8 pm (11 am to 7 pm on Sunday in winter). Its Web site is at www.paris-touristoffice.com. On Minitel, key in 3615 or 3617 OTPARIS.

The tourist office has branches (with the

same ☎ and fax) in Gare de Lyon (Map 5), open 8 am to 8 pm Monday to Saturday, and at the base of the Eiffel Tower (Map 4), open 11 am to 6 pm daily from 2 May to September.

For details of the Espace du Tourisme d'Île de France, which is responsible for the areas around Paris, see the Excursions chapter.

Tourist Offices Abroad

French-government tourist offices (usually called Maisons de la France) can provide every imaginable sort of tourist information on Paris, as well as the rest of the country, most of it in the form of brochures. They include:

Australia (☎ 02-9231 5244, fax 9221 8682, @ ifrance@internetezy.com.au) 25 Bligh St, 22nd floor, Sydney, NSW 2000. Open 9 am to 5 pm weekdays.

Belgium (☎ 02-513 5886, fax 514 3375, @ maisondelafrance@pophost.eunet.be) 21 ave de la Toison d'Or, 1050 Brussels. Open 10 am to 5 pm weekdays.

Canada (☎ 514-288 4264, fax 845 4868, @ mfrance@mtl.net) 1981 McGill College Ave, Suite 490, Montreal, Que H3A 2W9. Open 9 am to 4 pm weekdays.

Germany (☎ 069-580 131, fax 745 556, @ maison_de_la_france@t-online.de) West-endstrasse 47, 60325 Frankfurt-am-Main. Open 9 am to 4.30 pm weekdays.

Ireland (☎ 01-679 0813, fax 679 0814, @ frenchtouristoffice@tinet.ie) 10 Suffolk St, Dublin 2. Open 9.30 am to 1.30 pm and 2 to 5 pm weekdays.

Italy (☎ 02 584 86 57, fax 02 58 48 62 22, @ info@turismofrancese.it) Via Larga 7, 20122 Milan. Open 9.30 am to 5.30 pm weekdays.

Netherlands (☎ 0900 112 2332, fax 020-620 3339, @ informatie@fransverkeersbureau.nl) Prinsengracht 670, 1017 KX Amsterdam. Open 10 am to 5 pm weekdays.

Spain (☎ 91 541 8808, fax 91 541 2412, @ maisondelafrance@mad.sericom.es) Alcalá 63, 28014 Madrid. Open 8 am to 3 pm weekdays (9 am to 1.30 pm and 4 to 7 pm outside summer).

Switzerland (☎ 01-211 3085, fax 212 1644, @ tourismefrance@bluewin.ch) Löwenstrasse 59, 8023 Zürich. Open 10 am to 1 pm and 2 to 5.30 pm weekdays.

UK (☎ 020-7399 3500, fax 7493 6594, @ piccadilly@mdlf.demon.co.uk) 178 Piccadilly, London W1V 0AL. Open 10 am to 6 pm Monday to Saturday (to 5 pm on Saturday).

USA (☎ 212-838 7800, fax 838 7855, @ info@francetourism.com) 444 Madison Ave, 16th floor, New York, NY 10022-6903. Open 9 am to 5 pm weekdays. (☎ 310-271 6665, fax 276 2835, @ fgto@gte.net) 9454 Wiltshire Blvd, Suite 715, Beverly Hills, CA 90212-2967

TRAVEL AGENCIES
General

The following agencies are among the largest in Paris and offer the best services and deals:

Forum Voyages (☎ 0 803 83 38 03) Forum has 10 branches in Paris, including one at 11 ave de l'Opéra (Map 6, ☎ 01 42 61 20 20, metro Pyramides) in the 1er and another at 81 blvd Saint Michel (Map 5, ☎ 01 43 25 80 58, metro Luxembourg) in the 5e. They are usually open 9.30 am to 7 pm weekdays and 10 am to 6 pm on Saturday. Forum's Web site is at www.forum-voyages.fr. On Minitel, key in 3615 FV.

Nouvelles Frontières (☎ 0 825 00 08 25) This agency has 14 outlets around the city, including one at 13 ave de l'Opéra (Map 6, metro Pyramides) in the 1er, open 9 am to 8 pm weekdays and to 7 pm on Saturday, and another at 66 blvd Saint Michel (Map 5, metro Luxembourg) in the 6e, open 9 am to 7 pm Monday to Saturday. Its Web site is at www.nouvelles-frontieres.fr. On Minitel, key in 3615 NF.

Voyageurs du Monde (Map 6, ☎ 01 42 86 16 00, metro Pyramides or Quatre Septembre) 55 rue Sainte Anne, 2e. 'World Travellers' is an enormous agency with more than seven departments dealing with different destinations. It's open 9.30 am to 7 pm Monday to Saturday. There's also a good travel bookshop (☎ 01 42 86 17 38) and the agency has its own restaurant next door (☎ 01 49 86 17 17) serving daily specialities from around the world (lunch only). The agency's Web site is at www.vdm.com.fr. On Minitel, key in 3615 VOYAGEURS.

Student

Paris travel agencies that cater for students and young people can supply discount tickets to travellers of all ages. Most issue ISIC student ID cards (60FF) and the Carte Jeunes (120FF), and sell Eurolines tickets.

OTU Voyages (☎ 01 40 29 12 12) Along with its branch opposite the Centre Pompidou (see Accommodation Services in the Places to Stay chapter), this agency has a branch at 39 ave Georges Bernanos (Map 5, ☎ 01 44 41 38 50, metro Port Royal) in the 5e, open 10 am to 6.30 pm weekdays. Its Web site is at www.otu.fr.

usit Connect (☎ 0 825 08 25 25 or 01 42 44 14 00) This Irish-owned agency has four branches in Paris: 6 rue de Vaugirard (Map 5, ☎ 01 42 34 56 90, metro Luxembourg) in the 6e, open 9.30 am (from 10 am on Tuesday) to 6.30 pm weekdays; 14 rue Vivienne (Map 6, ☎ 01 44 55 32 60, metro Bourse) in the 2e, open 9.30 am to 6 pm weekdays (to 8 pm on Thursday in summer); 85 blvd Saint Michel (Map 5, ☎ 01 43 29 69 50, metro Luxembourg) in the 5e, open 10 am to 6 pm Monday to Saturday; and 31 bis rue Linné (Map 5, ☎ 01 44 08 71 20, metro Jussieu), also in the 5e, open noon to 7 pm Monday to Saturday. Its Web site is at www.usitconnect.fr.

Discount

The following are some cyber travel agencies offering discount air fares and package deals:

Anyway	www.anyway.fr
	Minitel 3615 ANYWAY
Dégriftour	www.degriftour.fr
e-mondial	www.e-mondial.com
QXL	www.qxl.fr
Réductour	www.reductour.fr
	Minitel 3615

DOCUMENTS

By law, everyone in France, including tourists, must carry some sort of ID at all times. For foreign visitors, this means a passport or, for citizens of EU countries where they're issued, a national ID card.

Visas

Tourist There are no entry requirements for nationals of EU countries. Citizens of Australia, the USA, Canada, New Zealand and Israel do not need visas to visit France as tourists for up to three months. Except for people from a handful of other European countries (including Switzerland and Poland), everyone else needs a 'Schengen Visa', named after the Schengen Agreement that abolished passport controls among Austria, Belgium, France, Germany, Greece, Italy, Luxembourg, the Netherlands and Portugal. A visa for any of these countries should, in theory, be valid throughout the Schengen area, but it pays to double-check with the embassy or consulate of each country you intend to visit.

Visa fees depend on the current exchange rate, but a transit visa should cost around US$9, a visa valid for stays of up to 30 days about $23 and a single- or multiple-entry visa for up to three months about US$32. You will need your passport (valid for a period of three months beyond the date of your departure from France), a return ticket, proof of sufficient funds to support yourself, proof of pre-arranged accommodation (possibly), two passport-size photos and the visa fee in cash.

If all the forms are in order, your visa will be issued on the spot (though in South Africa visas usually take two days to process). You can also apply for a French visa after arriving in Europe – the fee is the same, but you may not have to produce a return ticket. If you enter France overland, your visa may not be checked at the border, but major problems can arise if you don't have one later on (eg, at the airport as you leave the country).

Long-Stay & Student If you'd like to work or study in France or stay for over three months, apply to the French embassy or consulate nearest where you live for the appropriate sort of *long séjour* (long-stay) visa. Unless you live in the EU, it's extremely difficult to get a visa that will allow you to work in France. For any sort of long-stay visa, begin the paperwork in your home country several months before you plan to leave. Applications cannot usually be made in a third country nor can tourist visas be turned into student visas after you arrive in France. People with student visas can apply for permission to work part-time (inquire at your place of study).

Au Pair For details of au pair visas, which must be arranged *before* you leave home (unless you're a resident of an EU country), see Au Pair Work in the Work section later in this chapter.

Carte de Séjour If you are issued a long-stay visa valid for six or more months, you'll probably have to apply for a *carte de séjour* (residence permit) within eight days of arrival in France. Students of all nationalities must apply for a carte de séjour at the Centre des Étudiants (Map 4, metro Cambronne or Ségur), 13 rue Miollis, 15e. It's open 8.45 am to 4.30 pm weekdays (to 4 pm on Friday).

EU passport-holders seeking a carte de séjour should apply to the visa office in the Salle Europe, which is on the ground floor next to *escalier C* (stairway C) in the Préfecture de Police (Map 6, ☎ 01 53 71 51 68 or 0 836 67 22 22, metro Cité), 1 place Louis Lépine, 4e. On Minitel, key in 3611 PREFECTURE DE POLICE. It opens 8.30 am to 4.30 pm weekdays (to 4 pm on Friday).

Foreigners with non-EU passports must go to specific offices, depending on the arrondissement in which they're staying:

1er, 2e, 3e, 4e, 5e, 10e, 19e
  Hôtel de Police, 80 blvd de Sébastopol, 3e (metro Réaumur-Sébastopol)
6e, 7e, 13e, 14e, 15e, 16e
  Hôtel de Police, 114-116 ave du Maine, 14e (metro Gaîté)
8e, 9e, 17e, 18e
  Hôtel de Police, 19-21 rue Truffaut, 17e (metro Place de Clichy or La Fourche)
11e, 12e, 20e
  Hôtel de Police, 163 rue de Charenton, 12e (metro Reuilly Diderot)

All are open 9 am to 4.30 pm weekdays (to 4 pm on Friday).

Visa Extensions Tourist visas *cannot* be extended except in emergencies (eg, medical problems). If you're in Paris and have an urgent problem, you should call the Préfecture de Police (☎ 01 53 71 51 68) for guidance.

If you don't need a visa to visit France, you'll almost certainly qualify for another automatic three-month stay if you take the train to, say, Geneva or Brussels and then re-enter France. The fewer recent French entry stamps you have in your passport the easier this is likely to be.

If you needed a visa the first time around, one way to extend your stay is to go to a French consulate in a neighbouring country and apply for another there.

Travel Insurance

You should seriously consider taking out travel insurance. This not only covers you for medical expenses and luggage theft or loss but also for cancellation or delays in your travel arrangements. Cover depends on your insurance and type of airline ticket, so ask both your insurer and your ticket-issuing agency to explain where you stand. Ticket loss is also covered by travel insurance. Citizens of EU countries on public health-insurance schemes should note that they're generally covered by reciprocal arrangements in France (see the Health section for more details).

Paying for your airline ticket with a credit card often provides limited travel-accident insurance, and you may be able to reclaim the payment if the operator doesn't deliver. In the UK, for instance, institutions issuing credit cards are required by law to reimburse consumers if a company goes into liquidation and the amount in contention is more than UK£100. Ask your credit-card company what it's prepared to cover.

Driving Licence & Permits

If you don't hold a European driving licence and plan to drive – God forbid! – in Paris, obtain an International Driving Permit (IDP) from your local motoring association before you leave – you'll need a passport photo and a valid licence. IDPs are usually inexpensive and valid for one year only. An IDP is not valid unless accompanied by your original driver's licence.

Hostel Card

A Hostelling International (HI) card is necessary only at official *auberges de jeunesse* (youth hostels), of which there are only two in central Paris, but it may get you small discounts at other hostels. If you don't pick one up before leaving home, you can buy one at almost any official French hostel for 70/100FF (depending on whether you're under 26/over 26 years of age). One-night membership (where available) costs 19FF, and a family card is 150FF. See the HI Web site at www.iyhf.org for further information.

Student, Youth & Teachers' Cards

An International Student Identity Card (ISIC) can pay for itself through half-price admissions, discounted air and ferry tickets, and cheap meals in student cafeterias. You must be a student and many places stipulate a maximum age, usually 24 or 25. In Paris, ISIC cards are issued by OTU and other student travel agencies for 60FF (see the Travel Agencies section in the Getting There & Away chapter). Visit the ISIC Web site at www.isic.org.

If you're aged under 26 but not a student, you can apply for a GO25 card issued by the Federation of International Youth Travel Organisations (FIYTO; 60FF), which entitles you to much the same discounts as an ISIC and is also issued by student unions and student travel agencies.

A Carte Jeunes (120FF) is available to anyone aged under 26 who has been in France for at least six months. It gets you discounts on things like air tickets, car rental, sports events, concerts and films. In France, details are available on ☎ 0 803 00 12 26; on Minitel, key in 3615 CARTE JEUNES.

Teachers, professional artists, museum conservators and certain categories of student are admitted to some museums free. Bring along proof of affiliation – for example, an International Teacher Identity Card (ITIC; 60FF from OTU).

Seniors' Cards

Reduced entry prices are charged for people aged over 60 at most cultural centres, including museums, galleries and public theatres. SNCF issues the Carte Senior to those aged over 60, which gives reductions of 25% to 50% on train tickets. It costs 140FF for a card (photo required) valid for purchasing four train tickets or 285FF for a card valid for one year.

Copies

The hassles brought on by losing your passport can be considerably reduced if you have a record of its number and issue date or, even better, photocopies of the relevant data pages. It's also a good idea to make photocopies of your credit cards, airline ticket and other travel documents, and a photocopy of your birth certificate can also be useful. Also make a note of the serial numbers of your travellers cheques (cross them off as you cash them). Keep all this emergency material separate from your passport, cheques and cash, and leave extra copies with someone you can rely on back home. Add some emergency money, say the equivalent of US$50 in cash, to this separate stash as well. If you do lose your passport, notify the police immediately to get a statement, and contact your nearest consulate.

Remember that you can store and protect vital information that you may need to access while travelling in the eKno 'virtual' travel vault (www.ekno.lonelyplanet.com).

EMBASSIES & CONSULATES
French Embassies & Consulates

Almost all of the French embassies listed below have information posted on the Web at www.france.diplomatie.fr.

Australia
Embassy: (☎ 02-6216 0100, fax 6216 0127, ✆ embassy@france.net.au) 6 Perth Ave, Yarralumla, ACT 2600
Consulate: (☎ 02-9262 5779, fax 9283 1210, ✆ cgsydney@france.net.au) 20th floor, St Martin's Tower, 31 Market St, Sydney, NSW 2000

Belgium
Embassy: (☎ 02-548 8711, fax 513 6871, ✆ amba@ambafrance.be) 65 rue Ducale, 1000 Brussels
Consulate: (☎ 02-229 8500, fax 229 8510, ✆ consulat.france@skynet.bruxelles.be) 12A place de Louvain, 1000 Brussels

Canada
Embassy: (☎ 613-789 1795, fax 562 3735, ✉ consulat@amba-ottowa.fr) 42 Sussex Drive, Ottawa, Ont K1M 2C9
Consulate: (☎ 416-925 8041, fax 925 3076, ✉ fsltto@direct.com) 130 Bloor St West, Suite 400, Toronto, Ont M5S 1N5

Germany
Embassy: (☎ 030-20 63 90 00, fax 20 63 90 10) Kochstrasse 6-7, 10969 Berlin
Consulate: (☎ 030-88 59 02 43, fax 882 52 95) Kurfürstendamm 211, 10719 Berlin

Ireland
Embassy: (☎ 01-260 1666, fax 283 0178, ✉ consul@ambafrance.ie) 36 Ailesbury Rd, Ballsbridge, Dublin 4

Italy
Embassy: (☎ 06 68 60 11, fax 06 686 01 360, ✉ france-italia@france-italia.it) Piazza Farnese 67, 00186 Rome
Consulate: (☎ 06 688 06 437, fax 06 686 01 260, ✉ consulfrance-rome@iol.it) Via Giulia 251, 00186 Rome

Netherlands
Embassy: (☎ 070-312 5800, fax 312 5854) Smidsplein 1, 2514 BT The Hague.
Consulate: (☎ 020-624 8346, fax 626 0841, ✉ consulfr@euronet.nl) Vijzelgracht 2, 1000 HA Amsterdam

New Zealand
(☎ 04-384 2555, fax 384 2577, ✉ consulfrance@actrix.gen.nz) Rural Bank Building, 34-42 Manners St, Wellington

Spain
Embassy: (☎ 91 423 8900, fax 91 423 8901) Calle de Salustiano Olozaga 9, 28001 Madrid
Consulate: (☎ 91 700 7800, fax 91 700 7801, ✉ creire@consulfrance-madrid) Calle Marques de la Enseñada 10, 28004 Madrid

Switzerland
Embassy: (☎ 031-359 2111, fax 352 2191, ✉ ambassade.fr@iprolink.ch) Schlosshaldenstrasse 46, 3006 Berne
Consulate: (☎ 01-268 8585, fax 268 8500, ✉ consulat.france.zurich@swissonline.ch), Mühlebachstrasse 7, 8008 Zürich

UK
Embassy: (☎ 020-7201 1000, fax 7201 1004, ✉ press@ambafrance.org) 58 Knightsbridge, London SW1X 7JT
Consulate: (☎ 020-7838 2000, fax 7838 2018) 21 Cromwell Rd, London SW7 2EN. The visa section is at 6A Cromwell Place, London SW7 2EW (☎ 020-7838 2051).

USA
Embassy: (☎ 202-944 6000, fax 944 6166, ✉ visas-washington@amb-wash.fr) 4101

Reservoir Rd NW, Washington, DC 20007
Consulate: (☎ 212-606 3688, fax 606 3620, ✉ visa@franceconsulatny.org) 934 Fifth Ave, New York, NY 10021

Embassies & Consulates in Paris

It's important to realise what your embassy can and cannot do to help you if you get into trouble. Generally speaking, it won't be much help in emergencies if the trouble you're in is remotely your own fault. Remember that you are bound by French law while travelling in France.

In genuine emergencies you might get some assistance, but only if other channels have been exhausted. For example, if you need to get home urgently, a free ticket home is exceedingly unlikely – the embassy would expect you to have travel insurance. If you have all your money and documents stolen, the embassy will assist with getting a new passport, but a loan for onward travel is almost always out of the question.

The locations of most of the embassies and consulates listed below are indicated on the colour maps at the back of the book. To find an embassy or consulate not listed here, consult the *Pages Jaunes* (Yellow Pages) under 'Ambassades et Consulats'.

Australia
(Map 4, ☎ 01 40 59 33 00, metro Bir Hakeim) 4 rue Jean Rey, 15e. The consular section opens 9.15 am to noon and 2 to 4.30 pm Monday to Friday.

Belgium
(☎ 01 44 09 39 39, metro Charles de Gaulle-Étoile) 9 rue de Tilsitt, 17e

Canada
(Map 2, ☎ 01 44 43 29 00, metro Franklin D Roosevelt) 35 ave Montaigne, 8e. Consular services are available 9 am to noon and 2 to 5 pm weekdays.

Germany
Embassy: (☎ 01 53 83 45 00, ✉ ambassade@amb-allemagne.fr, metro Franklin D Roosevelt) 13 ave Franklin D Roosevelt, 8e
Consulate: (☎ 01 53 83 45 00, metro Iéna) 34 ave d'Iéna, 16e

Ireland
(Map 2, ☎ 01 44 17 67 00, or 01 44 17 67 67 after hours, Minitel 3615 IRLANDE, metro Argentine) 4 rue Rude, 16e. The chancellery

opens 9.30 am to noon Monday to Friday or by appointment.

Italy
Embassy: (☎ 01 49 54 03 00, metro Rue du Bac) 51 rue de Varenne, 7e
Consulate: (☎ 01 44 30 47 00, metro La Muette) 5 blvd Émile Augier, 16e

Netherlands
(☎ 01 40 62 33 00, metro Saint François Xavier) 7 rue Eblé, 7e

New Zealand
(Map 2, ☎ 01 45 01 43 43, metro Victor Hugo) 7 ter rue Léonard de Vinci, 16e. Consular services are available 9 am to 1 pm and 2 to 5.30 pm weekdays (8.30 am to 2 pm on Friday in July and August).

South Africa
(Map 4, ☎ 01 53 59 23 23, metro Invalides) 59 quai d'Orsay, 7e

Spain
(☎ 01 44 43 18 00, metro Alma Marceau) 22 ave Marceau, 8e

Switzerland
(☎ 01 49 55 67 00, metro Varenne) 142 rue de Grenelle, 7e

UK
Embassy: (Map 2, ☎ 01 44 51 31 00, ✆ ambassade@amb-grandebretagne.fr, metro Concorde) 35 rue du Faubourg Saint Honoré, 8e
Consulate: (Map 2, ☎ 01 44 51 31 02, metro Concorde) 18 bis rue d'Anjou, 8e. The consulate opens 9 am to noon and 2.30 to 5 pm.

USA
Embassy: (Map 2, ☎ 01 43 12 22 22, ✆ ambassade@amb-usa.fr, metro Concorde) 2 ave Gabriel, 8e
Consulate: (Map 2, ☎ 01 43 12 23 47, metro Concorde) 2 rue Saint Florentin, 1er. The American Services Section opens 9 am to 3 pm weekdays.

CUSTOMS

The usual allowances apply to duty-free goods purchased at airports or on ferries originating outside the EU: 200 cigarettes, 50 cigars or 250g of loose tobacco; 1L of strong liquor or 2L of less than 22% alcohol by volume, *and* 2L of wine; 500g of coffee (or 200g of extracts) *and* 100g of tea (or 40g of tea extracts); and 50g of perfume *and* 0.25L of eau de toilette.

Do not confuse these with *duty-paid* items (including alcohol and tobacco) bought at normal shops and supermarkets in another EU country and brought into France, where

certain goods might be more expensive. Then the allowances are more than generous: 800 cigarettes, 200 cigars or 1kg of loose tobacco; and 10L of spirits (more than 22% alcohol by volume), 20L of fortified wine or aperitif, 90L of wine or 110L of beer.

Note that duty-free shopping within the EU has been abolished. This means that you can still enter an EU country with duty-free items from countries outside the EU, but that you can't buy duty-free goods in, say, France and take them to the UK.

MONEY
Currency

The national currency is the French franc, abbreviated in this book to FF. One franc (1FF) is divided into 100 centimes.

French coins come in denominations of 5, 10, 20 and 50 centimes (0.5FF) and 1FF, 2FF, 5FF, 10FF and 20FF. Banknotes are issued in denominations of 20FF, 50FF, 100FF, 200FF and 500FF. It can be difficult getting change for a 500FF note.

Exchange Rates

Exchange rates at the time of research were:

country	unit		francs
Australia	A$1	=	4.21FF
Canada	C$1	=	4.95FF
euro	€1	=	6.56FF
Germany	DM1	=	3.35FF
Japan	¥100	=	6.89FF
New Zealand	NZ$1	=	3.13FF
UK	UK£1	=	10.63FF
USA	US$1	=	7.29FF

Exchanging Money

Changing or accessing your money presents few problems in Paris.

Cash In general, cash is not a very good way to carry money. Not only can it be stolen, but in France it doesn't attract an optimal exchange rate. The Banque de France, for instance, France's central bank, usually pays about 2.5% above its quoted rate for travellers cheques, more than making up for the 1% commission usually charged for buying the cheques in the first place.

euro currency converter   10FF = €1.52

Bring along the equivalent of about US$100 in low-denomination notes, which make it easier to change small sums of money if necessary (eg, at the end of your stay).

Travellers Cheques & Eurocheques

The most flexible travellers cheques are those issued by American Express (AmEx; in US dollars or French francs) and Visa (in French francs), as they can be changed at many post offices. Keep a record of cheque numbers, where they were purchased and which ones you've cashed separate from the cheques themselves.

AmEx offices don't charge commission on their own travellers cheques (though they charge 4% on other brands). If your AmEx travellers cheques are lost or stolen in Paris, call ☎ 0 800 90 86 00, a 24-hour toll-free number. Reimbursements can be made at the main AmEx office (Map 2, ☎ 01 47 77 77 75, metro Auber or Opéra), 11 rue Scribe, 9e, from 9.30 am to 6.30 pm weekdays and from 10 am to 5.30 pm on Saturday. Other AmEx outlets are at 38 ave de Wagram, 8e (Map 2, ☎ 01 42 27 58 80), and at 26 ave de l'Opéra, 1er (Map 6, ☎ 01 53 29 40 39).

If you lose your Thomas Cook cheques, contact any Thomas Cook bureau – for example, the one in Gare du Nord (Map 3, ☎ 01 42 80 11 50), open 6 am to 11 pm daily, or the one at 4 blvd Saint Michel, 6e (Map 6, ☎ 01 46 34 23 81) – for replacements. Thomas Cook's customer service bureau can be contacted toll-free on ☎ 0 800 90 83 30.

Eurocheques, available if you have a European bank account, are guaranteed up to a certain limit. When cashing them (eg, at post offices), you will be asked to show your Eurocheque card bearing your signature and registration number, and perhaps a passport or ID card. Eurocheques are not very popular with shops and hotels because of the bank charges attached.

ATMs Automatic teller machines (ATMs), which are known as DABs (*distributeurs automatiques de billets*) or *points d'argent*

Bonjour Euro, Adieu Franc

You'll come across two sets of prices at hotels, restaurants, department stores and so on while visiting Paris. Since 1999 both the franc and Europe's new currency – the euro – have been legal tender, and businesses must now list prices in both currencies. Along with the franc, the currencies of 10 other EU members are being phased out as part of European Monetary Union; the advent of the cash euro will end the 650-year reign of the franc, which began in 1360 when King Jean le Bon struck coins to signify that his part of France was *franc des anglois* (free of English domination).

Euro coins and banknotes will be introduced in January 2002; before that time payment in euros can only be made by credit card or cheque. Both the euro and the franc will remain in circulation until July 2002, when the franc will be withdrawn and prices displayed in euros only.

Fortunately, the euro has many benefits – cross-border travel will become easier, and prices in the 11 'euro-zone' countries will be immediately comparable. Also, once euro notes and coins are issued, you won't need to change money when travelling within most of the EU.

The EU has a dedicated euro Web site at europa.eu.int/euro, and you can also check the currency converter at www.oanda.com for the latest rates.

Australia	A$1	=	€0.64
Canada	C$1	=	€0.72
France	10FF	=	€1.52 (fixed)
Germany	DM1	=	€0.51 (fixed)
Japan	¥100	=	€1.02
New Zealand	NZ$1	=	€0.50
Spain	100 ptas	=	€0.60 (fixed)
UK	UK£1	=	€1.62
USA	US$1	=	€1.07

FACTS FOR THE VISITOR

in French, can be used to draw on your home bank account at a superior exchange rate. There are plenty of ATMs in Paris linked to the Cirrus, Plus and Maestro networks. Most ATMs will also give you a cash advance on your Visa or MasterCard credit card (see the following section).

euro currency converter €1 = 6.56FF

Some ATMs won't accept PIN codes with more than four digits – ask your bank how to handle this. If you normally remember your PIN code as a string of letters, translate it back into numbers, as keyboards may not have letters indicated.

Credit Cards One of the least expensive ways to take your money with you to France is by credit card. Visa (Carte Bleue) is the most widely accepted credit card in Paris, followed by MasterCard (Eurocard). AmEx cards are useful at more upmarket establishments and allow you to get cash at certain ATMs. In general, all three cards can be used for train travel, restaurant visits and cash advances.

When you get a cash advance against your Visa or MasterCard credit card account, your issuer charges a transaction fee, which can be as high as US$10 *plus* interest; check with your card issuer before leaving home. Also, many banks charge a commission of 30FF or more for an advance. But you can deposit funds into your account ahead of time, effectively turning your credit card into an interest-bearing bank account.

It may be impossible to get a lost Visa or MasterCard reissued until you get home, so two different credit cards are safer than one.

If your Visa card is lost or stolen in Paris, call Carte Bleue on ☎ 0 836 69 08 80 or 0 800 90 20 33 (24 hours). To get a replacement card you'll have to deal with the issuer.

Report a lost MasterCard or Eurocard to Eurocard France (☎ 01 45 67 53 53, 01 45 67 84 84 or 0 800 90 23 90, metro Sèvres Lecourbe), 16 rue Lecourbe, 15e (open 9.30 am to 5.30 pm weekdays).

If your AmEx card is lost or stolen, call ☎ 01 47 77 72 00 or 01 47 77 70 00 (both 24 hours). Replacements can be arranged at any AmEx office (see the earlier Travellers Cheques & Eurocheques section).

A lost Diners Club card should be reported on ☎ 01 49 06 17 50 or 01 47 62 75 75.

International Transfers Telegraphic transfers are not very expensive but, despite their name, can be quite slow. Be sure to specify the name of the bank and the name and address of the branch where you'd like to pick the money up.

It's quicker and easier to have money wired via AmEx, which costs about US$50 for US$1000. Western Union's Money Transfer system (☎ 01 43 54 46 12) and the MoneyGram service (☎ 01 47 58 21 00 or 0 800 90 53 11) used by Thomas Cook are also popular.

Moneychangers Banks, post offices and bureaux de change often give a better rate for travellers cheques than for cash. Paris' train stations and fancy hotels also have exchange facilities, which usually operate in the evening, at the weekend and during public holidays, but the rates are usually poor.

Post offices often offer the best exchange rates, and accept banknotes in various currencies as well as travellers cheques issued by AmEx or Visa. The commission for travellers cheques is 1.5% (minimum 25FF).

The Banque de France used to offer the country's best exchange rates, but nowadays the post offices offer a better deal. Branches open for exchange on weekday mornings only. The bank's headquarters (Map 6, ☎ 01 42 92 22 27, metro Palais Royal-Musée du Louvre) is at 31 rue Croix des Petits Champs, 1er, three blocks north of the Louvre. Other branches include the Bastille branch (Map 7, ☎ 01 44 61 15 30, metro Bastille), 3 bis place de la Bastille, 4e, directly across from Opéra Bastille; the

Money, money, money: bureaux de change are sprinkled liberally throughout Paris.

euro currency converter 10FF = €1.52

Raspail branch (Map 4, ☎ 01 49 54 27 27,
metro Sèvres Babylone), 48 blvd Raspail,
6e; and the Monceau branch (Map 2, ☎ 01
42 27 78 14, metro Monceau), 1 place du
Général Catroux, 17e, a block north of Parc
de Monceau.

Commercial banks usually charge a stiff
20FF to 35FF per foreign-currency transaction (eg, BNP charges 3.3% or a minimum
of 25FF). The rates offered vary, so it pays
to compare. Banks charge something like
22FF to 35FF to cash travellers cheques
(eg, BNP charges 1.5% with a minimum
charge of 25FF). Hours are usually from
8 or 9 am to sometime between 11.30 am
and 1 pm, and from 1.30 or 2 pm to 4.30 or
5 pm, Monday to Friday or Tuesday to Saturday. Exchange services may end half an
hour before closing time.

In Paris, bureaux de change are faster and
easier, open longer hours and give better
rates than most banks. It's best to famil-
iarise yourself with the rates offered by the
post office and compare them with those on
offer at bureaux de change, which are not
generally allowed to charge commissions.
On small transactions, even exchange
places with less-than-optimal rates may
leave you with more francs in your pocket.

Bureaux de change at both of Paris' airports are open 6 or 6.30 am to 11 or 11.30 pm
daily. All of Paris' six major train stations
have bureaux de change – mostly run by
Thomas Cook – but their rates are less than
stellar. Changing money at the bureau-de-
change chains like Chequepoint and Exact
Change is only slightly less foolish than making your travellers cheques into paper aero-
planes and launching them into the Seine;
they offer about 10% less than a fair rate.

When using bureaux de change, shop
around and beware of the small print – for
example, some bureaux on the rue de Rivoli
specialise in offering good rates that only
apply if you're changing the equivalent of
US$3000 or more. The CCF (☎ 01 49 52 53
47) exchange office at the main tourist office
takes no commission, offers a decent rate
and is open 9 am to 7.30 pm daily.

Among some of the better bureaux de
change are the following:

Louvre (Maps 2 & 6)
Paris Vision (Map 2, ☎ 01 42 60 30 01, metro
Tuileries) 214 rue de Rivoli, 1er. Open 7 am to
10 pm daily (to 9 pm outside summer).
Le Change du Louvre (Map 6, ☎ 01 42 97 27
28, metro Palais Royal-Musée du Louvre) 151
rue Saint Honoré, 1er, on the north side of Le
Louvre des Antiquaires. Open 10 am to 6 pm
weekdays, 10.30 am to 4.30 pm on Saturday.
Le Change de Paris (Map 2, ☎ 01 42 60 30 84,
metro Tuileries) 2 place Vendôme, 1er. Open
10 am to 6 pm Monday to Saturday.

Les Halles (Map 6)
Best Change (☎ 01 42 21 46 05, metro Louvre-
Rivoli) 21 rue du Roule, 1er, three blocks
south-west of Forum des Halles. Open 10 am
to 8 pm Monday to Saturday.

Latin Quarter (Map 6)
La Société Touristique de Service (STS;
☎ 01 43 54 76 55, metro Saint Michel)
2 place Saint Michel, 6e. Open 9 am to 9 pm
Monday to Saturday and 11 am to 8 pm on
Sunday.
Change de Paris (☎ 01 46 34 70 46) 1 rue
Hautefeuille, 6e, near the southern end of
place Saint Michel. Open 9 am to 9 pm daily.

Champs-Élysées & Madeleine (Map 2)
Bureau de Change (☎ 01 42 25 38 14, metro
Franklin D Roosevelt) 25 ave des Champs-
Élysées, 8e. Open 9 am to 8 pm daily.
Office de Change de Paris (☎ 01 42 66 25 33,
metro Madeleine or Concorde) 13 rue Royale,
8e, near La Madeleine. Open 9 am to 6 pm
weekdays and from 10 am on Saturday.
Thomas Cook (☎ 01 47 20 25 41, metro
George V) 125 ave des Champs-Élysées, 8e,
next to the main tourist office. Open 9.15 am
to 7.15 pm weekdays, 10 am to 10 pm at the
weekend.

Montmartre (Map 8)
Bureau de Change (☎ 01 42 52 67 19, metro
Abbesses) 6 rue Yvonne Le Tac, 18e. Open
10 am to 6.30 pm weekdays and 10.30 am to
6 pm on Saturday (and Sunday from June to
September).

Security
Overall Paris is a pretty safe city but pickpocketing can be a problem (see the Dangers & Annoyances section later in this
chapter). Don't carry more money than you
need, and keep your credit cards, passport

euro currency converter €1 = 6.56FF

and other documents in a concealed pouch or in a hotel safe or safe-deposit box. Always keep some spare travellers cheques or cash in a safe place for an emergency.

Costs

If you stay in a hostel or in a showerless, toiletless room in a bottom-end hotel and have picnics rather than dining out, it is possible to stay in Paris for the equivalent of US$35 a day per person. A couple staying in a two-star hotel and eating one cheap restaurant meal each day should count on spending at least US$65 a day per person. Eating out frequently, ordering wine and treating yourself to any of the many luxuries on offer in Paris will increase these figures considerably.

Discounts Museums, cinemas, the SNCF, ferry companies and other institutions offer all sorts of price breaks to people under the age of 26 (ie, holders of a GO25 card or Carte Jeunes), students with ISIC cards (age limits may apply) and seniors (*le troisième age*; ie, people aged over 60 or, in some cases, 65). Look for the words *demi-tarif* or *tarif réduit* (half-price tariff or reduced rate) on rate charts and then ask if you qualify.

Those aged under 18 get an even wider range of discounts, including free entry to the *musées nationaux* (national museums run by the government). For information on the Carte Musées et Monuments, which allows entry to around 70 places in Paris and the Île de France, see the boxed text 'Ah, la Carte!' in the Things to See & Do chapter.

Tipping & Bargaining

French law requires that restaurant, café and hotel bills include the service charge, which is usually between 12% and 15%. A word of warning: *service compris* (service included, often abbreviated to *s.c.* at the bottom of a restaurant bill) means that the service charge is built into the price of each dish; *service non-compris* (service not included) or *service en sus* (service in addition) means that the service charge is calculated *after* the food and drink you've ordered has been added up. In either case

you pay only the total of the bill so a *pour boire* (tip) on top of that is neither necessary nor expected in most cases. However, mos people leave a few francs in restaurants, un less the service was very bad. They rarely tip in cafés and bars when they've just had a coffee or a drink. In taxis, the usual tip is 2FF no matter what the fare, with the max imum about 5FF.

People in France rarely bargain except a flea markets.

Taxes & Refunds

France's TVA (*taxe sur la valeur agoutée* sales tax) is now 19.6% on most goods except medicine and books, for which it's 5.5%. Prices that include TVA are often marked *TTC* (*toutes taxes comprises*; literally 'all taxes included').

If you are not an EU resident, you can get a TVA refund provided that: you're over 15; you'll be spending less than six months in France; you purchase goods (not more than 10 of the same item) worth at least 1200FF (tax included) at a single shop; and the shop offers *vente en détaxe* (duty-free sales). Present a passport at the time of purchase and ask for a *bordereau de vente à l'exportation* (export sales invoice). Most shops will refund 12% or 13% of the purchase price rather than the full 17% you are entitled to in order to cover the time and expense involved in the refund procedure. As you leave France or another EU country, have all three pages (yellow, pink and green) of the bordereau validated by the country's customs officials at the airport or border. The officials will take the yellow and pink sheets and the stamped self-addressed envelope provided by the shop; the green sheet is your receipt. The pink sheet is then sent to the shop where you made your purchase, which will then make a *virement* (fund transfer) in the form you have requested, such as by cheque (in francs) or directly into your account. Be prepared for waits of up to three months.

For more information contact the customs information centre at ☎ 01 53 24 68 24.

Instant Refunds If you're flying out of Orly or Roissy Charles de Gaulle, certain

hops (which have arrangements with Trav-
lex, the company with the exchange con-
cessions at the airports) can arrange for you
to receive your refund as you're leaving the
country. You must make all the arrangements at the time of purchase.

When you arrive at the airport you have
to do three things:

- Up to three hours before your long-haul flight
  leaves (two hours for other flights), bring your
  bordereau, passport, air ticket and the things you
  purchased (keep them apart from your checked-
  in luggage) to the *douane* (customs) office so
  that they can stamp all three pages of the bordereau (one of which they'll keep).
- Go to an Aéroports de Paris (ADP) information
  counter, where they will check the figures and
  again stamp the pages of the bordereau.
- Go to the *douane de détaxe* (customs refund)
  window or the bureau de change indicated on
  your bordereau (open 24 hours) to pick up your
  refund.

POST & COMMUNICATIONS
Post
Most post offices in Paris are open 8 am to
7 pm weekdays and till noon on Saturday.
Tabacs (tobacconists) usually sell postage
stamps.

The main post office (Map 6, ☎ 01 40 28
20 00, metro Sentier or Les Halles), 52 rue
du Louvre, 1er, five blocks north of the east
end of the Louvre, is open 24 hours, seven
days a week, but only for sending mail,
telegrams and domestic faxes and for picking up poste restante mail (window No 6;
3FF per letter). Other services, including
currency exchange, are available only during regular opening hours. Be prepared for
long queues after 7 pm. Poste restante mail
not specifically addressed to a particular
branch post office will be delivered here.

The post office branch (Map 2, ☎ 01 53
89 05 80, metro George V) at 71 ave des
Champs-Élysées, 8e, has somewhat extended hours (8 am to 7.30 pm weekdays,
10 am to 7 pm on Saturday); here you can
send letters, telegrams and faxes and
change money.

Each arrondissement has its own five-
digit postcode, formed by prefixing the arrondissement number with '750' or '7500'

(eg, 75001 for the 1st arrondissement,
75019 for the 19th). The only exception is
the 16th, which has two postcodes: 75016
and 75116. All mail to addresses in France
must include the postcode. The abbreviation
'CEDEX' after the postcode and the word
'Paris' simply means that mail sent to that
address is collected at the post office rather
than delivered to the door.

Postal Rates Domestic letters up to 20g
cost 3FF. Postcards and letters up to 20g
cost 3FF within the EU; 3.80FF to the rest
of Europe; 3.90FF to Africa; 4.40FF to the
USA, Canada and the Middle East; and
5.20FF to Australasia. Packages weighing
over 2kg are handled by the *poste principale*
(main post office) of each arrondissement.

Telephone
Some three decades ago, Paris had one of the
worst telephone systems in Western Europe
and people still sent messages to one another
via the *pneumatique*, a system of vacuum
tubes that dispersed telegrams throughout the
city. But thanks to massive investment in the
late 1970s and early 1980s, the city now has
one of the most modern and sophisticated
telecommunications systems in the world.

A Parisian postbox, with destinations shown
under each slot for stress-free letter-sending

euro currency converter €1 = 6.56FF

Calling Paris To call the Paris area from outside France, dial your country's international access code, then 33 (France's country code), and then the 10-digit local number, omitting the initial 0.

Domestic Calls Local calls are quite cheap – costing from 0.74FF (from a home phone, 0.81FF from a phone box) for the first three minutes – depending on the time the call is made, the length of time taken and the distance covered. Additional minutes cost 0.14FF to 0.28FF. There are no area codes in France – you always dial the 10-digit number. Paris numbers always start with 01.

Note that while numbers beginning with 0 800 (*numéro vert*) are toll-free in France, other, similar numbers are not. A *numéro azur* (0 801, 0 810) is charged at local rates while a *numéro indigo* can cost 0.79FF (0 802, 0 820) or 0.99FF (0 803, 0 825) per minute. The ubiquitous 0 836 numbers (such as the SNCF's national information number) are always billed at 2.23FF per minute, whenever you call.

Calling Abroad To call someone outside France, dial the international access code (00), the country code, the area code (without the initial zero if there is one) and the local number. International direct dial (IDD) calls to almost anywhere in the world can be placed from public telephones.

To make a reverse-charges (collect) or person-to-person call, dial 00 then 33 plus the country code of the place you're calling (for the USA and Canada, dial 11 instead of 1).

For directory enquiries concerning numbers outside France, dial 00 then 33 12 and finally the relevant country code (again, 11 instead of 1 for the USA and Canada). But be careful when using this service from a private line: it costs a breathtaking 11.13FF. Consult the phone book on the Web (www.pagesi.com) or Minitel (3617 PAGES I) instead.

International Rates Daytime calls to other parts of Europe cost from 1.70FF to 3.60FF a minute. Reductions of from 20%

generally apply Monday to Thursday from 7 pm to 8 am, from 7 pm on Friday to 8 am on Monday, and all day on public holidays.

Full-price calls to continental USA and Canada are 1.70FF a minute on weekdays from 1 to 7 pm. The price then drops to 1.25FF. The rate to Alaska, Hawaii, Puerto Rico and the Virgin Islands is a whopping 9.30FF a minute (7.40FF discount rate).

Full-price calls to Australia, New Zealand, Japan and Hong Kong are 4.30FF a minute (discount rate 3.40FF). To Singapore the full/discount rates are 5.50/4.40FF.

Calls to other parts of Asia and non Francophone Africa are generally 9.30/7.40FF a minute. To South America count on 5.50/4.40FF.

Public Phones Almost all public telephones in Paris require phonecards, which can be purchased at post offices, tabacs, supermarket check-out counters, SNCF ticket windows, metro stations and anywhere you see a blue sticker reading '*télécarte en vente ici*'. Cards worth 50/120 calling units cost 49/97.50FF.

Many cafés and restaurants have privately owned and coin-operated Point Phones. To find a Point Phone, look for a blue-on-white window sticker bearing the Point Phone emblem.

All public phones except Point Phones can receive both domestic and international calls. If you want someone to call you back just give them France's country code and the 10-digit number, usually written after the words '*Ici le ...*' or '*No d'appel*' on the tariff sheet or on a little sign inside the phone box. When there's an incoming call the words '*décrochez – appel arrivé*' will appear in the LCD window.

For France Telecom's *service des renseignements* (directory enquiries or assistance), dial ☎ 12. Don't be surprised if the operator does not speak English. The call is free from a public phone and 3.73FF to 4.46FF from a private phone, depending on the time of day.

Telephone Cards You can buy prepaid phonecards in France that are better value or calling abroad than the standard télé-carte. Carte Intercall Monde, Carte Astuce and Eagle Télécom International are among the more popular cards, and all reduce standard French international call rates by up to 50%. They're available in 50FF and 100FF denominations from tabacs, newsagents, phone shops and other sales points, especially in ethnic areas such as rue du Faubourg Saint Denis (10e), Chinatown (13e) and Belleville (19e & 20e). A card worth 100FF will buy you up to 400 minutes of chat to the UK, 300 minutes to the USA and 220 minutes to Australia.

Lonely Planet's eKno Communication Card is aimed specifically at independent travellers and provides budget international calls, a range of messaging services, free email and travel information – for local calls, you're usually better off with a local card. You can join on-line at www.ekno .lonelyplanet.com, or by phone from Paris by dialling ☎ 0 800 91 26 77. Once you've joined, dial ☎ 0 800 91 20 66 to use eKno from France.

Country Direct Services Country Direct lets you phone home by billing the long-distance carrier you use at home. The numbers can be dialled from public phones without inserting a phonecard; with some models, you're meant to dial even if there's no dial tone. The numbers listed below will connect you, free of charge, with an operator in your home country:

Australia	(Telstra)	☎ 0 800 99 00 61
	(Optus)	☎ 0 800 99 20 61
Canada		☎ 0 800 99 00 16
		☎ 0 800 99 02 16
Ireland		☎ 0 800 99 03 53
New Zealand		☎ 0 800 99 00 64
UK	(BT)	☎ 0 800 99 00 44
		☎ 0 800 99 02 44
		☎ 0 800 99 60 44
	(Mercury)	☎ 0 800 99 09 44
USA	(AT&T)	☎ 0 800 99 00 11
		☎ 0 800 99 00 12
	(MCI)	☎ 0 800 99 00 19
	(Sprint)	☎ 0 800 99 00 87
	(IDB)	☎ 0 800 99 00 13

Mobile Phones France uses GSM 900/1800, which is compatible with the rest of Europe and Australia but not with the North American GSM 1900 (though some North Americans have GSM 1900/900 phones that do work in France) or the totally different system in Japan. If you have a GSM phone, check with your service provider about using it in France, and beware of calls being routed internationally.

A prepaid Mobicarte is a cheaper alternative. Sold by France Telecom, this package deal costs about 270FF and includes a cellular phone, a local cellular phone number and 144FF of prepaid connection time. For more time you can buy a recharge card for 70FF, 140FF or 250FF (including 30FF extra talk time) from tabacs and other places you'd buy a télécarte. Per-minute costs depend on which rate scheme you choose; the *classique* plan charges you 4.20FF per minute (24 hours). There are also schemes geared towards heavy evening and weekend use. Check out the Mobicarte Web site at www.mobicarte.tm.fr.

Minitel Minitel is a screen-based information service peculiar to France that was set up by the Socialist government in the 1980s. It's useful but can be expensive to use, and the growing popularity of the Internet is giving Minitel a run for its money. The most basic variety, with a B&W monitor and a clumsy keyboard, is free to telephone subscribers. Newer Minitel models have colour screens, and many people now access the system using a home computer and a modem.

Minitel numbers consist of four digits and a string of letters. Home users pay a per-minute access charge, but consulting the *annuaire* (directory) is free. Most of the Minitel terminals in post offices are also free for directory inquiries (though some require a 1FF or 2FF coin), and many of them can access pay-as-you-go on-line services.

Fax

Most Paris post offices and telephone shops can send and receive domestic and international faxes. It costs 13FF to send a one-page

FACTS FOR THE VISITOR

fax within France. Prices vary for international faxes depending on the destination but count on 60FF to 75FF per page.

Email & Internet Access

Some 80 post offices in Paris have Cyberposte Internet centres where a rechargeable chip card costs 50FF for one hour's connection time. When the card's exhausted you can recharge it for 30FF, good for a second hour and the use of a printer. The centres are generally open 9 am to 7 pm weekdays and till noon on Saturday, including the one at the main post office north of the Louvre (see the previous Post section). For a complete list check out www.cyberposte.com on the Web.

Commercial cybercafés in Paris include the following:

Café Orbital (Map 5, ☎ 01 43 25 76 77,
❷ info@orbital.fr, metro Luxembourg) 13 rue de Médicis, 6e. Open 9 am to 10 pm Monday to Saturday, from noon on Sunday (1/55FF per minute/hour, 200/300FF for five/10 hours). Its Web site is at www.cafeorbital.com.
Cyberbe@ubourg Internet C@fé (Map 7,
☎/fax 01 42 71 49 89, metro Châtelet-Les Halles) 38 rue Quincampoix, 4e. Open 9 am to 10 pm daily (1/48FF per minute/hour, 190/290FF for five/10 hours).
Village Web (Map 6, ☎ 01 44 07 20 15,
❷ infos@village-web.net, metro Saint Michel or Maubert Mutualité) 18 rue de la Bûcherie, 5e. Open 10 am to 10 pm daily (1/45FF per minute/hour, 200/300FF for five/10 hours). Its Web site is at www.village-web.net.
Web Bar (Map 6, ☎ 01 42 72 66 55,
❷ webbar@webbar.fr, metro Temple or République) 32 rue de Picardie, 3e. Open 8.30 am to 2 am weekdays, from 11 am at the weekend (25/45FF per half-hour/hour, 300FF for 10 hours). Its Web site is at www.webbar.fr.

INTERNET RESOURCES

The World Wide Web is a rich resource for travellers. You can research your trip, hunt down bargain air fares, book hotels, check on weather conditions and chat with locals and other travellers about the best places to visit (or avoid).

There's no better place to start your Web explorations than the Lonely Planet Web site (www.lonelyplanet.com). Here you'll find succinct summaries on travelling to most places on earth, postcards from other travellers and the Thorn Tree bulletin board where you can ask questions before you go or dispense advice when you get back. You can also find travel news and updates to many of our most popular guidebooks, and the subWWWay section links you to the most useful travel resources elsewhere on the Web.

Useful English-language Web sites on both Paris and France include:

France Diplomatie Includes lists of embassies and consulates with visa information.
www.france.diplomatie.fr
La France Gaie & Lesbienne 'Queer resources directory' for gay and lesbian travellers.
www.france.qrd.org
French Government Tourism Office Official tourism site with all manner of information on and about travel in France.
www.francetourism.com
Good Morning Paris Good for accommodation.
www.goodmorningparis
Maison de la France The main tourist office site.
www.maison-de-la-france.fr
Meteo France Two-day weather forecasts and current conditions.
www.meteo.fr
Metropole Paris
www.metropoleparis.com
The Paris Pages Good links to museums.
www.paris.org
Paris Tourist Office Fantastic site with more links than you thought imaginable.
www.paris-touristoffice.com
Pariscope The capital's foremost on-line entertainment-listings weekly.
www.pariscope.fr

BOOKS

Most books are published in different editions by different publishers in different countries. Fortunately, bookshops and libraries search by title or author, so your local bookshop or library should be able to advise you on the availability of the following recommendations without too many problems.

There are so many excellent books on Paris that it's hard to choose just a few to recommend, though the list has been short-

Read 'em and weep: second-hand books for sale near Pont Neuf

ELLIOT DANIEL

ned considerably by limiting the selection lmost exclusively to works available in aperback. See the Shopping chapter for etails of bookshops in Paris.

onely Planet

onely Planet also publishes *France*, which rovides information for those planning to avel around the rest of the country. *Paris 'ondensed* is a pocket guide written for iose on shorter visits to the capital, while *ut to Eat – Paris* describes an enormous election of the city's best eateries. LP's *rench phrasebook* is a complete guide to *i langue française*. *World Food: France* 'ill take you on a culinary tour of Paris and ie Île de France as well as the rest of the ountry. The *Paris* video provides a visual omplement to this book, while *CitySync 'aris* offers a digital guide to the city spe- ially designed for handheld computers. *ravel Photography: A Guide to Taking 'etter Pictures* is full of useful advice for ll photographers.

iuidebooks

xcellent walking guides to Paris include *'aris Step by Step* by Christopher Turner nd *Walking Paris: 30 Original Walks* by *iilles Desmons*. *Paris: A Literary Com- .anion* by Ian Littlewood escorts you past ie buildings where literary personalities nce lived. *Paris Pas Cher* by Anne Riou, pdated annually, lists inexpensive shop- ing options. The *Food Lover's Guide to* *Paris* by Patricia Wells, *la doyenne de la cuisine française* in English, is essential reading for those looking for more specific restaurant and food-shop recommendations than we have room for in this book.

History & Politics

The Sun King by Nancy Mitford is a classic work on Louis XIV and the country he ruled from Versailles. Alistair Horne's *The Fall of Paris* deals with the siege of the cap- ital and the Commune of 1870-1; *Citizens: A Chronicle of the French Revolution* by Simon Schama is a highly acclaimed and truly monumental work, which examines the first few years after the storming of the Bastille in 1789. Christopher Hibbert's *The Days of the French Revolution* is a highly readable social account of the same period.

Larry Collins and Dominique Lapierre's *Is Paris Burning?* is a dramatic account of the liberation of Paris in 1944. Horne's *To Lose a Battle: France 1940* deals with the defeat and capitulation of Paris. *Paris after the Liberation* by Anthony Beevor and Artemis Cooper brings post-WWII Paris to life; it's out of print but you may find it in the library.

One of the most interesting social ac- counts of Paris and France in general is Julian Barnes' *Cross Channel*, a witty collection of key moments in shared Anglo- French history – from Joan of Arc to trav- elling from London to Paris on Eurostar.

General

The French by Theodore Zeldin is a highly acclaimed survey of French passions, pecu- liarities and perspectives. *France Today* by John Ardagh is a good introduction to mod- ern-day France, its politics, its people and their idiosyncrasies. Also look out for Ardagh's *Cultural Atlas of France*, a su- perb, illustrated synopsis of French culture and history. Fernand Braudel's two-volume *The Identity of France* is a comprehensive look at the country and its people, though it's just gone out of print.

Past Imperfect: French Intellectuals, 1944-1956 by Tony Judt is an examination of the lively intellectual life of postwar

France. *The Food of France* by Waverley Root is a superb, very literary introduction to French cuisine.

FILMS

Paris has provided popular settings for scores of English-language films. Some of the better ones include:

Dangerous Liaisons (USA, 1988). An Oscar-winning, beautifully acted tale of two jaded aristocrats who play games of sexual intrigue.

The Hunchback of Notre Dame (USA, 1939). A superb version of Victor Hugo's novel about a deformed bell-ringer who saves a Gypsy girl from his master's evil-doings.

Les Misérables (USA, 1935). Wrongly sentenced to years in the galleys, Jean Valjean emerges to rebuild his life but is tormented by a police officer. A classic.

Round Midnight (USA, 1986). The last days of a black American jazz musician in Paris, with plenty of atmospheric club scenes.

Victor/Victoria (USA, 1982). A girl singer poses as a female impersonator in a Paris nightclub of the 1930s, causing complications in her love life.

NEWSPAPERS & MAGAZINES

France's main daily newspapers are *Le Figaro* (right-wing; aimed at professionals, businesspeople and the bourgeoisie), *Le Monde* (centre-left; popular with businesspeople, professionals and intellectuals), *Le Parisien* (centre; middle-class and easy to read if your French is basic), *France Soir* (right-wing; working and middle-class), *Libération* (left-wing; popular with students and intellectuals) and *L'Humanité* (communist; working-class). *L'Équipe* is a daily devoted exclusively to sport.

Among English-language newspapers widely available in Paris are the *International Herald Tribune* (10FF), which is edited in Paris and has very good coverage of French and international news; the *Guardian*; the *Financial Times*; the *Times*; and the colourful (if lightweight) *USA Today*. English-language news weeklies widely available include *Newsweek*, *Time* and the *Economist*.

The Paris-based *France USA Contacts* (or *FUSAC*), issued every fortnight, consists of hundreds of ads placed by both companies and individuals. It is distributed free at Paris' English-language bookshops (see the Shopping chapter), Anglophone embassies and the American Church (Ma 4, ☎ 01 40 62 05 00, metro Pont de l'Alma at 65 quai d'Orsay, 7e, and can be very helpful if you're looking for au pair work, short-term accommodation etc. To place an ad, contact FUSAC (☎ 01 56 53 54 54, fax 01 56 53 54 55, metro Alésia) at 26 rue Bernard, 14e, from 10 am to 7 pm weekdays. You can also advertise via their Web site (www.fusac.fr).

RADIO & TV
Radio

You can pick up a mixture of the BBC World Service and BBC for Europe in Paris and northern France on 648kHz AM. The Voice of America (VOA) is on 1197kHz AM. In Paris, you can pick up an hour of Radio France Internationale (RFI) news in English at noon, 2 and 4 pm daily on 738kHz AM. France Info broadcasts the news headlines in French every few minutes. It can be picked up on 105.5MHz FM in Paris.

Pocket-size short-wave radios make it easy to keep abreast of the world news in English wherever you are. The BBC World Service can be heard on 6195kHz, 9410kHz and 12095kHz (a good daytime frequency), depending on the time of day. BBC Radio 4 broadcasts on 198kHz long wave, and carries BBC World Service programming in the wee hours of the morning. The VOA broadcasts in English at various times of the day on 7170kHz, 9535kHz, 9760kHz, 9770kHz, 11805kHz, 15205kHz and 15255kHz. RFI can be picked up in English on 6175kHz at 2, 4 and 6 pm daily.

Internet Many local and international radio stations broadcast their programs via the Web, to be picked up by surfers using software such as RealAudio, which can be easily downloaded. Station Web sites often include write-ups of the latest news and are an excellent source of short-wave schedules.

TV

Upmarket hotels often offer cable and satellite TV, including CNN, BBC Prime, Sky and other networks. Canal+ (ka-**nahl** loose), a French subscription TV station that you'll find in many mid-range hotels, sometimes screens nondubbed English films.

A variety of TV listings weeklies are sold at newsstands, including *Télérama* (10FF), which also includes a detailed supplement on the best films of the month. Foreign films that haven't been dubbed and are shown in their original language with subtitles are marked 'VO' or 'v.o.' *(version originale)*.

VIDEO SYSTEMS

Unlike the rest of Western Europe and Australia, which use PAL, French TV broadcasts in SECAM *(système électronique couleur avec mémoire)*. North America and Japan use a third (and incompatible) system called NTSC. Non-SECAM TVs will not work in France, and French video cassettes cannot be played on video-cassette recorders and TVs that lack a SECAM capability.

PHOTOGRAPHY & VIDEO

Colour-print film produced by Kodak and Fuji is widely available in supermarkets, photo shops and Fnac stores. At Fnac, a 36-exposure roll of Kodak Gold costs 37FF while a packet of two films is 68FF. Developing costs 20FF per roll plus 2.50FF per photo.

For *diapositives* (slides), count on paying at least 46/54/68FF for a 36-exposure roll of Ektachrome rated at 100/200/400 ASA; developing costs 28/32FF for 24/36 exposures. A packet of three 36-exposure rolls of Fuji Sensia 100 ASA costs 134FF.

Photography is rarely forbidden, except in museums and art galleries. When photographing people, it is a basic courtesy to ask permission. If you don't know any French, smile while pointing at your camera and they'll get the picture.

Lonely Planet's *Travel Photography: A Guide to Taking Better Pictures*, written by travel photographer Richard I'Anson, is full of useful advice for improving your photography.

TIME

France uses the 24-hour clock in most cases, with the hours separated from the minutes by a lower-case 'h'. Thus, 15h30 is 3.30 pm, 21h50 is 9.50 pm, 00h30 is 12.30 am and so on.

France is on Central European Time, which is one hour ahead of (ie, later than) GMT/UTC. During daylight-saving time, which runs from the last Sunday in March to the last Sunday in October, France is two hours ahead of GMT/UTC.

Without taking daylight-saving time into account, when it's noon in Paris it's 11 am in London, 6 am in New York, 3 am in San Francisco, 9 pm in Sydney and 11 pm in Auckland.

Quelle heure est-il? This sculpture outside Gare Saint Lazare will leave you none the wiser.

MARTIN MOOS

FACTS FOR THE VISITOR

ELECTRICITY

France runs on 220V at 50Hz AC. Plugs are the standard European type with two round pins.

While the usual travel transformers allow North American appliances to run in France without blowing out, they cannot change the frequency, which determines – among other things – the speed of electric motors. As a result, tape recorders not equipped with built-in adapters may function poorly.

There are two types of adapters; mixing them up will destroy either the transformer or your appliance, so be warned. The 'heavy' kind, usually designed to handle 35W or less (see the tag) and often metal-clad, is designed for use with small electrical devices such as radios, tape recorders and razors. The other kind, which weighs much less but is rated for up to 1500W, is for use only with appliances that contain heating elements, such as hair dryers and irons.

The best place to seek out adapters and other electrical goods is the BHV department store near the Hôtel de Ville; see Department Stores in the Shopping chapter for details.

WEIGHTS & MEASURES
Metric System

France uses the metric system, which was invented after the Revolution by the French Academy of Sciences at the request of the National Assembly and adopted by the French government in 1795. Inspired by the same rationalist spirit in whose name churches were ransacked and turned into 'Temples of Reason', the metric system replaced a confusing welter of traditional units of measurement that lacked all logical basis and made conversion complicated and commerce chaotic. For a conversion chart, see the inside back cover.

Numbers

For numbers with four or more digits, the French use full stops (periods) or spaces where writers in English would use commas – one million therefore usually appears as 1.000.000 or 1 000 000. For decimals, on the other hand, the French use commas, so 1.75 comes out as 1,75.

LAUNDRY

There's a *laverie libre-service* (self-service laundrette) around every corner in Paris; your hotel or hostel can point you to one in the neighbourhood. Parisian laundrettes usually cost around 22FF for a 6kg or 7kg load and 2/5FF for five/12 minutes of drying. Some laundrettes have self-service *nettoyage à sec* (dry-cleaning) machines.

Change machines are sometimes out of order, so come prepared. Coins of 2FF are especially handy for the *séchoirs* (dryers) and the *lessive* (laundry powder) and *javel* (bleach) dispensers. In general, you deposit coins into a *monnayeur central* (central control box) – not the machine itself – and push a button that corresponds to the number of the machine you wish to operate. These gadgets are sometimes programmed to deactivate the washing machines an hour or so before closing time.

Among centrally located self-service laundrettes are the following:

Louvre (Map 6)
Laverie Libre Service (metro Louvre-Rivoli) 7 rue Jean-Jacques Rousseau, 1er, near the BVJ Paris-Louvre hostel. Open 7.30 am to 10 pm daily.

Marais (Map 7)
Laverie (metro Saint Paul) 40 rue du Roi de Sicile, 4e. Open 7.30 am to 8.30 pm.
Laverie Libre-Service (metro Hôtel de Ville) 35 rue Sainte Croix de la Bretonnerie, 4e. Open 7 or 7.30 am to 10 pm daily.
Laverie Libre Service (metro Saint Paul) 25 rue des Rosiers, 4e. Open 7 or 7.30 am to 10 pm daily.

Bastille (Map 6)
Miele (metro Bastille) 2 rue de Lappe, 11e. Open 7 am to 10 pm daily.

Latin Quarter (Map 5)
Laverie (metro Luxembourg) 216 rue Saint Jacques, 5e, three blocks south-west of the Panthéon. Open 7 am to 10 pm daily.
Lavomatique (metro Monge) 63 rue Monge, 5e, just south of the Arènes de Lutèce. Open 6.30 am to 10 pm daily.
Le Bateau Lavoir (metro Cardinal Lemoine) 1 rue Thouin, 5e, near place de la Contrescarpe. Open until 10 pm daily.

Saint Germain & Odéon (Map 6)

Julice Laverie (metro Mabillon) 56 rue de Seine, 6e. Open 7 am to 10.30 pm daily.
Julice Laverie (metro Saint André des Arts) 22 rue des Grands Augustins, 6e. Open 7 am to 9 pm daily.

Gare de l'Est (Map 3)

Lav' Club (metro Gare de l'Est) 55 blvd de Magenta, 10e, near the Franprix supermarket. Open 7 am to 10 pm daily.
Laverie (metro Château d'Eau) 6 rue des Petites Écuries, 10e. Open 7 am to 10 pm daily.

Montmartre (Map 8)

Laverie (metro Abbesses) 92 rue des Martyrs, 9e. Open 7.30 am to 10 pm daily.
Laverie Libre Service (metro Blanche) 4 rue Burq, 18e, west of the Butte de Montmartre. Open 7.30 am to 10 pm daily.

PUBLIC BATHS

Before WWII, a very high percentage of Paris' working-class flats lacked bathroom facilities. Even today, some Parisians live in showerless flats, which is why the municipality runs 20 or so *bains-douches municipaux* (municipal bathhouses), where a shower costs 7.50FF (3.70FF per person for large families). Facilities for both men and women are available.

Near the Centre Pompidou, the Bains-Douches Municipaux (Map 7, ☎ 01 42 77 71 90, metro Rambuteau), 18 rue du Renard, 4e, is open noon to 7 pm on Wednesday, 7 am to 7 pm on Thursday and Saturday, 8 am to 7 pm on Friday and 8 am to noon on Sunday.

On Île Saint Louis, the Bains-Douches Municipaux (Map 6, ☎ 01 43 54 47 40, metro Pont Marie), 8 rue des Deux Ponts, 4e, is open noon to 7 pm on Thursday, 8 am to 7 pm on Friday, 7 am to 7 pm on Saturday and 8 am to noon on Sunday. The Bains-Douches Municipaux (Map 5, ☎ 01 45 35 46 63, metro Monge), 50 rue Lacépède, 5e, just east of place de la Contrescarpe, and the Bains-Douches Oberkampf (Map 6, metro Parmentier), 42 rue Oberkampf, 11e, keep the same hours.

TOILETS

Public toilets are signposted as *toilettes* or *WC*. The tan-coloured, self-cleaning cylindrical toilets you see on Paris pavements are open 24 hours and cost 2FF. In general, café owners do not appreciate you using their facilities if you are not a customer. If you are desperate, try ducking into a fast-food place, a major department store, Forum des Halles or the underground toilets in front of Notre Dame.

In older cafés and hotels, the amenities may consist of a *toilette à la turque* (Turkish-style toilet), which is what the French call a squat toilet.

LEFT LUGGAGE

All the train stations in Paris (see the Getting There & Away chapter) have either left-luggage offices (eg, Gare Montparnasse) or lockers (eg, Gare du Nord). They cost between 10FF and 30FF for 72 hours (the maximum time allowed), depending on the size of the bag or the locker. You can store your bike at train station left-luggage offices for 35FF a day.

HEALTH

Your main health risk in Paris is likely to be an upset stomach from eating and drinking too much. You might experience mild stomach problems if you're not used to copious amounts of rich cream and olive-oil-based sauces, but you'll get used to it after a while.

Predeparture Planning

Organise a visit to your dentist before departure and arrange travel insurance with good medical cover. If you wear glasses, take along a spare pair and your prescription. If you require medicine available only on prescription in your own country, take an adequate supply (though French pharmacies may dispense medication that's available only on prescription elsewhere). No jabs are required to travel to France.

Travel Health Guides

There are a number of excellent travel-health sites on the Internet. From the Lonely Planet Web site (www.lonelyplanet.com) there are links to the World Health Organization (WHO) and the US Centers for Disease Control and Prevention, as well as to many other useful sources of health information.

Health System

France has an extensive public health-care system. Anyone (including foreigners) who is sick, even mildly so, can receive treatment in the *service des urgences* (casualty ward or emergency room) of any public hospital. Hospitals try to have people who speak English in the casualty wards, but this is not done systematically. If necessary, the hospital will call in an interpreter. It's an excellent idea to ask for a copy of the diagnosis – in English, if possible – in case your doctor back home needs it.

Getting treated for illness or injury in a public hospital costs much less in France than in many other Western countries, especially the USA: being seen by a doctor (a *consultation*) costs about 150FF (235FF to 250FF on Sunday and on public holidays, 275FF to 350FF from 8 pm to 8 am). Seeing a specialist is a bit more expensive. Blood tests and other procedures, each of which has a standard fee, will increase this figure. Full hospitalisation costs from 3000FF a day. Hospitals usually ask that visitors from abroad settle accounts right after receiving treatment.

Citizens of EU countries are covered for emergency medical treatment in France on presentation of an E111 form, though charges are likely for medication, dental work and secondary examinations including X-rays and laboratory tests. Ask about the E111 at your national health service at least a few weeks before you go. Claims must be submitted to a local *caisse primaire d'assurance-maladie* (sickness insurance office) before you leave France.

The coverage provided by most private US health-insurance policies continues if you travel abroad, at least for a limited period. Canadians covered by the Régie de l'Assurance-Maladie du Québec, and who have a valid Assurance-Maladie du Québec card, can benefit from certain reimbursement agreements with France's national health-care system. Australian Medicare provides absolutely no coverage in France.

Medical Services

There are some 50 *assistance publique* (public health service) hospitals in Paris. If you need an ambulance, call ☎ 15 or 01 4 67 50 50; the multilingual emergency number is ☎ 115. For emergency treatment, ca Urgences Médicales on ☎ 01 53 94 94 94 o SOS Médecins on ☎ 01 47 07 77 77. Bot offer 24-hour house calls.

Some hospitals in Paris are:

Hôtel Dieu (Map 6, ☎ 01 42 34 81 31, metro Cité) place du Parvis Notre Dame, 4e. After 8 pm use the emergency entrance on rue de la Cité. The 24-hour emergency room can refer you to the hospital's emergency gynaecological services in cases of sexual assault.
American Hospital (Map 1, ☎ 01 46 41 27 37, metro Anatole France) 63 blvd Victor Hugo, 92202 Neuilly. Offers emergency 24-hour medical and dental care.
Hôpital Franco-Britannique (Map 1, ☎ 01 46 39 22 22, metro Anatole France) 3 rue Barbès 92300 Levallois-Perret. This is a less expensive English-speaking option.

Dental Care

For emergency dental care contact:

Hôpital La Pitié-Salpêtrière (Maps 5 & 9, ☎ 01 42 16 00 00, or 01 42 17 72 47 in an emergency, metro Chevaleret) rue Bruant, 13e This is the only dental hospital with extended hours. The night-time entrance (5.30 pm to 8.30 am) is at 83 blvd de l'Hôpital, 13e (Map 5, metro Gare d'Austerlitz).
SOS Dentistes (Map 1, ☎ 01 43 37 51 00, metro Port Royal) 87 blvd de Port Royal, 14e. This is a private dental office that offers services when most dentists are off-duty: from 8.30 to 11 pm weekdays and from 9.30 am to 11 pm at the weekend.

Pharmacies

Some pharmacies with extended hours include:

Pharmacie Derhy (Map 2, ☎ 01 45 62 02 41, metro George V) inside the shopping arcade at 84 ave des Champs-Élysées, 8e. Open 24 hours year round.
Pharmacie Européenne (Map 2, ☎ 01 48 74 65 18, metro place de Clichy) 6 place de Clichy, 17e. Open 24 hours year round.

harmacie Première (Map 6, ☎ 01 48 87 62
30, metro Châtelet) 28 blvd de Sébastopol, 4e.
Open 8.30 to 2 am daily.

HIV/AIDS Organisations

For information on free and anonymous
HIV-testing centres *(centres de dépistage)*
in and around Paris, ring the SIDA Info
Service on ☎ 0 800 84 08 00 (toll-free, 24
hours). Its Web site is at www.sida.info
service.org. Information is also available
in the Marais at Le Kiosque (☎ 01 44 78 00
00, metro Saint Paul) at 36 rue Geoffroy
l'Asnier, 4e, and at another Le Kiosque
☎ 01 44 78 00 00, metro Maubert Mutual-
té) in the Latin Quarter at 6 rue Dante, 5e.
Both are open 10 am to 12.30 pm and 1 to
7 pm weekdays and 2 to 7 pm on Saturday.
AIDS patients under care may ring SIDA
Info Soignants (☎ 0 801 63 05 15) from
5 to 8 pm weekdays.

The offices of AIDES (☎ 01 44 52 00 00,
metro Télégraphe), 247 rue de Belleville,
19e, an organisation that works for the prevention of AIDS and assists AIDS sufferers,
are staffed from 10 am to 1.30 pm and 2 to
5 pm weekdays (and in addition from 7 to
10 pm on Thursday).

FACTS-Line (☎ 01 44 93 16 69), which
operates from 6 to 10 pm on Monday, Wednesday and Friday, is an English-language
helpline for those with HIV or AIDS.

WOMEN TRAVELLERS

Attitudes Towards Women

Women were given the right to vote in 1945
by de Gaulle's short-lived postwar government, but until 1964 a woman still needed
her husband's permission to open a bank
account or get a passport. Younger French
women especially are quite outspoken and
emancipated, but self-confidence has yet to
translate into equality in the workplace,
where women are often kept out of senior
and management positions.

Safety Precautions

Women attract more unwanted attention
than men, but female travellers need not
walk around Paris in fear, as people are
rarely assaulted on the street. However, the

French seem to have given relatively little
thought to *harcèlement sexuel* (sexual har-
assment), and many men still think that to
stare suavely at a passing woman is to pay
her a compliment.

Using the metro until late at night is generally OK, but there are certain stations to
avoid. See the Dangers & Annoyances section later in this chapter.

In an emergency, you can always call the
police (☎ 17), who will take you to the hospital. Medical, psychological and legal services are available to people referred by
the police at the 24-hour Service Médico-
Judiciaire of the Hôtel Dieu (☎ 01 42 34
84 46).

Organisations

France's women's liberation movement
flourished along with its counterparts in
other Western countries in the late 1960s
and early 1970s but by the mid-1980s was
pretty moribund. For reasons that have more
to do with French society than anything else,
few women's groups function as the kind of
supportive social institutions that have been
formed in the USA, the UK and Australia.

The women-only Maison des Femmes
(Map 5, ☎ 01 43 43 41 13, metro Reuilly
Diderot), 163 rue Charenton, 12e, is a meeting place for women of all ages and nationalities. It is staffed from 9 am to 1 pm on
Monday and Thursday, and from 4 to 7 pm
on Wednesday, Friday and Saturday.

France's national rape-crisis hotline (☎ 0
800 05 95 95) can be reached toll-free from
any telephone without using a phonecard.
Staffed by volunteers from 10 am to 6 pm
weekdays, it's run by a women's organisation called Viols Femmes Informations,
whose Paris office is at 9 villa d'Este, 13e
(metro Porte d'Ivry).

GAY & LESBIAN TRAVELLERS

France is one of Europe's most liberal countries when it comes to homosexuality – in
part because of the long French tradition of
public tolerance towards groups of people
who don't live by conventional social codes
– and the capital is its epicentre.

Paris is home to thriving gay and lesbian

FACTS FOR THE VISITOR

communities, and same-sex couples are a common sight on its streets. In 1999 the Jospin government, despite strong opposition from conservative forces, enacted its PACS legislation, designed to give homosexual couples the same legal protection (eg, regarding inheritance) as married heterosexuals.

The lesbian scene here is much less public than its gay counterpart and centres around a few cafés and bars in the Marais (see Gay & Lesbian Venues in the Entertainment chapter).

Organisations

Most of France's major gay organisations are based in Paris; they include:

Act Up-Paris (☎ 01 48 06 13 89 or 01 49 29 44 75, ✉ actup@actupp.org). Advice by phone is available from 2 to 6 pm on Wednesday and meetings are held every Tuesday at 7 pm at the École des Beaux-Arts (Map 6, metro Saint Germain des Prés), 14 rue Bonaparte, 6e.

Association des Médecins Gais (☎ 01 48 05 81 71). The Association of Gay Doctors, based in the CGL, deals with gay-related health issues. It's staffed from 6 to 8 pm on Wednesday and from 2 to 4 pm on Saturday.

Centre Gai et Lesbien (CGL; Map 5, ☎ 01 43 57 21 47, metro Ledru Rollin) 3 rue Keller, 11e. The CGL normally opens 2 to 8 pm Monday to Saturday.

Écoute Gaie (☎ 01 44 93 01 02). This hotline for gays and lesbians is staffed from 6 to 10 pm on weekdays and from 6 to 8 pm on Saturday.

SOS Homophobie (☎ 01 48 06 42 41). This hotline accepts anonymous calls concerning discriminatory acts against gays and lesbians from 8 to 10 pm weekdays.

Gay Publications

Têtu is a monthly national magazine available at newsstands everywhere (30FF). Among the more serious gay publications are Act Up-Paris' monthly called *Action* (free) and the CGL's *3 Keller*, which appears about once a month. Be on the lookout for *e.m@le*, which has interviews, gossip and articles (in French) and among the best listings of gay clubs, bars, associations and personal classifieds. It is available free at gay venues or for 5FF at newsagents.

Guidebooks listing pubs, restaurants, discotheques, beaches, saunas, sex shops and cruising areas include the following (available from Les Mots à la Bouche in Paris; see Bookshops in the Shopping chapter):

Guide Gai Pied A predominantly male, French- and English-language annual guide (79FF) to France (about 80 pages devoted to Paris), published by Les Éditions du Triangle Rose (☎ 01 43 14 73 00).
Spartacus International Gay Guide A male-only guide (190FF) to the world with more than 100 pages devoted to France and 28 pages on Paris.

Lesbian Publications

The monthly national magazine, *Lesbia* (25FF), gives a rundown of what's happening around the country. *Les Nanas*, a freebie appearing every other month, is for women only. *Damron's Women's Traveller* by Bob Damron is an English-language guide (109FF) for lesbians.

DISABLED TRAVELLERS

Paris is not particularly well equipped for *les handicapés* (disabled people): kerb ramps are few and far between, older public facilities and bottom-end hotels often lack lifts, and the metro, most of it built decades ago, is hopeless. But physically challenged people who would like to visit Paris can overcome these problems. Most hotels with two or more stars are equipped with lifts, and Michelin's *Guide Rouge* indicates hotels with lifts and facilities for disabled people. Both the Foyer International d'Accueil de Paris Jean Monnet and the Centre International de Séjour de Paris Kellermann have facilities for disabled travellers (see under Hostels in the Places to Stay chapter).

In recent years the SNCF has made efforts to make its trains more accessible to people with physical disabilities. A traveller in a wheelchair (*fauteuil roulant*) can travel in the wheelchair in both TGV and regular trains provided they make a reservation by phone or at a train station at least a few hours before departure. Details are available in SNCF's booklet *Guide du Voyageur à Mobilité Réduite*. You can also contact SNCF Accessibilité on ☎ 0 800 15 47 53 (toll-free).

In some places conveyances adapted for people in wheelchairs provide transport within the city. Details are available from the Groupement pour l'Insertion des Personnes Handicapées Physiques (see Organisations below).

Access in Paris by Gordon Crouch and Ben Roberts is a 245-page guide to the French capital for the disabled, published by Quiller Press in London, but the latest edition (1994) is already quite dated. In the UK it is available from the Royal Association for Disability and Rehabilitation (RADAR; ☎ 020-7250 3222), 12 City Forum, 250 City Rd, London EC1V 8AF.

Organisations

The following organisations can provide information to disabled travellers:

Association des Paralysées de France (☎ 0 800 85 49 76 or 01 40 78 69 00) 17 blvd Auguste Blanqui, 13e. Brochures on wheelchair access to accommodation in Paris.
Comité Nationale Française de Liaison pour la Réadaptation des Handicapées (CNRH; ☎ 01 53 80 66 66) 236 bis rue de Tolbiac, 13e. An information centre that publishes guides for disabled travellers.
Groupement pour l'Insertion des Personnes Handicapées Physiques (☎ 01 41 83 15 15) 98 rue de la Porte Jaune, 92210 Saint Cloud. Provides vehicles outfitted for people in wheelchairs within the city.

SENIOR TRAVELLERS

Seniors are entitled to discounts in France on things such as public transport, museum admission fees and so on, provided they show proof of their age. In some cases they might need a special pass. See Seniors' Cards in the earlier Documents section.

PARIS FOR CHILDREN

Paris abounds in places that will delight children. Family visits to many areas of the city can be designed around a rest stop (or picnic) at the following places (see the Things to See & Do chapter for further details, and the Ex-

cursions chapter for information on Parc Astérix and Disneyland Paris):

- Bastille, 4e (Map 5): playground at the Port de Plaisance de Paris-Arsenal
- Bois de Boulogne (Map 1): Jardin d'Acclimatation; Exploradôme
- Bois de Vincennes (Maps 1 & 9): Parc Zoologique de Paris
- Champs-Élysées, 8e (Map 2): Palais de la Découverte
- La Défense (La Défense map, page 159): Dôme IMAX
- Eiffel Tower, 7e (Map 4): Champ de Mars
- Jardin des Plantes, 5e (Map 5): Ménagerie; Musée National d'Histoire Naturelle
- Luxembourg, 6e (Map 5): Jardin du Luxembourg
- Montmartre, 18e (Map 8): playground
- La Villette, 19e (Map 1): Parc de la Villette; Cité des Sciences et de l'Industrie; Géode; Cinaxe

The weekly entertainment magazine *L'Officiel des Spectacles* (2FF), which appears every Wednesday, lists *gardes d'enfants* (babysitting services) available in Paris. These include:

Après la Classe (☎ 01 44 78 05 05) From 39.50FF per hour.
Baby Sitting Services (☎ 01 46 21 33 16) From 35FF per hour plus 60FF subscription.
Étudiants de l'Institut Catholique (☎ 01 45 48 31 70) From 35FF per hour plus 10FF for each session.

Lonely Planet's *Travel with Children* by Maureen Wheeler includes all sorts of useful advice for those travelling with their little ones.

Parc de la Villette abounds with opportunities for kids to get their kicks.

LIBRARIES

Both French and foreign libraries in Paris are open to foreigners.

American Library in Paris (Map 4, ☎ 01 53 59 12 61, metro Pont de l'Alma or École Militaire) 10 rue du Général Camou, 7e. This is among the largest English-language lending libraries in Europe, with some 100,000 volumes of classic and contemporary fiction and nonfiction, and some 450 magazines. Membership costs 570FF a year (460FF for students), 240/350FF for four/six months and 70FF a day (50FF for students; reading privileges only). It opens 10 am to 7 pm Tuesday to Saturday with limited hours in summer.

Bibliothèque Nationale de France François Mitterrand (Map 9, ☎ 01 53 79 53 79, metro Bibliothèque) 11 quai François Mauriac, 13e. This national library contains some 10 million tomes stored on some 420km of shelves, and can accommodate 2000 readers and 2000 researchers. It opens to the public (20/200FF per day/year) 10 am to 8 pm Tuesday to Saturday, and noon to 7 pm on Sunday.

Bibliothèque Publique d'Information (BPI; Map 7, ☎ 01 44 78 12 33 or 01 44 78 47 86, metro Rambuteau) Centre Pompidou, 4e. This huge, nonlending (and free) library is spread over three floors of the Centre Pompidou, with its entrance on the mezzanine level. The 2500 periodicals include 150 daily newspapers (many

Reading on the roof: a striking view from the top of the Bibliothèque Nationale de France

of them in English) and 150 magazines from around the world. It opens noon to 10 pm on Monday and Wednesday to Friday, and from 11 am at the weekend. Queues can be enormous; the best times to visit are between 1 and 1.30 pm and after 7 pm.

British Council (Map 4, ☎ 01 49 55 73 23, metro Invalides) 9-11 rue de Constantine, 7e. The British Council has a lending library that costs 160/300FF to join for six months/a year (130/250FF with a student card); the reference library costs 30FF a day to use. It opens 11 am to 6 pm weekdays (to 7 pm on Wednesday). See the following Cultural Centres section for more information.

UNIVERSITIES

The University of Paris, founded under papal protection in about 1215, was decentralised and split into 13 autonomous universities following the violent student protests of 1968 (see The Fifth Republic under History in the Facts about Paris chapter). The most celebrated of these is the Sorbonne (Map 5; see the Latin Quarter section in the Things to See & Do chapter). Unless you're studying in Paris or taking your meals at one of the 'restos U' (see University Restaurants in the Places to Eat chapter), you'll have little occasion to visit the University of Paris; none of the student residence halls welcome nonstudents during holiday breaks, for example.

CULTURAL CENTRES
British Council

The British Council (Map 4, ☎ 01 49 55 73 00, metro Invalides), 9-11 rue de Constan-

ASA ANDERSON

Design is an open book: the inspiration for the glass towers of the Bibliothèque Nationale de France came from François Mitterrand.

tine, 7e, has reference and lending libraries (see the Libraries section), and also runs language courses through the British Institute.

American Church

The American Church (Map 4, ☎ 01 40 62 05 00, metro Pont de l'Alma or Invalides), 65 quai d'Orsay, 7e, functions as a community centre for English-speakers and is an excellent source of information on accommodation, jobs and so on. Reception is staffed from 9 am till noon and 1 to 10.30 pm Monday to Saturday, and to 7.30 pm on Sunday. The church has four bulletin boards: an informal board downstairs on which people post all sorts of announcements at no charge, and three identical official ones – one near reception, another outside and one downstairs – listing flats, items for sale and jobs, especially work for au pairs, baby-sitters and English-language teachers. The American Church sponsors a variety of classes, workshops, concerts (at 6 pm most Sundays) and other cultural activities.

Service Culturel

France's Service Culturel (Cultural Service) has reams of information on studying in France, as do French-government tourist offices and consulates. In Paris, you might also contact the International Cultural Organisation (ICO; ☎ 01 42 36 47 18, fax 01 40 26 34 45, metro Châtelet), 55 rue de Rivoli, 1er, which is sponsored by the Ministry of Tourism. Its postal address is 55 rue de Rivoli, BP 2701, 75027 Paris CEDEX.

Among the offices of the French Cultural Service, many of them attached to embassies, are the following:

Australia (☎ 02-6216 0100, fax 6216 0127, @ embassy@france.net.au) 6 Perth Ave, Yarralumla, ACT 2600
Belgium (☎ 02-548 8711, fax 514 1772, @ ambafr@linkline.be) 42 blvd de Régent, 1000 Brussels
Canada (☎ 416-925 0025, fax 925 2560, @ kulto@idirect.com) 175 Bloor St East, Suite 606, Toronto, Ont M4W 3R8
Germany (☎ 030-885 9020, fax 882 1287, @ info@if-berlin.b.shuttle.de) Kurfürstendamm 211D, 10719 Berlin

Ireland (☎ 01-676 7116, fax 676 4077) 1 Kildare St, Dublin 2
Italy (☎ 06 686 011, fax 06 686 01 331, @ france-italia@inet.it) Piazza Farnese 67, 00186 Rome
Netherlands (☎ 020-622 4936, fax 623 3631, @ mdescart@ambafrance.nl) Vijzelgracht 2a, 1017 HR Amsterdam
New Zealand (☎ 09-524 9401, fax 524 9403) 27 Gilles Ave, Newmarket, PO Box 99, Auckland
Spain (☎ 91 308 4958, fax 91 319 6401, @ institutofrances@mad.servicom.es) Calle Marques de la Ensenada 12, 28004 Madrid
Switzerland (☎ 031-359 2111, fax 359 2192, @ ambassade.fr@iprolink.ch) Schlosshaldenstrasse 46, 3006 Berne
UK (☎ 020-7838 2055, fax 7838 2088, @ scientec@scientec.demon.co.uk) 23 Cromwell Rd, London SW7 2EL
USA (☎ 212-439 1400, fax 439 1455, @ new-york-culture@diplomatie.fr) 972 Fifth Ave, New York, NY 10021

DANGERS & ANNOYANCES

In general, Paris is a safe city and random street assaults are rare. La Ville Lumière (the City of Light), as Paris calls itself, is generally well lit, and there's no reason not to use the metro before it stops running at some time between 12.30 and 12.45 am. As you'll notice, women *do* travel alone on the metro late at night in most areas, though not all who do so report feeling 100% comfortable.

Metro stations that are probably best avoided late at night include: Châtelet-Les Halles and its endless corridors; Château Rouge, in Montmartre; Gare du Nord; Strasbourg Saint Denis; Réaumur Sébastopol; and Montparnasse Bienvenüe. *Bornes d'alarme* (alarm boxes) are located in the centre of each metro/RER platform and in some station corridors. Keep out of the Bois de Boulogne and the Bois de Vincennes after dark.

Nonviolent crime (such as pickpocketing and thefts from handbags and packs) is a problem wherever there are crowds, especially crowds of tourists. Places to be especially careful include Montmartre, Pigalle, around Forum des Halles and the Centre Pompidou, on the metro at rush hour and the Latin Quarter.

euro currency converter €1 = 6.56FF

FACTS FOR THE VISITOR

Lost Property

All objects found anywhere in Paris – except those picked up on trains or in train stations – are eventually brought to the city's Bureau des Objets Trouvés (Lost Property Office; Map 1, ☎ 01 55 76 20 20, fax 01 40 02 40 45, metro Convention), 36 rue des Morillons, 15e, run by the Préfecture de Police. Since telephone inquiries are impossible, the only way to find out if a lost item has been located is to go all the way down there and fill in the forms. The office opens 8.30 am to 5 pm on Monday, Wednesday and Friday, and to 8 pm on Tuesday and Thursday. In July and August it closes at 3.45 pm on Wednesday and Friday and at 4.45 pm on Tuesday and Thursday.

Items lost on the metro (☎ 01 40 30 52 00 for information) are held by station agents for one day before being sent to the Bureau des Objets Trouvés. Anything found on trains or in train stations is taken to the *objets trouvés* bureau – usually attached to the left-luggage office – of the relevant station. Telephone inquiries (in French) are possible:

Gare d'Austerlitz	☎ 01 53 60 71 98
Gare de l'Est	☎ 01 40 18 88 73
Gare de Lyon	☎ 01 53 33 67 22
Gare Montparnasse	☎ 01 40 48 14 24
Gare du Nord	☎ 01 55 31 58 40
Gare Saint Lazare	☎ 01 53 42 05 57

Litter

In theory Parisians can be fined 1000FF for littering but we've never seen (or heard of) anyone ever having to pay up. And – *merde, alors* – then there are all those dirty dogs (see the boxed text 'Remembrance of Dogs Past and Present' in the Things to See & Do chapter). Don't be nonplussed if you see locals drop paper wrappings or other detritus along the side of the pavement; the gutters in every quarter of Paris are washed and swept out daily and Parisians are encouraged to use them if litter bins are not available.

EMERGENCIES

The following are the numbers to be dialled in an emergency:

Ambulance (SAMU)	☎ 15
	☎ 01 45 67 50 50
Fire brigade	☎ 18
Police	☎ 17
Rape crisis hotline	☎ 0 800 05 95 95
Urgences Médicales de Paris (24-hour house calls)	☎ 01 53 94 94 94
	☎ 01 48 28 40 04
SOS Médecins (24-hour house calls)	☎ 01 47 07 77 77

LEGAL MATTERS
Police

Thanks to the Napoleonic Code on which the French legal system is based, the police can pretty much search anyone they want to at any time – whether or not there is probable cause.

France has two separate police forces. The Police Nationale, under the command of departmental prefects (and, in Paris, the Préfet de Police), includes the Police de l'Air et des Frontières (PAF), the border police. The Gendarmerie Nationale, a paramilitary force under the control of the Ministry of Defence, handles airports, borders and so on. During times of crisis (eg, a wave of terrorist attacks), the army may be called in to patrol public places.

The dreaded Compagnies Républicaines de Sécurité (CRS) – riot police heavies – are part of the Police Nationale. You often see hundreds of them, equipped with the latest riot gear, at strikes or demonstrations.

Police with shoulder patches reading 'Police Municipale' are under the control of the local mayor.

If asked a question, cops are likely to be correct and helpful but no more than that (though you may get a salute). If the police stop you for any reason, be polite and remain calm. They have wide powers of search and seizure and, if they take a dislike to you, they may choose to use them. The police can, without any particular reason, decide to examine your passport, visa, carte de séjour and so on.

French police are very strict about security, especially at airports. Do not leave baggage unattended; they're serious when they warn that suspicious objects will be summarily blown up.

euro currency converter 10FF = €1.52

Drinking & Driving

As elsewhere in the EU, the laws are very tough when it comes to drinking and driving, and for many years the slogan has been: '*Boire ou conduire, il faut choisir*' (To booze or to drive, you have to choose). The acceptable blood-alcohol limit is 0.05%, and drivers exceeding this amount face fines of up to 30,000FF (or a maximum of two years in jail). Licences can also be immediately suspended.

Drugs

Importing or exporting drugs can lead to a 10- to 30-year jail sentence. The fine for possession of drugs for personal use can be as high as 500,000FF.

Smoking

By nature many French people do not take seriously laws they consider stupid or intrusive; whether others feel the same is another matter. Laws banning smoking in public places do exist, for example, but no-one pays much attention to them. Diners will often smoke in the nonsmoking sections of restaurants – and the waiter will happily bring them an ashtray.

BUSINESS HOURS

Most museums are closed on either Monday or Tuesday. A few places (eg, the Louvre and the Musée d'Orsay) stay open until almost 10 pm on one night a week.

Small businesses are open daily, except Sunday and often Monday. Hours are usually 9 or 10 am to 6.30 or 7 pm, with a midday break from noon or 1 pm to 2 or 3 pm.

Banks are usually open 8 or 9 am to sometime between 11.30 am and 1 pm, and 1.30 or 2 pm to 4.30 or 5 pm, Monday to Friday or Tuesday to Saturday. Exchange services may end half an hour before closing time.

Post offices are generally open 8.30 or 9 am to 5 or 6 pm weekdays, perhaps with a one- to 1½-hour break at midday, and on Saturday morning.

Supermarkets and hypermarkets are open Monday to Saturday; a few open on Sunday morning in July and August. Small food-shops are mostly closed on Sunday and often Monday too, so Saturday afternoon may be your last chance to stock up on provisions until Tuesday, unless you come across a supermarket. Many restaurants in Paris are closed on Sunday.

Local laws require that most business establishments close for one day a week. Exceptions include family-run businesses, such as grocery stores and small restaurants, and places large enough to rotate staff so everyone has a day off. Since you can never tell which day of the week a certain shopkeeper or restaurateur has chosen to take off, this book includes, where possible, details of weekly closures.

PUBLIC HOLIDAYS & SPECIAL EVENTS

The following holidays are observed in Paris:

New Year's Day *(Jour de l'An)* 1 January
Easter Sunday *(Pâques)* Late March/April
Easter Monday *(Lundi de Pâques)* Late March/April
May Day *(Fête du Travail)* 1 May
Victory in Europe Day *(Victoire 1945)* 8 May
Ascension Thursday *(L'Ascension)* May (40th day after Easter)
Pentecost/Whit Sunday *(Pentecôte)* Mid-May to mid-June (7th Sunday after Easter)
Whit Monday *(Lundi de Pentecôte)* Mid-May to mid-June (7th Monday after Easter)
Bastille Day/National Day *(Fête Nationale)* 14 July
Assumption Day *(L'Assomption)* 15 August
All Saints' Day *(La Toussaint)* 1 November
Armistice Day/Remembrance Day *(Le onze Novembre)* 11 November
Christmas *(Noël)* 25 December

Innumerable cultural and sporting events take place in Paris throughout the year; weekly details appear in *Pariscope* and *L'Officiel des Spectacles* (see Listings in the Entertainment section). The mayor's office produces a *Progamme des Manifestions* each season with major events listed; check its Web site at www.paris-france.org. You can also find them listed on the tourist office's site (www.paris-touristoffice.com).

FACTS FOR THE VISITOR

FACTS FOR THE VISITOR

The following abbreviated list gives you a taste of what to expect.

31 December–1 January

New Year's Eve Blvd Saint Michel (5e), place de la Bastille (11e), the Eiffel Tower (7e) and especially ave des Champs-Élysées (8e) are the places to be.

La Grande Parade de Paris The city's New Year's Day parade originated in Montmartre but now takes place in different venues (eg, along the Grands Boulevards) each year. Check its Web site at www.parisparade.com.

Late January/early February

Chinese New Year Dragon parades and other festivities are held in Chinatown, the area of the 13e between ave d'Ivry and ave de Choisy (metro Porte de Choisy or Tolbiac), with an abridged version along rue Au Maire (metro Arts et Métiers) in the 3e.

Late February/early March

Salon International de l'Agriculture A 10-day international agricultural fair with lots to eat, including dishes from all over France. Held at the Parc des Expositions at Porte de Versailles in the 15e (metro Porte de Versailles).

Late February–March

Banlieues Bleues 'Suburban Blues' jazz and blues festival held in Saint Denis and other Paris suburbs, attracting big-name talent.

Early March

Jumping International de Paris Showjumping tournament at the Palais Omnisports de Paris-Bercy in the 12e (metro Bercy).

Early April

Marathon International de Paris The Paris International Marathon starts on the place de la Concorde, 1er, and finishes on ave Foch, 16e.

Late April/early May

Foire de Paris Huge food and wine fair at the Parc des Expositions at Porte de Versailles in the 15e (metro Porte de Versailles) with a 10-day jazz festival held concurrently.

May–September

Paris Jazz Festival Free jazz concerts every Saturday and Sunday afternoon in the Parc Floral (metro Château de Vincennes), south of the Château de Vincennes on route de la Pyramide.

Late May–early June

Internationaux de France de Tennis (French Open Tennis Tournament) A glitzy tennis tournament held at Stade Roland Garros (metro Porte d'Auteuil) at the southern edge of the Bois de Boulogne in the 16e.

Late June/early July

La Course des Garçons et Serveuses de Café A Sunday afternoon 8km foot race along the Grands Boulevards and Saint Germain des Prés with some 500 waiters and waitresses balancing a glass and a bottle on a small tray. Spilling or breaking anything results in disqualification.

Late June

Gay Pride A colourful, Saturday afternoon parade through the Marais to celebrate Gay Pride Day. Various bars and clubs sponsor floats.

21 June

Fété de la Musique A music festival that caters for a great diversity of tastes and features impromptu live performances all over the city.

OLIVIER CIRENDINI

Tight squeeze: Gay Pride festivities in the Marais every June

Early July
La Goutte d'Or en Fête World-music festival (raï, reggae, rap and so on) at place de Léon in the 18e (metro Barbès Rochechouart).

14 July
Bastille Day Paris is *the* place to be on France's national day. Late on the night of the 13th, *bals des sapeurs-pompiers* (dances sponsored by Paris' fire brigades, who are considered sex symbols in France) are held at fire stations around the city. At 10 am on the 14th, there's a military and fire-brigade parade along ave des Champs-Élysées, accompanied by a fly-over of fighter aircraft and helicopters. In the evening, a huge display of *feux d'artifice* (fireworks) is held at around 11 pm on the Champ de Mars, 7e.

Late July
Tour de France The last stage of the world's most prestigious cycling event ends with a dash up ave des Champs-Élysées on the 3rd or 4th Sunday of the month.

Mid-September–December
Festival d'Automne 'Autumn Festival' of arts – including painting, music and theatre – held in venues throughout the city.

September/October
Foire Internationale d'Art Contemporain (FIAC) Huge contemporary-art fair with some 160 galleries represented. Usually held at the Grand Palais (metro Champs-Élysées Clemenceau) in the 8e.

24–25 December
Christmas Eve Mass Celebrated at midnight on Christmas Eve at many Paris churches, including Notre Dame, but get there by 11 pm to find a place in a pew.

DOING BUSINESS
France is not the easiest country in which to do business, as the legal and tax systems are quite complicated. The best advice is to find a lawyer who specialises in international matters.

To rent a fully equipped office, you can expect to pay a minimum of about 500FF a day plus about 200FF per hour to rent a meeting room. Faxes cost 13FF per page to send internally, 60FF to 75FF per page internationally. Email access averages about 45FF an hour. The rate for a bilingual secretary is around 160FF an hour; an English translator charges around 400FF per page.

One outfit that can supply all your office and secretarial needs is NewWorks (Map 2, ☎ 01 53 30 32 00, fax 01 52 30 32 01, ✉ production@newworks.net, metro Auber or Havre-Caumartin), 12 rue Auber, 9e, which can serve as your office away from your office 24 hours a day, seven days a week. Staff speak English. Check its Web site (www.newworks.net) for new locations around the city.

Before you leave home, it's a good idea to contact one of the main commercial offices or your embassy's trade office in Paris. These include:

American Chamber of Commerce (☎ 01 56 43 45 67, fax 01 56 43 45 60) 156 blvd Haussmann, 75008 Paris. Its membership directory costs 984FF (1036FF for the one listing American firms based in France as well).
Web site: www.amchamfrance.org

Australian Embassy Trade Office (☎ 01 40 59 33 00, fax 01 40 59 33 10) 4 rue Jean Rey, 75017 Paris

Canadian Embassy, Department of Commercial & Economic Affairs (☎ 01 44 43 29 00, fax 01 44 43 29 98) 35 ave Montaigne, 75008 Paris
Web site: www.amb-canada.fr

Chambre de Commerce et d'Industrie de Paris (CCI; ☎ 01 55 65 55 65, or 01 55 65 75 75 for the legal department, fax 01 55 65 78 68) 27 ave de Friedland, 75008 Paris

Franco-British Chamber of Commerce & Industry (☎ 01 53 30 81 30, fax 01 53 30 81 35) 31 rue Boissy d'Anglas, 75008 Paris
Web site: www.fbcci.com

Irish Embassy Trade Office (☎ 01 44 17 67 00, fax 01 44 17 67 60, ✉ irembparis@wanadoo.fr) 4 rue Rude, 75016 Paris

New Zealand Embassy Trade Office (☎ 01 45 01 43 10, fax 01 45 01 43 11) 7 ter rue Léonard de Vinci, 75116 Paris

UK Embassy Trade Office (☎ 01 44 51 34 56, fax 01 44 51 34 01) 35 rue du Faubourg Saint Honoré, 75008 Paris
Web site: www.amb-grandebretagne.fr

US Embassy Business Information Department (☎ 01 43 12 25 32, fax 01 43 12 21 72)

US Embassy Trade Office (☎ 01 43 12 22 22, fax 01 43 12 21 72) 2 ave Gabriel, 75008 Paris

FACTS FOR THE VISITOR

WORK

The number of unemployed in France has fallen to below 10% of the workforce after several years of double-digit unemployment figures. Although there are laws preventing people who aren't nationals of EU countries from working in France, it's increasingly possible to work 'in the black' (ie, without the legally required documents). Au pair work is popular and can be done legally even by non-EU nationals.

For practical information on employment in France, you might want to pick up *Working in France: The Ultimate Guide to Job Hunting and Career Success à la Française* by Carol Pineau and Maureen Kelly. Two other titles with extensive sections on France (including Paris) are *Summer Jobs Abroad*, edited by David Woodworth, and *Living and Working in France: A Survival Handbook* by David Hampshire.

To work legally in France you must have a carte de séjour (see Visas in the Documents section). Getting one is now almost automatic for nationals of EU countries and almost impossible for anyone else except full-time students.

Non-EU nationals cannot work legally unless they obtain an *autorisation de travail* (work permit) before arriving in France. This is no easy matter, as a prospective employer has to convince the authorities that there is no French or other EU national who can do the job being offered to you.

The Agence Nationale pour l'Emploi (ANPE), France's national employment service, has lists of job openings; on Minitel, key in 3615 ANPE. The ANPE has branches throughout the city; the branch (☎ 01 42 71 24 68, metro Hôtel de Ville) at 20 bis rue Sainte Croix de la Bretonnerie, 4e, deals with those people residing in the 1er, 2e and 12e arrondissements, for example.

Centre d'Information et de Documentation Jeune (CIDJ) offices have information on housing, jobs, professional training and educational options. The Paris headquarters (☎ 01 44 49 12 00, fax 01 40 65 02 61, metro Champ de Mars-Tour Eiffel) is at 101 quai Branly, 15e; check its Web site at www.cidj.asso.fr. These offices sometimes have noticeboards with work possibilities.

The fortnightly *FUSAC* (see the Newspapers & Magazines section) is an excellent source for job-seekers; check out the classified ads under Employment & Careers.

If you play an instrument or have some other talent you could try busking. Busking is a common sight in front of the Centre Pompidou, around Sacré Cœur and on the metro, where the RATP police are in charge. To avoid hassles, talk to other street artists before you start.

Au Pair Work

Under the au pair system, single young people (aged 18 to about 27) who are studying in France can live with a French family and receive lodging, full board and a bit of pocket money in exchange for taking care of the kids, babysitting, doing light housework and perhaps teaching English to the children. Most families prefer young women, but a few positions are also available for young men. Many families want au pairs who are native English-speakers, but knowing at least some French may be a prerequisite.

For practical information, pick up *The Au Pair and Nanny's Guide to Working Abroad* by Susan Griffith and Sharon Legg.

By law, au pairs must have one full day off a week. In Paris, some families also provide weekly or monthly metro passes. The family must also pay for French social security, which covers about 70% of medical expenses (it's a good idea to get supplementary insurance).

Residents of the EU can easily arrange for an au pair job and a carte de séjour after arriving in France. Non-EU nationals who decide to look for an au pair position after entering the country cannot do so legally and won't be covered by the protections provided for under French law.

Check the bulletin boards at the American Church (see the Cultural Centres section) as well as *FUSAC* (see the Newspapers & Magazines section) for job ads. In the latter, you'll find au pair work listed under Childcare. The Paris tourist office also has a list of au pair placement agencies.

Getting There & Away

AIR

Paris has two main airports: Aéroport d'Orly, 18km south of central Paris, and Aéroport Roissy Charles de Gaulle, which is 30km north of the city centre. A third airport at Beauvais, 80km north of Paris, handles certain charter flights and Ryanair's Dublin–Paris flights.

For information on transport options between the city and the airports, see the Getting Around chapter.

Departure Tax

International flights from Paris attract a departure tax that varies according to the destination (about 135FF to Italy, for example, and 400FF to the USA). The tax is always built into the price of the ticket.

Other Parts of France

France's long-protected domestic airline industry is being opened up to competition, so a mode of transport once limited to businesspeople on expense accounts is now an option even for budget travellers. Carriers with domestic flights include Air Bretagne, Air France, Air Liberté (owned by British Airways), AOM, Air Littoral, Corsair (run by the Nouvelles Frontières travel agency), Corse Méditerranée and Proteus.

All of France's major cities – and many minor ones – have airports. Thanks to the high-speed TGV trains, however, travel between some cities (eg, Paris and Lyons) is faster and easier by rail than by air, particularly if you consider the time and hassle involved in getting to and from the airports.

Domestic Airfares The cheapest, off-season, one-way youth fares on Air France (www.airfrance.fr) from Paris include:

destination	fare (FF)
Ajaccio/Bastia	440
Bordeaux	440
Biarritz	290
Nice	325

Adult tickets cost 1¼ to six times as much depending on restrictions and when you fly. In general, the longer in advance that you book (eg, seven or 14 days ahead) the cheaper the fare, and the cheaper the ticket the more cumbersome the restrictions. You can often find last-minute promotional fares on the Internet; see Discount under Travel Agencies in the Facts for the Visitor chapter.

The UK

Return fares on the London–Paris route can be as low as UK£50; with the larger companies, expect to pay from UK£88. Some of the best deals are offered by Buzz (www .buzzaway.com) and Ryanair (www.ryanair .ie). British Airways (www.britishairways .com) and Air France (www.airfrance.co .uk), whose fares are often quite reasonable (especially for young people), link London and a variety of other British cities (eg, Birmingham, Edinburgh and Manchester) with Paris. Other airlines that may have decent prices include British Midland (www .britishmidland.com) and British European (www.jea.co.uk). Belfast–Paris youth and student fares start at UK£50/92.

Popular discount travel agencies include STA Travel (☎ 020-7361 6145, www .statravel.co.uk), whose offices around the UK include one at 86 Old Brompton Rd, London SW7, and usit Campus (☎ 0870 240 1010, www.usitcampus.co.uk), whose many branches include one at 52 Grosvenor Gardens, London SW1. Other recommended travel agencies include: Trailfinders (☎ 020-7937 5400, www.trailfinders.co .uk), 194 Kensington High St, London W8; Bridge the World (☎ 020-7734 7447, www.b-t-w.co.uk), 4 Regent Place, London W1; and Flightbookers (☎ 020-7757 2000, www.ebookers.com), 177-178 Tottenham Court Rd, London W1.

Ireland

The discount travel agency usit Now (☎ 01-602 1600, www.usitnow.ie) has changeable

Air Travel Glossary

Cancellation Penalties If you have to cancel or change a discounted ticket, there are often heavy penalties involved; insurance can sometimes be taken out against these penalties. Some airlines impose penalties on regular tickets as well, particularly against 'no-show' passengers.

Courier Fares Businesses often need to send urgent documents or freight securely and quickly. Courier companies hire people to accompany the package through customs and, in return, offer a discount ticket which is sometimes a phenomenal bargain. However, you may have to surrender all your baggage allowance and take only carry-on luggage.

Full Fares Airlines traditionally offer 1st class (coded F), business class (coded J) and economy class (coded Y) tickets. These days there are so many promotional and discounted fares available that few passengers pay full economy fare.

Lost Tickets If you lose your airline ticket an airline will usually treat it like a travellers cheque and, after inquiries, issue you with another one. Legally, however, an airline is entitled to treat it like cash and if you lose it then it's gone forever. Take good care of your tickets.

Onward Tickets An entry requirement for many countries is that you have a ticket out of the country. If you're unsure of your next move, the easiest solution is to buy the cheapest onward ticket to a neighbouring country or a ticket from a reliable airline which can later be refunded if you do not use it.

Open-Jaw Tickets These are return tickets where you fly out to one place but return from another. If available, this can save you backtracking to your arrival point.

Overbooking Since every flight has some passengers who fail to show up, airlines often book more passengers than they have seats. Usually excess passengers make up for the no-shows, but occasionally somebody gets 'bumped' onto the next available flight. Guess who it is most likely to be? The passengers who check in late.

Promotional Fares These are officially discounted fares, available from travel agencies or direct from the airline.

Reconfirmation If you don't reconfirm your flight at least 72 hours prior to departure, the airline may delete your name from the passenger list. Ring to find out if your airline requires reconfirmation.

Restrictions Discounted tickets often have various restrictions on them – such as needing to be paid for in advance and incurring a penalty to be altered. Others are restrictions on the minimum and maximum period you must be away.

Round-the-World Tickets RTW tickets give you a limited period (usually a year) in which to circumnavigate the globe. You can go anywhere the carrying airlines go, as long as you don't backtrack. The number of stopovers or total number of separate flights is decided before you set off and they usually cost a bit more than a basic return flight.

Transferred Tickets Airline tickets cannot be transferred from one person to another. Travellers sometimes try to sell the return half of their ticket, but officials can ask you to prove that you are the person named on the ticket. On an international flight tickets are compared with passports.

Travel Periods Ticket prices vary with the time of year. There is a low (off-peak) season and a high (peak) season, and often a low-shoulder season and a high-shoulder season as well. Usually the fare depends on your outward flight – if you depart in the high season and return in the low season, you pay the high-season fare.

and refundable Dublin–Paris flights for students and under-26s for IR£55/99 one way/return (a bit more in summer). Ryanair (www.ryanair.ie) often has cheap promotional fares to Beauvais.

Continental Europe

Fares on some routes have been dropping as deregulation kicks in. Air France offers many of the best under-26 and student rates. Sample one-way/return Paris youth and student fares include: Amsterdam f158/279; Berlin DM282/461; Copenhagen 740/1480 kr (adult return from 1800 kr); Madrid 16,000/31,000 ptas (adult return from 25,000 ptas); Oslo 1416/2645 kr; Rome L229,000/486,000 (adult return from L350,000); and Stockholm 1212/2406 kr.

The USA

You should be able to fly from New York to Paris and back for about US$475 in the low season and US$775 in the high season. Tickets from the West Coast are US$150 to US$250 higher.

Reliable discount-travel chains in the USA include Council Travel (☎ 1-800-226 8624, www.counciltravel.com) and STA Travel (☎ 1-800-781 4040, www.sta-travel.com). San Francisco-based Ticket Planet (☎ 1-800-799 8888, www.ticketplanet.com) is an online agency with lots of round-the-world offers. A popular US auction-based ticket service is www.priceline.com.

If your schedule is flexible, flying standby can work out to be very reasonable. Airhitch (☎ 1-800-326 2009 in New York, 310-574 0090 in Los Angeles and 01 47 00 16 30 in Paris, www.airhitch.org) specialises in this sort of thing and can get you to/from Europe (but not necessarily Paris) for US$169/219/249 each way from the East Coast/Midwest/West Coast, plus tax.

Another very cheap option is a courier flight – as little as US$300 for a New York-Paris return arranged at the last minute. You can find out more about courier flights and fares from the Colorado-based Air Courier Association (☎ 1-800-282 1202, www.aircourier.org), which charges US$39 for one year's membership; the International Association of Air Travel Couriers (☎ 561-582 8320, fax 561-582 1581, www.courier.org); and Now Voyager Travel (☎ 212-431 1616, fax 212-334 5243, www.nowvoyagertravel.com).

Canada

Travel CUTS (☎ 604-659 2887 in Vancouver and 416-614 2887 in Toronto, www.travelcuts.com), known as Voyages Campus in Quebec, has offices in all major Canadian cities. From Toronto or Montreal, return flights to Paris are available from about C$900 in the low season; prices are C$300 or C$400 more from Vancouver.

Australia

Flight Centre (☎ 131 600 Australia-wide, www.flightcentre.com.au) and STA Travel (☎ 131 776 Australia-wide, www.statravel.com.au) are major dealers in cheap air fares. From Melbourne or Sydney one-way/return Paris tickets cost from A$981/1504 (low season) to A$1009/2110 (high season – ie, June to August and around Christmas). Airlines offering good deals include Kuwait Airways, Qantas Airways, Thai Airways International, Royal Jordanian and Malaysia Airlines. Fares from Perth are about A$200 cheaper.

New Zealand

STA Travel (☎ 09-309 0458) and Flight Centre (☎ 09-309 6171) are also represented in New Zealand. On Thai Airways International, one-way/return fares from Auckland (via Bangkok) range from NZ$1169/2015 (low season) to NZ$1315/2319 (high season). Other carriers with attractive fares include Royal Jordanian, Kuwait Airways, Qantas Airways and Malaysia Airlines.

Africa & Asia

Charter fares from Morocco and Tunisia can be quite cheap – if you're lucky enough to find a seat. Many of the cheapest fares from Asia to Europe are offered by Eastern European or Middle Eastern carriers. STA Travel has branches in Hong Kong, Tokyo, Singapore, Bangkok and Kuala Lumpur.

GETTING THERE & AWAY

Airline Offices

The following is a list of selected airlines that have offices in Paris. Details of airline offices can also be found in the Paris *Pages Jaunes* (Yellow Pages) under 'Transports aériens'.

Air Canada	☎ 01 44 50 20 20
Air France	☎ 0 802 80 28 02
	(information and
	reservations)
	☎ 0 836 68 10 48
	(recorded information on
	arrivals and departures)
	Minitel 3615 or 3616 AF
	Web site: www.airfrance.fr
Air Liberté	☎ 0 803 80 58 05
	Minitel 3615 AIR
	LIBERTE
	Web site: www.air-liberte.fr
Air Littoral	☎ 0 803 83 48 34
Air New Zealand	☎ 01 40 53 82 23
Air UK	☎ 01 44 56 18 08
	Minitel 3615 AIR UK
American Airlines	☎ 0 801 87 28 72
	(toll-free)
British Airways	☎ 0 825 82 54 00
British Midland	☎ 01 48 62 55 52 or
	☎ 01 41 91 87 04
Continental	
Airlines	☎ 01 42 99 09 09
	Minitel 3615
	CONTINENTAL
Delta Air Lines	☎ 01 47 68 92 92
easyJet	☎ 0 825 08 25 08
KLM-Royal	
Dutch Airlines	☎ 01 44 56 18 18
Lufthansa Airlines	☎ 0 802 02 00 30
Northwest	
Airlines	☎ 01 42 66 90 00
Qantas Airways	☎ 0 803 84 68 46
Ryanair	☎ 03 44 11 41 41
Scandinavian	
Airlines (SAS)	☎ 0 801 25 25 25
	Minitel 3615 FLY SAS
Singapore Airlines	☎ 01 53 65 79 00
South African	
Airways	☎ 01 49 27 05 50
Thai Airways	
International	☎ 01 44 20 70 80
United Airlines	☎ 0 801 72 72 72
	Minitel 3615
	UNITED
	Web site: www.ualfrance.fr

BUS

Long-haul bus travel within France is not really an option, but neighbouring countries and the UK are well served by Eurolines (www.eurolines.com), an association of 31 bus companies that links Paris with points all over Western and Central Europe, Scandinavia and Morocco. Buses are slower and less comfortable than trains, but they are cheaper, especially if you qualify for the 10% discount available to those aged under 26 or over 60, or take advantage of the discount fares that are on offer from time to time.

The Eurolines ticket office (Map 6, ☎ 01 43 54 11 99 or 0 836 69 52 52, metro Cluny-La Sorbonne), 55 rue Saint Jacques, 5e, is open 9.30 am to 6.30 pm weekdays and 10 am to 5 pm on Saturday. Its Web site is at www.eurolines.fr. On Minitel, key 3615 EUROLINES. The Gare Routière Internationale de Paris-Gallieni (international bus terminal; Map 1, ☎ 0 836 69 52 52, metro Gallieni) is at 28 ave du Général de Gaulle, 20e, in the inner suburb of Bagnolet.

Other Parts of France

Because French transport policy is biased in favour of the excellent state-owned rail system, SNCF, the country has only extremely limited inter-regional bus services. However, buses are used quite extensively for short-distance travel within departments, especially in rural areas with relatively few train lines (eg, Brittany and Normandy).

The UK

Eurolines (☎ 01582-404511, www.eurolines .co.uk) has coach services from London's Victoria Coach Station to Paris (7½ hours) for UK£32/45 one way/return (a bit less if you qualify for a discount, a bit more in summer) via Dover and Calais. Bookings can be made at any office of National Express (☎ 0990 808080, www.nationalexpress.co .uk).

Intercars (☎ 01582-404311 in the UK, 01 42 19 99 35 in France) has a Manchester–London–Paris service. Its Web site is at www.intercars.fr.

GETTING THERE & AWAY

Continental Europe

Eurolines' direct buses link Paris with destinations including Amsterdam (195FF, 7½ hours), Barcelona (485FF, 15 hours), Berlin (450FF, 14 hours), Budapest (515FF, 23 hours), Madrid (530FF, 17 hours), Prague (400FF, 16 hours) and Rome (450FF, 23 hours). These are one-way fares for young people and seniors – adults pay about 10% more. Return tickets cost about 20% less than two one-ways. In summer, it's not a bad idea to make reservations at least two days in advance.

Eurolines-affiliated companies can be found across Europe, including Amsterdam (☎ 020-560 8787), Barcelona (☎ 93 490 4000), Berlin (☎ 030-860 960), Brussels (☎ 02-203 0707), Copenhagen (☎ 33 25 12 44 or 99 34 44 88), Gothenburg (☎ 031-100 240 or 020-98 73 77), Hamburg (☎ 040-24 98 18 or 24 71 06), Madrid (☎ 91 528 1105 or 91 327 1381), Rome (☎ 06 442 33 928) and Vienna (☎ 01-712 0453).

Intercars (see the previous section) links Paris with Berlin and Eastern Europe. It has a Paris office at 139 bis rue de Vaugirard, 15e (metro Falguière).

TRAIN

Paris has six major train stations: Gare d'Austerlitz, Gare de l'Est, Gare de Lyon, Gare du Nord, Gare Montparnasse and Gare St Lazare; each station handles passenger traffic to different parts of France and the rest of Europe. SNCF (Société Nationale des Chemins de Fer Français) train information is available for mainline services on ☎ 0 836 35 35 35 and for suburban services on ☎ 01 53 90 20 20 or 0 836 67 68 69; its Web site is at www.sncf.fr. On Minitel, key 3615 SNCF (3615 SNCFIDF for suburban services).

Other Parts of France

France's superb rail network, operated by SNCF, reaches almost every part of the country. Many towns and villages not on the SNCF train and bus network are linked with nearby railheads by intra-departmental buses called *cars*.

France's most important train lines radi-

ate from Paris like the spokes of a wheel, making rail travel between provincial towns situated on different spokes infrequent and rather slow. In some cases (though these days less and less frequently) you have to transit through Paris, which sometimes requires transferring from one of the six train stations to another.

The pride and joy of the SNCF is the world-renowned TGV (*train à grande vitesse*, or 'high-speed train'; pronounced teh-zheh-veh). There are now three TGV lines, which link Paris with northern France, Amsterdam, Brussels and London; south-east France, the Mediterranean and Geneva; and western and south-western France, including Brittany and the Atlantic Coast.

One-way, 2nd-class fares to destinations around France from Paris include:

EDWARD SNIJDERS

Graceful, chic and incredibly fast:
the legendary TGV

euro currency converter €1 = 6.56FF

destination	fare (FF)	duration (hours)
Annecy	363	3½
Lille	208	1*
Lyons	318	2*
Marseilles	379	4¼*
Nantes	297	2*
Nice	455	6*
Strasbourg	220	4
Toulouse	455	5½*

*by TGV

The UK

There are two distinctly different rail services via the Channel Tunnel. Eurostar operates between London and Paris carrying passengers, while Eurotunnel operates only between Folkestone and Coquelles (5km south-west of Calais) carrying cars, motorcycles and bicycles with their passengers or riders.

Eurostar The highly civilised Eurostar (☎ 0990 186186 in the UK, ☎ 0 836 35 35 39 in France) takes three hours (not including the one-hour time change) to get from London to Paris. There are between 16 and 18 departures a day from London, some of which also pick up passengers at Ashford in Kent.

A full-fare, 2nd-class one-way/return ticket from London to Paris costs a whopping UK£155/270, but prices for return travel drop precipitously if you stay over on a Saturday night: UK£69/80 if you book 14/seven days ahead, UK£100 to UK£140

if you don't. Frequent special offers reduce prices still further. Tickets for under-26s cost UK£45/75 one way/return. Kids aged under 12 pay UK£29/58. Student travel agencies often have youth fares not available directly from Eurostar. With the cheapest tickets you cannot change your travel dates or get a reimbursement.

The Eurostar Web site is at www.eurostar .com. In the UK you can also book Eurostar tickets through Rail Europe (☎ 0990 848848), whose Web site is at www.raileurope.co.uk.

Eurotunnel High-speed Eurotunnel shuttle trains (☎ 0990 353535 in the UK, ☎ 03 21 00 61 00 in France, www.eurotunnel .com) transport cars, motorbikes, bicycles and coaches from Folkestone through the Channel Tunnel to Coquelles in soundproofed and air-conditioned comfort. Shuttles run 24 hours a day, every day of the year, with up to five departures an hour during peak periods (one an hour from 1 to 5 am).

Prices vary with market demand, but the regular one-way fare for a car, including all passengers, ranges from UK£110 in winter to UK£175 in summer; return fares are twice as much. Five-day return fares cost UK£139 to UK£229. The fee for a bicycle, including its rider, is UK£15 return; advance reservations (☎ 01303-288680) are mandatory. To take advantage of promotional fares you must book at least one day ahead.

Gard du Nord, terminus for Eurostar: the elegant façade...

...and the hustle and bustle inside one of Paris' busiest stations

euro currency converter 10FF = €1.52

Rail/Ferry Eurostar has eclipsed many of the long-established rail/ferry links, but they are still the cheapest option for crossing the Channel.

There are train-boat-train services in association with Hoverspeed (☎ 0990 240241, www.hoverspeed.co.uk) and others from London's Charing Cross station to Paris' Gare du Nord via Dover that take between seven and eight hours and cost £44/59 one way/return. This is obviously cheaper than Eurostar but takes a lot longer, and you've got to mess around transferring by bus between the train station and the ferry terminal on both sides.

Continental Europe

Rail services link Paris with every country in Europe; schedules are available from major train stations. Because of different track gauges and electrification systems, you sometimes have to change trains at the border (eg, from Spain). The TGV service to Paris' Gare du Nord from Amsterdam, Brussels and Cologne is known as Thalys. Youth fares are half (or less) of the regular adult fare; seniors also get discounts.

One-way, 2nd-class fares to destinations in Continental Europe from Paris include:

destination	fare (FF)	duration (hours)
Amsterdam	479	4¼*
Berlin	1084	11
Brussels	354	1½*
Cologne	439	4*
Copenhagen	1132	16
Geneva	420	3½*
Madrid	647	16
Prague	1066	16
Rome	660	12

*by TGV

CAR & MOTORCYCLE

Taking a car or motorcycle to Paris is quick and convenient if you want to brave the traffic. From the UK to France you can cross under the Channel by Eurotunnel (see the previous Train section) or sail over by various ferry routes (see the later Boat section). Once in France, modern *autoroutes* will get you to Paris quickly if

Flowers can help soothe a motorcyclist's frayed nerves in Paris.

rather expensively, as tolls are charged on 'A'-designated roads (but not on ones beginning with 'N'). The Périphérique ring road encircles central Paris, and it's often quicker to follow it round to the closest point to your destination before diving into the city traffic. For a list of car-hire agencies see Rental under Car & Motorcycle in the Getting Around chapter.

BICYCLE

France is an eminently cycleable country, thanks in part to its extensive network of secondary and tertiary roads, many of which carry relatively light traffic. One drawback: they rarely have proper verges (shoulders). Paris now has a network of 130km of *pistes cyclables* (bicycle paths). See under Bicycle in the Getting Around chapter for more information.

It's easy to rent a bike in Paris nowadays but just as easy to bring your own bike with you by air (in a packing case or simply wheeled to the check-in desk and checked in as a piece of baggage), by cross-Channel ferry (usually free but a fee of UK£5 or 50FF may apply, especially from April to September) or by Eurotunnel (on which a bicycle and its rider pay UK£15 return).

European Bike Express (☎ 01642-251440, www.bikeexpress.co.uk) transports cyclists and their bikes from the UK to places all over France, including Paris. Depending on your destination, return fares cost UK£139 to UK£169 (UK£10 less for members of the Cyclists' Touring Club).

euro currency converter €1 = 6.56FF

SIMON BRACKEN

GETTING THERE & AWAY

HITCHING

Hitching is never entirely safe in any country, and we don't recommend it. Travellers who decide to hitch should understand that they are taking a small but potentially serious risk. People who do choose to hitch will be safer if they travel in pairs and let someone know where they are planning to go.

Getting out of Paris by hitching near highway entrance ramps or at petrol stations doesn't work very well. Your best bet is probably to take an RER train out to the far suburbs and try from there. Eurotunnel motorists can take a car full of passengers through the Channel Tunnel without any extra charge so you can hitch to/from France for nothing. Channel ferry services sometimes include a number of passengers free with each car carried as well, but usually in the low or shoulder seasons only.

An organisation in Paris that matches travellers and drivers heading for the same destination is Allôstop Provoya (Map 3, ☎ 01 53 20 42 42, metro Cadet), 8 rue Rochambeau, 9e. It can also be reached via its Web site (www.ecritel.fr/allostop) and on Minitel (key in 3615 ALLOSTOP). Sample fares are Paris to Rennes (75FF), Marseilles (169FF), Hamburg (195FF) and Berlin (300FF). Annual membership costs 40FF. The office opens 9 am to 6.30 pm weekdays and 9 am to 1 pm and 2 to 6 pm on Saturday.

BOAT

Tickets for ferry travel from the UK and Ireland to France are available from most travel agencies in each country. Except where noted, the prices given in this section are for standard one-way tickets; in some cases, return fares cost less than two singles. Children aged four to somewhere between 12 and 15 (depending on the company) travel for one-half to two-thirds of an adult fare.

The UK

Fares vary widely according to the day of the week and the season. Three- or five-day excursion (return) fares generally cost about the same as regular one-way tickets; special promotional return fares, often requiring advance booking, are sometimes cheaper than one-way tickets.

Ferry companies usually make it hard on people who use super-cheap one-day return tickets for one-way passage. A large backpack is a dead giveaway that you're not on the ferry for an afternoon in Calais.

The fastest way to cross the English Channel is between Dover (Douvres in French) and Calais on one of Hoverspeed's SeaCat catamarans (50 minutes, six to 14 a day). For foot passengers, a one-way trip (or a return trip completed within five days) costs UK£24 (243FF). Depending on the season, a car with up to nine passengers pays UK£109 to UK£175 one way, UK£135 to UK£225 for a five-day return. All sorts of incredibly cheap promotional fares are often available, including same-day return fares for pedestrians for as little as UK£5.

Another quick crossing, handled by Hoverspeed's SeaCats, is the Folkestone–Boulogne route (55 minutes, four times a day). Foot passengers pay the same as for Dover–Calais; car crossings are a bit cheaper.

The Dover–Calais crossing is also made by car ferries run by SeaFrance (1½ hours, 15 a day) and P&O Stena (one to 1¼ hours, 29 a day). With SeaFrance, foot passengers pay UK£15 for a one-way or five-day return ticket; day trips are sometimes available for just UK£5 or UK£10. A car with up to nine passengers pays UK£122.50 to UK£170 one way, double that for a return. A five-day return is UK£150 to UK215. Prices are a bit cheaper via its Web site (www.seafrance.com). If you don't book ahead there's a surcharge at the port. With P&O Stena, foot passengers pay UK£24 for a one-way or five-day return ticket; a car with up to nine people pays a minimum of UK£122.50.

Other routes across the Channel include Newhaven to Dieppe; Plymouth to Roscoff; Poole to Cherbourg; Portsmouth to Caen (Ouistreham), Cherbourg, Le Havre or Saint Malo; Southampton to Cherbourg; and Weymouth to Saint Malo. There are also ferry services linking the Channel Islands with Saint Malo.

Ireland

Irish Ferries has overnight runs from Rosslare to either Cherbourg (18 hours) or Roscoff (16 hours) every other day (three times a week from mid-September to October, with a possible break in services from November to February). Foot passengers pay IR£40 to IR£80 (IR£32 to IR£66 for students and seniors). A two-bed cabin costs IR£26 to IR£34. A car with two passengers is charged IR£129 to IR£319.

From April to September, Brittany Ferries operates a car ferry every Saturday from Cork (Ringaskiddy) to Roscoff (14 hours), and every Friday in the other direction. Foot passengers pay IR£35 to IR£69; a car with two adults costs IR£115 to IR£319 one way.

Freight ferries run by P&O Irish Sea link Rosslare with Cherbourg (18 hours, three times a week). A car with two passengers pays IR£110 to IR£260 one way. Foot passengers are not accepted.

GETTING THERE & AWAY

Getting Around

THE AIRPORTS
Orly

Aéroport d'Orly, the older and smaller of Paris' two major international airports, is 18km south of the city. Air France and some other international carriers (eg, Iberia and TAP Air Portugal) use Orly-Ouest (the west terminal), so the old rule of thumb – Orly-Sud (the south terminal) for international flights, Orly-Ouest for domestic services – no longer holds. A driverless overhead rail-line linking Orly-Ouest with Orly-Sud – part of the Orlyval system (see later in this section) – functions as a free shuttle between the terminals.

For flight and other information call ☎ 01 49 75 15 15 or 0 836 25 05 05. On Minitel, key in 3615 HORAV.

To/From Orly There are half a dozen public-transport options linking Orly with Paris. Apart from RATP (Régie Autonome des Transports Parisians) bus No 183, all services call at both terminals. Tickets for the bus services are sold on board. With certain exceptions, children aged between four or five and 10 or 12 pay half-price.

Orlybus
This RATP bus (☎ 01 44 36 32 74; 35FF, 30 minutes) runs to/from Denfert Rochereau metro station (Map 1) in the 14e. It runs every 12 minutes from 6.30 am to 11.30 pm and makes several stops in the eastern 14e in each direction.

Jetbus
With the exception of the slow public bus, this is the cheapest way to get into the city (☎ 01 69 01 00 09; 26.50FF, 20 minutes). Running every 12 to 15 minutes from about 6 am to about 10 pm, it runs to/from Villejuif Louis Aragon metro station, which is a bit south of the 13e on the city's southern fringe. From there a regular metro ticket will get you into the centre of Paris.

Air France Bus No 1
This bus (☎ 01 41 56 89 00; 45FF, 30 to 45 minutes) runs to/from the eastern side of Gare Montparnasse in the 15e (Map 4, metro Montparnasse Bienvenüe), along rue du Commandant René Mouchotte, as well as Aérogare des

Invalides in the 7e (Map 4, metro Invalides). I runs every 12 minutes from 6 am to 11.30 pr (5.45 am to 11 pm *to* the airport). On your wa into the city, you can request to get off at Port d'Orléans or Duroc metro station.

RATP Bus No 183
This is a slow public bus that links Orly-Su (only) with Porte de Choisy metro station (Ma 1), at the southern edge of the 13e. The cost i just 8FF or one metro/bus ticket. It runs every 3 minutes or so from 5.35 am to 12.30 am daily.

Orlyval
This service links the airport with the city cen tre via the RER (Réseau Express Régional; se the later Public Transport section) and a shuttl train (☎ 0 836 68 77 14; 57FF, 35 minutes). A completely automated shuttle train runs to/from Antony RER station on RER line B in eigh minutes; to get to Antony from the city, take lin B4 towards Saint-Rémy-lès-Chevreuse. Orlyva tickets are valid for 1st-class passage on th RER and for metro travel within the city. Orly val runs from 6 am to 10.30 pm Monday to Sat urday and from 7 am to 11 pm on Sunday.

Orlyrail
Orlyrail links the airport with RER line C (32.50FF, 50 minutes). An airport shuttle bus which runs every 15 minutes from 5.30 am t 9 pm and then every half-hour to 11.30 pm takes you to/from Pont de Rungis-Aéropor d'Orly RER station; from the city, take a C. train code-named ROMI or MONA (indicate both on the train and on the lightboard) toward Pont de Rungis or Massy-Palaiseau. Tickets are valid for onward travel on the metro.

Apart from public transport the followin options are available:

Shuttle Van
ParisShuttle (☎ 01 43 90 91 91, @ parishuttle@ aol.com), Paris Airports Service (☎ 01 49 62 7 78, @ pas@magic.fr) and Airport Shuttle (☎ 0 45 38 55 72, www.airportshuttle.fr) all provide door-to-door service for around 125FF for a sin gle person, or 75FF per person for two or mor people. Book in advance and allow for numer ous pick-ups and drop-offs.

Taxi
A standard taxi to/from central Paris will cos between 120FF and 175FF and take 20 to 3 minutes, depending on traffic conditions.

Roissy Charles de Gaulle

Aéroport Roissy Charles de Gaulle, 30km north-east of the city centre in the suburb of Roissy, consists of three terminal complexes. Aérogare 2 has five semicircular terminals that face each other in pairs (2A, 2B, 2C, 2D and 2F); a sixth one – 2E – is scheduled to open in 2003. Aérogare 2 is used by Air France for both international and domestic flights as well as by a number of foreign carriers, but the majority of international carriers use the cylindrical Aérogare 1. Aérogare T9 is used by charter companies and domestic airlines.

Flight and other information is available in English or French (24 hours) on ☎ 01 48 62 22 80 or 0 836 25 05 05. On Minitel, key in 3615 HORAV.

To/From Roissy Charles de Gaulle

Roissy Charles de Gaulle has two train stations: Aéroport Charles de Gaulle 1 (CDG1), which is linked to other parts of the airport complex by a free shuttle bus, and the sleek Aéroport Charles de Gaulle 2 (CDG2) at Aérogare 2. Both are served by commuter trains on RER line B3 (known as Roissyrail), which is on the TGV link that connects the TGV Nord line with the TGV Sud-Est line, and is also connected with the TGV Atlantique line.

Airport shuttle buses link Aérogare 1 with both train stations and Aérogare 2. Shuttle buses also go to Aérogare T9.

There are four public-transport options for travel between Aéroport Roissy Charles de Gaulle and Paris. Tickets for the bus services are sold on board. With certain exceptions, children aged between four or five and 10 or 12 pay half-price.

Roissybus
This RATP-run bus (☎ 01 48 04 18 24; 48FF, about 45 minutes) links Aérogares 1 & 2 with place de l'Opéra (Maps 2 & 3, metro Opéra) in the 9e.

Air France Bus Nos 2 & 4
Air France bus No 2 (☎ 01 41 56 89 00; 60FF, 35 to 50 minutes) links the airport with two locations on the Right Bank: outside 1 ave Carnot near the Arc de Triomphe (Map 2, metro Charles de Gaulle-Étoile) in the 17e, and the Palais des Congrès de Paris at blvd Gouvion Saint Cyr at Porte Maillot (Map 2, metro Porte Maillot), also in the 17e. Buses run every 12 to 20 minutes from 5.45 am to 11.30 pm (to 11 pm to the airport). Air France bus No 4 (70FF, 45 to 55 minutes) links the airport with Gare de Lyon (Map 5) at 20 bis blvd Diderot, and Gare Montparnasse (Map 4, metro Montparnasse Bienvenüe) in the 15e. Buses leave the airport every half-hour from 7.30 am to 9 pm; there are departures from the city every half-hour from 7 am to 9.30 pm.

RATP Bus Nos 350 & 351
RATP bus No 350 (24FF or three metro/bus tickets, one hour) links Aérogares 1 & 2 with Porte de la Chapelle in the 18e and stops at Gare du Nord (Map 3) at 184 rue du Faubourg Saint Denis, 10e, and Gare de l'Est (Map 3) on rue du 8 Mai 1945, 10e. RATP Bus No 351 goes to ave du Trône, on the eastern side of place de la Nation (Map 1, metro Nation) in the 11e and runs every half-hour or so until 9.30 pm (8.20 pm from the city to the airport).

Roissyrail (RER Line B3)
This rail line (49FF, 35 minutes) links both of the airport's train stations with the city. To get to the airport, take any RER line B train whose four-letter destination code begins with E (eg, EIRE). Regular metro ticket windows can't always sell Roissyrail tickets, so you may have to buy one at the RER station where you board. Trains run every 15 minutes from 5.30 am to around 11 pm.

In addition to the public transport options you can use the following:

Shuttle Van
The three companies listed under Shuttle Van in the Orly section will take you from Roissy Charles de Gaulle to your hotel for about 150FF for a single person, or 85FF per person for two or more people. Book in advance.

Taxi
Taxis to/from the city centre cost 200FF to 280FF, depending on the traffic and time of day.

Between Orly & Roissy Charles de Gaulle

Air France bus No 3 (☎ 01 41 56 89 00, 75FF) runs between the two airports every 20 to 30 minutes from 6 am to 11 or 11.30 pm; the service is free for Air France passengers making flight connections. When traffic is not heavy, the ride takes 50 to 60 minutes.

Taking a combination of Roissyrail and Orlyval costs 106FF and takes about an hour. A taxi from one airport to the other should cost around 350FF.

Beauvais

The city of Beauvais is 80km north of Paris and its airport is used by charter companies and the discount airline Ryanair for its flights between Paris and Dublin.

To/From Beauvais An express bus, which leaves and picks up from outside the James Joyce pub (Map 2, ☎ 01 44 09 70 32, metro Porte Maillot), 71 blvd Gouvion Saint Cyr, 17e, departs 2½ hours prior to each Ryanair departure and leaves the airport 20 minutes after each arrival. Tickets (50FF) can be purchased from Ryanair at the airport and the James Joyce pub (open 7 am to 2 am daily). The trip takes about one hour.

PUBLIC TRANSPORT

Paris' public transport system, most of which is operated by RATP, is one of the cheapest and most efficient in the Western world. RATP's map No 1, the *Plan de Paris* – showing metro, RER and bus routes – is available free at most metro-station ticket windows and RATP information desks, and will meet most travellers' requirements.

Metro & RER

Paris' underground network consists of two separate but linked systems: the Métropolitain, known as the *métro*, which now counts 14 lines (with the opening of the ultramodern, driverless Météor linking Madeleine station with Bibliothèque station and RER line C) and over 300 stations; and the RER, a network of suburban services that pass through the city centre. When we provide the names of specific stations in this book, the term 'metro' is used to cover both the Métropolitain and the RER system within Paris proper.

Information Metro maps of various sizes and degrees of detail are available for free

RICHARD NEBESKY

The Métropolitain, indispensable for getting around the city

at metro ticket windows. For information on the metro, RER and bus system, call the RATP's 24-hour inquiries number on ☎ 0 836 68 77 14 (in French) or 0 836 68 41 14 (in English). Its Web site is www.ratp.fr; on Minitel, key in 3615 RATP. For a useful tool on Minitel, key in 3615 SITU: enter your destination in Paris or the Île de France and you'll get an immediate response on the quickest and easiest public transport route.

Information on SNCF's suburban services (including certain RER lines) is available on ☎ 01 53 90 20 20 or 0 836 67 68 69. SNCF's Web site is at www.sncf.fr; on Minitel, key in 3615 SNCFIDF.

Metro Network Each metro train is known by the name of its terminus, which means that trains on the same line have different names depending on the direction in which they are travelling. Each line also has

Art in the Metro

There are more modern underground railways than the Paris metro, but few are as convenient, as reasonably priced or, at the better stations, more elegant. To mark what was both the start of the new millennium *and* the centenary of the Métropolitain, the Régie Autonome des Transports Parisians (RATP) set up themed displays in nine different stations – from Health at Pasteur and Cinema at Bonne Nouvelle to Creation at Saint Germain des Prés and Europe at (where else?) Europe. Many of the exhibits are meant to last (and evolve) over the next few years.

At the same time some 175 metro stations have been given a face-lift, with their lighting improved and their permanent decorations spruced up and/or rearranged. The following list is just a sample of the most interesting stations from an artistic point of view. The true train (station) spotters among you – and we know you're out there – will want to pick up a copy of *Promenades dans le Métro* (Excursions on the Metro), which highlights some 17 of the best stations and is available free from RATP information desks.

Abbesses (Map 8, line No 12) The noodle-like pale-green metalwork and glass canopy of the station entrance is one of the finest examples of the work of Henri Guimard (1867-1942), the best-known French Art-Nouveau architect, whose signature style once graced most metro stations. Another fine example can be found at the **Porte Dauphine** station entrance (Map 1, line No 2).
Arts et Métiers (Map 6, line No 11 platform) The copper panelling, portholes and mechanisms of this station recall Jules Verne, Captain Nemo and the nearby Musée des Arts et Métiers.
Bastille (Map 6, line No 5 platform) A large ceramic fresco features scenes taken from newspaper engravings published during the Revolution.
Bibliothèque (Map 9, line No 14) This enormous new station (1998) – all screens, steel and glass, and the terminus of the driverless Météor metro train – resembles a high-tech cathedral.
Champs-Élysées Clemenceau (Map 2, transfer corridor between line Nos 1 & 13) The elegant frescoes in blue, enamelled faïence recall Portuguese *azulejos* tiles and so they should: they were done by Manuel Cargaleiro as part of a cultural exchange between Paris and Lisbon.
Cluny-La Sorbonne (Map 6, line No 10 platform) A large ceramic mosaic replicates the signatures of intellectuals, artists and scientists from the Latin Quarter.
Concorde (Map 2, line No 12 platform) On the walls of the station, what look like children's building blocks in white and blue ceramic spell out the text of the *Déclaration des Droits de l'Homme and du Citoyen* (Declaration of the Rights of Man), the document setting forth the principles of the French Revolution.
Louvre-Rivoli (Map 6, line No 1 platform and corridor) Statues, bas-reliefs and photographs offer a small taste of what's to come at the nearby Musée du Louvre.

a number (from 1 to 14), and these are being used more and more by Parisians these days.

Though there are plans afoot to change the colour schemes, at present blue-on-white *direction* signs in metro and RER stations indicate the way to the correct platform. On lines that split into several branches, the terminus served by each train is indicated on the cars with back-lit panels.

Black-on-orange *correspondance* (transfer) signs show how to get to connecting trains. In general, the more lines that stop at a station, the longer the correspondance will take – and some (eg, those at Châtelet) are *very* long indeed.

White-on-blue *sortie* signs indicate the station exits from which you have to choose.

The last metro train on each line begins its run some time between 12.25 and 12.45 am. Metro travel is free after midnight and the barriers are left open. The metro starts up again around 5.30 am.

RER Network The RER is faster than the metro, but the stops are farther apart. Some parts of the city, such as the Musée d'Orsay, the Eiffel Tower and the Panthéon, can be reached far more conveniently by the RER than by metro.

RER lines are known by an alphanumeric combination – the letter (from A to E) refers to the line, the number to the spur it will follow somewhere out in the suburbs. As a rule of thumb, even-numbered RER lines head for Paris' southern or eastern suburbs while odd-numbered ones go north or west. All trains whose four-letter codes (indicated both on the train and on the lightboard) begin with the same letter have the same terminus. Stations served are usually indicated on electronic destination boards above the platform. Unlike the metro, the RER has 1st- and 2nd-class cars.

Suburban Services The RER and the SNCF's commuter lines serve suburban destinations outside the city (ie, those in zones 2 to 8). Purchase a special ticket *before* you board the train or you won't be able to get out of the station when you arrive. You are not allowed to pay the additional fare when you get there.

If you are issued with a full-sized SNCF ticket for travel to the suburbs, validate it in one of the orange time-stamp pillars before boarding the train. You may also be given a *contremarque magnétique* (magnetic ticket) to get through any metro/RER-type turnstiles on the way to/from the platform. If you are travelling on a multi-zone Carte Orange, Paris Visite or Mobilis pass, do *not* punch the magnetic coupon in one of SNCF's orange time-stamp machines. Some – but not all – RER/SNCF tickets purchased in the suburbs for travel to the city allow you to continue your journey by metro.

For some destinations, tickets can be purchased at any metro ticket window, but for others you'll have to go to an RER station on the line you need in order to buy a ticket. If you're trying to save every franc and have a Carte Orange, Paris Visite or Mobilis pass, you could get off the train at the last station covered by your coupon and then

ROB FLYNN

The RER can be an even faster way of getting across the city than the metro.

purchase a separate ticket for the rest of your journey from there.

Tickets & Fares The same RATP tickets are valid on the metro, the RER (for travel within the city limits) and buses as well as on trams (eg, in the northern suburb of Saint Denis) and the Montmartre funicular. They cost 8FF if bought individually and 55FF for a carnet of 10. Children aged four to 11 pay half the fare. Tickets are sold at every metro station, though not always at each and every entrance. At some stations, you can pay by credit card if the bill comes to at least 35FF; vending machines accept most cards.

One metro/bus ticket lets you travel between any two metro stations for a period of two hours, no matter how many transfers are required. You can also use it on the RER for travel within Paris (ie, within zone 1). However, a single ticket cannot be used to transfer from the metro to a bus, from a bus to the metro or between buses.

GETTING AROUND

Always keep your ticket until you exit from your station.

Bus

Regular bus services in Paris operate from between 5.45 and 7 am to 12.30 am daily. Services are drastically reduced on Sunday, on public holidays and after 8.30 pm, when a system of night buses (distinct from the Noctambus services described later in this section) is put into operation.

Tickets & Fares Short bus rides (ie, rides in one or two bus zones) cost one metro/bus ticket (see Tickets & Fares in the Metro & RER section); longer rides require two tickets. Transfers to other buses or the metro are not allowed on the same ticket. Travel to the suburbs costs up to three tickets, depending on the zone. Special tickets valid only on the bus can be purchased from the driver.

Whatever kind of single-journey ticket you have, you must cancel *(oblitérer)* it in the *composteur* (cancelling machine) next to the driver. If you have a Carte Orange, Mobilis or Paris Visite pass (see the later Travel Passes and Tourist Passes sections), just flash it at the driver when you board. Do *not* cancel your magnetic coupon.

Night Buses After the metro closes (between 12.25 and 12.45 am), the Noctambus network links the area just west of the Hôtel de Ville (Map 7) in the 4e with most parts of the city. Look for the symbol of a little black owl silhouetted against a yellow quarter moon. All 18 Noctambus lines depart every half-hour from 1 to 5.30 am daily.

Noctambus services are free if you have a Carte Orange, Mobilis or Paris Visite pass for the zones in which you are travelling. Otherwise, a single ride costs 15FF and allows one immediate transfer onto another Noctambus.

Travel Passes

The cheapest and easiest way to use public transport is to get a Carte Orange, a combined metro, RER and bus pass whose accompanying magnetic coupon comes in weekly and monthly versions. You can get tickets for travel in two to eight urban and suburban zones, but unless you'll be using the suburban commuter lines extensively, the basic ticket valid for zones 1 and 2 should be sufficient.

A weekly ticket costs 82FF for zones 1 and 2 and is valid from Monday to Sunday. Even if you'll be in Paris for only three or four days, it may work out cheaper than buying carnets, and it will certainly cost less than buying a daily Mobilis or Paris Visite pass (see the following Tourist Passes section). The monthly Carte Orange ticket (279FF for zones 1 and 2) begins on the first day of each calendar month. Both are on sale in metro and RER stations from 6.30 am to 10 pm and at certain bus terminals. You can also buy your Carte Orange coupon from vending machines and even via the RATP Web site (www.ratp.fr), though you'll need a French postal address for the latter.

To buy your first Carte Orange, take a passport-size photograph of yourself to any metro or RER ticket window (four photos are available from automatic booths in train and many metro stations for 25FF). Request a Carte Orange (which is free) and the kind of coupon you'd like. To prevent tickets from being used by more than one person, you must write your surname *(nom)* and first name *(prénom)* on the Carte Orange, and the number of your Carte Orange on each weekly or monthly coupon you buy (next to the words 'Carte No').

Tourist Passes

The rather pricey Mobilis and Paris Visite passes are valid on the metro, the RER, the SNCF's suburban lines, buses, night buses, trams and the Montmartre funicular railway. They do not require a photo, though you should write your card number on the ticket.

The Mobilis card and its coupon allows unlimited travel for one day in two to eight zones (32FF to 110FF). It is on sale at all metro and RER ticket windows as well as SNCF stations in the Paris region, but you would have to make at least six metro trips in a day (based on the carnet price) to break even on this pass.

GETTING AROUND

Paris Visite passes, which allow the holder discounted entry to certain museums and activities as well as discounts on transport fares, are valid for one, two, three or five consecutive days of travel in either three, five or eight zones. The version covering one to three zones costs 55/90/120/175FF for one/two/three/five days. Children aged four to 11 pay half-price. They can be purchased at larger metro and RER stations, at SNCF bureaus in Paris and at the airports.

CAR & MOTORCYCLE

The easiest way to turn a stay in Paris into an uninterrupted series of hassles is to arrive by car. If driving the car doesn't destroy your holiday sense of spontaneity, parking the damn thing will. In many parts of Paris you have to pay 10FF or 15FF an hour to park your car on the street. Large municipal parking garages usually charge 15FF an hour, 130FF for up to 10 hours and 200FF for 24 hours.

Parking fines are 75FF or 230FF, and parking attendants dispense them with great abandon (and glee, some would add). You pay them by purchasing a *timbre amende* (fine stamp) for the amount written on the ticket from any *tabac* (tobacconist), affixing the stamp to the pre-addressed coupon and dropping it in a letter box. We know all about it – we've been there many times.

But while driving in Paris is nerve-wracking, it is not impossible, except for the faint-hearted or indecisive. The fastest way to get across the city is usually via the blvd Périphérique (Map 1), the ring road that encircles the city.

Rental

A small car (eg, a Peugeot 106) for one day without insurance and no kilometres costs 290FF from Hertz, but there are deals from smaller agencies from as little as 269FF a day with 100km, 569FF for a weekend with 800km and 999FF for five days with 1000km.

Most of the larger companies listed below have offices at the airports, and several are also represented at Aérogare des Invalides in the 7e (Map 4, metro Invalides):

Avis	☎ 0 802 05 05 05
	☎ 01 42 66 67 58
Budget	☎ 0 800 10 00 01
Europcar	☎ 0 803 35 23 52
Hertz	☎ 01 39 38 38 38
National/Citer	☎ 01 42 06 06 06
Thrifty	☎ 0 801 45 45 45

For other rental operators check the Yellow Pages under 'Location d'Automobiles Tourisme et Utilitaires'. The following are some local companies offering more reasonable rates. It's a good idea to reserve at least three days ahead, especially for holiday weekends and during the summer.

ADA (☎ 0 836 68 40 02, www.ada-location.com) ADA has some 18 bureaus in Paris, including ones at 72 rue de Rome, 8e (Map 2, ☎ 01 42 93 65 13, metro Rome); 97 blvd Magenta, 10e (Map 3, ☎ 01 47 70 06 06, metro Gare du Nord); and 34 ave de la République, 11e (Map 6, ☎ 01 48 06 58 13, metro Parmentier).

Rent A Car Système (☎ 0 836 69 46 95) Rent A Car has a dozen branches in Paris, including ones at 115 blvd Magenta, 10e (Map 3, ☎ 01 42 80 31 31, metro Gare du Nord); 79 rue de Bercy, 12e (Map 9, ☎ 01 43 45 98 99, metro Bercy); and 84 ave de Versailles, 16e (Map 1, ☎ 01 42 88 40 04, metro Mirabeau). Its Web site is at www.rentacar.fr; on Minitel, key in 3615 RENTACAR.

There's an outfit called Rollerland Paris (🄮 rollerland@wanadoo.fr) that hires out electric-powered mini-scooters for 299FF a day; there's a branch (Map 5, ☎ 01 40 27 90 97, metro Bastille) at 3 blvd Bourdon, 4e.

TAXI

The *prise en charge* (flag fall) in a Parisian taxi is 13FF. Within the city limits, it costs 3.53FF per kilometre for travel between 7 am and 7 pm Monday to Saturday (Tarif A), and 5.83FF per kilometre at night, on Sunday and on public holidays (Tariff B).

There's an extra 8FF charge for taking a fourth passenger, but most drivers refuse to take more than three people because of insurance constraints. Each piece of baggage over 5kg costs 6FF extra and for pick-up from SNCF mainline stations there's a 5FF

ASA ANDERSON

6, ☎ 01 53 46 43 77, fax 01 40 28 01 00, metro Les Halles) at the Forum des Halles, 95 bis rue Rambuteau, 1er. Bicycles cost a mere 20/75FF per hour/day or 115/225FF for a weekend/week, insurance included. The deposit is 1000FF along with some form of identification. The office opens 9 am to 7 pm daily. On Sunday from March to October Roue Libre bikes can also be rented from Cyclobus, parked in half a dozen locations around the city, including place de la Concorde, 8e, and place Denfert Rochereau, 14e.

Other outfits that hire out bicycles (usually for around 80FF a day) include:

Bike 'n' Roller (Map 6, ☎ 01 44 07 35 89, metro Saint Michel) 6 rue Saint Julien le Pauvre, 5e. This place also hires out rollerblades (in-line skates).
Paris Cycles (Map 1, ☎ 01 47 47 22 37 for bookings, or 01 47 47 76 50 for a recorded message) This outfit hires out bicycles from two locations in the Bois de Boulogne, 16e (see the Bois de Boulogne section in the Things to See & Do chapter for details).
Paris à Vélo, C'est Sympa! (Map 6, ☎ 01 48 87 60 01, ✉ info@parisvelosympa.com, metro Bastille) 37 blvd Bourdon, 4e
Paris Vélo (Map 5, ☎ 01 43 37 59 22, metro Censier Daubenton) 2 rue du Fer à Moulin, 5e

Bicycles are not allowed on the metro. You can take your bicycle out to the suburbs on some RER lines at the weekend and on public holidays (all day), and on weekdays before 6.30 am, between 9 am and 4.30 pm, and after 7 pm. More lenient rules apply to SNCF commuter services.

supplement. The usual tip is 2FF, with the maximum about 5FF.

Radio-dispatched taxi companies, on call 24 hours a day, include:

Alpha Taxis	☎ 01 45 85 85 85
Artaxi	☎ 01 42 03 50 50
Taxis 7000	☎ 01 42 70 00 42
Taxis Bleus	☎ 01 49 36 10 10
Taxis-Radio Étoile	☎ 01 42 70 41 41
Taxis G7	☎ 01 47 39 47 39

BICYCLE

Paris now counts some 130km of bicycle lanes running throughout the city, and a lane running parallel to the blvd Périphérique is planned. Many are not particularly attractive or safe, but cyclists can be fined (250FF) for failing to use them. The tourist office distributes a useful (and free) brochure-map produced by the mayor's office called *Paris à Vélo*.

There's plenty of space for cyclists in the Bois de Boulogne (16e), the Bois de Vincennes (12e) and along Canal Saint Martin (10e) to Parc de la Villette (19e) and then along the south bank of the 108km Canal de l'Ourcq. The quays along the Seine on the Right Bank and the quai d'Orsay on the Left Bank are closed to motor vehicles from 9 am to 4 pm on Sunday.

The best place to rent a bicycle is the RATP-sponsored Maison Roue Libre (Map

BOAT

From mid-April to early November, the Batobus river shuttle (☎ 01 44 11 33 99, fax 01 45 56 07 88) docks at the following seven stops:

Eiffel Tower (Map 4) Port de la Bourdonnais (next to the Pont d'Iéna), 7e
Musée d'Orsay (Map 4) Port de Solférino, 7e
Saint Germain des Prés (Map 6) quai Malaquais, 6e
Notre Dame (Map 6) quai Montebello, 5e
Hôtel de Ville (Map 7) quai de l'Hôtel de Ville, 4e
Musée du Louvre (Map 6) quai du Louvre, 1er
Champs-Élysées (Map 2) Port des Champs-Élysées, 8e

GETTING AROUND

Urban Orienteering

In Paris, when a building is put up in a location where they've run out of consecutive street numbers, a new address is formed by fusing the number of an adjacent building with the notation *bis* (twice), *ter* (thrice) or, very rarely, *quater* (four times). Therefore, the street numbers 17 bis and 89 ter are the equivalent of 17A and 89B.

The street doors of most apartment buildings in Paris can be opened only if someone has given you the entry code, which is changed periodically; the days of the *concierges*, who would vet each and every caller before they would allow them entry, are well and truly over. In some buildings the entry-code device is deactivated during the day, but to get in (or out) you still have to push a button (usually marked *porte*) to release the electric catch.

The doors of many apartments are unmarked: not only are the occupants' names nowhere in sight, but there isn't even an apartment number. To know which door to knock on, you'll usually be given cryptic instructions, such as *cinquième étage, premier à gauche* (5th floor, first on the left) or *troisième étage, droite droite* (3rd floor, turn right twice).

In France (and in this book), the 1st floor is the floor above the *rez-de-chaussée* (ground floor).

In both directions, the boats come by every 25 minutes from about 10 am to 7 pm (to 9 pm in July and August). A one/two-day pass costs 60/80FF (children aged under 12 35/40FF). There's a seasonal pass available for 250FF.

WALKING

Paris is a wonderful city to walk around (see the Marais, Literary and Passages walking tours in the Things to See & Do chapter) and is surprisingly pedestrian-friendly, in part because it is relatively compact. It's also a fairly level city, so apart from toiling up to Montmartre, there's no hill-climbing involved. Traffic can be a problem, though – cars will only stop for you if you absolutely assert your rights on pedestrian crossings.

And then there's those damn dogs; see the boxed text 'Remembrance of Dogs Past & Present' in the Things to See & Do chapter.

ORGANISED TOURS

If you can't be bothered making your own way around Paris or don't have the time, consider a tour by helicopter, bus, boat or bicycle or on foot.

Helicopter

It's not within everyone's budget but it will certainly be a view of Paris you'll never forget. Paris Hélicoptère (☎ 01 48 35 90 44, ✉ pariheli@club-internet.fr) offers 80km circular flights of Paris every Sunday from its base at Aéroport du Bourget. The trip lasts 25 minutes and costs 800FF per person. You can reach Le Bourget by RER line B3 or B5 (station: Le Bourget) or by RATP bus No 350 (stop: Musée de l'Air) from Gare du Nord (Map 3) at 184 rue du Faubourg Saint Denis, 10e, and in front of Gare de l'Est (Map 3) on rue du 8 Mai 1945, 10e.

Bus

From 1 pm to just before 9 pm on Sunday from April to late September, RATP's Balabus follows a 50-minute route from Gare de Lyon to the Grande Arche in La Défense that passes by many of central Paris' most famous sights. Buses depart about every 20 minutes and cost one metro/bus ticket.

L'Open Tour (☎ 01 43 46 52 06, fax 01 43 46 53 06) runs open-deck buses along three circuits (central Paris, Montmartre and Bercy) year-round, which allow you to jump on and off at more than 30 stops. Tickets cost 135FF for a day (110FF if you've got a Carte Orange, Paris Visite or Batobus pass) and 150FF for two consecutive days. Schedules vary, but on the 'Grand Tour' of central Paris with some 20 stops between Notre Dame and the Arc de Triomphe, buses depart every 15 to 25 minutes from 10 am to 6 or 6.30 pm.

Cityrama (Map 6, ☎ 01 44 55 61 00, metro Tuileries), 4 place des Pyramides, 1er, opposite the western end of the Louvre, runs two-hour tours of the city daily (150FF), accompanied by taped commentaries in a dozen or so languages.

Taking it easy: cruising around town on L'Open Tour bus...

...and along the Seine on one of the many river tours on offer

Boat

Be it on the Seine – '*la ligne de vie de Paris*' ('the lifeline of Paris'), as it's called – or the canals to the north-east, a boat cruise is the most relaxing way to watch the city glide by.

Seine Cruises From its base just north of the Eiffel Tower at Port de la Bourdonnais, 7e, Bateaux Parisiens (Map 4, ☎ 01 44 11 33 44, metro Pont de l'Alma) runs one-hour river circuits (50/25FF for adults/under-12s) and lunch/dinner cruises (300/580FF) year-round. From May to October, boats also depart from the dock opposite Notre Dame, on quai de Montebello, 5e (Map 6, metro Maubert Mutualité).

Bateaux Mouches (Map 2, ☎ 01 42 25 96 10, or 01 40 76 99 99 for an English-language recording, metro Alma Marceau), based on the Right Bank just east of Pont de l'Alma, 8e, runs 1000-seat tour boats, the biggest on the Seine. From mid-March to mid-November boats depart every half-hour from 10 am to 12.30 pm and from 1.30 to 11.30 pm. The rest of the year there are sailings at 11 am, 2.30 pm and 3.15 pm and on the hour from 4 to 9 pm daily, with additional cruises at 1 and 9.30 pm depending on demand. The 1½-hour cruise with commentary costs 40FF (under-14s 20FF).

Vedettes du Pont Neuf (Map 6, ☎ 01 46 33 98 38, metro Pont Neuf), whose home dock is at the far western tip of Île de la Cité, 1er, offers one-hour boat excursions year-round. Between March and October, boats generally leave every half-hour from

10 am to noon and from 1.30 to 8 pm; night cruises depart every 30 minutes from 9 to 10.30 pm. From November to February there are about a dozen cruises on weekdays (when night services stop at 10 pm) and up to 18 at the weekend. A ticket costs 50FF (children aged under 12 25FF).

Canal Cruises From March to October, Canauxrama (Map 6, ☎ 01 42 39 15 00) barges travel between Port de Plaisance de Paris-Arsenal, 12e, and Parc de la Villette, 19e, along the charming Canal Saint Martin and Canal de l'Ourcq. Departures are at around 9.45 am and 2.30 pm from Bassin de la Villette, 13 quai de la Loire, 19e, and at 9.45 am and 2.30 pm from Port de l'Arsenal, 50 blvd de la Bastille, 12e. The cost is 80FF (students 60FF and children aged six to 11 50FF, except on Sunday and on public holidays when everyone pays 80FF).

Paris Canal Croisières (☎ 01 42 40 96 97) has daily three-hour cruises from late March to mid-November from quai Ana-tole France, just north-west of the Musée d'Orsay (Map 4), leaving at 9.30 am and departing from Parc de la Villette for the re-turn trip at 2.30 pm. There are extra trips at 2.35 pm (from the museum) and 6.15 pm (from the park) from mid-July to August. The cost is 100FF for adults, 75FF for those aged 12 to 25 or over 60 (excluding Sunday afternoons and public holidays), and 55FF for children aged four to 11. In winter it runs sporadic themed cruises; visit its Web site at www.pariscanal.com for details.

euro currency converter €1 = 6.56FF

Bicycle

Both Roue Libre and Paris à Vélo, C'est Sympa! (see the main Bicycle section earlier in this chapter) offer between seven and 10 bicycle tours of Paris lasting about three hours and departing between 10 am and 3 pm at the weekend, and on weekdays depending on the demand. Tours run by Paris à Vélo cost 185FF (under-26s 160FF) while Roue Libre's are 135FF (85FF for children aged four to 12). Both include a guide, the bicycle and insurance. A short, 1½-hour tour run by Paris à Vélo at 11 am on Sunday costs 100/60FF.

An English-speaking outfit that has received good reports from readers is Bullfrog Bike Tours (mobile ☎ 06 09 98 08 60, ✉ bullfrogbikes@hotmail.com), which offers day tours of the city (150FF) at 11 am and 3.30 pm from early May to late August (at 11 am only from late August to mid-September), departing from ave Gustave Eiffel, 7e, just opposite the Eiffel Tower at the start of the Champ de Mars. Night bicycle tours (170FF) leave from the same location at 8 pm Sunday to Thursday from early May to mid-September.

Walking

An outfit called Paris Walking Tours (☎ 0 48 09 21 40, fax 01 42 43 75 51, ✉ paris@ pariswalkingtours.com) has tours in English (60FF, students aged under 25 40FF, children 30FF) of several different districts and themes, including Montmartre at 10.30 am on Sunday and Wednesday (leaving from Abbesses metro station) and the Marais at 2.30 pm on Sunday and Thursday and at 10.30 am on Tuesday (departing from Saint Paul metro station). A tour by the name of Hemingway's Paris departs from Cardinal Lemoine metro station at 10 am on Tuesday.

If your French is up to scratch, the sky's the limit on specialised and themed walking tours. Both *Pariscope* and *L'Officiel des Spectacles* (see Listings in the Entertainment chapter) list a number of themed walks each week under the heading 'Conférences'. They are usually both informative and entertaining, particularly those run by Paris aux Cents Visages (☎ 01 44 67 92 33) and Paris Passé, Présent (☎ 01 42 58 95 99).

Things to See & Do

Paris is hardly a daunting city for the uninitiated. It's a nice, oval-ish shape, the Seine divides it neatly in two, the 20 *arrondissements* (districts) spiral clockwise from the centre in a logical fashion and no two metro stations are ever farther apart than 500m.

If you want a general overview of Paris before striking out on your own, however, take one of the tours described in the Organised Tours section of the Getting Around chapter; jump-on/jump-off bus tours are particularly useful for this purpose, and even grizzled old guidebook writers like us often use them to get a handle on a city. Failing that you can always go up to look down – see Views in the following Highlights section.

But the unrepentant couch potatoes among you – and we know you're out there – will head for **Paris-Story** (Map 2, ☎ 01 42 66 62 06, metro Auber or Opéra), 11 bis rue Scribe, 9e, a 45-minute audio-visual romp through Paris' 2000-year history that is also known as Paristoric. There's headset commentary in a dozen different languages, and admission costs 50FF (30FF for students and under-18s). Shows begin on the hour from 9 am to 6 pm (to 8 pm from April to October) daily. Its Web site is at www.paris-story.com.

HIGHLIGHTS

Paris has a wealth of wonderful places to visit, but some features are so outstanding that they deserve a special mention. Though it's all a matter of taste and personal interest, here are a dozen museums, monuments and other sights that should not be missed:

Eiffel Tower

Stand under the illuminated Eiffel Tower at night, look up, and enjoy what is arguably the most beautiful, the most evocative cliché in the world.

Reaching for the skies: the golden roof of the Église du Dôme rises above the rooftops.

Centre Pompidou
Visit the renovated centre's new video area, expanded exhibition space, cutting-edge cinema and spectacular rooftop view.

Louvre
Have a look at one of the new collections (eg, primitive art) before the requisite visits to old favourites such as the *Mona Lisa* and the *Venus de Milo*.

Musée d'Orsay
Marvel at this beautiful museum's incomparable collection of impressionist art.

Sainte Chapelle
Admire the Holy Chapel's sublime stained glass on a sunny day.

Notre Dame
Attend an organ concert and watch the rose windows change colour in the light.

Marais
Check out the sublime *hôtels particuliers* (private mansions) by day (see the Marais walking tour later in this chapter) and the throbbing bars and clubs after dark.

Bercy
See what's happening in the burgeoning southeast of the city with its new national library, Bercy Village, a lovely park and a plethora of floating clubs and restaurants on the Seine.

Musée National du Moyen Age
Visit this museum devoted to the Middle Ages primarily to see the sublime series of tapestries

known as *La Dame à la Licorne* (The Lady with the Unicorn).

Views
Enjoy Paris from on high from the Eiffel Tower, the Centre Pompidou, Sacré Cœur, La Samaritaine department store, the Tour Montparnasse, Parc des Buttes-Chaumont or the Grande Arche de la Défense.

Cimetière du Père Lachaise
Visit the very rich and/or very famous – but invariably very dead – residents of this leafy Valhalla.

Musée Rodin
Go for the art, of course, but don't overlook the delightful villa housing it and its wonderful gardens.

LOUVRE (Maps 2, 4 & 6)

The Louvre area of the 1er contains some of the most important sights for visitors to Paris and has long been a chic residential area for people of means.

Musée du Louvre

The vast Palais du Louvre (Map 6, ☎ 01 40 20 53 17, or 01 40 20 51 51 for a recording, metro Palais Royal-Musée du Louvre) was constructed around 1200 as a fortress and rebuilt in the mid-16th century for use as a royal palace. It began its career as a public museum in 1793. The museum's Web site is at www.louvre.fr. On Minitel, key in 3615 LOUVRE.

The paintings, sculptures and artefacts on display have been assembled by French governments over the past five centuries. Among them are works of art and artisanship from all over Europe and important collections of Assyrian, Etruscan, Greek, Coptic and Islamic art and antiquities. Traditionally the Louvre's *raison d'être* is to present Western art from the Middle Ages to about the year 1848 (at which point the Musée d'Orsay picks up the torch) as well as the works of ancient civilisations that formed the starting point for Western art, but all that is changing as the world's most famous museum confronts the 21st century and discovers it actually rather likes it.

The Louvre may be the most actively avoided museum in the world. Daunted by the richness and sheer size of the place (the side facing the Seine is some 700m long), both visitors and locals often find the prospect of an afternoon at a smaller museum far more inviting. Eventually, most people do their duty and come, but many leave overwhelmed, unfulfilled, exhausted and frustrated at having got lost on their way to Da Vinci's *La Joconde*, better known to us as *Mona Lisa*. Since it takes several serious visits to get anything more than a brief glimpse of the works on offer, your best bet – after checking out a few you really want to see – is to choose a particular period or section of the Louvre and pretend that the rest is in another museum somewhere across town.

The most famous works from antiquity include the *Seated Scribe*, the *Jewels of Rameses II* and that armless duo, the *Winged Victory of Samothrace* and the *Venus de Milo*. From the Renaissance, don't miss Michelangelo's *Slaves* and works by Raphael, Botticelli and Titian. French masterpieces of the 19th century include Ingres' *La Grande Odalisque*, Géricault's *The Raft of the Medusa* and the work of David and Delacroix.

When the museum opened in the late 18th century it contained 2500 paintings; today some 30,000 are on display. The 7-billion-franc 'Grand Louvre' project inaugurated by the late President Mitterrand in 1989 has doubled the museum's exhibition space, breathing new life into the museum with many new and renovated galleries now open to the public. Seven new rooms containing furniture, silver, clocks and Sèvres porcelain opened in late 1999. In the spring of 2000 a controversial (given the museum's traditional focus) and permanent four-room exhibit devoted to primitive art collected from Africa, Asia, Australasia and the Americas was unveiled in the Pavillon des Sessions in the Denon wing.

Orientation The main entrance and ticket windows in the Cour Napoléon are covered by a 21m-high **glass pyramid** designed by the Chinese-born American architect IM Pei. You can avoid the queues outside the pyramid by entering the Louvre complex

Crystal light: the celebrated (or infamous, depending on your viewpoint) glass pyramid

via the Carrousel du Louvre shopping area (Map 6), 99 rue de Rivoli, or by following the 'Louvre' exit from the Palais Royal-Musée du Louvre metro station.

The Louvre is divided into four sections: Sully, Denon, Richelieu and Hall Napoléon. **Sully** forms the four sides of the Cour Carrée (literally 'square courtyard') at the eastern end of the building. **Denon** stretches along the Seine to the south. **Richelieu** is the northern wing along rue de Rivoli.

The split-level public area under the glass pyramid is known as the **Hall Napoléon**. It has an exhibit on the history of the Louvre, a bookshop, a restaurant, a café and auditoriums for concerts, lectures and films. The centrepiece of the **Carrousel du Louvre** shopping centre (open 8.30 am to 11 pm daily), which runs underground from the pyramid to the Arc de Triomphe du Carrousel (see later in this section), is an **inverted glass pyramid**, also by Pei.

Free maps in English of the complex *(Louvre Plan/Information)* are available at the information desk in the pyramid. The best publication for a general overview is *Louvre: First Visit* (20FF), which leads you to some 50 works of art, including the Code of Hammurabi stele, Vermeer's *The Lacemaker* and the Apollo Gallery, which contains the French crown jewels as well as the *Winged Victory of Samothrace*, the *Venus de Milo* and, of course, the *Mona Lisa*, who is soon to be accommodated in her own private room. The more comprehensive *Louvre: The Visit* (60FF) illustrates and describes more than 160 works of art. Both publications are available in the museum gift shop.

Opening Hours & Tickets The Louvre opens Wednesday to Monday, although it closes on certain public holidays. The hours are 9 am to 6 pm Thursday to Sunday, and 9 am to 9.45 pm on Monday and Wednesday. On Wednesday virtually the entire museum remains open after 6 pm but on Monday evening there's only a *circuit court* (short tour) of selected galleries in the three wings. The Hall Napoléon opens 9 am to 9.45 pm Wednesday to Monday.

Museum Closing Times

The vast majority of museums in Paris close on Monday though some (such as the Louvre and the Centre Pompidou) are closed on Tuesday. It is also important to remember that *all* museums and monuments in Paris shut their doors or gates between half an hour and an hour before their actual closing times (the ones listed in this chapter). If a museum or monument closes at 6 pm, for example, don't count on getting in much later than 5 pm.

Admission to the permanent collections costs 45FF (26FF after 3 pm and all day Sunday); the first Sunday of every month is free. There are no discounts for students or seniors, but those aged under 18 get in free. Admission to temporary exhibits varies. Tickets are valid for the whole day, so you can come and go as you please. Entry to just the Hall Napoléon costs 30FF for everyone. A *billet jumelé* (combination ticket) for the permanent collections and the Hall Napoléon costs 60FF before 3 pm and 40FF after 3 pm and all day Sunday. Those in the know buy their tickets in advance at the *billeteries* (ticket offices) of Fnac (see under Booking Agencies in the Entertainment chapter) or of any of the department stores listed in the Shopping chapter for an extra 6FF and walk straight in without queuing at all.

Guided Tours English-language guided tours (☎ 01 40 20 52 63) lasting 1½ hours depart from the area marked 'Accueil des Groupes' under the glass pyramid three to five times daily, depending on the season, but just once on Sunday at 11.30 am. Tickets cost 38FF (22FF for those aged 13 to 18, free for under-12s) in addition to the cost of admission. Groups are limited to 30 people, so it's a good idea to sign up at least 30 minutes before departure time.

Recorded, self-paced tours in six languages, available until 4.30 pm, can be rented for 30FF under the pyramid at the entrance to each wing. The tour should take about 1½ hours.

Other Palais du Louvre Museums

In addition to the Musée du Louvre, the Palais du Louvre contains three other museums (Map 6, ☎ 01 44 55 57 50, metro Palais Royal-Musée du Louvre) revamped or created under the Grand Louvre scheme. All are at the western end of the Richelieu wing and can be entered from 107 rue de Rivoli, 1er.

The **Musée des Arts Décoratifs** (Museum of Applied Arts) on the 3rd floor displays furniture, jewellery and such *objets d'art* as ceramics and glassware from the Middle Ages and the Renaissance through to the Art Nouveau and Art Deco periods. The **Musée de la Publicité** (Advertising Museum), which shares the same floor, contains everything from 19th-century posters touting elixirs to electronic publicity. On the 1st and 2nd floors is the **Musée de la Mode et du Textile** (Museum of Fashion and Textiles). The museums are open 11 am to 6 pm Tuesday to Friday (to 9 pm on Wednesday) and 10 am to 6 pm at the weekend. Admission to all three costs 35FF (25FF for those aged 18 to 25).

Église Saint Germain L'Auxerrois

Built between the 13th and 16th centuries in a mixture of Gothic and Renaissance styles, this parish church (Map 6, metro Louvre-Rivoli or Pont Neuf) stands on a site at the eastern end of the Louvre that has been used for Christian worship since about 500 AD. After being mutilated by 18th-century churchmen intent on 'modernisation' and by vandals during the Revolution, it was restored by the Gothic Revivalist architect Viollet-le-Duc in the mid-19th century and has some fine stained glass. It is open 8 am to 8 pm daily.

Arc de Triomphe du Carrousel

Built by Napoleon to celebrate his battlefield successes of 1805, this triumphal arch (Map 6), which is set in the Jardin du Carrousel at the eastern end of the Jardin des Tuileries, was once crowned by the *Horses of Saint Mark's*, 'borrowed' from Venice by Napoleon but returned after his defeat at Waterloo. The quadriga (a two-wheeled

Imperial grandeur: Napoleonic memories abound at the Arc de Triomphe du Carrousel.

RICHARD I'ANSON

chariot drawn by four horses) on the top, added in 1828, celebrates the return of the Bourbons to the French throne after Napoleon's downfall. The sides of the arch are adorned with depictions of Napoleonic victories and eight pink marble columns, atop each of which stands a soldier of the emperor's Grande Armée.

Jardin des Tuileries

The formal, 28-hectare Tuileries Garden (Maps 2 & 4), which begins just west of the Jardin du Carrousel, was laid out in its present form (more or less) in the mid-17th century by André Le Nôtre, who also created the gardens at Vaux-le-Vicomte and Versailles (see the Excursions chapter). The Tuileries soon became the most fashionable spot in Paris for parading about in one's finery. The gardens are open 7 am (7.30 am in winter) to between 7.30 and 9 pm daily, depending on the season.

The **Voie Triomphale** (also known as the **Grand Axe** or 'Great Axis'), the western continuation of the Tuileries' east-west axis, follows the ave des Champs-Élysées to the Arc de Triomphe and, ultimately, to the Grande Arche in the skyscraper district of La Défense (see later in this chapter).

Orangerie

The Musée de l'Orangerie des Tuileries (Orangerie Museum; Map 4, ☎ 01 42 97 48 16, metro Concorde), in the south-west corner of the Jardin des Tuileries at place de la Concorde, 1er, has important impressionist works, including a series of Monet's *Décorations des Nymphéas* (Water Lilies) and paintings by Cézanne, Matisse, Picasso, Renoir, Sisley, Soutine and Utrillo. The museum closed in the spring of 1999 for major structural renovations and will reopen at the end of 2001.

Jeu de Paume

The Galerie Nationale du Jeu de Paume (Map 2, ☎ 01 42 60 69 69, metro Concorde) is housed in an erstwhile *jeu de paume* (real – or royal – tennis court) built in 1861 during the reign of Napoleon III in the northwest corner of the Jardin des Tuileries. Once the home of a good part of France's national collection of impressionist works (now housed in the Musée d'Orsay), it now serves as a gallery for innovative short-term exhibitions of contemporary art and is the venue for exhibiting the work of artists invited to the Festival d'Automne (see the Public Holidays & Special Events section in the Facts for the Visitor chapter). It's open noon to 9.30 pm on Tuesday, noon to 7 pm Wednesday to Friday, and 10 am to 7 pm at the weekend. Admission is 38FF (28FF for those aged 13 to 18 or over 60 and students aged under 26).

Place Vendôme

Octagonal place Vendôme (Map 2, metro Tuileries) and the arcaded and colonnaded buildings around it were built between 1687 and 1721. In March 1796, Napoleon married Josephine in the building at No 3.

Today, the buildings around the square house the posh Hôtel Ritz (see Deluxe in the Places to Stay chapter) and some of Paris' most fashionable and expensive boutiques, more of which can be found along nearby rue de Castiglione, rue Saint Honoré and rue de la Paix (see the Shopping chapter). The Ministry of Justice has been at Nos 11 to 13 since 1815.

The 43.5m-tall **Colonne Vendôme** in the centre of the square consists of a stone core wrapped in a 160m-long bronze spiral made from 1250 Austrian and Russian cannons captured by Napoleon at the Battle of Austerlitz in 1805. The bas-reliefs on the spiral celebrate Napoleon's victories between 1805 and 1807. The statue on top depicts Napoleon as a Roman emperor and dates from 1873.

Jardin du Palais Royal

The **Palais Royal** (Map 6, metro Palais

Remembrance of Dogs Past & Present

The Paris municipality spends nearly 70 million francs a year to keep the city's pavements relatively free of dog dirt, and the technology it employs – most notably the distinctive *moto-crottes* (motorised pooper-scooters) driven by the city's *chevaliers du trottoir* (knights of the pavement) – is undeniably impressive. But it would seem that repeated campaigns to get people to clean up after their pooches have been less than a howling success. Evidence to this effect takes the form of 'souvenirs' left by recently walked poodles and other breeds, often found smeared along the pavement by daydreaming strollers, one assumes, or guidebook writers absorbed in jotting down something important. And it gets more serious than that: more than 600 people are admitted to hospital each year after slipping on a *crotte*. Until that far-off day when Parisians – and their beloved canines – change their ways, the word on the street remains the same: watch your step.

Royal-Musée du Louvre), which briefly housed a young Louis XIV in the 1640s, lies to the north of place du Palais Royal and the Louvre. Construction was begun in the 17th century by Cardinal Richelieu, though most of the present neoclassical complex dates from the latter part of the 18th century. It now contains the governmental Conseil d'État (State Council) and is closed to the public. The colonnaded building facing place André Malraux is the **Comédie Française** (see under Theatre in the Entertainment chapter), founded in 1680 and the world's oldest national theatre.

Just north of the palace is the Jardin du Palais Royal, a lovely park surrounded by arcades. Nowadays **Galerie de Valois** on the eastern side shelters designer fashion shops, art galleries and jewellers, though Guillaumot Graveur, an engraver's at Nos 151 to 154 that's been trading since 1785, seems to have hung on somehow. **Galerie de Montpensier** on the western side has a few old shops remaining, selling things like colourful Légion d'Honneur-style medals (shop Nos 3-4 and 6-7) and lead toy soldiers (shop No 13-15). Le Grand Véfour, one of Paris' oldest and most beautiful restaurants (see under Louvre & Les Halles in the Places to Eat chapter), is at the northern end. At the southern end there's a controversial **sculpture** of black-and-white striped columns of various heights (Daniel Buren, 1986).

The park opens daily from 7 am (7.30 am from October to March) to between 8.30 pm in winter and 11 pm in summer.

Le Louvre des Antiquaires

This impressive building at 2 place du Palais Royal (Map 6, metro Palais Royal-Musée du Louvre) houses some 250 elegant antique shops filled with *objets d'art*, furniture, clocks and classical antiquities affordable for anyone with a king's ransom to spare. It opens 11 am to 7 pm Tuesday to Sunday (Tuesday to Saturday in July and August).

LES HALLES (Maps 6 & 7)

The mostly pedestrian zone between the Centre Pompidou, 1er, and the Forum des Halles with rue Étienne Marcel to the north

and rue de Rivoli to the south is always filled with people, just as it was for the 850-odd years part of the area served as Paris' main marketplace *(halles)*. During the day, the main attractions are museums, art galleries, shops and places to eat, while at night – and into the wee hours of the morning – restaurants, theatres and discos draw Parisians out for a night on the town.

Centre Pompidou

It's all change at the Centre Georges Pompidou (Map 7, ☎ 01 44 78 12 33, metro Rambuteau) following a huge 550-million-franc renovation that took more than two years to complete and was finished just in time for the new millennium. The result is a stunning reworked façade on the west side – all white and light – and, inside, expanded exhibition space, a new cinema, a CD and video centre, dance and theatre venues, a cybercafé, a restaurant that has to be seen to be believed,

OLIVIER CIRENDINI

Making a splash: the captivating fountains on place Igor Stravinsky

work and play areas for children and a startling view of Paris from the terraces of the 5th and 6th floors.

The Centre Pompidou, also known as the Centre Beaubourg, has amazed and delighted visitors since it was inaugurated in 1977 not just for its outstanding collection of modern art, but for its radical (at the time) architectural statement. It is the most popular attraction in the city and attracts more than 20,000 visitors a day. Its Web site is at www.centrepompidou.fr. On Minitel, key in 3615 BEAUBOURG.

In order to keep the exhibition halls as spacious and uncluttered as possible, architects Renzo Piano from Italy and Richard Rogers from the UK put the building's 'insides' outside. The purpose of each of the ducts, pipes and vents that enclosed the centre's glass walls could be divined from the paint job: escalators and lifts in red, electrical circuitry in yellow, the plumbing in green and the air-conditioning system in blue. But it all began to look somewhat *démodé* by the late 1990s and hence the refit, including the now gleaming-white western façade.

The 4th and 5th floors of the centre are dedicated to exhibiting some of the 40,000-plus works of the **Musée National d'Art Moderne** (MNAM; National Museum of Modern Art), France's national collection of 20th-century art, including the work of the Fauvists, surrealists and cubists as well as pop and op art and contemporary works. The **Atelier Brancusi**, the studio of the Romanian-born sculptor Constantin Brancusi (1876-1957) on place Georges Pompidou to the west, contains almost 140 examples of his work as well as drawings, paintings and glass photographic plates. The centre also contains the **Bibliothèque Publique d'Information** (BPI); for details see the Libraries section in the Facts for the Visitor chapter.

Place Georges Pompidou on the west side of the centre and the nearby pedestrian streets attract buskers, street artists, musicians, jugglers and mime artists and can be as much fun as the centre itself. The fanciful **mechanical fountains** (Map 7) of skeletons, dragons, G clefs and a big pair

of ruby-red lips, south of the centre on place Igor Stravinsky, were created by Jean Tinguely and Niki de Saint-Phalle. They are a positive delight.

The **Forum du Centre Pompidou**, the open space at ground level with temporary exhibits and information desks, opens 11 am to 10 pm Wednesday to Monday (free). The MNAM's permanent collection opens 11 am to 9 pm on the same days and costs 30FF (20FF for students, seniors and those aged 18 to 26; free for under-18s, and for everyone on the first Sunday of the month). Admission to the Atelier Brancusi, open 1 to 9 pm Wednesday to Monday, costs 20FF. A combination ticket including access to the museum, atelier and rooftop costs 40FF/30FF while a 'passe-partout' valid for the day and allowing entry to the temporary exhibits as well costs 50/40FF. There's even an annual pass for 240/120FF.

Forum des Halles

Les Halles, Paris' main wholesale food market, occupied the area just south of the Église Saint Eustache from the early 12th century until 1969, when it was moved to the suburb of Rungis near Orly. In its place, the unspeakable Forum des Halles (Map 6, ☎ 01 44 76 96 56, metro Les Halles or Châtelet Les Halles), rue Pierre Lescaut, 1er, a huge underground shopping centre, was constructed in the glass-and-chrome style of the early 1970s. It all looks a bit frayed more than three decades on.

Atop the Forum des Halles is a popular **park** where you can picnic, people-watch and sunbathe on the lawn while gazing at the flying buttresses of the Église Saint Eustache (see the following entry). During the warmer months, street musicians, fire-eaters and other performers display their talents throughout the area, especially at **place du Jean du Bellay**, whose centre is adorned by a multi-tiered Renaissance fountain, the **Fontaine des Innocents** (Map 6), erected in 1549. The square and the fountain are named after the Cimetière des Innocents, a cemetery on this site from which two million skeletons were disinterred and transferred to the Catacombes in

RICHARD I'ANSON

Underneath the arches: the gorgeous Église Saint Eustache, seen from Les Halles

stops and 8000 pipes is used for concerts, long a tradition here. The church opens 9 am to 7 pm (to 8 pm in summer) Monday to Saturday and 9 am to 12.30 pm and 2.30 to 7 pm (to 8 pm in summer) on Sunday.

Tour de Jean sans Peur

The Gothic, six-floor, 29m-high Tower of John the Fearless (Map 6, ☎ 01 40 26 20 28, metro Étienne Marcel), 20 rue Etienne Marcel, 2e, was built by the Duke of Bourgogne in the early 15th century so he could hide at the very top, safe from his enemies, and has only recently opened for visits. You can climb to the top too from 1.30 to 6 pm Tuesday to Sunday (Wednesday, Saturday and Sunday only during school terms) and admission costs 30FF (20FF for students and seven- to 18-year-olds).

La Samaritaine Rooftop Terrace

For an amazing 360° panoramic view of central Paris, head for the roof of La Samaritaine department store's main building (Map 6, ☎ 01 40 41 20 20, metro Pont Neuf), rue de la Monnaie, 1er. The 11th-floor lookout opens from 9.30 am to 7 pm Monday to Saturday (to 10 pm on Thursday).

Tour Saint Jacques

The Flamboyant Gothic, 52m-high Tower of Saint James (Map 6, metro Châtelet) on the north-east side of place du Châtelet, 4e, is all that remains of the Église Saint Jacques la Boucherie, built by the powerful butchers' guild in 1523. The tower, topped by a weather station, is not open to the public.

Hôtel de Ville

After having been gutted during the Paris Commune of 1871, Paris' city hall (Map 7, ☎ 01 42 76 40 40, metro Hôtel de Ville) was rebuilt in the neo-Renaissance style (1874-82). The ornate façade is decorated with 108 statues of noteworthy Parisians. The visitors entrance is at 29 rue de Rivoli, 4e, where there's a hall used for temporary exhibitions (open 9.30 am to 6 pm Monday to Saturday).

The Hôtel de Ville faces the majestic

the 14e (see the 13e & 14e Arrondissements section later in this chapter) after the Revolution. One block south of the fountain is **rue de la Ferronnerie**, where in 1610, while passing house No 11 in his carriage, Henri IV was assassinated by a Catholic fanatic named François Ravaillac.

Église Saint Eustache

This majestic church (Map 6, ☎ 01 42 36 31 05, metro Les Halles), one of the most beautiful in Paris, is just north of the gardens atop the Forum des Halles. Constructed between 1532 and 1640, Saint Eustache's dominant style is Gothic though a neoclassical façade was added on the west side in the mid-18th century. Inside, there are some exceptional Flamboyant Gothic arches holding up the ceiling of the chancel, though most of the interior ornamentation is Renaissance and classical. The gargantuan organ above the west entrance with 101

place de l'Hôtel de Ville, used since the Middle Ages to stage many of Paris' celebrations, rebellions, book-burnings and public executions. Known as place de Grève (Strand Square) until 1830, it was in centuries past a favourite gathering place of the unemployed, which is why a strike is, to this day, called *une grève* in French.

MARAIS (Map 7)

The Marais (literally 'marsh'), the area of the Right Bank directly north of Île Saint Louis, was in fact a swamp until the 13th century, when it was put to agricultural use. In the early 17th century, Henri IV built place des Vosges, turning the area into Paris' most fashionable residential district and attracting wealthy aristocrats who then erected their own luxurious but understated *hôtels particuliers* (private mansions); see the Marais walking tour for a fuller treatment of these glorious structures, many of which now house museums or government institutions.

When the aristocracy moved out of Paris to Versailles and Faubourg Saint Germain, 7e, during the late 17th and the 18th centuries, the Marais and its townhouses passed into the hands of ordinary Parisians. The 110-hectare area was given a major face-lift in the late 1960s and early 1970s. Today, the Marais is one of the few neighbourhoods of Paris that still has most of its pre-Revolution architecture; indeed, the oldest house in Paris still intact (1407) is at 51 rue de Montmorency, 3e. In recent years the area has become trendy, but it remains home to a long-established Jewish community and is the centre of Paris' gay life.

Place des Vosges

Place des Vosges, 4e (metro Saint Paul or Bastille), inaugurated in 1612 as place Royale, is an ensemble of 36 symmetrical houses with ground-floor arcades (now occupied by upmarket art galleries, antique shops and places to eat and drink), steep slate roofs and large dormer windows, arranged around a large square. Only the earliest houses were built of brick; to save time, the rest were given timber frames and

faced with plaster, which was later painted to resemble brick.

The beloved author Victor Hugo lived at the Hôtel de Rohan-Guéménée (No 6) from 1832 to 1848, moving here a year after the publication of *Notre Dame de Paris* (The Hunchback of Notre Dame). **Maison de Victor Hugo** (☎ 01 42 72 10 16), now a municipal museum devoted to the life and times of the celebrated novelist and poet, opens 10 am to 5.40 pm Tuesday to Sunday. Admission (including a mandatory guided tour) costs 22FF (15FF for students and seniors, free for those aged under 26).

Hôtel de Sully

While in the vicinity of Place des Vosges, it's well worth ducking into the Hôtel de Sully (metro Saint Paul), 62 rue Saint Antoine, 4e, a superb, early-17th-century aristocratic mansion that now houses the Caisse Nationale des Monuments Historiques et des Sites (a body responsible for many of France's historical monuments). See the Marais walking tour for details.

Musée Carnavalet

Also known as the Musée de l'Histoire de Paris (Paris History Museum; ☎ 01 44 59 58 58 or 01 42 72 21 13, metro Saint Paul), 23 rue de Sévigné, 3e, this museum is housed in two hôtels particuliers: the mid-16th-century, Renaissance-style Hôtel Carnavalet, once home to the 17th-century writer Madame de Sévigné, and the Hôtel Le Peletier de Saint Fargeau, which dates from the late 17th century. The artefacts on display in the museum's sublime rooms chart the history of Paris from the Gallo-Roman period to the 20th century. Some of France's most important documents, paintings and other objects from the French Revolution are here as is Fouquet's Art Nouveau jewellery shop from the rue Royale and Marcel Proust's cork-lined bedroom from his apartment on blvd Haussmann.

The museum opens 10 am to 5.40 pm Tuesday to Sunday. Admission costs 30FF (20FF for students; free for those aged under 26 or over 60, and for everyone from 10 am to 1 pm on Sunday).

euro currency converter 10FF = €1.52

MEDIEVAL MEANDERINGS IN THE MARAIS

Monks and the Knights Templar settled in the Marais as early as the 13th century, which explains the religious nature of many of its street names (eg, rue du Temple, rue des Blancs Manteaux). But it wasn't until Henri IV began construction of place Royale (today's place des Vosges) in the

ASA ANDERSSON

early 17th century that aristocrats began building the *hôtels particuliers* (private mansions) so characteristic of the district.

These golden and cream-coloured brick buildings are among the most beautiful Renaissance structures in the city. Because so many were built at more or less the same time, the Marais enjoys an architectural harmony unknown elsewhere in Paris.

The Golden Age of the Marais' hôtels particuliers was the 17th century, though construction continued into the first half of the 18th. The removal of the royal court lock, stock and gilded slipper to Versailles sounded the death knell for the Marais, and the mansions passed into the hands of commoners, who used them as warehouses, markets and shops.

The Marais was given a major face-lift in the late 1960s and early 1970s and today many of the hôtels particuliers house government offices, libraries and museums. We provide opening hours for those that are open to the public; details of the four museums mentioned in this walking tour, as well as the Hôtel de Sully, where exhibitions are sometimes held, are given in the Marais section of this chapter.

Begin the tour at Saint Paul metro station on rue François Miron, 4e, facing rue de Rivoli. Walk south on narrow rue du Prévôt (Provost St) to rue Charlemagne, once called rue des Prestres (Street of the Priests). To the west on the corner of rue des Nonnains Hyères and rue de Jouy stands the majestic **Hôtel d'Aumont (1)**, 7 rue de Jouy, 4e, and its geometrical gardens, built around 1650 for a financier and considered one the most beautiful private mansions in the Marais. It now contains offices of the Tribunal Administratif, the body that deals with – God save us! – internal disputes in the bloated French civil service. Opposite Hôtel d'Aumont, at the corner of rue de Jouy and rue de Fourcy, is a wonderful **17th-century relief of a winemaker (2)**.

Continue south on rue des Nonnains Hyères and head east on rue de l'Hôtel de Ville. On the left is **Hôtel de Sens (3)**, 1 rue du Figuier, 4e, the oldest mansion in the Marais (begun around 1475), built as the Paris digs for the powerful archbishops of Sens, under whose authority Paris

distance: 2km
start & finish: rue François Miron (metro Saint Paul)

fell. When Paris became an archdiocese of its own, it was rented out to coach drivers, fruit sellers, and even a hatter. It was heavily restored in mock Gothic style (complete with turrets) in 1911; today it is the **Bibliothèque Forney** (☎ 01 42 78 14 60), open 1.30 to 8 pm Tuesday to Friday, and 10 am to 8.30 pm on Saturday (though you can enjoy the lovely courtyards anytime).

Continue east on rue de l'Ave Maria and then go north along rue des Jardins Saint Paul. The twin towers on the left are all that remain of **Philippe-Auguste's fortified wall (4)**, built around 1190 and interrupted by 39 towers. They are now part of the prestigious Lycée Charlemagne. To the right along rue des Jardins Saint Paul is the entrance to **Village Saint Paul (5)**, a courtyard of antique and crafts sellers.

Cross over rue Charlemagne and duck into rue Eginhard, a street with a tiny courtyard and fountain built during the reign of Louis XIII. The street doglegs into rue Saint Paul; at the corner with rue Neuve Saint Pierre are the remains of the medieval **Église Saint Paul (6)**. Tiny passage Saint Paul leads to the side entrance of the **Église Saint Louis-Saint Paul (7)**, a Jesuit church completed during the Counter-Reformation (open from between 7.30 and 9 am to 8 pm daily). Notice the 'bridge of sighs' with a tiny room above the passage.

Rue Saint Paul debouches into rue Saint Antoine. Turn west, passing the front entrance of the Église Saint Louis-Saint Paul at No 99, and cross over rue de Rivoli (looking eastwards to catch a fine view of Opéra Bastille) to rue Malher and head north. A **former *pâtisserie* (8)** at No 13 (now a clothes shop) has a fine old shop sign advertising *gateaux secs* (biscuits).

Rue Malher runs into rue Pavée, the first 'paved' (ie, cobbled) street in Paris. Take a quick detour south to No 10 and the Art Nouveau **Guimard synagogue (9)**; see the Marais section in this chapter for details. At 24 rue Pavée stands **Hôtel Lamoignon (10)**, built between 1585 and 1612 for Diane de France (1538-1619), duchess of Angoulême and legitimised daughter of Henri II. It is a fine example of late-Renaissance architecture; note the Corinthian capitals, the hunting scenes (recalling Diana, goddess of the hunt) in high relief on the pediments and the symbolic mirror (truth) and snake (prudence) above the main gate. Hôtel Lamoignon now houses the **Bibliothèque Historique de la Ville de Paris** (Historical Library of the City of Paris; ☎ 01 44 59 29 40) and is open 9.30 am to 6 pm Monday to Saturday.

The large initials 'SC' at the corner of rue Pavée and rue des Francs Bourgeois mark the site of the medieval **priory of Sainte Catherine (11)**; to the west, at 31 rue des Francs Bourgeois, 4e, is **Hôtel d'Albret (12)**, among the last of the great hôtels particuliers (1740) to be built. Cross over rue des Francs Bourgeois and walk up rue Payenne. The buildings on the right are the mid-16th-century, Renaissance-style **Hôtel Carnavalet (13)**, built between 1548 and 1654 and home to the letter-writer Madame de Sévigné (1626-96), and **Hôtel Le Pel-**

etier de Saint Fargeau **(14)**, which dates from the late 17th century. They are now both part of the Musée Carnavalet.

From the grille next to the **Chapelle de l'Humanité (15)**, 5 rue Payenne, 3e, a 'temple of reason' dating from the 18th century (the quote on the façade reads: 'Love as the principal, order as the base, progress as the goal'), you can see the rear of **Hôtel Donon (16)**, 8 rue Elsévir, 4e, built in 1598 and now the Musée Cognacq-Jay. At 11 rue Payenne is the lovely **Hôtel de Marle (17)**, built at the end of the 16th century, which now serves as a pretty posh Swedish Cultural Institute.

Opposite is a pretty green space called **square George Cain (18)** with the remains of what was once the Hôtel de Ville. Have a look at the relief of Judgement Day on the tympanum (façade beneath the roof). A short distance to the west and the north-west are two spectacular 17th-century hôtels particuliers that now contain museums: **Hôtel de Libéral Bruant (19)**, 1 rue de la Perle, 3e, which houses the Musée de la Serrure (Lock Museum), and **Hôtel Aubert de Fontenay (20)**, also called Hôtel Salé, 5 rue de Thorigny, 3e, whose three floors and vaulted cellars house the beloved Musée Picasso.

Retrace your steps to rue du Parc Royal; you'll pass three hôtels on the short stretch east before turning south down rue de Sévigné, all of which date from about 1620 and now do civic duty as archives and historical libraries: **Hôtel de Croisille (21)** at No 12, **Hôtel de Vigny (22)** at No 10 and **Hôtel Duret de Chevry (23)** at No 8.

We've already seen the two hôtels on rue de Sévigné from the back – Hôtel Le Peletier de Saint Fargeau at No 29 and Hôtel Carnavalet at No 23. Take the time to check out the complicated monogram of the former's original owner, Michel Le Peletier de Souzy, on the front gate, and the exterior courtyard of the latter, with its wonderful reliefs – to the north are Roman gods and goddesses, to the south the elements, and to the west are reliefs for the four seasons attributed to the Renaissance sculptor Jean Goujon (1510-68), who created the Fontaine des Innocents near the Forum des Halles in 1549. In the centre is a statue of Louis XIII placed in front of the Hôtel de Ville on 14 July 1689 – a century to the day before an armed mob attacked the Bastille prison and sparked the revolution that would change the course of history.

Follow rue des Francs Bourgeois eastwards to the sublime **place des Vosges**, with its four symmetrical fountains and an 1829 copy of a mounted statue of Louis XIII, originally placed here in 1639. In the south-east corner at No 6 is **Hôtel de Rohan-Guéménée (24)**, home to Victor Hugo for 16 years in the first half of the 19th century and now the Maison de Victor Hugo. Madame de Sévigné was born at **No 1 (25)** in 1626.

In the south-west corner of the place des Vosges is the **back entrance (26)** to **Hôtel de Sully (27)**, 62 rue Saint Antoine, 4e, a perfectly restored aristocratic mansion built in 1624 and now housing (appropriately enough) the Caisse Nationale des Monuments Historiques et des Sites, the body responsible for many of France's historical monuments.

The rear entrance takes you through two beautifully decorated late Renaissance-style courtyards, both of which are festooned with allegorical reliefs of the seasons and the elements. In the first look to the south side for spring (horns of plenty) and summer (wheat); in the second turn to the north side for autumn (grapes) and winter, with a symbol representing both the end of the year and life. On the west side of the second courtyard are air on the left and fire on the right. On the east side look for earth on the left and water on the right.

Saint Paul metro station is just a short distance to the west.

Musée Picasso

The Picasso Museum (☎ 01 42 71 25 21, metro Saint Paul or Chemin Vert), 5 rue de Thorigny, 3e, housed in the mid-17th-century Hôtel Aubert de Fontenay (or Hôtel Salé), is one of Paris' best-loved art museums. Displays include more than 3500 of the *grand maître*'s engravings, paintings, ceramic works and drawings, and an unparalleled collection of sculptures. You can also see part of Picasso's personal art collection, which includes works by Braque, Cézanne, Matisse and Degas.

The museum opens 9.30 am to 6 pm Wednesday to Monday (to 8 pm on Thursday); from October to March it closes at 5.30 pm. Admission costs 30FF (20FF for those aged 18 to 25, and for everyone on Sunday; free for under-18s, and for everyone on the first Sunday of the month). When there are special exhibits (which is often), admission costs 38/28FF.

Musée de la Serrure

The Lock Museum (☎ 01 42 77 79 62, metro Saint Paul or Chemin Vert), 1 rue de la Perle, 3e, also known as the Musée Bricard, showcases a fine collection of locks, keys and door knockers. One lock, made around 1780, traps your hand in the jaws of a bronze lion if you try to use the wrong key. Another one, created in the 19th century, shoots anyone whose key doesn't fit. Resist the temptation to gain entry. The museum is open 2 to 5 pm on Monday and 10 am to noon and 2 to 5 pm Tuesday to Friday. Admission costs 30FF (15FF for students and seniors, free for under-18s).

Musée Cognacq-Jay

This museum (☎ 01 40 27 07 21, metro Saint Paul), in the Hôtel de Donon at 8 rue Elzévir, 3e, brings together oil paintings, pastels, sculpture, *objets d'art*, jewellery, porcelain and furniture from the 18th century. The objects on display, assembled by Ernest Cognacq (1839-1928), founder of La Samaritaine department store, give a pretty good idea of upper-class tastes during the Age of Enlightenment. It opens 10 am to 5.40 pm Tuesday to Sunday and costs 30FF (15FF for 18- to 25-year-olds, free for under-18s).

Archives Nationales

France's National Archives (☎ 01 40 27 60 96, metro Rambuteau) are housed in the impressive, early-18th-century Hôtel de Soubise, 60 rue des Francs Bourgeois, 3e. The complex also contains the **Musée de l'Histoire de France** (Museum of French History), where you can view documents dating from the Middle Ages. The ceiling and walls of the interior are extravagantly painted and gilded in the rococo style. The museum opens noon to 5.45 pm on Monday and from Wednesday to Friday, and 1.45 to 5.45 pm at the weekend. Admission costs 20FF (15FF for under-25s and those aged over 60; free on the first Sunday of each month).

Jewish Neighbourhood

The area around **rue des Rosiers** and **rue des Écouffes** (metro Saint Paul), traditionally known as the Pletzl, is one of Paris'

The Oval Room in the sumptuous Hôtel de Soubise, home of the Archives Nationales

liveliest Jewish neighbourhoods. Jewish and kosher cuisines from North Africa, Central Europe and Israel are served at a variety of eateries; see under Marais in the Places to Eat chapter for details.

When renovation of the Marais began in the late 1960s, the area – long home to a poor but vibrant Jewish community – was pretty run-down. Now trendy and expensive boutiques sit side-by-side with Jewish bookshops and *cacher* (kosher) grocery shops, butcher's shops and restaurants. The area is very quiet on the Sabbath (Saturday).

The Art Nouveau **Guimard synagogue**, 10 rue Pavée, 4e, was designed by Hector Guimard in 1913, designer of the famous metro entrances (see the boxed text 'Art in the Metro' in the Getting Around chapter). The interior is closed to the public.

Musée d'Art et d'Histoire du Judaïsme

Recently transferred from their modest digs in Montmartre to the stunning Hôtel de Saint Aignan (1650) in the heart of the Marais, the crafts, paintings and ritual objects from Eastern Europe and North Africa of the Musée d'Art Juif (Jewish Art Museum) have been combined with medieval Jewish artefacts from the Musée National du Moyen Age (see the Latin Quarter section later in this chapter) to create the Art and History of Judaism Museum (☎ 01 53 01 86 60, metro Rambuteau), 71 rue du Temple, 3e. The museum traces the evolution of Jewish communities from the Middle Ages to the present, with particular emphasis on the history of the Jews in France. Highlights include documents relating to the Dreyfus Affair (see The Third Republic & the Belle Époque under History in the Facts about Paris chapter) and works by Chagall, Modigliani and Soutine. It opens 11 am to 6 pm on weekdays, and from 10 am on Sunday. Admission (including a cassette tour) costs 40FF (25FF for students and those aged 18 to 26, free for under-18s).

Mémorial du Martyr Juif Inconnu

The Memorial to the Unknown Jewish Martyr (☎ 01 42 77 44 72, metro Pont Marie or Saint Paul), 17 rue Geoffroy l'Asnier, 4e, established in 1956, includes a memorial to the victims of the Holocaust, various temporary exhibits and small permanent exhibits on the 1st, 2nd and 3rd floors. It is open 10 am to 1 pm and 2 to 6 pm Sunday to Thursday, and to 4.30 pm on Friday. Entry to the museum and crypt is 15FF.

Maison Européenne de la Photographie

Housed in the rather overworked Hôtel Hénault de Cantorbe dating from the early 18th century, the European House of Photography (☎ 01 44 78 75 00, metro Saint Paul or Pont Marie), 5-7 rue de Fourcy, 4e, has cutting-edge temporary exhibits (a recent example was a retrospective of Brazilian photographer Sebastiaõ Salgado) and a permanent collection on the history of photography connected with France. The museum opens 11 am to 8 pm Wednesday to Sunday; admission costs 30FF (15FF for those aged nine to 25 or over 60; free for those aged eight or under, and for everyone after 5 pm on Wednesday).

Musée de la Curiosité et de la Magie

The delightful Museum of Curiosity and Magic (☎ 01 42 72 13 26, metro Saint Paul), in the *caves* (cellars) of the house of the Marquis de Sade at 11 rue Saint Paul, 4e, examines the ancient arts of magic, optical illusion and sleight of hand. Magic shows are included in the entry price (45FF; 30FF for children). The museum opens 2 to 7 pm on Wednesday, Saturday and Sunday.

Musée des Arts et Métiers

Recently reopened after a hiatus of six years, the Arts and Crafts Museum (Map 6, ☎ 01 53 01 82 00, metro Arts et Métiers), 60 rue de Réaumur, 3e, is a must for anyone with a scientific bent. Instruments, machines and working models from the 18th to 20th centuries are displayed over three floors, with Foucault's original pendulum (1855) – which he introduced to the world with the words, 'Come and see the world turn' – taking pride of place. The museum opens 10 am to 6 pm Tuesday to Sunday and costs 35FF (reduced rate 25FF).

BASTILLE (Maps 5, 6 & 7)

After years as a run-down immigrant neighbourhood notorious for its high crime rate, the Bastille area, which encompasses mostly the 11e and 12e but also the easternmost part of the 4e, has undergone a fair degree of gentrification, largely due to the opening of the Opéra Bastille in 1989. The area east of place de la Bastille retains its lively atmosphere and ethnicity.

Bastille

The Bastille, built during the 14th century as a fortified royal residence, is the most famous monument in Paris that doesn't exist: the infamous prison – the quintessential symbol of monarchical despotism – was demolished shortly after a mob stormed it on 14 July 1789 and all seven prisoners were freed. The site where it once stood, place de la Bastille, 12e (Map 7, metro Bastille), is now a very busy traffic roundabout.

In the centre of place de la Bastille is the 52m-high **Colonne de Juillet** (July Column), whose shaft of greenish bronze is topped by a gilded and winged figure of Liberty. It was erected in 1833 as a memorial to the people killed in the street battles that accompanied the July Revolution of 1830; they are buried in vaults under the column. It was later consecrated as a memorial to the victims of the February Revolution of 1848.

Opéra Bastille

Paris' giant 'second' opera house (Map 6, ☎ 0 836 69 78 68 or 01 44 73 13 99, metro Bastille), 2-6 place de la Bastille, 12e, designed by the Canadian Carlos Ott, was inaugurated on 14 July 1989, the 200th anniversary of the storming of the Bastille. For details of the 1¼-hour guided tours of the building (50FF; 30FF for students, seniors and children aged under 16), which depart most days at 1 or 5 pm, call ☎ 01 40 01 19 70. See the Entertainment chapter for information on buying tickets for performances.

Viaduc des Arts

The arches beneath this railway viaduct (Map 5) south-east of place de la Bastille along ave Daumesnil, 12e, which was taken out of service in 1969, is now a showcase for trendy designers and artisans; if you need your Gobelins tapestry restored, an antique copper saucepan patched

Mystic delights at the Musée de la Curiosité et de la Magie

From the twee to the chic, there's a plethora of inviting artists' workshops at the Viaduc des Arts.

euro currency converter €1 = 6.56FF

or a frame regilded, this is the place for you. The top of the viaduct forms a leafy, 4km-long promenade called the **Promenade Plantée**, which offers excellent views of the surrounding area. It's open 8 am (9 am at the weekend) to 5.30 pm (9.30 pm from May to August). Don't miss the spectacular Art Deco police station at 85 ave Daumesnil, opposite rue de Rambouillet, which is topped with a dozen huge marble torsos.

ÎLE DE LA CITÉ (Map 6)

The site of the first settlement in Paris around the 3rd century BC and later the centre of the Roman town of Lutèce (Lutetia), the Île de la Cité remained the centre of royal and ecclesiastical power even after the city spread to both banks of the Seine during the Middle Ages. The buildings on the middle part of the island were demolished and rebuilt during Baron Haussmann's great urban renewal scheme of the late 19th century.

Cathédrale de Notre Dame de Paris

The Cathedral of Our Lady of Paris (☎ 01 42 34 56 10, metro Cité), place du Parvis Notre Dame, 4e, is the true heart of Paris. Notre Dame is not only a masterpiece of French Gothic architecture, but has also been Catholic Paris' ceremonial focus for seven centuries.

Built on a site occupied by earlier churches – and, some two millennia ago, a Gallo-Roman temple – it was begun in 1163 and completed around 1345. Viollet-le-Duc carried out extensive renovations in the 19th century. The interior is 130m long, 48m wide and 35m high, and can accommodate over 6000 worshippers. Some 12 million people visit the cathedral each year.

Notre Dame is known for its sublime balance, although if you look closely you'll see all sorts of minor asymmetrical elements introduced to avoid monotony, in accordance with standard Gothic practice. These include the slightly different shapes of each of the

The Hunchback of Notre Dame

The story of the Hunchback of Notre Dame as told by Victor Hugo in his romantic novel *Notre Dame de Paris* – and not some silly musical or the Disney cartoon version with a happy ending – goes something like this. It's 15th-century Paris during the reign of Louis XI. A Gypsy girl called Esmeralda is in love with Captain Phoebus, but the evil and jealous archdeacon, Claude Frollo, denounces her as a witch. The hunchbacked bell-ringer Quasimodo is devoted to Esmeralda and saves her (for a while) when she seeks protection from the mob in the belfry of Notre Dame. We won't give the ending away but suffice it to say that everyone comes to a tragic end – including Captain Phoebus, who marries someone else.

Was *Notre Dame de Paris*, which is pure fiction, just a good story or a commentary on the times? Hugo began the book during the reign of the unpopular and reactionary Charles X who, with the guidance of his chief minister, had abolished freedom of the press and dissolved parliament. The ascent of Louis-Philippe, a bourgeois king with liberal leanings, in the July Revolution of 1830 took place shortly before the book was published. The novel can thus be seen as a condemnation of absolutism (ie, of Charles X) and of a society that allows the likes of Frollo and Phoebus to heap scorn and misery on unfortunate characters such as Esmeralda and Quasimodo.

Hugo's evocation of the colourful and intense life of the late 15th century is seen by some as a plea for the preservation of Gothic Paris and its decaying architecture. Indeed, the condition of Notre Dame in the early 19th century was so bad that artists, politicians and writers, including Hugo, beseeched Louis-Philippe to rectify the situation. Hugo was appointed to the new Commission for Monuments and the Arts, on which he sat for 10 years. In 1845 the Gothic revivalist architect Viollet-le-Duc began his renovation of Notre Dame, during which he added the steeple and gargoyles (among other things). The work continued for almost two decades.

three main entrances. One of the best views of Notre Dame is from **square Jean XXIII**, the lovely little park south and east of the cathedral, where you can see the tangle of ornate **flying buttresses** that encircle the chancel and support its walls and roof.

Inside, exceptional features include three spectacular **rose windows**, the most renowned of which is the 10m-wide one over the west façade, and the window on the north side of the transept, which has remained virtually unchanged since the 13th century. The central choir with its carved wooden stalls and statues is also noteworthy. The 7800-pipe organ was restored between 1990 and 1992.

Notre Dame opens 8 am to 6.45 pm daily. The **trésor** (treasury) in the south-east transept contains liturgical objects and works of art and opens 9.30 to 11.30 am and 1 to 5.30 or 6.30 pm Monday to Saturday, depending on the season; admission costs 15FF (10FF for students, 5FF for children). There are free **guided tours** of the cathedral in English at noon on Wednesday and Thursday and at 2.30 pm on Saturday (daily in August).

Distances from Paris to every part of metropolitan France are measured from **place du Parvis Notre Dame**, the square in front of Notre Dame. A bronze star, set in the pavement across the street from the cathedral's main entrance, marks the exact location of *point zéro des routes de France* (point zero of French roads).

North Tower The entrance to Notre Dame's north tower (☎ 01 44 32 16 72) is on rue du Cloître Notre Dame – to the right and round the corner as you walk out of the cathedral's main doorway. Climbing the 387 spiralling steps brings you to the top of the **west façade**, where you'll find yourself face-to-face with many of the cathedral's most frightening gargoyles – and a spectacular view of Paris. From April to September the tower opens 9.30 am to 7.30 pm Monday to Thursday, and to 10 pm Friday to Sunday; the rest of the year it opens 10 am to 6 or 6.30 pm daily, depending on the season. Tickets cost 35FF (23FF for those aged 12 to 25, free for children under 12).

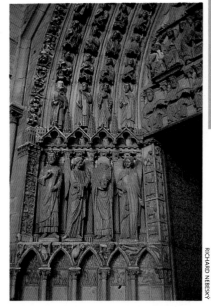

RICHARD NEBESKÝ

Statues peer down at you (and 12 million other visitors each year) as you enter Notre Dame.

Notre Dame's Kestrels

Birdwatchers estimate that about 40 pairs of kestrels *(Falco tinnunculus)* currently nest in Paris, preferring tall old structures like the towers at Notre Dame. Four or five pairs of kestrels regularly breed in niches and cavities high up in the cathedral, and once a year (usually in late June) local ornithologists set up a public kestrel-watching station behind the cathedral, with telescopes and even a camera transmitting close-up pictures of one of the kestrels' nesting sites. The birds form their partnerships in February, eggs are laid in April, the kestrel chicks hatch in May and are ready to depart by early July. In late June, birdwatchers may spot the adult kestrels returning to their young with a tasty mouse or sparrow. Unfortunately, Paris' pigeons – those dirty flying rats – are too large for a kestrel chick to handle.

Crypte Archéologique

Under the square in front of Notre Dame, the Archaeological Crypt (☎ 01 43 29 83 51), also known as the Crypte du Parvis, displays *in situ* the remains of structures from the Gallo-Roman and later periods. It was under renovation at the time of research but usually opens 10 am to 6 pm (to 5 pm from October to March) Tuesday to Sunday.

Sainte Chapelle

The most exquisite of Paris' Gothic monuments, Sainte Chapelle (Holy Chapel; ☎ 01 53 73 78 51, metro Cité), 4 blvd du Palais, 1er, is tucked away within the walls of the **Palais de Justice** (Law Courts). In stark contrast to the buttressed hulk of nearby Notre Dame, Sainte Chapelle is a masterpiece of delicacy and finesse. The 'walls' of the **upper chapel** are sheer curtains of richly coloured and finely detailed **stained glass**, which bathe the chapel in an extraordinary light.

Built in just under three years (compared with nearly 200 for Notre Dame), Sainte Chapelle was consecrated in 1248. The chapel was conceived by Louis IX (Saint Louis) to house his collection of holy relics, including what was then believed to be Jesus' crown of thorns and part of John the Baptist's skull (for which he paid several times the cost of building the chapel itself). The relics were relocated to Notre Dame after the Revolution.

Sainte Chapelle opens 9.30 am to 6.30 pm daily from April to September and 10 am to 5 pm the rest of the year. Admission costs 35FF (23FF for those aged 12 to 25, free for children under 12). A ticket valid for both Sainte Chapelle and the Conciergerie (see the following entry) costs 50/25FF.

Conciergerie

The Conciergerie (☎ 01 53 73 78 50, metro Cité), 1 quai de l'Horloge, 1er, was a luxurious royal palace when it was built in the 14th century, but it later lost favour with the kings of France and was turned into a prison. During the Reign of Terror (1793-4), the Conciergerie was used to incarcerate alleged enemies of the Revolution before they were brought before the Revolutionary Tribunal in the Palais de Justice next door. Among the 2600 prisoners held in the **cachots** (dungeons) here before being sent in tumbrels to the guillotine were Queen Marie-Antoinette

---

Circling the Squares

Postcard views of Paris are often constructed around pretty little squares, arrayed with café tables where happy imbibers quaff wine in the spring sunshine. A perfect example is **place du Marché Sainte Catherine** (Map 7), in the colourful Marais district, 4e. **Place des Vosges** (Map 7) is only a few minutes' stroll away if you want a more formal version of a *place parisienne*. And while you're in the Marais, search out the intricate courtyards of the **Village Saint Paul**, just off the antique-dealer stronghold of rue Saint Paul (Map 7).

CHRISTOPHER WOOD

Place des Vosges: beauty through harmony

On the Left Bank, **place de la Contrescarpe** (Map 5) in the 5e is a lively and picturesque little roundabout surrounded by cafés, bars and shops. Once upon a time this area was just outside the city walls, and there are chunks of medieval city wall still standing off rue du Cardinal Lemoine and rue Clovis. Over in the 6e, what is now called **rue de Furstemberg** (Map 6) takes on a special life on summer evenings, when magnolias scent the air and buskers serenade lovers under the old-fashioned street lamp. It will always be lovely little *place* de Furstemberg as far as we're concerned.

---

and, as the Revolution began to turn on its own, the Revolutionary radicals Danton and Robespierre and, finally, the judges of the tribunal themselves.

The huge Gothic **Salle des Gens d'Armes** (Cavalrymen's Hall) dates from the 14th century and is a fine example of the Rayonnant Gothic style. It is the largest surviving medieval hall in Europe. The **Tour de l'Horloge**, the tower on the corner of blvd du Palais and quai de l'Horloge, has held a public clock aloft since 1370 but the last time we looked it was *still* not keeping the correct time. Opening hours and admission fees at the Conciergerie are the same as those at Sainte Chapelle (see the previous entry).

Marché aux Fleurs

The Île de la Cité's famous flower market (metro Cité), the oldest in Paris, has been at place Louis Lépine, the square just north of the Préfecture de Police, since 1808. It opens 8 am to about 7 pm Monday to Saturday (and on public holidays when they fall on a Sunday). On Sunday, the flower market is transformed into a **marché aux oiseaux** (bird market), open 9 am to 7 pm.

Mémorial des Martyrs de la Déportation

At the south-eastern tip of the Île de la Cité, behind Notre Dame, is the Memorial to the Victims of Deportation, erected in 1962. It's a haunting monument to the 200,000 French people – including 76,000 Jews – who were killed in Nazi concentration camps. A single barred 'window' separates the bleak, rough concrete courtyard from the waters of the Seine. The Tomb of the Unknown Deportee is flanked by 200,000 bits of back-lit glass and the walls are etched with inscriptions from celebrated writers and poets. The memorial is open 10 am to noon and 2 to 8 pm (to 5 pm from October to March).

Pont Neuf

The now sparkling-white stone spans of Paris' oldest bridge, Pont Neuf (literally 'New Bridge'), link the western end of the Île de la Cité with both banks of the Seine. Begun in 1578, Pont Neuf was completed in 1607. The arches are decorated with humorous and grotesque figures of street dentists, pickpockets, loiterers and the like.

ÎLE SAINT LOUIS (Map 6)

The smaller of the Seine's two islands, Île Saint Louis is just downstream from the Île de la Cité. In the early 17th century, when it was actually two uninhabited islets – Île Notre Dame and Île aux Vaches – and sometimes used for duels, a building contractor and two financiers worked out a deal with Louis XIII to create one island out of the two and build two stone bridges to the mainland. In exchange they would receive the right to subdivide and sell the newly created real estate. This they did with great success, and between 1613 and 1664 the entire island was covered with fine new houses.

Today, the island's 17th-century, greystone houses and the small-town shops that line the streets and quays impart a village-like, provincial calm. The central thoroughfare, rue Saint Louis en l'Île, is home to a number of upmarket art galleries, boutiques and tea rooms. The area around **Pont Saint Louis**, the bridge linking the island with the Île de la Cité, and **Pont Louis-Philippe**, the bridge to the Marais, is one of the most romantic spots in all of Paris.

Église Saint Louis en l'Île

The French Baroque Church of Saint Louis on the Island (☎ 01 46 34 11 60, metro Pont Marie), 19 bis rue Saint Louis en l'Île, 4e, was built between 1656 and 1725 and opens 9 am to noon and 3 to 7 pm Tuesday to Sunday.

SIMON BRACKEN

Pont Neuf by night: Paris' oldest bridge, and its first without houses

JARDIN DES PLANTES (Map 5)

This lush, very picturesque area is due east of the Latin Quarter (see the following section).

Jardin des Plantes

Paris' botanical garden (☎ 01 40 79 30 00, metro Gare d'Austerlitz or Jussieu), 57 rue Cuvier, 5e, was founded in 1626 as a medicinal herb garden for Louis XIII. The first greenhouse, constructed in 1714, was home to an African coffee tree whose offspring helped establish the first coffee plantations in South America. The gardens are open 7.30 am to some time between 5.30 and 8 pm, depending on the season.

The **Serres Tropicales** (Tropical Greenhouses), also known as the Jardin d'Hiver (Winter Garden), are open 1 to 5 pm on Monday and Wednesday to Friday, and 10 am to 6 pm (to 5 pm from October to March) at the weekend. Admission costs 15FF (10FF for those aged 16 to 25 or over 60). The **Jardin Alpin** (Alpine Garden) and the gardens of the **École de Botanique** (Botanical School), both of which are free, are open 1 to 5 pm on Monday and Wednesday to Friday, April to September.

Ménagerie du Jardin des Plantes The northern section of the Jardin des Plantes is taken up by the Menagerie (☎ 01 40 79 37 94, metro Jussieu), a medium-sized zoo founded in 1794. During the Prussian siege of Paris in 1870, most of the animals were eaten by starving Parisians. The **Microzoo** open to everyone aged over 10, features microscopic animals. The zoo opens 9 am to 6 pm Monday to Saturday and to 6.30 pm on Sunday, April to September, and to 5 pm the rest of the year. Admission costs 30FF (20FF for students, seniors and children aged six to 15).

Musée National d'Histoire Naturelle The National Museum of Natural History (☎ 01 40 79 30 00, metro Censier Daubenton or Gare d'Austerlitz), created by a decree of the Revolutionary Convention in 1793, was the site of important scientific research in the 19th century. It is housed in four different buildings along the southern edge of the Jardin des Plantes.

The five-level **Grande Galerie de l'Évolution** (Grand Gallery of Evolution), 36 rue Geoffroy Saint Hilaire, 5e, has some imaginative exhibits on evolution and mankind's effect on the global ecosystem; the African parade, as if Noah had lined up his cargo for the ark, is quite something. The Salle des Espèces Menacées et des Espèces Dis-

Green & Open Spaces

Though upwards of 90,000 trees (mostly plane trees and horse chestnuts) line the streets of Paris, the city can often feel excessively built-up. However, you don't have to escape to the **Bois de Boulogne** (Map 1) in the 16e or the **Bois de Vincennes** (Map 1) in the 12e, the city's 'green lungs' to the west and south-east, to get a bit of grass under your feet and leaves over your head; there are over 400 parks to choose from – some not much bigger than a beach blanket, others the size of a small village.

The **Jardin du Luxembourg** (Map 5) in the 6e and the **Jardin des Tuileries** (Maps 2 & 4) in the 1er, while small, formal affairs, can give you the illusion of countryside. **Parc des Buttes-Chaumont** (Map 3), 19e, and **Parc de Monceau** (Map 2), 8e, on the other hand, are fully fledged green open spaces.

Over the past decade or so the city government has spent millions of francs transforming vacant lots and derelict industrial land into new parks. Some of the better ones are **Parc de Bercy** (Map 9) and the **Promenade Plantée** (Map 5), the 'planted promenade' above the Viaduc des Arts, both in the 12e; the **Jardin de l'Atlantique** (Map 4), behind the Gare Montparnasse, and **Parc André Citroën** (Maps 1 & 4) on the banks of the Seine, both in the 15e; **Parc de la Villette** (Map 1), 19e; and **Parc de Belleville** (Map 3), 20e.

arues on level 2 displays extremely rare specimens of endangered and extinct species of animal. The Salles de Découverte (Discovery Rooms) house interactive exhibits for kids. The gallery is open 10 am to 6 pm Wednesday to Monday (to 10 pm on Thursday). Entry costs 40FF (30FF for students, seniors and those aged 18 to 26). There's a guided tour in English (30FF) at 2.30 pm on Saturday.

The **Galerie de Minéralogie, de Géologie et de Paléobotanie**, 36 rue Geoffroy Saint Hilaire, which covers mineralogy, geology and palaeobotany (ie, fossilised plants), has an amazing exhibit of giant natural crystals and a basement display of jewellery and other objects made from minerals. It opens 10 am to 5 pm Wednesday to Monday (to 6 pm at the weekend from April to October) and costs 30/20FF. The **Galerie d'Entomologie**, in a modern building opposite the park at 45 rue Buffon, 5e, focuses on the study of insects (open 1 to 5 pm weekdays) and costs 5/10FF. The **Galerie d'Anatomie Comparée et de Paléontologie**, 2 rue Buffon, has displays on comparative anatomy and palaeontology (the study of fossils). It has the same hours and admission fees as the Galerie de Minéralogie, de Géologie et de Paléobotanie.

Mosquée de Paris

Paris' central mosque (☎ 01 45 35 97 33, metro Censier Daubenton or Place Monge), place du Puits de l'Ermite, 5e, was built in 1926 in the ornate Moorish style popular at the time. Guided tours take place from 9 am to noon and 2 to 6 pm Saturday to Thursday and cost 15FF (10FF for students and children). Visitors must remove their shoes at the entrance to the prayer hall and must be modestly dressed. The complex includes a North African-style *salon de thé* and a restaurant (for details of both see North African and Middle Eastern in the Latin Quarter section of the Places to Eat chapter), and a **hammam** (Turkish bath; ☎ 01 43 31 18 14) – all of which can be entered from 39 rue Geoffroy Saint Hilaire. The hammam (85FF) opens

SIMON BRACKEN

Once used only by scholars, the Mosquée de Paris is now open to all.

to men 2 to 9 pm on Tuesday and 10 am to 9 pm on Sunday only; on other days it is reserved for women and opens 10 am to 9 pm (on Friday from 4 pm). Massage costs 55FF per 10 minutes. The *formule orientale*, which includes entry to the hammam, a massage and a couscous meal with drink, costs 300FF.

Institut du Monde Arabe

The Arab World Institute (☎ 01 40 51 38 38, metro Cardinal Lemoine or Jussieu), 1 rue des Fossés Saint Bernard, 5e, established by France and some 20 Arab countries to promote cultural contacts between the Arab world and the West, is housed in a wonderful building (1987) that successfully mixes modern and traditional Arab and Western elements. The thousands of *mushrabiyah* (incredibly costly aperture-like mechanisms built into the glass walls), inspired by the traditional latticed wooden windows found throughout the Arab world that let you see out without being seen, are opened and closed by electric motors in order to regulate the amount of light and heat that reaches the interior of the building.

The 7th-floor **museum** displays 9th- to 19th-century art and artisanship from all over the Islamic world as well as instruments from astronomy and other fields of scientific endeavour in which Arab technology once led the world. It opens 10 am to 6 pm Tuesday to Sunday. Admission costs 25FF (20FF for students, under-25s and seniors). Temporary exhibitions (enter from quai Saint Bernard) usually costs 40/30FF.

Arènes de Lutèce

The Lutetia Arena (metro Place Monge), a Roman amphitheatre dating from the 2nd century, could once seat around 10,000 people for gladiatorial combats and other events. Discovered in 1869 and heavily reconstructed, it is now used by neighbourhood youths playing football and *boules*. There are entrances at 49 rue Monge and opposite 7 rue de Navarre, 5e. It is open (free) from 9 am (8 am in winter) to between 5.30 and 9.30 pm, depending on the season.

LATIN QUARTER (Maps 5 & 6)

Known as the Quartier Latin because all communication between students and professors here took place in Latin until the Revolution, this area has been the centre of Parisian higher education since the Middle Ages. It still has a large population of students and academics affiliated with the Sorbonne (now part of the University of Paris system), the Collège de France, the École Normale Supérieure and other institutions of higher learning, but in recent years has become increasingly touristy.

For details of the area's literary connections, see the Literary walking tour.

Musée National du Moyen Age

The National Museum of the Middle Ages (Map 6, ☎ 01 53 73 78 00, metro Cluny-La Sorbonne or Saint Michel), also known as

the Musée de Cluny, is housed in two structures: the *frigidarium* (cooling room) an other remains of Gallo-Roman baths datin from around AD 200, and the late-15th century **Hôtel de Cluny**, considered th finest example of medieval civil architec ture in Paris. The spectacular displays in clude statuary, illuminated manuscripts arms, furnishings and objects made of gold ivory and enamel. A sublime series of late 15th-century tapestries from the souther Netherlands known as *La Dame à l Licorne* (The Lady with the Unicorn) i hung in a round room on the 1st floor. A medieval garden and **Forêt de la Licorn** (Unicorn Forest) has recently been laid ou to the north and east of the museum base on the illustrations in the tapestries.

The museum, the entrance to which is a 6 place Paul Painlevé, 5e, opens 9.15 am t 5.45 pm Wednesday to Monday. Admissio costs 38FF (28FF for those aged 18 to 25 and for everyone on Sunday; free for under 18s, and for everyone on the first Sunda of the month). There are 1½-hour English language tours (56/25FF for adults/under 18s) at 11 am on Wednesday and Saturda in April, May and June.

Sorbonne

Paris' most renowned university, the Sor bonne (Map 5, metro Luxembourg o Cluny-La Sorbonne) was founded in 1253 by Robert de Sorbon, confessor of Loui IX, as a college for 16 impoverished theol ogy students. Closed in 1792 by the Revo lutionary government after operating fo centuries as France's premier theologica school, it was reopened under Napoleon Today, the Sorbonne's main comple (bounded by rue de la Sorbonne, rue de Écoles, rue Saint Jacques and rue Cujas, 5e and other buildings in the vicinity house most of the 13 autonomous universities tha were created when the University of Pari was reorganised following the violent stu dent protests of 1968.

Place de la Sorbonne links blvd Sain Michel and **Chapelle de la Sorbonne** (Ma 5), the university's gold-domed church buil between 1635 and 1642.

BOOKWORMING THROUGH THE LEFT BANK

ASA ANDERSSON

Writers have found their way to Paris ever since that 16th-century hedonist François Rabelais forsook his monastic vows and hightailed it to the capital. The 1920s saw the greatest influx of outsiders, though, particularly Americans. Many assume it was Paris' reputation for liberal thought and its relaxed morals that attracted the likes of Hemingway, Fitzgerald, Ezra Pound and so on, but that's just part of the story. Paris was cheap (there were 18FF to US$1 in 1922, for example) and in France, unlike Prohibition-era America, you could get drunk to your heart's content.

For some inspiration before you head off, see the boxed text 'Strangers in Paris' in the Facts about Paris chapter for appropriate reading material. Note that this is a very long walk; it can easily be done in sections as you'll pass many metro stations and bus stops along the way.

Begin at Cardinal Lemoine metro station, where rue du Cardinal Lemoine meets rue Monge, 5e. It's not the most convenient station in Paris, but it's a good beginning.

Walk south-west along rue du Cardinal Lemoine, ducking down the **passageway at No 71 (1)**, until recently the illustrious offices of Lonely Planet Paris. James Joyce (1882-1941) lived in the courtyard flat marked 'E' when he first arrived in Paris in 1921, and it was here that he finished editing *Ulysses*, which he began some seven years earlier. Farther south at **No 74 (2)** is the 3rd floor apartment where Ernest Hemingway (1899-1961) lived with his first wife Hadley and son 'Bumpy' in 1922 and 1923. The flat figures prominently in his book of memoirs, *A Moveable Feast*, from which the quotation on the wall plaque (in French) is taken: 'This is how Paris was in the early days when we were very poor and very happy'. Below the flat was the **Bal au Printemps**, a popular *bal musette* (dancing club), which served as the model for the one where Jake Barnes meets Brett Ashley in Hemingway's *The Sun Also Rises*.

Hemingway lived on rue du Cardinal Lemoine, but he actually wrote in a top-floor room of a hotel round the corner at **39 rue Descartes (3)**, the very hotel where the poet Verlaine died in 1896. The plaque incorrectly states that Hemingway lived here from 1921 to 1925.

Rue Descartes runs south into **place de la Contrescarpe**, a well scrubbed square with Judas trees and a fountain, but once a 'cesspool' (or so Hemingway said), especially the Café des Amateurs, now a pleasant pub called **La Chope (4)** at No 2-4. The **Nègre Joyeux (5)** at No 12, with its large mural of a jolly black man, was another popular music club at the time.

distance: 7km
start: rue du Cardinal Lemoine & rue Monge, 5e (metro Cardinal Lemoine)
finish: blvd du Montparnasse, 6e (metro Vavin)

Rue Mouffetard (from *mofette*, the French word for 'skunk') runs south of place de la Contrescarpe. Turn west at the first street on the right (rue du Pot de Fer); in 1928 one Eric Blair – better known to the world as George Orwell (1903-50) – stayed in a cheap and dirty **boarding house at No 6 (6)** called the Hôtel des Trois Moineaux and wrote all about it and the street, which he called 'rue du Coq d'Or', in *Down and Out in Paris and London*.

Turn north on rue Tournefort (the street where much of Balzac's *Père Goriot* takes place) to rue de l'Estrapade. The large building in front is the prestigious **Lycée Henri IV**; the tower in the north-east part of the school is the 13th-century **Tour Clovis (7)**, all that remains of an abbey founded by Clovis I.

From here follow Hemingway's own directions provided in *A Moveable Feast*: 'I walked down past the Lycée Henri Quatre and the ancient church of **St-Étienne-du-Mont (8)** and the windswept Place du Panthéon and cut in for shelter to the right and finally came out on the lee side of the Boulevard St-Michel and worked on down it past the **Cluny (9)** and the Boulevard St-Germain until I came to a good café that I knew in the Place St-Michel.'

The cafés on place Saint Michel were taken over by tourists decades ago and **Shakespeare & Company (10)**, round the corner at 37 rue de la Bûcherie, 5e, has nothing to do with the real bookshop of that name; that comes later in the tour. Instead, follow the Seine to the west along quai des Grands Augustins. Hemingway used to buy books from the *bouquinists* **(11)** (second-hand booksellers) who still line the embankment. At No 9 of tiny rue Gît le Cœur is the **Relais Hôtel du Vieux Paris (12)**, a favourite of beat writer Jack Kerouac (1922-69) and the poet Allen Ginsberg (1926-97) in the 1950s.

Pablo Picasso (1881-1973) had his studio at **7 rue des Grands Augustins (13)**, which also runs south from the quai, from 1936 to 1955. This *hôtel particulier* (private mansion) was also the setting for Balzac's *Le Chef d'Œuvre Inconnu* (The Unknown Masterpiece).

Walk south to rue Saint André des Arts, follow it westwards – Kerouac drank at a bar called **Le Gentilhomme (14)** at No 28 – and then turn south on rue de l'Ancienne Comédie. At No 12 on rue de l'Odéon, its continuation over blvd Saint Germain, stood the original **Shakespeare & Company (15)**, where founder/owner Sylvia Beach (1887-1962) lent books to Hemingway; edited, retyped and published *Ulysses* for Joyce; and hid from the Nazis for two years during WWII.

Return to blvd Saint Germain and walk westwards to the 11th-century **Église Saint Germain des Prés (16)**. Just opposite is **Les Deux Magots (17)** and beyond it **Café de Flore (18)**, favourite hang-outs of postwar Left Bank intellectuals such as Jean-Paul Sartre and Simone de Beauvoir.

From place Sartre-Beauvoir walk north along rue Bonaparte to the **Café Pré aux Clercs (19)** at No 30, a Hemingway hang-out. If you continue north on rue Bonaparte and turn east onto rue des Beaux-Arts, walking down to No 13, you reach **L'Hôtel (20)**, the former Hôtel d'Alsace, where Oscar Wilde died of meningitis in 1900.

Rue Jacob, which runs perpendicular to rue Bonaparte, has several literary associations – from the sublime to the completely ridiculous. At No 44, the **Hôtel Angleterre (21)** is where Hemingway spent his first night in Paris (in room No 14 in December 1921, to be precise). A few doors down at No 56, the former **Hôtel d'York (22)** is of great historic, if not literary, significance – this is where George III's representative met with Benjamin Franklin, John Adams and John Hay on 3 September 1783 to sign the treaty recognising American independence.

At the corner of rue Saint Jacob and rue des Saints Pères is a nondescript café called **Le Comptoir des Saints Pères (23)**, which under

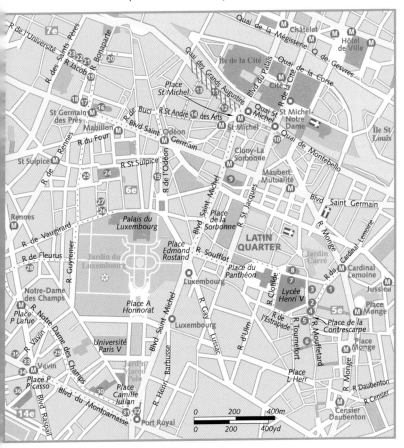

normal circumstances you would not glance at twice. But this was the fashionable restaurant Michaud's, where Hemingway stood outside watching Joyce and his family eat dinner and, later, when he was on the inside looking out, where a memorable event may or may not have taken place. According to *A Moveable Feast*, F Scott Fitzgerald (1896-1940), concerned about not being able to satisfy his wife sexually, asked Hemingway to inspect him in the café's toilet. 'It is not basically a question of the size in repose...' Hemingway advised him, in what is surely the greatest example of the Big Lie in American literary history. Sadly, the old Art Deco-style loo was recently removed and when we explained to the owner that he had thrown a footnote of American literature on the scrapheap, he looked incredulous.

Return to rue Bonaparte and follow it south this time past the **Église Saint Sulpice (24)** and the **Fontaine des Quatre Évêques (25)**. Its continuation, allée du Séminaire, leads to the north-west corner of the **Jardin du Luxembourg** and rue de Vaugirard. This is the area where Hemingway and many other members of the so-called Lost Generation moved after slumming it for a few years in the Latin Quarter. William Faulkner (1897-1962) spent a few months at **42 rue de Vaugirard (26)** in 1925. Hemingway lived his last few years in Paris in a rather grand flat at **6 rue Férou (27)**, within easy striking (the operative word, no doubt, as they had fallen out by then) distance of **27 rue de Fleurus (28)**, where the American novelist Gertrude Stein and her companion, Alice B Toklas, lived for 26 years, entertaining such luminaries as Matisse, Picasso, Braque, Gauguin, Ezra Pound and of course the young Hemingway and Hadley, who were treated as though they were 'very good, well-mannered and promising children'. Pound (1885-1972) lived not far away in a flat filled with Japanese paintings and with packing crates serving as furniture at **70 bis rue Notre Dames des Champs (29)**, as did Katherine Anne Porter in the same flat in 1934. Hemingway's first apartment in this part of town was above a **sawmill at No 113 (30)**, now part of the École Alsacienne. If you were to carry on eastwards you'd soon reach **La Closerie des Lilas (31)** on blvd du Montparnasse (described in more detail in the Entertainment chapter), where Hemingway often met John Dos Passos or just sat alone, contemplating the **statue of Marshall Ney (32)** in front.

Port Royal metro station is just opposite La Closerie des Lilas; to the west and clustered around place Pablo Picasso and Vavin metro station is a triad of café-restaurants that have hosted more literary luminaries than any others in the world: **La Rotonde (33)**, **Café du Dôme (34)** and, as Jake Barnes puts it in *The Sun Also Rises*, 'that new dive, **the Select (35)**'. But round the corner at No 10 of the otherwise nondescript rue Delambre is the **Auberge de Venise (36)**, once the Dingo Bar. It was here that Hemingway, the ambitious, middle-class kid from the Midwest, and Fitzgerald, the well-heeled, dissolute Princetonian, met for the first time, became friends of sorts and went on to change the face of American literature. For one of us, at least, the erstwhile Dingo remains a church.

Panthéon

The domed landmark now known as the Panthéon (Map 5, ☎ 01 44 32 18 00, metro Luxembourg), place du Panthéon, 5e, was commissioned around 1750 as an abbey church, but because of financial problems wasn't completed until 1789, not a good year for churches to open in France. Two years later, the Constituent Assembly converted it into a secular mausoleum for the *grands hommes de l'époque de la liberté française* (great men of the era of French liberty), removing all Christian symbols and references. The Panthéon's ornate marble interior is gloomy in the extreme and, while renovations to the nave have been completed, the upper levels remain closed. Permanent residents of the crypt include Voltaire, Louis Braille, Jean-Jacques Rousseau, Victor Hugo, Émile Zola, Jean Moulin and Nobel Prize-winner Marie Curie, who was reburied here (along with her husband, Pierre) in 1995.

The Panthéon, final resting place for a number of Parisian notables

The Panthéon opens 9.30 am to 6.30 pm daily, April to September, and 10 am to 6.15 pm the rest of the year. Admission costs 35FF (23FF for those aged 18 to 25).

Église Saint Étienne du Mont

The lovely Church of Mount Saint Stephen (Map 5, metro Cardinal Lemoine), place de l'Abbé Basset, 5e, was built between 1492 and 1655. The most exceptional feature of the Gothic interior is its marble **rood screen** separating the chancel from the nave. During the late Renaissance, all of Paris' rood screens were removed because they prevented the faithful assembled in the nave from seeing the priest celebrate Mass. This is a copy of one of the finest examples. Also of interest is the carved **wooden pulpit** (1650) held aloft by a figure of Samson, the 16th- and 17th-century **stained glass** and, in the south-east corner, a highly decorated **reliquary** containing the finger of Saint Geneviève, the patron saint of Paris and namesake of the hillock on which you're standing.

SAINT GERMAIN & LUXEMBOURG (Maps 5 & 6)

Centuries ago, the Église Saint Germain des Prés and its affiliated abbey owned most of the 6e and 7e. The neighbourhood around the church began to get built up in the late 17th century, and these days – under the name Saint Germain des Prés – it is celebrated for its 19th-century charm. Cafés such as Les Deux Magots and Café de Flore (see under Saint Germain & Odéon in the Pubs, Bars & Cafés section in the Entertainment chapter) were favourite hang-outs of postwar Left Bank intellectuals and the places where existentialism was born. Indeed, in the spring of 2000 place Saint Germain des Prés, the little square in front of the church facing Les Deux Magots, was renamed place Sartre-Beauvoir.

Église Saint Germain des Prés

The Romanesque-style Church of Saint Germanus of the Fields (Map 6, metro Saint Germain des Prés), the oldest (though hardly the most interesting) church in Paris,

NEIL SETCHFIELD

was built in the 11th century on the site of a 6th-century abbey. It has since been altered many times, but the **Chapelle de Saint Symphorien**, to the right as you enter, was part of the original abbey and is the final resting place of Saint Germanus (496-576), the first bishop of Paris. The **bell tower** over the west entrance has changed little since AD 1000, apart from the addition of the spire in the 19th century.

France's Merovingian kings were buried here during the 6th and 7th centuries, but their tombs disappeared during the Revolution. The interior is disfigured by truly appalling polychrome paintings and frescoes from the 19th century. The church, which is often used for concerts, is open 8 am to 7 pm daily.

Musée National Eugène Delacroix

The Eugène Delacroix Museum (Map 6, ☎ 01 44 41 86 50, metro Mabillon or Saint Germain des Prés), 6 rue de Furstemberg, 6e, was the artist's home and studio at the time of his death in 1863. It is open 9.30 am to 5 pm Wednesday to Monday. Admission costs 30FF (23FF for students and seniors, and for everyone on Sunday; free for under-18s, and for everyone on the first Sunday of the month).

Institut de France

This august body was created in 1795 by bringing together five of France's academies of arts and sciences. The most famous of these is the **Académie Française**, founded in 1635. Its 40 members, known as the Immortels (Immortals), are charged with the Herculean task of safeguarding the purity of the French language.

The domed building housing the Institut de France (Map 6, ☎ 01 44 41 44 41, metro Mabillon or Louvre-Rivoli), a masterpiece of French neoclassical architecture from the mid-17th century, is at 23 quai de Conti, across the Seine from the eastern end of the Louvre. There are usually tours (50FF) at 10.30 am or 3 pm at the weekend; call beforehand for information. You must write in advance if you want the tour in English.

Opposite is the **Bibliothèque Mazarine** (Mazarine Library; ☎ 01 44 41 44 06), 25 quai de Conti, 6e, founded in 1643 and the oldest public library in France. You can visit the bust-lined, late-17th-century reading room or consult the library's collection of 500,000 items from 10 am to 6 pm weekdays (closed during the first half of August). A two-day entry pass is free, but you must leave your ID at the office (to the left of the entryway). Annual membership to borrow books costs 100FF (a 'carnet' of 10 visits costs 50FF).

Musée de la Monnaie

The Museum of Coins (Map 6, ☎ 01 40 46 55 30, metro Pont Neuf), 11 quai de Conti, 6e, traces the history of French coinage from antiquity to the present and as well as coins and medals includes presses and other minting equipment. It opens 11 am to 5.30 pm Tuesday to Friday, and from noon at the weekend. Admission costs 20FF (15FF for students and seniors; free for under-16s, and for everyone on Sunday).

The **Hôtel des Monnaies**, which houses the museum, became a royal mint during the 18th century and is still used by the Ministry of Finance to produce commemorative medals. Except in August, French-language tours of the mint's workshops (☎ 01 40 46 55 35) leave at 2.15 pm on Wednesday and Friday (20FF).

Jardin du Luxembourg

When the weather is warm Parisians of all ages flock to the formal terraces and chestnut groves of the 23-hectare Luxembourg Gardens (Map 5, metro Luxembourg) to read, relax and sunbathe. It opens 7 am to 9.30 pm in summer and 8 am to sunset in winter.

Palais du Luxembourg Luxembourg Palace (Map 5), at the northern end of the Jardin du Luxembourg along rue de Vaugirard, 5e, was built for Marie de Médicis (queen of France from 1600 to 1610) to assuage her longing for the Pitti Palace in Florence, where she spent her childhood. Just east of the palace is the Italianate

GREG ELMS

Flower power in the ever-popular Jardin du Luxembourg

Fontaine des Médicis, a long, ornate gold-fish pond built around 1630. The palace has housed the Sénat (Senate), the upper house of the French parliament, since 1958. There are tours of the interior (☎ 01 44 61 21 69 for reservations) at 10 am on the first Sunday of each month, but you must book by the preceding Wednesday.

Musée du Luxembourg The Luxembourg Museum (Map 5, ☎ 01 42 34 25 94, metro Luxembourg or Saint Sulpice), 19 rue de Vaugirard, 6e, opened at the end of the 19th century in the orangery of the Palais du Luxembourg and was dedicated to presenting the work of artists still living; for many years it housed the work of the impressionists. It now hosts temporary art exhibitions, often from different regions of France. It opens 11 am to 6 pm Tuesday to Sunday (to 8 pm on Thursday); admission usually costs 31FF (reduced price and for everyone on Tuesday 21FF) but depends on the exhibit.

Activities for Children The Jardin du Luxembourg offers all of the delights of a Parisian childhood a century ago and is one of the best places in Paris to take kids. The atmosphere of bygone days is enhanced by the kepi-topped Senate guards at the Palais du Luxembourg.

At the octagonal pond called the **Grand Bassin**, **model sailboats** – many of them old enough to have been sailed by today's grandparents when they were children – can be rented (18FF) from 2 pm until sometime between 4.30 pm (in winter) and 7 pm (in spring and summer) on Wednesday, Saturday and Sunday (daily during school holidays, including July and August).

About 200m south-west of the pond, at the pint-sized **Théâtre du Luxembourg** (☎ 01 43 26 46 47), visitors are treated to a complete theatre experience in miniature; in a hall filled with child-sized seats, **marionettes** put on shows whose antics can be enjoyed even if you don't understand French. The puppets put on several performances (24FF) – one of which starts at 3 pm – on Wednesday, Saturday, Sunday and public holidays, and daily during the school holidays.

THINGS TO SEE & DO

Next to the Théâtre du Luxembourg, the modern **playground** – one half for kids aged up to seven, the other half for children aged seven to 12 – costs 15FF per child (9FF for adults). Not far away, the vintage **swings** cost 7FF per child, as does the old-time **merry-go-round** (carousel).

A hundred metres north of the theatre, kids of up to 35kg can ride **Shetland ponies** (14FF, or 35FF for three rides) from 11 am (2 pm on Monday, Tuesday, Thursday and Saturday). **Carriage rides** cost 11FF.

Église Saint Sulpice

The Church of Saint Sulpicius (Map 6, metro Saint Sulpice), its interior lined with chapels, is a block north of the Jardin du Luxembourg at place Saint Sulpice and was built between 1646 and 1780 on the site of earlier churches dedicated to the eponymous 6th-century archbishop of Bourges. The Italianate façade, designed by a Florentine architect, has two rows of superimposed columns and is topped by two towers. The neoclassical décor of the vast interior reflects the influence of the Counter-Reformation. The frescoes in the **Chapelle des Saints Anges** (Chapel of the Holy Angels), the first to the right as you enter, were painted by Eugène Delacroix between 1855 and 1861. The monumental **organ loft** dates from 1781. The 10.30 am Mass on Sunday is accompanied by organ music.

Place Saint Sulpice is adorned with a very energetic fountain, **Fontaine des Quatre Évêques** (Map 6), dating from 1844.

MONTPARNASSE (Map 4)

After WWI, writers, poets and artists of the avant-garde abandoned Montmartre and crossed the Seine, shifting the centre of artistic ferment to the area around blvd du Montparnasse. Chagall, Modigliani, Léger, Soutine, Miró, Picasso, Kandinsky, Stravinsky, Hemingway, Pound, Henry Miller and Cocteau, as well as such political exiles as Lenin and Trotsky, all used to hang out in the cafés and brasseries for which the quarter became famous. Montparnasse remained a creative centre until the mid-1930s.

Although the trendy Latin Quarter crowd considers the area hopelessly nondescript, blvd du Montparnasse (on the southern border of the 6e) and its many fashionable restaurants, cafés and cinemas attract large numbers of people in the evening.

Tour Montparnasse

The 209m-high Montparnasse Tower (☎ 01 45 38 52 56, metro Montparnasse Bienvenüe), 33 ave du Maine, 15e, built in 1974 with steel and smoked glass, affords spectacular views of the city. The lift to the 56th-floor indoor observatory, with shops, an exhibition and a video about Paris, costs 40FF (35FF for students and seniors, 27FF for under-14s). If you want to combine the lift trip with a hike up the stairs to the 59th-floor **open-air terrace**, the cost is 48/40/32FF. The tower opens 9.30 am to 11.30 pm daily, April to September, and 9.30 am to 10.30 pm Sunday to Thursday and 9.30 am to 11 pm on Friday, Saturday and public holidays during the rest of the year.

BRENDA TURNNIDGE

Serge Gainsbourg is just one of the French luminaries in Cimetière du Montparnasse.

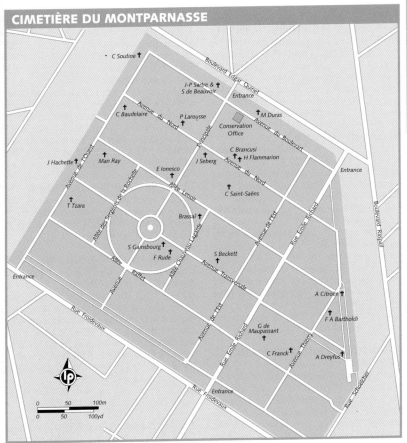

CIMETIÈRE DU MONTPARNASSE

Cimetière du Montparnasse

Montparnasse Cemetery (☎ 01 44 10 86 50, metro Edgar Quinet or Raspail), accessible from blvd Edgar Quinet and from rue Froidevaux, 14e, was opened in 1824. It contains the tombs of such illustrious personages as Charles Baudelaire, Guy de Maupassant, Samuel Beckett, François Rude, Frédéric August Bartholdi, Constantin Brancusi, Chaim Soutine, Man Ray, Camille Saint-Saëns, André Citroën, Alfred Dreyfus, Jean Seberg, Simone de Beauvoir and Jean-Paul Sartre. If Père Lachaise has Jim Morrison, Montparnasse has Serge Gainsbourg (division No 1); fans place metro tickets with their names inscribed on them atop the late crooner's tombstone – a reference to one of his more famous songs. Maps showing the location of the tombs of the dead and famous are posted near the entrances and are available free from the conservation office at 3 blvd Edgar Quinet, 14e. The cemetery opens 9 am to 6 pm daily, April to October (to 5.30 pm the rest of the year).

Musée Bourdelle

Due north of Gare Montparnasse, the Bourdelle Museum (☎ 01 49 54 73 73, metro

euro currency converter €1 = 6.56FF

Falguière), 18 rue Antoine Bourdelle, 15e, contains monumental bronzes in the very house and workshop where the sculptor Antoine Bourdelle (1861-1929) lived and worked. The three sculpture gardens are particularly lovely. It is open 11 am to 5.40 pm Tuesday to Sunday; admission costs 22FF (15FF for students, free for those aged under 26 or over 60).

Musée de la Poste

Much to the joy of philatelists, the Postal Museum (☎ 01 42 79 23 45, metro Montparnasse Bienvenüe), a few hundred metres south-west of the Tour Montparnasse at 34 blvd de Vaugirard, 15e, has reopened with some pretty impressive exhibits illustrating the history of the French postal service – a matter of particular importance in a highly centralised state like France. The exhibition rooms showcase the original designs of French stamps, antique postal and telecommunications equipment and models of postal conveyances. The museum is open 10 am to 6 pm Monday to Saturday. Admission costs 30FF (20FF for students and seniors, free for under-12s).

FAUBOURG SAINT GERMAIN (Map 4)

Faubourg Saint Germain in the 7e, the area between the Musée d'Orsay and, 1km to the south, rue de Babylone, was Paris' most fashionable neighbourhood in the 18th century. Some of the most interesting mansions, many of which now serve as embassies, cultural centres and government ministries, are along three streets running east to west: rue de Lille, rue de Grenelle and rue de Varenne. The **Hôtel Matignon**, the official residence of the French prime minister since the start of the Fifth Republic (1958), is at 57 rue de Varenne.

Musée d'Orsay

The Musée d'Orsay (☎ 01 40 49 48 48, or 01 45 49 11 11 for a recording, metro Musée d'Orsay or Solférino), facing the Seine at 1 rue de la Légion d'Honneur, 7e, displays France's national collection of paintings, sculptures, *objets d'art* and other works produced between the 1840s and 1914, including the fruits of the impressionist, postimpressionist and Art Nouveau movements. It is spectacularly housed in a former train station, built in 1900 and opened as a museum in 1986.

Many visitors head straight to the upper level (lit by a skylight) to see the famous **impressionist paintings** by Monet, Renoir, Pissarro, Sisley, Degas, Manet, Van Gogh and Cézanne and the **postimpressionist works** by Seurat, Matisse and so on, but there's also a great deal to see on the ground floor, including some early works by Manet, Monet, Renoir and Pissarro. The middle level has some magnificent **Art Nouveau rooms**. The museum's Web site is at www.musee-orsay.fr. On Minitel, key in 3615 ORSAY or 3615 CULTURE.

Opening Hours & Tickets The Musée d'Orsay opens 10 am (9 am on Sunday) to 6 pm (to 9.45 pm on Thursday) Tuesday to Sunday from late September to late June. In summer the museum opens at 9 am. Admission to the permanent exhibits cost 40FF (30FF for those aged 18 to 25 or over 60, and for everyone on Sunday; free for under-18s, and for everyone on the first Sunday of the month); tickets are valid all day so you can leave and re-enter the museum as you please. There are separate fees for temporary exhibitions.

Guided Tours General English-language tours begin at 11.30 am Tuesday to Saturday, with an additional one at 7 pm on Thursday. There's a tour focusing on the impressionists at 2.30 pm on Tuesday. Tickets (40FF in addition to the entry fee, no discounts) are sold at the information desk to the left as you enter the building. The 1½-hour cassette tour, available in six languages, points out 80 major works – many of which had a revolutionary impact on 19th-century art – that the uninitiated might easily miss. It can be rented for 30FF (no discounts) on the right just past the ticket windows. The excellent English-language full-colour *Guide to the Musée d'Orsay* costs 95FF.

Assemblée Nationale

The National Assembly, the lower house of the French parliament, meets in the 18th-century **Palais Bourbon** (☎ 01 40 63 60 00, metro Assemblée Nationale) at 33 quai d'Orsay, 7e. There are usually free guided tours in French (☎ 01 46 36 41 13) at 2.15 pm every Saturday. Admission is on a first-come, first-served basis (each tour has only 30 places), so join the queue early. A national ID card or passport is required.

The Second Empire-style **Ministère des Affaires Étrangères** (Ministry of Foreign Affairs), built between 1845 and 1855 and popularly referred to as the 'Quai d'Orsay', is next door at 37 quai d'Orsay.

Musée Rodin

The Musée Auguste Rodin (☎ 01 44 18 61 10, metro Varenne), 77 rue de Varenne, 7e, often listed by visitors as their favourite museum in Paris, is also one of the most relaxing spots in the city. Rooms on two floors of this 18th-century residence display extraordinarily vital bronze and marble sculptures by Rodin and Camille Claudel, including casts of some of Rodin's most celebrated works: *The Hand of God*, *The Burghers of Calais*, *Cathedral*, that perennial crowd-pleaser *The Thinker* and – we have tears in our eyes as we reflect upon it – the sublime, the incomparable *The Kiss*. There's a delightful **garden** round the back filled with sculptures and shade trees.

ASA ANDERSON

The museum opens 9.30 am to 5.45 pm daily, April to September (to 4.45 pm the rest of the year). Admission costs 28FF (18FF for those aged 18 to 25 or over 60, and for everyone on Sunday; free for under-18s, and for everyone on the first Sunday of each month). Visiting just the garden, which closes at 5 pm, costs 5FF.

INVALIDES (Map 4)

A 500m-long expanse of lawn called the **Esplanade des Invalides** (metro Invalides, Varenne or La Tour Maubourg) separates Faubourg Saint Germain from the Eiffel Tower area. At the southern end of the esplanade, which was laid out between 1704 and 1720, is the final resting place of the man many French people consider to be their greatest hero.

Hôtel des Invalides

The Hôtel des Invalides, 7e (metro Varenne or La Tour Maubourg), was built in the 1670s by Louis XIV to provide housing for 4000 *invalides* (disabled war veterans). On 14 July 1789, a mob forced its way into the building and, after fierce fighting, seized 28,000 rifles before heading on to the prison at Bastille and revolution.

North of the Hôtel des Invalides' main courtyard, which is called the **Cour d'Honneur**, is the **Musée de l'Armée** (☎ 01 44 42 37 72), 129 rue de Grenelle, 7e, a huge military museum; to the south of it is the **Église Saint Louis des Invalides** and the **Église du Dôme** (metro Varenne or La Tour Maubourg), with its sparkling dome (1677-1735), which is considered to be one of the finest religious edifices erected under Louis XIV. The church's career as a mausoleum for military leaders began in 1800, and in 1861 it received the remains of Napoleon, encased in six coffins that fit into one another like a Russian *matryoshka* doll.

The Musée de l'Armée and the very extravagant **Tombeau de Napoléon 1er** (Napoleon's Tomb) inside the church are open 10 am to 6 pm daily, April to September (to 5 pm the rest of the year). Admission costs 38FF (28FF for students and seniors, free for under-12s).

euro currency converter €1 = 6.56FF

EIFFEL TOWER AREA
(Maps 2 & 4)

Paris' most prominent and recognisable landmark, the Eiffel Tower is surrounded by open areas on both banks of the Seine, which take in both the 7e and 16e. There are several outstanding museums in this part of the Right Bank.

Musée des Égouts de Paris

The Paris Sewers Museum (Map 4, ☎ 01 47 05 10 29, metro Pont de l'Alma or Alma-Marceau) is a working museum whose entrance – a rectangular maintenance hole topped with a kiosk – is across the street from 93 quai d'Orsay, 7e. Raw sewage flows beneath your feet as you walk through 480m of odoriferous tunnels, passing artefacts illustrating the development of Paris' waste-water disposal system. It'll take your breath away, it will. The sewers are open 11 am to 6 pm Saturday to Wednesday, May to September (to 5 pm the rest of the year), except – God forbid – when rain threatens to flood the tunnels. Admission costs 25FF (20FF for students, seniors and children; free for kids under five).

Eiffel Tower

The Tour Eiffel (Map 4, ☎ 01 44 11 23 23, metro Champ de Mars-Tour Eiffel or Trocadéro) faced massive opposition from Paris' artistic and literary elite when it was built for the 1889 Exposition Universelle (World Fair), marking the centenary of the Revolution. It was almost torn down in 1909 but was spared for purely practical reasons: it proved an ideal platform for the transmitting antennas needed for the new science of radiotelegraphy. It was the world's tallest structure until the Chrysler building in New York was completed in 1930.

The Eiffel Tower, named after its designer, Gustave Eiffel, is 320m high, including the television antenna at the very tip. This figure can vary by as much as 15cm, however, as the tower's 7000 tonnes of iron, held together by 2.5 million rivets,

Admiring the paintwork: 40 tonnes of paint are used on the Eiffel Tower every four years.

expand in warm weather and contract when it's cold.

When you're done peering upwards through the girders, you can choose to visit any of the three levels open to the public. The lift (west and north pillars), which follows a curved trajectory, costs 22FF to the 1st platform (57m above the ground), 44FF to the 2nd (115m) and 62FF to the 3rd (276m). Children aged four to 12 pay 13/23/32FF respectively; there are no youth or student discounts. You can avoid the lift queues by taking the escalators (18FF) in the south pillar to the 1st and 2nd platforms.

The tower lifts operate 9.30 am to 11 pm daily (9 am to midnight from mid-June to August); the escalators run 9.30 am to 6.30 pm (to 9 pm May to June, and to 11 pm July to August).

Champ de Mars

Running south-east from the Eiffel Tower, the grassy 'Field of Mars' (Mars was the Roman god of war) was originally a parade ground for the cadets of the 18th-century École Militaire (Military Academy; Map 4), the vast, French-classical building at the south-east end of the park, which counts Napoleon among its graduates.

In 1783 the Champ de Mars (Map 4, metro École Militaire or Champ de Mars-Tour Eiffel) was the site of one of the world's first balloon flights. During the Revolutionary period, two important mass ceremonies were held here: the Fête de la Fédération (Federation Festival), held on 14 July 1790 to celebrate the first anniversary of the storming of the Bastille, and the Fête de l'Être-Suprême (Festival of the Supreme Being) of 1794, at which Robespierre presided over a ceremony that established a revolutionary state religion.

When the weather is fine, young Parisians flock to the Champ de Mars to skateboard or roller-skate; it's also an excellent place for a picnic. For the young at heart, the **Marionettes du Champ de Mars** (Map 4, ☎ 01 48 56 01 44, metro École Militaire) stage puppet shows (17FF) in the park at 3.15 and 4.15 pm on Wednesday, Saturday, Sunday and public holidays and daily during school holidays (including July and August).

Jardins du Trocadéro

The Trocadéro Gardens (Map 4, metro Trocadéro), whose fountains and statue garden are grandly illuminated at night, are in the posh 16e, accessible across Pont d'Iéna from the Eiffel Tower. They are named after the Trocadéro, a Spanish stronghold near Cádiz captured by the French in 1823.

Palais de Chaillot

The two curved, colonnaded wings of the Palais de Chaillot, 16e (Map 4, metro Trocadéro), built for the 1937 World Exhibition held here, and the terrace in between them afford an exceptional panorama of the Jardins du Trocadéro, the Seine and the Eiffel Tower. Anyone who has seen the newsreels from WWII will recognise the terrace as the place where Adolf Hitler danced a little jig and admired 'his' Paris after France capitulated in June 1940.

This vast complex houses a couple of interesting museums. The **Musée de l'Homme** (Museum of Mankind; ☎ 01 44 05 72 72), 17 place du Trocadéro, 16e, contains anthropological and ethnographical exhibits from Africa, Asia, Europe, the Arctic, the Pacific and the Americas. It opens 9.45 am to 5.15 pm Wednesday to Monday (30/20FF adult/reduced rate). The **Musée de la Marine** (Maritime Museum; ☎ 01 53 65 69 69), known for its beautiful model ships, opens 10 am to 5.45 pm Wednesday to Monday (38/28FF).

At the far eastern tip of the Palais de Chaillot is the main branch of the **Cinémathèque Française** (see under Cinema in the Entertainment chapter).

Musée Guimet

The Guimet Museum (Map 2, ☎ 01 47 23 88 11, metro Iéna), 6 place d'Iéna, 16e, midway between the Eiffel Tower and the Arc de Triomphe, is Paris' foremost repository for Asian art and has sculptures, paintings, *objets d'art* and religious articles from Afghanistan, India, Nepal, Pakistan, Tibet, Cambodia, China, Japan and Korea. However, until massive renovations are completed at the end of 2000, part of the collection is housed at the **Musée du**

Panthéon Bouddhique (Buddhist Pantheon Museum; Map 2, ☎ 01 40 73 88 11, metro Iéna), the Guimet annexe a short distance to the north at 19 ave d'Iéna, 16e. It contains Chinese and Japanese Buddhist paintings and sculptures brought to Paris in 1876 by collector Émile Guimet, and a wonderful Japanese garden. It opens 10.15 am to 1 pm and 2.30 to 6 pm Wednesday to Monday. Admission costs 16FF (12FF for students, seniors and those aged 18 to 25, and for everyone on Sunday; free for under-18s).

Musée d'Art Moderne de la Ville de Paris

The right wing of the **Palais de Tokyo**, 11 ave du Président Wilson, 16e, which was built for the World Exhibition of 1937, houses the Modern Art Museum of the City of Paris (Map 2, ☎ 01 53 67 40 00, or 01 40 70 11 10 for a recording, metro Iéna or Alma-Marceau), established in 1961. Its collections include representatives of just about every major artistic movement of the 20th century: Fauvism, cubism, Dadaism, surrealism, the School of Paris, expressionism, abstractionism and so on. Artists with works on display include Matisse, Picasso, Braque, Soutine, Modigliani, Chagall and Dufy. Part of the museum is being rebuilt as the **Palais du Cinema**.

The museum is open 10 am to 5.30 pm Tuesday to Sunday. Admission costs 30FF (20FF for students; free for those aged under 26 or over 60, and for everyone 10 am to 1 pm on Sunday).

Musée de la Mode et du Costume

The Fashion and Clothing Museum (Map 2, ☎ 01 47 20 85 23, metro Iéna or Alma-Marceau), housed in the **Palais Galliera**, which can be entered from 10 ave Pierre 1er de Serbie, 8e, and is sometimes called the Musée Galliera, contains some 70,000 outfits and accessories from the 18th century to the present day. The striking Italianate building and gardens are in themselves worth a visit. The museum is open 10 am to 5.40 pm Tuesday to Sunday and admission costs 45FF (reduced price 32FF).

Princess Diana Memorial

East of the Musée Guimet and the Musée du Panthéon Bouddhique is place de l'Alma (Map 2, metro Alma-Marceau), an insignificant square that would go unnoticed by most travellers if not for the automobile accident that occurred in the underpass running parallel to the Seine on 31 August 1997, killing Diana, Princess of Wales, her companion, Dodi Fayed, and their chauffeur, Henri Paul. The only reminder of the tragedy is the bronze **Flame of Liberty** (Map 2, metro Alma-Marceau) – a replica of the one atop the torch of the Statue of Liberty, placed here by Paris-based US firms in 1987 on the centenary of the *International Herald Tribune* newspaper as a symbol of friendship between France and the USA – which has become something of a memorial to Diana and is decorated with flowers, photographs, graffiti and personal notes.

PLACE DE LA CONCORDE AREA (Map 2)

The cobblestone expanses of place de la Concorde, 8e, are sandwiched between the Jardin des Tuileries and the parks at the eastern end of ave des Champs-Élysées. There are plans to turn the entire square into a pedestrian zone.

Place de la Concorde

Place de la Concorde was laid out between 1755 and 1775. The 3300-year-old pink granite **obelisk** in the middle of the square was given to France in 1831 by Muhammad Ali, viceroy and pasha of Egypt. Weighing 230 tonnes and towering 23m over the cobblestones, it once stood in the Temple of Ramses at Thebes (today's Luxor). The female statues adorning the four corners of the square represent France's eight largest cities.

In 1793, Louis XVI's head was lopped off by a guillotine set up in the north-west corner of the square, near the statue representing Brest. During the next two years, another guillotine – this one near the entrance to the Jardin des Tuileries – was used to behead 1343 more people, including Queen Marie-Antoinette and, six months later, the Revolutionary leaders Danton and Robespierre.

The square was given its present name after the Reign of Terror, in the hope that it would be a place of peace and harmony.

The two imposing buildings on the north side of place de la Concorde are the **Hôtel de la Marine**, headquarters of the French navy, and the **Hôtel de Crillon**, one of Paris' swankiest hotels (see Deluxe in the Places to Stay chapter).

Église de la Madeleine
The neoclassical Church of Saint Mary Magdalen (metro Madeleine), known simply as La Madeleine, is 350m north of place de la Concorde along rue Royale. Built in the style of a Greek temple, it was consecrated in 1842 after almost a century of design changes and construction delays. It is surrounded by 52 Corinthian columns, each standing 20m tall. The marble and gilt interior, topped by three sky-lit cupolas, opens 7.45 to 11 am and 12.25 to 6.30 pm Monday to Saturday and 7.30 am to 1 or 1.30 pm and 3.30 to 7 pm on Sunday. You can hear the massive organ being played at Mass at 6 pm on Saturday and at 11 am and 12.30 and 6 pm on Sunday.

CHAMPS-ÉLYSÉES AREA (Map 2)
Ave des Champs-Élysées, 8e, whose name means 'Elysian Fields' (Elysium was where happy souls dwelt after death, according to Greek mythology), links place de la Concorde with the Arc de Triomphe. The avenue has symbolised the style and *joie de vivre* of Paris since the mid-19th century.

Ave des Champs-Élysées
Popular with the aristocracy of the mid-19th century as a stage for parading their wealth, the 2km-long ave des Champs-Élysées was, after WWII, taken over by airline offices, cinemas, car showrooms and fast-food restaurants. In recent years, however, the municipality's 330-million-franc investment to regain some of the 72m-wide avenue's former sparkle and prestige has paid off and the Champs-Élysées is a more popular destination than ever.

Rue du Faubourg Saint Honoré
Rue du Faubourg Saint Honoré, 8e, the western extension of rue Saint Honoré some 400m north of ave des Champs-Élysées, links rue Royale (metro Concorde) with place des Ternes (metro Ternes). It is home to some of Paris' most renowned couture houses, jewellers and antique shops.

The most remarkable of the avenue's 18th-century mansions is the **Palais de l'Élysée**, at the intersection of rue du Faubourg Saint Honoré and ave de Marigny, 8e, now the official residence of the French president.

Straight as an arrow: a view from the Arc de Triomphe

Even better than the real thing: imitation fast food along ave des Champs-Élysées

euro currency converter €1 = 6.56FF

Musée du Petit Palais

The Petit Palais (☎ 01 42 65 12 73, metro Champs Élysées Clemenceau), ave Winston Churchill, 8e, built for the 1900 Exposition Universelle, houses the **Musée des Beaux-Arts de la Ville de Paris**, the Paris municipality's Museum of Fine Arts, with medieval and Renaissance *objets d'art* (porcelain, clocks etc), tapestries, drawings and 19th-century French painting and sculpture. It opens 10 am to 5.40 pm Tuesday to Sunday (to 8 pm on Thursday) and admission costs 30FF (reduced price 20FF, free for those aged under 26 or over 60), but it is expected to close for refurbishment in late 2000.

Grand Palais

West of the Petit Palais, the Grand Palais (☎ 01 44 13 17 17, metro Champs Élysées Clemenceau), 3 ave du Général Eisenhower, 8e, houses the **Galeries Nationales du Grand Palais**, which hosts special exhibitions lasting three or four months. Also erected for the 1900 Exposition Universelle, the Grand Palais has an iron frame and a huge, Art Nouveau-style glass roof. It is usually open 1 to 8 pm Wednesday to Monday (to 10 pm on Wednesday). The cost of admission varies but count on 50FF (35FF for students and seniors, and for everyone on Monday; free for under-18s, and for everyone on the first Sunday of the month).

Palais de la Découverte

The Palace of Discovery (☎ 01 56 43 20 21, metro Champs Élysées Clemenceau), ave Franklin D Roosevelt, 8e, is a fascinating science museum with interactive exhibits on astronomy, biology, medicine, chemistry, mathematics, computer science, physics and earth sciences. It opens 9.30 am to 6 pm Tuesday to Saturday, and 10 am to 7 pm on Sunday; admission costs 30FF (20FF for students, and those aged under 18 or over 60; free for under-fives). The **planetarium**, which has four shows a day (in French), costs an extra 15FF.

Arc de Triomphe

The Arc de Triomphe (☎ 01 55 37 73 77,

The Arc de Triomphe is Paris' traditional starting point for victory celebrations and parades.

euro currency converter 10FF = €1.52

metro Charles de Gaulle-Étoile) is 2.2km north-west of place de la Concorde in the middle of place Charles de Gaulle (also known as place de l'Étoile), the world's largest traffic roundabout and the meeting point of a dozen different avenues. It was commissioned in 1806 by Napoleon to commemorate his imperial victories but remained unfinished when he started losing – first battles and then entire wars. It was not completed until 1836.

Since 1920, the body of an **Unknown Soldier** from WWI, taken from Verdun in Lorraine, has lain beneath the arch; his fate and that of countless others is commemorated by a memorial flame that is rekindled each evening around 6.30 pm.

The most celebrated of the arch's four **relief panels** is to the right as you face it from the ave des Champs-Élysées side. Entitled *Départ des Volontaires de 1792* and also known as *La Marseillaise*, it is the work of François Rude. Higher up, a frieze running round the whole monument depicts hundreds of figures, each one 2m high.

From the viewing platform on top of the arch (284 steps and well worth the climb) you can see the 12 avenues – many of them named after Napoleonic victories and illustrious generals – radiating towards every part of Paris. The platform can be reached 9.30 am to 11 pm daily, April to September, and 10 am to 10.30 pm the rest of the year. Tickets cost 40FF (25FF for those aged 12 to 25, free for children) and are sold in the underground passageway.

Ave Foch

Ultra-exclusive ave Foch (which rhymes with 'posh') in the 16e is Paris' widest boulevard, linking the Arc de Triomphe with the Bois de Boulogne. Grassy areas with shaded paths – perfect for walking neurotic little dogs – separate the main lanes of traffic from the stately (and *very* expensive) apartment buildings along either side. Laid out in 1854, the avenue is named after Marshal Ferdinand Foch (1851-1929), commander of the Allied forces during the last few difficult months of WWI.

PARC DE MONCEAU AREA (Map 2)

The elegant residential districts that surround Parc de Monceau, 8e, are a bastion of Paris' *haute bourgeoisie*.

Parc de Monceau

Pass through one of the gates in the elaborate wrought-iron fence round the 8.25-hectare Parc de Monceau (metro Monceau) and you find yourself amid Paris' most immaculately tended lawns, flowerbeds, trees and pseudo-classical statues. From the many benches, you can observe the city's best-dressed children out with their nannies or on their way home from expensive private schools. Nearby streets are lined with opulent mansions and grand apartment buildings from the mid-19th century. The world's first parachute jump – from a balloon – was made here in 1797. The park is open 7 am to 8 pm (to 10 pm from April to October).

Musée Cernuschi

The Cernuschi Museum (☎ 01 45 63 50 75, metro Monceau or Villiers), 7 ave Vélasquez, 8e, houses a collection of ancient Chinese art (funerary statues, bronzes, ceramics) and works from Japan assembled during an 1871-3 world tour by the banker and philanthropist Henri Cernuschi (1821-96). It is open 10 am to 5.40 pm Tuesday to Sunday. Admission costs 30FF (20FF reduced price).

Musée Nissim de Camondo

The Nissim de Camondo Museum (☎ 01 53 89 06 40, metro Monceau or Villiers), 63 rue de Monceau, 8e, displays 18th-century furniture, wood panelling, tapestries, porcelain and other *objets d'art* collected by Count Moïse de Camondo, who established this museum in memory of his son Nissim, a soldier killed in 1917 during WWI. It is open 10 am to 5 pm Wednesday to Sunday; tickets cost 30FF (20FF for those aged 18 to 25 and seniors, free for under-18s).

Musée Jacquemart-André

The Jacquemart-André Museum (☎ 01 42 89 04 91, metro Miromesnil), 158 blvd Haussmann, 8e, is housed in an opulent residence built during the mid-19th century. The collection includes furniture, tapestries and enamels but is most noted for its paintings by Rembrandt and Van Dyck and some Italian Renaissance works by Bernini, Botticelli, Carpaccio, Donatello, Mantegna, Tintoretto, Titian and Uccello. The museum opens 10 am to 6 pm daily, and entrance costs 48FF (reduced price 36FF, free for under-sevens), including a cassette tour in one of six languages.

OPÉRA (Map 2)

The Palais Garnier, 9e, Paris' world-famous opera house, abuts the Grands Boulevards, the broad thoroughfares whose *belle époque* elegance has only partially been compromised by the traffic and pedestrian tumult of modern Paris.

Palais Garnier

This renowned opera house (metro Opéra), place de l'Opéra, 9e, designed in 1860 by Charles Garnier to showcase the splendour of Napoleon III's France, is one of the most impressive monuments erected during the Second Empire. It also contains the **Bibliothèque-Musée de l'Opéra** (Opera Library-Museum; ☎ 01 47 42 07 02), which opens 10 am to 5 pm daily and costs 30FF (20FF for under-26s, students and seniors; free for under-10s), including a visit to the opera house itself as long as there's not a daytime rehearsal or performance going on.

Blvd Haussmann

Blvd Haussmann, 8e and 9e, just north of Palais Garnier, is the heart of a commercial and banking district and is known for having some of Paris' most famous department stores, including **Galeries Lafayette** at No 40 and **Le Printemps** at No 64 (see Department Stores in the Shopping chapter).

Chapelle Expiatoire

The austere neoclassical Atonement Chapel (☎ 01 44 32 18 00, metro Saint Augustin), 29 rue Pasquier, 8e, sits atop the section of a cemetery where Louis XVI and Marie-Antoinette were buried after their executions in 1793. It was erected by the restored Bourbon king Louis XVIII in 1815.

GRANDS BOULEVARDS (Maps 2 & 3)

The eight contiguous Grands Boulevards (Great Boulevards) – Madeleine, Capucines, Italiens, Montmartre, Poissonnière, Bonne Nouvelle, Saint Denis and Saint Martin – stretch from elegant place de la Madeleine (Map 2) in the 8e eastwards to the less-than-luxurious place de la République (Map 3), where the 3e, 10e and 11e meet, a distance of just under 3km. The Grands Boulevards were laid out in the 17th century on the site of obsolete fortifications and served as a centre of café and theatre life in the 18th and 19th centuries, reaching the height of fashion during the *belle époque*.

Shopping Arcades

Walking through the *passages* (covered shopping arcades) off blvd Montmartre is the best way to step back into early-19th-century Paris; see the Passages walking tour on the opposite page.

Musée Grévin

This waxworks museum (Map 3, ☎ 01 47 70 85 05, metro Grands Boulevards) is most notable for its location – it's inside passage Jouffroy (enter from 10 blvd Montmartre, 9e). To be honest, the collection of 450 wax figures is not as good as that at Madame Tussaud's but would you get to see the death masks of French Revolutionary leaders in London? It opens 1 to 7 pm (from 10 am during school holidays) daily. Admission costs an outrageous 58FF (38FF for children aged six to 14).

10e ARRONDISSEMENT (Map 3)

The lively working-class area around blvd de Strasbourg and rue du Faubourg Saint Denis (metro Château d'Eau or Strasbourg Saint Denis), especially south of blvd de Magenta, is home to large communities of Indians, Bangladeshis, Pakistanis, West Indians, Africans, Turks and Kurds. Strolling through **passage Brady** (metro Château d'Eau) is almost like stepping into a back alley in Bombay.

TIME PASSAGES OF THE RIGHT BANK

ASA ANDERSSON

Stepping into the *passages couverts* (covered shopping arcades) or *galeries* of the Right Bank is probably the simplest way to get a feel for the Paris of the early 19th century. The passages couverts emerged during the period of relative peace and prosperity under the restored House of Bourbon after the fall of Napoleon, and the rapid growth of the new industrial classes. In a city without sewers, pavements or sheltered walkways, these arcades allowed shoppers to stroll from boutique to boutique protected from the elements and the filth of the streets.

The passages quickly became among Paris' top attractions – provincials made them their first port of call to kit themselves out for the capital – and by the mid-19th century Paris counted some 150 of these sumptuously decorated temples to mammon. As well as shopping, visitors could dine and drink, play billiards, bathe (all the passages had public baths), attend the theatre and, at night (the passages were open 24 hours in those days), engage in activities of a carnal nature; the passages were notorious for attracting prostitutes after dark and there were rooms available on the 1st level.

The demise of the passages came about for a number of reasons, but the most important was the opening of the first of the capital's department stores, Au Bon Marché, in 1852. Today a total of only 18 arcades remain – mostly in the 1er, 2e and 9e – in various states of repair. They are among the best places to get an idea of how Parisians and their tastes have changed over the years, with traditional millinery and cane shops mixing happily with postmodern designer fashion, and hand-worked printing presses sitting next to computer shops. And if you really wanted to you could spend your entire time in Paris under the glass roofs of the passages; they still contain everything you need – from restaurants, bars and theatres to hotels and, of course, shops.

distance: 2.75km
start: rue de Rivoli, 1er (metro Louvre-Rivoli)
finish: rue du Faubourg Montmartre, 9e (metro Le Peletier)

From Louvre-Rivoli metro station on rue de Rivoli, 1er, walk north along rue du Louvre, turn west onto rue Saint Honoré and then north again on rue Jean-Jacques Rousseau. The entrance to the **Galerie Véro Dodat (1)**, built in 1823 by two well-heeled *charcutiers*, is at No 19. The arcade retains its 19th-century skylights, ceiling murals, Corinthian columns, tiled floor and shop fronts, among the most interesting of which are the Marini France stained-glass workshop at No 28, the Capia shop with antique dolls and gramophones at No 23 and No 24-26, the Luthier music store with guitars and violins at

No 17 and the *papeterie-imprimerie* (stationer-printer's) at No 2-4, in place since 1848. For places to eat, see the Louvre & Les Halles section in the Places to Eat chapter.

The galerie's west exit gives onto rue Croix des Petits Champs. Walk north to the corner with rue du Colonel Driant – the massive building ahead of you is the headquarters of the **Banque de France** – and turn west. At the end of the road is one of the entrances to the **Galeries du Palais Royal (2)**. Strictly speaking, these galeries are not passages as they are arcaded rather than covered, but since they date from 1786 they are considered to be the prototypes of what was to come. The **Café de Foy**, from where the revolution sparked on a warm July day just three years after the galeries opened, once stood on the west side, what is today's **Galerie de Montpensier (3)**. Charlotte Corday, Marat's assassin, once worked in a shop in the **Galerie de Valois (4)**.

The tiny arcade that doglegs from the north of the Galeries du Palais Royal into rue de Beaujolais is **passage du Perron (5)**; the writer Colette (1873-1954) lived the last years of her life in a flat above here (9 rue de Beaujolais, 1er). Diagonally opposite from where you emerge at 4 rue des Petits Champs are the entrances to two of the most stunningly restored passages in Paris: **Galerie Vivienne (6)** and the interconnecting **Galerie Colbert (7)**.

Galerie Vivienne (1823), with stucco bas-reliefs, floor mosaics and a glass rotunda decorated with snakes (signifying prudence), anchors (for hope) and beehives (symbolising industry), was and still is one of the poshest of the passages. As you enter, look to the stairwell to the left at No 13 with its false marble walls; François Eugène Vidocq (1775-1857), master burglar *and* the chief of detectives in Paris in the early 19th century, lived upstairs. Some of the shops to check out are milliner Lola Prusac at No 11; Wolff et Descourtis with their fancy silk scarves at No 12; the Librairie Ancienne & Moderne at No 45, which Colette frequented; L'Atelier Emilio Robbo, one of the most beautiful flower shops in Paris, at No 33; and designer Jean-Paul Gaultier's first boutique (the main entrance is outside at 6 rue Vivienne, 2e).

The major draw of the overly restored Galerie Colbert (1826) is its huge glass dome and rotunda, which served as a car workshop and garage as recently as the early 1980s. There aren't a lot of shops here, but there is the *belle époque* brasserie Le Grand Colbert (see the Louvre & Les Halles section in the Places to·Eat chapter). Check out the bizarre fresco above the rue des Petits Champs exit; it's totally out of proportion.

Walk west along rue des Petits Champs – passing the original home of the **Bibliothèque Nationale**, with its curiously leaning **statue of Sartre (8)** in the courtyard (enter from rue Vivienne) – to No 40 and the entrance to **passage Choiseul (9)**.

Passage Choiseul (1828), some 45m long and containing 80 shops, is tatty but vibrant, especially during the week. Abandoned by the Japanese designer Kenzo after he'd made it in Paris in the early 1980s,

Choiseul houses discount clothing and shoe shops (Nos 7, 9, 16 and 18), Greek and Asian food shops (eg, No 59), second-hand bookshops and (at No 61) the actor Jean-Claude Brialy's **Théâtre des Bouffes Parisiens**, where comedies are performed. And it's got a long literary history: Paul Verlaine (1844-96) drank absinthe here and Céline (1894-1961) grew up in his mother's shop at No 62.

Leave passage Choiseul at 23 rue Saint Augustin and walk eastwards to rue du Quatre Septembre. The **building covered in graffiti (10)** at

No 2 housed squatters until recently; across the square is the **Bourse (11)**, built in 1826 and the future home of the no doubt crowd-pulling Musée de la Finance (Finance Museum). Turn north up rue Vivienne and east onto rue Saint Marc. The entrance to the maze-like **passage des Panoramas (12)** is at No 10.

Passage des Panoramas is the oldest covered arcade in Paris (1800) and was the first to receive gas lighting (1817). It was expanded in 1834 with the addition of four other interconnecting passages: Feydeau, Montmartre, Saint Marc and Variétés. It's a bit faded around the edges but keep an eye open for Jean-Paul Belmondo's **Théâtre des Variétés** at No 17, the erstwhile vaudeville Théâtre d'Offenbach, from where spectators would come out to shop during the interval; the engraver's Stern at No 47, which has been here since 1834; Le Croquenote, a restaurant famed for its *chansonniers* (cabaret singers), at No 22 (see French Chansons in the Entertainment chapter); and L'Arbre à Cannelle, a lovely tearoom (see the Louvre & Les Halles section in the Places to Eat chapter).

Leave at 11 blvd Montmartre. Directly across the road, at No 10-12, is the entrance to **passage Jouffroy (13)**.

Passage Jouffroy, the last major passage to open in Paris (1847) but the first to use metal and glass in its skylights and to have central heating, remains a personal favourite; no other passage offers so much or feels so alive. There are two hotels here, including the Hôtel Chopin (see Gare Saint Lazare & Grands Boulevards under Mid-Range in the Places to Stay chapter), as well as the Musée Grévin (see the Grands Boulevards section in this chapter). There are also some wonderful boutiques, including the bookshops Librairie du Passage (Nos 48 and 62) and Paul Vulin (No 50); M&G Segas (No 34), where Toulouse Lautrec bought his walking sticks; and the rococo Thomas Boog (No 36), where everything seems to be made of shells.

You can leave passage Jouffroy at 9 rue de la Grange Batelière, cross the road to No 6, and enter **passage Verdeau (14)**, the last and most modest of this stretch. Verdeau was never particularly successful because of its 'end-of-the-line' location. Nevertheless there's lots to explore: lead soldiers at Brocéliande (No 20), daguerreotypes at Photo Verdeau (No 14), books and prints at Gerard Ganet (No 10) and 1950s comic books at Roland Buret (No 6).

The northern exit from passage Verdeau will deposit you on the corner of rue du Faubourg Montmartre and rue Richer. Walk north along the former and you'll soon reach Le Peletier metro station. East along rue Richer are a number of kosher restaurants and, at No 32, the *Folies-Bergère* cabaret (see the boxed text 'They Certainly Can Cancan' in the Entertainment chapter).

Porte Saint Denis & Porte Saint Martin

Porte Saint Denis (metro Strasbourg Saint Denis), the 24m-high triumphal arch at the intersection of rue du Faubourg Saint Denis and blvd Saint Denis, was built in 1672 to commemorate Louis XIV's campaign along the Rhine. On the north side, carvings represent the fall of Maastricht in 1673.

Two blocks east, at the intersection of rue du Faubourg Saint Martin and blvd Saint Denis, is another triumphal arch, the 17m-high Porte Saint Martin, erected two years later to commemorate the capture of Besançon and the Franche-Comté region by Louis XIV's armies.

Musée Baccarat

The glittering, incredibly pricey Baccarat showroom (☎ 01 47 70 64 30, metro Château d'Eau) in the CIAT (Centre International des Arts de la Table) building at 30

Immortal Reminders

The French immortalise their heroes with statues and monuments. Père Lachaise, Montmartre and Montparnasse cemeteries are bursting with wonderfully evocative likenesses of heroes and villains, poets and philosophers, and revolutionaries and autocrats, and there's a resident stone or bronze celebrity in even the tiniest park. The following is a selection of the larger-than-life characters you might bump into on your way around Paris.

Saint Denis, patron saint of France (also known as Dionysius of Paris), introduced Christianity to Paris and was beheaded by the Romans for his pains. You can see him carrying his head under his arm on the carved western portal of Notre Dame (Map 6), place du Parvis Notre Dame, 4e.

Sainte Geneviève, patroness of Paris, turned Attila the Hun away from Paris in AD 451. Now she stands, ghostly pale, turning her back on the city from high above the Pont de la Tournelle (Map 6), just south of Île St Louis in the 5e. Plucky **Jeanne d'Arc** (Joan of Arc)

RICHARD I'ANSON

The infamously amorous Henri IV rides forth.

tried unsuccessfully to wrest Paris from the English almost a millennium later (1429); her gilded likeness now stands in place des Pyramides next to 192 rue de Rivoli (Map 6) and is a favourite rallying point for royalists and parties of the extreme right.

Henri IV, known as the *Vert Galant* ('jolly rogue' or 'dirty old man', depending on your perspective), sits astride his white stallion on the Pont Neuf (Map 6) in the 1er, exactly as he did when he inaugurated the 'New Bridge' in 1607. **Charlemagne**, emperor of the Francs, rides his steed under the trees in front of Notre Dame (Map 6), while a poor imitation of the Sun King, **Louis XIV**, prances in place des Victoires (Map 6) in the 2e. **Napoleon**, horseless and in Roman drag, stands atop the column in place Vendôme (Map 2) in the 1er.

But it's not just the holy and the regal who are immortalised. **Georges Danton**, a leader of the Revolution and later one of its victims, stands very much with his head intact near the site of his house at carrefour de l'Odéon (Map 6) in the 6e. An illuminated bronze replica of the **Statue of Liberty** – recently returned from a year in Tokyo Harbour – faces New York from an artificial island in the Seine (Map 4). And have a look at the impressive **Centaur** statue (1985) in the centre of place Le Corbusier (Map 4), which was made by César Baldaccini (known as César to the world), whose best-known work is the little statue handed to actors at the Césars, French cinema's equivalent to the Oscars. Impossible to miss, the statue of the mythological half-horse, half-man creature has disproportionate gonads the size of grapefruits. Now that's what we call larger than life.

bis rue de Paradis is a fine example of Napoleon III-era industrial architecture. The attached Baccarat Museum is filled with some 1000 stunning pieces of crystal, many of them custom-made for princes and dictators of desperately poor ex-colonies. The museum opens 10 am to 6 pm Monday to Saturday; admission costs 15FF (reduced price 10FF).

Canal Saint Martin

The tranquil, 4.5km-long Saint Martin Canal (metro République, Jaurès and others) links the 10e with Parc de la Villette, 19e, via the Bassin de la Villette and Canal de l'Ourcq. Its shaded towpaths – speckled with sunlight filtering through the plane trees – are a wonderful place for a romantic stroll or a bike ride and take you past nine **locks**, metal bridges and ordinary Parisian neighbourhoods. Parts of the waterway – built in 1806 to link the Seine with the 108km-long Canal de l'Ourcq – are higher than the surrounding land. The two canals, along with the Canal Saint Denis, are slated to undergo a massive 600 million FF renovation that will take six years.

Between the Port de Plaisance de Paris-Arsenal (the pleasure-boat marina next to place de la Bastille) and square Frédéric Lemaître, 10e, Canal Saint Martin disappears under reinforced concrete vaults for over 2km. The northern, open-air half of the canal, which links square Frédéric Lemaître with Parc de la Villette, 19e, was saved from the same fate thanks to the failure of a plan – mooted in the early 1970s – to pave it over and turn it into an autoroute. For information on barge rides, see Organised Tours in the Getting Around chapter.

BERCY (Maps 5 & 9)

Long cut off from the rest of the city by railway tracks and the Seine but now joined with the Left Bank by the 240-million-franc (and quite ordinary-looking) Pont Charles de Gaulle (1996) and the new driverless Météor metro line, Bercy in the 12e has some of Paris' most important new buildings. These include the octagonal **Palais Omnisports de Paris-Bercy** (Map 9), blvd

Just cruising: taking it easy along Canal Saint Martin

de Bercy, 12e, designed to serve as both an indoor sports arena and a venue for concerts, ballet and theatre, and the giant **Ministry of Finance** (Map 5), also on blvd de Bercy. Across the Seine in the 13e is the new Bibliothèque Nationale de France François Mitterrand.

The development of **Bercy Village** (Map 9, metro Cour Saint-Émilion) – a series of former wine warehouses dating from 187 that now house bars and trendy restaurants – and the arrival of river barges fitted out with more glitzy eateries and music clubs has turned the 12e into a seriously happening district. The new **Marina de Bercy** (Map 9, ☎ 01 43 43 40 30) and something called **Sable en Seine** (Sand on the Seine; Map 9) – a miniature (and ephemeral, as it appears sporadically at the weekend in the warmer months) 'beach' where you can rent umbrellas and Lilos (air mattresses) and stretch out on fine white sand to sunbathe – are helping the quarter to reclaim its share of the river. **Parc de Bercy** (Map 9), linking the Palais Omnisports with Bercy Village, is a particularly attractive park. On an island in he centre of one of its large ponds is the **Maison du Lac du Parc de Bercy** (☎ 01 53 46 19 34), a small centre with temporary exhibitions (open 10 am to 6 pm daily).

13e & 14e ARRONDISSEMENTS (Maps 1 & 9)

The 13e (Map 1) begins a few blocks south of the Jardin des Plantes, 5e, and is beginning to undergo something of a renaissance following the opening of the Bibliothèque Nationale de France François Mitterrand, the new high-speed Météor metro line (No 14) and, across the Seine in the 12e, Bercy Village. The less-than-thrilling 14e is best known for the Cimetière du Montparnasse (see the Montparnasse section earlier in this chapter), but it also boasts one of Paris' more unusual attractions.

Bibliothèque Nationale de France François Mitterrand

Right across the river from Bercy are the four glass towers of the controversial, 13.6-billion-franc National Library of France (Map 9, ☎ 01 53 79 59 59 or 01 53 79 53 79, metro Bibliothèque), 11 quai François Mauriac, 13e, conceived by the late president François Mitterrand as a 'wonder of the modern world' and opened in 1998. No expense was spared to carry out a plan that many said defied logic. While many of the more than 10 million books and historical documents are shelved in the sun-drenched, 18-storey towers – shaped like half-open books – visitors sit in artificially lit basement halls built round a 'forest courtyard' of 140 50-year-old pines, trucked in from the countryside. For details of how to use the library, see Libraries in the Facts for the Visitor chapter.

Manufacture des Gobelins

The celebrated Gobelins Factory (Map 1, ☎ 01 44 61 21 69, metro Les Gobelins), 42 ave des Gobelins, 13e, which has been weaving *haute lisse* (high-relief) tapestries on specialised looms since the 18th century along with Beauvais-style *basse lisse* (low-relief) ones and Savonnerie rugs, can be visited on a guided tour at 2 and 2.45 pm

Tuesday to Thursday. Admission costs 50FF (reduced price 40FF, free for under-sevens).

Chinatown

The area concentrated around ave de Choisy, ave d'Ivry and blvd Masséna is Paris' high-rise Chinatown (Map 1, metro Porte d'Ivry, Porte de Choisy or Tolbiac), owing its distinctly Franco-Chinese ambience to the scores of Asian restaurants, shops and travel agencies. For details see the special section 'Paris Mondial' after the Facts about Paris chapter.

Catacombes

In 1785, it was decided to solve the hygiene and aesthetic problems posed by Paris' overflowing cemeteries by exhuming the bones and storing them in the tunnels of three disused quarries. One ossuary created in 1810 is now known as the Catacombes (Map 1, ☎ 01 43 22 47 63, metro Denfert Rochereau) and is without doubt the most macabre place in Paris. After descending 20m from street level, visitors follow 1.6km of underground corridors in which the bones and skulls of millions of Parisians are neatly stacked along the walls. During WWII, these tunnels were used as a headquarters by the Resistance.

The route through the Catacombes begins at the small green building at 1 place Denfert Rochereau, 14e. It opens 2 to 4 pm Tuesday to Friday, and 9 to 11 am and 2 to 4 pm at the weekend. Tickets cost 33FF (22FF for students, free for those aged under 26 or over 60). It's a good idea to bring along a torch (flashlight). Flash photography is allowed but tripods are not.

The exit (metro Mouton Duvernet), where a guard will check your bag for stolen bones, is on rue Remy Dumoncel, 700m south-west of place Denfert Rochereau.

MONTMARTRE (Map 8)

During the 19th century the bohemian lifestyle of Montmartre, 18e, attracted artists and writers whose presence turned the area into Paris' most important centre of creativity. Although the activity shifted to

THINGS TO SEE & DO

Montparnasse after WWI, Montmartre retains an upbeat ambience that all the tourists in the world couldn't spoil.

In English-speaking countries, Montmartre's mystique of unconventionality has been magnified by the supposed notoriety of the **Moulin Rouge**, a nightclub on the edge of the Pigalle district that was founded in 1889 and is known for its scantily clad chorus girls. For details, see the boxed text 'They Certainly Can Cancan' in the Entertainment chapter.

Basilique du Sacré Cœur

Sacred Heart Basilica (☎ 01 53 41 89 00, metro Anvers), 35 rue du Chevalier de la Barre, 18e, perched at the very top of Butte de Montmartre, was built from contributions pledged by Parisian Catholics as an act of contrition after the humiliating Franco-Prussian War of 1870-1. Construction began in 1873, but the basilica was not consecrated until 1919.

Some 234 spiralling steps lead you to the basilica's **dome** (15FF; 8FF for students aged under 25 and children), which affords one of Paris' most spectacular panoramas; they say you can see for 30km on a clear day. The chapel-lined **crypt** (same admission charges), down the stairs to the right as you exit the basilica, is huge but not very interesting.

The basilica opens 7 am to 11 pm daily, and the dome and crypt 9 am to 7 pm daily, April to September (to 6 pm the rest of the year).

Place du Tertre

Half a block west of the **Église Saint Pierre de Montmartre**, parts of which date from the 12th century, is place du Tertre (metro Abbesses), once the main square of the village of Montmartre. These days it's filled with cafés, restaurants, portrait artists and tourists and is always animated. Look for the two **windmills** to the west on rue Lepic.

Espace Montmartre-Salvador Dalí

Over 300 works by Salvador Dalí (1904-89), the flamboyant Catalan surrealist print-

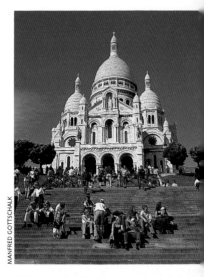
MANFRED GOTTSCHALK

Rhapsody in white: the tourist magnet that is the Basilique du Sacré Cœur

maker, painter, sculptor and self-promoter are on display at this spooky surrealist-style museum (☎ 01 42 64 40 10, metro Abbesses), 9-11 rue Poulbot, 18e, just round the corner from place du Tertre. It is open 10 am to 6.30 pm daily, and admission costs 40FF (30FF reduced rate).

Musée de Montmartre

The Montmartre Museum (☎ 01 46 06 61 11, metro Lamarck Caulaincourt), 12 rue Cortot, 18e, displays paintings, lithographs and documents mostly relating to the area's rebellious and bohemian/artistic past. It's hard to appreciate what the big deal is (and to justify the admission fee) unless you care about Montmartre's mythology. There's a lush little garden at the back. The museum opens 11 am to 6 pm Tuesday to Sunday and costs 25FF (20FF for students and seniors).

Musée d'Art Naïf-Max Fourny

The Museum of Naive Art, founded in 1986, is housed in Halle Saint Pierre (☎ 01 42 58 72 89, metro Anvers), 2 rue Ronsard, 18e, across from square Willette and the ase of the funicular. The colourful, vivid aintings – gathered from around the world are immediately appealing, thanks in part o their whimsical and generally optimistic erspective on life. The museum, whose hemed exhibitions change frequently, is ›pen 10 am to 6 pm daily. Entrance is a ricey 40FF (30FF for students, seniors and eachers; 20FF for children).

Cimetière de Montmartre

Montmartre Cemetery (Maps 2 & 8, ☎ 01 43 ɔ7 64 24, metro Place de Clichy), estab-ished in 1798, is perhaps the most famous emetery in Paris after Père Lachaise. It con-ains the graves of Zola, Alexandre Dumas he younger, Stendhal, Heinrich Heine, acques Offenbach, Hector Berlioz, Degas, François Truffaut and Vaslav Nijinsky.

The entrance nearest Butte de Mont-nartre is at 20 ave Rachel, down the stairs rom 10 rue Caulaincourt. The cemetery ›pens 9 am (8.30 am on Saturday) to 6 pm laily, mid-March to early November, and ɔ.30 am to 5.30 pm the rest of the year.

Getting Around

The RATP's sleek funicular, travelling up and down the southern slope of Butte de Montmartre (Montmartre Hill), whisks vis-tors from square Willette (metro Anvers) to Sacré Cœur. It runs until 12.40 am daily and costs one metro/bus ticket each way. Carte Orange, Paris Visite and Mobilis ›asses are valid on it.

Montmartrobus, also run by the RATP, akes a circuitous route all over Mont-nartre; maps are posted at bus stops.

PIGALLE (Map 8)

Only a few blocks south-west of the tran-quil, residential streets of Montmartre is ively, neon-lit Pigalle, 9e and 18e, one of Paris' two main sex districts (the other, which is much more low-rent, is along rue Saint Denis, 1er, north of Forum des Halles). But Pigalle is more than just a sleazy red-light district: though the area around blvd de Clichy between Pigalle and Blanche metro stations is lined with erotica shops and striptease parlours, there are also

plenty of trendy night spots, including clubs and cabarets.

Musée de l'Érotisme

The Museum of Erotic Art (☎ 01 42 58 28 73, metro Blanche), 72 blvd de Clichy, 18e, tries to put some 2000 titillating statuary and stimulating sexual aids from days gone by on a loftier plane, with erotic art both antique and modern from four continents spread over seven floors. But we know why we're here. Its Web site is at www.erotic-museum.com and offers a sneak preview. It opens 10 am to 2 am daily and costs 40FF (30FF for students).

Musée Gustave Moreau

The Gustave Moreau Museum (Map 3, ☎ 01 48 74 38 50, metro Trinité), about 500m south-west of place Pigalle at 14 rue de La Rochefoucauld, 9e, is dedicated to the eponymous symbolist painter's work. Housed in what was once Moreau's studio, the two-storey museum is crammed with paintings, drawings and sketches. It is open 11 am to 5.15 pm on Monday and Wednes-day and 10 am to 12.45 pm and 2 to 5.15 pm Thursday to Sunday. Admission costs 22FF (15FF for students and those aged over 60, free for under-18s).

LA VILLETTE AREA (Map 1)

The 19e is of interest to visitors mainly be-cause of Parc de la Villette, with its won-derful museums and other attractions. You can go boating on Canal de l'Ourcq (see Organised Tours in the Getting Around Chapter).

Parc de la Villette

This whimsical, 30-hectare park in the city's far north-eastern corner, which opened in 1993, stretches for 600m from the Cité des Sciences et de l'Industrie (metro Porte de la Villette) southwards to the Cité de la Musique (metro Porte de Pantin). Split into two sections by the Canal de l'Ourcq, its lawns are enlivened by shaded walkways, imaginative public furniture, a series of themed gardens and fanciful, bright-red building-sculptures known as *folies* (follies).

For kids, there's a **merry-go-round** near the Cinaxe, a **playground** between the Géode and the nearest bridge, and two large play areas: the **Jardin des Vents** (Wind Garden) and the adjacent **Jardin des Dunes** (Dune Garden). Divided into three areas for children of different ages, they are across Galerie de la Villette (the covered walkway) from the **Grande Halle**, a wonderful old abattoir of wrought iron and glass now used for concerts, theatre performances, expositions and conventions.

For information on barge rides to Parc de la Villette from the Port de Plaisance de Paris-Arsenal and from quai Anatole France near the Musée d'Orsay, see Organised Tours in the Getting Around chapter.

Cité des Sciences et de l'Industrie

The enormous City of Sciences and Industry (☎ 01 40 05 80 00, or 01 40 05 12 12 for reservations, metro Porte de la Villette), 30 ave Corentin Cariou, 19e, at the northern end of Parc de la Villette, has all sorts of high-tech exhibits. Visit its Web site at www.cite-sciences.fr. On Minitel, key in 3615 VILLETTE.

Musée Explora The huge, rather confusing main museum opens 10 am to 6 pm Tuesday to Sunday (to 7 pm on Sunday). A ticket good for Explora, the planetarium, a 3-D film and the French-navy submarine *Argonaute*, commissioned in 1957 and drydocked in the park, costs 50FF (35FF for those aged eight to 25, seniors and teachers, and for everyone on Saturday; free for under-sevens) and allows you to enter and exit up to four times during the day. Various combination tickets valid for the Cité des Sciences, the Géode and Cinaxe are available.

A free map-brochure in English and the detailed, 80-page *Guide to the Permanent Exhibitions* are available from the round information counter at the Cité des Sciences' main entrance.

Cité des Enfants & Techno Cité The highlight of the Cité des Sciences is the brilliant Cité des Enfants, whose colourful and imaginative hands-on demonstrations c basic scientific principles are divided int two sections: one for three- to five-yea olds, the other for five- to 12-year-olds. I the former, kids can explore, among othe things, the conduct of water (waterproof la ponchos provided), while in the latter chil dren can build toy houses with industri robots and stage news broadcasts in a T studio equipped with real video cameras The new Techno Cité is devoted to teachin kids how to use computers.

Visits lasting 90 minutes begin four time a day at two-hour intervals from 9.30 (Tues day, Thursday and Friday) or 10.30 an (Wednesday, Saturday and Sunday). Eac child is charged 25FF and must be accom panied by an adult. During school holiday it's a good idea to make reservations two o three days in advance by telephone, on th Web or on Minitel.

Géode

Just south of the Cité des Sciences at 26 av Corentin Cariou is the Géode (☎ 01 40 05 7 99), a 36m-high sphere whose mirror-lik surface made of thousands of polished, stain less-steel triangles has made it one of the a chitectural calling-cards of modern Paris Inside, high-resolution, 45-minute, 70mm films – on virtual reality, special effects, na ture etc – are projected onto a 180° scree that gives viewers a sense of being sur rounded by the action. Films are shown fron 10 am to 6 pm Tuesday to Sunday, with a special double feature at 6.30 pm; hours var on Monday. Headsets that pick up an Englis soundtrack are available for no extra charge

Tickets to the Géode cost 57FF (44FF fo under-25s and seniors, except at the week end and on public holidays from 2 to 5 pm) the double feature at 6.30 pm is 65FF.

Cinaxe

The Cinaxe (☎ 01 42 09 86 04, or 01 40 05 12 12 for reservations), a cinema with hy draulic seating for 60 people that moves i synchronisation with the action on the screen, is right across the walkway from the south-western side of the Cité des Sciences This example of proto-virtual-reality tech

ology opens 11 am to 5 pm Tuesday to
Sunday and costs 34FF (29FF for students,
seniors and those aged 12 to 17, 25FF for
under-12s). Shows begin every 15 minutes.

Cité de la Musique
On the southern edge of Parc de la Villette,
the City of Music (☎ 01 44 84 44 84, metro
Porte de Pantin), 221 ave Jean Jaurès, 19e, is
a striking triangular concert hall whose brief
is to bring non-elitist music from around the
world to Paris' multiethnic masses. Some
900 rare musical instruments are on display
in its fascinating **Musée de la Musique**
(Music Museum); you can hear many of
them being played through the earphones included in the admission. The museum opens
noon to 6 pm Tuesday to Thursday, noon to
7.30 pm on Friday and Saturday and 10 am
to 6 pm on Sunday. Admission costs 35FF
(25FF for students, seniors and those aged 18
to 25, 10FF for those aged six to 18). Nearby
is the prestigious **Conservatoire Nationale
de la Danse et de la Musique** (National
Conservatory of Dance and Music).

Parc des Buttes-Chaumont
Encircled by tall apartment blocks, the 25-
hectare Buttes-Chaumont Park (Map 3,
metro Buttes-Chaumont or Botzaris) in the
19e is the closest thing in Paris to Manhattan's Central Park. Great for jogging,
cycling or sunbathing, the park's lush,
forested slopes hide grottoes and artificial
waterfalls. The romantic **lake** is dominated
by a temple-topped **island** linked to the
mainland by two footbridges. Once a quarry
and rubbish tip, the park – bordered by rue
Manin and rue Botzaris – was given its
present form by Baron Haussmann in the
1860s. It's open 7 am to 9 pm (to 11 pm
May to September) daily.

MÉNILMONTANT & BELLEVILLE (Maps 1 & 3)
The area of Ménilmontant in the 11e is
growing trendier by the day, thanks to the
surfeit of restaurants, bars and clubs, while
Belleville, 20e, remains for the most part
unpretentious and working-class. Paris'
most famous necropolis lies just south.

Belleville
This inner-city 'village', centred around
blvd de Belleville (Map 3, metro Belleville),
is home to large numbers of immigrants,
especially Muslims and Jews from North
Africa and Vietnamese and ethnic Chinese
from Indochina; see the special section
'Paris Mondial' after the Facts about Paris
chapter for more details. In recent years,
the area's none-too-solid, late-19th-century
workers' flats have become popular with
artists in search of cheap housing and the
cachet that comes with slumming it.

Parc de Belleville (Map 3, metro Couronnes), which opened in 1992 a few blocks
east of blvd de Belleville, occupies a hill
almost 200m above sea level. It offers superb views of the city.

Cimetière du Père Lachaise
The world's most visited cemetery, Père
Lachaise (Map 1, ☎ 01 43 70 70 33,
metro Philippe Auguste, Gambetta or Père

**A touch of class: Frédéric Chopin's grave at
Cimetière du Père Lachaise**

SIMON BRACKEN

Lachaise) was founded in 1805. Its 70,000 ornate (some even ostentatious) tombs of the rich and/or famous form a verdant, open-air sculpture garden. Among the one million people buried here are Chopin, Molière, Apollinaire, Oscar Wilde, Balzac, Proust, Gertrude Stein, Colette, Simone Signoret, Pissarro, Seurat, Modigliani, Sarah Bernhardt, Yves Montand, Delacroix, Edith Piaf, Isadora Duncan and even those immortal 12th-century lovers, Abélard and Héloïse (see the boxed text 'Star-Crossed Lovers' under History in the Facts about Paris chapter). One particularly frequented (and now guarded) grave is that of 1960s rock star **Jim Morrison**, who died in an apartment (Map 7) at 17-19 rue Beautreillis, 4e, in the Marai in 1971 and is buried in division No 6.

On 27 May 1871, the last of the Communard insurgents, cornered by government forces, fought a hopeless, all-night battle among the tombstones. In the morning, the 147 survivors were lined up against the **Mur des Fédérés** (Wall of the Federalists) and shot. They were buried where they fell in a mass grave.

The cemetery, which has four entrance (two of them on blvd de Ménilmontant)

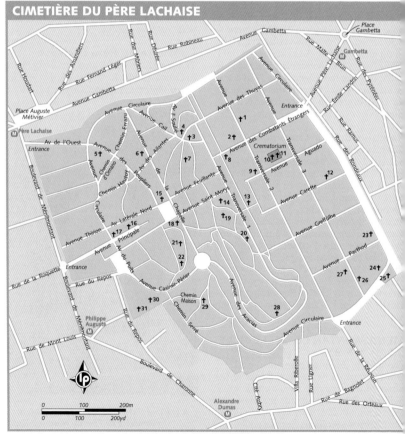

CIMETIÈRE DU PÈRE LACHAISE

pens 8 am (8.30 am on Saturday, 9 am on
unday) to 6 pm, mid-March to early No-
ember (to 5.30 pm the rest of the year).
Maps indicating the location of noteworthy
raves are posted around the cemetery and
an be obtained free at all the entrances, in-
luding the conservation office at 16 rue
u Repos, 20e, on the western side of the
emetery. Newsstands and flower kiosks in
he area sell the *Plan Illustré du Père
Lachaise* (Illustrated Map of Père Lachaise)
or 10FF. Two-hour English-language tours
(☎ 01 40 71 75 60; 38/26FF adult/reduced
ate) leave from the conservation office at
 pm on Saturday, June to September.
They're available in French (both themed
nd general) throughout the year at various
imes, but there's usually one at 2.30 pm on
aturday.

BOIS DE VINCENNES (Map 1)
Paris' largest English-style park, the 995-
hectare Vincennes Wood is in the 12e in the
ar south-eastern corner of the city. The **Parc
Floral** (Floral Park; metro Château de Vin-
ennes), just south of the Château de Vin-
ennes, is on route de la Pyramide; the
Jardin Tropical (Tropical Garden; metro
Nogent-sur-Marne) is at the park's eastern
dge on ave de la Belle Gabrielle. They are
open from 9.30 am to sometime between
 and 9 pm daily; entry costs 10FF (5FF for
hose aged six to 17).

Each year from the end of March to early
May, a huge amusement park known as the
Foire du Trône installs itself on the Pélouse
de Reuilly at the western end of the Bois de
Vincennes.

Château de Vincennes
The Vincennes Chateau (☎ 01 48 08 31 20,
metro Château de Vincennes), at the northern edge of the Bois de Vincennes, is a
bona fide royal chateau complete with
massive fortifications and a moat. Louis
XIV spent his honeymoon at the mid-17th-
century **Pavillon du Roi**, the westernmost
of the two royal pavilions flanking the
Cour Royale (Royal Courtyard). The 52m-
high **dungeon**, completed in 1369, was
used as a prison during the 17th and 18th
centuries.

You can walk round the grounds for
free, but the only way to see the Gothic
Chapelle Royale (Royal Chapel), built between the 14th and 16th centuries, is to
take a guided tour (in French, with an information booklet provided in English).
Tickets cost 32FF (reduced price 21FF) for
a long tour, and 25FF (15FF) for a short
one; they're free for those aged under 18.
There are five long and five short tours a
day from April to September, when the
chateau opens 10 am to noon and 1.15 to
6 pm daily, and four of each the rest of the
year, when it opens 10 am to noon and
1.15 to 5 pm.

Parc Zoologique de Paris
The zoo (☎ 01 44 75 20 10, metro Porte
Dorée), just east of Lac Daumesnil and
its two islets, was established in 1934. It
opens 9 am to 6 pm (to 5 pm in winter)
Monday to Saturday, and to 6.30 pm (to
5.30 pm in winter) on Sunday. Admission
costs 40FF (reduced tariff 30FF, 10FF for
children).

CIMETIÈRE DU PÈRE LACHAISE

1	Marcel Proust	11	Max Ernst	22	Frédéric Chopin
2	Guillaume Apollinaire	12	Oscar Wilde	23	Gertrude Stein
3	Eugène Delacroix	13	Sarah Bernhardt	24	Paul Éluard
4	Honoré de Balzac	14	Dominique Ingres	25	Mur des Fédérés
5	Georges Seurat	15	Jacques Louis David	26	Edith Piaf &
6	Georges Bizet	16	Georges Haussmann		Théo Sarapo
7	Hilaire Belloc	17	Sidonie Colette	27	Amedéo Modigliani
8	Hippolyte Kardec	18	Théodule Géricault	28	Beaumarachais
9	Yves Montand &	19	Jean-Baptiste Corot	29	Jim Morrison
	Simone Signoret	20	Molière	30	Abélard & Héloïse
10	Isadora Duncan	21	Vincenzo Bellini	31	Camile Pissarro

Musée National des Arts d'Afrique et d'Océanie

The National Museum of African and Oceanic Art (☎ 01 44 74 84 80, metro Porte Dorée), just within the wood at 293 ave Daumesnil, 12e, is devoted to the art of the South Pacific as well as North, West and Central Africa. It opens 10 am to 5.30 pm Wednesday to Monday (to 6 pm at the weekend) and costs 30FF (20FF for students, seniors and those aged 18 to 25; free for under-18s, and for everyone on the first Sunday of the month).

BOIS DE BOULOGNE (Map 1)

The 845-hectare Boulogne Wood, on the western edge of the city in the 16e, owes its informal layout to its designer, Baron Haussmann, who took his inspiration from London's Hyde Park rather than the more geometric French models.

The southern reaches of the wood take in **Stade Rolland Garros**, home of the French Open tennis tournament, and two horse-racing tracks, the **Hippodrome de Long-champ** for flat races and the **Hippodrome d'Auteuil** for steeplechases. For details, see Horse Racing under Spectator Sports in the Entertainment chapter.

Baron Haussmann

Few town planners anywhere in the world have had as great an impact on the city of their birth as Baron Georges-Eugène Haussmann (1809-91) had on Paris. As prefect of the Seine *département* under Napoleon III for 17 years, Haussmann and his staff of architects and engineers completely rebuilt huge swathes of Paris. He is best known – and most bitterly attacked – for having demolished much of medieval Paris, replacing the chaotic narrow streets, which were easy to barricade in an uprising, with the handsome, arrow-straight thoroughfares for which the city is so famous. He also revolutionised Paris' water supply and sewerage systems and laid out many of the city's loveliest parks, including large areas of the Bois de Boulogne, 16e, and the Bois de Vincennes, 12e.

Gardens

The enclosed **Parc de Bagatelle**, in the north western corner of the wood, is renowned for its beautiful gardens, which surround the **Château de Bagatelle**, built in 1775. There are areas dedicated to irises (which bloom in May), roses (June to October) and water lilies (August).

The **Pré Catalan** (Catalan Meadow) includes a **Jardin Shakespeare** in which you can see plants, flowers and trees mentioned in Shakespeare's plays. It's open 8.30 am to 7 or 7.30 pm daily.

At the southern end of the wood is the **Jardin des Serres d'Auteuil** (☎ 01 40 71 7 23), a garden with impressive conservatories that opened in 1898. They are open 10 am to 6 pm (to 5 pm from October to March) daily and cost 10FF (reduced price 5FF).

Musée National des Arts et Traditions Populaires

Just outside the borders of the Jardin d'Acclimatation but still in the wood, the National Museum of Popular Arts and Traditions (☎ 01 44 17 60 00, metro Les Sablons), 6 ave du Mahatma Gandhi, 16e, has displays illustrating life in rural France before and during the Industrial Revolution. It opens 9.45 am to 5.15 pm Wednesday to Monday and costs 30FF (23FF for students, seniors and those aged 18 to 25; free for under-18s, and for everyone on the first Sunday of the month).

Musée Marmottan-Claude Monet

Two blocks east of the Bois de Boulogne between Porte de la Muette and Porte de Passy, the Marmottan-Claude Monet Museum (☎ 01 42 24 07 02, metro La Muette), 2 rue Louis Boilly, 16e, has the world's largest collection of works by the impressionist painter as well as paintings by Gauguin, Sisley, Pissarro and Renoir. It opens 10 am to 5.30 pm Tuesday to Sunday. Entrance costs 40FF (reduced price 25FF).

Rowing Boats & Bicycles

Rowing boats can be hired (☎ 01 42 88 04 69) at **Lac Inférieur** (metro Avenue Henri

Martin), the largest of the wood's lakes and ponds, for 56FF an hour from 10 am to 6 pm (to 7 pm in summer) daily. Paris Cycles ☎ 01 47 47 76 50 for a recorded message or 01 47 47 22 37 to book) hires out bicycles at two locations: on ave du Mahatma Gandhi (metro Les Sablons), across from the Porte Sablons entrance to the Jardin d'Acclimatation amusement park, and near the Pavillon Royal (metro Avenue Foch) at the northern end of Lac Inférieur. Except when it rains, bicycles are available from 10 am to sundown daily, mid-April to mid-October, and during the same hours on Wednesday, Saturday and Sunday only the rest of the year. The rental cost is 20/30FF for 30/60 minutes and 60/80FF for a half/full day.

Jardin d'Acclimatation

This kids-oriented amusement park (☎ 01 40 67 90 82, metro Les Sablons) on ave du Mahatma Gandhi, whose name is another word for 'zoo' in French, now also includes the high-tech **Exploradôme**, a tented structure in the western section devoted to science, the media and the Internet. The park opens 10 am to 6 pm daily and admission costs 13FF (reduced price 6.50FF). Entry to both the park and Exploradôme costs 10/20FF; a carnet valid for entry to 13/16 attractions costs 130/150FF.

To the south-west is Bowling de Paris (☎ 01 53 64 93 00), a bowling alley open 9 am to 3 am (to 5 am at the weekend) where games cost 13FF to 37FF per person, depending on the time and the day (the highest tariffs apply after 8 pm and at the weekend).

LA DÉFENSE

La Défense, Paris' skyscraper district, is 3km west of the 17e. Set on the sloping west bank of the Seine, its ultramodern architecture and multistorey office blocks are so strikingly different from the rest of centuries-old Paris that it's well worth a brief visit to put it all in perspective.

The development of La Défense, one of the world's most ambitious civil-engineering projects, began in the late 1950s. Its first major structure was the triangular-shaped Centre des Nouvelles Industries et Technologies (Centre for New Industries & Technologies), better known as the **CNIT**, inaugurated in 1958 and renovated some three decades later. During the mid-1970s, when skyscrapers fell out of fashion, office space in La Défense became hard to sell or lease: buildings stood empty and the whole project appeared doomed.

Things picked up in the 1980s and 1990s, and today La Défense has some 60 buildings, the highest of which is the 45-storey, 178m-tall **Framatome**. The head offices of more than half of France's 20 largest corporations are housed here, and a total of 1200 companies of all sizes employ some 150,000 people.

Information

Just north-west of the computer-controlled **Agam fountain**, Info-Défense (☎ 01 47 74 84 24, fax 01 47 78 17 93) at 15 place de la Défense (open 10 am to 6 pm daily) has a guide to the area's monumental art (15FF), a *Guide to Architecture* (35FF) and details on cultural activities. It also contains a museum of the development of La Défense

In Defence of Paris

La Défense is named after *La Défense de Paris*, a sculpture erected here in 1883 to commemorate the defence of Paris during the Franco-Prussian War of 1870-1. Removed in 1971 to facilitate construction work, it was placed on a round pedestal just west of the Agam fountain in 1983.

Many people don't like the name La Défense, which sounds rather militaristic, and it has caused some peculiar misunderstandings over the years. A high-ranking official of the authority that manages the project was once denied entry into Egypt because his passport indicated he was the 'managing director of La Défense', which Egyptian officials apparently assumed was part of France's military-industrial complex. And a visiting Soviet general once expressed admiration at how well the area's military installations had been camouflaged!

through the years with drawings, architectural plans and scale models.

There are banks with ATMs everywhere in La Défense, including BNP (☎ 0 801 63 06 06) at 19 place des Reflets (open 9 am to 5.15 pm weekdays) and CIC (☎ 0 836 68 75 20), 11 place de la Défense (open 8.45 am to 4.45 pm weekdays). There's a post office at the south-eastern corner of the CNIT.

Grande Arche

The remarkable, cube-like Grande Arche (☎ 01 49 07 27 57), designed by Danish architect Otto von Spreckelsen and housing government and business offices, is made of white marble and glass and measures 112m along each side. Inaugurated on 14 July 1989, it marks the western end of the 8km-long **Grand Axe**, the 'Great Axis' stretching from the Louvre's glass pyramid through the Jardin des Tuileries and along the ave des Champs-Élysées to the Arc de Triom-

phe, Porte Maillot and finally the fountains, shaded squares and plazas of La Défense' Esplanade du Général de Gaulle. The structure, which symbolises a window open to the world, is ever-so-slightly out of alignment with the Grand Axe.

Neither the view from the rooftop nor the temporary exhibitions relating to human rights housed in the top storey justify the ticket price of 46FF (33FF for students those aged six to 18 and seniors). Both are open 10 am to 7 pm daily.

Parvis & Esplanade

The Parvis, place de la Défense and Esplanade du Général de Gaulle, which together form a pleasant, kilometre-long pedestrian walkway, have been turned into a **garden of contemporary art**. The nearly 70 monumental sculptures and murals here – and west of the Grande Arche in the **Quartier du Parc** and **Jardins de l'Arche**, 2km-long westward extension of the Gran

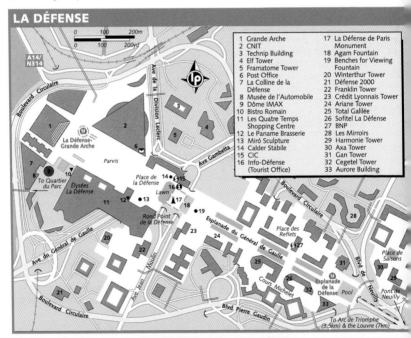

LA DÉFENSE

1 Grande Arche	17 La Défense de Paris Monument
2 CNIT	18 Agam Fountain
3 Technip Building	19 Benches for Viewing
4 Elf Tower	Fountain
5 Framatome Tower	20 Winterthur Tower
6 Post Office	21 Défense 2000
7 La Colline de la Défense	22 Franklin Tower
8 Musée de l'Automobile	23 Crédit Lyonnais Tower
9 Dôme IMAX	24 Ariane Tower
10 Bistro Romain	25 Total Galilée
11 Les Quatre Temps Shopping Centre	26 Sofitel La Défense
12 Le Paname Brasserie	27 BNP
13 Miró Sculpture	28 Les Mirroirs
14 Calder Stabile	29 Harmonie Tower
15 CIC	30 Axa Tower
16 Info-Défense (Tourist Office)	31 Gan Tower
	32 Cegetel Tower
	33 Aurore Building

Axe – include colourful and imaginative works by Calder, Miró, Agam, Torricini and others.

In the south-east corner of place de la Défense and opposite the Info-Défense office is a much older monument honouring the defence of Paris during the Franco-Prussian War of 1870-1 (see the boxed text 'In Defence of Paris').

Colline de la Défense

This complex, just south of the Grande Arche and west of Les Quatre Temps shopping centre, houses the huge **Dôme IMAX** (☎ 01 46 92 45 50), a 460-seat, 180° cinema that screens the usual 2-D and 3-D IMAX films – documentaries about travel, space and wildlife that thrill, shock and frighten for a little while and then get rather dull and repetitive. Tickets cost 57FF (44FF for students, seniors and under-16s) and 40FF for the second film. A double feature on Saturday costs 80/70FF. Screenings are from 12.30 to 5.45 pm (10.45 am to 7.30 pm at the weekend).

Musée de l'Automobile

Of more conventional interest is the Car Museum (☎ 01 46 92 71 71), 1 place du Dôme, whose outstanding collection of 110 vintage cars includes lots of very early French models. It opens 12.15 to 7 pm daily, and admission costs 40FF (reduced price 30FF).

Getting There & Away

The La Défense-Grande Arche metro station is the western terminus of metro line No 1; the ride from the Louvre takes about 15 minutes. If you take the faster RER line A remember that La Défense is in zone three and you must pay a supplement (11.50FF) if you are carrying a travel pass for zones 1 & 2.

La Défense: soaring skyscrapers, sublime sculpture...

MARTIN MOOS

...and a chance to chill out under the Grande Arche

RACHEL IMESON

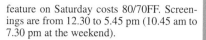

euro currency converter €1 = 6.56FF

MUSÉE DE L'AIR ET DE L'ESPACE

The Aeronautics and Space Museum (☎ 01 49 92 71 99) in Paris' northern suburb of Le Bourget has some 180 military and civilian aircraft, dozens of rockets and spacecraft, and other displays that chart the history of flight and space exploration. It opens 10 am to 5 pm (to 6 pm May to October) Tuesday to Sunday. Entrance costs 40FF (30FF for students and those aged eight to 16).

You can reach Le Bourget by RER line B3 or B5 (station: Le Bourget) or by RATP bus No 350 (stop: Musée de l'Air) from Gare du Nord (Map 3) at 184 rue du Faubourg Saint Denis, 10e, and in front of Gare de l'Est (Map 3) on rue du 8 Mai 1945, 10e.

ACTIVITIES

The entertainment weeklies *Pariscope* and *L'Officiel des Spectacles* (see under Listings in the Entertainment chapter) have up-to-date information in French on every imaginable sort of activity. For information (in French) on Paris' sporting activities and facilities, contact Allô Sports (☎ 01 42 76 54 54); on Minitel, key in 3615 PARIS. It is staffed 10.30 am to 5 pm weekdays (to 4.30 pm on Friday).

Swimming

Paris has some 34 swimming pools open to the public – ask at your hotel for the nearest one. Most are short-length pools and finding a free lane for lengths is nigh on impossible. Opening times vary widely, but avoid Wednesday afternoon and Saturday when kids off from school take the plunge. The cost is generally 16FF (reduced price 9FF), but some of the bigger and better ones charge more. Among some of the better venues are:

Piscine de la Butte aux Cailles (Map 1, ☎ 01 45 89 60 05, metro Tolbiac) 5-7 place Paul Verlaine, 13e. This positively stunning pool built in 1924 and now listed takes advantage of the warm water issuing from a nearby artesian well. It's open 2 to 7 pm on Monday, 7 am to 7 pm Tuesday to Saturday and 8 am to 5.30 pm on Sunday.

Piscine Pontoise-Quartier Latin (Map 6, ☎ 0 55 42 77 88, metro Maubert Mutualité) 19 ru de Pontoise, 5e. This beautiful Art Deco-styl pool in the heart of the Latin Quarter measure 33m by 15m. The complex also includes a gyr and squash courts. It's open 9 am to 10 pm dail and entry costs 26FF (reduced price 23FF).

Piscine Suzanne Berlioux (Map 6, ☎ 01 42 36 9 44, metro Les Halles) Level –3, Forum de Halles, rue Pierre Lescaut, 1er. This 50m b 20m pool is surrounded by a tropical garden in side Paris' largest shopping centre. It's alway busy but fun nonetheless. It's open 10 am t 10 pm daily and entry costs 25/20FF.

If you're into water parks, Paris can oblig with **Aquaboulevard** (Map 1, ☎ 01 40 60 1(00, metro Balard), 4 rue Louis Armand 15e, a huge recreational centre in south west Paris with a wide range of activitie for adults and kids, including a swimmin; pool, a 'beach' and aquatic park, tennis squash, golf practice, a gym, restaurant and so on. It's a real saviour for parents o a hot summer's day. It's open 9 am to mid night daily; admission costs 78FF (58FF fo children aged under 12).

Boating

The three rivers in or around Paris (the Seine, Marne and Oise) and its two mair canals (Saint Martin and l'Ourcq) offer unique vantage point from which to enjo the delights of Paris. A one- or two-wee rental – less expensive than many hotels i there are four or more of you – can easil be split between quiet canal/river cruise and days spent moored in the city. Withir Paris proper, the only places you can sta overnight are Bassin de la Villette (Map 3) 19e, and Port de Plaisance de Paris-Arsena (Map 5) in the 4e and 12e, but it's possible to stop for an hour or two at a number o quays along the Seine.

Europ' Yachting (Map 5, ☎ 01 43 44 6(77, fax 01 43 44 74 18, metro Quai de la Rapée), on the ground floor of the Capi tainerie du Port de Plaisance de Paris Arsenal at 11 blvd de la Bastille, 12e, rent out boats for four to seven people. From mid-March to mid-October you can rent b; the weekend (ie, Friday night to Sunday

JOHN HAY

Sail away: luxurious yachts for hire in the Jardin des Tuileries

night) for 2000FF to 5000FF, by the working week (Monday to Friday) for 3000FF to 7000FF or by the full week (Saturday night to Saturday morning) for 4000FF to 9000FF. Hiring a pilot costs 4500FF for up to three hours, 8500FF for the day. Bookings should be made three weeks in advance, though boats are sometimes available at the last minute. The office opens 10 am to 1 pm and 2.30 to 7 pm Monday to Saturday.

COURSES

The Service Culturel (see Cultural Centres in the Facts for the Visitor chapter) has reams of information on studying in France, as do French government tourist offices and consulates. The Paris tourist office also has a list of courses of instruction that have been well received.

Language

All manner of French-language courses, lasting from two weeks to nine months, are available in Paris and many places begin new courses every month or so. Some of the organisations detailed below can also arrange homestays or other accommodation.

Among the many French-language schools in the capital are:

Alliance Française (Map 4, ☎ 01 42 84 90 00, ✉ info@alliancefrancaise.fr, metro Saint Placide) 101 blvd Raspail, 6e. This is the Paris headquarters of the venerable institution whose brief is to promote French language and civilisation around the world. Month-long French courses at all levels begin on the first working day of each month; registration (250FF) takes place five days before. If there's space, it's possible to enrol for just two weeks. *Intensif* courses, which meet for four hours a day, cost 3200FF a month; *extensif* courses, which involve two hours of class a day, cost 1600FF a month. The registration office is open 9 am to 5 pm weekdays. Bring your passport and a passport-size photo. Payment, which must be made in advance, can be by travellers cheque or credit card. The Alliance Française's Web site is at www.alliancefrancaise.fr.

Cours de Langue et Civilisation Françaises de la Sorbonne (Map 5, ☎ 01 40 46 22 11, 🖂 ccfs@paris4.sorbonne.fr) 47 rue des Écoles, 5e. The Sorbonne's prestigious French Language and Civilisation Course, from which one of the authors graduated sometime in the early Middle Ages, caters for students at all levels. Costs vary, but a four-week summer course should cost from about 5300FF while 16 to 20 hours a week of lectures and tutorials costs between 7000FF and 8000FF per semester. The instructors take a very academic (though solid) approach to language teaching; don't expect to learn how to haggle in a market or to cuss about road hogs even after a year here.

Eurocentre (Map 6, ☎ 01 40 46 72 00, 🖂 par-info@ieurocentres.com, metro Odéon) 13 passage Dauphine, 6e. This is the Paris branch of the Zürich-based, nonprofit Eurocentre chain, which has schools in 10 countries. Two/four-week intensive courses with 12 to 15 participants, favourably reviewed by Lonely Planet readers, cost 3820/7640FF, including 25 50-minute lessons, three lectures and five to 10 hours in the multimedia learning centre per week. There are also intensive 12-week courses for 20,400FF. New courses begin every two weeks. The registration fee is 500FF.

Institut Parisien de Langue et de Civilisation Françaises (Map 4, ☎ 01 40 56 09 53, 🖂 institut.parisien@dial.oleane.com, metro Dupleix) 87 blvd de Grenelle, 15e. Four-week courses with a maximum of 12 students per class cost 2640/3960/6600FF for 10/15/25 hours a week; six-week courses are 3920/5880/

9800FF. The office is open 8.30 am to 5 pm weekdays.

Langue Onze (Map 6, ☎ 01 43 38 22 87, 🖂 langue11@club-internet.fr, metro Parmentier) 15 rue Gambey, 11e. This small, independent language school gets good reports from readers. Two/four-week intensive courses of four hours' instruction a day cost 1900/3200FF (1900/3400 July to September), evening classes start at 2000FF a trimester (48 hours) and individual lessons are around 120FF an hour. Classes have a maximum of nine students.

Cooking

The major cooking schools in Paris include École Le Cordon Bleu (☎ 01 53 68 22 50, fax 01 48 56 03 96, metro Vaugirard or Convention), 8 rue Léon Delhomme, 15e; École de Gastronomie Française-Ritz Escoffier (☎ 01 43 16 30 50, 🖂 ecole@ritzparis.com, metro Concorde), 38 rue Cambon, 1er and La Toque d'Or (☎ 01 45 44 86 51, youngsg@aol.com, metro Varenne), 55 rue de Varenne, 7e. The cost of tuition varies widely (1360FF to 3400FF), but the highly popular Cours de Cuisine Françoise Meunier (☎ 01 40 26 14 00, 🖂 fmeunier@easynet.fr, metro Bourse or Sentier), 7 rue Paul Lelong, 2e, offers three-hour courses at 10.30 am Tuesday to Saturday and a 7.30 pm on Wednesday for 450FF. 'Carnets' of 5/10/20 courses cost 2000/3800/7200FF

Places to Stay

Paris has a very wide choice of accommodation options that caters for all budgets in most sections of the city. When calculating accommodation costs in Paris assume you'll spend close to 100FF per person per night in a hostel and about 150FF for a washbasin-equipped double in a bottom-end hotel. Bear in mind that in budget hotel rooms without en suite shower or bath, you may be charged from 10FF to as much as 30FF each time you use the hall shower. If you can't go without your daily ablutions it is often a false economy staying at such places.

Mid-range places in Paris charge between 300FF and 600FF for a double and offer excellent value, especially at the higher end. Top-range places will cost two people up to about 1200FF a night and anything above that falls into the deluxe category.

Accommodation Services

The main Paris tourist office (Map 2, ☎ 0 836 68 31 12, fax 01 49 52 53 00, metro George V), 127 ave des Champs-Élysées, 8e, and its annexe at Gare de Lyon can find you a place to stay for the night of the day you stop by. It also has a number of brochures on homestays, including one on *pensions de famille*, which are similar to B&Bs. Recommended pensions de famille in Paris include the following:

Pension Ladagnous *(Map 4, ☎ 01 43 26 79 32, 78 rue d'Assas, 6e, metro Vavin or Notre Dame des Champs)*. Singles/doubles with half-board are 260/395FF.

Pension Les Marroniers *(Map 4, ☎ 01 43 26 37 71, fax 01 43 26 07 72, 78 rue d'Assas, 6e, metro Vavin or Notre Dame des Champs)*. Half-board singles/doubles cost from 270/495FF. Monthly rates are 20% less; vegetarian meals are available.

Pension Au Palais Gourmand *(Map 4, ☎ 01 45 48 24 15, fax 01 42 22 33 41, 120 blvd Raspail, 6e, metro Vavin or Notre Dame des Champs)*. Half-board singles are 290FF to 374FF, doubles 442FF to 495FF.

Résidence Cardinal *(Map 2, ☎ 01 48 74 16 16, 4 rue Cardinal Mercier, 9e, metro Liège or Place de Clichy)*. Singles with breakfast cost 160FF to 190FF, doubles 260FF to 320FF.

Some travel agencies, especially student ones (see Travel Agencies in the Facts for the Visitor chapter), can book you reasonably priced accommodation. OTU (Map 7, ☎ 01 40 29 12 12, ✉ otuvoyage@terranet.fr, metro Rambuteau), at 119 rue Saint Martin, 4e, directly across the square from the Centre Pompidou, can *always* find you accommodation, even in the summer. It works like this: you come in on the day (or the day before) you need a place to stay and pay for the accommodation (plus a 20FF fee). The staff then give you a voucher to take to the hotel. Prices for singles are around 270FF, doubles start at about 300FF. This OTU branch opens 10 am to 6.30 pm weekdays, and to 5 pm on Saturday. Be prepared for long queues.

Homestays

Under an arrangement known as *hôtes payants* (literally 'paying guests') or *hébergement chez l'habitant* (lodging with the occupants of private homes), students, young people and tourists can stay with French families. In general you rent a room and have access (sometimes limited) to the family's kitchen and telephone. Many language schools (see Courses in the Things to See & Do chapter) arrange homestays for their students.

For details of each agency's prices and conditions, it's a good idea to call, write or fax at least six weeks in advance, though last-minute arrangements are sometimes possible.

Students and tourists alike should count on paying 3000FF to 5500FF a month, 1200FF to 1500FF a week or 130FF to 300FF a day for a single room, including breakfast.

Accueil Familial des Jeunes Étrangers (☎ 01 42 22 50 34, fax 01 45 44 60 48, metro Sèvres

Babylone) 23 rue du Cherche Midi, 6e. This organisation can find you a room with a family for 3000FF to 3500FF a month, including breakfast. For stays of less than a month, expect to pay from 140FF a day. There's a subscription fee of 150FF per month on longer stays.

France Lodge (☎ 01 53 20 02 54, fax 01 53 20 01 25, metro Le Peletier) 41 rue La Fayette, 9e. This nonprofit organisation arranges accommodation in private homes and apartments. Prices start at about 150FF a night per person (cheaper by the month). Annual membership costs 100FF.

Apartments & Flats

For details of accommodation for longer stays, see Long-Term Rentals at the end of this chapter.

PLACES TO STAY – BUDGET
Camping

Camping du Bois de Boulogne (☎ 01 45 24 30 81, fax 01 42 24 42 95, 2 allée du Bord de l'Eau, 16e), the only camp site within the Paris city limits, lies along the Seine at the far western edge of the Bois de Boulogne opposite the Île de Puteaux. Two people with a tent pay 67FF to 88FF (105FF to 143FF with a vehicle), depending on the season, and reception at this seven-hectare site is staffed 24 hours a day. It's very crowded in the summer, but there's always space for a small tent. Fully equipped caravans accommodating four people are available for rent for between 285FF and 399FF, depending on the type and the season. Porte Maillot metro station (Map 2), 4.5km to the north-east through the wood, is linked to the site by RATP bus No 244 (which runs 6 am to 8.30 pm) and, from April to October, by a privately operated shuttle bus (10FF).

Paris' main tourist office and its Web site (see Tourist Offices in the Facts for the Visitor chapter) have a list of dozens of other camp sites in the Île de France.

Hostels

Accommodation in hostels doesn't come cheaply in Paris. Beds under 100FF are few and far between, so two people who don't mind sleeping in the same bed may find basic rooms in budget hotels a less expensive proposition. Groups of three or four willing to share two or three beds in a budget hotel will save even more. Showers are always free at hostels in Paris.

Some hostels allow guests to stay a maximum of three nights, particularly in the summer. Places that have upper age limits (eg, 30) tend not to enforce them. Only the official *auberges de jeunesse* (youth hostels) require guests to present Hostelling International (HI) cards or their equivalent. Curfew – if enforced – is generally at 1 or 2 am. Only a few hostels accept telephone reservations from individuals; those that do are indicated.

Louvre & Les Halles (Map 6) You can't get any more central than the area of the 1er between the Louvre and the Forum des Halles.

Centre International BVJ Paris-Louvre (☎ 01 53 00 90 90, fax 01 53 00 90 91, 20 rue Jean-Jacques Rousseau, 1er, metro Louvre-Rivoli). This modern, 200-bed hostel run by the Bureau des Voyages de la Jeunesse charges 130FF (including breakfast) for a bunk in a single-sex room for two to 10 people. Guests should be aged under 35. Rooms are accessible from 2.30 pm on the day you arrive and all day after that. There are no kitchen facilities. There is usually space in the morning, even in the summer. The hostel's Web site is at www.bvjhotels.com.

Marais (Map 7) The Marais is one of the liveliest parts of the Right Bank and its hostels are among the city's finest. The Maison Internationale de la Jeunesse et des Étudiants (MIJE) runs three hostels in attractively renovated 17th- and 18th-century *hôtels particuliers* (private mansions).

Costs are the same for all three. A bed in a shower-equipped, single-sex dorm for four to eight people is 145FF (155/175/240FF in a triple/double/single), including breakfast. Rooms are closed noon to 3 pm; curfew is from 1 to 7 am.

Individuals can make reservations for all three MIJE hostels by calling or faxing the central switchboard (☎ 01 42 74 23 45, fax 01 40 27 81 64); they'll hold you a bed till

Affordable digs in the heart of the Latin Quarter at the Young & Happy Hostel

noon, and the maximum stay is seven nights. During the summer and other busy periods, there may not be space after about mid-morning. There's an annual membership fee of 15FF. The MIJE Web site is at www.mije.com.

MIJE Fourcy (*6 rue de Fourcy, 4e, metro Saint Paul*). This 207-bed branch is the largest of the three. There's a cheap restaurant with a three-course *menu* with a drink for 60FF and a plat du jour plus drink for 50FF.

MIJE Fauconnier (*11 rue du Fauconnier, 4e, metro Saint Paul or Pont Marie*). This 111-bed hostel is two blocks south of MIJE Fourcy.

MIJE Maubuisson (*12 rue des Barres, 4e, metro Hôtel de Ville*). This 114-bed place, the pick of the three in our opinion, is half a block south of the *mairie* (town hall) of the 4e.

Latin Quarter (Map 5) The lively Latin Quarter, in the northern section of the 5e and close to the Seine, is popular with students and young people.

Centre International BVJ Paris-Quartier Latin (*☎ 01 43 29 34 80, fax 01 53 00 90 91, 44 rue des Bernardins, 5e, metro Maubert Mutualité*). This 138-bed hostel has the same rules as the Centre International BVJ Paris-Louvre (see under Louvre & Les Halles in this section), though the rates are a bit different. Individuals pay 160/140/130FF per person in rooms with one/two/five bed(s). Its Web site is at www.bvjhotels.com.

Young & Happy Hostel (*☎ 01 45 35 09 53, fax 01 47 07 22 24,* ✉ *smile@youngandhappy.fr, 80 rue Mouffetard, 5e, metro Place Monge*). This friendly place is in the most happening area of the Latin Quarter and very popular with a younger crowd. The rooms are closed 11 am to 4 pm, but reception is always open. A bed in a smallish room with washbasin for three or four people costs 117FF (137FF per person in a double), including breakfast. The 2 am curfew is strictly enforced. In the summer, the best way to get a bed is to stop by at about 9 am.

Bastille (Maps 5 & 6) The relatively untouristed 11e is generally made up of unpretentious, working-class areas and is a good way to see 'real' Paris up close.

Auberge de Jeunesse Jules Ferry (*Map 6, ☎ 01 43 57 55 60, fax 01 43 14 82 09,* ✉ *auberge@easynet.fr, 8 blvd Jules Ferry, 11e, metro République or Goncourt*). This official hostel, three blocks east of place de la République, is a bit institutional, but the atmosphere is fairly relaxed. Beds cost 115FF in a four- or six-person room and 120FF in a double, including breakfast. Rooms are locked from 10.30 am to 2 pm. You must have an HI card to stay here or pay an extra 19FF per night. Internet access costs 5FF. The only other official hostel in central Paris is the Auberge de Jeunesse Le D'Artagnan (see under 20e Arrondissement in this section).

Auberge Internationale des Jeunes (*Map 5, ☎ 01 47 00 62 00, fax 01 47 00 33 16,* ✉ *aij@aijparis.com, 10 rue Trousseau, 11e, metro Ledru Rollin*). This clean and very friendly hostel, 700m east of place de la Bastille, attracts a young, international crowd and gets very full in the summer. Beds in dorms for two to six people cost 81FF from November to February and 91FF from March to October, including breakfast. Rooms are closed for cleaning between 10 am and 3 pm.

Maison Internationale des Jeunes pour la Culture et la Paix (*Map 5, ☎ 01 43 71 99 21, fax 01 43 71 78 58,* ✉ *mij.cp@wanadoo.fr, 4 rue*

Titon, 11e, metro Faidherbe Chaligny). The 150-bed MIJCP, 1.3km east of place de la Bastille, charges 110FF for a bed in a spartan dorm for up to eight people, including breakfast. Curfew is from 2 to 6 am. The upper age limit of 30 is not strictly enforced. Telephone reservations are accepted, but your chance of finding a bed is greatest if you call or stop by between 8 and 10 am. The maximum stay is theoretically three days, but you can usually stay for a week if there is room.

Résidence Bastille (Map 5, ☎ 01 43 79 53 86, fax 01 43 79 35 63, 151 ave Ledru Rollin, 11e, metro Voltaire). This 150-bed hostel is about 900m north-east of place de la Bastille. Beds in rooms for two to four people cost 125FF (110FF from November to February), including breakfast, and there are singles for 175FF (160FF in the low season). Check-in is from 7 am to 12.30 pm and 2 to 10 pm. Curfew is at 1 am.

Gare du Nord & Gare de l'Est (Map 3)

The areas east and north-east of these two train stations have always had a more ample selection of hotels, but until recently there wasn't a hostel to be found.

Peace & Love Hostel (☎ 01 46 07 65 11, fax 01 42 05 47 50, ✆ pl@paris-hostels.com, 245 rue La Fayette, 10e, metro Jaurès). This groovy hostel, which attracts a crowd that appreciates all the gifts of Mother Nature, is one of the cheapest around, with beds in rooms for two, three or four people costing a uniform 85FF in the winter and 97FF in the summer. Facilities are limited, but there's Internet access and a full bar on the ground floor (open till 2 am) that boasts the cheapest beer in Paris.

Gare de Lyon & Nation (Maps 1 & 5)

The development of Bercy Village has done much to resuscitate the 12e.

Blue Planet Hostel (Map 5, ☎ 01 43 42 06 18, fax 01 43 42 09 89, ✆ general@hostelblueplanet .com, 5 rue Hector Malot, 12e, metro Gare de Lyon). If you like the idea of rolling out of bed directly onto your southbound train, this new 43-room hostel is for you: you couldn't find a place closer to Gare de Lyon. A bed in a room for two people costs 150FF per person (in a room for three to five people 100FF), including breakfast. Rooms are locked between 11 am and 3 pm and there's no curfew. Internet access costs 1FF a minute.

Centre International de Séjour de Paris Maurice Ravel (Map 1, ☎ 01 44 75 60 06, fax 01 43 44 45 30, ✆ 100616.2215@compuserve.com, 4-6 ave Maurice Ravel, 12e, metro Porte de Vincennes). The 230-bed CISP Maurice Ravel, on the south-eastern edge of the city due east of place de la Nation, charges 126FF in a room for two to four people, 156FF in a double and 206FF in a single, including breakfast. Meals cost 50FF to 55FF. If you stay more than a week the nightly rates are 116FF, 146FF and 196FF respectively. There is no age limit. Reception is open 6.30 am to 1.30 am. Individuals (as opposed to groups, which predominate) can make telephone reservations up to two days ahead. To get there from Porte de Vincennes metro station, walk south on blvd Soult, turn left onto rue Jules Lemaître and then go right onto rue Maurice Ravel. Its Web site is at www.cisp.asso.fr.

Chinatown & Montparnasse (Maps 1 & 4)

The southern 13e, 14e and 15e are not particularly exciting, but they're not too far from the Left Bank's major sights.

Aloha Hostel (Map 4, ☎ 01 42 73 03 03, fax 01 42 73 14 14, ✆ friends@aloha.fr, 1 rue Borromée, 15e, metro Volontaires). Run by the same people as the Three Ducks (see later in this section) and charging the same prices, the Aloha is much more laid-back and quieter than its sister hostel to the west. The rooms, which have two to six beds and sometimes showers, are closed 11 am to 5 pm, but reception is always open. Curfew is at 2 am. Kitchen facilities and safe-deposit boxes are available.

Centre International de Séjour de Paris Kellermann (Map 1, ☎ 01 44 16 37 38, fax 01 43 44 45 30, ✆ 100616.2215@compuserve.com, 17 blvd Kellermann, 13e, metro Porte d'Italie). The 350-bed CISP Kellermann has beds in dorms for two to four people for 126FF (101FF for those with eight beds). Basic singles are 146FF, or 196FF with shower and toilet. A double with facilities costs 312FF. Except on Friday and Saturday night, curfew is at 1.30 am. The maximum stay is five or six nights. Kitchen facilities are not available. Telephone reservations can be made up to 48 hours before you arrive. Facilities for disabled people are available.

Foyer International d'Accueil de Paris Jean Monnet (Map 1, ☎ 01 43 13 17 00, fax 01 45 81 63 91, ✆ fiapadmi@fiap.assoc.fr, 30 rue Cabanis, 14e, metro Glacière). FIAP Jean Monnet, a few blocks south-east of place Denfert Rochereau, has modern, carpeted rooms – pretty luxurious by hostel standards – for five to eight people for 139FF per person, for three to four for 172FF per person and for two for 194FF per person (including breakfast); singles are 301FF. Rooms specially outfitted for disabled people are available. Curfew is from 2 to 6 am. Telephone reservations are accepted up to 15 days ahead, but priority is given to groups.

Maison des Clubs UNESCO *(Map 1, ☎ 01 43 36 00 63, fax 01 45 35 05 96, clubs.unesco.paris@ wanadoo.fr, 43 rue de la Glacière, 13e, metro Glacière).* This rather institutional place charges 130FF for a bed in a large, unsurprising room for three or four people; singles/doubles are 180/300FF. In the multibed rooms, priority is given to 18- to 30-year-olds. Beds booked by telephone are usually held until 2 pm.

Three Ducks Hostel *(Map 4, ☎ 01 48 42 04 05, fax 01 48 42 99 99, backpack@3ducks.fr, 6 place Étienne Pernet, 15e, metro Félix Faure).* Named after three ducks who used to live in the courtyard, this friendly, down-to-earth hostel at the southern end of rue du Commerce is a favourite with young backpackers looking to party. It can apparently get pretty noisy at night (the new bar is open till 1 am) so if you're in Paris to sleep, stay somewhere else. A bunk bed in a very basic room for two to eight people costs 117FF (97FF from November to April), including breakfast. Telephone reservations are accepted on the day of arrival. Kitchen facilities

and Internet access are available. Rooms are closed between noon and 5 pm and there's a 2 am curfew. Its Web site is at www.3ducks.fr.

Montmartre & Pigalle (Maps 3 & 8)
The 9e and 18e each have a fine hostel.

Le Village Hostel *(Map 8, ☎ 01 42 64 22 02, fax 01 42 64 22 04, ✆ bonjour@villagehostel.fr, 20 rue d'Orsel, 18e, metro Anvers).* This fine 26-room hostel with beamed ceilings and views of Sacré Cœur has beds in rooms for two to six people for 117FF (97FF from November to February) and doubles/triples/quads for 147/137/127FF per person (137/127/117FF in winter), including breakfast. All rooms have showers and toilet. Kitchen facilities are available, and there is a bar and a lovely outside terrace. Curfew is at 2 am.

Woodstock Hostel *(Map 3, ☎ 01 48 78 87 76, fax 01 48 78 01 63, flowers@woodstock.fr, 48 rue Rodier, 9e, metro Anvers).* This hostel is just down the hill from raucous Pigalle in a quiet, residential quarter. A dorm bed in a room for four to six people costs 77FF in the winter, a bed in a double room costs 87FF; both prices include breakfast. In summer prices rise to 97FF and 107FF respectively. There's a 2 am curfew and rooms are shut from noon to 4 pm. There's a kitchen and Internet access.

Montmartre: one of Paris' most picturesque districts, with a handy hostel just down the hill

euro currency converter €1 = 6.56FF

20e Arrondissement (Map 1) This hostel is away from the centre of the action but just one metro stop from the Gare Routière Internationale de Paris-Gallieni (international bus terminal).

Auberge de Jeunesse Le D'Artagnan (☎ 01 40 32 34 56, fax 01 40 32 34 55, ✆ paris .le-d'artagnan@fuaj.org, 80 rue Vitruve, 20e, metro Porte de Bagnolet). This official hostel has rooms with two to eight beds, big lockers, laundry facilities, Internet access and even a bar and cinema. It has the same rules and rates as the Auberge de Jeunesse Jules Ferry (see under Bastille).

Hotels

Paris may not be able to boast the number of cheap hotels it did even a decade ago, but the choice is still more than ample, especially in the Marais, around Bastille and near the major train stations off the Grands Boulevards. Places with one star or the designation 'NN' (Nouvelle Norme), which signifies that a hotel is awaiting its rating but assures you of a certain standard of comfort, are much of a muchness. Remember: the consideration at these places is cost not quality.

Louvre & Les Halles (Map 6) This area of the 1er may be very central, but don't expect to find tranquillity or many bargains left. Both airports are linked to nearby Châtelet-Les Halles metro station by Roissy-rail and Orlyval.

Hôtel de Lille (☎ 01 42 33 33 42, 8 rue du Pélican, 1er, metro Palais Royal-Musée du Louvre). Clean singles/doubles at this 13-room hotel down a quiet side street come with washbasin, bidet and cheap ceiling tiles and cost 210/ 240FF. Doubles with shower are 290FF. A shower costs an expensive 30FF.

Marais (Map 7) This district is one of the liveliest and trendiest in Paris and, despite gentrification, still has some cheapies left.

CHRISTINE OSBORNE

The Marais: an eminently desirable quarter that still has a few budget options

euro currency converter 10FF = €1.52

PLACES TO STAY

Hôtel de la Herse d'Or (☎ 01 48 87 84 09, fax 01 48 87 94 01, 20 rue Saint Antoine, 4e, metro Bastille). This friendly, 35-room place has unsurprising, serviceable singles with washbasin for 170FF and with basin and toilet for 210FF; doubles with toilet and a small shower are 290FF to 305FF. Hall showers are 10FF.

Hôtel Moderne (☎ 01 48 87 97 05, 3 rue Caron, 4e, metro Saint Paul). The less-than-salubrious singles/doubles at this small hotel off lovely place du Marché Sainte Catherine come with washbasin and start at 160FF; doubles with shower are 260FF (300FF with shower and toilet). Triples cost 400FF. There's a shower (15FF) on the stairs halfway between each floor.

Hôtel Pratic (☎ 01 48 87 80 47, fax 01 48 87 40 04, 9 rue d'Ormesson, 4e, metro Saint Paul). This 23-room hotel round the corner from the Hôtel Moderne has renovated singles/doubles with washbasin and toilet for 250/305FF (370/390FF with shower). Singles/doubles with bath and toilet are 420/450FF.

Hôtel Rivoli (☎ 01 42 72 08 41, 44 rue de Rivoli, 4e, metro Hôtel de Ville). This hotel is not as cheap as it was, but it's still a good deal. Basic and somewhat noisy rooms with washbasin start at 200FF. Singles with shower are 210FF; doubles with bath but no toilet are 230FF (with toilet 300FF). The hall shower (20FF) is sometimes lukewarm. The front door is locked from 2 to 7 am.

Hôtel Sully (☎ 01 42 78 49 32, fax 01 44 61 76 50, 48 rue Saint Antoine, 4e, metro Bastille). You'll find basic doubles with washbasin for 230FF, with shower for 280FF, and with shower and toilet for 300FF at this hotel, which is only one block south of delightful place des Vosges. A two-bed triple with shower and toilet costs 320FF.

Île de la Cité (Map 6)

Believe it or not, the only hotel on the Île de la Cité is a budget one.

Hôtel Henri IV (☎ 01 43 54 44 53, 25 place Dauphine, 1er, metro Pont Neuf or Cité). This old-fashioned, very popular hotel is a bit tattered and worn but has 21 adequate rooms: one-bed rooms with nothing are 125FF to 155FF and with sink 170FF to 210FF; two beds with washbasin cost 215FF and a room for three to four people is 295FF. Showers in the hall cost 15FF, and breakfast is included. The four rooms with their own showers cost 270FF to 295FF. Reception is open until 8 pm, but you should make reservations a month in advance.

Latin Quarter (Maps 1 & 5)

Real cheapies have almost gone the way of the dodo in the Latin Quarter but a couple remain.

Hôtel de Médicis (Map 5, ☎ 01 43 54 14 66, 214 rue Saint Jacques, 5e, metro Luxembourg). This is exactly how a dilapidated Latin Quarter dive for impoverished students and travellers has always looked. Very basic singles are 90FF to 100FF, but they're usually occupied; doubles/triples are 180/250FF.

Port Royal Hôtel (Map 1, ☎ 01 43 31 70 06, fax 01 43 31 33 67, 8 blvd de Port Royal, 5e, metro Les Gobelins). The 46 clean, quiet and well kept singles/doubles at this older place start at 180/245FF (380FF with shower and toilet). Hall showers are 15FF.

Gare du Nord (Map 3)

This may not be one of the city's most attractive districts, but it's not dangerous and it has some pretty good budget deals. Gare du Nord is linked to Charles de Gaulle airport by Roissyrail and RATP bus No 350 and to Orly airport by Orlyval.

Hôtel Bonne Nouvelle (☎ 01 48 74 99 90, 125 blvd de Magenta, 10e, metro Gare du Nord). The 'Good News' is a modest hotel with simple, clean, shower-equipped doubles from 160FF to 240FF. Hall toilets are on the landing.

Grand Hôtel Magenta (☎ 01 48 78 03 65, fax 01 48 78 41 64, 129 blvd de Magenta, 10e, metro Gare du Nord). Clean, spacious rooms are available with washbasin and bidet from 150FF to 190FF, with shower from 250FF, and with shower and toilet from 300FF. Larger rooms for three to five people are 350FF to 450FF. Hall showers are 20FF.

Hôtel de Milan (☎ 01 40 37 88 50, fax 01 46 07 89 48, 17-19 rue de Saint Quentin, 10e, metro Gare du Nord). This friendly, old-fashioned 50-room place is equipped with an ancient lift. Clean, quiet but basic singles are available from 160FF to 180FF, doubles are 200FF. Doubles with toilet and shower cost from 280FF, triples cost from 430FF. Hall showers cost 18FF.

Hôtel La Vieille France (☎ 01 45 26 42 37, fax 01 45 26 99 07, 151 rue La Fayette, 10e, metro Gare du Nord). This is a 34-room place with spacious, pleasant and soundproofed doubles with washbasin and bidet for 245FF, and with bath or shower and toilet from 355FF to 390FF. Triples are 430FF to 480FF. Hall showers cost 15FF.

Gare de l'Est (Map 3) This lively, working-class area of the 10e has its own attractions even if you're not on a train pulling into Gare de l'Est. RATP bus No 350 to/from Charles de Gaulle airport stops right in front of the station. The 10e has some of Paris' grungiest dosshouses, but the few diamonds in the rough offer some bargains.

Hôtel d'Alsace, Strasbourg & Magenta (☎ *01 40 37 75 41, 85 blvd de Strasbourg, 10e, metro Gare de l'Est).* An old, but well maintained, 30-room hostelry with bright, clean singles/doubles/triples with washbasin for 134/187/250FF. Doubles with shower are 247FF. The fireplaces give the rooms a bit of old-time charm. Hall showers cost 10FF. The entrance is on the left-hand side of the passageway.

Hôtel du Brabant (☎ *01 47 70 12 32, fax 01 47 70 20 32, 18 rue des Petits Hôtels, 10e, metro Poissonnière or Gare de l'Est).* This bargain place, with a wonderful Art Nouveau mosaic on the front, is convenient for both Gare de l'Est and Gare du Nord. Simple singles/doubles are 160/200FF, with toilet 190/220FF and with shower 260/280FF.

Hôtel Liberty (☎ *01 42 08 60 58, fax 01 42 40 12 59, 16 rue de Nancy, 10e, metro Château d'Eau).* Clean, plain singles/ doubles in this 1st-floor hotel start at 150/180FF (190/230FF with shower, 220/275FF with shower and toilet). Hall showers are 10FF.

Hôtel Pacific (☎ *01 47 70 07 91, fax 01 47 70 98 43, 70 rue du Château d'Eau, 10e, metro Château d'Eau).* An older place with 23 rooms, the Pacific has unpretentious but clean singles for 153FF to 173FF; doubles/triples are 186/259FF (276/309FF with shower). Hall showers are 15FF.

Hôtel du Prado (☎ *01 40 22 97 91 or 01 47 70 11 49, 12 rue du Faubourg Saint Denis, 10e, metro Strasbourg Saint Denis).* This cheapie, which you enter from inside passage du Prado, 18-20 blvd Saint Denis, 10e, has very basic singles/doubles for 160/260FF.

Sibour Hôtel (☎ *01 46 07 20 74, fax 01 46 07 37 17,* 🖂 *sibour.hotel@wanadoo.fr, 4 rue Sibour, 10e, metro Gare de l'Est).* This friendly hotel has 45 well kept rooms, including old-fashioned singles/doubles from 180/200FF (290/320FF for a double with shower/bath, toilet and TV). Hall showers cost 15FF.

Bastille (Maps 1, 5 & 6) The area just east of place de la Bastille (ie, around rue de Lappe) gets busy after dark, ever since the arrival of the Opéra Bastille. Farther east is a mostly ungentrified, typically Parisian working-class neighbourhood whose hotels cater mainly for French businesspeople of modest means. Place de la Nation (Map 1) is linked to Charles de Gaulle airport by RATP bus No 351.

The 11e has Paris' best selection of respectable, old-time cheapies. The best deals are away from place de la Bastille.

Hôtel des Alliés (*Map 5,* ☎ *01 44 73 01 17, 90 rue du Faubourg Saint Antoine, 12e, metro Ledru Rollin).* This uninspiring, 37-room place offers one of the better deals in the Bastille neighbourhood, with singles/doubles/triples/quads from 90/150/195/240FF (130/180/210/280FF in the high season). Some rooms have their own showers.

Hôtel Bastille Opéra (*Map 6,* ☎ *01 43 55 16 06, 6 rue de la Roquette, 11e, metro Bastille).* This ageing, 20-room place, just off place de la Bastille, has basic singles for 130FF to 140FF and doubles for 180FF. Showers are free. Reception (open 24 hours) is on the 1st floor.

Hôtel Baudin (*Map 5,* ☎ *01 47 00 18 91, fax 01 48 07 04 66, 113 ave Ledru Rollin, 11e, metro Ledru Rollin).* This once-grand, old-fashioned hostelry has 17 partially renovated singles/doubles from 170/230FF (220/290FF with shower, 260/320FF with shower and toilet); triples are 350FF to 400FF. Hall showers are free.

Hôtel Camélia (*Map 1,* ☎ *01 43 73 67 50, 6 ave Philippe Auguste, 11e, metro Nation).* This family-run, 30-room establishment has well kept singles/doubles from 175/250FF. Doubles with shower/bath and toilet cost 280/350FF. Hall showers cost 20FF.

Hôtel Central (*Map 1,* ☎ *01 43 73 73 53, 16 ave Philippe Auguste, 11e, metro Nation).* This quiet and clean place just north of place de la Nation has singles/doubles/quads with washbasin and bidet for 165/185/270FF. Hall showers cost 20FF.

Hôtel Familial (*Map 5,* ☎ *01 43 67 48 24, 33 rue Richard Lenoir, 11e, metro Voltaire).* This family-run, old-time cheapie has basic, run-down singles with washbasin for 80FF to 100FF and doubles for 115FF to 120FF. Hall showers are 15FF.

Hôtel de France (*Map 5,* ☎ *01 43 79 53 22, 159 ave Ledru Rollin, 11e, metro Voltaire).* Decent, well maintained singles/doubles/triples with shower go for 150/220/280FF at this establishment. All the toilets are off the hall. Reception is in the Restaurant de France next door.

Hôtel de Saint Amand *(Map 5, ☎ 01 47 00 90 55, 6 rue Trousseau, 11e, metro Ledru Rollin).* The linoleum-floored, washbasin-equipped rooms spread over six floors (there's no lift) are nothing fancy, but the prices begin at only 100/120FF (170FF with shower). Hall showers are 20FF.

Hôtel de Savoie *(Map 5, ☎ 01 43 72 96 47, 27 rue Richard Lenoir, 11e, metro Voltaire).* Nondescript but serviceable singles/doubles start at 150/180FF; showers are free. Rooms with shower are 180/250FF.

Vix Hôtel *(Map 5, ☎ 01 48 05 12 58, fax 01 48 06 15 09, 19 rue de Charonne, 11e, metro Bastille or Ledru Rollin).* This place is a bit dreary and not exactly spotless, but it has plenty of basic singles/doubles from 130/200FF; hall showers are 15FF. Doubles with shower cost 220FF and with shower and toilet 250FF.

Chinatown (Map 1)

Paris' original Chinatown is south of place d'Italie along ave d'Ivry and ave de Choisy. The 13e may not be electrifying, but it has some good deals and there are plenty of decent Chinese restaurants around.

Arian Hôtel *(☎ 01 45 70 76 00, fax 01 45 70 85 53, ✉ arianhotel@aol.com, 102 ave de Choisy, 13e, metro Tolbiac).* This motel-like 30-room place has simple singles for 170FF (250FF with shower). Doubles/triples with shower and toilet cost 300/400FF.

Hôtel des Beaux-Arts *(☎ 01 44 24 22 60, 2 rue Toussaint Féron, 13e, metro Tolbiac).* Singles/doubles at this 25-room hotel start at 160/190FF and go up to 250FF with shower and 390FF with bath and toilet.

Hôtel Tolbiac *(☎ 01 44 24 25 54, fax 01 45 85 43 47, email htolbiac@club-internet.fr, 122 rue de Tolbiac, 13e, metro Tolbiac).* Well lit, quiet and spotlessly clean singles/doubles with washbasin go for 140/170FF (270FF with shower and toilet). Hall showers are free.

Montparnasse (Maps 1 & 4)

Though untouristed and less than thrilling, the 14e and the easternmost corner of the 15e do have a number of good deals on offer. Gare Montparnasse is served by Air France buses from both airports. Place Denfert Rochereau is also linked to both airports by Orlybus, Orlyval and Roissyrail. The bud-

get places in the 14e don't usually see many foreign tourists.

Celtic Hôtel *(Map 4, ☎ 01 43 20 93 53, fax 01 43 20 66 07, 15 rue d'Odessa, 14e, metro Edgar Quinet).* The 29-room Celtic is an old-fashioned place that has undergone only partial modernisation. It has bare singles/doubles at 230/260FF, and doubles/triples with shower at 300/410FF.

Hôtel de l'Espérance *(Map 4, ☎ 01 43 21 63 84, 45 rue de la Gaîté, 14e, metro Gaîté).* This 14-room place along a street lined with sex shops has slightly frayed doubles with washbasin for 170FF, with shower for 185FF to 215FF and with shower and toilet for 220FF. A bed for a third person is 50FF. Hall showers cost 15FF.

Hôtel de l'Espérance *(Map 1, ☎ 01 43 21 41 04, fax 01 43 22 06 02, 1 rue de Grancey, 14e, metro Denfert Rochereau).* This similarly named but unrelated 17-room hotel has basic rooms from 200FF, 275FF with shower.

Montmartre & Pigalle (Map 8)

Montmartre, encompassing the 18e and the northern part of the 9e, is one of the most charming neighbourhoods in Paris. The flat area around the base of the hill has some surprisingly good deals. The lively, ethnically mixed area east of Sacré Cœur can be a bit rough – some say it's prudent to avoid Château Rouge metro station at night.

Hôtel Audran *(☎ 01 42 58 79 59, fax 01 42 58 39 11, 7 rue Audran, 18e, metro Abbesses).* Basic singles/doubles start at 120/160FF; doubles with shower start at 180FF (with shower and toilet 250FF). The 1st and 3rd floors have showers (10FF).

Hôtel Bonséjour *(☎ 01 42 54 22 53, fax 01 42 54 25 92, 11 rue Burq, 18e, metro Abbesses).* We've had quite a few letters from readers praising this place (no lift) at the end of a quiet cul-de-sac in Montmartre, and we liked what we saw the last time we visited. Basic singles are 120FF to 140FF, doubles 180FF; a hall shower costs 10FF. Doubles/triples with shower are a bargain 230/270FF and some rooms (Nos 14, 23, 33, 43 & 53) have little balconies.

Hôtel de Carthage *(☎/fax 01 46 06 27 03, 10 rue Poulet, 18e, metro Château Rouge).* This 40-room place has singles and twins with shower for 250FF, doubles with shower and toilet for 300FF. They lock the doors at 1 am, though.

Hôtel Eldorado *(Map 2, ☎ 01 45 22 35 21, fax 01 43 87 25 97, 18 rue des Dames, 17e, metro*

PLACES TO STAY

Place de Clichy). This welcoming, well run place has rooms in a main building on a quiet street and in a villa annexe with a private garden at the back. Singles/doubles/triples start at 150/300/400FF.

Hôtel de Rohan *(☎ 01 42 52 32 57, fax 01 55 79 79 63, 90 rue Myrha, 18e, metro Château Rouge)*. Basic, tidy rooms at this 25-room establishment go for 120/150FF. Doubles with shower and TV are 220FF. Showers in the hall cost 20FF.

Hôtel Saint Pierre *(☎ 01 46 06 20 73, 3 rue Seveste, 18e, metro Anvers)*. This friendly, family-run establishment in a renovated 150-year-old building with 36 simple but serviceable rooms charges from 120/180FF for basic singles/doubles (170/190FF with shower and toilet, 230FF with bath and toilet). With busy blvd de Rochechouart so close, it can be a bit noisy here.

PLACES TO STAY – MID-RANGE

Mid-range hotels in Paris offer some of the best value for money in Europe.

Louvre & Les Halles (Map 6)

This area is more disposed to welcoming top-end travellers, but there are some mid-range places to choose from.

Hôtel Saint Honoré *(☎ 01 42 36 20 38, fax 01 42 21 44 08, 85 rue Saint Honoré, 1er, metro Châtelet)*. This upgraded hotel at the eastern end of a very upmarket shopping street offers cramped doubles/quads from 290/480FF; more spacious doubles are 380FF to 420FF.

Marais (Map 7)

There's an excellent choice of one- and two-star hotels in the buzzy Marais.

Hôtel Castex *(Map 6, ☎ 01 42 72 31 52, fax 01 42 72 57 91, ✉ info@castexhotel.com, 5 rue Castex, 4e, metro Bastille)*. This cheery, 29-room establishment, equidistant from Bastille and the heart of the Marais, has been run by the same family since 1919. Quiet, old-fashioned but immaculate singles/doubles with shower cost 240/320FF (290FF to 360FF with toilet as well). Triples/quads are 460/530FF. Reserve well in advance.

Hôtel Le Compostelle *(☎ 01 42 78 59 99, fax 01 40 29 05 18, 31 rue du Roi de Sicile, 4e, metro Hôtel de Ville)*. This tasteful 25-room place at the more tranquil end of the Marais has singles/doubles with shower, toilet and TV for 330/490FF. Doubles with bath are 530FF.

Grand Hôtel Jeanne d'Arc *(☎ 01 48 87 62 11, fax 01 48 87 37 31, 3 rue de Jarente, 4e, metro*

Grand Hôtel Jeanne d'Arc: an excellent base for exploring the buzziest corners of the Right Bank

euro currency converter 10FF = €1.52

PLACES TO STAY

Saint Paul). This 36-room hotel near lovely place du Marché Saint Catherine is a great little pied-à-terre for your peregrinations among the museums, bars and restaurants of the Marais, Village Saint Paul and Bastille. Small singles/doubles are 320/325FF; larger ones are 410/425FF. Triples/quads are 550/620FF.

Hôtel de Nice *(☎ 01 42 78 55 29, fax 01 42 78 36 07, 42 bis rue de Rivoli, 4e, metro Hôtel de Ville).* The English-speaking owner of this especially warm, family-run place has 23 comfortable singles/doubles/triples/quads for 380/450/550/680FF. Many rooms have balconies high above busy rue de Rivoli.

Hôtel de la Place des Vosges *(☎ 01 42 72 60 46, fax 01 42 72 02 64, ✉ hotel.place.des.vosges@ gofornet.fr, 12 rue de Birague, 4e, metro Bastille).* Superbly situated due south of sublime place des Vosges, this 16-room place has rather average singles from 365FF (495FF in the summer) and doubles with bathroom from 545FF to 690FF, including breakfast. There's a tiny lift from the 1st floor.

Hôtel du Septième Art *(☎ 01 44 54 85 00, fax 01 42 77 69 10, 20 rue Saint Paul, 4e, metro Saint Paul).* Somewhat reminiscent of a love hotel in Tokyo, this is a fun place for film buffs, with a black-and-white-movie theme throughout, right down to the tiled floors and bathrooms. Basic singles cost 295FF; doubles with shower or bath and toilet range from 430FF to 690FF.

Latin Quarter (Maps 5 & 6)

There are dozens of two- and three-star hotels, including a cluster near the Sorbonne and another group along the lively rue des Écoles. Mid-range hotels in the Latin Quarter are popular with visiting academics so rooms are hardest to find when conferences and seminars are scheduled, which is usually March to July and in October.

The Luxembourg and Port Royal RER stations are linked to both airports by Roissyrail and Orlyval.

Hôtel Cluny Sorbonne *(Map 5, ☎ 01 43 54 66 66, fax 01 43 29 68 07, ✉ cluny@club-internet.fr, 8 rue Victor Cousin, 5e, metro Luxembourg).* The lift in this 23-room hotel, which has pleasant, well kept singles/doubles/triples for 450/480/700FF, is the size of a telephone box but will accommodate most travellers and their hatboxes.

Hôtel de l'Espérance *(Map 5, ☎ 01 47 07 10 99, fax 01 43 37 56 19, 15 rue Pascal, 5e, metro Censier Daubenton).* Just a couple of minutes' walk south of lively rue Mouffetard, this quiet and immaculately kept 38-room hotel has singles/doubles with shower and toilet for 400/450FF. Larger rooms with two double beds cost 600FF. Breakfast costs 38FF.

Hôtel Esmeralda *(Map 6, ☎ 01 43 54 19 20, fax 01 40 51 00 68, 4 rue Saint Julien le Pauvre, 5e, metro Saint Michel).* This 19-room gem, tucked away in a quiet street with full views of Notre Dame, has been everyone's secret 'find' for years now. A simple single with washbasin is 180FF; doubles with shower and toilet cost 350FF and with bath and toilet from 450FF to 520FF. Triples/quads start at 580/650FF. Book well in advance.

Familia Hôtel *(Map 5, ☎ 01 43 54 55 27, fax 01 43 29 61 77, 11 rue des Écoles, 5e, metro Cardinal Lemoine).* This exceptionally welcoming and well situated hotel has 21 rooms attractively decorated with murals of Parisian landmarks. Eight have balconies, from which you can catch a glimpse of Notre Dame. Singles/doubles/triples/quads with shower or bath go for 385/465/615/765FF.

Hôtel Gay Lussac *(Map 5, ☎ 01 43 54 23 96, fax 01 40 51 79 49, 29 rue Gay Lussac, 5e, metro*

Familia Hôtel: rooms with a view (not to mention a balcony) in the Latin Quarter

Luxembourg). This family-run, 35-room hotel with a lot of character and a lift has small singles starting as low as 170FF but averaging 220FF; rooms with toilet cost 240FF to 260FF, and rooms with shower or bath and toilet are 310FF to 360FF. Fairly large doubles/quads with shower, toilet and high ceilings start at 360/450FF.

Grand Hôtel du Progrès *(Map 5, ☎ 01 43 54 53 18, fax 01 56 24 87 80, 50 rue Gay Lussac, 5e, metro Luxembourg)*. Washbasin-equipped singles at this older, 26-room hotel are 160FF to 180FF; large, old-fashioned doubles with a view and morning sun are 240FF to 290FF (320FF to 350FF with shower and toilet), including breakfast. Hall showers are free.

Hôtel Marignan *(Map 6, ☎ 01 43 54 63 81, 13 rue du Sommerard, 5e, metro Maubert Mutualité)*. This friendly, 30-room place has pleasant, old-fashioned singles/doubles/triples/quads with washbasin for 250/320/460/500FF. Doubles with shower are 490FF to 520FF, triples 530FF to 560FF and quads 600FF to 670FF. About half of the rooms have toilets. Guests also have free use of a fridge, microwave, washing machine and clothes dryer.

Hôtel Minerve *(Map 5, ☎ 01 43 26 26 04, fax 01 44 07 01 96, 13 rue des Écoles, 5e, metro Cardinal Lemoine)*. Sister hotel to the Familia, the 54-room Minerve has been completely renovated and the reception area is kitted out in Oriental carpets and antique books, which owner/manager Erich collects. Some of the rooms have frescoes of French monuments and reproduction 18th-century wallpaper. Singles with shower and toilet cost 390FF to 540FF, doubles 460FF to 540FF and triples 620FF to 650FF. Some 10 rooms have small balconies, eight have views of Notre Dame and two have tiny courtyards that are swooningly romantic.

Hôtel Saint Jacques *(Map 5, ☎ 01 44 07 45 45, fax 01 43 25 65 50, ✉ hotelstjacques@wanadoo .fr, 35 rue des Écoles, 5e, metro Maubert Mutualité)*. Audrey Hepburn and Cary Grant, who filmed some scenes of *Charade* here, would commend the mod cons that now complement the original 19th-century detailing (ornamented ceilings, iron staircase) of this adorable 35-room hotel, whose balconies overlook the Panthéon. Spacious singles are 260FF to 480FF, doubles 450FF to 610FF and triples 680FF.

ROB FLYNN

Hôtel Esmeralda is phenomenally handy for Notre Dame.

euro currency converter 10FF = €1.52

Saint Germain & Odéon (Map 6)

Saint Germain des Prés is a delightful area, but it is quite expensive given the modest comforts offered by most mid-range hotels. The places listed here are the least expensive mid-range hotels the 6e has to offer.

Hôtel des Académies (Map 4, ☎ 01 43 26 66 44, fax 01 43 26 03 72, 15 rue de la Grande Chaumière, 6e, metro Vavin). This truly charming 21-room hotel has been run by the same friendly family since 1920 and has immaculate singles with washbasin for 230FF, and shower-equipped doubles for 315FF (360FF to 375FF with shower and toilet).

Delhy's Hôtel (☎ 01 43 26 58 25, fax 01 43 26 51 06, 22 rue de l'Hirondelle, 6e, metro Saint Michel). This 21-room hotel, through the arch from 6 place Saint Michel, has neat, simple, washbasin-equipped singles/doubles for 220/300FF; doubles with toilet are 300FF and with shower 390FF. Hall showers cost 25FF. Breakfast (35FF) is usually obligatory during the summer and holiday periods.

Hôtel du Globe (☎ 01 43 26 35 50, fax 01 46 33 62 69, 15 rue des Quatre Vents, 6e, metro Odéon). The 15 rooms in this eclectic hotel – each with its own theme – cost 410FF to 495FF with shower and toilet and 595FF with bath and toilet.

Hôtel de Nesle (☎ 01 43 54 62 41, 7 rue de Nesle, 6e, metro Odéon or Mabillon). The Nesle is a relaxed, colourfully decorated hotel (with an Arabian Nights theme) in a quiet street west of place Saint Michel. It's no longer the bargain it once was but singles/doubles with shower are 275/350FF; a double with shower/bath and toilet is 400/450FF. Reservations are not accepted – the only way to get a bed is to stop by in the morning.

Hôtel Petit Trianon (☎ 01 43 54 94 64, 2 rue de l'Ancienne Comédie, 6e, metro Odéon). This less-than-sensitively redecorated 15-room hotel has basic singles with washbasin for 180FF; the showers in the hall are free. Doubles with shower begin at 380FF and with shower and toilet at 450FF; triples are 550FF. There's a discount after a stay of more than four nights.

Hôtel Saint André des Arts (☎ 01 43 26 96 16, fax 01 43 29 73 34, ✉ hsaintand@minitel .net, 66 rue Saint André des Arts, 6e, metro Odéon). Rooms at this 31-room hotel, on a lively, restaurant-lined thoroughfare, start at 380/490/600/670FF for one/two/three/four people, including breakfast.

Hôtel Saint Michel (☎ 01 43 26 98 70, fax 01 40 46 95 69, 17 rue Gît le Cœur, 6e, metro Saint Michel). Comfortable but pretty standard, soundproofed singles/doubles start at 228/256FF with washbasin, at 328/356FF with shower and 368/396FF with shower and toilet. The hall shower costs 12FF.

Gare Saint Lazare & Grands Boulevards (Maps 2 & 3)

The avenues around blvd Montmartre are a popular nightlife area. The better deals are away from Gare Saint Lazare, but there are several places along rue d'Amsterdam (beside the station).

Hôtel des Arts (Map 3, ☎ 01 42 46 73 30, fax 01 48 00 94 42, 7 cité Bergère just off rue Bergère, 9e, metro Grands Boulevards). This cheap and funky 26-room hotel with loads of character (and resident parrot) is in a little alley near the Grands Boulevards. Gay readers might like to know that the largest and steamiest sauna in town is just round the corner. Singles with shower/bath go for 370/390FF, doubles for 390/410FF and triples for 550FF.

Hôtel Britannia (Map 2, ☎ 01 42 85 36 36, fax 01 42 85 16 93, 24 rue d'Amsterdam, 9e, metro Saint Lazare). This 46-room place with narrow hallways and pleasant, clean rooms has singles/doubles with shower for 395/490FF; doubles with bath are 490FF. The triples (565/610FF with shower/bath) are a bit on the small side.

Hôtel Chopin (Map 3, ☎ 01 47 70 58 10, fax 01 42 47 00 70, 46 passage Jouffroy with entrance at 10 blvd Montmartre, 9e, metro Grands Boulevards). This 36-room hotel is down one of Paris' most delightful 19th-century *passages* (covered shopping arcades). It may be a little faded around the edges, but it's still enormously evocative of the *belle époque* and the welcome is always warm. The top floors are the most comfortable. Basic singles start at 355FF; shower-equipped singles/doubles/triples cost from 405/450/595FF. After the arcade closes at 10 pm, ring the *sonnette de nuit* (night doorbell).

Hôtel Peletier-Haussmann-Opéra (Map 3, ☎ 01 42 46 79 53, fax 01 48 24 12 01, ✉ peletier .haussmann@wanadoo.fr, 15 rue Le Peletier, 9e, metro Richelieu Drouot). This friendly 24-room hotel just off blvd Haussmann has shower-equipped singles/doubles/triples/quads for 405/460/575/620FF.

euro currency converter €1 = 6.56FF

Gare du Nord & Gare de l'Est (Map 3)

There are quite a few two- and three-star places around the train stations in the 10e.

Hôtel Français (☎ 01 40 35 94 14, fax 01 40 35 55 40, 13 rue du 8 Mai 1945, 10e, metro Gare de l'Est). This is a 71-room place with attractive, almost luxurious singles/doubles/triples (some with balconies) from 405/450/550FF. Parking in the hotel garage costs 40FF.

Grand Hôtel de Paris (☎ 01 46 07 40 56, fax 01 42 05 99 18, 72 blvd de Strasbourg, 10e, metro Gare de l'Est). This well run establishment has 49 pleasant, soundproofed singles/doubles/triples/quads (320/380/500/620FF) and a tiny lift. If you stay at least four days in the off-season, they may throw in breakfast (normally 30FF) for free.

Nord Hôtel (☎ 01 45 26 43 40, fax 01 42 82 90 23, ✉ nordhotel@wanadoo.fr, 37 rue de Saint Quentin, 10e, metro Gare du Nord). This 46-room hotel, right across from Gare du Nord, has clean and quiet singles/doubles/triples with shower or bath for 320/410/620FF, including breakfast.

Nord-Est Hôtel (☎ 01 47 70 07 18, fax 01 42 46 73 50, 12 rue des Petits Hôtels, 10e, metro Poissonnière). This unusual 30-room hotel is situated in an attractive villa set away from the street and fronted by a small garden. It is convenient for both Gare de l'Est and Gare du Nord and costs 370/400FF for singles/doubles in the low season and 400/460FF in the high season.

Bastille (Maps 5, 6 & 7)

Two-star comfort is less expensive in the 11e than in the inner arrondissements.

Hôtel Bastille (Map 6, ☎ 01 47 00 06 71, fax 01 43 57 07 23, 24 rue de la Roquette, 11e, metro Bastille). The youthful staff at this friendly, 20-room hotel offer neat and modern singles/doubles/triples for 350/400/500FF, including breakfast. From June to September and around Christmas, a bed in a single-sex shared triple with shower and toilet costs 122FF, including breakfast.

Hôtel Lyon Mulhouse (Map 7, ☎ 01 47 00 91 50, fax 01 47 00 06 31, ✉ hotelyonmulhouse@wanadoo.fr, 8 blvd Beaumarchais, 11e, metro Bastille). This renovated 40-room hotel offers quiet though predictable singles from 340FF, and doubles with shower and toilet from 530FF; there are also triples (550FF to 580FF) and quads (600FF to 640FF).

Hôtel Pax (Map 5, ☎ 01 47 00 40 98, fax 01 43 38 57 81, 12 rue de Charonne, 11e, metro Bastille or Ledru Rollin). Large, spotless rooms with shower range from 250FF to 270FF (270FF to 450FF with toilet and shower).

Hôtel Royal Bastille (Map 6, ☎ 01 48 05 62 47, fax 01 49 23 07 58, 14 rue de la Roquette, 11e, metro Bastille). More upmarket than most of the hotels along rue de la Roquette, this pleasant 26-room place has good-value singles/doubles/triples/quads from 400/450/580/700FF.

13e Arrondissement (Map 9)

This district is where you'll find the new Bibliothèque Nationale de France François Mitterrand as well as plenty of restaurants and night spots both along the river and over in the Bercy Village area.

Factôtel Tolbiac (☎ 01 53 61 62 00, fax 01 53 61 62 01, 15 rue de Tolbiac, 13e, metro Bibliothèque). This 87-room conversion stands out not so much for its amenities but for its location – it's a stone's throw from the new national library and the péniches (barges) on the Seine fitted out with music clubs and restaurants. ingles/doubles start at 400/460FF.

Montparnasse (Map 1)

Just east of Gare Montparnasse, there are a number of two- and three-star places on rue Vandamme and rue de la Gaîté; the latter street is rife with sex shops.

Hôtel de Blois (☎ 01 45 40 99 48, fax 01 45 40 45 62, 5 rue des Plantes, 14e, metro Mouton Duvernet). This 25-room establishment offers smallish singles/doubles with washbasin and bidet for 240/250FF. Doubles are 280FF with shower, and 350FF with shower and toilet. Fully equipped triples are 370FF.

Hôtel Floridor (☎ 01 43 21 35 53, fax 01 43 27 65 81, 28 place Denfert Rochereau, 14e, metro Denfert Rochereau). Shower-equipped singles/doubles go for 289/317FF (307/335FF with toilet as well), including breakfast. Triples are 423FF.

Petit Palace Hôtel (☎ 01 43 22 05 25, fax 01 43 21 79 01, 131 ave du Maine, 14e, metro Gaîté). The same family has run this friendly, ambitiously named, 44-room hotel for half a century. It has smallish but spotless doubles/triples for 250/320FF with washbasin and bidet, and from 440FF with shower and toilet. Hall showers are 20FF.

ASA ANDERSSON

Montmartre & Pigalle (Map 8)

The attractive two-star places on rue Aristide Bruant are generally less full in July and August than in the spring and autumn.

Hôtel des Arts (☎ 01 46 06 30 52, fax 01 46 06 10 83, 5 rue Tholozé, 18e, metro Abbesses). This is a friendly, attractive 50-room place with singles/doubles from 360/460FF (490FF for a twin). Breakfast costs 35FF.

Hôtel Avenir (☎ 01 48 78 21 37, fax 01 40 16 92 62, 39 blvd Rochechouart, 9e, metro Anvers). This 42-room place on noisy blvd Rochechouart has singles/doubles/triples from 300/420/460FF. All rooms have a bath or shower and the rates include breakfast.

Hôtel des Capucines Montmartre (☎ 01 42 52 89 80, fax 01 42 52 29 57, ☻ capucines@compuserve.com, 5 rue Aristide Bruant, 18e, metro Abbesses). Singles with TV and minibar cost 250FF to 325FF, doubles 300FF to 350FF and triples 350FF to 420FF.

Hôtel Luxia (☎ 01 46 06 84 24, fax 01 46 06 10 14, 8 rue Seveste, 18e, metro Anvers). This 45-room hotel mainly takes groups, but at least a few rooms are almost always left for independent travellers. Plain, clean singles/doubles/triples with shower, toilet and TV are 280/300/390FF.

Hôtel du Moulin (☎ 01 42 64 33 33, fax 01 46 06 42 66, ☻ moulin.hotel@worldnet.fr, 3 rue Aristide Bruant, 18e, metro Abbesses). This 27-room place has singles/doubles with toilet and bath or shower for 250/300FF in the winter and 350/440FF in the summer.

Timhôtel Montmartre (☎ 01 42 55 74 79, fax 01 42 55 71 01, ☻ montmartre@timhotel.fr, 11 rue Ravignan and place Émile Goudeau, 18e, metro Abbesses). This is a good choice if you place more value on location than room size. The 60 neat, modern rooms of this branch of the Timhôtel chain cost 680FF for singles and doubles; triples are 810FF. Some of the rooms on the 4th and 5th floors have stunning views of the city (100FF extra). Buffet breakfast costs 50FF.

Hôtel Utrillo (☎ 01 42 58 13 44, fax 01 42 23 93 88, ☻ adel.utrillo@wanadoo.fr, 7 rue Aristide Bruant, 18e, metro Abbesses). Singles/doubles at this 30-room hotel are 305/380FF in the low season and 360/420FF in the summer. A double with bath and toilet is 420FF (450FF in the summer). Breakfast costs 40FF.

Airports

Both airports have a wide selection of places, including mid-range Ibis hotels and, at Charles de Gaulle, a rather unusual form of accommodation if you just need to rest.

Cocoon (☎ 01 48 62 06 16, fax 01 48 62 56 97). This strange place – below departure level (Hall 36) at Charles de Gaulle (Aérogare 1) – has 60 'cabins' where you can sleep for up to 16 hours – but no longer than that. The single/double day rates (check in any time between 8 am and 6 pm) are 150/250FF, overnight rates are 250/300FF. All cabins have TVs, telephones with fax and, most importantly, alarm clocks.

Hôtel Ibis CDG Aéroport (☎ 01 49 19 19 19, fax 01 49 19 19 21). This large, modern, chain hotel – next to Aéroport Charles de Gaulle 1 train station – with two stars and 556 rooms has singles and doubles from 455FF and triples from 595FF. The hotel is linked to the terminals by shuttle bus.

Hôtel Ibis Orly Aéroport (☎ 01 46 87 33 50, fax 01 46 87 29 92). This 299-room chain hotel at Orly airport is linked to both terminals by the Navette ADP (airport shuttle bus). Rooms for up to three people start at 415FF; quads start at 500FF.

PLACES TO STAY – TOP END

There's a wide price range at hotels bearing three or four stars in Paris.

Louvre & Les Halles (Maps 2 & 6)

The 1er is the area to come to if you really want to blow the budget.

PLACES TO STAY

Hôtel Brighton (Map 2, ☎ 01 47 03 61 61, fax 01 42 60 41 78, ✆ hotel.brighton@wanadoo.fr, 218 rue de Rivoli, 1er, metro Tuileries). This is a three-star, 70-room establishment with lovely singles/doubles/triples starting at 530/670/955FF and climbing to 875/905/1055FF, depending on the season and the room. The rooms that overlook the Jardin des Tuileries are the most popular; those on the 4th and 5th floors afford views over the trees to the Seine.

Grand Hôtel de Champagne (Map 6, ☎ 01 42 36 60 00, fax 01 45 08 43 33, 17 rue Jean Lantier, 1er, metro Châtelet). This very comfortable, three-star hotel has 42 rooms, with singles costing 596FF to 920FF and doubles 652FF to 1045FF, depending on the season.

Marais (Map 7)

There are top-end hotels in the heart of the Marais as well as in the vicinity of the elegant place des Vosges.

Hôtel Axial Beaubourg (☎ 01 42 72 72 22, fax 01 42 72 03 53, 11 rue du Temple, 4e, metro Hôtel de Ville). The name of this place says it all: modern mixed with historic. It's in the heart of the Marais and charges from 500/650FF for singles/doubles with shower.

Hôtel Central Marais (☎ 01 48 87 56 08, fax 01 42 77 06 27, 2 rue Sainte Croix de la Bretonnerie, 4e, metro Hôtel de Ville). This sevenroom hotel, mostly catering for gay men, also welcomes lesbians. Singles and doubles with one bathroom for every two rooms are 535FF; suites for one or two are 650FF, for three or four 795FF. After 3 pm reception is round the corner in the bar at 33 rue Vieille du Temple. Reservations should be made four to six weeks ahead.

Grand Hôtel Malher (☎ 01 42 72 60 92, fax 01 42 72 25 37, ghmalher@yahoo.fr, 5 rue Malher, 4e, metro Saint Paul). The 31 nicely appointed rooms at this family-run establishment start at 490/590FF for singles/doubles (100FF more in the high season).

Île Saint Louis (Map 6)

The smaller of the two islands in the Seine is an easy walk from central Paris but the hotels are pricey.

Hôtel des Deux Îles (☎ 01 43 26 13 35, fax 01 43 29 60 25, 59 rue Saint Louis en l'Île, 4e, metro Pont Marie). This excellent 17-room hotel has small singles from 770FF and doubles from 890FF. Breakfast costs 55FF.

BRENDA TURNNIDGE

Chilling out on Île Saint Louis, the secluded location of some fine hotels

Hôtel de Lutèce (☎ 01 43 26 23 52, fax 01 43 29 60 25, 65 rue Saint Louis en l'Île, 4e, metro Pont Marie). This exquisite 23-room hotel, more country than city, is under the same friendly and helpful management as the Hôtel des Deux Îles. The comfortable rooms are tastefully decorated and the location is probably the most desirable in all of France. Rates are similar to those at the Hôtel des Deux Îles.

Hôtel Saint Louis (☎ 01 46 34 04 80, fax 01 46 34 02 13, 75 rue Saint Louis en l'Île, 4e, metro Pont Marie). Singles/doubles (from 695/895FF) at this 21-room establishment are appealing but unspectacular, though the public areas are lovely. The breakfast room in the basement dates from the early 17th century; breakfast costs 49FF.

Latin Quarter (Map 5)

The Latin Quarter generally offers better top-end value than the nearby 6e.

Hôtel des Grandes Écoles (☎ 01 43 26 79 23, fax 01 43 25 28 15, ✆ hotel.grandes.ecoles@

PLACES TO STAY

wanadoo.fr, 75 rue du Cardinal Lemoine, 5e, metro Cardinal Lemoine). This wonderful 51-room hotel just north of place de la Contrescarpe has one of the loveliest situations in the Latin Quarter, tucked away in a courtyard off a medieval street with its own garden (James Joyce lived in one of the courtyard flats in 1921). Singles are 550FF, doubles 720FF and an extra bed is 100FF.

Grand Hôtel Saint Michel (☎ 01 46 33 33 02, fax 01 40 46 96 33, ✉ grand.hotel.st.michel@ wanadoo.fr, 19 rue Cujas, 5e, metro Luxembourg). This well situated 45-room hotel is far away from the din of blvd Saint Michel, making it feel almost remote. Singles/doubles (some with balcony) cost 690/890FF, while triples are 1290FF. The attached *salon de thé* is quite pleasant.

Hôtel Au Royal Cardinal (☎ 01 43 26 83 64, fax 01 44 07 22 32, royalcardinal@multi.micro .com, 1 rue des Écoles, 5e, metro Cardinal Lemoine or Jussieu). We've heard good things about this very central, 36-room hotel near the Sorbonne. Singles are 460FF to 510FF, doubles 500FF to 550FF and triples 735FF to 785FF.

Résidence Monge (☎ 01 43 26 87 90, fax 01 43 54 47 25, ✉ hotel-monge@gofornet.com, 55 rue Monge, 5e, metro Place Monge). This clean, well managed hotel with 36 rooms right in the thick of things is an expensive choice if you're alone (singles cost 380FF to 480FF) but a good deal if you've got a companion or two: doubles are 500FF to 550FF, triples 600FF to 650FF.

Hôtel Saint Christophe (☎ 01 43 31 81 54, fax 01 43 31 12 54, hotelstchristophe@compuserve .com, 17 rue Lacépède, 5e, metro Place Monge). A classy small hotel with 31 well equipped singles/doubles at 550/680FF, although discounts are often available.

Saint Germain & Odéon (Maps 4 & 6)

The three-star hotels in this area are around Saint Germain des Prés.

Hôtel des Deux Continents (Map 6, ☎ 01 43 26 72 46, fax 01 43 25 67 80, 25 rue Jacob, 6e, metro Saint Germain des Prés). This 41-room establishment has spacious singles for 775FF, doubles from 845FF to 895FF and triples for 1100FF; breakfast costs 60FF.

Hôtel Lenox Saint Germain (Map 4, ☎ 01 42 96 10 95, fax 01 42 61 52 83, ✉ hotel@ lenoxsaintgermain.com, 9 rue de l'Université, 7e, metro Rue du Bac). Simple, uncluttered and comfortable rooms upstairs and a late-opening 1930s-style bar downstairs attract a chic clien-

tele. The Art Deco décor is magnificent. Doubles with shower/bath start at 700/850FF.

Hôtel des Marronniers (Map 6, ☎ 01 43 25 30 60, fax 01 40 46 83 56, 21 rue Jacob, 6e, metro Saint Germain des Prés). This 37-room place at the back of a small courtyard has less-than-huge singles/doubles/triples from 610/805/1100FF and a magical garden round the back.

Hôtel Michelet Odéon (Map 6, ☎ 01 53 10 05 60, fax 01 46 34 55 35, hotel@micheletodeon.com, 6 place de l'Odéon, 6e, metro Odéon). Opposite the Odéon Théâtre de l'Europe and just a minute's walk from the Jardin du Luxembourg, this 42-room place has tasteful, generously proportioned singles for 430FF, doubles with shower/bath for 510/580FF, triples from 700FF and quads from 770FF.

Gare Saint Lazare & Grands Boulevards (Maps 2 & 3)

There are a few reasonably priced top-end hotels in this area.

Atlantic Opéra Hôtel (Map 2, ☎ 01 43 87 45 40, fax 01 42 93 06 26, 44 rue de Londres, 8e, metro

Hôtel Saint Christophe: a classy hang-out in the Latin Quarter

ROB FLYNN

PLACES TO STAY

euro currency converter €1 = 6.56FF

Saint Lazare or Europe). On the northern side of the train station, this stylishly renovated 85-room hotel has singles at 580FF, doubles from 780FF and triples for 995FF.

Hôtel Favart *(Map 3, ☎ 01 42 97 59 83, fax 01 40 15 95 58, ✆ favart.hotel@wanadoo.fr, 5 rue Marivaux, 2e, metro Richelieu Drouot).* This stylish Art Nouveau hotel facing the Opéra Comique has 37 rooms, with singles/doubles costing from 530/665FF.

Montparnasse (Map 4)

The area around Gare Montparnasse is better known for budget and mid-range accommodation but there are some top-end hotels.

Hôtel Miramar *(☎ 01 45 48 62 94, fax 01 45 48 68 73, 6 place Bienvenüe, 15e, metro Montparnasse Bienvenüe).* Soundproofed, smallish and typically three-star singles/doubles/triples here cost 486/512/818FF.

Montmartre & Pigalle (Map 3)

There is a bunch of top-end hotels in the area, including one within easy reach of Pigalle.

Hôtel des Trois Poussins *(☎ 01 53 32 81 81, fax 01 53 32 81 82, ✆ h3p@les3poussins.com, 15 rue Clauzel, 9e, metro Saint Georges).* This lovely hotel due south of place Pigalle has singles/doubles from 680/780FF (750/850FF in the high season), but more than half of its 40 rooms are small studios with their own cooking facilities. They cost from 780/880FF for a single/double (850/950FF in the high season).

PLACES TO STAY – DELUXE

Paris' most opulent – and famous – four-star and four-star+ (the French equivalent of five-star) hotels are in or near the 1er (Map 2).

Hôtel Costes *(☎ 01 42 44 50 00, fax 01 45 44 50 01, 239 rue Saint Honoré, 1er, metro Concorde).* Jean-Louis Costes' eponymous 83-room hotel, opened in 1995, offers a 'luxurious and immoderate home away from home' to the visiting style mafia. Outfitted by Jacques Garcia in camp Second Empire castoffs, it's the current darling of the rich and famous. Doubles range from 2000FF to 3500FF (remember: size counts among the rich); suites start at 5500FF. Breakfast costs 170FF.

Hôtel de Crillon *(☎ 01 44 71 15 00, fax 01 44 71 15 02, crillon@crillon-paris.com, 10 place de la Concorde, 8e, metro Concorde).* The colonnaded, 200-year-old Crillon, whose sparkling public areas (including Les Ambassadeur restaurant, with two Michelin stars) are sumptuously decorated with chandeliers, original sculptures, gilt mouldings, tapestries and inlaid furniture, is the epitome of French luxury. Spacious singles/doubles with pink-marble bathrooms start at 2950/3500FF. The cheapest suites are 4950FF, larger ones go for 7300FF to 8300FF. Breakfast is another 185FF (continental) or 275FF (American).

Hôtel Ritz *(☎ 01 43 16 30 30, fax 01 43 16 36 68, resa@ritzparis.com, 15 place Vendôme, 1er, metro Opéra).* As one of the world's most celebrated and expensive hotels, the 142-room, 45-suite Ritz has sparkling rooms starting at 3000/3600FF (3300/4000FF from May to June and September to October). Junior suites begin a 5000FF (5400FF); regular suites start at 6500FF (7700FF). The hotel restaurant, L'Espadon, has two Michelin stars, and the renovated Hemingway Bar is where the American author imbibed once he'd made it.

SIMON BRACKEN

Putting on the Ritz:
the epitome of Parisian sophistication

LONG-TERM RENTALS

If you intend to stay in Paris for more than a week or so, consider staying in a serviced flat or even renting a furnished flat through one of the many agencies listed under the heading 'Location Appartements Meublés' on sheets distributed by the Paris tourist office and on its Web site. Organisations that can help find accommodation for students who will be in Paris for at least a semester are listed under 'Logements pour Étudiants'.

Finding a Flat

The hardest time to find an apartment – especially a cheap one – in Paris is in September and October, when everyone is back from their summer holidays and students are searching for digs for the academic year. Moderately priced places are easiest to come by towards the end of university semesters – ie, between Christmas and early February and over the summer (July to September).

About 2500FF a month will get you a tiny garret room (9 sq metres minimum) with a washbasin but no telephone, no proper place to cook and no private toilet. There may not even be a communal shower. These rooms, often occupied by students, are often converted *chambres de bonne* (maids' quarters) on the 6th or 7th floors of old apartment buildings without lifts but in decent neighbourhoods.

Small (15 to 30 sq metres), unfurnished/furnished studios with attached toilet start at about 100FF per sq metre a month. The per-metre cost theoretically goes down the larger the place is, the farther away it is from the city centre and depending on whether or not it has a lift.

If you've exhausted your word-of-mouth sources (expats, students, compatriots living temporarily in Paris), it's a good idea to check out the bulletin boards at the American Church (see Cultural Centres in the Facts for the Visitor chapter). People who advertise there are unlikely to fear renting to foreigners, will probably speak some English and might be willing to sign a relatively short-term contract. *FUSAC*, a free periodical issued every two weeks (see Newspapers & Magazines in the Facts for the Visitor chapter) is another good source.

If you know some French (or someone who does), you'll be able to consult several periodicals available from newsagents: *De Particulier à Particulier* (16F) and *Se Loger* (14FF), both issued on Thursday, *L'Hebdo Immobilier* (12FF) on Wednesday as well as *À Vendre à Louer* (7FF). You'll have to do your calling in French though. If you have access to a telephone, you could place an apartment-wanted ad in *De Particulier à Particulier* and have people call you.

Rental Agencies

Allô Logement Temporaire (Map 7, ☎ 01 42 72 00 06, fax 01 42 72 03 11, 🖂 alt@ claranet.fr, metro Rambuteau), 64 rue du Temple, 3e, is a nonprofit organisation that liaises between flat-owners and foreigners looking for furnished apartments for periods of one week to one year. Small furnished studios of about 25 to 30 sq metres cost 3000FF to 5000FF a month, depending on the location. October, when university classes resume, is the hardest month in which to find a place, but over summer it's usually possible to find something within a matter of days. Before any deals are signed, the company will arrange for you to talk to the owner by phone, assisted by an interpreter if necessary. There is a 300FF annual membership fee and, in addition to the rent and one month's deposit (paid directly to the owner), a charge of 200FF for each month you rent. The office opens noon to 8 pm weekdays.

Another nonprofit organisation that can help you find a flat is France Lodge Locations (☎ 01 53 20 09 09, fax 01 53 20 01 25, metro Le Peletier), 41 rue La Fayette, 9e. Prices start at about 150FF per person per night (cheaper by the month) and annual membership costs 100FF.

Serviced Flats

Serviced flats – like staying in a hotel without all the extras – are an excellent option for those on a budget, particularly those in small groups. There are several locations around Paris.

euro currency converter €1 = 6.56FF

Citadines Apart'hotels (✉ *res@citdines.com*). This hotel chain with studios and apartments has some 18 properties in Paris, including the following four: ***Bastille Nation*** *(Map 5, ☎ 01 40 04 43 50, fax 01 40 04 43 99, 14-18 rue de Chaligny, 12e, metro Reuilly Diderot)*; ***Montmartre*** *(Map 8, ☎ 01 44 70 45 50, fax 01 45 22 59 10, 16 ave Rachel, 18e, metro Blanche)*; ***Opéra Drouot*** *(Map 3, ☎ 01 40 15 14 00, fax 01 40 15 14 15, 18 rue Favart, 2e, metro Richelieu Drouot)*; and ***Raspail Montparnasse*** *(Map 4, ☎ 01 43 35 46 35, fax 01 40 47 43 01, 121 blvd du Montparnasse, 6e, metro Vavin)*. Prices vary depending on the time of year and the property but in general a small studio for one person with cooking facilities ranges in price from 505FF to 875FF, a studio accommodating two people is 600FF to 975FF and a one-bedroom flat sleeping four costs 850FF to 1600FF. For stays longer than six days there's a discount of about 10%, and for over a month of about 25%.

Flatôtel International *(Map 4, ☎ 01 45 75 6₂ 20,* fax 01 45 79 73 30, 14 rue du Théâtre, 15e, metro Charles Michels)*. Kitchen-equipped studios measuring 40 sq metres cost 680FF to 900FF a day and one-bedroom flats 980FF to 1300FF; rates are much lower by the month.

Résidence des Arts *(Map 6, ☎ 01 55 42 71 11, fax 01 55 42 71 00, ✉ residencedesarts@hotma .com, 14 rue Gît le Cœur, 6e, metro Saint Michel)*. This lovely place in a 15th-century hôtel particulier just west of place Saint Michel feels more like a hotel than a flat but has studios for 750FF to 950FF, suites for 1200FF to 1500FF and apartments from 1800FF to 2300FF.

Résidence Pierre & Vacances Paris Montmartre *(Map 8, ☎ 01 42 57 14 55, fax 01 42 54 48 87, ✉ ydarsa@pierre-vacances.fr, 10 place Charles Dullin, 18e, metro Abbesses)*. One of several branches of a new serviced-flat chain, this one charges 570FF to 910FF a night for a studio and 900FF to 1115FF for a one-bedroom flat. There's a 10% discount on stays of more than eight days and 30% on stays of more than 28 days.

Places to Eat

FOOD

The French think mainly about two things
– their two main meals,' one well-fed *bon
vivant* friend in Paris told us. 'Everything
else is in parentheses.' And it's true. Eating
well is still of prime importance to most
people here, who spend an amazing amount
of time thinking about, talking about and
consuming food. And why not? The cuisine
of France is remarkably varied, with a
great many regional differences based on
the produce and gastronomy of each region.

Lonely Planet's *World Food: France* will
take you on a culinary tour of Paris as well
as the rest of the country.

Ethnic Cuisine

Paris has a considerable population of immigrants from France's former colonies and
protectorates, and ethnic food has become as
Parisian as onion soup. The *nems* (spring
rolls) and *pâtés impériaux* (spring or egg
rolls) of Vietnam and China, the couscous
and *tajines* of North Africa, *boudin antillais*
(West Indian blood pudding) from the
Caribbean and the *yassa* (meat or fish grilled
in onion and lemon sauce) of Senegal are all
eaten with relish throughout the capital.

Vegetarians & Vegans

Vegetarians and vegans make up a small
minority in a country where *viande* (meat)
once also meant 'food' and they are not
very well catered for, as specialist vegetarian restaurants are few and far between. Unfortunately, very few set menus include
vegetarian options.

Meals in France

Parisians start the day with a *petit déjeuner*
(breakfast; see the boxed text 'The Very
Petit Déjeuner' on the next page), usually
consisting of a light bread roll or half a
baguette (often left over from dinner the
night before) with butter and jam, followed
by a *café au lait* (coffee with lots of hot
milk), a small black coffee or hot chocolate.

Contrary to what many foreigners think, the
French do not eat croissants every day but
usually reserve them for a weekend treat.

For many people, *déjeuner* (lunch) is still
the main meal of the day, with *dîner* (dinner)
often something lighter – almost a supper.

Eating Out

Restaurants & Brasseries Parisian restaurants usually specialise in a particular
variety of food (eg, traditional French,
regional French, North African or Vietnamese), whereas brasseries serve more
standard French and Alsatian fare. Most
restaurants open for lunch and dinner only
(from noon to 2.30 pm or so and from 7 or
7.30 pm to sometime between 10 and
11 pm). Brasseries usually stay open from
morning till late at night and many remain
open on Sunday.

Can you resist? An enticing menu
in a restaurant window

GREG ELMS

Lonely Planet's *Out to Eat – Paris* has a huge selection of recommended eateries for those seriously interested in the city's food scene.

University Restaurants Stodgy but filling cafeteria food is available in copious quantities at Paris' 15 *restaurants universitaires* (student cafeterias), run by the Centre Régional des Œuvres Universitaires et Scolaires (CROUS; ☎ 01 40 51 36 00). Tickets for three-course meals cost 14.50FF for students with ID (an ISIC is unacceptable). Guests pay between 22FF and 26FF, depending on the CROUS branch. CROUS restaurants (usually called 'restos U') have variable opening times that change according to university holiday schedules and weekend rotational agreements; check the schedule posted outside *Assas (Map 5, ☎ 01 46 33 61 25, metro Port Royal or Notre Dame des Champs)*, 92 rue d'Assas, 6e; *Bullier (Map 5, ☎ 01 43 54 93 38, metro Port Royal)*, 39 ave Georges Bernanos, 5e; *Châtelet*

(Map 5, ☎ 01 43 31 51 66, metro Censier Daubenton), 8 rue Jean Calvin, 5e, just off rue Mouffetard; or *Mabillon (Map 6, ☎ 01 43 2. 66 23, metro Mabillon)*, 3 rue Mabillon, 6e.

Cafés The café is an integral part of man Parisians' day-to-day existence but onl basic food such as sandwiches is availabl at most traditional ones. Many of the pubs bars and less traditional cafés listed in th Entertainment chapter also serve snacks an light meals.

Fast-Food & Chain Restaurants Ameri can fast-food companies have busy branche all over Paris as does the local hamburg chain Quick.

A number of restaurants have several out lets around Paris with standard menus They're a definite step up from the fast-foo outlets and can be good value in areas such a ave des Champs-Élysées, where restaurant tend to be expensive or bad value (or both).

The Very Petit Déjeuner

French breakfast *(petit déjeuner)* is not every Anglo-Saxon's cup of tea. For many, a croissant, a bit of leftover baguette with butter and jam and a cup of over-milked coffee do not a breakfast make. Masters of the kitchen throughout the rest of the day, French chefs don't seem up to it in the morning. The whole idea is not to fill up – petit déjeuner means 'little lunch' and the real *déjeuner* (lunch) is just round the corner!

The following are some good choices for breakfast or brunch in Paris. Be advised, though, that you're here for the atmosphere and/or the scenery (be it a park or on two legs) and not necessarily the petit déjeuner as such.

Café Beaubourg (Map 7, ☎ 01 48 87 63 96, 43 rue Saint Merri, 4e, metro Châtelet-Les Halles). This minimalist café draws an arty crowd for breakfast (70FF) and Sunday brunch (120FF) on the terrace, and there's always free entertainment on the *parvis* (large square) opposite in front of the Centre Pompidou. It's open 8 am to 1 am Monday to Thursday and on Sunday, and to 2 am on Friday and Saturday.

Ma Bourgogne (Map 7, ☎ 01 42 78 44 64, 19 place des Vosges, 4e, metro Saint Paul or Bastille). Overlooking what is arguably the most beautiful square in Paris, 'My Burgundy' is a wonderful place to wake up to over breakfast. The plat du jour is 100FF and there's a *menu* for 195FF. It's open 8 am till 1.30 am daily.

Le Viaduc Café (Map 5, ☎ 01 44 74 70 70, 43 ave Daumesnil, 12e, metro Gare de Lyon). The terrace of this ever-so-*branché* (trendy) café in one of the glassed-in arches of the Viaduc des Arts, a disused railway bridge, is an excellent spot to while away the early hours. The jazz brunch from noon to 4 pm on Sunday (*menus* 125FF and 135FF) is very popular. It's open 9 am to 4 am daily and you can order food until an hour before closing.

Bistro Romain
This increasingly popular chain, with some 21 branches around the city, has *menus* (fixed-price meals) available from 49FF (lunch) to 99FF. They are usually open 11.30 am to 1 am but the Champs-Élysées branch *(Map 2, ☎ 01 43 59 93 31, 122 ave des Champs-Élysées, 8e, metro George V)* stays opens later.

Buffalo Grill
This national newcomer took over many of the former Batifol restaurants and now counts 10 branches in Paris proper, including one opposite Gare du Nord *(Map 3, ☎ 01 40 16 47 81, 9 blvd de Denain, 10e, metro Gare du Nord)*. The emphasis is on grills (49FF to 84FF) and steak – T-bone (93FF) and even ostrich (86FF) – and set meals start at 63FF. The restaurants are open 11 am to 11 pm daily.

Hippopotamus
There are about 19 branches in Paris of this hugely popular national chain, which specialises in solid, steak-based meals. *Menus* range from 52FF (lunch) to 143FF and branches are typically open 11.30 am to 1 am daily (to 1.30 am on Friday and Saturday). Five branches, however, are open to 5 am daily, including one facing place de la Bastille *(Map 7, ☎ 01 44 61 90 40, 1 blvd Beaumarchais, 4e, metro Bastille)*.

Léon de Bruxelles
The 13 branches of this restaurant chain are dedicated to one thing only: *moules* (mussels). Meal-size bowls of the bivalves, served with chips and fresh bread, start at 50FF; there are *menus* available at 66FF, 70FF and 99FF. They're open 11.30 am to 1 am daily (to 2 am on Saturday), including the one near Forum des Halles *(Map 6, ☎ 01 42 36 18 50, 120 rue Rambuteau, 1er, metro Châtelet-Les Halles)*.

Self-Catering
One of Paris' delights is stocking up on fresh bread, pastries, cheese, fruit, vegetables and prepared dishes and sitting down for a gourmet *pique-nique*. However many food shops are closed on Sunday afternoon and Monday, and almost all supermarkets are closed all day on Sunday.

Fresh bread is baked and sold at *boulangeries* (see the boxed text 'The Stuff of Life' later in this chapter); mouth-watering pastries are available at *pâtisseries*; a *fromagerie* can supply you with cheese that is *fait* (ripe) to the exact degree that you request; a *charcuterie* offers sliced meat,

ASA ANDERSSON

pâtés and so on; and fresh fruit and vegetables are sold at *épiceries* (greengrocers), supermarkets and open-air markets.

A *boucherie* is a general butcher, but for specialised poultry you have to go to a *marchand de volaille*. A *boucherie chevaline*, easily identifiable by the gilded horse's head above the entrance, sells horse meat, which some people prefer to beef or mutton. Fresh fish and seafood are available from a *poissonnerie*.

Paris' neighbourhood food-markets offer the freshest and best-quality fruit, vegetables, cheese, prepared salads and so on at the lowest prices. For details of the best see the special section 'The Markets of Paris' after this chapter.

DRINKS
Nonalcoholic Drinks
The most commonly drunk nonalcoholic beverages in France today are coffee and mineral water. Fruit juices, soft drinks and tea trail far behind.

Coffee A cup of coffee can take various forms, but the most ubiquitous is the espresso. A small, black espresso is called a *café noir*, an *express* or simply a *café*. You can also ask for a *grand* (large) version.

A *café crème* is an espresso with steamed milk or cream. A small café crème is a *petit*

euro currency converter €1 = 6.56FF

crème. A *café au lait* is lots of hot milk with a little coffee served in a large cup or even a small bowl. A *noisette* (literally 'hazelnut') is an espresso with just a dash of milk. A coffee in a café can be as little as 8FF if you drink it standing up at the counter. Sit down and the price will double.

Water Tap water in Paris is safe to drink, so there is no real need to buy bottled water. Tap water that is not drinkable (eg, at most public fountains) will usually have a sign reading '*eau non potable*'.

If you prefer to have tap water with your meal rather than a soft drink or wine, don't be put off if the waiter scowls: by law restaurants must serve tap water to clients who request it. Otherwise you can order mineral water (*eau minérale*), which comes flat (*plate*) or carbonated (*gazeuse*). Spring water (*eau de source*) is usually flat.

GREG ELMS

Water, water, everywhere: *eau minérale* is available in abundance in Paris.

Alcoholic Drinks

Wine is not the only alcohol drunk with meals in France and people don't just drink alcohol with food; it comes before and after too.

Wine Two regions produce the most celebrated wines in France: Bordeaux and Burgundy. Burgundy of the right vintage can be extraordinary, but Bordeaux is generally more reliable. Beaujolais, a light Burgundy can be drunk as young as two months old.

Aperitifs & Digestifs Meals are often preceded by an appetite-stirring aperitif such as kir (white wine sweetened with a blackcurrant liqueur) or pastis, which is aniseed flavoured and turns cloudy when you add water.

France's most famous brandies are Armagnac and Cognac. The various other sorts of brandies are known collectively as *eaux-de-vie* (literally 'waters of life'). Calvados is an apple brandy that ages beautifully. Popular liqueurs include Cointreau, Bénédictine and Chartreuse.

Beer *Bière*, which is usually served by the *demi* (about 0.33L) in bars and cafés, is usually one of the national brands such as Kronenbourg or 33 and totally forgettable. Be on the lookout for beers from Alsace and the north of France. A draught beer is a *bière à la pression*.

LOUVRE & LES HALLES (Map 6)

The area between Forum des Halles and the Centre Pompidou is filled with scores of trendy restaurants, but few of them are particularly good or inexpensive. Streets lined with places to eat include rue des Lombards, the pedestrians-only rue Montorgueil, and the narrow streets north and east of Forum des Halles.

There are a number of worthwhile places in the *passages couverts* (covered shopping arcades; see the Passages walking tour in the Things to See & Do chapter) in this area. In the Galerie Véro Dodat (Map 6), *Café de l'Époque* (☎ 01 42 33 40 70) at No 35-37 (or 2 rue du Bouloi) has drinks

The Stuff of Life

Nothing is more French than *pain* (bread), and more than 80% of all French people eat it at every meal. Don't worry about buying too much; most *boulangeries* (bakeries) will sell you half a loaf. But you'll probably be able to eat a whole one in any case.

French bakeries offer an infinite variety of breads; one smallish one we happened to pass listed no fewer than 28 types. All bakeries have baguettes (or *flûtes*), which are long and thin, and wider loaves simply called *pains*; both these kinds are at their best if eaten within four hours of baking. You can store them for longer in a plastic bag, but the crust becomes soft and chewy; if you leave them out, they'll soon be hard – which is the way many French people like them at breakfast the next day. The pain is softer on the inside and has a less crispy crust than the baguette, and is slightly cheaper by weight. If you're not very hungry, ask for half a loaf: a *demi baguette* or a *demi pain*.

Bread has experienced a renaissance in France in recent years, and most bakeries also carry heavier, more expensive breads made with all sorts of grains and cereals; you will also find loaves studded with nuts, raisins or herbs. Other types of bread, which come in a wide range of sizes and shapes, vary from shop to shop, but as they are all on display, making a selection is easy. These heavier breads keep much longer than baguettes and standard white-flour breads. To extend the life of them, do like the French and wrap the loaf snugly in a tea towel or dish cloth.

Bread is baked at various times during the day, so it's available fresh as early as 6 am and also in the afternoon. Most bakeries close for one day a week, but the days are staggered so that a neighbourhood is never left without a place to buy a loaf (except, perhaps, on Sunday afternoon). Places that sell bread but don't bake it on the premises are known as *dépôts de pain*. You can always ask for your baguette or loaf to be *coupé en deux* (cut in two) or, for a small fee, sliced.

Along with bread, bakeries usually sell croissants, brioches, *pains au chocolat* and so on – baked goods that are lumped together under the term *viennoiserie*.

and light meals (58FF to 84FF), while the more elaborate **Restaurant Véro Dodat** (☎ 01 45 08 92 86) at No 19 has entrées/main courses/desserts for 25/85/35FF and a decent *menu* at 115FF. In Galerie Colbert (Map 6), **Le Grand Colbert** (☎ 01 42 86 87 88), which can also be entered from 2-4 rue Vivienne, 2e, has lots of atmosphere and a *menu* at 160FF. At No 57 in passage des Panoramas (Map 3), **L'Arbre à Cannelle** (☎ 01 43 31 68 31) is a lovely tearoom with *tartes salées* (savoury pies; 41FF to 44FF), salads (41FF to 58FF) and scrumptious, original 19th-century décor.

French

The 1er and 4e have a diverse selection of French eating establishments.

L'Amazonial (☎ 01 42 33 53 13, 3 rue Sainte Opportune, 1er, metro Châtelet). The food at this predominantly gay restaurant is nothing to write home about, but the *formules* (fixed-price meals with a choice of courses) are only 68FF (lunch) and, at night, 85FF and 129FF. It's open noon to 1 or 1.30 am daily. Weekend brunch is from noon to 6 pm.

Café Marly (☎ 01 46 26 06 60, cour Napoléon, 93 rue de Rivoli, 1er, metro Palais Royal-Musée du Louvre). Nibbling and sipping under the colonnades of the Louvre, overlooking the glowing pyramid on a warm spring evening... well, it ain't gonna get much better than this. The Marly serves contemporary French fare, tending towards white meat, fish and salad, with a great fruit salad to finish. It's open 11 am to 1 am daily.

Aux Crus de Bourgogne (☎ 01 42 33 48 24, 3 rue de Bachaumont, 2e, metro Les Halles or Sentier). This excellent bistro on a pedestrian street serves great seafood and has a 130FF *menu* (expect to pay 200FF à la carte). It's open for lunch and dinner till 11.30 pm weekdays only.

L'Épi d'Or (☎ 01 42 36 38 12, 25 rue Jean-Jacques Rousseau, 1er, metro Louvre-Rivoli). This oh-so-Parisian bistro east of Les Halles serves classic, well prepared dishes such as *gigot d'agneau* (leg of lamb) cooked for seven hours to a surprisingly well-heeled crowd.

euro currency converter €1 = 6.56FF

There's a *menu* for 105FF. It's open for lunch and dinner Monday to Friday and on Saturday evening.

Le Grand Véfour (☎ *01 42 96 56 27, 17 rue de Beaujolais, 1er, metro Pyramides*). This 18th-century jewellery box of a restaurant on the northern edge of the Jardin du Palais Royal has been a dining favourite of the Paris elite since 1784. And chef Guy Martin's traditional French and Savoyard creations are so close to perfection that we suspect heaven will be somewhat disappointing. Count on spending from 800FF per person for dinner. A lunch *menu* is available for 390FF. It's open for lunch and dinner to 10.15 pm weekdays only.

Le Monde à L'Envers (☎ *01 40 26 13 91, 35 rue Tiquetonne, 2e, metro Étienne Marcel*). Another gay place, but one that takes its food more seriously, the 'World Upside Down' has a good-value three-course *menu* for 140FF. It's open for lunch and dinner till midnight Tuesday to Sunday.

Le Petit Mâchon (☎ *01 42 60 08 06, 158 rue Saint Honoré, 1er, metro Palais Royal-Musée du Louvre*). This bistro has Lyons-inspired specialities, with starters from 39FF to 85FF, main

courses from 68FF to 118FF, and a *menu* fo 98FF. It's open for lunch and dinner to 11 pi Tuesday to Sunday.

Willi's Wine Bar (☎ *01 42 61 05 09, 13 rue de Petits Champs, 1er, metro Bourse*). Willi's is civilised yet convivial wine bar run by two Britis expats who introduced the wine-bar concept t Paris in the mid-1980s. The lunch *menu* is 158FI dinner is 195FF. À la carte starters average 65FI main courses 95FF and desserts 45FF. It's ope noon to 11 pm Monday to Saturday.

Asian

Japanese businesspeople in search of rea sushi and *soba* flock to rue Sainte Anne an other streets of Paris' Japantown, which i just west of the Jardin du Palais Roya There are also some good-value restaurant serving other Asian cuisine.

Higuma (☎ *01 47 03 38 59, 32 bis rue Saint Anne, 1er, metro Pyramides*). Stepping into thi place is like ducking into a corner noodle-sho in Tokyo. A meal-sized bowl of soup noodle costs 40FF to 48FF and there are *menus* fo 63FF to 70FF. It's open 11.30 am to 10 pr daily.

La Maison Savoureuse (*Map 3,* ☎ *01 42 60 0. 22, 62 rue Sainte Anne, 2e, metro Quatre Sep tembre*). This cheap and cheerful little plac serves excellent-value Vietnamese food at th table (lunch/dinner *menus* from 37/46FF tc 62FF) or you can take your nems (10FF) anc vermicelli noodles to square Louvois, a pretty little park to the south-east, for a picnic.

Other Cuisines

This part of Paris is a fast-food lover's paradise, with a variety of chain outlets close to the Centre Pompidou and Les Halles.

Joe Allen (☎ *01 42 36 70 13, 30 rue Pierre Lescot, 1er, metro Étienne Marcel*). A friendly American bar-restaurant with a great atmosphere and a good selection of Californian wines Joe Allen's has two/three course *menus* for 112/140FF and Sunday brunch for 90FF to 105FF. It's open noon to 1.30 am daily.

Le Loup Blanc (☎ *01 40 13 08 35, 42 rue Tiquetonne, 2e, metro Étienne Marcel*). This place does some relatively pricey but decent fusion main courses, such as Thai-style prawns and squid with anise (65FF to 98FF). It's open 7.30 pm to midnight Monday to Thursday, to 12.30 am on Friday, to 1 am on Saturday and 11 am to 4.30 pm on Sunday.

CHRISTOPHER GROENHOUT

Café life – and where better to watch the world go by than outside the Louvre?

Self-Catering

There are a number of options along ave de
l'Opéra and rue de Richelieu, as well as
around Forum des Halles, including a
*Monoprix supermarket (21 ave de l'Opéra,
1e)*, open 9 am to 10 pm weekdays, and to
9 pm on Saturday; a *Franprix supermarket
(35 rue Berger, 1er)*, open 8.30 am to 8 pm
Monday to Saturday; and an *Ed l'Épicier
supermarket (Map 7, 80 rue de Rivoli, 4e)*,
open 9 am to 8 pm Monday to Saturday.
Fine food shops can be found on rue de
Richelieu, 1er, including a *fromagerie* at
No 38 (open Tuesday to Saturday) and
Évrard, a *traiteur* (delicatessen) across the
street at No 41 (open to 7.30 pm weekdays).

MARAIS (Maps 6 & 7)

The Marais, filled with small restaurants
of every imaginable type, is one of Paris'
premier neighbourhoods for eating out.
Pretty little place du Marché Sainte Cath-
rine is surrounded by small restaurants,
some with outside seating.

French

The French places in this area tend to be
small and intimate.

*Amadéo (Map 7, ☎ 01 48 87 01 02, 19 rue
François Miron, 4e, metro Saint Paul or Hôtel
de Ville)*. This chic Mozart-mad restaurant is
decidedly gay, although straight diners are very
welcome. The food is stylish and delicious
modern French with entrées/main courses/
desserts at 55/105/45FF, lunch *menus* at 75FF
and 95FF and an evening *menu* at 185FF
(110FF on Tuesday evening, including a kir). A
highlight is the Thursday *dîner lyrique* with a
live opera or operetta performance with a *menu*
at 285FF. It opens for lunch Tuesday to Friday
and for dinner Monday to Saturday till 11 pm.

*Au Bascou (Map 6, ☎ 01 42 72 69 25, 38 rue
Réaumur, 3e, metro Arts et Métiers)*. This popular eatery serves Basque classics such as
pipérade (peppers, onions, tomatoes and ham
cooked with scrambled eggs), *ttoro* (Basque
bouillabaisse) and Bayonne ham in all its
guises. The 90FF lunch *menu* is good value; expect to pay about 180FF at dinner. It's open for
lunch weekdays and for dinner until 10.30 pm
Monday to Saturday.

*Chez Jenny (Map 6, ☎ 01 42 74 75 75, 39 blvd
du Temple, 3e, metro République)*. We suspect

that most people come to this cavernous 1930s-
style brasserie (part of the Flo chain of restaurants) to admire the stunning marquetry of
Alsatian scenes on the first floor, but the *choucroute garnie* (sauerkraut cooked in wine and
served with assorted prepared meats) for 92FF
is gargantuan and quite good. It's open 11.30 am
to 1 pm daily.

*Le Petit Picard (Map 7, ☎ 01 42 78 54 03, 42 rue
Sainte Croix de la Bretonnerie, 4e, metro Hôtel
de Ville)*. This popular restaurant serves very
traditional French cuisine, with *menus* at 64FF
(lunch) and 89FF; there's also a *menu* of Pic-
ardy specialities for 129FF. It's open for lunch
weekdays and for dinner Tuesday to Sunday.

*Robert et Louise (Map 7, ☎ 01 42 78 55 89, 64
rue Vieille du Temple, 3e, metro Saint Sébastien
Froissart)*. This 'country inn' – complete with
red gingham curtains – offers delightful, un-
fussy and inexpensive French food prepared by
a husband-and-wife team, including *côte de
bœuf* cooked on an open fire (200FF for two).
Starters are 20FF to 60FF, main courses 70FF to
120FF, with a plat du jour at 80FF. It's open for
lunch weekdays and for dinner till 10 pm Monday to Saturday.

*Le Trumilou (Map 7, ☎ 01 42 77 63 98, 84 quai
de l'Hôtel de Ville, 4e, metro Hôtel de Ville)*. If
you're looking for an authentic, *very* inexpensive French meal, you won't do better than this
Parisian institution, which has been here for
over a century. *Menus* are 80FF and 98FF, and
it's open for lunch and dinner to 11 pm daily (to
10.30 pm on Sunday).

*Le Valet du Carreau (Map 6, ☎ 01 42 72 72 60,
2 rue Dupetit Thouars, 3e, metro Temple or
République)*. While this restaurant justifiably attracts its diners with such dishes as charlotte of
salmon and duck *galette*, the main draw here is
the wonderful terrace under the chestnut trees
facing the old Carreau du Temple market. The
lunch formule is 75FF, the dinner *menu* 180FF.
Entrées are between 45FF and 58FF and main
courses from 78FF to 102FF; expect to pay
180FF to 200FF à la carte. It's open for lunch
weekdays and for dinner to 10.30 pm Monday
to Saturday.

*Vins des Pyrénées (Map 7, ☎ 01 42 72 64 94, 25
rue Beautreillis, 4e, metro Bastille)*. In a former
wine warehouse a couple of doors down from
where Jim Morrison of the Doors died in 1971
(No 17-19), this bistro is a good place to splurge
on a French meal, with starters from 35FF to
60FF and main courses from around 70FF to
110FF; count on spending about 170FF. It's
open for lunch daily and for dinner to 11.30 pm
Monday to Saturday.

North African & Middle Eastern

The Marais boasts two of Paris' top *restaurants maghrébins*.

404 (*Map 6, ☎ 01 42 74 57 81, 69 rue des Gravilliers, 3e, metro Arts et Métiers*). The upbeat 404, as comfortable a Maghrebi caravanserai as you'll find in Paris, has excellent couscous and tajine (a meat and vegetable stew cooked in a domed earthenware pot) from 85FF to 130FF. It also has excellent grills from 98FF to 135FF, aniseed bread and a lunch *menu* at 89FF. The weekend *brunch berbère* (Berber brunch; 120FF) is available noon to 4 pm. The 404 opens for lunch/brunch and dinner till midnight daily.

Chez Omar (*Map 6, ☎ 01 42 72 36 26, 47 rue de Bretagne, 3e, metro Arts et Métiers*). Long a favourite of show biz and fashion types, this is another excellent choice for couscous (65FF to 120FF) and *pastillas* (from 55FF). It opens for lunch Monday to Saturday and for dinner till midnight daily.

Jewish & Kosher

The kosher and kosher-style restaurants along rue des Rosiers serve specialities from North Africa, Central Europe and Israel. Many are closed on Friday evening, Saturday and Jewish holidays. Takeaway falafel and *shwarma* (kebabs) are available at several places along the street.

Chez Hanna (*Map 7, ☎ 01 42 78 23 09, 54 rue des Rosiers, 4e, metro Saint Paul*). Israeli dishes, including the *assiette royale* (a plate of seven salads and meze; 60FF), are served 11 am to 2 am daily.

Chez Marianne (*Map 7, ☎ 01 42 72 18 86, 2 rue des Hospitalières Saint Gervais, 4e, metro Saint Paul*). This place is a Sephardic alternative to the Ashkenazi Jo Goldenberg (see later in this section). Plates with four/five/six different meze (eg, falafel, hummus) and purées of eggplant, chickpeas and so on cost 65/75/85FF; a *plat dégustation* (sampling platter) is 115FF. The window of the adjoining deli dispenses killer takeaway falafel sandwiches for 25FF. Chez Marianne opens 11 am till midnight daily.

Hammam Café (*Map 7, ☎ 01 42 78 04 45, 4 rue des Rosiers, 4e, metro Saint Paul*). Positively the grooviest strictly kosher place we've ever eaten in (and our in-laws have dragged us to quite a few over the years), the Hammam Café is bright and airy, with the original Art Nouveau mosaics of an old Turkish bar, and designer-furnished. Dishes include kosher pizzas (45FF to 98FF), *gratins* (45FF to 65FF) and galette (from 29FF). It's open for lunch Sunday to Friday and for dinner till midnight daily except Friday (to 2 am on Saturday).

Jo Goldenberg (*Map 7, ☎ 01 48 87 20 16, 7 rue des Rosiers, 4e, metro Saint Paul*). Founded in 1920, this kosher-style deli/restaurant is Paris' most famous Jewish eatery. The mixed starter (32FF) and apple strudel (30FF) are excellent but the plats du jour (79FF to 89FF) don't measure up to even a generic New York deli. The restaurant opens noon till midnight daily.

Pitchi Poï (*Map 7, ☎ 01 42 77 46 15, 7 place du Marché Sainte Catherine, 4e, metro Saint Paul*). This Eastern European Jewish restaurant beamed down onto a picturesque little square on the edge of the Marais will warm the cockles with its trademark *tchoulent* (cholent; slowly simmered duck with vegetables), *datcha* (smoked salmon served with a baked-potato cream) and chopped chicken liver. There's a *menu* for 119FF. It's open for lunch and dinner to 11 pm daily.

Vegetarian

The Marais is one of the few neighbourhoods in Paris actually to offer a choice of meatless restaurants.

Aquarius (*Map 7, ☎ 01 48 87 48 71, 54 rue Sainte Croix de la Bretonnerie, 4e, metro Rambuteau*). The calming atmosphere of this healthy restaurant, which has been around since the days of *Hair* and the 'Age of Aquarius' (1974), is perfect if you're in the mood for something light and green. The two-course lunch *menu* is 64FF; at dinner it costs 95FF for three courses. It's open noon to 10.15 pm Monday to Saturday.

Piccolo Teatro (*Map 7, ☎ 01 42 72 17 79, 6 rue des Écouffes, 4e, metro Saint Paul*). The menus at this intimate place with stone walls, a beamed ceiling and cosy little tables cost 63FF and 85FF at lunch and 90FF and 125FF at dinner; the tasty *assiette végétarienne* (vegetarian plate) is 70FF. It's open for lunch and dinner Tuesday to Sunday.

Other Cuisines

The Marais has a good selection of ethnic places. If you're looking for authentic Chinese food but can't be bothered going all the way to Chinatown in the 13e or Belleville in the 20e, check out any of the small *noodle shops and restaurants* along rue Au Maire, 3e (Map 6, metro Arts et Métiers), which is south-east of the new Musée des Arts et Métiers.

Caves Saint Gilles *(Map 7, ☎ 01 48 87 22 62, 4 rue Saint Gilles, 3e, metro Chemin Vert).* This trendy Spanish wine bar north-east of place des Vosges is the best place on the Right Bank for tapas (82FF for a platter), paella (at the weekend; 102FF) and sangria (130FF for 1L). The red, upholstered benches are always full of diners, and it's open for lunch and dinner till midnight daily.

L'Enoteca *(Map 7, ☎ 01 42 78 91 44, 25 rue Charles V, 4e, metro Pont Marie).* This attractive place in the historic Village Saint Paul quarter serves *haute cuisine à l'italienne,* and there's an excellent list of Italian wines by the glass (20FF to 48FF). The weekday lunch *menus* are good value at 75FF and 100FF; the plat du jour is around 60FF. Expect to pay from 160FF à la carte.

Minh Chau *(Map 7, ☎ 01 42 71 13 30, 10 rue de la Verrerie, 4e, metro Hôtel de Ville).* For a mere 26FF to 32FF you can enjoy tasty main dishes (grilled chicken with lemon grass, roast duck) at this tiny but welcoming Vietnamese place in the heart of the Marais. It opens for lunch and dinner till 11 pm Monday to Saturday.

La Perla *(Map 7, ☎ 01 42 77 59 40, 26 rue François Miron, 4e, metro Saint Paul or Hôtel de Ville).* A favourite with younger Parisians, this Californian-style Mexican bar-restaurant serves guacamole (35FF), *nachos* (31FF to 41FF) and burritos (from 48FF). It's open for lunch and dinner to 11 pm weekdays and non-stop from noon to 11 pm at the weekend.

Thanksgiving *(Map 7, ☎ 01 42 77 68 28, 20 rue Saint Paul, 4e, metro Saint Paul).* OK, you didn't come all the way to Paris for *jumbalaya,* gumbo and other Cajun dishes, but Thanksgiving gives you the option. *Menus* are 89FF (lunch), 148FF and 200FF. It's open for lunch Tuesday to Sunday and for dinner to 10.30 or 11 pm Tuesday to Saturday.

Self-Catering

There are several *food shops* and *Asian delicatessens* on the odd-numbered side of rue Saint Antoine, 4e (Map 7), between the *Monoprix supermarket* at No 71 (open 9 am to 9 pm Monday to Saturday) and the *Supermarché G20* at No 115 (open 9 am to 8.30 pm Monday to Saturday). There's a *Franprix supermarket* at No 135 on the same street (open 8.30 am to 7.45 pm Monday to Saturday, and 9 am to 12.45 pm on

Ma Bourgogne on the gorgeous place des Vosges – a wonderful place for a leisurely breakfast

Sunday). **Flo Prestige** (Map 7, ☎ 01 53 01 91 91, 10 rue Saint Antoine, 4e, metro Bastille), a branch of the famous traiteur chain at the corner of rue des Tournelles, has picnic supplies and some of the most delectable pastries in Paris (open 8 am to 11 pm daily). You'll also find a **Franprix** (Map 6, 49 rue de Bretagne, 3e, metro Arts et Métiers) in the northern Marais (open 9 am to 8.30 pm Tuesday to Saturday, and to 1.30 pm on Sunday).

ÎLE SAINT LOUIS (Maps 6 & 7)
Famed for its ice cream as much as anything else, the Île Saint Louis is generally an expensive place to eat. It's best suited to those looking for a light snack or ingredients for lunch beside the Seine. Rue Saint Louis en l'Île, 4e (Map 6, metro Pont Marie), has several *salons de thé* (tearooms), including the lovely **La Charlotte en Île** (Map 6, ☎ 01 43 54 25 83, metro

Paris' finest ice cream? Decide for yourself at Berthillon, Île Saint Louis.

GREG ELMS

Pont Marie) at No 24, and there are lots of restaurants both on and just off this street.

French
Berthillon (Map 6, ☎ 01 43 54 31 61, 31 rue Saint Louis en l'Île, 4e, metro Pont Marie). This *glacier* is reputed to have Paris' most delicious ice cream. While the fruit flavours are justifiably renowned, the chocolate, coffee, *marron glacés* (candied chestnuts), Agenaise (Armagnac and prunes) and *nougat au miel* (honey nougat) are much richer. The takeaway counter opens 10 am to 8 pm Wednesday to Sunday with one/two/three small scoops costing 9/16/20FF. The *salon dégustation* (sit-down area) opens 1 pm (2 pm at the weekend) to 8 pm on the same days.

Brasserie de l'Isle Saint Louis (Map 7, ☎ 01 43 54 02 59, 55 quai de Bourbon, 4e, metro Pont Marie). Founded in 1870, this spectacularly situated brasserie features choucroute garnie and other Alsatian dishes for under 100FF (average total: 150FF), but you can enjoy the location by ordering coffee/beer (7/15FF at the bar, 14/20FF at a table or on the terrace). It opens 11.30 am to 1 am Thursday to Tuesday (from 6 pm on Thursday).

Les Fous de l'Île (Map 6, ☎ 01 43 25 76 67, 33 rue des Deux Ponts, 4e, metro Pont Marie). This friendly and down-to-earth establishment has a lunch *menu* for 78FF and serves à la carte meals in the evening for between 120FF and 150FF per person. It's open noon to 11 pm Tuesday to Friday, from 3 pm on Saturday and noon to 7 pm on Sunday.

Self-Catering
Along rue Saint Louis en l'Île there are a number of **fromageries** and **groceries** (usually closed on Sunday afternoon and Monday). There are more **food shops** on rue des Deux Ponts.

LATIN QUARTER (Maps 5 & 6)
Rue Mouffetard, 5e (Map 5, metro Place Monge or Censier Daubenton), is filled with scores of places to eat. It's especially popular with students, in part because of the number of stands selling baguette sandwiches, *panini* (Italian toasted bread with fillings) and crepes.

Avoid rue de la Huchette (Map 6; see the boxed text 'La Ruelle de la Bactérie') unless you're after shwarma, available at several places, including Nos 14 and 17.

French

he Latin Quarter has a good selection of French places both reasonably priced and otherwise.

es Bouchons de François Clerc (Map 6, ☎ 01 43 54 15 34, 12 rue de l'Hôtel Colbert, 5e, metro Maubert Mutualité). Along with excellently prepared French dishes (137FF for a two-course formule at lunch including wine, 227FF for four courses at dinner), the draws here are the wonderful wines sold at almost wholesale prices and an excellent cheese selection. It's open for lunch weekdays and for dinner Monday to Saturday.

hez Léna et Mimille (Map 5, ☎ 01 47 07 72 47, 32 rue Tournefort, 5e, metro Censier Daubenton). The two/three-course lunch *menus* are 98/138FF and the dinner one is 198FF at this cosy but elegant French restaurant with live piano music most nights. The fabulous terrace overlooks a lovely little park. It opens for lunch and dinner to 11 pm daily (in winter it opens for lunch weekdays and for dinner Monday to Saturday).

'Étoile du Berger (Map 5, ☎ 01 43 26 38 87, 42 rue de la Montagne Sainte Geneviève, 5e, metro Maubert Mutualité). This Savoyard restaurant, decorated like a mountain chalet, specialises in *raclette* and fondue (85FF to 105FF). There are *menus* for 89FF and 120FF. It's open for lunch on Saturday and Sunday and for dinner till midnight daily.

e Navigator (Map 6, ☎ 01 43 54 35 86, 63 rue Galande, 5e, metro Maubert Mutualité). This restaurant serves very traditional French cuisine at lunch and dinner to 11 pm Tuesday to Saturday. Four *menus* are available (120FF to 220FF).

'erraudin (Map 5, ☎ 01 46 33 15 75, 157 rue Saint Jacques, 5e, metro Luxembourg). If you fancy classics such as *bœuf bourguignon, gigot d'agneau* or *confit de canard* (all 59FF), try this reasonably priced traditional French restaurant, which hasn't changed much since the late 19th century. At lunch time there's a 65FF *menu* and 25cL of wine is 10FF. It's open for lunch weekdays and for dinner to 10.15 pm Monday to Saturday.

e Vigneron (Map 5, ☎ 01 47 07 29 99, 18-20 rue du Pot de Fer, 5e, metro Place Monge). Arguably the best French restaurant in the Mouffetard quarter, the 'Wine Grower' specialises in south-west cuisine, with lunch *menus* at 60FF and 80FF and dinner ones for 118FF and 158FF. À la carte prices range from 65FF to 110FF for starters, 95FF to 125FF for main dishes, and

La Ruelle de la Bactérie

One of Paris' largest concentrations of ethnic restaurants is squeezed into a labyrinth of narrow streets in the 5e across the Seine from Notre Dame. The Greek, North African and Middle Eastern restaurants between rue Saint Jacques, blvd Saint Germain and blvd Saint Michel attract mainly foreign tourists, who appear to be unaware that some people refer to rue de la Huchette and nearby streets such as rue Saint Séverin and rue de la Harpe as 'Bacteria Alley'. To add insult to injury, many of the poor souls who eat here are under the impression that this little maze is the famous Latin Quarter. You'll be better off looking for ethnic food elsewhere: blvd de Belleville in the 20e for Middle Eastern; nearby rue de Belleville in the 19e for Asian (especially Thai and Vietnamese); and Chinatown in the 13e for Chinese, especially ave de Choisy, ave d'Ivry and rue Baudricourt.

55FF to 75FF for desserts. It opens for lunch and dinner till midnight daily.

Les Vignes du Panthéon (Map 5, ☎ 01 43 54 80 81, 4 rue des Fossés Saint Jacques, 5e, metro Luxembourg). With the dearth of quality French restaurants in the Panthéon quarter, this restaurant owned and managed by a husband-and-wife team stands out for its south-west-inspired food (starters around 60FF, main courses just over 100FF) and choice of wines, but service is chaotic at best. *Menus* are 85/160FF at lunch/dinner. It's open for lunch and dinner weekdays only.

North African & Middle Eastern

The Latin Quarter is a good area for couscous and tajines as well as meze. The Mosquée de Paris complex *(Map 5, place du Puits de l'Ermite, 5e, metro Censier Daubenton or Place Monge)*, to the east of the Latin Quarter, includes a North African-style *salon de thé*, open 9 am to 11.30 pm daily, and a *restaurant (☎ 01 43 31 38 20)*, with excellent couscous and tajines (60FF to 110FF), open for lunch and dinner to 10.30 pm daily. Both can be entered from 39 rue Geoffroy Saint Hilaire.

Al Dar (Map 6, ☎ 01 43 25 17 15, 8-10 rue Frédéric Sauton, 5e, metro Maubert Mutualité).

PLACES TO EAT

This Lebanese restaurant has lunch *menus* for 89FF and 150FF; à la carte main courses are 64FF to 75FF and the plat du jour is 70FF. It's open for lunch and dinner till midnight daily. The excellent deli section, with little pizzas (15FF), sandwiches (from 22FF) and stuffed grapevine leaves (5FF each), opens 7 am to midnight daily.

Founti Agadir *(Map 5, ☎ 01 43 37 85 10, 117 rue Monge, 5e, metro Censier Daubenton)*. This Moroccan restaurant has some of the best cous-cous and tajines (75FF to 89FF) and pastillas (40FF to 42FF) on the Left Bank and there are lunch *menus* for 75FF and 89FF. It's open for lunch and dinner to 11 pm Tuesday to Sunday.

Koutchi *(Map 5, ☎ 01 44 07 20 56, 40 rue du Cardinal Lemoine, 5e, metro Cardinal Lemoine)*. The décor of this Afghan restaurant is reminiscent of a Central Asian caravanserai. Specialities include Afghan salads (25FF to 30FF), meat dishes (65FF to 85FF) and desserts (25FF to 30FF). The lunch-time *menu* costs 55FI, the evening one 98FF. It's open for lunch weekdays and for dinner to 11 pm Monday to Saturday.

Asian

There's an abundance of Asian restaurants in the Latin Quarter.

Chez Maï *(Map 6, ☎ 01 43 54 05 33, 65 rue Galande, 5e, metro Maubert Mutualité)*. This hole-in-the-wall Vietnamese place straight out of a Saigon back lane (with cook to match) has main courses (including excellent shrimp ones) for 25FF to 30FF; soup is 20FF. It's open for lunch and dinner to 11 pm daily.

Tashi Delek *(Map 5, ☎ 01 43 26 55 55, 4 rue des Fossés Saint Jacques, 5e, metro Luxembourg)*. Paris abounds in Tibetan restaurants – 'that would be with yak butter, monsieur?' – and while the food at this intimate little place (whose name approximates *tashi dele*, 'bonjour' in Tibetan) is not gourmet it's cheap, with a lunch *menu* at 65FF and a dinner one at 105FF, including 25cL of wine. There are some seven vegetarian choices (37FF to 51FF). It opens for lunch and dinner to 11 pm Monday to Saturday.

Tao *(Map 5, ☎ 01 43 26 75 92, 248 rue Saint Jacques, 5e, metro Luxembourg)*. Decidedly upmarket with Zen-ish décor, Tao serves some of the best Vietnamese cuisine in the Latin Quarter; try the warm beef noodle salad or grilled minced prawns. Dishes are in the 60FF to 95FF range. It opens for lunch Monday to Saturday and for dinner till 11 pm on Monday and Wednesday to Saturday.

Vegetarian

The choice for vegetarians is not as gre here as in the Marais, but there are a coup of decent options.

Jardin des Pâtes *(Map 5, ☎ 01 43 31 50 71, 4 ru Lacépède, 5e, metro Cardinal Lemoine)*. O the cosy 'Garden of Pastas' is not strictly veg tarian but it's 100% *bio* (organic) and it has many types of noodle as you care to nam (wholemeal, buckwheat, chestnut and so o from 39FF to 77FF and fresh vegetable jui from 17FF to 24FF. It's open for lunch and di ner to 11 pm daily. A branch of **Jardin des Pât** *(Map 1, ☎ 01 45 35 93 67, 33 blvd Arago, 13 metro Les Gobelins)* keeps the same hours Mo day to Saturday.

Le Petit Légume *(Map 5, ☎ 01 40 46 06 8 36 rue des Boulangers, 5e, metro Cardin Lemoine)*. This tiny place is a great choice f homemade vegetarian fare, with *menus* at 50F 64FF and 75FF. It's open for lunch and dinn to 10 pm Monday to Saturday.

Other Cuisines

The Chipper *(Map 5, ☎ 01 43 26 05 55, 14 ru Thouin, 5e, metro Place Monge)*. Shame c you! But, hey, we all need a cheap fix of chip battered cod and mushy peas from time to tim – even in Paris – and this is the real McCo Trust us. It's open till midnight daily.

Fogon Saint Julien *(Map 6, ☎ 01 43 54 31 3. 10 rue Saint Julien le Pauvre, 5e, metro Sai. Michel)*. The real treat at this relatively price (average 220FF) Spanish restaurant is the seve authentic paellas, including vegetable, rabb chicken and seafood. But go for the *arroz negr* black with squid ink and hiding shrimps an chunks of fish. *Menus* cost 90FF and 120FF lunch and 175FF at dinner. It's open for lunc and dinner to 2 am Monday to Saturday.

Machu Picchu *(Map 5, ☎ 01 43 26 13 13, 9 ru Royer Collard, 5e, metro Luxembourg)*. Doe Peruvian food just mean guinea-pig fricassee Apparently not always and this small plac serves up excellent main grilled meat an seafood dishes from 58FF to 88FF and has bargain-basement 48FF lunch *menu*. It's ope for lunch weekdays and for dinner to 11 p Monday to Saturday.

Tea Caddy *(Map 6, ☎ 01 43 54 15 56, 14 ru Saint Julien le Pauvre, 5e, metro Saint Michel* A fine place to enjoy an English-style tea (fro 32FF) in the shadow of Notre Dame; light mea run from 37FF to 49FF and salads from 30FF t 55FF. It's open noon to 7 pm daily.

elf-Catering

lace Maubert, 5e (Map 6), is transformed
ito a lively *food market* three mornings a
veek (see the special section 'The Markets
f Paris' after this chapter). *Food shops* are
lso found here, including the *fromagerie
Crémerie des Carmes* (☎ 01 43 54 50 93,
'7 ter blvd Saint Germain, 5e, metro
Maubert Mutualité)*.

There's a particularly lively *food market*
long rue Mouffetard; again see the special
ection 'The Markets of Paris' after this
hapter. The nearby *Franprix supermarket
Map 5, 82 rue Mouffetard, 5e, metro Cen-
ier Daubenton or Place Monge)* opens
am to 8 pm Monday to Saturday, and to
pm on Sunday.

The smaller *food market* on place
Monge, 5e (Map 5, metro Place Monge),
ppens from about 7 am to 1 pm on Wednes-
lay, Friday and Sunday. Nearby there's a
*hopi supermarket (Map 5, 34 rue Monge,
5e, metro Place Monge)* open 8.30 am to
pm Monday to Saturday and an *Ed
'Épicier (Map 5, 37 rue Lacépède, 5e)*
ppen 9 am to 7.30 pm Monday to Saturday.

For picnic fare to take to the Jardin du
Luxembourg, try the popular hole-in-the-
wall *Douce France (Map 5, 7 rue Royer
Collard, 5e, metro Luxembourg)*, where the
unch-time line of students is testament to
he quality of the sandwiches (13.50FF) and
fruit juices (6FF). It's open 11 am to 4 pm
weekdays.

**Jardin des Plantes: one of central Paris' many
excellent picnic spots**

SAINT GERMAIN & ODÉON (Map 6)

Rue Saint André des Arts (metro Saint
Michel or Odéon) is lined with restaurants,
including a few down the covered passage
between Nos 59 and 61. There are lots of
places between the Église Saint Sulpice and
the Église Saint Germain des Prés, especially along rue des Canettes, rue Princesse
and rue Guisarde. Carrefour de l'Odéon
(metro Odéon) has a cluster of lively bars,
cafés and restaurants.

French

Place Saint Germain des Prés is home to
celebrated cafés such as Les Deux Magots
and Café de Flore (see Pubs, Bars & Cafés
in the Entertainment chapter) as well as an
equally celebrated brasserie.

Brasserie Lipp (☎ 01 45 48 53 91, 151 blvd Saint
  Germain, 6e, metro Saint Germain des Prés).
  Politicians rub shoulders with intellectuals and
  editors while waiters in dinner jackets serve
  pricey à la carte dishes (choucroute garnie,
  102FF; plats du jour, 115FF to 120FF) at this
  old-time, wood-panelled café-brasserie. The
  menu touristique costs 196FF (including 25cL
  of wine). Many people make a big fuss about
  sitting downstairs rather than upstairs, which
  is the nonsmoking section and considered
  nowheresville. It's open continuously 11.30 am
  to 1 am daily.
Cour de Rohan (☎ 01 43 25 79 67, 59-61 rue
  Saint André des Arts, 6e, metro Mabillon).
  Local writers and publishers seek peace, quiet
  and homemade scones in this slightly faded tearoom, with its assortment of exquisite furniture
  and *objets d'art*. Mixed salads and daily spe-
  cials complement the aromatic teas, while three
  chefs keep the dessert cart piled with delicacies.
  It's open noon to 7.30 pm weekdays, and to
  11 pm at the weekend.
Fish la Poissonnerie (☎ 01 43 54 34 69, 69 rue
  de Seine, 6e, metro Mabillon). This hybrid of a
  place run by a Kiwi and a Cuban-American has
  surely taken its cue from London, where restaurants serving simply prepared fish (eg, grilled
  tuna, 98FF here) with a variety of sauces are all
  the rage. It's housed in an old fishmonger's
  (that's the *poissonnerie* part); dig the wonderful
  old mosaic on the front. It's open for lunch and
  dinner to 11 pm Wednesday to Sunday.
Le Mâchon d'Henri (☎ 01 43 29 08 70, 8 rue
  Guisarde, 6e, metro Saint Sulpice). This very

JULIET COOMBE

PLACES TO EAT

Parisian bistro in a street awash with bars serves up Lyons-inspired dishes such as lentil salad, *rosette du mâconnais* (large pork slicing-sausage prepared with red wine) and *clafoutis* (fruit covered with a thick batter and baked until puffy). Starters are 35FF to 40FF, main courses 60FF to 80FF and desserts 35FF to 40FF. It's open for lunch and dinner until 11.30 pm daily.

Le Petit Zinc (☎ 01 42 61 20 60, 11 rue Saint Benoît, 6e, metro Saint Germain des Prés). This wonderful (and expensive, with entrées 48FF to 119FF and main courses 99FF to 170FF) bistro serves both traditional French cuisine and regional specialities from the south-west in true Art Nouveau splendour. There are *menus* at 148FF and 188FF. It's open noon to 2 am daily.

Polidor (☎ 01 43 26 95 34, 41 rue Monsieur le Prince, 6e, metro Odéon). A meal at this *crémerie-restaurant* is like a quick trip back to Victor Hugo's Paris – the restaurant and its décor date from 1845 – but everyone knows about it, and the place is pretty touristed. Still, *menus* of tasty, family-style French cuisine are available for 55FF (lunch) and 110FF. Specialities include *bœuf à la provençal* (60FF), *blanquette de veau* (veal in white sauce; 68FF) and the most famous *tarte Tatin* (caramelised apple pie; 25FF) in Paris. It's open for lunch and dinner till 12.30 am daily (to 11 pm on Sunday).

Vegetarian

Guen Maï (☎ 01 43 26 03 24, 2 bis rue de l'Abbaye, 6e, metro Saint Germain des Prés or Mabillon). Macrobiotic, totally organic plats du jour (64FF), soups (around 27FF) and main courses (50FF to 57FF) are available at this cosy place from 11.45 am to 3.30 pm Monday to Saturday.

Other Cuisines

The cuisines of southern Europe and Asia are well represented in the 6e.

Chez Albert (☎ 01 46 33 22 57, 43 rue Mazarine, 6e, metro Odéon). Authentic Portuguese food is not easy to come by in Paris despite the large Portuguese population, but this place has it in spades: *cataplana* (Algarve-style shellfish cooked with ham in a covered casserole), numerous *bacalhau* (salt-dried cod) dishes, prawns sautéed in lots of garlic and a good selection of Portuguese wines. *Menus* are 95FF for two courses till 8 pm and 135FF for three courses at night. It's open for lunch Tuesday to Saturday and for dinner till 11.30 pm Monday to Saturday.

BRENDA TURNNIDGE

Feel the angst: the Café de Flore has been an intellectual haunt since the days of Sartre et al.

Le Golfe de Naples (☎ 01 43 26 98 11, 5 rue de Montfaucon, 6e, metro Mabillon). Italian residents say this restaurant-pizzeria has the best pizza and homemade pasta in Paris, which is not generally celebrated for its Italian food (Parisians consider it lightweight). Pizzas range from 54FF to 61FF, and don't forget to try the *assiette napolitaine*, a plate of grilled fresh vegetables (85FF).

Indonesia (Map 5, ☎ 01 43 25 70 22, 12 rue de Vaugirard, 6e, metro Luxembourg). One of only two Indonesian restaurants in the whole city, this nonprofit cooperative has all the standards – from an elaborate, multicourse *rijsttafel* to *nasi goreng*, *rendang* and *gado-gado*. *Menus* (numbering six) are 49FF to 89FF at lunch, 79FF to 129FF at dinner. It opens for lunch and dinner to 11 pm daily.

Self-Catering

With the Jardin du Luxembourg nearby, this is the perfect area for a picnic lunch. There is a large cluster of *food shops* on rue de Seine and rue de Buci, 6e (metro Mabillon). The renovated and covered *Marché Saint*

Germain (rue Lobineau, 6e, metro Mabillon), just north of the eastern end of the Église Saint Germain des Prés, has a huge array of produce and prepared food.

Champion (79 rue de Seine, 6e, metro Mabillon). This supermarket opens 8.40 am to 9 pm Monday to Saturday. There's a superb fromagerie just next door.

Chez Jean-Mi (☎ 01 43 26 89 72, 10 rue de l'Ancienne Comédie, 6e, metro Odéon). This boulangerie (with a restaurant at the back) opens 24 hours a day, 365 days a year.

Monoprix (52 rue de Rennes, 6e, metro Saint Germain des Prés). This department store's supermarket, at the back of the basement level, opens 9 am to 10 pm Monday to Saturday.

CHAMPS-ÉLYSÉES (Map 2)

Few places along touristy ave des Champs-Élysées offer good value, but some of the restaurants in the surrounding areas are excellent.

French

Generally, you're unlikely to find cheap French eats in this area, but there are more than a few places offering excellent food.

L'Ardoise (☎ 01 42 96 28 18, 28 rue du Mont Thabor, 1er, metro Concorde or Tuileries). This little bistro has no menu as such (ardoise means 'blackboard', which is all there is), but who cares? The food – rabbit and hazelnut terrine, and beef fillet with morels, prepared dexterously by chef Pierre Jay (ex-Tour d'Argent) – is superb and the 175FF menu offers excellent value. It's open for lunch and dinner until 11.30 pm Tuesday to Sunday.

L'Étoile Verte (☎ 01 43 80 69 34, 13 rue Brey, 17e, metro Charles de Gaulle-Étoile). When one of us was a student in Paris (you know, back when the prehistoric Lascaux cave paintings in Périgord were still wet), this was the place for both Esperanto speakers (étoile verte means 'green star', which is their symbol) and students on a splurge, and it still feels like it did way back then. All the old classics remain – the onion soup, the snails, the rabbit – and there are menus for 74FF (available at lunch), 110FF (with 25cL of wine) and 155FF (with aperitif, wine and coffee). À la carte soups/entrées start at 35/60FF, main courses average 90FF. It's open for lunch weekdays and for dinner to 11 pm daily.

Ladurée (☎ 01 40 75 08 75, 75 ave des Champs Élysées, 8e, metro George V). The salons of this sumptuous belle époque tearoom (1862) are named after the mistresses of Napoleon III: Mathilde, Castiglione and Paeva. But it's difficult to imagine any of them being as luscious as the pastries Ladurée serves. Mixed salads and light lunches are available; the dinner menu is 195FF. It's open 7.30 am to 1 am daily.

Maison Prunier (☎ 01 44 17 35 85, 16 ave Victor Hugo, 16e, metro Charles de Gaulle-Étoile). This venerable restaurant, founded in 1925, is as famed for its Art Deco interior as for its exquisite fish and seafood dishes. First courses go for 90FF to 250FF, main courses 160FF to 280FF; count on 500FF a head. It's open for lunch Tuesday to Saturday and for dinner to 11 pm Monday to Saturday.

Other Cuisines

Man Ray (☎ 01 54 88 36 36, 34 rue Marbeuf, 8e, metro Franklin D Roosevelt). This is the restaurant that everyone has been talking (and talking and talking) about since the start of the new millennium, named after our main man Man Ray, the surrealist photographer. But being seen eating lacklustre Asian fusion food (even if it does involve knocking elbows with Leonardo DiCaprio) has been done to death – if you want a lot of form over little substance, go to London. Menus are 120FF and 140FF at lunch, 250FF and 350FF at dinner. It's open for lunch and dinner to 12.45 am daily.

Spoon, Food & Wine (☎ 01 40 76 34 44, 14 rue de Marignan, 8e, metro Franklin D Roosevelt). Three-star Michelin chef Alain Ducasse invites diners to mix and match their own main courses and sauces – grilled calamari, say, with a choice of satay, curry and Béarnaise sauces. Controversially (this is France, remember), the cellar features wines from the USA, Australia and other parts of Europe, with only a small proportion being French. SFW opens for lunch and dinner till midnight weekdays only.

Self-Catering

Place de la Madeleine, 8e (metro Madeleine), is the luxury food centre of one of the world's food capitals (see Food & Wine in the Shopping chapter). The delicacies on offer don't come cheap, but even travellers on a modest budget can turn a walk around La Madeleine into a gastronomic odyssey.

Lina's (☎ 01 40 15 94 95, 4 rue Cambon, 1er, metro Concorde). This branch of the six-outlet

MARTIN MOOS

Going alfresco on ave des Champs-Élysées

lunch chain has upmarket sandwiches in the 21FF to 47FF range and salads for 25FF to 35FF. There are also branches at 9 ave de l'Opéra, 1er (Map 6, ☎ 01 47 03 30 29, metro Pyramides), and at 5 & 7 rue Princess, 6e (Map 6, ☎ 01 43 25 55 55, metro Mabillon).

Monoprix (62 ave des Champs-Élysées, 8e, metro Franklin D Roosevelt). The large supermarket section in the basement opens 9 am to midnight Monday to Saturday.

GARE SAINT LAZARE & GRANDS BOULEVARDS (Map 3)
The neon-lit blvd Montmartre (metro Grands Boulevards or Richelieu Drouot) and nearby sections of rue du Faubourg Montmartre (neither of which are anywhere near the neighbourhood of Montmartre) form one of Paris' most animated café and dining districts.

French
This area has a couple of French restaurants that could (or should) be declared national monuments.

Restaurant Arthur (☎ 01 42 08 34 33, 25 rue du Faubourg Saint Martin, 10e, metro Strasbourg

Saint Denis). This old-fashioned wood-panelle bistro has simple dishes (*gigot d'agnear poêlon de champignons* and so on) and simpl prices to match, with two/three-course *men*u for 115/139FF. It's open for lunch weekday and for dinner Tuesday to Saturday.

Chartier (☎ 01 47 70 86 29, 7 rue du Faubour Montmartre, 9e, metro Grands Boulevards). real gem that is justifiably famous for its 33(seat *belle époque* dining room, virtually un altered since 1896. With starters from 9FF t 33FF, main courses from 34FF to 54FF and bottle of cider/wine for 14/20FF, you shoul spend no more than 85FF per person, thoug there are more elaborate *menus* for 74FF, 110F and 190FF. It opens for lunch and dinner t 10 pm daily. Reservations are not accepted, s expect a queue.

Julien (☎ 01 47 70 12 06, 16 rue du Faubour Saint Denis, 10e, metro Strasbourg Sair Denis). You wouldn't cross town for Julien food or the less-than-salubrious neighbour hood, but – *mon Dieu!* – the décor and the at mosphere: it's an Art Nouveau extravaganz perpetually in motion and a real step back i time. Three-course *menus* go for 138FF (afte 10 pm) and 189FF at dinner; both includ wine. It's open for lunch and dinner to 1.30 ar daily.

ewish & North African

here's a large selection of kosher Jewish nd North African restaurants on rue icher, rue Cadet and rue Geoffroy Marie, e, south of Cadet metro station.

es Ailes (☎ 01 47 70 62 53, 34 rue Richer, 9e, metro Cadet). Just next door to the Folies-Bergère (think of the convenience!), this kosher Tunisian place has superb couscous with meat or fish starting at about 100FF and a good selection of North African salads. It's open for lunch Sunday to Friday and for dinner till 11.30 pm Sunday to Thursday. Pre-ordered, pre-paid *shabbas* meals taken at the restaurant cost 250FF per person and are positive blowouts.

ally le Saharien (☎ 01 42 85 51 90, 36 rue Rodier, 9e, metro Saint Georges or Cadet). Wally's is a cut above most Maghrebi restaurants in Paris, offering couscous in its pure Saharan form – without stock or vegetables, just a finely cooked grain served with a delicious sauce. The rich Moorish coffee is a fitting finish. It's open for lunch and dinner to 10.30 pm Tuesday to Saturday.

)ther Cuisines

hez Haynes (☎ 01 48 78 40 63, 3 rue Clauzel, 9e, metro Saint Georges). This legendary and very funky African-American-run hang-out dishes up genuine shrimp gumbo, fried chicken, barbecued ribs and cornbread (75FF to 85FF). There's usually a lively crowd for the jazz sessions at 8 pm on Friday and Saturday. It's open for dinner to 12.30 am Tuesday to Saturday.

;ARE DU NORD & GARE DE 'EST (Map 3)

his area offers all types of food but most otably Indian and Pakistani, which can be lusive cuisines in Paris.

rench

here's a cluster of brasseries and bistros pposite the façade of Gare du Nord. hey're decent options for a first (or final) neal in the City of Light.

erminus Nord (☎ 01 42 85 05 15, 23 rue de Dunkerque, 10e, metro Gare du Nord). The copper bar, white tablecloths, brass fixtures and mirrored walls look much as they did when the Nord opened in 1925. Breakfast (39.50FF) is available 8 to 11 am daily, full meals are served continuously 11 am to 12.30 am. The 138FF

faim de nuit (night hunger) menu is available after 10 pm.

Other Cuisines

The tiny restaurants off blvd de Strasbourg, many open throughout the afternoon, serve the city's most authentic Indian and Pakistani food.

Paris-Dakar (☎ 01 42 08 16 64, 95 rue du Faubourg Saint Martin, 10e, metro Gare de l'Est). Specialities at this authentic but relatively pricey Senegalese restaurant include *assiette sénégalaise* (mixed starters; 38FF), *tiéboudienne* (rice, fish and vegetables; 99FF), *yassa* (chicken or fish marinated in lime juice and onion sauce; 79FF) and *maffé Cap Vert* (lamb sautéed in peanut sauce; 76FF). *Menus* cost 59FF (lunch only, including 25cL of wine) and 149FF to 199FF at dinner. It's open for lunch Tuesday to Thursday and at the weekend, for dinner till midnight Tuesday to Sunday.

Passage Brady (between 43 rue du Faubourg Saint Denis and 58 blvd de Strasbourg, 10e, metro Château d'Eau). This derelict covered *passage* (arcade) could easily be in Calcutta. Its incredibly cheap Indian, Pakistani and Bangladeshi places offer among the best cheap lunches in Paris (meat curry, rice and a tiny salad from 30FF, chicken or lamb biryani for about 50FF); there are dinner *menus* for 49FF to 65FF. There are lots of places to choose from but the pick of the crop are *Pooja* (☎ 01 48 24 00 83) at No 91 and *Yasmin* (☎ 01 45 23 04 25) at Nos 71 to 73.

Passage du Prado (between 12 rue du Faubourg Saint Denis and 18-20 blvd Saint Denis, 10e, metro Strasbourg Saint Denis). This equally neglected passageway nearby has several ethnic cafés and small restaurants, including the Mauritian *Le Filao* (☎ 01 48 24 17 17).

Self-Catering

Rue du Faubourg Saint Denis, 10e (metro Strasbourg Saint Denis or Château d'Eau), which links blvd Saint Denis and blvd de Magenta, is one of the cheapest places in Paris to buy food, especially fruit and vegetables (shop Nos 18, 23 and 27 to 29). It has a distinctively Middle Eastern air, and quite a few of the groceries offer Turkish, North African and Subcontinental specialities. Many of the *food shops*, including the *fromagerie* at No 54, are open Tuesday to noon Sunday. The *Franprix supermarket* (7-9 rue des Petites

Écuries, 10e, metro Château d'Eau) opens 9 am to 7.50 pm Monday to Saturday as does the **Franprix** *(25 rue du Faubourg Saint Denis, 10e, metro Strasbourg Saint Denis)* to the south.

Farther north, you'll find **Marché Saint Quentin** *(metro Gare de l'Est)* – see the special section 'The Markets of Paris' after this chapter – and another **Franprix** *(57 blvd de Magenta, 10e, metro Gare de l'Est)*, which opens 9 am to 8 pm Monday to Saturday.

BASTILLE (Maps 5, 6 & 7)

The area around Bastille is chock-a-block with restaurants. Narrow, scruffy rue de Lappe, 11e (Maps 5 & 6), may not look like much during the day, but it's one of the most popular streets for cafés and nightlife in Paris and attracts a young, alternative crowd.

French

Traditional French food in all price ranges can be found in the Bastille area.

Le Bistrot du Dôme Bastille *(Map 7, ☎ 01 48 04 88 44, 2 rue de la Bastille, 4e, metro Bastille).* This superb restaurant, a distant cousin of **Le Dôme** (Map 4, metro Vavin) on blvd du Montparnasse, 14e, specialises in superbly prepared (and pricey) fish dishes. The blackboard menu has starters from 55FF to 80FF and main courses from 105FF to 130FF, so count on about 210FF each. Wines are all 99FF. It's open for lunch and dinner till 11.30 pm daily.

Bofinger *(Map 7, ☎ 01 42 72 87 82, 5-7 rue de la Bastille, 4e, metro Bastille).* This is reputedly the oldest brasserie in Paris (founded in 1864), with polished Art Nouveau brass, glass and mirrors throughout. Specialities include *choucroute à l'alsacienne* (86FF to 118FF) and seafood dishes (from 116FF). There are *menus* at 119FF, 178FF and 189FF (the last one includes a half-bottle of wine). It opens noon to 3 pm and 6.30 pm to 1 am weekdays and continuously from noon to 1 am at the weekend.

Chez Paul *(Map 5, ☎ 01 47 00 34 57, 13 rue de Charonne, 11e, metro Ledru Rollin).* This is a convivial and extremely popular bistro with traditional French main courses, handwritten on a yellowing menu, from 62FF to 95FF, so count on paying about 170FF for a meal. It's open for lunch and dinner to 12.30 am daily.

Crêpes Show *(Map 5, ☎ 01 47 00 36 46, 51 rue de Lappe, 11e, metro Ledru Rollin).* This un-

pretentious little restaurant specialises in swe crepes and savoury buckwheat galettes (18FF 45FF) and has *menus* at 43FF (lunch), 55FF ar 63FF. There are lots of vegetarian choices, i cluding salads from 39FF. It opens for lunc weekdays and for dinner to 1 or 2 am dai (closed on Sunday in winter).

L'Encrier *(Map 5, ☎ 01 44 68 08 16, 55 rue Tr versière, 12e, metro Ledru Rollin).* If you' looking for lunch south of Bastille, you won do better than the 'Inkwell', which serves a excellent-value, three-course lunch *menu* fo 65FF and dinner ones for 78FF and 108FF. It open for lunch weekdays and for dinner t 11 pm Monday to Saturday.

Les Galopins *(Map 5, ☎ 01 47 00 45 35, 24 ru des Taillandiers, 11e, metro Bastille).* This cu little neighbourhood bistro serves simple b high-quality starters (37FF to 60FF) and mai courses (69FF to 85FF) such as rabbit with mus tard and green salad with pâté de foie gra there's a lunch *menu* at 68FF. It opens for lunc on weekdays and for dinner to 11 pm Monda to Saturday.

Bistrot à Vin Jacques Mélac *(Map 5, ☎ 01 43 7 59 27, 42 rue Léon Frot, 11e, metro Charonne* Wine-bar owner and vintner Jacques Méla takes his wine very seriously, offering a wid choice by the glass (22FF to 28FF) or bottl (90FF to 125FF). Light meals (omelettes 54F salads 38FF to 42FF, plat du jour 80FF) ar available at lunch Monday to Saturday and dinner to 10.30 pm Tuesday to Saturday.

Le K *(Map 5, ☎ 01 53 36 03 96, 20 rue Kelle 11e, metro Bastille or Voltaire).* This high-tec restaurant is the flagship of up-and-comin rue Keller, which some think is the new ru Oberkampf. It has *menus* for 100FF and 120F and there's live entertainment in the form c *chansons françaises* several nights a week. It open for dinner from midnight Tuesday to Sunday

La Maison d'Or *(Map 5, ☎ 01 44 68 04 68, 13 rue du Faubourg Saint Antoine, 11e, metr Ledru Rollin).* Corsican cuisine – such as stu fatu (mutton stew cooked with ham, tomato and white wine) and *brocciu* (a soft whit cheese) – is surprisingly elusive in a city wher every other cop seems to come from Ajaccic but this simple place has what it takes. Expec to pay about 140FF per person. It's open fc lunch and dinner to 11 pm Monday to Saturday

Le Square Trousseau *(Map 5, ☎ 01 43 43 06 0C 1 rue Antoine Vollon, 12e, metro Ledru Rollin* This vintage bistro, with its etched glass, zin bar and polished wood panelling, is comfortabl rather than trendy and attracts a jolly and ver mixed clientele. But most people come to enjo the lovely terrace overlooking a small park. The two/three-course lunch *menus* are 100/135FF; à la carte starters are 40FF to 106FF and main courses 88FF to 125FF at night, so expect to pay about 180FF a head. It's open for lunch and dinner to 11.30 pm daily.

Lire entre les Vignes (Map 5, ☎ 01 43 55 69 49, 38 rue Sedaine, 11e, metro Bastille or Bréguet Sabin). Hidden away in a nondescript Bastille backstreet, 'Read Between the Vines' is an oasis of conviviality, reminiscent of a comfortable and spacious country kitchen, and a great spot to dine with friends. The food is fresh, imaginative and tasty, and prepared before your eyes in the corner kitchen. It's open for lunch and dinner till 10.30 pm weekdays.

Les Sans-Culottes (Map 6, ☎ 01 48 05 42 92, 27 rue de Lappe, 11e, metro Bastille). This museum-like bistro, with its bare wooden floors and zinc bar surrounded by mirrors and etched glass, is a wonderful place for a romantic dinner or for lunch on Sunday. There's a two-course formule at 80FF and a three-course *menu* for 130FF. It's open for lunch Wednesday to Monday and for dinner to 11 pm Tuesday to Sunday.

North African & Middle Eastern

Café Le Serail (Map 6, ☎ 01 43 38 17 01, 10 rue Sedaine, 11e, metro Bastille). This trendy North African café-restaurant is a lounge-lizard's paradise, with deep over-stuffed sofas where you can sit and sip mint tea or a cocktail before or after your meal. Couscous is 85FF to 135FF and tajines 85FF to 105FF; expect to pay about 200FF à la carte at dinner. At lunch the plat du jour is 48FF and there's a *menu* for 100FF. It's open 10 am to 12.30 am (to 2 am at the weekend).

Le Mansouria (Map 5, ☎ 01 43 71 00 16, 11 rue Faidherbe, 11e, metro Faidherbe Chaligny). We didn't eat the best couscous of our lives when we visited this beautifully decorated Moroccan restaurant, but the milk-fed steamed lamb, the lovely surroundings and the excellent service are impressive. The *menus* are 182FF and 280FF (including wine). It's open for lunch Tuesday to Saturday and for dinner to 11.30 pm Monday to Saturday.

Asian

Blue Elephant (Map 5, ☎ 01 47 00 42 00, 43 rue de la Roquette, 11e, metro Bastille). Paris' most

Dining by streetlamp is an attractive option in Paris.

euro currency converter €1 = 6.56FF

famous (if not its best) Thai restaurant is part of a hip international chain. Although it has become a little too successful for its own good, the indoor tropical rainforest and well prepared spicy dishes are still worth the inflated prices, with *menus* at 150FF (lunch, Monday to Friday) and 275FF. It's open for lunch Sunday to Friday and for dinner to 11 pm or midnight daily.

Chez Heang *(Map 6,* ☎ *01 48 07 80 98, 5 rue de la Roquette, 11e, metro Bastille).* You cook your food on a gas grill in the middle of your table at this Korean barbecue restaurant. *Menus* are 58FF at lunch and 68FF to 148FF at dinner; the *fondue maison* – a kind of spicy hotpot in which you dip and cook your food – is 135FF per person (minimum two people). It's open for lunch and dinner till midnight daily.

Other Cuisines

Cuisines from all over the world can be found along rue de la Roquette and rue de Lappe, just east of place de la Bastille, but Latin American, Tex-Mex and that vague term 'international' predominate.

Café de l'Industrie *(Map 6,* ☎ *01 47 00 13 53, 16 rue Saint Sabin, 11e, metro Bréguet Sabin).* At this very popular international restaurant with a neocolonial décor, main courses are in the 50FF to 85FF bracket and the desserts (notably *tartes*) are 24FF to 34FF. It's open 11 am to 2 am Sunday to Friday.

Havanita Café *(Map 6,* ☎ *01 43 55 96 42, 11 rue de Lappe, 11e, metro Bastille).* This bar-restaurant is decorated with posters and murals inspired – like the food and drink – by Cuba. Cocktails are from 48FF, starters 38FF to 57FF and excellent main courses 69FF to 94FF. Happy hour, when cocktails are 28FF, is 5 to 8 pm. It opens 5 pm to 2 am daily (from noon on Sunday).

Suds *(Map 5,* ☎ *01 43 14 06 36, 55 rue de Charonne, 11e, metro Ledru Rollin).* No, not a trendy laundrette but a very hip bar-restaurant with a name that means 'Souths'. The cuisine here is anything and everything from the south – from Mexican and Peruvian to Portuguese and North African. There's a lunch *menu* for 70FF, the plat du jour is 72FF to 88FF and the vegetarian plate is 52FF. À la carte starters range from 29FF to 45FF, main courses from 64FF to 88FF and desserts from 34FF to 39FF, so expect to pay about 150FF per person. It opens for lunch Tuesday to Friday and for dinner to 1.30 am Tuesday to Sunday.

Tex-Mex is as tasty in Paris as it is everywhere else in the world.

euro currency converter 10FF = €1.52

Self-Catering
There are lots of *food shops* along rue de la Roquette (Maps 5 & 6, metro Voltaire or Bastille) up towards place Léon Blum and a *Monoprix supermarket* (*Map 5, 97 rue du Faubourg Saint Antoine, 11e, metro Ledru Rollin*) open 9 am to 9 pm Monday to Saturday.

MÉNILMONTANT & BELLEVILLE (Maps 3, 5, 6 & 7)
In the northern part of the 11e and into the 19e and 20e, rue Oberkampf and its extension, rue de Ménilmontant, are becoming increasingly popular with diners and denizens of the night. Rue de Belleville and the streets running off it are dotted with Chinese, South-East Asian and a few Turkish places; blvd de Belleville has loads of kosher couscous restaurants, most of which are closed on Saturday.

French
French restaurants run the gamut here – from the sublime to the ridiculously cheap.

Le Baratin (*Map 3, ☎ 01 43 49 39 70, 3 rue Jouye-Rouve, 20e, metro Pyrénées*). This animated wine bistro, just a step away from a stunning vista over Paris and the lively Belleville quarter, offers some of the best food in the 20e. The wine selection (by the glass or carafe) is excellent. The weekday lunch *menu* is 73FF; an à la carte dinner shouldn't set you back more than 175FF. It's open noon to midnight weekdays and from 6 pm on Saturday.

Le Clown Bar (*Map 6, ☎ 01 43 55 87 35, 114 rue Amelot, 11e, metro Filles du Calvaire*). This wonderful wine bar next to the Cirque d'Hiver is like a museum, with painted ceilings, mosaics on the wall and a lovely zinc bar. The food is simple and unpretentious traditional French, with starters 38FF to 58FF and main courses 65FF to 88FF; expect to pay from 150FF per person. It's open for lunch Monday to Saturday and for dinner till 11.30 pm daily.

Le Pavillon Puebla (*Map 3, ☎ 01 42 08 92 62, corner of ave Simon Bolivar and rue Botzaris, 19e, metro Buttes-Chaumont*). This exquisite restaurant in a Second Empire-style pavilion in Parc des Buttes-Chaumont attracts people not so much for its wonderful seafood and fish dishes but for its open terrace in the summer. *Menus* are 180FF and 250FF. For dessert, don't miss the *millefeuille aux fraises* (strawberries in layers of flaky pastry). It's open for lunch and dinner to 10.30 pm Tuesday to Saturday.

Le Repaire de Cartouche (*Map 7, ☎ 01 47 00 25 86, 8 blvd des Filles du Calvaire and 99 rue Amelot, 11e, metro Saint Sébastien Froissart*). This old-fashioned place takes a very modern approach to French food under the direction of a talented young chef. Innovative starters cost 40FF to 60FF, main courses 85FF to 120FF and desserts 30FF to 40FF. Wines average about 160FF a bottle. It's open for lunch and dinner till 11 pm Tuesday to Saturday.

Au Trou Normand (*Map 6, ☎ 01 48 05 80 23, 9 rue Jean-Pierre Timbaud, 11e, metro Oberkampf*). Hosted by several grannies, this cosy, very French restaurant has some of the lowest prices in Paris. Starters range from 10FF to 15FF (the vegetable *potage* is particularly good), main courses from 29FF to 39FF and desserts are under 10FF, so you won't spend a lot more than 60FF per person. It's open for lunch weekdays and for dinner till 11 pm Monday to Saturday.

Le Villaret (*Map 6, ☎ 01 43 57 89 76, 13 rue Ternaux, 11e, metro Parmentier*). This excellent neighbourhood bistro, an easy walk from Marché Bastille (see the special section 'The Markets of Paris' after this chapter), has diners coming from across Paris till late to sample the house specialities. Starters cost 45FF to 55FF, main courses 85FF to 110FF and desserts are from 45FF. The lunch *menus* are 120/150FF for two/three courses, and the plat du jour is 90FF. It opens for lunch weekdays and for dinner to 1 am Monday to Saturday.

Asian
Krung Thep (*Map 3, ☎ 01 43 66 83 74, 93 rue Julien Lacroix, 20e, metro Pyrénées*). The kitsch 'Bangkok' is a small (some might say cramped) place with all our favourites: green curries, *tom yam gung* and fish or chicken steamed in banana leaves. The steamed shrimp ravioli and stuffed crab will hit the spot. Expect to pay between 130FF and 150FF per person. It's open for dinner till midnight daily.

New Nioullaville (*Map 3, ☎ 01 40 21 96 18, 32 rue de l'Orillon, 11e, metro Belleville*). Whenever we get nostalgic for South-East Asia we head for this cavernous, 500-seat place that resembles the Hong Kong Stock Exchange on a busy day. The food is a bit of a mishmash – *dim sum* sits comfortably next to beef satay, as does fresh scallops with black bean alongside Singapore noodle. But order carefully and you'll approach authenticity. Count on 160FF per person. It's open for lunch and dinner to 1 am daily.

Thai Classic *(Map 3, ☎ 01 42 40 78 10, 41 rue de Belleville, 19e, metro Belleville).* One of the most authentic Thai eateries we've found in Paris, Thai Classic offers soups for 40FF to 45FF and all our favourite Thai dishes (and a few Laotian ones, too) for 45FF to 50FF. About half a dozen of the choices are vegetarian. It's open for lunch and dinner to 11.30 pm Monday to Saturday.

Vegetarian

La Ville de Jagannath *(Map 3, ☎ 01 43 55 80 81, 101 rue Saint Maur, 11e, metro Parmentier).* This New Age-inspired place has imaginative (and good-value) Indian vegetarian *thali* dishes and *menus* for 90FF, 130FF and 160FF. It's open for lunch Monday to Saturday and for dinner to 11.30 pm daily (to 12.30 am at the weekend).

Other Cuisines

The cuisines of southern Europe, North Africa and Asia are well represented here as is 'café food'.

Le Charbon *(Map 3, ☎ 01 43 57 55 13, 109 rue Oberkampf, 11e, metro Parmentier).* With its remarkable antique-cum-postmodern ambience, the Charbon was the first – and is arguably still the best – of the hip cafés and bars to sprout up in Ménilmontant. The plat du jour is 66FF to 69FF, there's a 68FF lunch *menu* and brunch at the weekend (11 am to 5 pm) is 75FF. It's open 9 am to 2 am daily.

Chez Lalou *(Map 3, ☎ 01 43 58 35 28, 78 blvd de Belleville, 20e, metro Couronnes).* The pick of the kosher couscous crop on blvd de Belleville, Chez Lalou has killer steamed semolina with the usual accompaniments and unusual stews and tajines from 65FF to 80FF, grills from 65FF to 75FF, *brick à l'oeuf* for 25FF and salads from 20FF to 40FF. The terrace is a lovely – and lively – place to dine in the warm weather. It's open for lunch and dinner till midnight daily.

Café Florentin *(Map 6, ☎ 01 43 55 57 00, 40 rue Jean-Pierre Timbaud, 11e, metro Parmentier).* Excellent Italian fare can be had here in cosy surroundings. The lunch *menu* is 65FF (including wine), à la carte starters are 24FF to 75FF and main courses are 60FF to 90FF. The two-dozen pasta dishes range from 45FF to 75FF. It opens for lunch weekdays and for dinner till 11 pm Monday to Saturday.

La Favela Chic *(Map 3, ☎ 01 43 57 15 47, 131 rue Oberkampf, 11e, metro Ménilmontant).* The day job of the people who co-host the hotter-than-hot Brazilian evenings at the Élysée-Montmartre in Pigalle on certain Saturdays (see the boxed text 'Salsa City' in the Entertainment chapter) is preparing authentic Brazilian dishes at this cosy cantina. Main courses, including a massive *feijoada*, are 50FF to 70FF. It's open noon to 2 am daily (from 7 pm on Saturday).

Le Kitch *(Map 6, ☎ 01 40 21 94 14, 10 rue Oberkampf, 11e, metro Filles du Calvaire).* The misspelled name says it all: curtains of plastic flowers, rubber carafes, Formica table-tops with mismatched cutlery. And the food? Well, curries, gazpacho – anything luridly coloured (about 120FF per person). Obviously a place to experience rather than digest. It's open for lunch weekdays and for dinner to 2 am daily.

La Piragua *(Map 5, ☎ 01 40 21 35 98, 6 rue Rochebrune, 11e, metro Saint Ambroise).* Colombian food and good Latin American music feature at this small, brightly coloured eatery. There are *menus* at 99FF and 112FF, à la carte starters such as *empañadas* and fried plantains for 25FF to 40FF and main courses from 60FF to 98FF. It opens for lunch and dinner to 10.30 pm Monday to Saturday.

Chez Vincent *(Map 3, ☎ 01 42 02 22 45, 5 rue du Tunnel, 19e, metro Botzaris).* This restaurant on the southern boundary of Parc des Buttes-Chaumont offers refined and rather expensive Italian cuisine (ordering à la carte won't leave you with much change from 250FF) in a lively environment. It's open for lunch Sunday to Friday and for dinner to 11 pm daily.

Self-Catering

Supermarkets in the area include two branches of **Franprix** *(Map 3, 28 blvd Jules Ferry, 11e, metro République or Goncourt;*

Map 6, 23 rue Jean-Pierre Timbaud, 11e, metro Oberkampf); both are open 8 am to 8 pm Monday to Saturday.

NATION (Maps 1 & 5)

There are loads of decent restaurants on the roads fanning out from place de la Nation.

French

The French restaurants in this area tend to be real finds.

Les Amognes (Map 5, ☎ 01 43 72 73 05, 243 rue du Faubourg Saint Antoine, 11e, metro Faidherbe Chaligny). A meal at Les Amognes is a quintessentially French – rather than Parisian – experience: haute cuisine at a reasonable 180FF set price, discreet service and an atmosphere that is *correcte* (proper), even provincial. The wines aren't cheap though (from 200FF for a less-than-stellar Burgundy). It's open for lunch Tuesday to Friday and for dinner to 10.30 pm Monday to Saturday (to 11.30 pm on Friday and Saturday).

Other Cuisines

Place de la Nation and the surrounding area has a large number of restaurants specialising in cuisines other than French.

À la Banane Ivoirienne (Map 5, ☎ 01 43 70 49 90, 10 rue de la Forge Royale, 11e, metro Ledru Rollin). This friendly place serves West African specialities, with entrées 20FF to 38FF and main courses in the 60FF to 90FF region. There's live African-Brazilian music from 10 pm on Friday. It's open 7 pm till midnight Tuesday to Saturday.

Café Canelle (Map 5, ☎ 01 43 70 48 25, 1 bis rue de la Forge Royale, 11e, metro Ledru Rollin). This festive Moroccan restaurant is run by Algerians who do couscous with a twist – how does it sound flavoured with cinnamon, orange-blossom water and almonds as a dessert? Couscous and tajines are 79FF to 95FF, pastilla is 79FF. It's open 8 pm to 12.30 am Tuesday to Sunday.

Khun Akorn (Map 1, ☎ 01 43 56 20 03, 8 ave de Taillebourg, 11e, metro Nation). In this airy Thai restaurant most starters are 40FF to 60FF, main courses 70FF to 90FF. Lunch/dinner menus are 125/195FF. It's open for lunch and dinner to 11 pm Tuesday to Sunday.

Le Réservoir (Map 5, ☎ 01 43 56 39 60, 16 rue de la Forge Royale, 11e, metro Ledru Rollin).

This warehouse turned bar-restaurant done up in modern kitsch serves Mediterranean dishes to celebrities and their hangers-on. Count on from 200FF a head and avoid the weekend unless you like techno-heads and large TV screens with videos of *sport extrême*. The restaurant is open 8 pm till midnight daily, the bar to 2 am.

GARE DE LYON & BERCY (Maps 5 & 9)

The waterfront south-west of Gare de Lyon has had a new lease of life in recent years with the opening of several *péniche* (barge) restaurants and the development of the old wine warehouses in Bercy Village (see Bercy in the Things to See & Do chapter), which attract winers and diners till the wee hours.

French

Some of the French restaurants in greater Bercy are trendsetters.

L'Oulette (Map 9, ☎ 01 40 02 02 12, 13-15 place Lachambeaudie, 12e, metro Cour Saint Émilion). This lovely restaurant with a terrace overlooks a pretty church and an admittedly rather busy roundabout, but it remains quintessentially Parisian. Entrées/main courses/desserts that hint of the South of France are a standard 96/138/55FF and there are *menus* at 165FF and 260FF. It's open for lunch weekdays and for dinner to 10.15 pm Monday to Saturday.

Au Pressoir (Map 9, ☎ 01 43 44 38 21, 257 ave Daumesnil, 12e, metro Michel Bizot or Porte Dorée). This luxurious French restaurant right next to the Bois de Vincennes is a welcoming and warm wood-panelled place that has become a favourite of well-heeled Bercy folk: count on 500FF per person or choose the three-course 420FF *menu*. It's open for lunch and dinner to 10.30 pm weekdays only.

Other Cuisines

Some of the restaurants in this area are decidedly un-French in their approach, serving unusual dishes, stocking New World wines and serving continuously throughout the day.

La Barge (Map 5, ☎ 01 40 02 09 09, port de la Rapée, 12e, metro Gare de Lyon). The food at this moored-barge restaurant is a mix of everything – Mediterranean, North African and even

Eastern European – and the smiling staff can explain all in most known languages. *Menus* are 120FF and 160FF. It's open for lunch and dinner to 11.30 pm daily.

La Compagnie du Ruban Bleu (*Map 5, ☎ 01 43 41 15 15, port de la Rapée, 12e, metro Bercy or Gare de Lyon*). Ironically the 'Blue Ribbon Company' feels more like a boat than La Barge (see the previous entry) and the couple who own it have sailed the seven seas in pursuit of wine, judging from the comprehensive list. The food is pretty international too – from kangaroo and ostrich to all kinds of seafood – with starters 55FF to 90FF and main courses 90FF to 145FF. There's a lunch menu for 80FF. It's open noon to 2 am Sunday to Friday, and from 6 pm on Saturday.

Le Vinéa Café (*Map 9, ☎ 01 44 74 09 09, 26-28 cour Saint Émilion, 12e, metro Cour Saint Émilion*). This is the main tenant – or so it would seem – of the cour Saint Émilion: a delightful wine bar-restaurant with starters 34FF to 68FF, main courses 78FF to 98FF and a lovely terrace to the back facing place des Vins de France. It's open 8 am till midnight weekdays, and from noon at the weekend.

Self-Catering
West of Parc de Bercy, the *Franprix supermarket* (*Map 9, 3 rue Baron le Roy, 12e, metro Cour Saint Émilion*) is open 9 or 9.30 am to 7.30 pm Monday to Saturday (with a break between 1 and 3 pm weekdays).

13e ARRONDISSEMENT & CHINATOWN (Maps 1 & 9)
Until the opening of the high-tech Météor metro line and the new Bibliothèque Nationale de France François Mitterrand, few travellers ventured as far south as this unless they were in search of authentic Chinese food. But all that is changing.

French
This area offers some excellent and very innovative French food.

L'Avant-Goût (*Map 1, ☎ 01 53 80 24 00, 26 rue Bobillot, 13e, metro Place d'Italie*). In this prototype of the Parisian 'neo-bistro' (classical yet modern), chef Christophe Beaufront serves some of the most inventive modern cuisine around (eg, courgette stuffed with fresh goat's cheese, lamb *confit* with rosemary and polenta and fig and apple tart). There's a remarkably affordable lunch *menu* at 59FF, and a dinner one for 145FF; à la carte dining will cost upwards of 170FF. It's open for lunch and dinner to 11 pm Tuesday to Saturday.

Chez Jacky (*Map 9, ☎ 01 45 83 71 55, 109 rue du Dessous des Berges, 13e, metro Bibliothèque*). In the shadow of the new national library, this Baroque palace run by three brothers serves exquisite veal and pâté de foie gras dishes, with starters from 98FF and main courses around 120FF. It's open for lunch and dinner to 10 pm weekdays only.

Paris-Orléans (*Map 9, ☎ 01 45 83 89 42, 2 rue de Patay, 13e, metro Tolbiac*). Our colleagues at Lonely Planet Paris tell us that 'one eats very well at Paris-Orléans in a somewhat disciplined atmosphere'. We didn't notice that – we were too busy eyeing the complex salads and fresh seafood dishes that go for a song (count on less than 100FF). It's open for lunch weekdays only.

Le Pet de Lapin (*Map 9, ☎ 01 45 86 58 21, 2 rue Dunois, 13e, metro Bibliothèque*). Don't let the unappetising name put you off; the 'Rabbit's Fart' promises quality food from south-west France and delivers – at very reasonable prices: spinach salad with bacon (25FF), chicken liver terrine (28FF) and pork loin in mustard sauce (49FF). It's open for lunch and dinner to 10 pm Tuesday to Saturday.

Asian
Dozens of North-East and South-East Asian restaurants – and not just Chinese ones – line the main streets of Paris' Chinatown, including ave de Choisy, ave d'Ivry and rue Baudricourt. The cheapest *menus*, which go for about 50FF, are usually available only at lunch on weekdays.

La Fleuve de Chine (*Map 1, ☎ 01 45 82 06 88, 15 ave de Choisy, 13e, metro Porte de Choisy*). Take it from those who know: this place, which can also be reached through the Tour Bergame housing estate at 130 blvd Masséna, has the most authentic Cantonese and Hakka food in Paris and, as is typical, both the surroundings and the service are as forgettable as the 1997 Hong Kong handover. Main courses range from 40FF to 95FF, but are around 40FF to 50FF for chicken, prawn and superb clay-pot dishes; expect to pay about 120FF a head. It opens for lunch and dinner to 11 pm Friday to Wednesday.

MONTPARNASSE (Map 4)

Since the 1920s, the area around blvd du Montparnasse has been one of the city's premier avenues for enjoying that most Parisian of pastimes: sitting in a café and checking out the passers-by. Many younger Parisians, however, now consider the area *démodé*.

As Gare Montparnasse is where Bretons looking for work in Paris would usually disembark (and apparently venture no further), there is no shortage of *creperies* in the area. There are three at 20 rue d'Odessa, and many, many more round the corner on rue du Montparnasse.

French

Blvd du Montparnasse, around Vavin metro station, is home to a number of legendary places, made famous between the wars by writers (see the Literary walking tour in the Things to See & Do chapter) and avant-garde artists (eg, Dalí, Cocteau). Before the Russian Revolution, these cafés attracted exiles such as Lenin and Trotsky.

La Coupole (☎ *01 43 20 14 20, 102 blvd du Montparnasse, 14e, metro Vavin*). La Coupole's famous mural-covered columns (decorated by such artists as Brancusi and Chagall), dark wood-panelling and indirect lighting have hardly changed since the days of Sartre, Soutine, Man Ray and Josephine Baker. Starters at this 450-seat brasserie, which opened in 1927, cost 29FF to 50FF, and main courses 78FF to 92FF, so count on spending about 200FF for a full meal. A lunch-time express *menu* is 98.50FF including 25cL of wine; evening *menus* are 138FF to 189FF. It opens noon to 1 or 1.30 am daily. There's dancing on some nights and tea dances at the weekend (see Clubs in the Entertainment chapter).

Le Select (☎ *01 42 22 65 27, 99 blvd du Montparnasse, 6e, metro Vavin*). Another Montparnasse legend, the Select's décor has changed very little since 1923. The *menu* costs 90FF, and *tartines* (slices of buttered bread with toppings) made with Poilâne bread start at 30FF. Breakfast/brunch is 55/80FF. Meals are served 11 am to 3 am daily (to 4 am on Friday and Saturday).

Le Caméléon (☎ *01 43 20 63 43, 6 rue de Chevreuse, 6e, metro Vavin*). If you want to eat at a '*nouveau*' bistro that serves fresh, innovative food in a traditional setting, you won't do better than Le Caméléon; its lobster ravioli (92FF) and the Auvergne sausage with *purée maison* (bangers and mash *à la française*) are worth the visit alone. Starters range from 35FF to 90FF, main courses from 88FF to 120FF, and there's a lunch-time *menu* for 120FF. It's open for lunch weekdays and for dinner to 10.30 pm Monday to Saturday.

The Birth of Restoration

In 1765 a certain Monsieur A Boulanger opened a small business in rue Bailleul, 1er, just off rue de Rivoli, selling soups, broths and later sheep's feet in white sauce. Above the door he hung a sign advertising these *restaurants* (restoratives, from the verb *se restaurer*, meaning 'to feed oneself'). The world had its first restaurant as we know it today – and a new name for an eating place.

Before that time not everyone cooked at home every day of the year. Hostelries and inns existed, but they only served guests set meals at set times and prices from the *table d'hôte* (host's table) while cafés only offered drinks. Boulanger's restaurant is thought to have been the first public place where diners could order a meal from a menu offering a range of dishes.

Other restaurants opened in the following decades, including a luxury one in Paris called La Grande Taverne de Londres in 1782. The 1789 Revolution at first stemmed the tide of new restaurants but when corporations and privileges were abolished in the 1790s, their numbers multiplied. By 1804 Paris counted some 500 restaurants, providing employment for many of the chefs and cooks who had once worked in the kitchens of the aristocracy. A typical menu at that time might have included 12 soups, two dozen hors d'oeuvre, between 12 and 30 entrées of beef, veal, mutton, fowl and game, 24 fish dishes, 12 types of patisserie and 50 desserts.

PLACES TO EAT

Other Cuisines

Tex-Mex on blvd du Montparnasse? *Pourquoi pas*?

Mustang Café (☎ *01 43 35 36 12, 84 blvd du Montparnasse, 14e, metro Montparnasse Bienvenüe)*. This café that *almost* never sleeps has passable Tex-Mex (combination platters and chilli from 47FF to 78FF, *fajitas* for 99FF). It's open from 8 am to 5 am.

Self-Catering

The ***Inno supermarket*** *(rue du Départ, metro Montparnasse Bienvenüe)* opposite the Tour Montparnasse is open 9 am to 10 pm weekdays, and to 9 pm on Saturday. The nearby ***food market*** on blvd Edgar Quinet is open from about 7 am to 1 pm on Wednesday and Saturday.

15e ARRONDISSEMENT (Maps 1 & 4)

There are quite a few places to eat to the south of blvd de Grenelle.

French

Parisians are always on the lookout for 'finds', and the names of the following two places were on everyone's lips the last time we were in town.

L'Os à Moëlle (Map 1, ☎ *01 45 57 27 27, 3 rue Vasco de Gama, 15e, metro Lourmel)*. The 'Marrowbone' is well worth a trip to the far-flung south-western 15e, and chef Thierry Faucher (ex-Hotel Crillon) offers one of the best and most affordable *menus dégustation* (sampling menus) in town at 155/190FF at lunch/dinner. Its four courses could include such delicacies as creamed scallops in the shell with coriander, bass in cumin-flavoured butter and half a quail prepared with endives and chestnuts, plus dessert. The wine list is very good and you can buy a bottle 'to go' at the Cave de l'Os à Moëlle across the street. The restaurant is open for lunch and dinner to 11.30 pm Tuesday to Saturday.

Le Troquet (Map 4, ☎ *01 45 66 89 00, 21 rue François Bonvin, 15e, metro Sèvres Lecourbe)*. The incomparable American food-writer Patricia Wells chose this place the last time we dined together so what better street cred can there be? Young chef Christian Etchebest takes 'ordinary' things and puts a spin on them: veal bouillon flavoured with aniseed and served with vegetable quenelles, caramelised pork on purée of vegetables, and sealed whiting on a bed of fresh green beans. The lunch/dinner *menu* offer pedigree courses for 130/170FF. It's open for lunch and dinner to 10 pm Tuesday to Saturday.

North African & Middle Eastern

Not surprisingly, these ever-popular cuisine can be found throughout the 15e.

Feyrous (Map 4, ☎ *01 45 78 07 02, 8 rue de Lourmel, 15e, metro Dupleix)*. This bright, busy and outgoing *traiteur-restaurant* has excellent Lebanese dishes, with *menus* at 60FF and 85FF at lunch and 105FF at dinner; the plat du jour is 79FF. It's open continuously from 7 am to 2 am daily.

Le Tipaza (Map 4, ☎ *01 45 79 22 25, 150 ave Émile Zola, 15e, metro Avenue Émile Zola)*. This classy restaurant has good couscous (65FF to 90FF), tajines (79FF to 82FF) and Moroccan grills done on a wood-burning stove (65FF to 103FF). *Menus* are 79FF at lunch and 130FF at dinner. It's open for lunch and dinner till midnight daily.

Self-Catering

There are plenty of supermarkets in this area, including an ***Atac*** *(Map 4, 12 rue Dupleix, 15e, metro La Motte Picquet-Grenelle)*, open 9 am to 8 pm Monday to Saturday; a ***Monoprix*** *(Map 4, 2 rue du Commerce, 15e, metro La Motte Picquet-Grenelle)*, open 9 am to 10 pm on the same days; and a ***Franprix*** *(Map 4, 32 rue de Lourmel, 15e, metro Dupleix)*, open 8.30 am to 8 pm, again on the same days.

MONTMARTRE & PIGALLE (Maps 1, 2 & 8)

The restaurants along rue des Trois Frères, 18e (Map 8), are a much better bet than their touristy counterparts in and around place du Tertre.

French

Some of Montmartre's French restaurants, like most everything else on the Butte de Montmartre, are slightly offbeat.

Le Bateau Lavoir (Map 8, ☎ *01 42 54 23 12, 8 rue Garreau, 18e, metro Abbesses)*. Named after the studio behind it on place Émile Goudeau where Picasso and co made art at the start of the 20th century, this wonderful old-style bistro has good-value salads (50FF) and lunch/dinner *menus* at 98/140FF and makes its own pâté de foie gras and *confit de canard*. It's open for lunch and dinner to 11 pm Thursday to Tuesday.

Le Refuge des Fondus *(Map 8, ☎ 01 42 55 22 65, 17 rue des Trois Frères, 18e, metro Abbesses or Anvers).* This establishment has been a Montmartre favourite since 1966. For 92FF you get an aperitif, hors d'oeuvre, red wine (or beer or soft drink) in a baby bottle and a good quantity of either *fondue savoyarde* (melted cheese) or *fondue bourguignonne* (meat fondue; minimum two people). It opens for dinner 7 pm to 2 am daily (last sitting at midnight or 12.30 am).

Macis et Muscade *(Map 2, ☎ 01 42 26 62 26, 110 rue Legendre, 17e, metro La Fourche).* This is an excellent example of a proper *restaurant du quartier* (neighbourhood restaurant), with a lunch-time formule at 75FF and a dinner *menu* at 130FF. À la carte entrées cost 37FF to 44FF and main courses 68FF to 85FF. It's open for lunch Sunday to Friday and for dinner till 11 pm Tuesday to Sunday.

Other Cuisines

French cuisine is not the only option in Montmartre.

Charlot *(Map 2, ☎ 01 53 20 48 00, 12 place de Clichy, 9e, metro Place de Clichy).* Some Parisians think that this Art Deco palace is the best place in town for no-nonsense seafood (eg, perfect oysters by the *douzaine*, grilled sardines, sole meunière); it bills itself as 'le Roi des Coquillages' (the King of Shellfish). Generous seafood platters are 208FF and 242FF; a *menu bouillabaisse* is 238FF. It's open for lunch and dinner till 1 am daily.

À la Grande Bleue *(Map 1, ☎ 01 42 28 04 26, 4 rue Lantiez, 17e, metro Brochant or Guy Moquet).* This is our latest discovery and we can't get enough of the *crêpes berbères* (38FF to 52FF), the unusual barley couscous (50FF to 98FF) prepared in the style of the Kabyles of eastern Algeria and the savoury-sweet *pastilla au poulet* (chicken pastilla; 85FF). Add to that the cool blue and yellow décor, the art on the walls and one of the warmest welcomes in Paris and you've got a winner. It's open for lunch weekdays and for dinner to 11 pm Monday to Saturday.

ROB FLYNN

Eating out in Montmartre, one of Paris' most delightful settings

euro currency converter €1 = 6.56FF

Il Duca (Map 8, ☎ 01 46 06 71 98, 26 rue Yvonne le Tac, 18e, metro Abbesses). An intimate little Italian restaurant with good, straightforward food including a three-course *menu* for 89FF and main courses from 80FF to 90FF. Home-made pasta dishes are 55FF to 76FF. It's open for lunch and dinner to 11 pm daily.

La Maffiosa (Map 2, ☎ 01 42 93 52 43, 16 rue des Dames, 17e, metro Place de Clichy). One of our more PC friends eschews this pizzeria because of its name but the 40-odd pizzas (34FF to 48FF) are just too good for us to stay away. It's open for lunch Monday to Saturday and for dinner to 11 pm daily.

Le Mono (Map 8, ☎ 01 46 06 99 20, 40 rue Véron, 18e, metro Abbesses or Blanche). Togolese and other West African specialities at Le Mono include *lélé* (flat, steamed cakes of white beans and shrimp served with tomato sauce; 25FF), *maffé* (beef or chicken served with peanut sauce; 50FF), *gbekui* (a sort of goulash made with spinach, onions, beef, fish and shrimp; 55FF) and *djenkoumé* (grilled chicken

with semolina noodles; 60FF). It opens for dinner only 7 to about 11.30 pm Thursday to Tuesday.

Self-Catering

Towards Pigalle there are lots of *groceries*, many of them open until late at night; try the side streets leading off blvd de Clichy (eg rue Lepic). Heading south from blvd de Clichy, rue des Martyrs, 9e (Map 3), is lined with food shops almost all the way to Notre Dame de Lorette metro station.

Supermarkets in the area include a *Franprix (Map 8, 44 rue Caulaincourt, 18e, metro Lamarck Caulaincourt)*, open 8.30 am to 7.25 pm Monday to Thursday, and to 7.45 pm on Friday and Saturday; and an *Ed l'Épicier (Map 8, 31 rue d'Orsel, 18e, metro Anvers)* a block south of the bottom of the funicular, open 9 am to 8 pm Monday to Saturday.

JULIET COOMBE

While strolling through Paris on a Saturday morning, should you notice throngs of basket-toting people passing you by with great determination, and others, laden with bags, going in the opposite direction at a more relaxed pace, then follow the former as you have stumbled upon that most Parisian of weekend pastimes, shopping at the street *marché alimentaire* (food market). There is no better way to be mistaken for a native; forsake that day at the Louvre, grab a basket and load up with fresh provisions.

The *marchés découverts* (open-air markets) – 57 of which pop up in public squares around the city two or three times a week – are open from about 7 am to 2 pm. The 18 *marchés couverts* (covered markets) are open 8 am to about 1 pm and from 3.30 or 4 to 7 or 7.30 pm Tuesday to Sunday lunch time. To find out when there's a market near your hotel or hostel, ask the staff or anyone who lives in the neighbourhood. Completing the picture are numerous independent *rues commerçantes*, pedestrian streets where the shops set up outdoor stalls.

Food markets in the capital offer the usual French stand-bys and more – fresh vegetables and fruit, meat, bread, patisserie, cheese, *charcuterie*, prepared dishes, pâté de foie gras, nuts, fish and flowers – all painstakingly arrayed in colour-coordinated displays beneath chalkboards with the prices marked in that characteristic French scrawl. Tradespeople and peddlers ply basket- and chair-repair services, Oriental carpets, sewing machines and kitchen utensils. Children sell 10FF bunches of fragrant, purple lilacs in spring.

But markets are far more than a cute picture postcard or a remembrance of Paris past. They are very much a symbol of Paris present and an integral part of modern life. Visiting them shows you a cross-section of the great variety of people that make up Paris today.

JULIET COOMBE

ELLIOT DANIEL

Title Page: Tomatoes decorate the colourful food stalls on rue Mouffetard, one of Paris' oldest street markets. (photograph: Juliet Coombe)

Top: Olives – no French salad would be complete without them.

Bottom Left: Stalls at Belleville market sell an incredible variety of food, including a wide range of fresh fish.

Bottom Right: Mouthwatering cherries on rue Mouffetard

Some people think that modernisation is taking its toll on the city's markets. While *les grandes surfaces* (immense shopping centres or hypermarkets) are banned within the city limits, moderately sized *supermarchés* abound, menacing the market with convenient one-stop shopping and longer opening hours. But the market still has many seductive advantages. Dependable quality is ensured by the intimate relationship of the vendors and their repeat customers. Market-garden culture brings fresh seasonal produce. The sometimes daunting number of competing stands allows you to pick and choose for quality and price. The flourishing immigrant population is bringing new blood to the old tradition with booming ethnic markets. Markets can be a lifesaver on Sunday, when all the large supermarkets close their doors. And the very Gallic desire to cling to *l'art de la gastronomie* for the sake of tradition (if not practicality) cannot be discounted.

The following is an alphabetical list of 10 Paris markets rated according to the variety of their produce, their ethnicity and the neighbourhood. They are *la crème de la crème*.

Marché d'Aligre

Although gentrification has brought rising rents and hip bars to neighbouring arrondissements, place d'Aligre (Map 5, metro Ledru Rollin) in the 12e remains a solidly Arab and North African enclave. Exotically garbed mothers carry babies on their backs as they bargain down the price of plantains. Competing vegetable vendors call out their prices in several different languages. Muslim butchers display whole sheep with their prices marked in Arabic. Browse in the adjoining covered **Marché Beauvau** and the large flea market, then take mint tea and a honey pastry at the North African La Ruche à Miel, a tearoom at 19 rue d'Aligre. Beauvau is open all day, Tuesday to Sunday.

Left: Spoilt for choice: legumes for sale on rue Montorgueil

Right: Out and about on market day

GREG ELMS

BRENDA TURNNIDGE

Marché Bastille

A subterranean canal runs under blvd Richard Lenoir, 11e, forming a wide, open space above that's perfect for what many consider to be Paris' quintessential neighbourhood market (Map 7, metro Bastille). It is also one of the biggest, with over a dozen stalls for every type of food on offer where you can observe locals exchanging *bises* (pecks on the cheek) and pleasantries with vendors over great piles of endives, courgettes, peppers and leeks. Buy a rich hunk of Gruyère and a crusty, floury *baguette à l'ancienne* for a picnic at the exquisite place des Vosges. The market is open Tuesday and Sunday mornings.

Batignolles-Clichy

This market (Map 2, blvd des Batignolles between rue des Batignolles and rue Puteaux, 17e, metro Place de Clichy or Rome) is one of three *marchés bio* (organic markets) in Paris and spreads out under the filtering light of the plane trees. The trade in *produits sans chimiques* (products without additives) is carefully government-regulated (though

still looked upon with suspicion by many stalwart traditionalists). Feast your eyes on hot *galettes de blé* (wheaten crêpes), hearty wholemeal breads and patisserie, rough and simple cheeses, yoghurt and healthy-looking vegetables. The market is open 9 am to 1.30 pm on Saturday. The other organic markets are **Raspail** (Map 4, blvd Raspail between rue de Rennes and rue du Cherche Midi, 6e, metro Rennes), open 9 am to 1.30 pm on Sunday, and **Saint Charles** (Map 4, rue Saint Charles around place Charles Michels, 15e, metro Charles Michels), open 9 am to 1 pm on Friday.

Belleville

Like Marché Beauvau at place d'Aligre, Belleville provides a fascinating entry into the large, vibrant ethnic communities of the *quartiers de l'est* (eastern neighbourhoods), home to African, Middle Eastern and Asian immigrants as well as artists and students (see the special section 'Paris Mondial' after the Facts about Paris chapter). The market (Map 3, blvd de Belleville between rue Jean-Pierre Timbaud and rue du Faubourg du Temple, 11e & 20e, metro Belleville or Couronne) is a joy to behold – what seems like kilometres of tables groaning with fantastic vegetables, miniature pineapples, lychees and fresh dates on their branches. Cheerful vendors, offering slices of mango and sparring

Left: Tempting-looking fruit and vegetables at one of Paris' organic markets

SIMON BRACKEN

JULIET COOMBE

light-heartedly with their competitors across the aisles, turn this market into a real show. The market is open Tuesday and Friday mornings.

Rue Cler

Rue Cler (Map 4, metro École Militaire) in the 7e is a breath of fresh air in a sometimes stuffy neighbourhood (most of the city's governmental buildings are nearby). A short, sunny market street near the Eiffel Tower, filled with the stands of the many upmarket food shops, the rue Cler market feels like a party at the weekend when the whole neighbourhood – from yuppies to housewives – turns out en masse. Have a *café grand crème* at the popular Café du Marché at No 38 and watch the dignified *grands-mères*, the heads of their pet poodles sticking out of their push carts, meeting friends and evaluating the produce. The market is open all day, Tuesday to noon on Sunday.

Grenelle

The Grenelle market (Map 4, blvd de Grenelle between rue de Lourmel and rue du Commerce, 15e, metro La Motte-Piquet Grenelle) runs below an elevated railway and is surrounded by stately Haussmann boulevards and elaborate Art Nouveau apartment blocks. On market days Parisian high society prepares for the week's dinner parties by picking up such goodies as olives, nuts and dates (for the apéritif, of course), stuffed scallops and *escargots*, buckets of paella and Alsatian *choucroute garnie* (sauerkraut with meat). The market is open Wednesday and Sunday mornings.

Place Maubert

Right: Have a slice: melons for sale (with ee samples) at Belleville market

A hop from the Seine, place Maubert (Map 6, metro Maubert Mutualité) in the 5e reigns over Saint Germain des Prés, the most upmarket part of the bohemian 5e. A small, cheerfully cramped group of stallholders spread over the pavements of this small triangle of intersecting streets. Pleasant cafés lining one side of the market provide a nice break from shopping. Tourists will appreciate Maubert's close proximity to the Île de la Cité, Notre Dame and the Jardin du Luxembourg. The market is open 7 am to 1.30 or 2 pm on Tuesday, Thursday and Saturday.

Rue Montorgueil

A plaque on colourful rue Montorgueil calls it an *haut lieu de la gastronomie et du commerce d'alimentation depuis le 13ème siècle* (bastion of gastronomy and the food trade since the 13th century). Well, even though Paris' 700-year-old wholesale market, Les Halles, was moved from this area to the southern suburb of Rungis in 1969, food remains the party line here (Map 6, rue Montorgueil between rue de Turbigo and rue Réaumur, 2e, metro Les Halles): witness the shops offering everything from live crayfish to vintage wines and the fantastic wholesale pâté de foie gras outlets on rue Montmartre. And don't miss the stunning patisserie Stohrer at No 51 and the historic restaurant Au Rocher de Cancale at No 78, where the characters in Balzac's *La Comédie Humaine* hung out. The market is open all day, Tuesday to noon on Sunday.

Rue Mouffetard

The endearingly rumpled rue Mouffetard, 5e, is home to the city's university students, whose lively bars rub shoulders with food shops on the narrow, hilly *rue commerçante* beloved by Ernest Hemingway. This is the city's most picturesque market street (Map 5, rue Mouffetard around rue de l'Arbalète, metro Censier Daubenton or Place Monge) – the place where Parisians send visitors. Pyramids of fruit, suspended rabbits and chickens, and wonderfully pungent cheese-shops make it a true moveable feast. Dine at a bargain *prix fixe* bistro (try rue du Pot de Fer) and finish with a drink where the students do, at a café (eg, La Chope) on the dreamy little place de la Contrescarpe. The market is open all day, Tuesday to noon on Sunday.

Left: Fine food at Comptoir de la Gastronomie on rue Montmartre, a stone's throw from rue Montorgueil

GREG ELMS

Top Left: Rue Mouffetard: the entrance to the market...

Top Right: ...a chef stocking up on fresh herbs...

Bottom: ...and an inviting selection of succulent fruit

Marché Saint Quentin

The wholesale Les Halles is long gone, but a handful of other iron-and-glass covered markets remain from the late 19th century. A welcome respite from the cold in winter, marchés couverts are a classier precursor of our modern-day shopping centres. Built in 1866, Saint Quentin (Map 3, 85 blvd de Magenta, 10e, metro Gare de l'Est) is a maze of corridors lined mostly with gourmet food stalls. A café counter, where vendors stand for an afternoon brew, and a fountain in the middle complete the illusion of a town within a city. It is open 8 am to 1 pm and 3.30 to 7.30 pm Tuesday to Sunday.

Emma Bland

Entertainment

LISTINGS

It's virtually impossible to sample the richness of Paris' entertainment scene without first perusing *Pariscope* (3FF) or *L'Officiel des Spectacles* (2FF), both of which come out on Wednesday and are available at any newsstand. *Pariscope* includes a six-page insert in English, courtesy of London's *Time Out* magazine, and can be found online at www.pariscope.fr.

For up-to-date information on clubs and the music scene, pick up a copy of *LYLO* (an acronym for *Les Yeux, Les Oreilles*, literally 'Eyes & Ears'), a free magazine with excellent listings of rock concerts and other live music that's available at certain cafés and bars; on Minitel, key in 3615 LYLO. The monthly magazines *Les Inrockuptibles* (15FF) and *Nova* (20FF) are good sources for information on clubs and the music scene; the latter's *Hot Guide* listings insert is particularly useful. Check out any of the Fnac outlets (see the following Booking Agencies section), especially the ones in the Forum des Halles shopping centre and Bastille, for free flyers and programs.

Two other excellent guides to what's on are Radio FG on 98.2MHz FM and Radio Nova on 101.5MHz FM.

BOOKING AGENCIES

You can buy tickets for many cultural events at several ticket outlets, among them Fnac (rhymes with 'snack') outlets and Virgin Megastores. Both accept reservations and ticketing by phone and take most credit cards. Tickets cannot be returned or exchanged unless a performance is cancelled.

Reservations for a wide variety of theatre and opera productions can be made on Minitel; key in 3615 THEA.

Fnac (☎ 0 803 80 88 03). Fnac has outlets with *billeteries* (ticket offices) throughout Paris (usually open 10 am to 7.30 pm Monday to Saturday), including Fnac Forum des Halles (Map 6, ☎ 01 40 41 40 00, metro Châtelet-Les Halles), Forum des Halles shopping centre, Level 3, 1-7 rue Pierre Lescot, 1er; Fnac Montparnasse (Map 4, ☎ 01 49 54 30 00, metro Saint Placide), 13 rue de Rennes, 6e; Fnac Musique Bastille (Map 6, ☎ 01 43 42 04 04, metro Bastille), 4 place de la Bastille, 12e, open 10 am to 8 pm Monday to Saturday (to 10 pm on Wednesday and Friday) and Fnac Étoile (Map 2, ☎ 01 44 09 18 00, metro Ternes), 26-30 ave des Ternes, 17e. You can purchase tickets via Fnac's Web site (www.fnac.com) or on Minitel (key in 3615 FNAC) with your credit card (commission 10FF to 20FF).

Virgin Megastore (Map 2, ☎ 01 49 53 50 00, metro Franklin D Roosevelt) 52-60 ave des Champs-Élysées, 8e. The billeterie (☎ 01 49 53 52 09) in the basement opens 10 am to midnight daily (from noon on Sunday). There's another Virgin Megastore (☎ 01 49 53 52 90) with a box office in the Carrousel du Louvre shopping centre (Map 6, metro Palais Royal-Musée du Louvre), 99 rue de Rivoli, 1er, next to the inverted glass pyramid. It opens 11 am to 8 pm daily (to 10 pm Wednesday to Saturday).

Other booking agencies include:

Agence des Théâtres (Map 2, ☎ 01 43 59 21 60, metro Franklin D Roosevelt) 78 ave des Champs-Élysées, 8e

Agence des Théâtres Marivaux (Map 3, ☎ 01 42 97 46 70, metro Richelieu Drouot) 7 rue de Marivaux, 2e

Comptoir Théâtral (Map 2, ☎ 01 42 60 58 31, metro Madeleine) 6 place de la Madeleine, 8e

Discount Tickets

On the day of a performance, Kiosque Théâtre outlets sell theatre tickets at half price (plus a commission of 16FF). The seats are almost always the most expensive ones in the stalls or 1st balcony. Tickets to concerts, operas and ballets might also be available.

Both outlets – one (Map 2, metro Madeleine) across from 15 place de la Madeleine, 8e, and the other (Map 4, metro Montparnasse Bienvenüe) on the parvis Montparnasse, halfway between Gare Montparnasse and the nearby Tour Montparnasse, 15e – are open 12.30 to 8 pm Tuesday to Saturday, and to 4 pm on Sunday.

Under the red windmill: the legendary Moulin Rouge

PUBS, BARS & CAFÉS

Like most other cities in Europe, Paris has been invaded by Irish pubs, which, though much of a muchness, have helped to bring the price of a pint of beer or a cocktail down to expensive, rather than extortionate, levels. You'll be able to find these on your own, but one of the better ones – with live music some nights – is *Coolin* (Map 6, ☎ 01 44 07 00 92, 15 rue Clément, 6e, metro Mabillon) in a renovated old covered market.

Les Halles (Map 6)

The area around Forum des Halles is filled with attractive places for a drink.

Le Tour du Table (☎ 01 42 96 47 54, 17 rue des Petits Champs, 1er, metro Bourse). This is an excellent place to sample wine, with glasses starting at about 15FF. It's open 11 am to midnight Monday to Friday and on Saturday evening.

Café Oz (☎ 01 40 39 00 18, 18 rue Saint Denis, 1er, metro Châtelet). An Aussie pub bubbling with the same Down Under enthusiasm as the original across the river (see the later Latin Quarter section). It opens 3 pm to 2 am daily (happy hour 6 to 8 pm).

Marais (Map 7)

The 4e has quite a few lively places for daytime and after-hours drinks.

La Chaise au Plafond (☎ 01 42 76 03 22, 10 rue du Trésor, 4e, metro Hôtel de Ville). Owned by the same people as Au Petit Fer à Cheval (see the next entry but one), the 'Chair on the Ceiling' is a warm, topsy-turvy place with tables outside on a pedestrian-only side street. It's open 9 am to 2 am daily.

Les Étages (☎ 01 42 78 72 00, 35 rue Vielle du Temple, 4e, metro Hôtel de Ville). Head upstairs to the two upper floors for grunge, with graffiti on the walls and big leather armchairs. The drinks aren't cheap (55FF to 65FF for spirits), but there's some serious pulling going on here.

euro currency converter €1 = 6.56FF

MANFRED GOTTSCHALK

ENTERTAINMENT

They Certainly Can Cancan

Paris' risqué cabaret revues – those dazzling, pseudo-bohemian productions featuring hundreds of performers, including female dancers both in and out of their elaborate costumes – are about as representative of the Paris of the 21st century as crocodile-wrestling is of Australia or bronco-busting is of the USA. But they do keep on drawing in the crowds, and the recent revival of the cancan at the Folies-Bergère may have set a retro-trend for the days of Toulouse-Lautrec.

Crazy Horse (Map 2, ☎ 01 47 23 32 32, 12 ave George V, 8e, metro Alma Marceau). The Crazy Horse, now approaching half a century of promoting *l'art du nu* (nudity), had its dressing (or un-dressing) rooms featured in Woody Allen's film *What's New Pussycat?* (1965). There are two shows (8.30 and 11 pm) Sunday to Friday and three (8 and 10.15 pm and 12.15 am) on Satur-day. Prices range from 290FF (at the bar) including two drinks to 750/980FF with dinner.

Folies-Bergère (Map 3, ☎ 01 44 79 98 98, 32 rue Richer, 9e, metro Cadet). This place is now cel-ebrated for its high-kicking, feather-clad cancan dancers but also stages musicals. There are shows at 9 pm (dinner at 7 pm) Tuesday to Sunday and matinees at 3 pm (lunch at noon) on Thursday and Sunday. Admission to the show costs 90FF to 350FF, dinner starts at 240FF (dinner plus show from 520FF).

Le Lido de Paris (Map 2, ☎ 01 40 76 56 10, 116 bis ave des Champs-Élysées, 8e, metro George V). The floor show of this cabaret (founded in 1946) gets top marks for its ambitious sets and lavish costumes. Nightly shows cost 560FF at 10 pm and 460FF (560FF on Friday and Saturday) at mid-night with half a bottle of champagne, 385FF to watch from the bar with two drinks and 815FF, 915FF and 1015FF with dinner, depending on the *menu* chosen.

Moulin Rouge (Map 8, ☎ 01 53 09 82 82, 82 blvd de Clichy, 18e, metro Blanche). Ooh la la... This legendary cabaret, whose dancers appeared in Toulouse-Lautrec's celebrated posters, sits under its trademark red windmill (actually a 1925 copy). The champagne dinner show (at 7 pm) costs 790FF, 890FF or 990FF. The show at 9 pm with half a bottle of champers costs 560FF; at 11 pm, it drops to 500FF.

Paradis Latin (Map 5, ☎ 01 43 25 28 28, 28 rue du Cardinal Lemoine, 5e, metro Cardinal Lemoine). This establishment is known for its extravagant, nonstop performances of songs, dances and night-club numbers. The staff, including the waiters, often participate. The show begins at 9.30 pm Wednesday to Monday and costs 465FF, including half a bottle of champagne or two drinks. A ticket including dinner at 8 pm costs 680FF, 865FF or 1250FF, depending on the *menu* you choose.

It's open 11 am to 2 am daily; happy hour is 5 to 9 pm.

Au Petit Fer à Cheval (☎ 01 42 72 47 47, 30 rue Vieille du Temple, 4e, metro Hôtel de Ville or Saint Paul). A slightly offbeat bar-restaurant named after its horseshoe-shaped counter, often filled to overflowing with friendly, mostly straight young regulars. The stainless-steel bathroom is straight out of a Flash Gordon film. It's open 9 am to 2 am (from 11 am at the week-end); happy hour is 6 to 8 pm. Food (plat du jour 60FF, sandwiches from 32FF) is available non-stop from noon to about 1.15 am.

Piment Café (☎ 01 42 74 33 75, 15 rue de Sévi-gné, 4e, metro Saint Paul). The mood at this small and cosmopolitan bar changes frequently during the evening, with tranquil moments punctuated by live music, art on show and good,

reasonably priced food (30FF to 50FF for light meals and salads, 38FF to 45FF for the plat du jour). It's open noon to 1 am daily (from 6 pm on Sunday).

Stolly's (☎ 01 42 76 06 76, 16 rue de la Cloche Percée, 4e, metro Hôtel de Ville). On a tiny street just off rue de Rivoli, this Anglophone bar is always crowded, particularly during the 4.30 to 8 pm happy hour, when a 1.6L pitcher of cheap *blonde* (house lager) is 55FF. It's open 4.30 pm to 1.30 am daily.

Île de la Cité (Map 6)

The island is not exactly hopping after dark, but there is a good wine bar here.

Taverne Henri IV (☎ 01 43 54 27 90, 13 place du Pont Neuf, 1er, metro Pont Neuf). A decent restaurant as well as a serious wine bar with a choice of 14 *tartines* (slices of bread with toppings or garnishes; 40FF), this place attracts lots of people in the legal profession from the nearby Palais de Justice. It's open noon to 9 pm weekdays, and to 4 pm on Saturday.

Latin Quarter (Maps 5 & 6)

The Latin Quarter has Paris' highest concentration of bars catering for Anglophones.

Café Oz (Map 5, ☎ 01 43 54 30 48 or 01 40 39 00 18, 184 rue Saint Jacques, 5e, metro Luxembourg). A casual Australian pub with Foster's on tap for 22FF (35FF for a 'schooner' or 400mL), and VB, Coopers, Cascade and Redback as well as other amber options, plus Australian wines from 20FF a glass. Pies start at 30FF. It opens 3 pm to 2 am Sunday to Thursday, to 3 am on Friday and noon to 3 am on Saturday. Happy hour is from 6 to 9.30 pm.

Le Cloître (Map 6, ☎ 01 43 25 19 92, 19 rue Saint Jacques, 5e, metro Saint Michel). A relaxed, unpretentious place – the mellow background music goes down well with the students who congregate here. It opens 3 pm to 2 am daily.

Polly Magoo (Map 6, ☎ 01 46 33 33 64, 11 rue Saint Jacques, 5e, metro Saint Michel). An informal, friendly, cult bar founded in 1967 and usually still spinning discs from that era (Doors, Jacques Brel etc). Beer starts at 13FF (19.50FF after 10 pm). It opens noon to 5 am Sunday to Thursday, and to 8 am on Friday and Saturday.

Le Violon Dingue (Map 5, ☎ 01 43 25 79 93, 46 rue de la Montagne Sainte Geneviève, 5e, metro Maubert Mutualité). A loud and lively American-style bar that attracts lots of English-speakers in their early twenties. A pint of beer costs 35FF, or 20FF during happy hour (6 to 10 pm), when most mixed drinks (usually 40FF to 45FF) are half-price. American sporting events such as the Superbowl and the NBA play-offs are shown on the large-screen TV. It's open 6 pm (cellar bar 8 pm) to 1.30 am Sunday to Thursday, and 8 pm to 4 am (cellar bar 10 pm to 4.30 am) on Friday and Saturday.

Saint Germain & Odéon (Map 6)

The 6e has some of Paris' most famous cafés and quite a few decent newcomers.

Café de Flore (☎ 01 45 48 55 26, 172 blvd Saint Germain, 6e, metro Saint Germain des Prés). This is an Art Deco café that's a bit less touristy than the Deux Magots (see the next entry but one), and where the red, upholstered benches,

mirrors and marble walls haven't changed since the days when Sartre, de Beauvoir, Camus and Picasso imbibed here. The terrace is a sought-after place to sip beer (42FF for 400mL), the house Pouilly Fumé wine (33FF) or coffee (24FF). It opens 7 am to 1.30 am daily.

Chez Georges (☎ 01 43 26 79 15, 11 rue des Canettes, 6e, metro Mabillon). This friendly bar, straight out of Orwell's *Down and Out in Paris and London*, is decorated with photos of musicians who played here in the 1960s and 1970s and is popular with people of all ages. Bottled beer starts at 18FF (22FF after 10 pm, 25FF in the cellar). It's open noon to 2 am Tuesday to Saturday and closes in August. The dank cellar, suffused with canned, mellow music at the weekend, opens at 10 pm.

Les Deux Magots (☎ 01 45 48 55 25, 170 blvd Saint Germain, 6e, metro Saint Germain des Prés). There's been a café here since 1885 but the present one – whose name derives from the two *magots* (grotesque figurines) of Chinese dignitaries at the entrance – dates from 1914. It is perhaps best known as the haunt of Sartre, Hemingway and André Breton. Coffee is 23FF, beer on tap 30FF and the famous steaming, homemade hot chocolate served in porcelain jugs 33FF. It's open 7.30 am to 2 am daily.

La Palette (☎ 01 43 26 68 15, 43 rue de Seine, 6e, metro Mabillon). This *fin de siècle* café, erstwhile stomping ground of Cézanne and Braque, attracts art dealers and collectors from the nearby galleries. It's open 8 am to 2 am Monday to Saturday.

Champs-Élysées (Map 2)

Once considered very out of fashion, the ave des Champs-Élysées and the area around it have had a new lease of life since their costly renovation in the mid-1990s.

Buddha Bar (☎ 01 53 05 90 00, 8 rue Boissy d'Anglas, 8e, metro Concorde). A wall of Buddhas greets you on your arrival at this bar-restaurant frequented by suits, supermodels and hangers-on. Everyone should go at least once for a look, but stick to the drinks (cocktails from 60FF); a Pacific Rim-style meal will cost you upwards of 300FF though there's a lunch *menu* for 190FF. It's open noon to 3 pm and 6 pm to 2 am daily.

The Cricketer (☎ 01 40 07 01 45, 41 rue des Mathurins, 8e, metro Saint Augustin). This genuine English pub, supposedly transported to Paris lock, stock and barrel from Ipswich, is a last refuge for homesick Brits, with darts, quiz

ENTERTAINMENT

nights and Adnams on tap (25FF). It's open 11 am to 2 am daily.

Grands Boulevards (Maps 2 & 6)

The bars and cafés on and just off the seemingly interminable Grands Boulevards are some of the best venues for a night on the town if you're restricting yourself to the Right Bank.

Café Noir (Map 6, ☎ 01 40 39 07 36, 65 rue Montmartre, 2e, metro Sentier). On the edge of the Sentier garment district, the 'Black' may be a bit off the beaten track but it draws both Anglo- and Francophones well into the night, attracted by the friendly ambience and reasonable prices. Its open 8 am to 2 am weekdays, and from 4 pm on Saturday.

Harry's New York Bar (Map 2, ☎ 01 42 61 71 14, 5 rue Daunou, 2e, metro Opéra). Back in the prewar years when there were several dozen American-style bars in Paris, Harry's was one of the most popular. Habitués included F Scott Fitzgerald and Hemingway, who no doubt sampled the bar's unique cocktail: the Bloody Mary. The Cuban mahogany interior dates from the mid-19th century and was brought over from a bar on Manhattan's Third Avenue in 1911. Beer costs 30FF (38FF after 10 pm). Drinks in the basement piano bar (soft jazz 10 pm to 2 or 3 am) cost 53FF to 77FF. It's open 10.30 am to 4 am daily. The copyrighted advertisement for Harry's in the *International Herald Tribune* still reads: 'Tell the Taxi Driver Sank Roo Doe Noo'.

Oberkampf & Ménilmontant (Maps 3 & 6)

South of place de la République, rue Oberkampf and its surrounding area, together with its eastern extension, rue Ménilmontant, are among the hottest areas in Paris at the moment, with a number of interesting cafés and bars.

L'Autre Café (Map 3, ☎ 01 40 21 03 07, 62 rue Jean Pierre Timbaud, 11e, metro Parmentier). This popular venue has already begun to move the centre of after-dark activity north of rue Oberkampf. With its long bar, open spaces, relaxed environment and reasonable prices, it attracts a mixed young crowd of locals, artists and party-goers. It's open 9 am to 2 am daily.

Cannibale Café (Map 3, ☎ 01 49 29 95 59, 93 rue Jean-Pierre Timbaud, 11e, metro Couronnes). A

SIMON BRACKEN

Les Deux Magots: haunt of numerous literary luminaries in its heyday

laid-back alternative to the pubs and bars on rue Oberkampf, the 'Cannibal' is the place to linger over a coffee (10FF) or grab a quick beer at the bar (13FF) or *à table* (17FF). It's open 8 am to 2 am daily (from 9 am at the weekend).

Chez Wolf Motown Bar (Map 3, ☎ 01 46 07 09 79, 81-83 blvd de Strasbourg, 10e, metro Gare de l'Est). This is the place to come in the lonely wee hours when you've got a thirst but, alas, no friends. It's open 24 hours, you can eat and drink at any time of day and both the staff and the patrons are exceptionally friendly. The place almost feels like a club.

Le Mécano (Map 3, ☎ 01 40 21 35 28, 99 rue Oberkampf, 11e, metro Parmentier). Housed in a former tool-shed, this ultra-cool café/bar is a good place to meet before heading elsewhere along rue Oberkampf to eat and party. It's open 9 pm to 2 am daily.

Le Sirena (Map 3, ☎ 01 43 55 93 53, 76 rue Jean-Pierre Timbaud, 11e, metro Parmentier). This little place, all blues and shaded light, attracts musicians from 5 pm to 2 am daily.

Satellit' Café (Map 6, ☎ 01 47 00 48 87, 44 rue de la Folie Méricourt, 11e, metro Oberkampf).

ENTERTAINMENT

This is the best place in the quarter for world music and is not as painfully trendy as some of its neighbours. Open daily till 5.30 am.

e Troisième Bureau (Map 6, ☎ 01 43 55 87 65, 74 rue de la Folie Méricourt, 11e, metro Oberkampf). A pub-cum-bistro with an interesting clientele where you can read, listen to music and even send or receive a fax from the phone box. Decent dishes are available for from 50FF to 85FF. It's open 11.30 am to 2 am daily (from 6.30 pm on Sunday).

Bastille (Maps 5 & 6)

The area north-east of place de la Bastille is enormously popular for dining, drinking and dancing all night long. To the south-east of the square there are a number of excellent after-dark venues.

Boca Chica (Map 5, ☎ 01 43 57 93 13, 58 rue de Charonne, 11e, metro Ledru Rollin). This is an enormous, almost industrial, place with three large bars on two floors and a friendly, lively crowd. Happy hour is 4 to 8 pm daily when 1L of sangria is 45FF and cocktails are half-price. It's open 11 am to 2 am daily.

Café des Phares (Map 7, ☎ 01 42 72 04 70, 7 place Bastille, 4e, metro Bastille). This is Paris' original *philocafé* (philosophers' café), where you can debate such fascinating topics as 'What is a fact?' and 'Can people communicate?' (hey, can we?) at 11 am on Sunday. Attempts to resurrect the Paris of Sartre on a commercial basis are very popular elsewhere in Paris; for a list of *philocafés* visit www.socrate.com on the Web.

Le Café du Passage (Map 5, ☎ 01 49 29 97 64, 12 rue de Charonne, 11e, metro Ledru Rollin). This is a modern yet laid-back wine bar where you can relax in upholstered armchairs while sampling 70 varieties of wine, 16 of them available by the glass (from 25FF to 42FF). Light food such as pâtés, risotto and salads (42FF to 85FF) is also available. It's open 6 pm to 2 am Monday to Friday, and from noon on Saturday.

China Club (Map 5, ☎ 01 43 43 82 02, 50 rue de Charenton, 12e, metro Ledru Rollin). If you've got a rich uncle or aunt in tow, have them take you to this stylish establishment behind the Opéra Bastille. It's got a huge bar with high ceilings on the ground floor, a *fumoir* (smoking room) for smoking cigars on the 1st floor and a jazz club called Le Sing Song done up to look like Shanghai circa 1930 in the cellar. Happy hour is 7 to 9 pm daily, when all drinks are 35FF. It's open 7 pm to 2 am (to 3 am on Friday and Saturday).

Iguana Café (Map 6, ☎ 01 40 21 39 99, 15 rue de la Roquette, 11e, metro Bastille). A chic, two-level café/pub that attracts trendy 20- to 30-year-olds. Cocktails are 48FF to 55FF (52FF to 59FF after 10 pm), beer on tap is 24FF to 28FF (or 28FF to 32FF in the evening). It's open 9 am to 5 am daily.

Sanz Sans (Map 5, ☎ 01 44 75 78 78, 49 rue du Faubourg Saint Antoine, 11e, metro Bastille). By night this full-on watering hole is one of the liveliest (OK, rowdiest) drinking spots on the Bastille beat: dress (or undress) to impress. By day the red velvet décor seems a tad overdone. It's open 9 am to 2 am daily.

Bercy (Map 9)

The converted wine warehouses in Bercy Village now house a variety of restaurants and bars. Across the Seine in the 13e, what better spot for a sundowner than a barge moored along the quay?

Blues Café (☎ 01 45 84 24 88, quai François Mauriac, 13e, metro Quai de la Gare or Bibliothèque). Another barge with a theme, this place has decent canned and live blues and jazz.

Nicolas (☎ 01 44 74 62 65, 24 cour Saint Émilion, 12e, metro Cour Saint Émilion). Nicolas, one of the largest wine retailers in Paris, has now decided to get in on the act and open its own place. Lower-shelf wines cost 11FF to 17FF a glass; the vintage stuff is 20FF to 43FF. Salads, cheese platters and other edibles go for 46FF to 81FF. It's open for lunch and dinner to 11.30 pm daily.

Montparnasse (Maps 5 & 6)

The most popular places to while away the hours over a drink or coffee in Montparnasse are the large café-restaurants such as *La Coupole* and *Le Select* on blvd du Montparnasse (see the Places to Eat chapter).

La Closerie des Lilas (Map 5, ☎ 01 40 51 34 50, 171 blvd du Montparnasse, 6e, metro Port Royal). Anyone who has read Hemingway will know that he did a lot of writing, drinking and eating of oysters here; little brass tags on the tables tell you exactly where he (and other luminaries such as Picasso and Apollinaire) whiled away the hours. It's open 11.30 am to 1 am daily.

Cubana Café (Map 4, ☎ 01 40 46 80 81, 47 rue Vavin, 6e, metro Vavin). This is the perfect place for a couple of 'starter' drinks before carrying

ENTERTAINMENT

on to the nearby Coupole, with cocktails (43FF) reduced to 29FF at happy hour (6 to 8 pm). Sunday Cuban brunch (noon to 7 pm) costs 98FF. For those who indulge in cigars, there's a fumoir equipped with a bunch of comfy sofas. It's open noon to 2 am daily.

Montmartre & Pigalle (Map 8)
In between the sleaze there are some interesting bars at the bottom of the Butte de Montmartre (Montmartre Hill).

Chào-Bà Café (☎ *01 46 06 72 90, 22 blvd de Clichy, 18e, metro Pigalle*). This café-restaurant, transformed from the old-style Café Pigalle into something straight out of *Indochine*, is open 9 am to 2 am Sunday to Wednesday, to 4 am on Thursday and to 5 am on Friday and Saturday.

Le Dépanneur (☎ *01 40 16 40 20, 27 rue Fontaine, 9e, metro Blanche*). This American diner with postmodern frills has plenty of tequila and fancy cocktails (40FF to 55FF). Beer is 28FF to 30FF though cheaper during happy hour (6 to 8 pm). The lunch *menu* is 75FF, the dinner one 99FF. It's open 24 hours a day, seven days a week; arrive here and you may never leave.

La Fourmi (☎ *01 42 64 70 35, 74 rue des Martyrs, 18e, metro Pigalle*). This trendy Pigalle hang-out buzzes all day and all night and is a convenient place to meet before heading for Le Divan du Monde (see the Rock section) just across the road. It's open 8.30 am to 2 am (from 10 am on Sunday).

Le Sancerre (☎ *01 42 58 08 20, 35 rue des Abbesses, 18e, metro Abbesses*). A popular, rather brash bistro/bar that's often crowded in the evening. The cheapest beers cost between 11FF (at the bar during the day) and 20FF (after 10 pm). Food, including two plats du jour (60FF), is served noon to 11 pm and there's brunch (60FF) at the weekend. It's open 7 am to 1.30 am daily.

20e Arrondissement (Map 1)
Should you be getting on or off an international bus or staying at the Auberge de Jeunesse Le D'Artagnan (see Hostels in the Places to Stay chapter), the following place should be your first port of call.

La Flèche d'Or (☎ *01 43 72 42 44, 102 bis rue de Bagnolet, 20e, metro Porte de Bagnolet or Alexandre Dumas*). This smoky music bar – in a disused train station south-east of Cimetière

du Père Lachaise – attracts a trendy and arty young crowd; this may as well be Berlin. There's a 65FF lunch *menu* (105FF and 125FF at dinner) and the big café here does a decent brunch noon to 3 pm on Sunday. It's open 10 am to 2 am daily.

CLUBS
The clubs and other dancing venues favoured by the Parisian 'in' crowd change frequently, and many are officially private. Single men may not be admitted – even if their clothes are subculturally appropriate – simply because they're men on their own. Women, on the other hand, get in for free on some nights. It's always easier to get into the club of your choice during the week when things may be hopping even more than they are at the weekend. The truly trendy crowd considers showing up before 1 am a serious breach of good taste.

Paris is a great music town and there are some fine DJs based here. Latin American and Cuban salsa and merengue are also particularly hot (see the boxed text 'Salsa City' later in this section). Theme nights are common; for more details consult any of the sources mentioned under Listings at the start of this chapter.

Les Bains (*Map 6, ☎ 01 48 87 01 80, 7 rue du Bourg l'Abbé, 3e, metro Étienne Marcel*). This club, in a refitted old Turkish bath, is still renowned for its surly, selective bouncers on the outside and both celebrity and star-struck revellers inside; it's hard to gain entry at the weekend. Music is house, garage and techno. It's open 11.30 pm to 6 am daily (entry 100FF to 130FF).

Batofar (*Map 9, ☎ 01 56 29 10 00, opposite 11 quai François Mauriac, 13e, metro Quai de la Gare or Bibliothèque*). What looks like a mild-mannered tugboat moored near the imposing Bibliothèque Nationale de France is a rollicking dancing spot that attracts some top international DJ talent. It's open 6 pm to 2 am Tuesday to Sunday (entrance up to 100FF).

Le Balajo (*Map 6, ☎ 01 47 00 07 87, 9 rue de Lappe, 11e, metro Bastille*). This vintage place has been a mainstay of Parisian nightlife since 1936. Wednesday (9 pm to 2 am) is live mambo night, Thursday live salsa (10 pm to 3 am) and DJs spin LPs and CDs (rock, 1970s disco, funk) on Friday and Saturday from 11.30 pm to 5 am. Admission costs 100FF (50FF on Wednesday) and includes one drink. From 2.30 to 6.30 pm

River rhythms: dance the night away, literally on the Seine, at Batofar.

on Thursday and 3 to 7 pm on Sunday, DJs play old-fashioned *musette* (accordion music) – waltz, tango, cha-cha – for aficionados of retro tea-dancing (50FF).

Cithéa (Map 3, ☎ 01 40 21 70 95, 114 rue Oberkampf, 11e, metro Parmentier). This ever-hopping place has bands playing soul, acid jazz, Latin and funk. Wine and beer cost 30FF, cocktails from 70FF. It's open 10 am to 5.30 am daily.

La Coupole (Map 4, ☎ 01 43 20 14 20, 102 blvd du Montparnasse, 14e, metro Vavin). La Coupole hosts one of the best salsa sessions in town on Tuesday night (see the boxed text 'Salsa City' on the next page); from 9.30 pm to 4 am on Friday and Saturday there's a retro disco (100FF), and from 3 to 7 pm on Saturday and 3 to 9 pm on Sunday there are tea dances (40FF).

Folies Pigalle (Map 8, ☎ 01 48 78 25 26 or 01 40 36 71 58, 11 place Pigalle, 9e, metro Pigalle). The Folies is a heaving, mixed place that is great for cruising from the balcony above the dance floor. It's open midnight till dawn Thursday to Saturday with concerts at 2 am (100FF to 150FF). Sunday night is ethnic gay night (40FF) with a Latin American music and drag show (100FF) from midnight till dawn.

Le Gibus (Map 3, ☎ 01 47 00 78 88, 18 rue du Faubourg du Temple, 11e, metro République). Once a cathedral of rock, the cave-like Gibus has undergone a metamorphosis, with Wednesday devoted to techno and the weekend to trance and house. It's open midnight to dawn (admission 20FF weekdays and 110FF at the weekend).

La Guinguette Pirate (Map 9, ☎ 01 56 29 10 20, opposite 11 quai François Mitterrand, 13e, metro Quai de la Gare or Bibliothèque). Another barge-based *boîte* (club), this time in a three-masted Chinese junk, the 'Pirate Dance Café' usually hosts some sort of concert at 9 or 10.30 pm (entry 40FF), and the crowd is young and energetic. It's open from about noon to 2 am daily.

La Locomotive (Map 8, ☎ 0 836 69 69 28 or 01 53 41 88 88, 90 blvd de Clichy, 18e, metro Blanche). An enormous, ever-popular disco on three levels that has long been one of the favourite dancing venues for teenage out-of-towners hot to bop. It opens 11 pm to 6 or 7 am (from midnight on Monday). Admission costs 70/55FF with/without a drink Monday to Thursday (women get in free before 12.30 am); on Friday and Saturday it costs 60FF without a drink before midnight and 100FF with one after that.

ENTERTAINMENT

Salsa City

Ay, que rico! Whether you're a Latin music aficionado, a salsa and merengue enthusiast or just a Hemingway wannabe in search of that perfect *mojito* (rum cocktail), you'll soon discover that Paris boasts enough sizzling, Cuba-inspired bars and *boîtes* (clubs) to more than rival its Hispanic neighbour to the south and some say even Havana itself.

What's more, the Latin American vibes don't stop when the temperature drops. New clubs are opening up all the time, established venues are adding salsa nights and virtually anyone who's anyone in the Latin world makes it to Paris eventually, including the Cuban *Buena Vista* veterans. So don your dancing shoes and let's dance till dawn.

For who and what is *caliente* (hot) in Latin American music, tune in to Radio Latina 99MHz FM, with repeated schedules from 6 and 10 am and 5 and 8 pm weekdays and 5 to 11 pm on Saturday. You can also check out its Web site at www.latina.fr. On Minitel, key in 3615 LATINA. *Pariscope* and *L'Officiel des Spectacles* (see Listings at the start of this chapter) also list concerts.

The following are the hottest, happeningest Latin dance venues in Paris at the moment. The price of admission often includes the first drink. Many clubs offer salsa and merengue classes in the early evening.

Le Balajo (Map 6, ☎ 01 47 00 07 87, 9 rue de Lappe, 11e, metro Bastille). Live salsa music and dancing are featured at this ancient ballroom 10 pm to 5 am on Thursday (100FF).

La Casa 128 (Map 3, ☎ 01 48 01 05 71, 128 rue La Fayette, 10e, metro Gare du Nord). This club has an excellent ambience and salsa 8 pm to 2 am Thursday to Sunday (50FF).

La Chapelle des Lombards (Map 6, ☎ 01 43 57 24 24, 19 rue de Lappe, 11e, metro Bastille). This place has Nuits Fauves (Wild Nights) on Wednesday, and tropical and Latin nights Thursday to Saturday (100FF).

La Coupole (Map 4, ☎ 01 43 20 14 20, 102 blvd du Montparnasse, 14e, metro Vavin). The Latin fever epidemic can be traced to La Coupole and the year 1993, when the now (in)famous Tuesday salsa night (8.30 pm to 3 am) with live big bands was launched. Admission costs 100FF (140FF including a dance class from 8.30 to 9.30 pm).

L'Opus (Map 3, ☎ 01 40 34 70 00, 167 quai de Valmy, 10e, metro Château Landon). Salsa, zouk (a blend of African and Latin American dance rhythms), jazz and rock are on offer after 9.30 pm on Friday and Saturday and after 7 pm on Sunday in this former officers' mess by the Canal Saint Martin.

Queen (Map 2, ☎ 01 53 89 08 90, 102 ave des Champs-Élysées, 8e, metro George V). The king (as it were) of gay discos in Paris now reigns even more supreme with special theme parties open to all (eg, the mixed Respect night on Wednesday), if they can get past the bouncers. It's open midnight to 6 am daily; the cover charge (Friday and Saturday nights only) is 100FF.

Rex Club (Map 3, ☎ 01 42 36 83 98 or 01 42 36 10 96, 5 rue Poissonnière, 2e, metro Bonne Nouvelle). This huge club is indisputably the hottest place in town for techno and attracts Paris' top DJ talent. It's open 11 pm till dawn Wednesday to Sunday; admission costs 60FF to 100FF, depending on the night.

La Scala de Paris (Map 6, ☎ 01 42 61 64 00, 188 bis rue de Rivoli, 1er, metro Palais Royal-Musée du Louvre or Pyramides). A large, touristy disco whose three dance floors (all playing the same music) and five bars are lit by laser lights. The patrons are mostly in the 18 to 30 age group and come from all over Western Europe and provincial France. It opens 10.30 pm to dawn daily. Entrance costs 80FF (100FF on Friday and Saturday nights), including one drink. Women get in for free Sunday to Thursday.

Slow Club (Map 6, ☎ 01 42 33 84 30, 130 rue de Rivoli, 1er, metro Châtelet). An unpretentious dance and jazz club, housed in a deep cellar once used to ripen Caribbean bananas, attracting a very mixed-age crowd. The music varies from night to night but includes jazz, boogie, bebop, swing and blues. It's open 10 pm to 3 am Tuesday to Thursday, and to 4 am on Friday and Saturday. Admission costs 60FF (80FF on Friday and Saturday with a drink); women get in free before midnight.

Salsa City

Le Divan du Monde (Map 8, ☎ 01 44 92 77 66 or 01 43 38 70 76, 75 rue des Martyrs, 18e, metro Pigalle). This place has world-music nights with at least one salsa night a week (admission varies).

L'Élysée-Montmartre (Map 8, ☎ 01 44 92 45 45 or 01 55 06 07 00, 72 blvd de Rochechouart, 18e, metro Anvers). This place co-hosts special Brazilian evenings (80FF) with the Favela Chic restaurant (see Ménilmontant & Belleville in the Places to Eat chapter) on some Saturdays; check Pariscope for details. On other Saturdays it becomes a salsa venue known as the Bal de l'Élysée-Montmartre.

Les Étoiles (Map 3, ☎ 01 47 70 60 56, 61 rue du Château d'Eau, 10e, metro Château d'Eau). Paris' first music hall (opened in 1856) features live Latin bands and an ambiente popular from 11 pm to 4 am Thursday to Saturday (60FF).

La Java (Map 3, ☎ 01 42 02 20 52, 105 rue du Faubourg du Temple, 10e, metro Belleville). The dance hall where Édith Piaf (see the boxed text 'The Urchin Sparrow') got her first break now reverberates to the sound of salsa 11 pm to 5 am Thursday to Saturday and 2 to 7 pm on Sunday (80FF to 100FF).

Latina Café (Map 2, ☎ 01 42 89 98 89, 114 ave des Champs-Élysées, 8e, metro George V). This recently opened restaurant/music club has something for everyone – from novices to well-honed Latin music lovers. There's a bodeguita (little bar) and tapas bar on the ground floor (demi of beer 21FF, cocktails 59FF), a restaurant and the Bar Hacienda on the 1st floor and a club with a stage and live bands in the basement. Radio Latina broadcasts from here live on Thursday. It's open 9 am to 5 am daily.

Los Latinos (Map 6, ☎ 01 43 55 12 45, 45 rue de Saint Sébastien, 11e, metro Richard Lenoir). This Latin restaurant has a small but intimate dance floor and a tropical atmosphere. Live bands play Thursday to Saturday nights (180FF for dinner and concert).

Montecristo Café (Map 2, ☎ 01 45 62 30 86, 68 ave des Champs-Élysées, 8e, metro Franklin D Roosevelt). This bar/restaurant brings mainstream Latin music to the Right Bank and the tourists love it. The music is good, there's a great bar and basement and it is open 11 am to 6 am daily, with a DJ and salsa from 10 pm (60FF to 100FF).

Brenda Turnnidge

Zed Club (Map 6, ☎ 01 43 54 93 78, 2 rue des Anglais, 5e, metro Maubert Mutualité). A vaulted basement where the DJs favour rock 'n' roll, jazz and swing. It's open 10.30 pm to 3 am on Wednesday and Thursday and 11 pm to 5.30 am on Friday and Saturday. Admission costs 60FF (100FF on Friday and Saturday), including a drink. Garçons non accompagnés (literally 'unaccompanied boys') may not get in.

GAY & LESBIAN VENUES

The Marais, especially those areas around the intersection of rue Sainte Croix de la Bretonnerie and rue des Archives and eastwards to rue Vieille du Temple, has been Paris' main centre of gay and lesbian nightlife for two decades. There are also a few bars and clubs within walking distance west of blvd de Sébastopol.

Amnésia Café (Map 7, ☎ 01 42 72 16 94, 42 rue Vieille du Temple, 4e, metro Hôtel de Ville). A cosy, warmly lit and very popular place, with comfy sofas and a mixed clientele. Beers start at 19FF, cocktails at 45FF. Breakfast is 75FF and brunch (noon to 4 pm daily) is 95FF and 135FF. It's open 9.30 am to 2 am daily.

L'Arène (Map 7, 80 quai de l'Hôtel de Ville, 4e, metro Hôtel de Ville). For those seriously OFB (out for business), this place can oblige. It's got dark rooms and cubicles on two levels and heats up (boils over, rather) from around midnight. Take the usual precautions. It's open 2 pm to 6 am daily (to 7 am at the weekend).

Banana Café (Map 6, ☎ 01 42 33 35 31, 13 rue de la Ferronnerie, 1er, metro Châtelet). This ever-popular cruise bar on two levels has a nice enclosed terrace with stand-up tables and attracts a young, buffed-up crowd. Happy hour is 4 to 9 pm. It's open 4.30 pm to 6 am daily.

La Champmeslé (Map 6, ☎ 01 42 96 85 20, 4 rue Chabanais, 2e, metro Pyramides). A relaxed, long-established place that plays mellow music for its patrons, about 75% of whom are lesbians

euro currency converter €1 = 6.56FF

(the rest are mostly gay men). The back room is reserved for women only. Beer or fruit juice costs 20FF to 30FF. It's open 5 pm to 5 am Monday to Saturday, and there's a cabaret of French *chansons* at 10 pm on Thursday.

Le Cox *(Map 7, ☎ 01 42 72 08 00, 15 rue des Archives, 4e, metro Hôtel de Ville)*. OK, we don't like the in-your-face name either but what's a boy to do? This small bar attracts an interesting (and interested) crowd throughout the evening. It's open 1 pm to 2 am (happy hour is 6 to 9 pm).

Full Metal *(Map 7, ☎ 01 42 72 30 05, 40 rue des Blancs Manteaux, 4e, metro Rambuteau)*. Heavy stuff most nights here till the wee hours, with a demanding fetishist dress code on Wednesday: leather, latex, jeans or uniforms. Admission costs 80FF; happy hour is 5 to 8 pm.

Mixer Bar *(Map 7, ☎ 01 48 87 55 44, 23 rue Sainte Croix de la Bretonnerie, 4e, metro Hôtel de Ville)*. The name says it all: techno and house music of all flavours, gay (with a hint of hetero) patrons. Beers are 16FF to 25FF. It's open 4 pm to 2 am.

Open Bar *(Map 7, ☎ 01 42 72 26 18, 17 rue des Archives, 4e, metro Hôtel de Ville)*. This is where most boyz of all ages head after work (or however they've spent the day). It's packed but more social than cruisy. It opens 11 am to 2 am (happy hour is 6 to 8 pm) and its small *coffee shop* next door (open noon till midnight) serves food.

QG *(Map 7, ☎ 01 48 87 74 18, 12 rue Simon Le Franc, 4e, metro Rambuteau)*. QG is not as popular as L'Arène but it's the same type of place, so come prepared. It's open 5 pm to 6 am daily (to 8 am at the weekend).

Quetzal *(Map 7, ☎ 01 48 04 83 02, 10 rue de la Verrerie, 4e, metro Hôtel de Ville)*. The Quetzal, just opposite rue des Mauvais Garçons (literally 'Bad Boys Street', which has been its name since 1540 when brigands congregated here), is a dimly lit, modern bar popular with thirty-something gay men and is still the cruisiest, most attitude-free place in the Marais. It's open 5 pm to 3 am (to 5 am on Friday and Saturday). Happy hour is 5 to 8 pm.

Les Scandaleuses *(Map 7, ☎ 01 48 87 39 26, 8 rue des Écouffes, 4e, metro Hôtel de Ville)*. Glossy and lively women-only bar in the Marais, popular with artists and designers. It's open 6 pm to 2 am daily.

Le Tango *(Map 6, ☎ 01 42 72 17 78, 13 rue au Maire, 3e, metro Arts et Métiers)*. Former Afro-Caribbean *club frotti/frotta* (roughly 'rub club') goes camping, with a mixed gay and lesbian crowd bent on doing the same. Entrance usually costs 40FF to 60FF. It's open 10.30 pm to 5 am daily but most popular Thursday to Saturday.

ROCK

There's rock at many bars, cafés and clubs around Paris, and a number of venues regularly host acts by international performers. It's often easier to see big-name Anglophone acts in Paris than in their home countries. The most popular stadiums or other big venues for international acts are the ***Palais Omnisports de Paris-Bercy*** *(Map 9, ☎ 01 44 68 44 68)* in the 12e, which hosts the likes of Ricky Martin and Tom Jones; the ***Stade de France*** *(☎ 01 55 93 00 00 or 01 44 68 44 44)* in Saint Denis (last seen: Tina Turner; see the Excursions chapter); and ***Le Zénith*** *(Map 1, ☎ 01 42 08 60 00)*, at the Cité de la Musique in the 19e, where groups such as The Cure perform.

Other venues – though not exclusively for rock – include:

Le Bataclan *(Map 6, ☎ 01 43 14 35 35 or 0 826 02 12 12, 50 blvd Voltaire, 11e, metro Saint Ambroise)*. A small concert venue with some big acts (eg, Oasis), Le Bataclan also masquerades as a theatre and dance hall. It's open from 8.30 pm for concerts (around 110FF to 195FF).

Café de la Danse *(Map 6, ☎ 01 47 00 57 59, 5 passage Louis-Philippe, 11e, metro Bastille)*. An auditorium with 300 to 500 seats, Café de la Danse is just a few metres from 23 rue de Lappe. Almost every day at 7.30 or 8.30 pm it plays host to rock and world-music concerts, dance performances, musical theatre and poetry readings. Tickets (60FF to 120FF) are available from Fnac.

La Cigale *(Map 8, ☎ 01 49 25 89 99 or 0 803 81 58 03, 102 blvd de Rochechouart, 18e, metro Anvers or Pigalle)*. An enormous old music hall that hosts international rock acts and occasionally jazz and folk groups (eg, the Dubliners). There's seating in the balcony and dancing up front. Admission costs 60FF to 180FF.

Le Divan du Monde *(Map 8, ☎ 01 44 92 77 66 or 01 43 38 70 76, 75 rue des Martyrs, 18e, metro Pigalle)*. One of the best concert venues in town, with good visibility and sound, Latin music features at least once a week (see the boxed text 'Salsa City'). It's also a popular club open most days 11.30 pm till dawn (30FF to 60FF).

L'Élysée-Montmartre *(Map 8, ☎ 01 44 92 45 45, 72 blvd de Rochechouart, 18e, metro Anvers)*. This huge old music hall is one of the better venues for one-off rock and indie concerts and opens 6 pm to 6 am Monday to Saturday (80FF to 120FF). For details of Brazilian and salsa

ENTERTAINMENT

nights see the boxed text 'Salsa City' earlier in this chapter.

Espace Voltaire (*Map 5*, ☎ *01 40 24 02 48, 4 rue Camille Desmoulin, 11e, metro Voltaire*). This large hall is hired out for special events and has some of the best musical entertainment in the city. Check any of the entertainment weeklies (see Listings at the start of this chapter) and keep an eye out for brochures and flyers.

JAZZ

After WWII, Paris was Europe's most important jazz centre and it is again very much à la mode; the city's better clubs attract top international stars. The Banlieues Bleues (☎ 01 49 22 10 10 for information), a jazz festival held in Saint Denis and other Paris suburbs in late February and March, attracts big-name talent.

Le Baiser Salé (*Map 6*, ☎ *01 42 33 37 71, 58 rue des Lombards, 1er, metro Châtelet*). This is one of a trio of very hip jazz clubs on the same street. The *salle de jazz* on the 1st floor has concerts of Afro-jazz, jazz fusion and so on from 10 pm to 3 am daily. The cover charge is 40FF to 100FF, depending on the act; it's free on Sunday (when young musicians play) and during jam sessions on Monday night. The bar on the ground floor is open 6 pm to 6 am daily.

Le Caveau de la Huchette (*Map 6*, ☎ *01 43 26 65 05, 5 rue de la Huchette, 5e, metro Saint Michel*). This place is a medieval *caveau* (cellar) – used as a courtroom and torture chamber during the Revolution – where virtually all the jazz greats have played since 1946. It's touristy – no doubt about that – but the atmosphere can often be more electric than at the more 'serious' jazz clubs. It opens 9.30 pm to 2.30 am daily (to 3.30 am on Friday, to 4 am on Saturday); sessions begin at 10.30 pm. The cover charge is 60FF (55FF for students) during the week, 70FF (no discounts) at the weekend.

Au Duc des Lombards (*Map 6*, ☎ *01 42 33 22 88, 42 rue des Lombards, 1er, metro Châtelet*). A cool venue decorated with posters of jazz greats (eg, the eponymous Duke) that attracts a far more relaxed (and less reverent) crowd than the other two jazz venues in the area. The ground floor bar vibrates 9 pm to 4 am nightly, with sets starting at 10 pm. The cover charge is 80FF to 100FF, depending on what's on.

New Morning (*Map 3*, ☎ *01 45 23 51 41, 7-9 rue des Petites Écuries, 10e, metro Château d'Eau*). An informal auditorium that hosts jazz concerts as well as blues, rock, funk, salsa, Afro-Cuban

and Brazilian music three to seven nights a week at 9 pm. The second set ends at about 1 am. Tickets (120FF to 150FF) are available at the box office (4.30 to 7.30 pm) as well as Fnac and Virgin Megastores, but can usually be purchased at the door.

Le Sunset (*Map 6*, ☎ *01 40 26 46 60, 60 rue des Lombards, 1er, metro Châtelet*). Musicians and actors (both film and theatre) are among the jazz fans who hang out at this trendy club, whose cellar hosts live concerts of funk, Latin American music, bebop and the like at 9 pm and 2 am daily. Admission costs 50FF to 120FF, depending on who's playing.

FRENCH CHANSONS

When French music comes to mind, most people hear accordions and *chansonniers* (cabaret singers) such as Edith Piaf, Jacques Brel, Georges Brassens and Léo Ferré. But though you may stumble upon buskers performing *chansons françaises* or playing *musette* (accordion music) in the market, it can sometimes be difficult to catch traditional French music in a more formal setting in Paris.

Chez Louisette (*Map 1*, ☎ *01 40 12 10 14, Marché aux Puces de Saint Ouen, 93400 Saint Ouen, metro Porte de Clignancourt*). This is one of the highlights of a visit to Paris' largest flea market (see Flea Markets in the Shopping chapter). Market-goers crowd around little tables to eat lunch (main dishes 65FF to 135FF) and hear an old-time chanteuse belt out Piaf numbers accompanied by accordion music. It

ASA ANDERSSON

The Urchin Sparrow

The singer Édith Piaf was a tragic, stoical figure who France took to its heart and never let go. Born Édith Giovanna Gassion to a street acrobat and a singer in Belleville in 1915, her early childhood was spent with her maternal grandmother, an alcoholic who neglected her, and later with her father's parents, who ran a brothel. At the age of nine she toured with her father, but she left home at 15 to sing alone in the streets of Paris. Her first employer, Louis Leplée, called her *la môme piaf* (the urchin sparrow) and introduced her to the cabarets of Pigalle. When Leplée was murdered, Piaf faced the streets again. But along came Raymond Asso, an ex-legionnaire who would become her Pygmalion, forcing her to break with her pimp and hustler friends, putting her in her signature black dress and inspiring her first big hit (*Mon Légionnaire*, 1937). When he got her a contract at one of the most famous Parisian music halls of the time, her career skyrocketed.

Singing about street life, drugs, death and prostitutes, Piaf seemed to embody all the miseries of the world yet sang in a husky, powerful voice with no self-pity. Her tumultuous love life earned her a reputation as a man-eater, but she launched the careers of several, including Yves Montand and Charles Aznavour. After suffering injuries in a car accident in 1951, Piaf began drinking heavily and became addicted to morphine. Her health declined quickly, but she continued to sing around the world and recorded some of her biggest hits (*Je Ne Regrette Rien*; *Milord*). In 1962, frail and once again penniless, Piaf married a young hairdresser called Théo Sarapo, recorded the duet *À Quoi Ça Sert l'Amour?* (What Use Is Love?) with him and left Paris for southern France, where she died the following year. Some two million people attended her funeral in Paris, and her grave at Cimetière du Père Lachaise is still visited and decorated by thousands of loyal fans each year.

opens noon to 6 pm Saturday to Monday. Chez Louisette is inside the maze of Marché Vernaison not far from 130 ave Michelet, the boulevard on the other side of the highway from Porte de Clignancourt metro station.

Le Croquenote (Map 3, ☎ 01 42 33 60 70, 22 passage des Panoramas, 2e, metro Grands Boulevards). An intimate French restaurant with dinner (180FF) at 8 pm and chansons – in the styles of Brel, Brassens, Ferré and Félix Leclerc – at around 10 pm Monday to Saturday (closed in August).

Au Lapin Agile (Map 8, ☎ 01 46 06 85 87, 22 rue des Saules, 18e, metro Lamarck Caulaincourt). This is a rustic cabaret venue that was favoured by artists and intellectuals in the early 20th century. These days, chansons are performed and poetry read 9 pm to 2 am Tuesday to Sunday. Entry costs 130FF (90FF for students, except on Saturday and public holidays), including a drink.

CLASSICAL MUSIC, OPERA & DANCE

The Opéra National de Paris (ONP) now splits its performances between Palais Garnier, its original home, built in 1875, and the modern Opéra Bastille, which opened in 1989. Both opera houses also stage ballets and classical music concerts performed by the ONP's affiliated orchestra and ballet companies. The opera season runs from September to July. The ONP Web site is at www.opera-de-paris.fr. On Minitel, key in 3615 OPERAPARIS.

Opéra Bastille (Map 6, ☎ 0 836 69 78 68 or 01 44 73 13 99, 2-6 place de la Bastille, 12e, metro Bastille). The box office, which is at 120 rue de Lyon, 11e, opens 11 am to 6.30 pm Monday to Saturday. Ticket sales begin 14 days before the date of the performance, but according to local opera buffs the only way to ensure a booking is by post some two months in advance (120 rue de Lyon, 75576 Paris CEDEX 12). Opera tickets cost 90FF to 670FF. To have a shot at the cheapest (ie, worst) seats in the house (45FF to 60FF), you have to stop by the ticket office the day tickets go on sale – exactly 14 days before the performance (on Monday if the performance is on a Sunday). Ballets cost 70FF to 420FF (45FF to 50FF for the cheapest seats), concerts are 85FF to 255FF (45FF). If there are unsold tickets, people aged under 25 or over 65 and students can get excellent seats for about 100FF only 15 minutes before the curtain goes up *(tarif spécial)*.

Opéra Comique (Map 3, ☎ 01 42 44 45 46, 5 rue Favart, 2e, metro Richelieu Drouot). A century-old hall that plays host to classic and less well known works of opera. Tickets, available from Fnac or Virgin, cost 100FF to 610FF; 50FF tickets with limited or no visibility are available up to 12 hours before the performance at the box office (opposite the theatre at 14 rue Favart), which opens 11 am to 6 or 7 pm Monday to Saturday and one hour before any performance. Subject to availability, students and those aged under 26 can purchase unsold tickets for around 50FF.

Palais Garnier (Map 2, ☎ 0 836 69 78 68, place de l'Opéra, 9e, metro Opéra). Ticket prices and conditions (including last-minute discounts) are almost exactly the same as those at the Opéra Bastille.

In addition to opera, Paris plays host to dozens of orchestral, organ and chamber-music concerts each week.

Cité de la Musique (Map 1, ☎ 01 44 84 45 45 or 01 44 84 45 00, 221 ave Jean Jaurès, 19e, metro Porte de Pantin). The oval, 1200-seat main auditorium at La Villette, whose blocks of seats can be reconfigured to suit different types of performance, hosts every imaginable type of music and dance, from Western classical to North African and Japanese. Tickets, usually available from Fnac and Virgin, cost 75FF to 200FF (60FF to 170FF reduced rate) for evening concerts. Concerts in the little auditorium on Friday, Saturday and Sunday cost 80/60FF. The Sunday afternoon performances, which usually start at 3 pm, cost 80FF. The ticket office, open noon to 6 pm Tuesday to Sunday, is opposite the main auditorium next to the Fontaine aux Lions (Lion Fountain). Visit its Web site at www.cite-musique.fr. On Minitel, key in 3615 CITEMUSIQUE.

Regard du Cygne (Map 1, ☎ 01 43 58 55 93, 210 rue de Belleville, 20e, metro Place des Fêtes). Many of Paris' young and daring talents in movement, music and theatre congregate around this interesting performance space in Belleville. If you're in the mood for some innovative modern dance – performance or participation – this is the place. Tickets cost around 70FF (discounts for students and seniors half an hour before curtain time).

Salle Pleyel (Map 2, ☎ 01 45 61 53 01, 252 rue du Faubourg Saint Honoré, 8e, metro Ternes). This is a highly regarded, 1920s-era hall that hosts many of Paris' finest classical music concerts and recitals. The box office opens 11 am to 6 pm Monday to Saturday. Tickets cost 80FF to 410FF.

Théâtre des Champs-Élysées (Map 2, ☎ 01 49 52 50 50, 15 ave Montaigne, 8e, metro Alma

A night at the opera: class acts at Palais Garnier

SIMON BRACKEN

Marceau). This is a prestigious Right Bank orchestral and recital hall with concerts held throughout the year. The box office opens 1 to 7 pm Monday to Saturday.

Théâtre Musical de Paris (Map 6, ☎ 01 40 28 28 40, 2 rue Édouard Colonne, 1er, metro Châtelet). Also called Théâtre du Châtelet, this hall hosts operas (200FF to 750FF for the better seats, 50FF to 80FF for seats with limited visibility), ballets (90FF to 200FF), concerts (including ones by the excellent Orchestre de Paris) and theatre performances. Classical music is performed at 11 am on Sunday (120FF) and at 12.45 pm on Monday, Wednesday and Friday (55FF). The ticket office opens 11 am to 7 pm daily (to 8 pm on performance nights); tickets go on sale 14 days before the performance date. Subject to availability, anyone aged under 26 or over 65 can get reduced-price tickets (opera 100FF, ballet 60FF, concerts 50FF) from 15 minutes before curtain time. There are no performances in July and August. You can also book via the theatre's Web site at www.chatelet-theatre.com. On Minitel, key in 3615 CHATELET.

Théâtre de la Ville (Map 6, ☎ 01 42 74 22 77, 2 place du Châtelet, 4e, metro Châtelet). This

ENTERTAINMENT

The shock of the new: the shiny, imposing hulk of Opéra Bastille

municipal hall plays host to theatre, dance and all kinds of music, with tickets from 95FF to 190FF. Depending on availability, people aged under 26 and students can buy up to two tickets at a 30% to 50% discount on the day of the performance. The ticket office is open 11 am to 7 pm on Monday, to 8 pm Tuesday to Saturday and an hour before curtain time on Sunday. There are no performances in July and August. On Minitel, key in 3615 THEAVILLE.

Church Venues
The churches of Paris are popular venues for classical music concerts and organ recitals. The concerts held at *Notre Dame Cathedral* (Map 6, ☎ 01 42 34 56 10) don't keep to any fixed schedule but are advertised on posters around town and usually cost 100/80FF for the full/reduced tariff. From April to October, classical concerts are also held in *Sainte Chapelle* (Map 6, ☎ 01 42 77 65 65 or 01 53 73 78 51) on Île de la Cité, 1er; the cheapest seats are around 110FF (80FF for students aged under 26). From December to June concerts (120/80FF) are also held at the delightful *Église Notre Dame du Val-de-*

Grâce (Map 5, fax 01 42 01 47 67, 277 bis rue Saint Jacques, 5e, metro Port Royal).

Other noted concert venues with similar admission fees are the Église Saint Eustache (Map 6) in the 1er; the Église Saint Étienne du Mont (Map 5) and Église Saint Julien le Pauvre (Map 6) in the 5e; the Église Saint Germain des Prés (Map 6) in the 6e; the American Church (Map 4) in the 7e; and the Église de la Madeleine (Map 2) in the 8e.

CINEMA
Pariscope and *L'Officiel des Spectacles* (see Listings at the start of this chapter) list Paris' cinematic offerings alphabetically by their French title followed by the English (or German, Italian, Spanish etc) one. Going to the cinema in Paris does not come cheaply: expect to pay between 40FF and 50FF for a ticket. Students and those aged under 18 or over 60 usually get discounts of about 25% except on Friday, Saturday and Sunday nights. On Wednesday (and sometimes Monday) most cinemas give discounts to everyone.

If a movie is labelled 'vo' or 'VO' (for *version originale*) it means it will be subtitled rather than dubbed (labelled 'vf', for *version française*), so English-language films marked 'vo' will still be in English.

Beyond the cinemas showing Hollywood blockbusters, the following are noteworthy:

Le Champo *(Map 6, ☎ 01 43 54 51 60, 51 rue des Écoles, 5e, metro Saint Michel or Cluny-La Sorbonne)*. One of the most popular of the many Latin Quarter cinemas, featuring classics and retrospectives along the lines of Hitchcock, Jacques Tati, Frank Capra and Woody Allen. Showings cost 43/33FF (matinee 27FF).

Cinéma des Cinéastes *(Map 2, ☎ 01 53 42 40 20, 7 ave de Clichy, 17e, metro Place de Clichy)*. Founded by the three Claudes (Miller, Berri and Lelouch) and *Betty Blue* director Jean-Jacques Beneix, this three-screen place is dedicated to quality cinema, whether French, foreign or avant-garde. Thematic seasons, documentaries and meet-the-director sessions round out the repertoire. Tickets cost 43/35FF.

Cinémathèque Française *(☎ 01 53 65 74 74, or 01 56 26 01 01 for a recording)*. This cultural institution almost always leaves its foreign offerings – often rarely screened classics – in their original versions. There are two cinemas, one *(Map 4, 7 ave Albert de Mun, 16e, metro Trocadéro or Iéna)* at the Palais de Chaillot and the other *(Map 3, 42 blvd Bonne Nouvelle, 10e, metro Bonne Nouvelle)* along the Grands Boulevards. Screenings (29/18FF) take place Tuesday to Sunday; its Web site (www.cinematheque.tm.fr) lists exact times.

THEATRE

Almost all of Paris' theatre productions, including those written in other languages, are performed in French. There are a few English-speaking troupes around, though; look for ads on metro poster boards and in English-language periodicals such as *FUSAC* (see Newspapers & Magazines in the Facts for the Visitor chapter). Apart from the celebrated Bouffes du Nord listed below, theatres that occasionally stage productions in English include **Théâtre de Nesle** *(Map 6, ☎ 01 46 34 61 04, 8 rue de Nesle, 6e, metro Odéon or Mabillon)*, **Théâtre Les Déchargeurs** *(Map 6, ☎ 01 42 36 00 02, 3 rue des Déchargeurs, 1er, metro Châtelet)* and **Théâtre de Ménilmontant**

ROB FLYNN

Le Champo: one of the finest of Paris' arthouse cinemas

(Map 1, ☎ 01 46 56 20 50, 15 rue du Retrait, 20e, metro Gambetta).

Among the best established and/or more innovative theatres in Paris are:

Théâtre de la Ville Les Abbesses *(Map 8, ☎ 01 42 74 22 77, 31 rue des Abbesses, 18e, metro Abbesses)*. The new neoclassical home for the Théâtre de la Ville is the venue for mainly contemporary theatre, music and dance. Tickets cost 95FF to 190FF and the box office is open 5 to 8 pm Tuesday to Saturday.

Bouffes du Nord *(Map 3, ☎ 01 46 07 34 50, 37 bis blvd de la Chapelle, 10e, metro La Chapelle)*. Best known as the Paris base of Peter Brooks' experimental theatre troupe, this theatre also hosts works by other directors, notably Stéphane Lissner, as well as classical and jazz concerts. Tickets average 70FF to 130FF (matinees 50FF to 110FF) and the box office is open 11 am to 6 pm Monday to Saturday.

Comédie Française *(Map 6, ☎ 01 44 58 15 15, 2 rue de Richelieu, 1er, metro Palais Royal-Musée du Louvre)*. Founded under Louis XIV, the Comédie Française bases its repertoire around the works of the classic French playwrights

euro currency converter €1 = 6.56FF

ENTERTAINMENT

Game for a laugh: Point Virgule is an excellent stand-up venue.

(Corneille, Molière, Racine etc), though contemporary and even non-French works have been staged in recent years. The box office is open 11 am to 6 pm daily. Tickets for regular seats cost 70FF to 190FF; tickets for places near the ceiling (30FF) go on sale one hour before curtain time (usually 8.30 pm), which is when those aged under 25 and students aged under 27 can purchase any of the better seats remaining for around 60FF. Tickets to Thursday night's performance are a uniform 50FF (except for the 30FF cheapies). The discount tickets are available from the window round the corner from the main entrance and facing rue de Montpensier. Its Web site is at www.comedie-francaise.fr.

Odéon Théâtre de l'Europe *(Map 6, ☎ 01 44 41 36 00, place de l'Odéon, 6e, metro Odéon).* This huge, ornate theatre, built in the early 1780s, often puts on foreign plays in their original languages (subtitled in French) and hosts theatre troupes from abroad (seats 30FF to 180FF). The box office (☎ 01 44 41 36 36) opens 11 am to 6 pm Monday to Saturday. People aged over 60 get a discount on the pricier tickets, while students and those aged under 26 with a Carte Jeunes can get good reserved seats for as little as 30FF to 50FF. On Thursday and Sunday 50 seats are available to everyone for 20FF 1½ hours before curtain time.

Théâtre de la Bastille *(Map 5, ☎ 01 43 57 42 14, 76 rue de la Roquette, 11e, metro Bastille or Voltaire).* This is arguably the best fringe theatre venue in town, with a variety of experimental works including text, movement and music. Tickets cost 120/80FF and the box office is open 10 am to 1 pm and 2 to 6.30 pm weekdays and in the afternoon at the weekend.

COMEDY

Though it may come as a surprise to some, Parisians do like to laugh. Such comedians as Bourvil, Fernandel, Bernard Blier, Louis de Funès, Francis Blanche, Jean Poiret and Michel Serrault have enjoyed enormous popularity over the years. Among contemporary stars are the Algerian-born French comics Elie Kakou and Guy Bedos (the latter is left-wing, which, among this generally conservative group, is comical in itself) and the French-Arab comedian Smaïn.

Comedy clubs in Paris include:

Café de la Gare *(Map 7, ☎ 01 42 78 52 51, 41 rue du Temple, 4e, metro Hôtel de Ville or Rambuteau).* This is one of the best and most innovative café-theatres in Paris, with acts ranging

Sport, concerts, ballet, theatre...the Palais Omnisports de Paris-Bercy has it all.

ROB FLYNN

from comic theatre and stand-up to reinterpreted classics. Tickets cost 100FF to 120FF (reduced price 50FF to 100FF).

Hôtel du Nord (Map 3, ☎ *01 48 06 01 20, 102 quai de Jemmapes, 10e, metro République*). The Hôtel du Nord hosts Laughing Matters at 8.30 pm on Sunday and Monday (100/80FF), the best place in town for English-language belly laughs, with a regular stream of stand-ups from across the Channel or drying out on the way back home from Edinburgh.

Point Virgule (Map 7, ☎ *01 42 78 67 03 or 01 39 91 62 10, 7 rue Sainte Croix de la Bretonnerie, 4e, metro Hôtel de Ville*). This popular spot in the Marais offers café-theatre at its best, with stand-up comics, performance artists, musical acts – you name it. The quality is variable, but it's great fun nevertheless. There are three shows daily at 8, 9.15 and 10.15 pm. Entry costs 90/130/150FF for one/two/three shows (students 70FF).

SPECTATOR SPORTS

Parisians are mad about sport. For details of upcoming sporting events, consult the sports daily *L'Équipe* (4FF) or *Figaroscope*, which is published with *Le Figaro* each Wednesday.

Football & Rugby

Le foot (football) has gained even more popularity since France won the World Cup at home in 1998 and then went on to win the 2000 European Championships, defeating Italy in the final in spectacular style, and Paris hosts its fair share of international events. Paris-Saint Germain play their home games at the *Parc des Princes* (Map 1, 24 rue du Commandant Guilbaud, 16e, metro Porte de Saint Cloud). Tickets (50FF to 600FF) are available through Fnac and Virgin Megastores (see Booking Agencies earlier in this chapter) as well as at the Parc des Princes box office (☎ 01 49 87 29 29), which opens 9 am to 8 pm weekdays and 10 am to 5 pm on Saturday. In Saint Denis, the 80,000-seat *Stade de France* (☎ 01 55 93 00 00 or 01 44 68 44 44) hosted the World Cup finals and is the major venue for both football and rugby (see the Excursions chapter for details).

Rugby is popular in South-West France and Paris-based Le Racing Club de France are the reigning champions. Their home ground is *Stade Yves du Manoir* (☎ 01 45 67 55 86) in Colombes, north-west of Paris.

ENTERTAINMENT

Tennis

In late May/early June the tennis world focuses on the clay surface of **Stade Roland Garros** *(Map 1, ☎ 01 47 43 48 00, 2 ave Gordon Bennett, 16e, metro Porte d'Auteuil)* in the Bois de Boulogne for Les Internationaux de France de Tennis (French Open), the second of the four Grand Slam tournaments. The capacity of the stadium's main section, Le Central, is about 16,500. Tickets are expensive and hard to come by; bookings must usually be made by March at the latest.

The top indoor tournament is the Open de Tennis de la Ville de Paris (Paris Tennis Open), which usually takes place sometime in late October/early November at the **Palais Omnisports de Paris-Bercy** *(Map 9, ☎ 01 44 68 44 68, 8-12 blvd de Bercy, 12e, metro Bercy).*

Cycling

Since 1974 the final stage of the Tour de France, the world's most prestigious cycling event, has ended on the ave des Champs-Élysées. The final day varies from year to year but is usually the 3rd or 4th Sunday in July, with the race finishing sometime in the afternoon. If you want to see this exciting event, find a spot at the barricades before noon.

The biggest indoor cycling event is the Grand Prix des Nations, held in October and pitting the best cyclists from the world's eight best cycling nations against one another on a 250m velodrome at the **Palais Omnisports de Paris-Bercy** (see the previous Tennis section).

Horse Racing & Showjumping

One of the cheapest ways to spend a relaxing afternoon in the company of Parisians of all ages, backgrounds and walks of life is to go to the races. The most accessible of Paris' six racecourses is **Hippodrome d'Auteuil** *(Map 1, ☎ 01 40 71 47 47 or 01 45 27 12 25, metro Porte d'Auteuil)* in the south-east corner of the Bois de Boulogne, which hosts steeplechases from February to early July and early September to early December.

Races are held on Sunday as well as some other days of the week, with half a dozen or so heats scheduled between 2 and 5.30 pm. There's no charge to stand on the *pelouse* (lawn) in the middle of the track; a seat in the *tribune* (stands) costs 25FF (40FF on Sunday and public holidays, 50FF during special events). Race schedules are published in almost all national newspapers. If you can read a bit of French, pick up a copy of *Paris Turf*, the horse-racing daily available at newsstands for 7FF.

Showjumping is all the rage in Paris and the Jumping International de Paris held in March at the **Palais Omnisports de Paris-Bercy** (see the previous Tennis section) attracts thousands of fans.

Shopping

Paris is a superb place to shop, whether you're someone who can afford an original Cartier diamond bracelet or you're an impoverished *lèche-vitrine* (literally 'window-licker'). From the ultra-chic couture houses of ave Montaigne to the flea-market bargains at Saint Ouen, from the vast underground shopping centre at Les Halles to the cubbyhole boutiques of the Marais, Paris is a city that knows how to make it, present it and charge for it.

WHAT TO BUY

Paris has everything for sale but stick to the tried and the true: fashion, jewellery, fine food and wine, professional kitchenware, quality gifts and souvenirs. Paris' flea markets are well-and-truly picked over but are still among the largest in the world and offer a great way to spend a weekend morning.

Opening hours in Paris are notoriously anarchic, with each store setting its own hours according to some ancient black art. Most stores will be open at least 10 am to 6 pm five days a week (including Saturday), but they may open earlier, close later, close for lunch (usually 1 to 2.30 pm) or for a full or half-day on Monday or Tuesday. Many larger stores also have a *nocturne* – one late night (usually to 10 pm) a week.

Antiques

For details of Le Louvre des Antiquaires (Map 6), see the Louvre in the Things to See & Do chapter.

In the 6e there are a number of shops selling antique maps and antiquarian books around rue Bonaparte and rue Jacob (Map 6, metro Saint Germain des Prés).

Clothing & Fashion Accessories

All of the major French couturiers have their own boutiques in the capital (some, such as Yves Saint Laurent, have several), but it's also possible to see impressive designer collections at major department stores such as Le Printemps, Galeries

ASA ANDERSSON

Lafayette and Au Bon Marché. The Right Bank is traditionally the epicentre of Parisian fashion. New collections are released twice a year – for spring/summer and autumn/winter.

Triangle d'Or Some of the fanciest clothes in Paris are sold by the *haute couture* houses of the Triangle d'Or, 1er and 8e (Map 2, metro Franklin D Roosevelt or Alma Marceau), an ultra-chic neighbourhood whose corners are at place de la Concorde, the Arc de Triomphe and place de l'Alma. Along the even-numbered side of ave Montaigne, 8e, you'll find Prada at No 10, Inès de la Fressange at No 14, Christian Lacroix at No 26 and Celine at No 38. On the odd side you'll pass Valentino at No 17, Nina Ricci at No 39 and Thierry Mugler at No 49. Givenchy is nearby at 3 ave George V, 8e; Hermès is at No 42 of the same street.

Rue du Faubourg Saint Honoré & Rue Saint Honoré There is another group of couture houses and exclusive clothing and accessories stores just north of place de la Concorde along rue du Faubourg Saint Honoré, 8e (Map 2, metro Madeleine or Concorde), and its eastern extension, rue

Saint Honoré (metro Tuileries). Lolita Lempicka is at 14 rue du Faubourg Saint Honoré, Guy Laroche at No 28 and Christian Lacroix at No 73.

Place des Victoires Trendy designer boutiques at place des Victoires, 1er and 2e (Map 6, metro Bourse or Sentier), include Kenzo at No 3, Cacharel at No 5 and Stephane Kélian at No 6. The postmodern designs of Jean-Paul Gaultier are on sale a few blocks west of place des Victoires at 6 rue Vivienne in the 2e.

Rue Étienne Marcel, which runs to the east of place des Victoires, is home to Comme des Garçons at Nos 40 (for men) and 42 (for women), Yohji Yamamoto at Nos 45 and 47, Chevignon at No 49, Kenzo at No 51 and Junko Shimada at No 54. Farther east towards Forum des Halles and near the Église Saint Eustache on rue du Jour, 1er, the modern, casual styles of Agnès B (metro Les Halles) are available at Nos 3 (for men) and 6 (for women).

Marais Rue des Rosiers, 4e (Map 7, metro Saint Paul), is attracting a growing number of fashionable clothing shops, including Tehen at No 5 bis and Martin Grant at No 32. Under the exclusive arcades of place des Vosges, 4e, Issey Miyake is tucked away at No 5. There are other interesting shops along rue des Francs Bourgeois, 3e and 4e, leading out of place des Vosges. For more everyday clothing, there are lots of shops along rue de Rivoli, which gets less expensive as you move east from the 1er into the 4e.

Saint Germain & Odéon The largest group of chic clothing boutiques in the fashionable 6e – many of them run by younger and more daring designers – is north-west of place Saint Sulpice (Map 6, metro Saint Sulpice or Saint Germain des Prés). Ultra-chic clothing, footwear and leather-goods shops along rue du Cherche Midi (Map 4) include Yves Saint Laurent at No 13 and Il Bisonte at No 17. Along blvd Saint Germain (Map 4), Sonia Rykiel has shops at Nos 175 (for women) and 194 (for men).

Rue de Rennes (Map 4) has Celine at No 58 and Kenzo at No 60. At place Saint Sulpice (Map 6) you can pop into Yves Saint Laurent Rive Gauche at No 6 and its Rive Gauche Homme at No 12.

A bit to the south-west, just south of Au Bon Marché department store, rue Saint Placide (Map 4, metro Sèvres Babylone) has lots of attractive shops selling clothes and shoes, mainly (but not exclusively) for women.

Reasonably priced clothing and shoe shops are legion along the southern half of rue de Rennes (Map 4, metro Rennes or Saint Placide).

Fashion shops offering creations and accessories from a variety of cutting-edge designers include:

Colette (Map 2, ☎ 01 55 35 33 90, metro Tuileries) 213 rue Saint Honoré, 1er. Probably the most talked-about shop in Paris in the last few years, Japanese-inspired Colette is an ode to style over all else. Its selection and display of clothes, accessories, and odds and ends is exquisite. Featured designers include Alexander McQueen, Alberta Ferretti and Lulu Guinness. It's open 10.30 am to 7.30 pm daily.

Kiliwatch (Map 6, ☎ 01 42 21 17 37, metro Étienne Marcel) 64 rue Tiquetonne, 2e. This enormous shop is filled with rack after rack of colourfully original street- and club-wear, plus a startling range of quality second-hand clothes and accessories. It's open 1 to 7 pm on Monday and 10.30 am to 9 pm Tuesday to Saturday.

Spleen (Map 7, ☎ 01 42 74 65 66, metro Saint Paul) 3 bis rue des Rosiers, 4e. This is a stunning showcase for a range of new *créateurs*, many from Italy and the UK, among them John Richmond, Lawrence Steele, Emilio Cavallin and Joerg Hartmann. It's open 3 to 7 pm on Monday, 11 am to 7 pm Tuesday to Saturday and 2 to 7 pm on Sunday.

Food & Wine

The food and wine shops of Paris are legendary and well worth seeking out.

Brûlerie des Ternes (Map 2, ☎ 01 46 22 52 79, metro Charles de Gaulle-Étoile) 10 rue Poncelet, 17e. This is probably the best coffee roaster, grinder and shop in Paris. It's open 9 am to 2 pm and 3.30 to 7.30 pm weekdays, 9 am to 7.30 pm on Saturday and 9 am to 1 pm on Sun-

GREG ELMS

Pure indulgence: tempting confectionery on display at Hédiard

day. There's a great open-air market along this street most days.

Cacao et Chocolat (Map 6, ☎ 01 46 33 77 63, metro Mabillon) 29 rue du Buci, 6e. Here's a contemporary exotic take on chocolate, showcasing the cocoa bean in all its guises, both solid and liquid. The added citrus flavours, spices and even chilli are guaranteed to tease you back for more. It's open 10.30 am to 7.30 pm Tuesday to Saturday.

Fauchon (Map 2, ☎ 01 47 62 60 11, metro Madeleine) 26-30 place de la Madeleine, 8e. Six departments sell the most incredibly mouthwatering (and expensive) delicacies, such as pâté de foie gras for 1000FF to 2000FF per kilogram. Fruit – the most perfect you've ever seen – includes exotic items from South-East Asia (mangosteens, rambutans etc). It's open 9.30 am to 7 pm Monday to Saturday.

Fromagerie Alléosse (Map 2, ☎ 01 46 22 50 45, metro Charles de Gaulle-Étoile) 13 rue Poncelet, 17e. This is probably the best cheese shop in Paris. It's open 9 am to 1 pm and 4 to 7 pm Tuesday to Saturday, and 9 am to 1 pm on Sunday.

Hédiard (Map 2, ☎ 02 43 12 88 88, metro Madeleine) 21 place de la Madeleine, 8e. This famous luxury food shop consists of two adjacent sections selling prepared dishes, tea, coffee, jam, wine, pastries, fruit, vegetables and so on. It's open 9.30 am to 9.30 pm Monday to Saturday.

Jadis et Gourmande (Map 5, ☎ 01 43 26 17 75, metro Port Royal) 88 blvd de Port Royal, 5e. This is one of four branches selling chocolate, chocolate and more chocolate in every conceivable shape and size. It's open 1 to 7 pm on Monday, and 9.30 am to 7 pm Tuesday to Saturday.

La Maison du Miel (Map 2, ☎ 01 47 42 26 70, metro Madeleine) 24 rue Vignon, 9e. This store stocks over 40 kinds of honey (19FF to 45FF for 500g). It opens 9.15 am to 7 pm Monday to Saturday.

La Maison de la Truffe (Map 2, ☎ 01 42 66 10 01, metro Madeleine) 19-21 place de la Madeleine, 8e. If you've always wanted to taste fine truffles – French black from late October to March, Italian white from mid-October to December (over 2000FF per 100g) – here's your chance. There's also a small sit-down area where you can sample dishes made with the prized fungus (375FF for the *menu*). It's open 9 am (eating area from 11.45 am) to 9 pm Monday to Saturday.

Mariage Frères (Map 7, ☎ 01 42 72 28 11, metro Hôtel de Ville) 30 rue du Bourg Tibourg, 4e. Paris' first and arguably finest tea shop (founded in 1854), with 500 varieties from more than 30 countries, Mariage Frères has a branch (Map 6, ☎ 01 40 51 82 50, metro Odéon) at 13 rue des Grands Augustins, 6e, and another (Map 2, ☎ 01 46 22 18 54, metro Tuileries) at 260 rue du Faubourg Saint Honoré, 8e. All are open 10.30 am to 7.30 pm daily.

À l'Olivier (Map 7, ☎ 01 48 04 86 59, metro Saint Paul) 23 rue de Rivoli, 4e. This is the place in Paris for oil – from olive to walnut – with a good selection of vinegars and olives too. It's open 9.30 am to 1 pm and 2 to 7 pm Tuesday to Saturday.

Le Palais des Thés (Map 7, ☎ 01 43 56 96 38, metro Hôtel de Ville or Saint Paul) 64 rue Vieille du Temple, 3e. This 'Palace of Teas' is not as well established as Mariage Frères but the selection is as large and the surroundings a tad more 21st century. It's open 10.30 am to 7.30 pm Tuesday to Saturday, and 2 to 7 pm on Sunday.

Poilâne (Map 4, ☎ 01 45 48 42 59, metro Sèvres Babylone) 8 rue du Cherche Midi, 6e. Truly a legend in its own lunch time, Poilâne – the most famous *boulangerie* in Paris – bakes perfect wholegrain bread (21.50FF for a small loaf) using traditional sourdough leavening and sea salt. Every loaf is an original. Poilâne is open 7.15 am to 8.15 pm Monday to Saturday. There's a branch (Map 4, ☎ 01 45 79 11 49, metro Dupleix) at 49 blvd de Grenelle, 15e, to the south-west.

Gifts & Souvenirs

Paris has a huge number of speciality shops offering gift items.

Album (Map 6, ☎ 01 43 25 85 19, metro Maubert Mutualité) 8 rue Dante, 5e. This shop specialises in *bandes dessinées* (comic books), which have an enormous following in France, with everything from *Tintin* to erotic comics and French editions of the latest Japanese *manga*. It's open 10 am to 8 pm Monday to Saturday.

Anna Joliet (Map 6, ☎ 01 42 96 55 13, metro Pyramides) passage du Perron, 9 rue de Beaujolais, 1er. This wonderful (and tiny) shop at the northern end of the Jardin du Palais Royal specialises in music boxes, both new and old, for romantics and children (or both). Just open the door and see if you aren't tempted in (or recognise the tune). It's open 1 to 7 pm on Monday and 10 am to 7 pm Tuesday to Saturday.

Bains Plus (Map 7, ☎ 01 48 87 83 07, metro Hôtel de Ville or Rambuteau) 51 rue des Francs Bourgeois, 3e. This bathroom supplier for the new millennium stocks luxurious robes and gowns, soaps and oils, shaving brushes and mirrors. It's open 11 am to 7.30 pm Tuesday to Saturday, and 2.30 to 7 pm on Sunday.

E Dehillerin (Map 6, ☎ 01 42 36 53 13, metro Les Halles) 18-20 rue Coquillière, 1er. This old shop (founded in 1820) carries the most incredible selection of professional-quality kitchenware – you're sure to find something even the most well equipped kitchen is lacking. It's open 8 am to 12.30 pm and 2 to 6 pm on Monday, and 8 am to 6 pm Tuesday to Saturday.

EOL' Modelisme (Map 6, ☎ 01 43 54 01 43, metro Maubert Mutualité) 62 blvd St Germain, 5e, with branches at Nos 55 and 70. This shop sells expensive toys for big boys and girls, including every sort of model imaginable – from radio-controlled aircraft to large wooden yachts. The main shop is open 1 to 7 pm on Monday, and 11 am to 1 pm and 2 to 7 pm Tuesday to Saturday.

Galerie Alain Carion (Map 6, ☎ 01 43 26 01 16, metro Pont Marie) 92 rue Saint Louis en l'Île, 4e. This shop has a stunningly beautiful collection of museum-quality minerals, crystals, fos-

sils and meteorites from 40 different countries, some of them in the form of earrings, brooches and pendants. Prices range from 5FF to 80,000FF (for a 60kg meteorite; 5200FF will get you one the size of a potato). It's open 10.30 am to 1 pm and 2 to 7.30 pm Tuesday to Saturday.

Il Pour l'Homme (Map 2, ☎ 01 42 60 43 56, metro Tuileries) 209 rue Saint Honoré, 1er. Housed in an old paint shop with 19th-century display counters and chests of drawers, 'It for the Man' has everything a man could want or not need – from tie clips and cigar cutters to DIY tools and designer tweezers. It's open 10.30 am to 7 pm Monday to Saturday.

Madeleine Gély (Map 4, ☎ 01 42 22 63 35, metro Saint Germain des Prés) 218 blvd Saint Germain, 7e. If you're in the market for a bespoke cane or umbrella, this vintage shop (founded in 1834) will supply it. It's open 10 am to 7 pm Tuesday to Saturday.

La Maison du Cerf-Volant (Map 5, ☎ 01 44 68 00 75, metro Ledru Rollin) 7 rue de Prague, 12e. Kites, kites and more kites – in every conceivable size, shape and colour. It's open 10 am to 7 pm Monday to Saturday.

Mélodies Graphiques (Map 7, ☎ 01 42 74 57 68, metro Pont Marie) 10 rue du Pont Louis-Philippe, 4e. This shop carries all sorts of items made from exquisite Florentine *papier à cuve* (paper hand-decorated with marbled designs). It opens 2 to 7 pm on Monday, and 11 am to 7 pm Tuesday to Saturday.

Robin des Bois (Map 7, ☎ 01 48 04 09 36, metro Saint Paul) 15 rue Fernand Duval, 4e. A shop strictly for environmentalists, this place sells everything and anything made from recycled things – from jewellery to stationery. It's open 10.30 am to 7.30 pm Monday to Saturday, and from 2 pm on Sunday.

A Simon (Map 6, ☎ 01 42 33 71 65, metro Étienne Marcel) 36 rue Étienne Marcel, 2e. This more modern kitchenware shop than nearby E Dehillerin has more pots, pans, mixing bowls and utensils than you thought imaginable. The professional annexe is opposite at 52 rue Montmartre. It's open 1.30 to 6.30 pm on Monday, and from 9 am Tuesday to Saturday.

Jewellery

Around place Vendôme, 1er (Map 2, metro Tuileries), Cartier has a shop at No 7, Patek Philippe at No 10 and Van Cleef & Arpels at No 22. There are more expensive jewellery shops along nearby rue de Castiglione, 1er, and rue de la Paix, 2e.

WHERE TO SHOP

Some of Paris' department stores are Art Nouveau extravaganzas, including Au Bon Marché, while others offer such things as fabulous views out over the rooftops of the city. But all offer quality and very stylish items that will go down a treat at home.

Certain streets in Paris still specialise in certain products. Rue du Pont Louis-Philippe, 4e (Map 7, metro Pont Marie), for example, has all manner of paper goods and stationery, while rue de Paradis, 10e (Map 3, metro Château d'Eau), is famed for its crystal, glass and tableware shops. If you're in the market for a sewing machine, turn south from rue de Paradis onto rue Martel – it's chock-a-block with the things. In the nearby passage de l'Industrie, shops specialise in equipment and tools for *coiffeurs* (hairdressers). Walk along rue Victor Massé, 9e (Map 3), and you'll see more musical instruments than you thought existed. The shops on rue Drouot in the 9e (Map 3) sell almost nothing but old postage stamps.

Bookshops

Paris has a number of bookshops that cater for English-speakers.

All that glitters: cutting-edge jewellery at Cécile et Jeanne

Less expensive jewellery is sold at various places around the city. Funky items, many of them imported, can be found in the Marais, including along rue des Francs Bourgeois, 3e and 4e (Map 7). Costume jewellery is available at the flea markets.

Cécile et Jeanne (Map 2, ☎ 01 42 61 68 68, metro Tuileries) 215 rue Saint Honoré, 1er. Cécile and Jeanne are two young jewellery designers making a splash in Paris with their colourful and arty jewellery and accessories. They have several places in the city. It's open 11 am to 7 pm Monday to Saturday.
Galerie d'Amon (Map 6, ☎ 01 43 26 96 60, metro Saint Sulpice) 28 place Saint Sulpice, 6e. This shop specialises in modern glass and jewellery with a medieval twist. It's open 11 am to 6.45 pm Tuesday to Saturday.
Sic Amor (Map 7, ☎ 01 42 76 02 37, metro Pont Marie) 20 rue du Pont Louis-Philippe, 4e. Sic Amor sells contemporary jewellery by local designers. It's open 10.30 am to 7.30 pm Monday to Saturday, and from noon on Sunday.

Abbey Bookshop (Map 6, ☎ 01 46 33 16 24, metro Cluny-La Sorbonne) 29 rue de la Parcheminerie, 5e. A mellow place, not far from place Saint Michel, and known for having free tea and coffee, a supply of Canadian newspapers and a good selection of new and used works of fiction. It opens 10 am to 7 pm Monday to Saturday and on some Sundays, according to the owner's whim.
Brentano's (Map 3, ☎ 01 42 61 52 50, metro Opéra) 37 ave de l'Opéra, 2e. Midway between the Louvre and Opéra Garnier, this is a good shop for tracking down books from the USA, including fiction, business titles and magazines. It also has a good range of kid's books. It opens 10 am to 7.30 pm Monday to Saturday.
Espace IGN (Map 2, ☎ 01 43 98 85 00, metro Franklin D Roosevelt) 107 rue La Boétie, 8e. This is the best place to find a full selection of Institut Géographique National (IGN) maps as well as atlases, globes, walking maps, wine-district maps, compasses, satellite images, historic maps and guidebooks. It's open 9.30 am to 7 pm weekdays and 11 am to 12.30 pm and 2 to 6.30 pm on Saturday.

euro currency converter €1 = 6.56FF

- **Librarie Gourmande** (Map 6, ☎ 01 43 54 37 27, metro Maubert Mutualité) 4 rue Dante, 5e. Not only do the French love to talk about food, they love to write – and read – about it as well, and Geneviève Baudon's tasteful bookshop is *the* place to discover the secrets of French food and wine and the culinary arts. It's open 10 am to 7 pm daily.
- **Les Mots à la Bouche** (Map 7, ☎ 01 42 78 88 30, metro Hôtel de Ville) 6 rue Sainte Croix de la Bretonnerie, 4e. Paris' premier gay bookshop opens 11 am to 11 pm Monday to Saturday and 2 to 8 pm on Sunday. Most of the back wall is devoted to English-language books, including lots of novels.
- **Shakespeare & Company** (Map 6, ☎ 01 43 26 96 50, metro Saint Michel) 37 rue de la Bûcherie, 5e. Paris' most famous English-language book-shop (but very much resting on its laurels) has a varied and unpredictable collection of new and used books in English, including paperback novels from as little as 10FF. It opens noon till midnight daily. Poetry readings are held at 8 pm on most Mondays, and there's a library on the 1st floor. This isn't the original Shakespeare & Company owned by Sylvia Beach – that was at 12 rue de l'Odéon and was closed by the Germans in 1941.
- **WH Smith** (Map 2, ☎ 01 44 77 88 99, metro Concorde) 248 rue de Rivoli, 1er. One block east of place de la Concorde, WH Smith opens 9 am to 7.30 pm Monday to Saturday, and from 1 pm on Sunday.
- **Ulysse** (Map 6, ☎ 01 43 25 17 35, metro Pont Marie) 26 rue Saint Louis en l'Île, 4e. For two decades Catherine Demain has been fuelling the wanderlust of Parisian travellers in this delight-ful store full of travel guides, maps, back issues of *National Geographic* and sage advice. It's open 2 to 8 pm Tuesday to Saturday.
- **Village Voice** (Map 6, ☎ 01 46 33 36 47, metro Mabillon) 6 rue Princesse, 6e. A helpful shop with an excellent selection of contemporary North American fiction and European literature in translation. It opens 2 to 8 pm on Monday, from 10 am Tuesday to Saturday, and 2 to 7 pm on Sunday.

Department Stores

Paris boasts a number of *grands magasins*, including the following. Sales *(soldes)* are generally held in January and June/July.

- **Bazar de l'Hôtel de Ville** (BHV; Map 7, ☎ 01 42 74 90 00, metro Hôtel de Ville) 14 rue du Tem-ple, 4e. BHV is a straightforward department store – apart from its enormous but hopelessly

Galeries Lafayette: the Louvre of Paris' department stores

SIMON BRACKEN

chaotic hardware/DIY department in the base-ment, with every type of hammer, power tool, nail, plug or hinge you could ask for (which is what you'll have to do as you'll never find it on your own). It opens 9.30 am to 7 pm Monday to Saturday (to 10 pm on Wednesday).

- **Au Bon Marché** (Map 4, ☎ 01 44 39 80 00, metro Sèvres Babylone) 24 rue de Sèvres, 7e. Paris' first department store, built by Gustav Eiffel, is less frenetic than its rivals across the river, but no less chic. Men's as well as women's fashions are well served. Its glorious grocery store, La Grande Épicerie de Paris, is next door at 26 rue de Sèvres. Au Bon Marché is open 9.30 am to 7 pm weekdays (to 10 pm on Thursday), and to 8 pm on Saturday; La Grande Épicerie de Paris is open 8.30 am to 9 pm on the same days.
- **Galeries Lafayette** (Map 2, ☎ 01 42 82 34 56, metro Auber or Chaussée d'Antin) 40 blvd Haussmann, 9e. This vast store, in two adjacent buildings linked by a pedestrian bridge over rue de Mogador, features over 75,000 brand-name items, and has a wide selection of fashion and accessories. There's a fine view from the

rooftop restaurant. It opens 9.30 am to 7 pm Monday to Saturday (to 9 pm on Thursday).

e Printemps (Map 2, ☎ 01 42 82 50 00, metro Havre Caumartin) 64 blvd Haussmann, 9e. Actually three separate stores – one each for women's and men's fashion and one for household goods – Printemps offers a staggering display of perfume, cosmetics and accessories, as well as established and up-and-coming designer wear. There's a fashion show at 10 am on Tuesday (and on Friday March to October) on the 7th floor under the cupola. Printemps opens 9.35 am to 7 pm Monday to Saturday (to 10 pm on Thursday).

a Samaritaine (Map 6, ☎ 01 40 41 20 20, metro Pont Neuf) in three buildings between Pont Neuf and 142 rue de Rivoli, 1er. The arrowhead-shaped building on rue de Rivoli is devoted solely to sports and games; the men's building has a big supermarket in the basement. The main store's biggest draw is the outstanding view from the rooftop. La Samaritaine opens 9.30 am to 7 pm Monday to Saturday (to 10 pm on Thursday).

ati (Map 8, ☎ 01 55 29 50 00, metro Barbès Rochechouart) 4 blvd Barbès, 18e. With its war-cry of *les plus bas prix* (the lowest prices) – and

quality to match, some would say – Tati has been Paris' great working-class department store for 50 years. Don't be surprised to see trendy Parisians searching for street cred and fighting for bargains hidden in the oddments crammed into bins and piled onto tables. It's open 10am to 7 pm on Monday, 9.30 am to 7 pm Tuesday to Friday, and 9.15 am to 7 pm on Saturday. There's a smaller branch at 13 place de la République, 3e (Map 6, ☎ 01 48 87 72 81, metro République).

Flea Markets

Paris' *marchés aux puces* (flea markets), easily accessible by metro, can be great fun if you're in the mood to browse for unexpected treasures among the *brocante* (second-hand goods) and bric-a-brac on display. Some new goods are also available, and a bit of bargaining is expected.

Marché d'Aligre (Map 5, metro Ledru Rollin) place d'Aligre, 12e. Smaller but more central than the other flea markets listed here, Marché d'Aligre is one of the best places in Paris to rummage through boxes filled with old clothes

CHRISTINE OSBORNE

Flea-market frenzy: rummaging for second-hand gems

euro currency converter €1 = 6.56FF

SHOPPING

and one-of-a-kind accessories worn decades ago by fashionable (and not-so-fashionable) Parisians. It opens early in the morning to 1 pm Tuesday to Sunday.

Marché aux Puces de Montreuil (Map 1, metro Porte de Montreuil) ave de la Porte de Montreuil, 20e. Established in the 19th century, this market is known for having good-quality, second-hand clothes and designer seconds. The 500 stalls also sell engravings, jewellery, linen, crockery, old furniture and appliances. It's open 7 am to about 7 pm on Saturday, Sunday and Monday.

Marché aux Puces de la Porte de Vanves (Map 1, metro Porte de Vanves) ave Georges Lafenestre & ave Marc Sangnier, 14e. This market is known for its fine selection of junk. Ave

Georges Lafenestre looks like a giant car-boot sale, with lots of 'curios' that aren't quite old (or classy) enough to qualify as antiques. Ave Marc Sangnier is lined with stalls selling new clothes, shoes, handbags and household items. It opens 7 am to 6 pm on Saturday and Sunday.

Marché aux Puces de Saint Ouen (Map 1, metro Porte de Clignancourt) rue des Rosiers, ave Michelet, rue Voltaire, rue Paul Bert & rue Jean-Henri Fabre, 18e. This vast flea market founded in the late 19th century and said to be Europe's largest, has 2000-odd stalls grouped into nine *marchés* (market areas), each with its own speciality (antiques, cheap clothing etc). It opens 7.30 am to 7 pm on Saturday, Sunday and Monday.

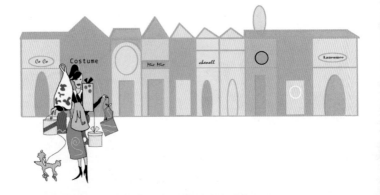

Excursions

Paris is encircled by the Île de France, the 2,000 sq km 'Island of France' shaped by five rivers: the Epte (in the north-west), the Aisne (north-east), the Eure (south-west), the Yonne (south-east) and the Marne (east). The Île de France was the seed from which France the kingdom grew, beginning in about AD 1100.

Today, the region's excellent rail and road links with the French capital and its exceptional sights – the cathedrals of Saint Denis, Chartres and Senlis; the chateaux of Versailles, Fontainebleau, Chantilly and Vaux-le-Vicomte; and, of course, every kid's favourite, Disneyland Paris – make it specially popular with day-trippers from Paris. The many woodland areas around the city, including the forests of Fontainebleau and Chantilly, offer unlimited outdoor activities within easy striking distance of the capital.

Information

The Espace du Tourisme d'Île de France (☎ 0 803 81 80 00, 01 44 50 19 98 from outside France, ✉ info@paris-ile-de-france .com), which is in the lower level of the Carrousel du Louvre shopping centre (Map 6; enter from 99 rue de Rivoli, 1er), opens 10 am to 7 pm Wednesday to Monday. You can also visit its bilingual Web site at www.paris-ile-de-france.com.

If you're visiting under your own steam, pick up a copy of Michelin's 1:200,000 scale *Île de France* map (No 237; 35FF) or the 1:100,000 scale *Environs de Paris* map (No 106; 26FF).

Organised Tours

If you're pressed for time or too lazy to do it yourself, several companies organise excursions outside Paris. Cityrama (Map 6, ☎ 01 44 55 61 00, metro Tuileries), 4 place des Pyramides, 1er, has half-day trips to Versailles (200FF) and full-day trips to Chartres (285FF), as well as many other options, while Paris Vision (Map 2, ☎ 01 42

60 30 01, metro Tuileries), 214 rue de Rivoli, 1er, has nine-hour trips to Vaux-le-Vicomte, Barbizon and Fontainebleau (460FF) and Versailles and Giverny (595FF). Children aged four to 11 pay half-price.

SAINT DENIS
postcode 93200 • pop 85,800
For 1200 years, Saint Denis was the burial place of the kings of France; today it is a quiet suburb just north of the 18e. The ornate royal tombs, adorned with some truly remarkable statuary, and the basilica that contains them are an easy half-day excursion by metro.

Saint Denis' more recent claim to fame is for being the home of the Stade de France, just south of the Canal de Saint Denis, the futuristic stadium where France beat Brazil in spectacular style to win the World Cup in July 1998.

Information
The tourist office (☎ 01 55 87 08 70, fax 01 48 20 24 11), 1 rue de la République, opens 9.30 am to 1 pm and 2 to 6 pm Monday to Saturday and 10 am to 1.30 pm on Sunday, October to March; and 9.30 am to 1 pm and 2.30 to 6.30 pm Monday to Saturday and 2 to 5.30 pm on Sunday the rest of the year. Visit its Web site at www.ville-saint-denis .fr. It has guided tours of the city (in French) at 3 pm on Saturday and 4 pm on Sunday from June to September (40FF; 30FF for students and under-18s).

Banks with ATMs include the Société Générale (☎ 01 43 20 86 39) at 11 place Jean Jaurès, which opens 9 am to 12.30 pm and 2 to 5 pm Tuesday to Saturday, and the BNP (☎ 01 48 13 53 49) near Saint Denis-Porte de Paris metro station at 6 blvd Anatole France (open 9.30 am to 6.15 pm Monday to Friday).

The post office at 59 rue de la République is open 8 am to 7 pm weekdays and 8 am to noon on Saturday.

AROUND PARIS

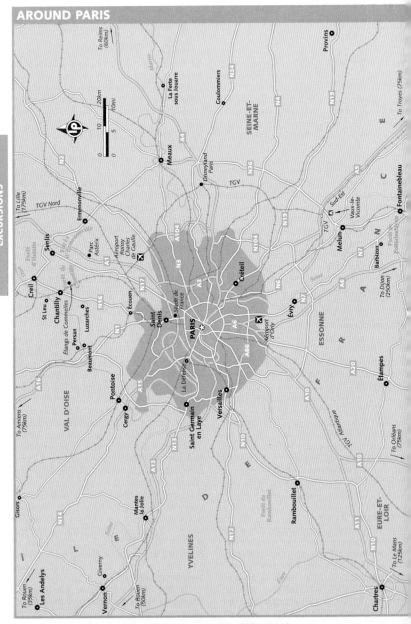

Basilique Saint Denis

The Basilica of Saint Denis (☎ 01 48 09 83 54), 1 rue de la Légion d'Honneur, served as the burial place for all but a handful of France's kings from Dagobert I (ruled 629-39) to Louis XVIII (ruled 1814-24). Their tombs and mausoleums constitute one of Europe's most important collections of funerary sculpture.

The present basilica, begun around 1135, changed the face of Western architecture. It was the first major structure to be built in the Gothic style, and served as a model for many other 12th-century French cathedrals, including the one at Chartres. Features illustrating the transition from Romanesque to Gothic can be seen in the **choir** and **ambulatory**, which are adorned with a number of 12th-century **stained-glass windows**. The **narthex** (the portico running along the western end of the basilica) also dates from this period. The nave and transept were built in the 13th century.

During the Revolution and the Reign of Terror, the basilica was devastated; human remains were removed from the royal tombs and dumped in two pits outside the church, but the mausoleums, put into storage in Paris, survived. They were brought back in 1816, and the royal bones were reburied in the crypt a year later. Restoration of the structure was begun under Napoleon, but most of the work was carried out by Viollet-le-Duc from 1858 until his death in 1879.

Tombs The tombs are decorated with life-size figures of the deceased. Those built after the Renaissance are adorned with *gisants* (recumbent figures). Those made after 1285 were carved from death masks and are thus fairly, well, lifelike; those made before under Louis IX (Saint Louis; ruled 1214-70) are depictions of how the rulers might have looked. The oldest tombs (dating from around 1230) are those of **Clovis I** (died 511) and his son **Childebert I** (died 558).

Opening Hours & Tickets You can visit the nave for free, but there's an admission fee of 32FF (21FF for those aged 12 to 25, students and seniors; free for under-12s) to visit the transept and crypt. The basilica opens 10 am (noon on Sunday) to 5 pm (to 7 pm April to September) daily. Self-paced 1¼-hour tours on CD-ROM headsets cost 25FF (35FF for two people sharing).

Stade de France

The 80,000-seat Stadium of France (☎ 01 55 93 00 00, fax 01 55 93 00 49), rue Francis de Pressensé, south of central Saint Denis and in full view from rue Gabriel Péri, was built for the 1998 World Cup, which France won by miraculously defeating Brazil 3-0. The futuristic and quite beautiful structure, with a roof the size of place de la Concorde in Paris, is now used for football and rugby matches as well as big-ticket music concerts.

The stadium can be visited on a self-guided tour (38FF; 30FF for those aged 6 to 17) from 10 am to 6 pm daily or on a more elaborate 1½-hour guided tour called 'Les Coulisses du Stade' (Behind the Scenes of the Stadium; 90/65FF) between 10 am and 4.30 pm in French and at 2.30 pm in English. Its Web site is at www.stadefrance .com; on Minitel, key in 3615 STADE DE FRANCE.

Musée d'Art et d'Histoire

Saint Denis' excellent Museum of Art & History (☎ 01 42 43 05 10), 22 bis rue Gabriel Péri, occupies a restored Carmelite convent founded in 1625 and later presided over by Louise de France, the youngest daughter of Louis XV. Displays include reconstructions of the Carmelites' cells, an 18th-century apothecary and, in the archaeology section, fascinating items found during excavations around Saint Denis. There's also a section on modern art as well as politically charged posters, cartoons, lithographs and paintings from the 1871 Paris Commune.

The museum opens 10 am to 5.30 pm on Monday and Wednesday to Saturday, and 2 to 6.30 pm on Sunday. Entry costs 20FF (10FF for students, teachers and seniors; free for under-16s).

EXCURSIONS

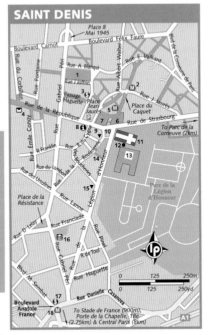

Places to Eat

There are a number of restaurants in the modern shopping area around Basilique de Saint Denis metro station and along rue de la Légion d'Honneur, including *Au Petit Breton* (☎ *01 48 20 11 58, 18 rue de la Légion d'Honneur*), with a *menu* for 65FF (open for lunch and dinner till 9 pm from Monday to Saturday afternoon).

A more expensive choice is *Les Mets du Roy* (☎ *01 48 20 89 74, 4 rue de la Boulangerie*), opposite the basilica, with an à la carte meal costing about 250FF. It opens for lunch weekdays and for dinner Monday to Saturday.

From 7 am to 1 pm on Tuesday, Friday and Sunday, there's a large, multiethnic *food market* – known in particular for its selection of spices – at place Jean Jaurès, across the street from the tourist office, and in the *Halle du Marché*, the large covered market a short stroll away to the north-west.

Getting There & Away

Take metro line No 13 to the penultimate station, Basilique de Saint Denis, for the basilica and tourist office, or to Saint Denis-Porte de Paris for the Musée d'Art et d'Histoire and the Stade de France; the latter can also be reached via RER line D1 (station Stade de France-Saint Denis). When taking metro line No 13, make sure you board a train heading for Saint Denis Université, not for Gabriel Péri/Asnières-Gennevilliers, as the line splits at La Fourche.

PARC ASTÉRIX

postcode 60128

A home-grown alternative to Disneyland Paris (see the following section), Parc Astérix (☎ 03 44 62 34 04) is 36km north-east of Paris, just beyond Roissy Charles de Gaulle Airport. Like Disneyland, it's divided into a number of 'regions' – the Village of the Gauls, the Roman Empire, Ancient Greece and so on – and there are lots of rides, including a particularly hair-raising roller coaster called Zeus' Thunder and the new Oxygenarium flume.

Opening times vary widely, but essentially visitors are welcome from 10 am to 7 pm daily from early April to early October. At the weekend from May to September, and daily from mid-July to August, it opens 9.30 am to 8 pm. All-inclusive admission costs 175FF (125FF for children aged 3 to 11). The park's Web site is at www.parcasterix.fr; on Minitel, key in 3615 PARC ASTERIX.

Getting There & Away
Take RER line B3 from Châtelet or Gare du Nord to Aéroport Charles de Gaulle 1 train station. From there Courriers Île-de-France buses depart for the park every half-hour from 9.30 am to 2 pm. They return from the park every half-hour from 4 pm until 30 minutes after the park closes. A ticket including admission and transport to/from the park, available at most RER and SNCF stations, costs 219/149FF for adults/children aged under 10.

DISNEYLAND PARIS
postcode 77777
It took some 30 billion francs and five years of work to turn the beet fields 32km east of the capital into Disneyland Paris, which opened in 1992 amid much fanfare and controversy. Although Disney stockholders were less than thrilled with the park's performance for the first few years, what was originally known as EuroDisney is now very much in the black, and the many visitors – mostly families with young children – can't seem to get enough. The park is now the single most popular fee-charging tourist attraction in Europe, welcoming some 12.5 million visitors in 1998 alone.

Orientation
Disneyland Paris consists of two main areas: commercial Disney Village, with shops, restaurants and clubs, and Disneyland Paris Theme Park. The two are separated by the RER and TGV train stations. Moving walkways whisk visitors from the far-flung car park.

Information
There are information booths scattered around the park, including one next to the RER station and another in City Hall, which can also make hostel reservations. In France, information is available on ☎ 01 60 30 60 30 (fax 01 60 30 30 99). In the UK

ring ☎ 0870 503 03 03 and in the USA ☎ 407-WDISNEY. The park's Web site is at www.disney.fr; on Minitel, key in 3615 DISNEYLAND.

There are several American Express exchange bureaus, including one (open 10 am to 6.30 pm daily) in the wing of the Disneyland Hotel nearest the main entrance to the theme park and another in Disney Village (open 9.30 am to 9.30 pm weekdays and 9 am to 10 pm at the weekend, with shorter hours outside summer).

The Disney Village post office opens 12.30 to 7 pm weekdays, 9.45 am to 6 pm on Saturday and 1 to 7 pm on Sunday. Summer hours are 8.30 am to 10.30 pm Monday to Saturday, and 1 to 7 pm on Sunday.

Disneyland Paris Theme Park
The theme park is divided into five *pays* (lands). **Main Street, USA**, just inside the main entrance and behind the Disneyland Hotel, is a spotless avenue reminiscent of Norman Rockwell's idealised small-town America, circa 1900. The adjoining **Frontierland** is a re-creation of the 'rugged, untamed American West'.

Adventureland, intended to evoke the Arabian Nights and the wilds of Africa (among other exotic lands portrayed in Disney films), is home to that old favourite, Pirates of the Caribbean, as well as the Indiana Jones and the Temple of Doom roller coaster. **Fantasyland** brings fairy-tale characters such as Sleeping Beauty, Pinocchio, Peter Pan and Snow White to life. **Discoveryland** features high-tech rides (including Space Mountain and Orbitron) and futuristic films that pay homage to Leonardo da Vinci, George Lucas and – for a bit of local colour – Jules Verne.

Opening Hours & Tickets Disneyland Paris opens daily. From early September to March the hours are 10 am to 6 pm (to 8 pm on Saturday, some Sundays and during some school holidays); in spring and early summer, the park opens 9 am to 8 pm (to 11 pm at the weekend). From early July to early September the hours are 9 am to 11 pm.

The one-day entry fee, which includes unlimited access to all rides and activities (except the shooting gallery and the video-games arcade), costs 220FF (170FF for children aged three to 11) April to early November and during the Christmas holidays. Prices drop to 165/135FF the rest of the year. Multiple-day passes are also available; two-day passes in the high season, for example, cost 425/330FF for adults/children, and three-day passes 595/460FF.

Places to Eat

There are some 50 restaurants at Disneyland Paris, including *Planet Hollywood* (☎ 01 60 43 78 27) in Disney Village, which opens 11 or 11.30 am to about midnight daily. Burgers, pasta and sandwiches are in the 74FF to 89FF range. You are not allowed to picnic inside the theme park.

OLIVIER CIRENDINI

Disneyland Paris: a little slice of America on Paris' doorstep

Getting There & Away

Marne-la-Vallée-Chessy (Disneyland's RER station) is served by RER line A4; trains run every 15 minutes or so from central Paris (38FF, 35 to 40 minutes). Trains that go all the way to Marne-la-Vallée-Chessy have four-letter codes beginning with the letter 'Q'. The last train back to Paris leaves at about 12.20 am.

VERSAILLES
postcode 78000 • pop 85,700

The prosperous, leafy and very bourgeois suburb of Versailles, 23km south-west of Paris, is the site of the grandest and most famous chateau in France. It served as the kingdom's political capital and the seat of the royal court for almost the entire period between 1682 and 1789, the year Revolutionary mobs massacred the palace guard and dragged Louis XVI and Marie-Antoinette back to Paris, where they eventually had their heads lopped off.

Because so many people consider Versailles a must-see destination, the chateau attracts more than three million visitors a year. The best way to avoid the queues is to arrive first thing in the morning; if you're interested in just the Grands Appartements, another good time to get here is around 3.30 or 4 pm.

Information

The tourist office (☎ 01 39 24 88 88, @ tourisme@ot-versailles.fr) is at 2 bis ave de Paris, just north of the Versailles-Rive Gauche train station and east of the chateau. It opens 9 am to 7 pm daily, April to October, and to 6 pm the rest of the year.

The Banque de France (☎ 01 39 24 55 49), 50 blvd de la Reine, opens for exchange 8.45 am till noon weekdays. The main post office, on the opposite side of ave de Paris from the tourist office, opens 8.30 am to 7 pm weekdays and to 12.30 pm on Saturday.

Château de Versailles

This enormous palace (☎ 01 30 83 78 00 or 01 30 83 77 77) was built in the mid-17th century during the reign of Louis XIV – the Roi Soleil (Sun King) – to project both a

euro currency converter 10FF = €1.52

VERSAILLES

PLACES TO EAT
11 Mandarin Royal
25 Crêperie Saint Louis
26 Pizzeria Via Veneto
27 Le Falher
38 Potager du Roy
39 À la Ferme

OTHER
1 Hameau de la Reine
2 Porte Saint Antoine
3 Petit Trianon
4 Grand Trianon

5 Bicycle Hire
6 Bassin d'Appolon
7 Grille de la Reine; Bicycle Hire
8 Grille de Neptune
9 Bassin de Neptune
10 Grille du Dragon
12 Banque de France
13 Musée Lambinet
14 Versailles-Rive Droite
   Train Station
15 Église Notre Dame
16 Open-Air & Covered
   Food Market

17 Château de Versailles
18 Cour Royale
19 Louis XIV Statue
20 Cour des Ministres
21 Les Grandes Heures
   du Parlement
22 Porte des Matelots
23 Orangerie
24 Jeu de Paume
28 Petites Écuries
29 Grandes Écuries;
   Musée des Carrosses
30 Post Office

31 Monoprix
   Supermarket
32 Préfecture
33 Tourist Office
34 Les Manèges
   Shopping Centre
35 Hôtel de Ville
36 Versailles-Rive Gauche
   Train Station
37 Local Bus Station
40 Cathédrale Saint Louis
41 Versailles-Chantiers
   Train Station

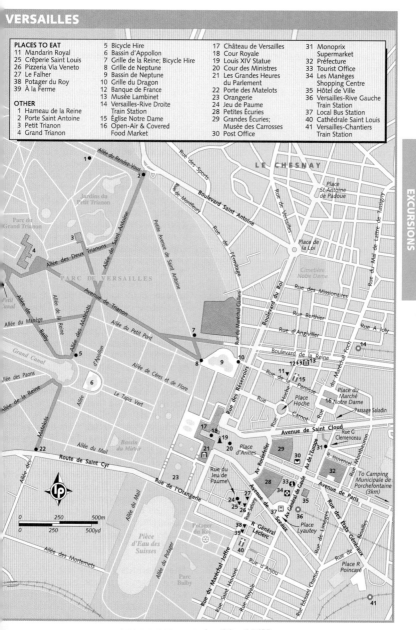

EXCURSIONS

home and abroad the absolute power of the French monarchy, then at the height of its glory. Its scale and décor also reflect Louis XIV's taste for profligate luxury and his near boundless appetite for self-glorification. Some 30,000 workers and soldiers toiled on the structure, the bills for which all but emptied the kingdom's coffers.

The chateau complex consists of four main sections: the palace building, a 580m-long structure with innumerable wings, grand halls and sumptuous bedchambers (only parts of which are open to the public); the vast gardens, canals and pools west of the palace; and two outbuildings, the Grand Trianon and, a few hundred metres to the east, the Petit Trianon. The chateau has undergone relatively few alterations since its construction, though almost all the interior furnishings disappeared during the Revolution, and many of the rooms were rebuilt by Louis-Philippe (ruled 1830-48).

History About two decades into his long reign (1643-1715), Louis XIV decided to enlarge the hunting lodge his father had built at Versailles and turn it into a palace big enough for the entire court, which numbered some 6000 people at the time. To accomplish this he hired four supremely talented men: the architect Louis Le Vau; Jules Hardouin-Mansart, who took over from Le Vau in the mid-1670s; the painter and interior designer Charles Le Brun; and the landscape artist André Le Nôtre, whose workers flattened hills, drained marshes and relocated forests as they laid out the seemingly endless gardens, ponds and fountains.

Le Brun and his hundreds of artisans decorated every moulding, cornice, ceiling and door of the interior with the most luxurious and ostentatious of appointments: frescoes, marble, gilt and woodcarvings, with the themes and symbols of many being drawn from Greek and Roman mythology. The **Grand Appartement du Roi** (King's Suite), for example, includes rooms dedicated to Hercules, Venus, Diana, Mars and Mercury. The opulence reaches its peak in the Galerie des Glaces, a 75m-long ballroom with 17 huge mirrors on one side and, on the other,

an equal number of windows looking out o the gardens.

Gardens & Fountains The section of th vast gardens nearest the palace, laid out be tween 1661 and 1700 in the formal Frenc style, is famed for its geometrically aligne terraces, flowerbeds, tree-lined paths, pond and fountains. The many statues of marble bronze and lead were made by the fines sculptors of the period. The English-styl **Jardins du Petit Trianon** are more pastora and have meandering, sheltered paths.

The **Grand Canal**, 1.6km long and 62n wide, is oriented to reflect the setting sun It is traversed by the 1km-long **Petit Cana** creating a cross-shaped body of water wit a perimeter of over 5.5km. Louis XIV use to hold boating parties here. From May t mid-October, you too can paddle around th Grand Canal: four-person rowing boat (☎ 01 39 54 22 00) cost 72FF an hour. Th dock is at the canal's eastern end. The Or angerie, built under the parterre du Mid (flowerbed) on the south side of the palace is used to store exotic plants in winter.

The gardens' largest fountains are th 17th-century **Bassin de Neptune** (Neptun Fountain), 300m north-west of the mai palace building, whose straight side abut a small, round pond graced by a winge dragon, and the **Bassin d'Apollon**, at th eastern end of the Grand Canal, in the cen tre of which Apollo's chariot, pulled b rearing horses, emerges from the water.

Each Saturday from July to Septembe and each Sunday from early April to earl October the fountains are turned on a 11 am for the hour-long **Grande Perspectiv** and from 3.30 to 5 pm for the longer an more elaborate **Grandes Eaux**. On the sam days the Bassin de Neptune flows for 1 minutes from 5.20 pm. All the perfor mances are accompanied by taped classica music.

The Trianons In the middle of the park about 1.5km north-west of the main build ing, are Versailles' two smaller palaces each surrounded by neatly tended flower beds. The pink-colonnaded **Grand Triano**

as built in 1687 for Louis XIV and his amily as a place of escape from the rigid :iquette of the court. Napoleon I had it reone in the Empire style. The much smaller, :hre-coloured **Petit Trianon**, built in the 760s, was redecorated in 1867 by Empress :ugénie (wife of Napoleon III), who added .ouis XVI-style furnishings similar to the ninspiring pieces that now fill its 1st-floor :ooms.

A bit farther north is the **Hameau de la ?eine** (Queen's Hamlet), a mock village f thatched cottages constructed from 775 to 1784 for the amusement of Marie-\ntoinette.

)pening Hours & Tickets The **Grands \ppartements** (State Apartments), the main ection of the palace that can be vis'ted vithout a guided tour, include the **Galerie les Glaces** (Hall of Mirrors), the **Appartenent de la Reine** (Queen's Suite) and the **Musée de l'Histoire de France** (Museum f French History). They are open 9 am to .30 pm (to 6.30 pm May to September)

Tuesday to Sunday. Admission costs 45FF (35FF after 3.30 pm, free for under-18s). Tickets are on sale at Entrée A (Entrance A), which is off to the right from the equestrian statue of Louis XIV as you approach the palace. The queues are worst on Tuesday, when many Paris museums are closed, and on Sunday. The chateau's Web site is at www.chateauversailles.fr. On Minitel, key in 3615 VERSAILLES.

A rather esoteric exhibit called **Les Grandes Heures du Parlement** (Landmarks in the History of the French Parliament; ☎ 01 39 67 07 73), which focuses on the history of France's Assemblée Nationale (National Assembly), is in the chateau's south wing. It keeps the same hours as the chateau. Entry costs 20FF (15FF for those aged 18 to 25, free for under-18s) including a taped commentary.

From April to October, the Grand Trianon (25FF; reduced price 15FF, free for under-18s) opens noon to 6.30 pm daily. During the rest of the year it closes at 5.30 pm. The Petit Trianon, open the same days and hours,

EXCURSIONS

Versailles: 'a masterpiece of bad taste and magnificence', according to Voltaire

euro currency converter €1 = 6.56FF

DIANA MAYFIELD

costs 15FF (reduced price 10FF, free for under-18s). A combined ticket for both costs 30FF (reduced price 20FF).

The gardens are open 7 am (8 am in winter) to dusk (between 5.30 and 9.30 pm, depending on the season) daily. Entry is free except when the fountains are in operation (30FF; 20FF for students).

If you have a Carte Musées et Monuments (see the boxed text 'Ah, la Carte!' in the Things to See & Do chapter), you don't have to wait in the queue – go straight to Entrée A2.

The entrance for disabled visitors is Entrée H, just north-west of Entrée A.

Guided Tours One of the best ways to get a sense of the Grands Appartements is to rent the audioguide available for 30FF at Entrée A, right behind the ticket booths. The excellent commentary lasts 80 minutes.

The **Appartement de Louis XIV** and the **Appartements du Dauphin et de la Dauphine** can be toured with a one-hour audioguide, available at Entrée C, for 25FF (free for children aged under 10). You can begin your visit between 9 am and 3.30 pm (4.15 pm May to September). This is also a good way to avoid the queues at Entrée A.

Several different guided tours (☎ 01 30 83 77 88 for information) are available in English from 9 am to 3.30 pm (to 4 pm May to September). They cost 25/37/50FF (17/26/34FF for those aged 10 to 17) for one/1½/two hours. Tickets are sold at Entrée D; tours begin across the courtyard at Entrée F.

All tours require you to purchase a ticket to the Grands Appartements. If you buy it at Entrée C or Entrée D you can later avoid the Grands Appartements queue at Entrée A by going straight to Entrée A2.

The Town of Versailles

Like its chateau, the attractive town of Versailles, crisscrossed by wide boulevards, is a creation of Louis XIV. However, most of today's buildings date from the 18th and 19th centuries.

Grandes & Petites Écuries Ave de Paris, ave de Saint Cloud and ave de Sceaux, the three wide thoroughfares that fan out eastwards from place d'Armes in front of the chateau, are separated by two large, late 17th-century stables: the Grandes Écuries (mostly occupied by the department archives) and the Petites Écuries, which contains an architectural unit and restoration workshops. The **Musée des Carrosses** (Carriage Museum; ☎ 01 30 83 77 88) in the Grandes Écuries, 1 ave Rockefeller, can be visited from 2 to 6.30 pm (to 5.30 pm October to April) on Saturday and Sunday (12FF; free for under-18s).

Jeu de Paume The Jeu de Paume (☎ 01 30 83 77 88), 350m south-east of the chateau on rue du Jeu de Paume, was built in 1686 and played a pivotal role in the Revolution less than a century later (see the boxed text 'The Tennis Court Oath'). It opens 2 to 5 pm on Saturday and Sunday from May to September (entry is free).

Potager du Roi The King's Kitchen Garden (☎ 01 39 24 62 62), south of the Jeu de Paume at 6 rue Hardy, was built on nine hectares of land in the late 17th century to meet the enormous catering requirements of the court. It retains its original patch divisions as well as some very old apple and pear orchards. It opens 10 am to 6 pm at the weekend from April to October (40FF; 20FF for students and under-18s).

Cathédrale Saint Louis This neoclassical (and slightly Baroque) cathedral at 4 place Saint Louis, a harmonious if austere work by Hardouin-Mansart, was built between 1743 (when Louis XV himself laid the first stone) and 1754 and was made a cathedral in 1802. It is known for its 3131-pipe Cliquot organ and is decorated with a number of interesting paintings and stained glass panels. It opens 9 am to noon and 2 to 6 or 7 pm.

Musée Lambinet Housed in a lovely 18th-century residence at 54 blvd de la Reine, the Musée Lambinet (☎ 01 39 50 30 32) displays 18th-century furnishings (ceramics, sculpture, paintings and furniture

The Tennis Court Oath

In May 1789, in an effort to deal with the huge national debt and to moderate dissent by reforming the tax system, Louis XVI convened at Versailles the États-Généraux (States General), a body made up of over 1000 deputies representing the three estates: the Nobility, the Clergy (most of whom were exempt from paying taxes) and the Third Estate, representing the middle classes.

When the Third Estate's representatives, who formed the majority of the delegates, were denied entry to the usual meeting place of the États-Généraux, they met separately in the Salle de Jeu de Paume (Royal Tennis Court), where, on 17 June, they constituted themselves as the National Assembly. Three days later they took the famous Tennis Court Oath, swearing not to dissolve the assembly until Louis XVI had accepted a new constitution. This act of defiance sparked demonstrations of support and, less than a month later, a mob in Paris would storm the Hôtel des Invalides and seize weapons before heading on to the prison at Bastille.

and objects connected with the history of Versailles (including the Revolutionary period). It opens 2 to 5 pm on Tuesday and Friday, 1 to 6 pm on Wednesday and Thursday, and 2 to 6 pm on Saturday and Sunday. Admission costs 25FF (reduced tariff 15FF).

Places to Eat

Restaurants The quiet and elegant *Le Falher* (☎ *01 39 50 57 43, 22 rue Satory*) has French gastronomic *menus* for 138FF and 175FF (including wine) at lunch and 168FF and 210FF at dinner. It's open for lunch Tuesday to Friday and on Sunday, and for dinner Monday to Saturday.

Traditional French *menus* at the refined *Potager du Roy* (☎ *01 39 50 35 34, 1 rue du Maréchal Joffre*) go for 135FF (weekday lunch only) and 178FF. There's also a four-course *menu dégustation* (sampling menu) with wine for 280FF. It's open for lunch Tuesday to Sunday and for dinner Tuesday to Saturday.

Next door the much cheaper and more relaxed *À la Ferme* (☎ *01 39 53 10 81, 3 rue du Maréchal Joffre*) specialises in grilled meats and the cuisine of South-West France. Two-course *formules* and *menus* cost 60FF to 93FF at lunch and 88FF to 118FF at dinner. It's open for lunch Wednesday to Sunday and for dinner Tuesday to Sunday.

The Breton specialities at the cosy *Crêperie Saint Louis* (☎ *01 39 53 40 12, 33 rue du Vieux Versailles*) include sweet and savoury crepes and *galettes* (18FF to 46FF), and there are *menus* for 52FF, 58FF and 75FF. It opens for lunch and dinner daily. There are lots of other restaurants in the immediate vicinity, including *Pizzeria Via Veneto* (☎ *01 39 51 03 89, 20 rue Satory*), which has pizzas (39FF to 53FF) and pasta dishes (50FF to 63FF) and opens for lunch and dinner daily.

The *Mandarin Royal* (☎ *01 39 50 48 03, 5 rue de Sainte Geneviève*), a Chinese restaurant with some Vietnamese dishes, has lunch *menus* for 49FF and 58FF and dinner ones for 68FF, 88FF and 118FF. It's open for lunch Tuesday to Sunday and for dinner Monday to Saturday.

Self-Catering The outdoor *food market* (*place du Marché Notre Dame*) opens 7.30 am to 2 pm on Tuesday, Friday and Sunday; if coming from the tourist office, enter via passage Saladin at 33 ave de Saint Cloud. The *food stalls* in the adjoining covered market are open 7 am to 7.30 pm daily (to 2 pm on Sunday).

The *Monoprix supermarket* (*rue Georges Clemenceau*) north of ave de Paris opens 8.30 am to 9 pm Monday to Saturday.

Getting There & Away

Bus No 171 (8FF or one metro/bus ticket, 35 minutes) links Pont de Sèvres, 15e, in Paris with the place d'Armes daily, but it's faster to go by train. Each of Versailles' three train stations is served by RER and/or SNCF trains coming from a different group of Paris stations.

RER line C4 takes you from Paris' Left Bank RER stations to Versailles-Rive Gauche station (14.50FF), which is only

euro currency converter €1 = 6.56FF

700m south-east of the chateau and close to the tourist office. From Paris, catch any train whose four-letter code begins with the letter 'V'. There are up to 70 trains a day (half that number on Sunday), and the last train back to Paris leaves shortly before midnight.

RER line C5 links Paris' Left Bank with Versailles-Chantiers station (14.50FF), a 1.3km walk from the chateau. From Paris, take any train whose code begins with 'S'. Versailles-Chantiers is also served by some three dozen SNCF trains a day (20 on Sunday) from Gare Montparnasse (14.50FF, 15 minutes); all trains on this line continue to Chartres.

From Paris' Gare Saint Lazare (20FF) and La Défense (12FF), the SNCF operates about 70 trains a day to Versailles-Rive Droite, which is 1.2km from the chateau. The last train to Paris leaves just after midnight.

Getting Around
From late February to December, bicycles can be hired for 32/64FF for a half/full day from kiosks at Petite Venise at the eastern end of the Grand Canal and next to Grille de la Reine (☎ 01 39 66 97 66). Opening hours are 10 am to at least 5 pm (later as the days get longer).

FONTAINEBLEAU
postcode 77300 • pop 15,900
The town of Fontainebleau, 65km south-east of Paris, is renowned for its elegant Renaissance chateau – one of France's largest royal residences – whose splendid furnishings make it particularly worth visiting. It's much less crowded and pressured than Versailles. The town itself has a number of fine restaurants and night spots – we always have a fine time in Fontainebleau – and is surrounded by the beautiful Forêt de Fontainebleau, a favourite hunting ground of a long line of French kings.

Information
The tourist office (☎ 01 60 74 99 99, fax 01 60 74 80 22), in a converted petrol station at 4 rue Royale, opens 10 am to 6.30 pm Mon-

day to Saturday, and to 4 pm on Sunday. They hire out bicycles (see Getting Around) and self-paced audioguide tours of the city in English lasting 1½ hours (20FF). Its Web site is at www.fontainebleau.org. On Minitel, key in 3615 FONTAINEBLEAU.

The Banque de France at 192 rue Grande opens for exchange from 8.30 am to noon weekdays. The main post office, at 2 rue de la Chancellerie, opens 8.15 am to 7 pm weekdays and till noon on Saturday.

Château de Fontainebleau
The enormous, 1900-room Château de Fontainebleau (☎ 01 60 71 50 70), whose list of former tenants reads like a who's who of French royal history, is one of the most beautifully decorated and furnished chateaux in France. Every centimetre of wall and ceiling space is richly adorned with wood panelling, gilded carvings, frescoes, tapestries and paintings. The parquet floors are of the finest woods, the fireplaces ornamented with exceptional carvings, and many of the pieces of furniture are Renaissance originals.

History The first chateau on this site was built sometime in the early 12th century and enlarged by Louis IX a century later. Only a single medieval tower survived the energetic Renaissance-style reconstruction undertaken by François I (ruled 1515-47) whose superb artisans, many of them brought over from Italy, blended Italian and French styles to create what is known as the First School of Fontainebleau. During this period, the *Mona Lisa* hung here amid other fine works of art in the royal collection.

During the latter half of the 16th century, the chateau was further enlarged by Henri II (ruled 1547-59), Catherine de Médicis and Henri IV (ruled 1589-1610), whose Flemish and French artists created the Second School of Fontainebleau. Even Louis XIV got in on the act: it was he who hired Le Nôtre to redesign the gardens.

Fontainebleau, which was not damaged during the Revolution (though its furniture was stolen or destroyed), was beloved by Napoleon, who did a fair bit of restoration.

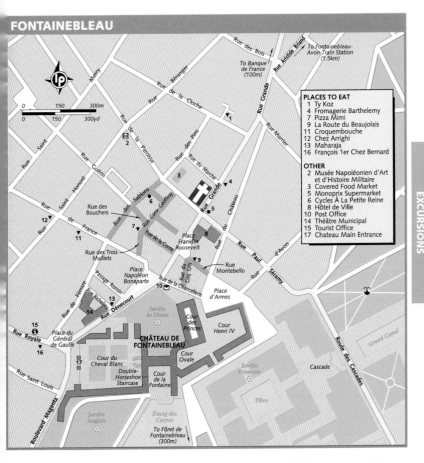

FONTAINEBLEAU

PLACES TO EAT
1 Ty Koz
4 Fromagerie Barthelemy
7 Pizza Mimi
9 La Route du Beaujolais
11 Croquembouche
12 Chez Arrighi
13 Maharaja
16 François 1er Chez Bernard

OTHER
2 Musée Napoléonien d'Art
   et d'Histoire Militaire
3 Covered Food Market
5 Monoprix Supermarket
8 Cycles À La Petite Reine
10 Post Office
14 Théâtre Municipal
15 Tourist Office
17 Chateau Main Entrance

work. Napoleon III was another frequent visitor.

During WWII, the chateau was turned into a German headquarters. Liberated in 1944 by General George Patton, part of the complex served as Allied and then NATO headquarters from 1945 to 1965.

Courtyards & Rooms As successive monarchs added their own wings to the chateau, five irregularly shaped courtyards were created. The oldest and most interesting is the **Cour Ovale** (Oval Courtyard), no longer oval but U-shaped due to Henri IV's

construction work. It incorporates the keep, the sole remnant of the medieval chateau. The largest courtyard is the **Cour du Cheval Blanc** (Courtyard of the White Horse), also known as the Cour des Adieux (Farewell Courtyard); it was from here that Napoleon, about to be exiled to Elba in 1814, bid farewell to his guards from the magnificent **double-horseshoe staircase**, built under Louis XIII in 1634.

The **Grands Appartements** (State Apartments) include a number of outstanding rooms. The spectacular **Chapelle de la Trinité** (Trinity Chapel), whose ornamentation dates from the first half of the 17th century, is where Louis XV married Marie Leczinska in 1725 and where the future Napoleon III was christened in 1810. **Galerie François 1er**, a gem of Renaissance architecture, was decorated from 1533 to 1540 by Il Rosso, a Florentine follower of Michelangelo. In the wood panelling, François I's monogram appears repeatedly along with his emblem, a dragon-like salamander.

The **Salle de Bal**, a 30m-long ballroom dating from the mid-16th century that was also used for receptions and banquets, is renowned for its mythological frescoes, marquetry floor and Italian-inspired coffered ceiling. The large windows afford views of the Cour Ovale and the gardens. The gilded bed in the 17th- and 18th-century **Chambre de l'Impératrice** was never used by Marie-Antoinette, for whom it was built in 1787. The gilding in the **Salle du Trône**, the royal bedroom before the Napoleonic period, is in three shades: golden, green and yellow.

The **Petits Appartements** were the private apartments of the emperor and empress. They do not have fixed opening hours but are usually open 9 am to 5 pm on Monday. There may be a separate admission fee to view them.

Museums The **Musée Napoléon 1er** within the chateau has a collection of personal effects (such as uniforms, hats, ornamented swords, coats) and knick-knacks that belonged to Napoleon and his relatives. At the time of research it was undergoing renovation.

The four rooms of the **Musée Chinois** (Chinese Museum) are filled with beautiful ceramics and other objects brought to France from eastern Asia during the 19th century. Some of the items, from the personal collection of Empress Eugénie, were gifts of a delegation that came from Siam (Thailand) in 1861. Others were stolen by a Franco-British expeditionary force sent to China in 1860.

Gardens On the north side of the chateau, the **Jardin de Diane**, a formal garden created by Catherine de Médicis, is home to a flock of noisy *paons* (peacocks). The marble fountain in the middle of the garden decorated with a statue of Diana, goddess of the hunt, and four urinating dogs, dates from 1603.

Le Nôtre's formal, 17th-century **Jardin Français** (French Garden), also known as the Grand Parterre, is east of the **Cour de la Fontaine** (Fountain Courtyard) and the **Étang des Carpes** (Carp Pond). The **Grand Canal** was excavated in 1609 and predates the canals at Versailles by over half a century. The informal **Jardin Anglais** (English Garden), laid out in 1812, is west of the pond. The **Forêt de Fontainebleau**, crisscrossed by paths, begins 500m south of the chateau.

Opening Hours & Tickets The interior of the chateau (enter from the Cour du Cheval Blanc) opens Wednesday to Monday; the hours are 9.30 am to 6 pm in July and August, 9.30 am to 5 pm in June and September, and 9.30 am to 12.30 pm and 2 to 5 pm the rest of the year. Tickets for the Grands Appartements and the Musée Chinois, valid for the day, cost 35FF (23FF for those aged 18 to 25 and, on Sunday, for everyone; free for under-18s). Conducted tours of the Grands Appartements in English depart several times a day from the staircase near the ticket windows.

The gardens (entry free) are open 9 am to 7 pm, May to September, and to about 5 pm the rest of the year.

Musée Napoléonien d'Art et d'Histoire Militaire

Fontainebleau's only museum of Napoleoniana while the one in the chateau is being renovated, the Napoleonic Museum of Art & Military History (☎ 01 60 74 64 89) is housed in a late-19th-century mansion at 88 rue Saint Honoré and has exhibits of military uniforms and weapons. It opens 2 to 5 pm Tuesday to Saturday and admission costs 10FF (free for under-12s). The museum's lovely gardens are open 10 am to 5 pm (to 7 pm from mid-March to mid-November) Tuesday to Saturday.

orêt de Fontainebleau

his 20,000-hectare forest, which sur-
ounds the town of Fontainebleau, is one
f the loveliest woods in the Paris region.
he many trails – including parts of the
R1 and GR11 – are excellent for jogging,
king, cycling, horse riding and climbing.
he area is covered by IGN's 1:25,000
cale *Forêt de Fontainebleau* map (No
417OT; 58FF). The tourist office sells
e *Guide des Sentiers de Promenades
ans le Massif Forestier de Fontainebleau*
50FF), whose maps and text (in French)
over almost 20 walks in the forest, as
ell as the more comprehensive *La Forêt
e Fontainebleau* (79FF), published by
e Office National des Forêts, with 33
alks.

laces to Eat

estaurants Two excellent choices are
st down the road from one another. *Chez
rrighi* (☎ *01 64 22 29 43, 53 rue de
rance*), whose Corsican two-course for-
ules are 120FF and 148FF and three-
ourse *menus* are 98FF, 145FF and 195FF,
open for lunch and dinner Tuesday to
unday. *Croquembouche* (☎ *01 64 22 01
7, 43 rue de France*), where the *menus* go
or 88FF and 125FF (at lunch), 135FF (till
0 pm) and 210FF, is open for lunch Friday
Tuesday and for dinner Thursday to
uesday.

François 1er Chez Bernard (☎ *01 64 22
4 68, 3 rue Royale*) has excellent speciali-
es from Normandy and Brittany (espe-
ially seafood) and *menus* at 98FF and
60FF. Expect to pay about 220FF per per-
on if ordering à la carte.

La Route du Beaujolais (☎ *01 64 22 27
8, 3 rue Montebello*) is no great shakes,
ut it's central, serves reliable food and
pens for lunch and dinner daily. Lyonnaise
menus are 75FF at lunch and 85FF and
30FF at dinner; expect to pay about 180FF
ordering à la carte.

Maharaja (☎ *01 64 22 14 64, 15 rue
Dénecourt*) has curries (46FF to 65FF) and
andoori dishes (35FF to 48FF) as well as
tandard starters such as pakoras and
amosas for 22FF to 26FF. There are lunch-

time *menus* for 59FF and 89FF and one at
dinner for 99FF. It's open for lunch and dinner Monday to Saturday.

For Breton crepes and galettes (15FF to
45FF), head for *Ty Koz* (☎ *01 64 22 00
55*), down a little alleyway from 18 rue de
la Cloche, which opens noon to 10 pm
daily.

Pizza Mimi (☎ *01 64 22 70 77, 17 rue des
Trois Maillets*) has pizzas (44FF to 56FF),
pastas (40FF to 57FF) and more elaborate
Italian main courses (69FF to 75FF) at
lunch and dinner daily.

Self-Catering Fontainebleau's covered
food market (*rue des Pins*) opens dawn to
4 pm on Tuesday, Friday and Sunday. The
Monoprix supermarket (*58 rue Grande*)
opens 8.45 am to 7.45 pm Monday to Saturday; the food section is on the 1st floor.
Fromagerie Barthelemy (☎ *01 64 22 21
64, 92 rue Grande*), just a few doors north,
is one of the finest cheese shops in the Île
de France. It's open 8 or 8.30 am to 12.30
or 1 pm and 3.30 to 7.30 pm Tuesday to
Saturday and on Sunday morning.

Getting There & Away

Up to three dozen daily commuter trains link
Paris' Gare de Lyon with Fontainebleau-
Avon station (48FF, 40 to 60 minutes); in
off-peak periods, there's about one train an
hour. The last train back to Paris leaves
Fontainebleau a bit after 9.45 pm (a little
after 10.30 pm on Sunday and public holidays). SNCF has a package that includes
return transport from Paris, bus transfers
and admission to the chateau for 125/100/
50FF for adults/children aged 10 to 17/
under-10s.

Getting Around

The tourist office hires out bikes for
80/100FF per half/full day. Cycles À La
Petite Reine (☎ *01 60 74 57 57*), at 32 rue
des Sablons, has mountain bikes for 30FF
per hour and 60/80FF for a half/full day
(80/100FF at the weekend). The weekly
rate is 350FF (2000FF deposit required).
The shop opens 9 am to 7.30 pm Monday
to Saturday, and to 6 pm on Sunday.

EXCURSIONS

VAUX-LE-VICOMTE

postcode 77950

This privately owned chateau (☎ 01 64 14 41 90) and its magnificent gardens, 20km north of Fontainebleau and 55km south-east of Paris, were designed and built by Le Brun, Le Vau and Le Nôtre between 1656 and 1661 as a precursor to their more ambitious work at Versailles.

Unfortunately, Vaux-le-Vicomte's beauty turned out to be the undoing of its owner Nicolas Fouquet, Louis XIV's minister of finance. It seems that Louis, seething with jealousy that he had been upstaged at the chateau's official opening, had Fouquet thrown into prison, where he died in 1680. Today visitors can view the interior of the chateau from 10 am to 1 pm and 2 to 5.30 pm daily from mid-March to mid-November; the **formal gardens** and the **Musée des Équipages** (Carriage Museum) are open 10 am to 6 pm daily. Admission costs 63FF (49FF for students and children aged six to 16).

On the second and the last Saturday of every month from April to October, there are elaborate *jeux d'eau* (fountain display) in the gardens from 3 to 6 pm. You can visit the chateau by candlelight (80/70FF) from 8 pm to midnight on Thursday and Saturday from May to mid-October. Vaux-le-Vicomte's Web site is at www.vaux-le-vicomte.com.

Getting There & Away

Vaux-le-Vicomte is not an easy place to reach. The chateau is 5km north-east of Melun, which is served by RER line D from Paris (48FF, 45 minutes). Bus No 2 (6.40FF) links the station (the stop is next to the Casino supermarket) with the chateau at 10.55 am daily from late April to mid-September, returning at 12.27 and 5.40 pm, but at other times you'll have to walk or take a taxi (between 100FF and 120FF). If you're travelling under your own steam, take the N6 from Paris (53km) or the N7 and the N36 from Fontainebleau.

A prelude to Versailles: the elegant Vaux-le-Vicomte

euro currency converter 10FF = €1.52

CHRISTOPHER WOOD

CHANTILLY

postcode 60500 • pop 10,900

The elegant town of Chantilly, 48km north of Paris, is best known for its heavily re-stored but imposing chateau, surrounded by gardens, lakes and a vast forest. The chateau is just over 2km east of the train station. The most direct route is to walk along ave de la Plaine des Aigles through a section of the Forêt de Chantilly, but you'll get a better sense of the town by taking ave du Maréchal Joffre and rue de Paris to rue du Connétable, Chantilly's principal thoroughfare.

Information

The tourist office (☎ 03 44 57 08 58, fax 03 44 57 74 64), 60 ave du Maréchal Joffre, opens 9 am to 7 pm daily, May to September. During the rest of the year the hours are 9.30 am to 12.30 pm and 2.15 to 6 pm Monday to Saturday. Its Web site is at www.ville-chantilly.fr.

Société Générale (☎ 03 44 62 57 00), 1 ave du Maréchal Joffre, opens 8.30 am to 12.15 pm and 1.45 to 5.25 pm weekdays, and to 4.15 pm on Saturday.

There's a post office at 26 ave du Maréchal Joffre, which opens 9 am to 12.15 pm and 1.45 to 6 pm weekdays and 9 am to 12.30 pm on Saturday.

Château de Chantilly

The chateau (☎ 03 44 62 62 62), left in a shambles after the Revolution, is of interest mainly because of its gardens and a number of superb paintings. It consists of two attached buildings entered through the same vestibule. The **Petit Château** was built around 1560 for Anne de Montmorency (1492-1567), who served six French kings as *connétable* (high constable), diplomat and warrior and died in battle against the Protestants. The attached Renaissance-style **Grand Château**, completely demolished during the Revolution, was rebuilt by the Duke of Aumale, son of King Louis-Philippe, in the late 1870s.

The Grand Château, to the right as you enter the vestibule, contains the **Musée Condé**. Its unremarkable 19th-century rooms are adorned with furnishings, paintings and sculptures haphazardly arranged according to the whims of the duke, who donated the chateau to the Institut de France at the end of the 19th century on the condition that the exhibits were not reorganised. The most remarkable works are hidden away in a small room called the **Sanctuaire**, including paintings by Raphael, Filippino Lippi and Jean Fouquet.

The Petit Château contains the **Appartements des Princes** (Princes' Apartments), which are straight ahead from the entrance. The highlight here is the **Cabinet des Livres**, a repository of 700 manuscripts and over 12,000 volumes including a Gutenberg Bible and a facsimile of the *Très Riches Heures du Duc de Berry*, an illuminated manuscript dating from the 15th century that illustrates the calendar year for both the peasantry and the nobility. The chapel, to the left as you walk into the vestibule, is made up of woodwork and windows dating from the mid-16th century and assembled by the duke in 1882.

Opening Hours & Tickets The chateau and Musée Condé are open 10 am to 6 pm Wednesday to Monday, March to October, and 10.30 am to 12.45 pm and 2 to 5 pm on the same days the rest of the year. Admission to the chateau and its park, which opens daily, costs 42FF (37FF for those aged 12 to 17, 15FF for children aged three to 11). Entry to the park alone costs 17FF (10FF).

Gardens The chateau's excellent but long-neglected gardens were once among the most spectacular in France. The formal **Jardin Français**, whose flowerbeds, lakes and Grand Canal were laid out by Le Nôtre in the mid-17th century, is directly north of the main building. To the west, the 'wilder' **Jardin Anglais** was begun in 1817. East of the Jardin Français is the rustic **Jardin Anglo-Chinois**, created in the 1770s. Its foliage and silted-up waterways surround the **Hameau** (Hamlet), a mock village whose mill and half-timbered buildings, built in 1774, inspired the Hameau de la Reine at

EXCURSIONS

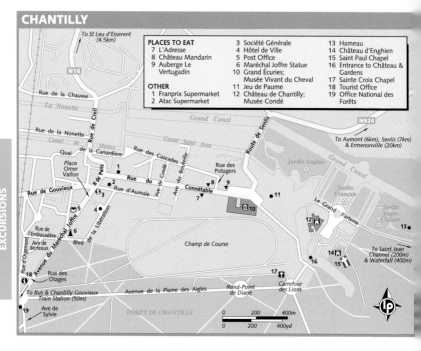

CHANTILLY

PLACES TO EAT
7 L'Adresse
8 Château Mandarin
9 Auberge Le Vertugadin

OTHER
1 Franprix Supermarket
2 Atac Supermarket

3 Société Générale
4 Hôtel de Ville
5 Post Office
6 Maréchal Joffre Statue
10 Grand Écuries; Musée Vivant du Cheval
11 Jeu de Paume
12 Château de Chantilly; Musée Condé

13 Hameau
14 Château d'Enghien
15 Saint Paul Chapel
16 Entrance to Château & Gardens
17 Sainte Croix Chapel
18 Tourist Office
19 Office National des Forêts

Versailles. Crème Chantilly – cream beaten with icing and vanilla sugar and dolloped on everything sweet that doesn't move in France – was born here (see the boxed text 'Château de Whipped Cream').

Activities There are a couple of attractions in the gardens that will keep the kids (and maybe even the adults) happy. The **Áerophile**, the world's largest hot-air balloon, takes on passengers and soars 150m up into the sky (it's attached to a cable), offering views as far as Paris (they say) on a clear day. The **Hydrophile**, an electric boat, silently slips along the Grand Canal. Admission to the Áerophile and park costs 66FF (60FF for those aged 12 to 17, 38FF for children aged three to 11). Admission to the Hydrophile and park costs 52/47/30FF. Both are open 10 am to 7 pm daily, March to October. Combination tickets including entry to the chateau, the Musée Vivant du Cheval (see the following entry)

and rides on either the balloon or the boat are available. For information ring ☎ 03 44 57 35 35.

Musée Vivant du Cheval The chateau's **Grandes Écuries** (stables), built from 1719 to 1740 to house 240 horses and over 400 hunting hounds, are next to Chantilly's famous **Champ de Course** (racecourse), inaugurated in 1834. They house the Living Horse Museum (☎ 03 44 57 40 40), whose equines live in luxurious **wooden stalls** built by Louis-Henri de Bourbon, the seventh Prince de Condé. Displays, in 31 rooms, include everything from riding equipment to horse toys and portraits of famous nags.

The museum opens 10.30 am to 5.30 pm daily (to 6 pm at the weekend) in May and June, and daily except for Tuesday morning in July and August, and Wednesday to Monday in April, September and October. From November to March it opens 2 to pm on Monday and Wednesday to Friday, and 10.30 am to 5.30 pm at the weekend. Entry costs 50FF (40FF for those aged 12 to 17, 35FF for children aged three to 11).

The 30-minute **Présentation Équestre Pédagogique** (Introduction to Dressage), included in the entry price, generally takes place at 11.30 am, and 3.30 and 5.15 pm (3.30 pm only from November to March). More elaborate, hour-long demonstrations of dressage (100FF; 90FF for children aged four to 12) are held on the first Sunday of the month at 3.30 pm from February to November.

Forêt de Chantilly

Chantilly Forest, once a royal hunting estate, covers some 15,000 hectares south of the chateau and is crisscrossed by a variety of walking and riding trails. In some areas, straight paths laid out centuries ago meet at multi-angled *carrefours* (crossroads). Long-distance trails that pass through the Forêt de Chantilly include the **GR11**, which links the chateau with the town of Senlis and its wonderful cathedral; the **GR1**, which goes from Luzarches (famed for its 16th-century cathedral) to Ermenonville; and the **GR12**, which goes north-eastwards from four lakes known as the **Étangs de Commelles** to the Forêt d'Halatte.

The area is covered by IGN's 1:25,000 scale *Forêts de Chantilly, d'Halatte and d'Ermenonville* map (No 2412OT; 58FF). The 1:100,000 scale *Carte de Découverte des Milieux Naturels et du Patrimoine Bâti* (40FF), available at the tourist office, indicates sites of interest (eg, churches, chateaux, museums and ruins). The Office National des Forêts (ONF; ☎ 03 44 57 03 88, fax 03 44 57 91 67), south-east of the tourist office at the start of ave de la Plaine des Aigles, publishes a good walking guide for families, *Promenons-Nous dans les Forêts de Picardie* (49FF). It also organises forest walks departing at 3 pm on Sunday from June to September.

Places to Eat

The restaurant at the *Auberge Le Vertugadin* (☎ 03 44 57 03 19, 44 rue du Con-

Château de Whipped Cream

Like every self-respecting French chateau in the 18th century, the one at Chantilly had its own hamlet complete with *laitier* (dairy) where the lady of the household and her guests could play at being milkmaids, as Marie-Antoinette did at Versailles. But the cows at Chantilly's dairy took their job rather more seriously than most of their fellow bovine actors at the other *faux* dairies, and news of the sweet cream served at the hamlet's teas became the talk (and envy) of aristocratic Europe. The future Habsburg Emperor Joseph II visited this *temple de marbre* (marble temple) incognito to try it in 1777, and when the Baroness of Oberkirch tasted the goods she cried: 'Never have I eaten such good cream, so appetising, so well prepared'.

Not to be outdone, an equally well heeled chateau to the south has lent its name to another sweet dairy product. Take some fromage frais, fold in Chantilly and – *voilà!* – you've got Fontainebleau, a triple-cream cheese.

nétable), with starters for around 50FF, main courses for 85FF and *menus* for 98FF and 150FF, is highly recommended.

Other restaurants nearby include the bistro-like *L'Adresse* (☎ 03 44 57 27 74, 49 rue du Connétable) and a Chinese place called *Château Mandarin* (☎ 03 44 57 00 29, 62 rue du Connétable). L'Adresse has starters from 40FF to 48FF, main courses for 75FF to 98FF, a two-course formule at 98FF and a *menu* for 145FF. It's open for lunch Tuesday to Sunday and for dinner Tuesday to Saturday. The Château Mandarin has starters in the 25FF to 35FF range, main courses for 40FF to 96FF and a 76FF lunch *menu*. It opens for lunch and dinner to 9.30 pm Tuesday to Sunday.

Midway between the train station and the chateau, the *Atac supermarket (place Omer Vallon)* opens 8.30 am to 7.30 pm Monday to Saturday. There's a *Franprix (132 rue du Connétable)* almost opposite, which opens 8.30 am to 7.30 pm Tuesday to Saturday and 8.45 am to 12.45 pm on Sunday.

EXCURSIONS

Getting There & Away

Paris' Gare du Nord is linked to Chantilly Gouvieux train station (42FF, 30 to 45 minutes) by a mixture of RER and SNCF commuter trains, a total of almost 40 a day (about two dozen on Sunday). In the morning, there are departures at least twice an hour; in the evening, there are generally trains back to Paris every hour or so until just before midnight.

The trains, signposted for a variety of destinations, including Compiègne, Saint Quentin, Amiens and Creil, use both the 'Grandes Lignes' (main line) and 'Banlieue' (suburban) platforms.

Chantilly's bus station is next to the train station.

SENLIS

postcode 60300 • pop 163,000

Senlis, just 10km north-east of Chantilly through the forest, is an attractive medieval town of winding cobblestone streets, Gallo-Roman ramparts and towers. It was a royal seat from the time of Clovis to Henri IV and contains four fine museums and an important 12th-century cathedral.

The Gothic **Cathédrale de Notre Dame**, which is entered through the south portal on place Notre Dame, was built between 1150 and 1191. The cathedral is unusually bright, but the stained glass, though original, is unexceptional. The magnificent carved stone **Grand Portal** (1170), on the west side facing place du Parvis Notre Dame, has statues and a central relief relating to the life of the Virgin Mary. It was the inspiration for the portal at the cathedral in Chartres.

The tourist office (☎ 03 44 53 06 40, fax 03 44 53 29 80) is on place du Parvis Notre Dame just opposite (and west of) the cathedral. It is open 10 am till noon and 2.15 to 6.15 pm Wednesday to Monday. Guided tours of the cathedral and town (30FF; 15FF for under-16s and those aged over 60) depart from here at 3 pm on Sunday from March to mid-November.

Places to Eat

There are several places to eat around the cathedral, including the upmarket *Le Scaramouche* (☎ 03 44 53 01 26, 4 place Notre Dame). You'll find cheaper eateries (pizzerias, creperies etc) as well as an open air *market* (Tuesday and Friday morning) along rue Saint Hilaire, south-west of the cathedral.

Getting There & Away

Buses (16FF, 25 minutes) link Senlis with Chantilly about every half-hour, with the last one returning to Chantilly just after 7 pm Monday to Saturday and at 9.50 pm on Sunday.

CHARTRES

postcode 28000 • pop 40,300

The magnificent 13th-century cathedral of Chartres, crowned by two very different spires – one Gothic, the other Romanesque – rises from rich farmland 88km south-west of Paris and dominates the medieval town around its base. The cathedral's varied collection of relics – particularly the Sainte Chemise, a piece of the blouse said to have been worn by the Virgin Mary when she gave birth to Jesus – attracted many pilgrims during the Middle Ages, who contributed to the building and extending of the cathedral.

Information

The tourist office (☎ 02 37 18 26 26, @ chartres.tourism@wanadoo.fr) is across place de la Cathédrale from the cathedral's main entrance. It opens 9 am to 7 pm Monday to Saturday and 9.30 am to 5.30 pm on Sunday, April to September; and 10 am to 6 pm Monday to Saturday and 10 am to 1 pm and 2.30 to 4.30 pm on Sunday the rest of the year.

The Banque de France, 32 rue du Docteur Maunoury, opens for exchange 9 am to 12.30 pm weekdays. There's a BNP (☎ 0 802 35 63 91) at 9 place des Épars, open 8.30 am till noon and 1.30 to 5.30 pm Tuesday to Friday, and to 4.30 pm on Saturday. The impressive neo-Gothic post office on place des Épars opens 8.30 am to 7 pm weekdays and 8.30 am to noon on Saturday.

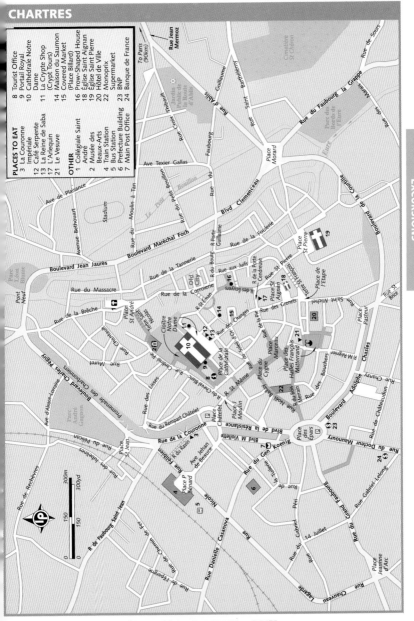

CHARTRES

PLACES TO EAT
3 La Couronne Impériale
12 Café Serpente
13 La Reine de Saba
17 L'Arlequin
21 Le Vesuve

OTHER
1 Collégiale Saint André
2 Musée des Beaux-Arts
5 Bus Station
6 Préfecture Building
7 Main Post Office
8 Tourist Office
9 Portail Royal
10 Cathédrale Notre Dame
11 La Crypte Shop (Crypt Tours)
14 Maison du Saumon
15 Covered Market (Place Billard)
16 Prow-Shaped House
18 Eglise Saint Aignan
19 Eglise Saint Pierre
20 Hôtel de Ville
22 Monoprix
23 BNP
24 Banque de France

EXCURSIONS

EXCURSIONS

Cathédrale Notre Dame

Chartres' 130m-long cathedral (☎ 02 37 21 75 02), one of the crowning architectural achievements of Western civilisation, was built in the Gothic style during the first quarter of the 13th century to replace a Romanesque cathedral that had been devastated – along with much of the town – by fire on the night of 10 June 1194. Because of effective fund-raising among the aristocracy and donations of labour by the common folk, construction took only 30 years, resulting in a high degree of architectural unity. It is France's best-preserved medieval cathedral, having been spared both postmedieval modifications and the ravages of war and the Revolution (see the boxed text 'Saved by Red Tape').

Opening Hours & Guided Tours The cathedral opens 7.30 am (8.30 am on Sunday) to 7.15 pm daily, except during Mass, weddings and funerals. There are excellent 1½-hour English-language tours (35FF; 25FF for students) conducted by Chartres expert Malcolm Miller (☎ 02 37 28 15 58, fax 02 37 28 33 03) that depart at noon and 2.45 pm Monday to Saturday from Easter to November. If you miss one of Miller's tours, his books are available at the gift shop inside the cathedral: *Chartres* (30FF) and *Chartres Cathedral* (110FF). Audioguide tours in English lasting 25 to 70 minutes (15FF to 30FF) can be hired from the cathedral bookshop.

Portals & Towers All three of the cathedral's entrances have superbly ornamented triple portals, but the west entrance, known as the **Portail Royal**, is the only one that predates the fire. Carved from 1145 to 1155, its superb statues, whose features are elongated in the Romanesque style, represent the glory of Christ in the centre, and the Nativity and Ascension to the right and left respectively. The structure's other main Romanesque feature is the 105m-high **Clocher Vieux** (Old Bell Tower), also known as the Tour Sud (South Tower), which was begun in the 1140s. It is the tallest Romanesque steeple still standing.

Saved by Red Tape

The cathedral at Chartres managed to survive the ravages of the Revolution and the Reign of Terror for the same reason that everyday life in France can often seem so complicated: the vaunted French bureaucratic approach to almost everything.

As antireligious fervour was nearing fever pitch in 1791, the Revolutionaries decided that the cathedral deserved something more radical than mere desecration: demolition. The question was how to accomplish that. To find an answer, they appointed a committee, whose admirably thorough members deliberated for four or five years. By that time the Revolution's fury had been spent, and the plan was shelved.

A visit to the 112m-high **Clocher Neuf** (New Bell Tower) – also known as the Tour Nord (North Tower) – is well worth the ticket price and the long, spiral climb. Access is via the north transept. A 70m-high platform on the lacy Flamboyant Gothic spire, built from 1507 to 1513 by Jehan de Beauce after an earlier wooden spire burned down, affords superb views of the three-tiered flying buttresses and the 19th-century copper roof, turned green by verdigris.

The Clocher Neuf opens 9 am to 6 pm Monday to Saturday and 1 to 6.30 pm on Sunday, May to August; and 9.30 or 10 am to 11.30 am and 2 to 5 pm (to 4 pm from November to February) Monday to Saturday and 1 to 2 pm on Sunday the rest of the year. Admission costs 25FF (15FF for those aged 12 to 25, free for under-12s and for everyone on certain Sundays).

Stained-Glass Windows The cathedral's 172 extraordinary stained-glass windows, almost all of which are 13th-century originals, form one of the most important ensembles of medieval stained glass in Europe. The three most important windows dating from before the 13th century are in the wall above the west entrance, below the rose window. Survivors of the fire of 1194 (they were made around 1150), the windows are renowned for the depth and intensity of their blue tones, which have become known as Chartres blue.

Treasury & Crypt Chapelle Saint Piat, up the stairs at the far end of the choir, houses the cathedral's *trésor* (treasury), where you'll find the Sainte Chemise, also known as the Voile de Notre Dame (Veil of Our Lady). At the time of research it was undergoing renovation.

The cathedral's 110m-long crypt, a tombless Romanesque structure built in 1024 around a 9th-century predecessor, is the largest in France. Guided tours in French (with a written English translation), lasting 30 minutes, start at La Crypte (☎ 02 37 21 56 33), the cathedral-run shop selling religious items and souvenirs at 18 Cloître Notre Dame. There are departures at 11 am and 4.15 or 4.30 pm daily year-round, with two or three additional tours a day from April to October. Tickets cost 15FF (10FF for students and seniors, free for under-sevens).

Musée des Beaux-Arts

The Fine Arts Museum (☎ 02 37 36 41 39), 29 Cloître Notre Dame (through the gate next to the cathedral's north portal), is housed in the former **Palais Épiscopal** (Bishop's Palace), most of which was built in the 17th and 18th centuries. Its collections include 16th-century enamels of the Apostles made by Léonard Limosin for François I, paintings from the 16th to 19th centuries and wooden sculptures from the Middle Ages.

It opens 10 am to noon and 2 to 5 pm on Monday and Wednesday to Saturday (to 6 pm on the same days from May to October) and on Sunday afternoon. Admission costs 15FF (7.50FF for students and those aged over 60).

Old City

Chartres' carefully preserved old city is north-east and east of the cathedral along the narrow western channel of the River Eure, which is spanned by a number of footbridges. From rue Cardinal Pie, the stairway called **Tertre Saint Nicolas** and **rue**

Chantault – the latter is lined with old houses – lead down to the empty shell of the 12th-century **Collégiale Saint André**, a Romanesque collegiate church closed in 1791 and severely damaged in the early 19th century and again in 1944.

Rue de la Tannerie and its extension **rue de la Foulerie** along the river's east bank are lined with flower gardens, millraces and the restored remnants of riverside trades: wash houses, tanneries and the like. **Rue aux Juifs** (Street of the Jews) on the west bank has been extensively renovated. Half a block down the hill there's a riverside promenade and up the hill **rue des Écuyers** has many structures dating from around the 16th century, including a half-timbered, **prow-shaped house** at No 26 with its upper section supported by beams. **Rue du Bourg** and **rue de la Poissonnerie** also have some old half-timbered houses; on the latter, look for the magnificent **Maison du Saumon** (Salmon House; 1500) with its fishy consoles.

From place Saint Pierre, you get a good view of the flying buttresses holding up the 12th- and 13th-century **Église Saint Pierre**. Once part of a Benedictine monastery founded in the 7th century, it was outside the city walls and thus vulnerable to attack; the fortress-like, pre-Romanesque **bell tower** attached to it was used as a refuge by monks and dates from around 1000. The fine, brightly coloured **clerestory windows** in the nave, choir and apse date from the mid-13th and early 14th centuries. It opens 10 am to noon and 2 to 5 pm daily.

Église Saint Aignan, place Saint Aignan, built in the early 16th century, is interesting for its wooden barrel-vault roof (1625) and its painted interior of faded blue and gold floral motifs (circa 1870). The stained glass and the Renaissance Chapelle de Saint Michel date from the 16th century. It's open 9 am to noon and 2 to 6.30 pm daily.

Places to Eat

Restaurants *L'Arlequin* (☎ 02 37 34 88 57, 8 rue de la Porte Cendreuse) features fish dishes for 72FF to 85FF, with starters for 33FF to 75FF and a lunch-time *menu* at 95FF. Evening *menus* are 120FF and 150FF.

EXCURSIONS

It's open for lunch Sunday to Friday and for dinner till 11 pm Tuesday to Saturday.

Café Serpente (☎ *02 37 21 68 81, 2 Cloître Notre Dame)*, a brasserie and *salon de thé* by the cathedral, serves meals from 10 am to 1 am daily. The plat du jour is 78FF to 98FF and salads are 69FF to 79FF.

La Reine de Saba (☎ *02 37 21 89 16, 8 Cloître Notre Dame)* has lunch *menus* for 69FF and 99FF. This casual French restaurant opens 11.30 am to 8 pm daily (to 9.30 or 10 pm at the weekend and from July to mid-September).

At *Le Vesuve* (☎ *02 37 21 56 35, 30 place des Halles François Mitterrand)*, pizzas (35FF to 60FF), salads (42FF to 48FF) and light meals are served at lunch and dinner to 11 pm daily.

La Couronne Impériale (☎ *02 37 21 87 59, 7-9 rue de la Couronne)* has Chinese and Vietnamese starters for 25FF to 50FF, main courses for 40FF to 66FF and dim sum for 26FF to 33FF. *Menus* are available for 60FF and 82FF. It's open for lunch and dinner Tuesday to Sunday.

Self-Catering There are a number of *food shops* around the *covered market (rue des Changes)*, which opens from about 7 am to 1 pm on Saturday. The *Monoprix supermarket (21 rue Noël Ballay)* opens 9 am to 7.30 pm Monday to Saturday.

Getting There & Away

There are some three dozen trains a day (20 on Sunday) from/to Paris' Gare Montparnasse (72FF, 55 to 70 minutes). The last train back to Paris leaves Chartres a bit after 9 pm weekdays, 7.40 pm on Saturday and sometime after 10 pm on Sunday and public holidays.

GIVERNY
postcode 27620 • pop 524
Situated between Paris and Rouen, this small village contains the Musée Claude Monet, the home (from 1883 to 1926) and flower-filled garden of one of the leading impressionist painters. Here Monet painted some of his most famous series of works, including *Décorations des Nymphéas* (Water Lilies).

CHRISTOPHER WOOD

A lasting impression: Monet's gorgeous house at Giverny
euro currency converter 10FF = €1.52

Musée Claude Monet

The hectare of land that Monet owned here has become two distinct areas, cut by the chemin du Roy, a small railway line that, unfortunately, was converted into what is now the busy D5 road.

The northern part is the **Clos Normand**, where Monet's famous pastel pink and green house and the **Water Lilies studio** stand. These days the studio is the entrance hall, adorned with precise reproductions of his works and ringing with cash-register bells from busy souvenir stands. Outside are the symmetrically laid-out gardens.

Giverny's gardens reflect the seasons. From early to late spring, daffodils, tulips, rhododendrons, wisteria and irises appear, followed by poppies and lilies. By June, nasturtiums, roses and sweet peas are in blossom. Around September, there are dahlias, sunflowers and hollyhocks.

From the Clos Normand's far corner, a tunnel leads under the D5 to the **Jardin d'Eau** (Water Garden). Having bought this piece of land in 1895, after his reputation had been established, Monet dug a pool (fed by the Epte, a tributary of the nearby Seine), planted water lilies and constructed the Japanese bridge, which has since been rebuilt. Draped with purple wisteria, the bridge blends into the asymmetrical foreground and background, creating the intimate atmosphere for which the 'Painter of Light' was famous.

The museum (☎ 02 32 51 28 21) opens 10 am to 6 pm Tuesday to Sunday from April to October. Admission to the house and gardens costs 35FF (25FF for students, 20FF for children).

Musée d'Art Américain

The American Art Museum (☎ 02 32 51 94 65) contains a fine collection of the works of many of the American impressionist painters who flocked to France in the late 19th and early 20th centuries. It's housed in an unsightly building at 99 rue Claude Monet, 100m down the road from the Musée Claude Monet, and keeps the same opening hours (except that on the first Thursday of each month it is open till 9 pm). Admission costs 35FF (20FF for students, 15FF for children aged seven to 12).

Getting There & Away

Giverny is 76km north-west of Paris. The nearest town is Vernon, nearly 7km to the north-west on the Paris-Rouen train line.

From Paris' Gare Saint Lazare (66FF, 50 minutes), there are two early-morning trains to Vernon. For the return trip there's roughly one train an hour between 5 and 9 pm. Once in Vernon it's still a hike to Giverny. Buses (☎ 02 35 71 32 99) meet most trains and cost 14/22FF for a single/return trip. Alternatively bikes can be hired from the train station for 55FF a day; a 1000FF deposit is required.

EXCURSIONS

Language

Around 122 million people worldwide speak French as their first language. Apart from in France, it is an official language in Belgium, Switzerland, Luxembourg, the Canadian province of Quebec and over two dozen other countries, most of them former French colonies in Africa.

You'll find that any attempt to communicate in French will be much appreciated. Your best bet is always to approach people politely in French, even if the only sentence you know is *Pardon, madame/monsieur/ mademoiselle, parlez-vous anglais?* (Excuse me, madam/sir/miss, do you speak English?).

For a more comprehensive guide to the French language get a copy of Lonely Planet's *French phrasebook*.

Grammar

All nouns in French are either masculine or feminine, and adjectives reflect the gender of the noun they modify. The feminine form of many nouns and adjectives is indicated by a silent *e* added to the masculine form, as in *étudiant* and *étudiante*, the masculine and feminine for 'student'. In the following phrases we have indicated both masculine and feminine forms where necessary. The masculine form comes first, separated from the feminine by a slash. The gender of a noun is often indicated by a preceding article: 'the/a/some', *le/un/du* (m), *la/une/ de la* (f); or a possessive adjective, 'my/ your/his/her', *mon/ton/son* (m), *ma/ta/sa* (f). With French, unlike English, the possessive adjective agrees in number and gender with the thing possessed: *sa mère* (his/her mother).

Pronunciation

Most letters in French are pronounced more or less the same as their English equivalents. A few which may cause confusion are:

j   as the 's' in 'leisure', eg *jour* (day)

c   before **e** and **i**, as the 's' in 'sit'; before **a**, **o** and **u** it's pronounced as English 'k'. When underscored with a 'cedilla' (ç) it's always pronounced as the 's' in 'sit'.

French has a number of sounds that are difficult for Anglophones to produce. These include:

- The distinction between the 'u' sound (as in *tu*) and 'oo' sound (as in *tout*). For both sounds, the lips are rounded and projected forward, but for the 'u' the tongue is towards the front of the mouth, its tip against the lower front teeth, whereas for the 'oo' the tongue is towards the back of the mouth, its tip behind the gums of the lower front teeth.

- The nasal vowels. With nasal vowels the breath escapes partly through the nose and partly through the mouth. These sounds occur where a syllable ends in a single **n** or **m**; the **n** or **m** is silent but indicates the nasalisation of the preceding vowel.

- The **r**. The standard **r** of Parisian French is produced by moving the bulk of the tongue backwards to constrict the air flow in the pharynx while the tip of the tongue rests behind the lower front teeth.

Greetings & Civilities

Hello/Good morning.	*Bonjour.*
Good evening.	*Bonsoir.*
Good night.	*Bonne nuit.*
Goodbye.	*Au revoir.*
Yes.	*Oui.*
No.	*Non.*
Maybe.	*Peut-être.*
Please.	*S'il vous plaît.*
Thank you.	*Merci.*
You're welcome.	*Je vous en prie.*
Excuse me.	*Excusez-moi.*
I'm sorry.	*Pardon.*
How are you?	*Comment allez-vous?* (polite)

How are you?	*Comment vas-tu?/*
	Comment ça va?
	(informal)
Fine, thanks.	*Bien, merci.*
What's your name?	*Comment vous*
	appelez-vous?
My name is ...	*Je m'appelle ...*
How old are you?	*Quel âge avez-vous?*
I'm ... years old.	*J'ai ... ans.*
Do you like ...?	*Aimez-vous ...?*
Where are you	*De quel pays*
from?	*êtes-vous?*

I'm from ...	*Je viens ...*
Australia	*d'Australie*
Canada	*du Canada*
England	*d'Angleterre*
New Zealand	*de Nouvelle Zélande*
the USA	*des États-Unis*

Language Difficulties

Do you speak	*Parlez-vous anglais?*
English?	
I understand.	*Je comprends.*
I don't understand.	*Je ne comprends pas.*
Could you please	*Est-ce que vous*
write it down?	*pouvez l'écrire?*

Getting Around

What time does	*À quelle heure*
the ... leave/arrive?	*part/arrive ...?*
bus (city)	*l'autobus*
bus (intercity)	*l'autocar*
ferry	*le ferry(-boat)*
train	*le train*

Where is (the) ...?	*Où est ...?*
bus stop	*l'arrêt d'autobus*
metro station	*la station de métro*
train station	*la gare*
ticket office	*le guichet*

I'd like a ... ticket.	*Je voudrais un billet ...*
one-way	*aller-simple*
return	*aller-retour*
1st class	*première classe*
2nd class	*deuxième classe*

| How long does | *Combien de temps* |
| the trip take? | *dure le trajet?* |

The train is ...	*Le train est ...*
delayed	*en retard*
on time	*à l'heure*
early	*en avance*

Do I need to ...?	*Est-ce que je dois ...?*
change trains	*changer de train*
change platform	*changer de quai*

left-luggage locker	*consigne automatique*
platform	*quai*
timetable	*horaire*

I'd like to hire ...	*Je voudrais louer ...*
a bicycle	*un vélo*
a car	*une voiture*

Around Town

I'm looking for ...	*Je cherche ...*
a bank/	*une banque/*
exchange office	*un bureau de*
	change
the city centre	*le centre ville*
the ... embassy	*l'ambassade de ...*
the hospital	*l'hôpital*
my hotel	*mon hôtel*
the market	*le marché*
the police	*la police*
the post office	*le bureau de poste/*
	la poste
a public phone	*une cabine*
	téléphonique
a public toilet	*les toilettes*
the tourist office	*l'office de tourisme*

What time does it open/close?	Quelle est l'heure d'ouverture/ de fermeture?
I'd like to make a telephone call.	Je voudrais téléphoner.
I'd like to change ... some money travellers cheques	Je voudrais changer ... de l'argent chèques de voyage

Directions

How do I get to ...?	Comment dois-je faire pour arriver à ...?
Is it near/far?	C'est près/loin?
Can you show me on the map/ city map?	Est-ce que vous pouvez me le montrer sur la carte/le plan?
Go straight ahead.	Continuez tout droit.
Turn left.	Tournez à gauche.
Turn right.	Tournez à droite.

Accommodation

I'm looking for ... the camp ground the hostel	Je cherche ... le camping l'auberge de jeunesse
a hotel	un hôtel
Where can I find a cheap hotel?	Où est-ce que je peux trouver un hôtel bon marché?
What's the address?	Quelle est l'adresse?
Do you have any rooms available?	Est-ce que vous avez des chambres libres?
I'd like to book ... a bed a single room	Je voudrais réserver ... un lit une chambre pour une personne
a double room	une chambre double
a room with a shower and toilet	une chambre avec douche et WC
I'd like to stay in a dormitory.	Je voudrais coucher dans un dortoir.
How much is it ...? per night per person	Quel est le prix ...? par nuit par personne

Emergencies

Help!	Au secours!
Call a doctor!	Appelez un médecin!
Call the police!	Appelez la police!
Leave me alone!	Fiche-moi la paix!
I've been robbed.	On m'a volé.
I've been raped.	On m'a violé(e)/ violée. (m/f)
I'm lost.	Je me suis perdu/ perdue. (m/f)

Can I see the room?	Est-ce que je peux voir la chambre?
Where is the toilet?	Où sont les toilettes?
Where is ...? the bathroom the shower	Où est ...? la salle de bains la douche

Shopping

How much is it?	C'est combien?
It's too expensive for me.	C'est trop cher pour moi.
Can I look at it?	Est-ce que je peux le/la voir? (m/f)
I'm just looking.	Je ne fais que regarder.
It's too big/small.	C'est trop grand/petit.
more/less	plus/moins
cheap	bon marché
cheaper	moins cher

Time & Dates

What time is it?	Quelle heure est-il?
It's (two) o'clock.	Il est (deux) heures.
When?	Quand?
today	aujourd'hui
tonight	ce soir
tomorrow	demain
day after tomorrow	après-demain
yesterday	hier
all day	toute la journée
in the morning	du matin
in the afternoon	de l'après-midi
in the evening	du soir

Monday	*lundi*
Tuesday	*mardi*
Wednesday	*mercredi*
Thursday	*jeudi*
Friday	*vendredi*
Saturday	*samedi*
Sunday	*dimanche*

January	*janvier*
February	*février*
March	*mars*
April	*avril*
May	*mai*
June	*juin*
July	*juillet*
August	*août*
September	*septembre*
October	*octobre*
November	*novembre*
December	*décembre*

Numbers

1	*un*
2	*deux*
3	*trois*
4	*quatre*
5	*cinq*
6	*six*
7	*sept*
8	*huit*
9	*neuf*
10	*dix*
11	*onze*
12	*douze*
13	*treize*
14	*quatorze*
15	*quinze*
16	*seize*
17	*dix-sept*
20	*vingt*
100	*cent*
1000	*mille*

| one million | *un million* |

Health

I'm sick.	*Je suis malade.*
I need a doctor.	*Il me faut un médecin.*
Where is the hospital?	*Où est l'hôpital?*

I'm ...	*Je suis ...*
diabetic	*diabétique*
epileptic	*épileptique*
asthmatic	*asthmatique*
anaemic	*anémique*

I'm allergic ...	*Je suis allergique ...*
to antibiotics	*aux antibiotiques*
to penicillin	*à la pénicilline*
to bees	*aux abeilles*

antiseptic	*antiseptique*
aspirin	*aspirine*
condoms	*préservatifs*
contraceptive	*contraceptif*
medicine	*médicament*
nausea	*nausée*
sunblock cream	*crème solaire haute protection*
tampons	*tampons hygiéniques*

FOOD

breakfast	*le petit déjeuner*
lunch	*le déjeuner*
dinner	*le dîner*
a starter (appetiser)	*une entrée*
a main course	*un plat principal*
a dessert	*un dessert*

I'd like the set menu.	*Je prends le menu.*
I'm a vegetarian.	*Je suis végétarien/ végétarienne.* (m/f)
I don't eat meat.	*Je ne mange pas de viande.*

Starters (Appetisers)

assiette anglaise
   plate of cold mixed meats and sausages
assiette de crudités
   plate of raw vegetables with dressings
soufflé
   a light, fluffy dish made with egg yolks, stiffly beaten egg whites, flour and cheese or other ingredients

Soup

bouillabaisse
   Mediterranean-style fish soup, originally from Marseille, made with several kinds of fish, including *rascasse* (scorpion fish); often eaten as a main course

bouillon
  broth or stock
potage
  thick soup made with puréed vegetables
soupe au pistou
  vegetable soup made with a basil and garlic paste
soupe de poisson
  fish soup
soupe du jour
  soup of the day

Meat, Chicken & Poultry

agneau	lamb
andouille or *andouillette*	sausage made from pork or veal tripe
bifteck	steak
bœuf	beef
bœuf haché	minced beef
boudin noir	blood sausage (black pudding)
brochette	kebab
canard	duck
charcuterie	cooked or prepared meats (usually pork)
chevreuil	venison
côte	chop of pork, lamb or mutton
côtelette	cutlet
cuisses de grenouilles	frogs' legs
entrecôte	rib steak
dinde	turkey
escargot	snail
faisan	pheasant
faux-filet	sirloin steak
filet	tenderloin
foie	liver
foie gras de canard	duck liver pâté
gibier	game
gigot d'agneau	leg of lamb
jambon	ham
langue	tongue
lapin	rabbit
lard	bacon
lièvre	hare
mouton	mutton
oie	goose
pieds de porc	pigs' trotters
porc	pork
poulet	chicken
rognons	kidneys
saucisson	large sausage
saucisson fumé	smoked sausage
steak	steak
tournedos	thick slices of fillet
tripes	tripe
veau	veal
viande	meat
volaille	poultry

Common Meat & Poultry Dishes

blanquette de veau
  veal stew with white sauce
bœuf bourguignon
  beef and vegetable stew cooked in red wine
cassoulet
  Languedoc stew made with goose, duck, pork or lamb fillets and haricot beans
choucroute garnie
  sauerkraut with sausage and other prepared meats
confit de canard or *d'oie*
  duck or goose preserved and cooked in its own fat
coq au vin
  chicken cooked in wine
fricassée
  stew with meat that has first been fried
grillade
  grilled meats
quenelles
  dumplings made of a finely sieved mixture of cooked fish or meat
steak tartare
  raw ground meat mixed with onion, raw egg yolk and herbs

Ordering a Steak

bleu
  nearly raw
saignant
  very rare (literally 'bleeding')
à point
  medium rare but still pink
bien cuit
  literally 'well cooked', but usually like medium rare

Fish & Seafood

anchois	anchovy
anguille	eel
brochet	pike
cabillaud	cod
calmar	squid
chaudrée	fish stew
coquille Saint-Jacques	scallop
crabe	crab
crevette	shrimp/prawn
fruits de mer	seafood
hareng	herring
homard	lobster
huître	oyster
langouste	crayfish
langoustine	very small saltwater 'lobster' (Dublin Bay prawn)
maquereau	mackerel
morue	cod
moules	mussels
palourde	clam
poisson	fish
raie	ray
rouget	mullet
sardine	sardine
saumon	salmon
sole	sole
thon	tuna
truite	trout

Vegetables, Herbs & Spices

ail	garlic
anis	aniseed
artichaut	artichoke
asperge	asparagus
aubergine	aubergine (eggplant)
basilic	basil
betterave	beetroot
cannelle	cinnamon
carotte	carrot
céleri	celery
cèpe	cep (boletus mushroom)
champignon	mushroom
chou	cabbage
concombre	cucumber
courgette	courgette (zucchini)
crudités	small pieces of raw vegetables
épice	spice
épinards	spinach
fenouil	fennel
gingembre	ginger
haricots	beans
haricots blancs	white beans
haricots verts	French (string) beans
herbe	herb
laitue	lettuce
légume	vegetable
lentilles	lentils
maïs	sweet corn
menthe	mint
oignon	onion
olive	olive
origan	oregano
persil	parsley
petit pois	pea
poireau	leek
poivron	green pepper
pomme de terre	potato
ratatouille	casserole of aubergines, tomatoes, peppers and garlic
riz	rice
salade	salad or lettuce
tomate	tomato
truffe	truffle

Cooking Methods

à la vapeur	steamed
au feu de bois	cooked over a wood-burning stove
au four	baked
farci	stuffed
fumé	smoked
gratiné	browned on top with cheese
grillé	grilled
rôti	roasted
sauté	sautéed (shallow fried)

Sauces & Accompaniments

béchamel	basic white sauce
huile d'olive	olive oil
moutarde	mustard

pistou
  pesto (pounded mix of basil, hard cheese, olive oil and garlic)
provençale
  tomato, garlic, herb and olive oil dressing or sauce
tartare
  mayonnaise with herbs
vinaigrette
  salad dressing made with oil, vinegar, mustard and garlic

Fruit & Nuts

abricot	apricot
amande	almond
ananas	pineapple
arachide	peanut
banane	banana
cacahuète	peanut
cassis	blackcurrant
cerise	cherry
citron	lemon
fraise	strawberry
framboise	raspberry
marron	chestnut
melon	melon
mirabelle	type of plum
myrtille	bilberry (blueberry)
noisette	hazelnut
orange	orange
pamplemousse	grapefruit
pêche	peach
pistache	pistachio
poire	pear
pomme	apple
prune	plum
pruneau	prune
raisin	grape

Desserts & Sweets

crêpe
  thin pancake
crêpes suzettes
  orange-flavoured crepes flambéed in liqueur
dragée
  sugared almond
éclair
  pastry filled with cream
flan
  egg-custard dessert
galette
  wholemeal or buckwheat pancake; also a type of biscuit
gâteau
  cake
gaufre
  waffle
glace
  ice cream
île flottante
  literally 'floating island'; beaten egg white lightly cooked, floating on a creamy sauce
macaron
  macaroon (sweet biscuit made of ground almonds, sugar and egg whites)
tarte
  tart (pie)
tarte aux pommes
  apple tart
yaourt
  yoghurt

Snacks

croque-monsieur
  a grilled ham and cheese sandwich
croque-madame
  a croque-monsieur with a fried egg
frites
  chips (French fries)
quiche
  quiche (savoury egg, bacon and cream tart)

Basics

beurre	butter
chocolat	chocolate
confiture	jam
crème fraîche	cream (naturally thickened)
farine	flour
huile	oil
lait	milk
miel	honey
œuf	egg
poivre	pepper
sel	salt
sucre	sugar
vinaigre	vinegar

Glossary

(m) indicates masculine gender, (f) feminine gender and (pl) plural

accueil (m) – reception

adjoint (m) – deputy mayor

alimentation (f) – grocer's shop

ancien régime (m) – literally 'old order'; France under the monarchy before the Revolution

arrondissement (m) – one of the 20 administrative divisions in Paris, indicated on signs by 1er (1st arrondissement), 2e or 2ème (2nd) and so on

auberge de jeunesse (f) – youth hostel

baguette (f) – standard long, crispy French loaf of bread weighing about 50g

bains-douches municipaux (m) – municipal bathhouses

bande dessinée (f) – comic strip or book

belle époque (f) – literally 'beautiful age'; era of elegance and gaiety characterising fashionable Parisian life in the period preceding WWI

bière (f) – beer

bière à la pression (f) – draught beer

bière blonde (f) – lager

billet (m) – ticket

billet jumelé (m) – combination ticket (ie, one valid for more than one site, museum etc)

billeterie (f) – ticket office or counter

biologique or **bio** – organic

boîte (f) – box; nightclub

borne d'alarme (f) – alarm used to summon assistance in metro and RER stations

boucherie (f) – butcher's

boucherie chevaline (f) – butcher's specialising in horse meat

boudin antillais (m) – West Indian blood pudding or sausage

boudin blanc (m) – a smooth sausage made of veal, pork or chicken and blended with milk, cream, flour and spices

boudin noir (m) – a 'black' or blood pudding made with pork blood, often flavoured with onions, rice, potatoes or fruit

boulangerie (f) – bakery

boules (f pl) – a game played with heavy metal balls on a sandy pitch; also called *pétanque*

brasserie (f) – brewery; restaurant usually serving food – including Alsatian specialities and seafood – all day

brick à l'œuf (m) – North African egg fritter

brocante (f) – second-hand goods

bureau de change (m) – currency exchange office

bureau de poste (m) – post office

bureau des objets trouvés (m) – lost and found office, lost property office

cacher or **casher** – kosher

café (m) – coffee; café

café au lait (m) – espresso coffee with lots of hot milk

café crème (m) – espresso coffee with cream

café noir (m) – black coffee, espresso

café noisette (m) – literally 'hazelnut coffee'; espresso coffee with a dash of milk

capitainerie (f) – harbour master's office

carnet (m) – a book of five or 10 bus, metro or other tickets sold at a reduced rate

carrefour (m) – crossroads

carte (f) – card; menu; map

carte de séjour (f) – residence permit

cave (f) – (wine) cellar

caveau (m) – vault; (jazz) cellar club

chai (m) – wine storehouse

chambre (f) – room

chambre de bonne (f) – maid's quarters

chambre d'hôte (f) – B&B

chanson française (f) – literally 'French song'; traditional musical genre where lyrics are paramount

chansonnier (m) – cabaret singer

charcuterie (f) – varieties of pork product that are cured, smoked or processed, including sausages, hams, pâtés and *rillettes*; the shop where these products are sold

cimetière (m) – cemetery

cohabitation (f) – political situation in

which the president represents one political party and the government another

coiffeur (m) – hairdresser's, barber's

consigne or **consigne manuelle** (f) – left-luggage office

consigne automatique (f) – luggage locker

correspondance (f) – linking tunnel or walkway (eg, in the metro); rail or bus connection

couchette (f) – sleeping berth on a train or ferry

cour (f) – courtyard

couscous (m) – grainy 'pasta' made from semolina (coarsely ground wheat flour); North African dish of steamed semolina garnished with chunks of meat and vegetables and served with *harissa*

crêpe (f) – large, paper-thin pancake with a filling of sugar, jam or fruit or flamed as a dessert, or filled with meat, fish or cheese as an entrée or main course (then usually called a *galette*)

dégustation (f) – tasting

demi (m) – half; 330mL glass of beer

demi-pension (f) – half-board (B&B with either lunch or dinner)

demi-tarif (m) – half-price

département (m) – administrative division of France

dépôt de pain (m) – shop where bread is sold but not baked

diapositive (f) – slide, transparency

digestif (m) – digestive; a drink served after a meal

distributeur automatique de billets or **DAB** (m) – automatic teller machine (ATM)

douane (f) – customs

eau (f) – water

eau de source (f) – spring water

eau-de-vie (f) – literally 'water of life'; any of a number of brandies made from fruit, berries or nuts

eau minérale (f) – mineral water

église (f) – church

embarcadère (m) – pier, jetty

entracte (m) – interval, intermission

entrée (f) – entrance; first course or starter

épicerie (f) – small grocer's shop

escalier (m) – stairway

espace (f) – space; outlet or branch

express (m) – espresso coffee

fête (f) – festival; holiday

ficelle (f) – string; thinner, crustier 200g version of the baguette not unlike a very thick breadstick

fin de siècle – literally 'end of the century'; characteristic of the last years of the 19th century and generally used to indicate decadence

fondue bourguignonne (f) – hot oil or broth for cooking meat at the table

fondue savoyarde (f) – pot of melted cheeses that diners dip bread into at the table

forêt (f) – forest

formule or **formule rapide** (f) – similar to a *menu* but with a choice of two of three courses (eg, starter and main course or main course and dessert)

foyer (m) – workers' or students' hostel

fromagerie (f) – cheese shop

fumoir (m) – smoking room or chamber

funiculaire (m) – funicular railway

galerie (f) – gallery; covered shopping arcade (also called *passage*)

galette (f) – pancake with a variety of (usually savoury) fillings; see also *crêpe*

gare or **gare SNCF** (f) – railway station

gare routière (f) – bus station

gaufre (f) – waffle with various toppings, usually eaten as a snack

gendarmerie (f) – police station; police force

glacier (m) – ice-cream maker or parlour

grand magasin (m) – department store

grande école (f) – prestigious educational institution offering training in such fields as business management, engineering and the applied sciences

Grands Boulevards – literally 'Great Boulevards'; broad thoroughfares that were a centre of café and theatre life in the 18th and 19th centuries

grand projet (m) – huge, public edifice erected by a government or politician, generally in an attempt to immortalise themselves

gratin (m) – dish cooked in the oven and browned with breadcrumbs or cheese forming a crust on the surface

halles (f pl) – central food market (usually covered)
halte routière (f) – bus stop
hameau (m) – hamlet
hammam (m) – steam room, Turkish bath
harissa (f) – North African hot red chilli sauce
haute couture (f) – literally 'high sewing'; the creations of the leading clothes designers
haute cuisine (f) – literally 'high cuisine'; classic French style of cooking typified by super-rich, elaborately prepared and beautifully presented multicourse meals
horaire (m) – timetable, schedule
hôte payant (m) – paying guest
hôtel de ville (m) – city or town hall
hôtes payants (m pl) or **hébergement chez l'habitant** (m) – homestay

intra-muros – literally 'within the walls' (Latin); central Paris

jardin (m) – garden
jardin botanique (m) – botanical garden
jeux d'eau (m pl) – fountain displays
jours fériés (m pl) – public holidays

képi (m) – cap with a flat round top and a stiff visor worn by French soldiers and certain police
kir (m) – white wine sweetened with blackcurrant (or other) liqueur

laverie (f) – laundrette
laverie libre-service (f) – self-service laundrette
lavomatique (m) – laundrette
lélé (m) – West African steamed cakes of white beans and shrimp, served with tomato sauce
lycée (m) – secondary school

maffé (m) – West African dish of lamb or beef sautéed in peanut sauce
mairie (f) – city or town hall
maison de la presse (f) – newsagent

maison du parc (f) – park headquarters or visitors' centre
marchand de volaille (m) – butcher's specialising in poultry
marché (m) – market
marché alimentaire (m) – food market
marché aux fleurs (m) – flower market
marché aux oiseaux (m) – bird market
marché aux puces (m) – flea market
marché couvert (m) – covered market
marché découvert (m) – open-air market
menu (m) – fixed-price meal with two or more courses; see *formule*
menu dégustation (m) – tasting or sampling menu of up to half a dozen small courses
musée (m) – museum
musée national (m) – national museum
musette (f) – accordion music

nem (m) – Vietnamese spring roll
navette (f) – shuttle bus, train or boat
nocturne (f) – late-night opening at a shop

orangerie (f) – orangery (conservatory for growing citrus fruit)

pain (m) – bread
palais de justice (m) – law courts
parlement (m) – parliament
parvis (m) – square in front of a church or public building
passage (m) – covered shopping arcade (also called *galerie*)
pastilla (f) – meat or poultry baked in filo pastry
pastis (m) – aniseed-flavoured aperitif that turns cloudy when you add water
pâté (m) – potted meat; thickish paste, often of pork or other meat, cooked in a ceramic dish and served cold (sometimes called *terrine*)
pâté impérial (m) – spring roll, egg roll
pâtisserie (f) – cakes and pastries; shop that sells them
pelouse (f) – lawn
péniche (f) – barge
pension de famille (f) – similar to B&B
pétanque (f) – see *boules*
pied-noir (m) – literally 'black foot'; French colonial born in Algeria

place (f) – place; square or plaza
plan (m) – city map
plan du quartier (m) – map of nearby streets (hung on the wall near metro station exits)
plat du jour (m) – daily special in a restaurant
plat principal (m) – main course
point d'argent (m) – ATM
poissonnerie (f) – fishmonger, fish shop
pont (m) – bridge
port (m) – harbour, port
port de plaisance (m) – pleasure-boat harbour or marina
porte (f) – door; gate in a city wall
poste (f) – post office
poste principale (f) – main post office, GPO
pression (f) – draught beer
prix fixe (m) – literally 'fixed price'; see *menu*

quai (m) – quay, railway platform
quartier (m) – quarter, neighbourhood, district

raclette (f) – hot melted cheese scraped from a block placed in front of a vertical grill and served with potatoes and gherkins
résidence (f) – residence; hotel for long-term stays
rez-de-chausée (m) – ground floor
rillettes (f pl) – type of potted meat or fish
rive (f) – bank of a river
riverain (m) – local resident
rond point (m) – roundabout
rue (f) – street or road

salon de thé (m) – tearoom
service compris (m) – service included, with the service charge built into the price of each dish (often abbreviated to 's.c.' at the bottom of a restaurant bill)
service des renseignements (m) – directory enquiries or assistance
service des urgences (f) – casualty ward, emergency room
service non-compris (m) – service not included, with the service charge calculated after the food and drink has been added up

(also called *service en sus*, or 'service in addition'); no extra tip is required
soldes (m pl) – sale, the sales
sonnette (f) – doorbell
sono mondiale (f) – world music
sortie (f) – exit
spectacle (m) – performance, play or theatrical show
square (m) – public garden
supplément (m) – supplement, additional cost
syndicat d'initiative (m) – tourist office

tabac (m) – tobacconist (also selling bus tickets, phonecards etc)
tajine (m) – meat and vegetables slow-cooked in a domed clay pot with dried fruit and spices; the pot itself
tarif réduit (m) – reduced price (for students, seniors, children etc)
tartine (f) – slice of bread with a topping or garnish, such as butter, jam, honey or cream cheese
taxe de séjour (f) – municipal tourist tax
télécarte (f) – phonecard
tiéboudienne (m) – West African dish of rice, fish and vegetables
toilettes (f pl) – toilet, bathroom (also *WC*)
tour (f) – tower
tour d'horloge (f) – clock tower
traiteur (m) – caterer or delicatessen
troisième age (m) – retirement years, seniors

vélo (m) – bicycle
version française or **v.f.** (m) – literally 'French version'; a film dubbed into French
version originale or **v.o.** (m) – literally 'original version'; a nondubbed film with French subtitles
vieille ville (f) – old town or city
vin de table (m) – table wine
voie (f) – way; train platform

WC (m pl) – toilet, bathroom (also *toilettes*)

yassa (m) – West African dish of meat or fish marinated in lime juice and onion sauce and grilled

LONELY PLANET

You already know that Lonely Planet publishes more than this one guidebook, but you might not be aware of the other products we have on this region. Here is a selection of titles that you may want to check out as well:

Corsica
ISBN 0 86442 792 1
US$15.95 • UK£9.99 • 120FF

Cycling France
ISBN 1 86450 036 0
US$19.99 • UK£12.99 • 149FF

France
ISBN 1 86450 151 0
US$24.99 • UK£14.99 • 189FF

French phrasebook
ISBN 0 86442 450 7
US$5.95 • UK£3.99 • 40FF

The Loire
ISBN 1 86450 097 2
US$17.99 • UK£11.99 • 140FF

Out to Eat Paris
ISBN 1 86450 107 3
US$14.99 • UK£7.99 • 99FF

Paris City Map
ISBN 1 86450 011 5
US$5.95 • UK£3.99 • 39FF

Paris condensed
ISBN 1 86450 044 1
US$9.95 • UK£5.99 • 59FF

Provence & the Côte d'Azur
ISBN 1 86450 196 0
US$17.99 • UK£11.99 • 139FF

South-West France
ISBN 0 86442 794 8
US$16.95 • UK£11.99 • 130FF

Walking in France
ISBN 0 86442 601 1
US$19.99 • UK£12.99 • 149FF

Available wherever books are sold.

Guides by Region

L onely Planet is known worldwide for publishing practical, reliable and no-nonsense travel information in our guides and on our Web site. The Lonely Planet list covers just about every accessible part of the world. Currently there are 16 series: Travel guides, Shoestring guides, Condensed guides, Phrasebooks, Read This First, Healthy Travel, Walking guides, Cycling guides, Watching Wildlife guides, Pisces Diving & Snorkeling guides, City Maps, Road Atlases, Out to Eat, World Food, Journeys travel literature and Pictorials.

AFRICA Africa on a shoestring • Cairo • Cairo City Map • Cape Town • Cape Town City Map • East Africa • Egypt • Egyptian Arabic phrasebook • Ethiopia, Eritrea & Djibouti • Ethiopian (Amharic) phrasebook • The Gambia & Senegal • Healthy Travel Africa • Kenya • Malawi • Morocco • Moroccan Arabic phrasebook • Mozambique • Read This First: Africa • South Africa, Lesotho & Swaziland • Southern Africa • Southern Africa Road Atlas • Swahili phrasebook • Tanzania, Zanzibar & Pemba • Trekking in East Africa • Tunisia • Watching Wildlife East Africa • Watching Wildlife Southern Africa • West Africa • World Food Morocco • Zimbabwe, Botswana & Namibia

Travel Literature: Mali Blues: Traveling to an African Beat • The Rainbird: A Central African Journey • Songs to an African Sunset: A Zimbabwean Story

AUSTRALIA & THE PACIFIC Auckland • Australia • Australian phrasebook • Australia Road Atlas • Bush-walking in Australia •Cycling New Zealand • Fiji • Fijian phrasebook • Healthy Travel Australia, NZ and the Pacific • Islands of Australia's Great Barrier Reef • Melbourne • Melbourne City Map • Micronesia • New Caledonia • New South Wales & the ACT • New Zealand • Northern Territory • Outback Australia • Out to Eat – Melbourne • Out to Eat – Sydney • Papua New Guinea • Pidgin phrasebook • Queensland • Rarotonga & the Cook Islands • Samoa • Solomon Islands • South Australia • South Pacific • South Pacific phrasebook • Sydney • Sydney City Map • Sydney Condensed • Tahiti & French Polynesia • Tasmania • Tonga • Tramping in New Zealand • Vanuatu • Victoria • Walking in Australia • Watching Wildlife Australia • Western Australia

Travel Literature: Islands in the Clouds: Travels in the Highlands of New Guinea • Kiwi Tracks: A New Zealand Journey • Sean & David's Long Drive

CENTRAL AMERICA & THE CARIBBEAN Bahamas, Turks & Caicos • Baja California • Bermuda • Central America on a shoestring • Costa Rica • Costa Rica Spanish phrasebook • Cuba • Dominican Republic & Haiti • Eastern Caribbean • Guatemala • Guatemala, Belize & Yucatán: La Ruta Maya • Healthy Travel Central & South America • Jamaica • Mexico • Mexico City • Panama • Puerto Rico • Read This First: Central & South America • World Food Mexico • Yucatán

Travel Literature: Green Dreams: Travels in Central America

EUROPE Amsterdam • Amsterdam City Map • Amsterdam Condensed • Andalucía • Austria • Baltic States phrasebook • Barcelona • Barcelona City Map • Berlin • Berlin City Map • Britain • British phrasebook • Brussels, Bruges & Antwerp • Brussels City Map • Budapest • Budapest City Map • Canary Islands • Central Europe • Central Europe phrasebook • Corfu & the Ionians • Corsica • Crete • Crete Condensed • Croatia • Cycling Britain • Cycling France • Cyprus • Czech & Slovak Republics • Denmark • Dublin • Dublin City Map • Eastern Europe • Eastern Europe phrasebook • Edinburgh • Estonia, Latvia & Lithuania • Europe on a shoestring • Finland • Florence • France • Frankfurt Condensed • French phrasebook • Georgia, Armenia & Azerbaijan • Germany • German phrasebook • Greece • Greek Islands • Greek phrasebook • Hungary • Iceland, Greenland & the Faroe Islands • Ireland • Istanbul • Italian phrasebook • Italy • Krakow • Lisbon • The Loire • London • London City Map • London Condensed • Madrid • Malta • Mediterranean Europe • Mediterranean Europe phrasebook • Moscow • Mozambique • Munich • the Netherlands • Norway • Out to Eat – London • Paris • Paris City Map • Paris Condensed • Poland • Portugal • Portuguese phrasebook • Prague • Prague City Map • Provence & the Côte d'Azur • Read This First: Europe • Romania & Moldova • Rome • Rome City Map • Russia, Ukraine & Belarus • Russian phrasebook • Scandinavian & Baltic Europe • Scandinavian Europe phrasebook • Scotland • Sicily • Slovenia • South-West France • Spain • Spanish phrasebook • St Petersburg • St Petersburg City Map • Sweden • Switzerland • Trekking in Spain • Tuscany • Ukrainian phrasebook • Venice • Vienna • Walking in Britain • Walking in France • Walking in Ireland • Walking in Italy • Walking in Spain • Walking in Switzerland • Western Europe • Western Europe phrasebook • World Food France • World Food Ireland • World Food Italy • World Food Spain

Travel Literature: Love and War in the Apennines • The Olive Grove: Travels in Greece • On the Shores of the Mediterranean • Round Ireland in Low Gear • A Small Place in Italy • After Yugoslavia

LONELY PLANET

Mail Order

onely Planet products are distributed worldwide. They are also available by mail order from Lonely Planet, so if you have difficulty finding a title please write to us. North and South American residents should write to 150 Linden St, Oakland, CA 94607, USA; European and African residents should write to 10a Spring Place, London NW5 3BH, UK; and residents of other countries to Locked Bag 1, Footscray, Victoria 3011, Australia.

INDIAN SUBCONTINENT Bangladesh • Bengali phrasebook • Bhutan • Delhi • Goa • Healthy Travel Asia & India • Hindi & Urdu phrasebook • India • Indian Himalaya • Karakoram Highway • Kerala • Mumbai (Bombay) • Nepal • Nepali phrasebook • Pakistan • Rajasthan • Read This First: Asia & India • South India • Sri Lanka • Sri Lanka phrasebook • Tibet • Tibetan phrasebook • Trekking in the Indian Himalaya • Trekking in the Karakoram & Hindukush • Trekking in the Nepal Himalaya
Travel Literature: The Age of Kali: Indian Travels and Encounters • Hello Goodnight: A Life of Goa • In Rajasthan • A Season in Heaven: True Tales from the Road to Kathmandu • Shopping for Buddhas • A Short Walk in the Hindu Kush • Slowly Down the Ganges

ISLANDS OF THE INDIAN OCEAN Madagascar & Comoros • Maldives • Mauritius, Réunion & Seychelles

MIDDLE EAST & CENTRAL ASIA Bahrain, Kuwait & Qatar • Central Asia • Central Asia phrasebook • Dubai • Hebrew phrasebook • Iran • Israel & the Palestinian Territories • Istanbul • Istanbul City Map • Istanbul to Cairo on a shoestring • Jerusalem • Jerusalem City Map • Jordan • Lebanon • Middle East • Oman & the United Arab Emirates • Syria • Turkey • Turkish phrasebook • World Food Turkey • Yemen
Travel Literature: Black on Black: Iran Revisited • The Gates of Damascus • Kingdom of the Film Stars: Journey into Jordan

NORTH AMERICA Alaska • Boston • Boston City Map • California & Nevada • California Condensed • Canada • Chicago • Chicago City Map • Deep South • Florida • Great Lakes • Hawaii • Hiking in Alaska • Hiking in the USA • Honolulu • Las Vegas • Los Angeles • Los Angeles City Map • Louisiana & The Deep South • Miami • Miami City Map • New England • New Orleans • New York City • New York City City Map • New York City Condensed • New York, New Jersey & Pennsylvania • Oahu • Out to Eat – San Francisco • Pacific Northwest • Puerto Rico • Rocky Mountains • San Francisco • San Francisco City Map • Seattle • Southwest • Texas • USA • USA phrasebook • Vancouver • Virginia & the Capital Region • Washington DC • Washington, DC City Map • World Food Deep South, USA • World Food New Orleans
Travel Literature: Caught Inside: A Surfer's Year on the California Coast • Drive Thru America

NORTH-EAST ASIA Beijing • Beijing City Map • Cantonese phrasebook • China • Hiking in Japan • Hong Kong • Hong Kong City Map • Hong Kong Condensed • Hong Kong, Macau & Guangzhou • Japan • Japanese phrasebook • Korea • Korean phrasebook • Kyoto • Mandarin phrasebook • Mongolia • Mongolian phrasebook • Seoul • Shanghai • South-West China • Taiwan • Tokyo
Travel Literature: In Xanadu: A Quest • Lost Japan

SOUTH AMERICA Argentina, Uruguay & Paraguay • Bolivia • Brazil • Brazilian phrasebook • Buenos Aires • Chile & Easter Island • Colombia • Ecuador & the Galapagos Islands • Healthy Travel Central & South America • Latin American Spanish phrasebook • Peru • Quechua phrasebook • Read This First: Central & South America • Rio de Janeiro • Rio de Janeiro City Map • Santiago • South America on a shoestring • Santiago • Trekking in the Patagonian Andes • Venezuela
Travel Literature: Full Circle: A South American Journey

SOUTH-EAST ASIA Bali & Lombok • Bangkok • Bangkok City Map • Burmese phrasebook • Cambodia • Hanoi • Healthy Travel Asia & India • Hill Tribes phrasebook • Ho Chi Minh City • Indonesia • Indonesian phrasebook • Indonesia's Eastern Islands • Jakarta • Java • Lao phrasebook • Laos • Malay phrasebook • Malaysia, Singapore & Brunei • Myanmar (Burma) • Philippines • Pilipino (Tagalog) phrasebook • Read This First: Asia & India • Singapore • Singapore City Map • South-East Asia on a shoestring • South-East Asia phrasebook • Thailand • Thailand's Islands & Beaches • Thailand, Vietnam, Laos & Cambodia Road Atlas • Thai phrasebook • Vietnam • Vietnamese phrasebook • World Food Thailand • World Food Vietnam

ALSO AVAILABLE: Antarctica • The Arctic • The Blue Man: Tales of Travel, Love and Coffee • Brief Encounters: Stories of Love, Sex & Travel • Chasing Rickshaws • The Last Grain Race • Lonely Planet Unpacked • Not the Only Planet: Science Fiction Travel Stories • Lonely Planet On the Edge • Sacred India • Travel with Children • Travel Photography: A Guide to Taking Better Pictures

LONELY PLANET

ON THE ROAD

Travel Guides explore cities, regions and countries, and supply information on transport, restaurants and accommodation, covering all budgets. They come with reliable, easy-to-use maps, practical advice, cultural and historical facts and a rundown on attractions both on and off the beaten track. There are over 200 titles in this classic series, covering nearly every country in the world.

 Lonely Planet Upgrades extend the shelf life of existing travel guides by detailing any changes that may affect travel in a region since a book has been published. Upgrades can be downloaded for free from **www.lonelyplanet.com/upgrades**

For travellers with more time than money, **Shoestring** guides offer dependable, first-hand information with hundreds of detailed maps, plus insider tips for stretching money as far as possible. Covering entire continents in most cases, the six-volume shoestring guides are known around the world as 'backpackers bibles'.

For the discerning short-term visitor, **Condensed** guides highlight the best a destination has to offer in a full-colour, pocket-sized format designed for quick access. They include everything from top sights and walking tours to opinionated reviews of where to eat, stay, shop and have fun.

CitySync lets travellers use their Palm™ or Visor™ hand-held computers to guide them through a city with handy tips on transport, history, cultural life, major sights, and shopping and entertainment options. It can also quickly search and sort hundreds of reviews of hotels, restaurants and attractions, and pinpoint their location on scrollable street maps. CitySync can be downloaded from **www.citysync.com**

MAPS & ATLASES

Lonely Planet's **City Maps** feature downtown and metropolitan maps, as well as transit routes and walking tours. The maps come complete with an index of streets, a listing of sights and a plastic coat for extra durability.

Road Atlases are an essential navigation tool for serious travellers. Cross-referenced with the guidebooks, they also feature distance and climate charts and a complete site index.

LONELY PLANET

ESSENTIALS

Read This First books help new travellers to hit the road with confidence. These invaluable predeparture guides give step-by-step advice on preparing for a trip, budgeting, arranging a visa, planning an itinerary and staying safe while still getting off the beaten track.

Healthy Travel pocket guides offer a regional rundown on disease hot spots and practical advice on predeparture health measures, staying well on the road and what to do in emergencies. The guides come with a user-friendly design and helpful diagrams and tables.

Lonely Planet's **Phrasebooks** cover the essential words and phrases travellers need when they're strangers in a strange land. They come in a pocket-sized format with colour tabs for quick reference, extensive vocabulary lists, easy-to-follow pronunciation keys and two-way dictionaries.

Miffed by blurry photos of the Taj Mahal? Tired of the classic 'top of the head cut off' shot? **Travel Photography: A Guide to Taking Better Pictures** will help you turn ordinary holiday snaps into striking images and give you the know-how to capture every scene, from frenetic festivals to peaceful beach sunrises.

Lonely Planet's **Travel Journal** is a lightweight but sturdy travel diary for jotting down all those on-the-road observations and significant travel moments. It comes with a handy time-zone wheel, world maps and useful travel information.

Lonely Planet's eKno is an all-in-one communication service developed especially for travellers. It offers low-cost international calls and free email and voicemail so that you can keep in touch while on the road. Check it out on **www.ekno.lonelyplanet.com**

FOOD & RESTAURANT GUIDES

Lonely Planet's **Out to Eat** guides recommend the brightest and best places to eat and drink in top international cities. These gourmet companions are arranged by neighbourhood, packed with dependable maps, garnished with scene-setting photos and served with quirky features.

For people who live to eat, drink and travel, **World Food** guides explore the culinary culture of each country. Entertaining and adventurous, each guide is packed with detail on staples and specialities, regional cuisine and local markets, as well as sumptuous recipes, comprehensive culinary dictionaries and lavish photos good enough to eat.

OUTDOOR GUIDES

For those who believe the best way to see the world is on foot, Lonely Planet's **Walking Guides** detail everything from family strolls to difficult treks, with 'when to go and how to do it' advice supplemented by reliable maps and essential travel information.

Cycling Guides map a destination's best bike tours, long and short, in day-by-day detail. They contain all the information a cyclist needs, including advice on bike maintenance, places to eat and stay, innovative maps with detailed cues to the rides, and elevation charts.

The **Watching Wildlife** series is perfect for travellers who want authoritative information but don't want to tote a heavy field guide. Packed with advice on where, when and how to view a region's wildlife, each title features photos of over 300 species and contains engaging comments on the local flora and fauna.

With underwater colour photos throughout, **Pisces Books** explore the world's best diving and snorkelling areas. Each book contains listings of diving services and dive resorts, detailed information on depth, visibility and difficulty of dives, and a roundup of the marine life you're likely to see through your mask.

LONELY PLANET

OFF THE ROAD

Journeys, the travel literature series written by renowned travel authors, capture the spirit of a place or illuminate a culture with a journalist's attention to detail and a novelist's flair for words. These are tales to soak up while you're actually on the road or dip into as an at-home armchair indulgence.

The new range of lavishly illustrated **Pictorial** books is just the ticket for both travellers and dreamers. Off-beat tales and vivid photographs bring the adventure of travel to your doorstep long before the journey begins and long after it is over.

Lonely Planet **Videos** encourage the same independent, tough-minded approach as the guidebooks. Currently airing throughout the world, this award-winning series features innovative footage and an original soundtrack.

Yes, we know, work is tough, so do a little bit of deskside dreaming with the spiral-bound Lonely Planet **Diary**, the tearaway page-a-day **Day-to-Day Calendar** or a Lonely Planet **Wall Calendar**, filled with great photos from around the world.

TRAVELLERS NETWORK

Lonely Planet Online. Lonely Planet's award-winning Web site has insider information on hundreds of destinations, from Amsterdam to Zimbabwe, complete with interactive maps and relevant links. The site also offers the latest travel news, recent reports from travellers on the road, guidebook upgrades, a travel links site, an online book-buying option and a lively traveller's bulletin board. It can be viewed at **www.lonelyplanet.com** or AOL keyword: lp.

Planet Talk is a quarterly print newsletter, full of gossip, advice, anecdotes and author articles. It provides an antidote to the being-at-home blues and lets you plan and dream for the next trip. Contact the nearest Lonely Planet office for your free copy.

Comet, the free Lonely Planet newsletter, comes via email once a month. It's loaded with travel news, advice, dispatches from authors, travel competitions and letters from readers. To subscribe, click on the Comet subscription link on the front page of the Web site.

Index

Text

Bold indicates maps.

Boxed Text & Walking Tours

MAP 1

See La Défense Map p160

La Défense
Grande Arch

La Défense
Esplanade
de la Défense

COURBEVOIE
Courbevoie

CLICHY
Clichy
Levallois

Pont de
Levallois Bécon

LEVALLOIS-PERRET

Porte
de Clichy

PUTEAUX

NEUILLY-SUR-SEINE

Pont de Neuilly

Av Charles de Gaulle

Les Sablons

Île de
Puteaux

Porte
Maillot

MAP 2

Blvd Pereire

17e

Blvd de Courcelles

Parc de
Monceau

Av de la Grand Armée

Arc de
Triomphe

8e

Blvd Hauss

Av des Champs Élysées

56 55
54 53

Allée de Longchamp

Porte
Dauphine

Av Foch

Av d'Iéna

TRIANGLE
D'OR

Place de la
Concorde

To Camping
du Bois de
Boulogne

51

50

52

Avenue
Foch

Lac
Inférieur

Av Victor Hugo

Av Kléber

MAP 4

Place du
Trocadéro

Jardins du
Trocadéro

Eiffel
Tower

Hôtel des
Invalides

Esplanade
des Invalides

7e

FAUBO
SAINT GE

LEFT BA

BOIS DE
BOULOGNE

Avenue
Henri Martin

16e

Parc du
Champ
de Mars

Av de la Motte Picquet

Av de Breteuil

Av de l'Hippodrome

La Muette

49

Hippodrome
de Longchamp

Boulainvilliers

Ranelagh

Jasmin

Hippodrome
d'Auteuil

To
Versailles

A13

Av de la Porte d'Auteuil

48 47

Michel Ange
Auteuil

Église
d'Auteuil

Mirabeau

Javel

Av Émile Zola

Blvd Garibaldi

Av du Mor

Porte
d'Auteuil

Michel Ange
Molitor

Chardon
Lagache

46

R de Vaugirard

R du Château

Exelmans

R Lecourbe

Gare
Montparnasse

Porte de
St Cloud

Bd Victor

R de la Convention

15e

To
Versailles

N10

Av Édouard Vaillant

Porte de
St Cloud

45

Balard

Convention

BOULOGNE-BILLANCOURT

Marcel
Sembat

Pernety

14e

Plaisance

R d'Alésia

Porte de
Versailles

43

Blvd Victor

Île St
Germain

Issy-Val-
de Seine

44

R Ernest Renan

ISSY-LES-MOULINEAUX

Corentin Celton

Mairie d'Issy

Porte de
Vanves

42

Porte de
Vanves

VANVES

Malakoff Plateau
de Vanves

Blvd Périphérique

Issy-Ville

MALAKOFF

Blvd Gabriel Péri

MONTROUGE

0   400   800m
0   400   800yd

LP

MAP 1

ROD HYETT

Fine art crops up in all kinds of places in Paris...

MAP 2

PLACES TO STAY
59 Hôtel Brighton
69 Hôtel Ritz
71 Hôtel Costes
76 Hôtel de Crillon
104 Hôtel Britannia
105 Atlantic Opéra Hôtel
110 Résidence Cardinal
115 Hôtel Eldorado

PLACES TO EAT
9 L'Étoile Verte
12 Maison Prunier
17 Bistro Romain
22 Ladurée
30 Man Ray
32 Spoon, Food & Wine
72 L'Ardoise
73 Lina's
113 Charlot
116 La Maffiosa
117 Macis et Muscade

PLACES TO DRINK
2 James Joyce Pub
  (Buses to Beauvais Airport)
18 Le Lido de Paris
19 Latina Café
20 Queen
26 Montecristo Café
44 Crazy Horse
68 Harry's New York Bar
79 Buddha Bar
101 The Cricketer

MUSEUMS & GALLERIES
46 Musée de la Mode et du
  Costume (Palais Galliera)
47 Musée du Panthéon
  Bouddhique
48 Musée Guimet
49 Musée d'Art Moderne de la
  Ville de Paris
53 Palais de la Découverte
54 Grand Palais;
  Galeries Nationales du Grand
  Palais
55 Petit Palais;
  Musée des Beaux-Arts de la
  Ville de Paris
57 Jeu de Paume
103 Musée Jacquemart-André
106 Musée Nissim de Camondo
107 Musée Cernuschi

OTHER
1 Palais des Congrès de Paris
3 Fnac Étoile
4 Fromagerie Alléosse
5 Brûlerie des Ternes
6 American Express
7 Mariage Frères
8 Salle Pleyel
10 Air France Buses
11 Irish Embassy
13 New Zealand Embassy
14 Main Tourist Office
15 Thomas Cook
16 Air France
21 Hermès
23 Pharmacie Derhy
24 Agence des Théâtres
25 Post Office
27 Monoprix Supermarket
28 Espace IGN
29 Virgin Megastore
31 Bureau de Change
33 Thierry Mugler
34 Chanel
35 Celine
36 Nina Ricci
37 Canadian Embassy
38 Christian Lacroix
39 Armenian Church
40 Inès de la Fressange
41 Prada
42 Valentino
43 Théâtre des Champs-Élysées
45 Givenchy
50 Flame of Liberty;
  Diana Memorial
51 Bateaux Mouches
52 Batobus Stop
56 Obelisk
58 WH Smith
60 Paris Vision
61 Il Pour l'Homme
62 Colette
63 Cécile et Jeanne
64 Le Change de Paris
65 Patek Philippe
66 Colonne Vendôme
67 Van Cleef & Arpels
70 Cartier
74 US Consulate
75 Hôtel de la Marine
77 US Embassy
78 Office de Change de Paris
80 Lolita Lempicka
81 Guy Laroche
82 British Embassy
83 Palais de l'Élysée
84 Christian Lacroix
85 British Consulate
86 Comptoir Théâtral
87 Église de la Madeleine
88 Kiosque Théâtre
89 La Maison de la Truffe
90 Hédiard
91 Fauchon
92 La Maison du Miel
93 American Express
94 Palais Garnier;
  Bibliothèque-Musée de
  l'Opéra
95 Paris-Story (Paristoric)
96 NewWorks
97 Galeries Lafayette
98 Le Printemps Department
  Store (Women)
99 Le Printemps Department
  Store (Household)
100 Le Printemps Department
  Store (Men)
102 Chapelle Expiatoire
108 Banque de France
109 ADA Car Rental
111 Batignolles-Clichy Organic
  Market
112 Pharmacie Européenne
114 Cinéma des Cinéastes

MAP 2

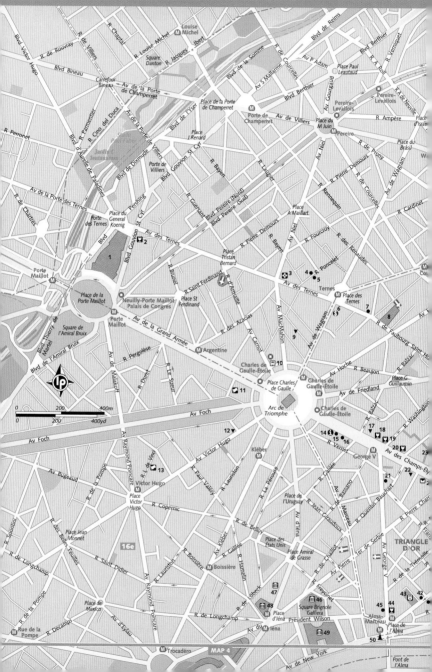

MAP 2

MAP 3

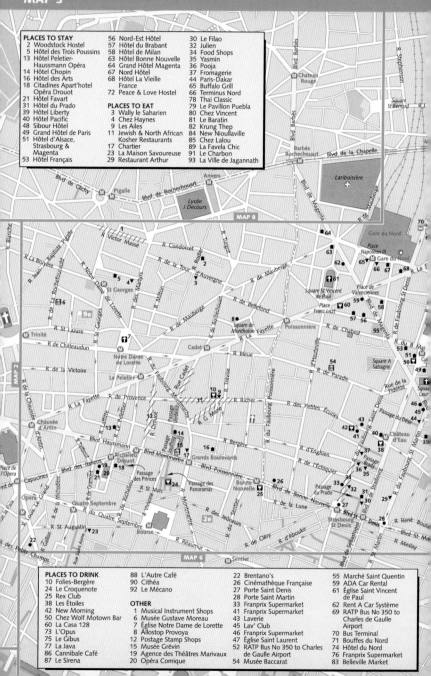

MAP 3

MAP 4

MAP 2

Rue de la Pompe
R. Decamps
Av d'Eylau
Av Georges Mandel

Place du Trocadéro
Trocadéro et du
11 Novembre

1

2

Cimetière
de Passy

Square
Yorktown

3

Jardins du
Trocadéro

Place de
Varsovie

4

Pont d'Iéna

Eiffel
Tower

5

Champ de Mars
Tour Eiffel

Parc du
Champ de Mars

Place
Jacques Rueff

Av du President Kennedy
Maison de Radio-France

Place de
Bolivie

71

Bir Hakeim

Pont de
Bir Hakeim

R. Jean Rey

72

Seine

73

74

75

76

77

69

70

66

67

68

65

Duplex

La Motte
Picquet
Grenelle

Avenue
Émile Zola

Av Émile Zola

Charles
Michels

Place du
Commerce

Commerce

Square
Violet

78

79

Félix
Fauré

Boucicaut

15e

Vaugirard

MAP 4

1er

Albert 1er — Cours la Reine

Tuileries

MAP 2

Pont des Invalides
Pont Alexandre III
Pont de la Concorde

Quai d'Orsay

13

Jardin des Tuileries

Quai des Tuileries

Orsay
7
8

Place de Finlande

9
Invalides
10

11

12

Quai Anatole France

14

Pont de Solférino

Assemblée Nationale

Quai d'Orsay

Musée d'Orsay

15

Seine

Quai des Tuileries

Quai Royal

R de l'Université

Place du Prés E Herriot
Place du Palais Bourbon

Blvd Saint Germain

R de Lille

R de Solférino

Légion d'Honneur

Pont Royal

Quai Voltaire

R de Lille

R de l'Université

R de Verneuil

16

Esplanade des Invalides

R Saint Dominique

Square S Rousseau

R Las Cases

Solférino

R du Bac

Les Saints Pères

MAP 6

Place Santiago du Chili

La Tour Maubourg

Square Santiago du Chili

7e

Square d'Ajaccio

17 Cour d'Honneur

Varenne

R de Grenelle

FAUBOURG SAINT GERMAIN

R du Bac

Blvd Saint Germain

23

22

Hôtel des Invalides

18

19

20

21

R de Varenne

Rue du Bac

24

25

Jardin de l'Intendant

Av de Tourville

Place Vauban

Lycée Victor Duruy

R Barbet de Jouy

R Vaneau

R du Bac

Blvd Raspail

Square des Missions Étrangères

Square Chaise Récamier

R de Grenelle

R des Saints Pères

R du Dragon

26

27

R du Four

Esplanade du Souvenir Français

Place André Tardieu

R de Babylone

Sèvres Babylone

R de Sèvres

St Sulpice

28

29

Vieux Colombier

Place du Prés

St François Xavier

Square de l'Abbé Esquerré

R Oudinot

R Rousselat

Jardin Catherine Labouré

Laennec

Vaneau

Square Boucicaut

33

32

Sèvres Babylone

30

31

R du Cherche Midi

R de Mézières

R de Cassette

R Madame

Place de Breteuil

R Duroc

R de l'Abbé Grégoire

R Saint Placide

34

35

Rennes

R de Vaugirard

Duroc
Place L P Fargue

6e

St Placide

36

R de Vaugirard

R de Rennes

R de Fleurus

Blvd Raspail

37

Necker

Place Camille Claudel

Falguière

Blvd du Montparnasse

Montparnasse Bienvenüe

Notre-Dame des Champs

Place P Lafue

38

61

Lycée Buffon

Lycée Pasteur

58

R Antoine Bourdelle

Montparnasse Bienvenüe

57

Place Bienvenüe

56

Place du 18 Juin 1940

Place R Dautry

55

52

Square Gaston Baty

47

46

45

48

43

Vavin

41

40

39

42

Place R Picasso

49

50

51

Edgar Quinet

R Delambre

Volontaires

59

Gare Montparnasse

Square Max Hymans

Jardin de l'Atlantique

54

Gaîté

53

14e

Raspail

Cimetière du Montparnasse

0   200   400m
0   200   400yd

Place des Cinq Martyrs du Lycée Buffon
Rue du Commandant René Mouchotte

MAP 4

RICHARD I'ANSON

Quick on the draw: if you'd like a portrait, you won't have to wait long.

MAP 5

PLACES TO STAY

- 4 Hôtel de Savoie
- 5 Hôtel Familial
- 6 Hôtel de France
- 7 Résidence Bastille
- 16 Hôtel Baudin
- 17 Vix Hôtel
- 20 Hôtel Pax
- 23 Hôtel des Alliés
- 27 Auberge Internationale des Jeunes
- 28 Hôtel Saint Amand
- 33 Maison Internationale des Jeunes pour la Culture et la Paix
- 43 Blue Planet Hostel
- 44 Citadines Apart'hotel Bastille Nation
- 55 Hôtel de l'Espérance
- 69 Hôtel Au Royal Cardinal
- 73 Résidence Monge
- 76 Hôtel Saint Christophe
- 79 Hôtel des Grands Écoles
- 82 Familia Hôtel
- 83 Hôtel Minerve
- 84 Centre International BVJ Paris-Quartier Latin
- 85 Hôtel Saint Jacques
- 92 Young & Happy Hostel
- 96 Grand Hôtel du Progrès
- 97 Hôtel Gay Lussac
- 100 Hôtel de Médicis
- 109 Grand Hôtel Saint Michel
- 110 Hôtel Cluny Sorbonne

PLACES TO EAT

- 1 La Piragua
- 3 Bistrot à Vin Jacques Mélac
- 9 Lire entre les Vignes
- 10 Blue Elephant
- 11 Les Galopins
- 12 Le K
- 14 Suds
- 18 Crêpes Show
- 21 Chez Paul
- 25 Le Square Trousseau
- 26 La Maison d'Or
- 29 Café Canelle
- 30 Á la Banane Ivoirienne
- 31 Le Réservoir
- 32 Le Mansouria

- 34 Les Amognes
- 38 L'Encrier
- 42 Le Viaduc Café
- 47 La Compagnie du Ruban Bleu
- 48 La Barge
- 54 Founti Agadir
- 70 Le Petit Légume
- 75 Jardin des Pâtes
- 81 Koutchi
- 86 L'Étoile du Berger
- 90 The Chipper
- 91 Le Vigneron
- 94 Châtelet University Restaurant
- 95 Chez Léna et Mimille
- 98 Tao
- 101 Douce France
- 102 Machu Picchu
- 103 Les Vignes du Panthéon
- 105 Tashi Delek
- 108 Perraudin
- 115 Indonesia
- 124 Assas University Restaurant
- 127 Bullier University Restaurant; OTU Voyages

PLACES TO DRINK

- 2 Espace Voltaire
- 15 Boca Chica
- 19 Le Café du Passage
- 22 Sanz Sans
- 37 China Club
- 68 Paradis Latin
- 87 Le Violon Dingue
- 107 Café Oz
- 128 La Closerie des Lilas

MUSEUMS & GALLERIES

- 58 Grande Galerie de l'Évolution
- 59 Galerie de Minéralogie, de Géologie et de Paléobotanie
- 60 Galerie d'Entomologie
- 61 Galerie d'Anatomie Comparée et de Paléontologie
- 116 Musée du Luxembourg

OTHER

- 8 Théâtre de la Bastille
- 13 Centre Gai et Lesbien
- 24 Monoprix Supermarket
- 35 Marché d'Aligre

- 36 La Maison du Cerf-Volant
- 39 Children's Playground
- 40 Rollerland Paris (Scooter Hire)
- 41 Capitainerie du Port de Plaisance de Paris-Arsenal; Europ' Yachting
- 45 Maison des Femmes
- 46 Ministry of Finance
- 49 Cour Départ
- 50 Cour d'Arrivée
- 51 Hôpital La Pitié-Salpêtrière
- 52 Hospital Night-Time Entrance
- 53 Paris Vélo
- 56 Mouffetard Food Market
- 57 Mosquée de Paris
- 62 École de Botanique
- 63 Serres Tropicales (Jardin d'Hiver)
- 64 Jardin Alpin
- 65 Ménagerie
- 66 Ménagerie Entrance
- 67 Institut du Monde Arabe
- 71 usit Connect
- 72 Arènes de Lutèce
- 74 Lavomatique
- 77 Ed l'Épicier Supermarket
- 78 Bains-Douches Municipaux
- 80 Shopi Supermarket
- 88 Église Saint Étienne du Mont
- 89 Le Bateau Lavoir
- 93 Franprix Supermarket
- 99 Laverie
- 104 Panthéon
- 106 Food Shops; Fromagerie
- 111 Chapelle de la Sorbonne
- 112 Cours de Langue et Civilisation Françaises de la Sorbonne
- 113 Sorbonne
- 114 usit Connect
- 117 Café Orbital
- 118 Fontaine des Médicis
- 119 Grand Bassin
- 120 Théâtre du Luxembourg
- 121 Forum Voyages
- 122 usit Connect
- 123 Nouvelles Frontières
- 125 Fontaine de l'Observatoire
- 126 Église Notre Dame du Val-de-Grâce
- 129 Jadis et Gourmande

MAP 5

MAP 5

MAP 6

MAP 6

MAP 3

MAP 7

MAP 3

MAP 5

MAP 5

MAP 6

PLACES TO STAY
29 Hôtel de Lille
30 Centre International BVJ
   Paris-Louvre
58 Hôtel Saint Honoré
66 Grand Hôtel de Champagne
98 Auberge de Jeunesse
   Jules Ferry
120 Hôtel Bastille
122 Hôtel Royal Bastille
123 Hôtel Bastille Opéra
128 Hôtel Castex
135 Hôtel des Deux Îles
136 Hôtel de Lutèce
137 Hôtel Saint Louis
148 Hôtel Marignan
167 Hôtel Esmeralda
175 Hôtel Henri IV
186 Hôtel de Nesle
190 Delhy's Hôtel
191 Hôtel Saint Michel
194 Résidence des Arts
196 Hôtel Saint André des Arts
202 Hôtel des Marronniers
203 Hôtel des Deux Continents
213 Hôtel Petit Trianon
228 Hôtel du Globe
229 Hôtel Michelet Odéon

PLACES TO EAT
7 Higuma
9 Willi's Wine Bar
11 Le Grand Véfour
12 Fine Food Shops;
   Fromagerie; Evrard
14 Lina's
24 Café Marly
27 Le Petit Mâchon
31 L'Épi d'Or
46 Aux Crus de Bourgogne
48 Le Loup Blanc
50 Le Monde à l'Envers
76 L'Amazonial
80 Léon de Bruxelles
81 Joe Allen
83 404
86 Au Bascou
87 Chinese Noodle Shops &
   Restaurants
89 Chez Omar
93 Le Valet du Carreau
95 Chez Jenny
96 Au Trou Normand
99 Café Florentin
104 Le Villaret
107 Le Clown Bar
109 Le Kitch
111 Café de l'Industrie
112 Café Le Serail
116 Les Sans-Culottes
118 Havanita Café

121 Chez Heang
130 La Charlotte en Île
133 Berthillon Ice Cream
134 Les Fous de l'Île
142 Les Bouchons de François
   Clerc
143 Al Dar
159 Le Navigator; Chez Maï
163 Tea Caddy
164 Fogon Saint Julien
197 Chez Albert
198 Fish la Poissonnerie
200 Guen Maï
204 Le Petit Zinc
207 Brasserie Lipp
212 Cour de Rohan
214 Chez Jean-Mi
216 Le Golfe de Naples
218 Mabillon University
   Restaurant
219 Lina's (Two Outlets)
222 Le Mâchon d'Henri
231 Polidor

PLACES TO DRINK
4 La Champmeslé
8 Le Tour du Table
17 La Scala de Paris
42 Café Noir
64 Slow Club
72 Café Oz
73 Au Duc des Lombards
74 Le Sunset;
   Le Baiser Salé
75 Banana Café
82 Les Bains
88 Le Tango
101 Le Troisième Bureau
105 Satellit' Café
110 Los Latinos
113 Iguana Café
114 Le Balajo
117 La Chapelle des Lombards
144 Zed Club
156 Le Cloître
161 Polly Magoo
165 Le Caveau de la Huchette
176 Taverne Henri IV
184 La Palette
205 Café de Flore
206 Les Deux Magots
217 Coolin
221 Chez Georges

MUSEUMS & GALLERIES
19 Musée des Arts Décoratifs;
   Musée de la Mode et du
   Textile; Musée de la Publicité
85 Musée des Arts et Métiers
153 Musée National du Moyen
   Age (Musée de Cluny)

179 Musée de la Monnaie
201 Musée National Eugène
   Delacroix

OTHER
1 Voyageurs du Monde
2 usit Connect
3 Jean-Paul Gaultier
5 American Express
6 Monoprix Supermarket
10 Anna Joliet
13 Forum Voyages
15 Nouvelles Frontières
16 Cityrama
18 Comédie Française
20 Entrance to Carrousel du
   Louvre; Virgin Megastore
21 Arc de Triomphe du Carrousel
22 Inverted Glass Pyramid
23 Glass Pyramid
25 Le Louvre des Antiquaires
26 Le Change du Louvre
28 Laverie Libre Service
32 Bourse de Commerce
33 E Dehillerin
34 Main Post Office
35 Chevignon
36 Kenzo
37 Cacharel
38 Kenzo
39 Louis XIV Memorial
40 Stepane Kélian
41 Junko Shimada
43 Comme des Garçons
   (Women)
44 Comme des Garçons (Men)
45 A Simon
47 Rue Montorgueil Market
49 Tour de Jean sans Peur
51 Kiliwatch
52 Yohji Yamamoto (Two Shops)
53 Agnès B (Women)
54 Agnès B (Men)
55 Église Saint Eustache
56 Piscine Suzanne Berlioux
57 Franprix Supermarket
59 Best Change
60 La Samaritaine (Men);
   Supermarket
61 Église Saint Germain
   L'Auxerrois
62 La Samaritaine Main Building;
   Rooftop Terrace
63 La Samaritaine (Sports)
65 Théâtre Les Déchargeurs
67 Théâtre Musical de Paris
68 Théâtre de la Ville
69 Noctambus (Night Bus) Stops
70 Tour Saint Jacques
71 Pharmacie Première
77 Fontaine des Innocents

MAP 6

This way for artistic overload: the gateway to the Louvre

RICHARD I'ANSON

MAP 7

QUARTIER
DE L'HORLOGE

R M Le Comte

R des Haudriettes

R des Archives

Blvd de Sébastopol

R Quincampoix

R St-Martin

R Beaubourg

Rambuteau

R des 4 F.

1

2

3

Place
Georges
Pompidou

Centre
Georges
Pompidou;
BPI

R Geoffroy l'Angevin

R Rambuteau

Rue du Temple

R de Brague

5

6

R Berger

Place E
Michelet

R Simon Le Franc

4

R Pecquay

R des Archives

7

10

R Beaubourg

8

9

R du Plâtre

R des Blancs   Manteaux

Notre Dame
des Blancs
Manteaux

11

Place Igor
Stravinsky

R St-Martin

R des Lombards

12

13

R du Renard

R du Temple

14   15

R Ste Croix

16   17

de la Bretonnerie

R des Archives

R Aubriot

52

R Vieille du Temple

53

R. des
Francs Bo.

51

R des Guillemites

20

19   18

R de la Verrerie

R des Archives

48

49   50

55

46

R du Bourg Tibourg

47

45

56   57

R des Ros

58

R St-Martin

R de Rivoli

21

44

Hôtel
de Ville

23

Hôtel
de Ville

R de Rivoli

24   25

R Vieille du Temple

Av Victoria

22

26

Hôtel
de Ville

Place de
l'Hôtel
de Ville

Hôtel
de Ville

R du Roi de Sicile

43

42

59

40   41

R des Écouffes

60

Quai de Gesvres

R de Lobau

27

Place
Baudoyer

39

R de Rivoli

61

R du Roi

Pont
d'Arcole

Place St
Gervais

Quai de l'Hôtel de Ville

R de Brosse

30

28   38

37

R François Miron

R d'Arcole

32

33

Voie Georges Pompidou

31

R des Barres

Rue Philippe

R du Pont-Louis-Philippe

29

Rue Grenier sur l'Eau

35

36

Geoffroy

4e

R du Jour

85

R Charonne

Seine

88

87

Quai aux Fleurs

Pont Louis-
Philippe

Square A
Schweltzer

R des Nonains d'Hyères

Voie Georges Pompidou

Pont Marie

Quai des Célestins

90

R du Cloître Notre Dame

Quai de Bourbon

34   R J du Bellay

MAP 7

R. Pastourelle

R. de Bretagne

R. de Poitou

R. de Turenne

R. Froissart

Blvd des Filles du Calvaire

R. du Pont aux Choux

St Sébastien Froissart

76

R. St Sébastien

R. Charlot

R. de Saintonge

R. Vieille du Temple

R. Debelleyme

Cathédrale Sainte Croix

R. Amelot

R. St Claude

Saint Denys du Saint Sacrement

R. de Thorigny

du Temple

R. de la Perle

75

R. Pelée

Blvd Beaumarchais

74

3e

R. Barbette

R. Villehardouin

R. Villehardouin

R. du

73

72

71

Square Léopold Achille

Parc Royal

R. de Turenne

R. St Gilles

Tournelles

R. Amelot

R. Etesvie

70

Square George Cain

77

69

R. Payenne

R. de Sévigné

R. des Minimes

Chemin Vert

MARAIS

68

67

78

R. des Tournelles

R. de béarn

R. du Chemin Vert

66

65

R. des Rosiers

80

R. des Francs Bourgeois

Blvd Beaumarchais

Pavée

81

79

107

Place des Vosges

R. Amelot

82

R. Mahler

R. de Sévigné

R. de Jarente

R. de Turenne

Rivoli

St Paul

105

106

Place du Marché Sainte Catherine

83

104

103

R. de Rivoli

108

R. des Tournelles

Église Saint Louis-Saint Paul

R. St Antoine

110

Passage St Paul

100

109

111

102

101

R. de Brague

Bastille

Blvd Richard Lenoir

Charlemagne

99

Marché Bastille

91

agne

R. Saint Paul

96

R. Neuve St Pierre

R. St Antoine

113

114

112

R. de la Bastille

Village St Paul

95

94

93

98

97

R. Beautreillis

115

116

Bastille

117

118

92

R. Castex

119

Place de la Bastille

MAP 7

PLACES TO STAY

- 20 Hôtel Axial Beaubourg
- 26 Hôtel Rivoli
- 27 Hôtel de Nice
- 29 MIJE Maubuisson
- 40 Hôtel Le Compostelle
- 46 Hôtel Central Marais
- 82 Grand Hôtel Malher
- 86 MIJE Fourcy
- 89 MIJE Fauconnier
- 95 Hôtel du Septième Art
- 99 Hôtel Sully
- 103 Hôtel Moderne
- 104 Hôtel Pratic
- 106 Grand Hôtel Jeanne d'Arc
- 109 Hôtel de la Place
  des Vosges
- 111 Hôtel Lyon Mulhouse
- 115 Hôtel de la Herse d'Or

PLACES TO EAT

- 10 Café Beaubourg
- 14 Aquarius
- 15 Le Petit Picard
- 24 Minh Chau
- 28 La Perla
- 32 Le Trumilou
- 34 Brasserie de l'Isle
  Saint Louis
- 38 Amadéo
- 54 Robert et Louise
- 55 Chez Hanna
- 57 Chez Marianne
- 60 Piccolo Teatro
- 63 Jo Goldenberg
- 65 Hammam Café
- 76 Le Repaire de Cartouche
- 77 Caves Saint Gilles
- 93 L'Enoteca
- 94 Thanksgiving
- 98 Vins des Pyrénées
- 102 G Millet Fromagerie
- 105 Pitchi Poï
- 107 Ma Bourgogne
- 112 Hippopotamus
- 113 Bofinger
- 114 Le Bistrot du Dôme
  Bastille

PLACES TO DRINK

- 4 QG
- 8 Full Metal
- 9 Café de la Gare
- 17 Open Bar
- 18 Mixer Bar
- 19 Le Cox
- 25 Quetzal
- 31 L'Arène
- 41 Stolly's
- 44 La Chaise au Plafond
- 45 Au Petit Fer à Cheval
- 50 Les Étages
- 51 Amnésia Café
- 59 Les Scandaleuses
- 79 Piment Café
- 117 Café des Phares

MUSEUMS & GALLERIES

- 3 Atelier Brancusi
- 5 Musée d'Art et d'Histoire du
  Judaïsme
- 7 Archives Nationales;
  Musée de l'Histoire de France
- 36 Mémorial du Martyr Juif
  Inconnu
- 69 Musée Cognacq-Jay
- 74 Musée de la Serrure
- 75 Musée Picasso
- 78 Musée Carnavalet
- 85 Maison Européenne de la
  Photographie
- 92 Musée de la Curiosité et de la
  Magie
- 110 Maison de Victor Hugo

OTHER

- 1 Cyberbe@ubourg
  Internet C@fé
- 2 OTU
- 6 Allô Logement Temporaire
- 11 Mechanical Fountains
- 12 Église Saint Merri
- 13 Bains-Douches Municipaux
- 16 Laverie Libre-Service
- 21 Ed l'Épicier Supermarket
- 22 Noctambus (Night Bus) Stops
- 23 Bazar de l'Hôtel de Ville (BHV)
- 30 Eglise Saint Gervais-Saint
  Protais
- 33 Batobus Stop
- 35 Mélodies Graphiques
- 37 Sic Amor
- 39 À l'Olivier
- 42 Laverie
- 43 Web 46 Internet Café
- 47 Mariage Frères
- 48 Point Virgule
- 49 Les Mots à la Bouche
- 52 Bains Plus
- 53 Le Palais des Thés
- 56 Laverie Libre-Service
- 58 Martin Grant
- 61 Laverie
- 62 Robin des Bois
- 64 Tehen
- 66 Hôtel Lamoignon
  (Bibliothèque Historique
  de la Ville de Paris)
- 67 Sainte Catherine Priory
  (Ruins)
- 68 Hôtel Albret
- 70 Hôtel de Marle
  (Swedish Cultural Institute)
- 71 Hôtel Duret de Chevry
- 72 Hôtel de Vigny
- 73 Hôtel de Croisille
- 80 Spleen
- 81 Guimard Synagogue
- 83 Supermarché G20
- 84 Franprix Supermarket
- 87 Winemaker Relief
- 88 Hôtel d'Aumont
  (Tribunal Administratif)
- 90 Hôtel de Sens
- 91 Medieval Fortified Wall
- 96 Église Saint Paul (Ruins)
- 97 House Where Jim Morrison
  Died
- 100 Hôtel de Sully
- 101 Monoprix
  Supermarket
- 108 Issey Miyake
- 116 Flo Prestige
- 118 Banque de France
- 119 Colonne de Juillet

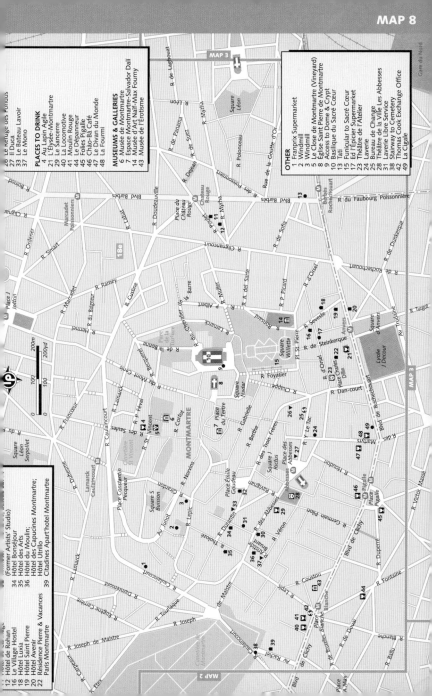

MAP 8

PLACES TO STAY
- 12 Hôtel de Rohan
- 16 Le Village Hostel
- 18 Hôtel Luxia
- 19 Hôtel Saint Pierre
- 20 Hôtel Avenir
- 22 Résidence Pierre & Vacances Paris Montmartre
- 34 (Former Artists' Studio)
- 34 Hôtel Bonséjour
- 35 Hôtel des...
- 36 Hôtel du Moulin; Hôtel des Capucines Montmartre; Hôtel Utrillo
- 39 Citadines Apart'hotel Montmartre

PLACES TO DRINK
- 26 Le Refuge des Fondus
- 27 Il Duca
- 33 Le Bateau Lavoir
- 37 Le Mono
- 4 Au Lapin Agile
- 21 L'Elysée-Montmartre
- 29 Le Sancerre
- 40 La Locomotive
- 41 Moulin Rouge
- 44 Le Dépanneur
- 45 Folies Pigalle
- 46 Chão-Bà Café
- 47 Le Divan du Monde
- 48 La Fourmi

MUSEUMS & GALLERIES
- 6 Musée de Montmartre
- 7 Espace Montmartre-Salvador Dalí
- 14 Musée d'Art Naïf-Max Fourny
- 43 Musée de l'Erotisme

OTHER
- 1 Franprix Supermarket
- 2 Windmill
- 3 Windmill
- 5 Le Clos de Montmartre (Vineyard)
- 8 Église Saint Pierre de Montmartre
- 9 Access to Dome & Crypt
- 10 Basilique du Sacré Cœur
- 13 Tati
- 15 Funicular to Sacré Cœur
- 17 Ed l'Épicier Supermarket
- 23 Théâtre de l'Atelier
- 24 Laverie
- 25 Bureau de Change
- 28 Théâtre de la Ville Les Abbesses
- 31 Laverie Libre Service
- 38 Stairway to Cemetery
- 49 Thomas Cook Exchange Office
- 49 La Cigale

MAP 9

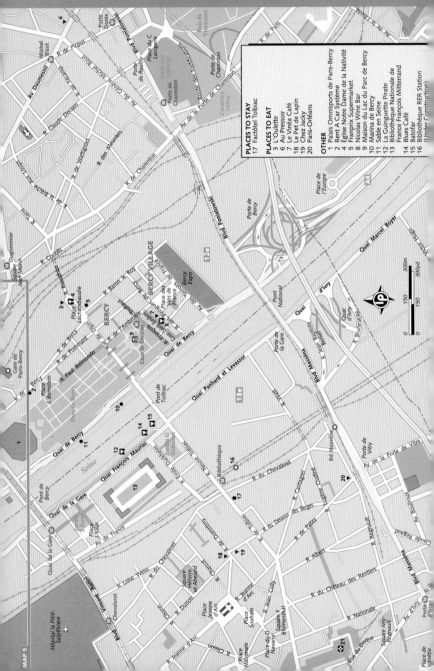

MAP 5

PLACES TO STAY
17 Factôtel Tolbiac

PLACES TO EAT
3 L'Oulette
6 Au Pressoir
7 Le Vinéa Café
18 Le Pet de Lapin
19 Chez Jacky
20 Paris-Orléans

OTHER
1 Palais Omnisports de Paris-Bercy
2 Rent A Car Système
4 Église Notre Dame de la Nativité
5 Franprix Supermarket
8 Nicolas Wine Bar
9 Maison du Lac du Parc de Bercy
10 Marina de Bercy
11 Sable en Seine
12 La Guinguette Pirate
13 Bibliothèque Nationale de France François Mitterrand
14 Blues Café
15 Batofar
16 Bibliothèque RER Station (Under Construction)

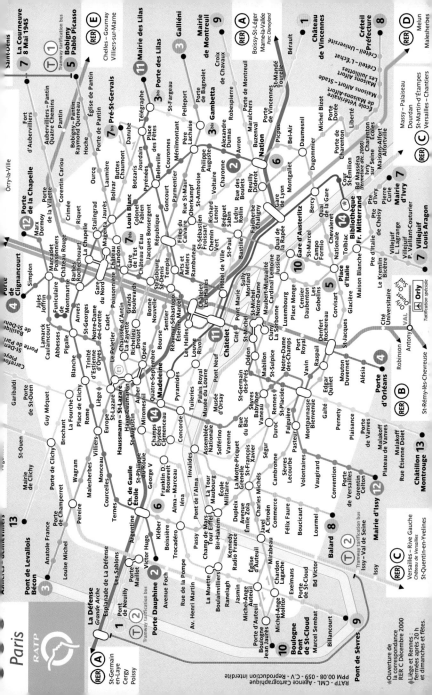

MAP LEGEND

BOUNDARIES

————————— Arrondissements

HYDROGRAPHY

Coastline

River, Creek

Lake

Canal

Building

Hotel

Urban Area

ROUTES & TRANSPORT

Autoroute

Primary Road

Secondary Road

Tertiary Road

Unsealed Road

City Autoroute

City Main Road

City Road

City Street, Lane

Pedestrian Area

Footbridge

Walking Tour

Train Route & Station

Cable Car or Chairlift

AREA FEATURES

Park, Gardens

Cemetery

Market

Forest

Beach

Key Area

MAP SYMBOLS

☼	**PARIS**	Capital City	✈	Airport	▲	Monument
●	**Versailles**	City or Large Town		Ancient or City Wall	🏛	Museum
●	**Barbizon**	Town	Θ	Bank or Bureau du Change	P	Parking Area
●	Giverny	Village	🚍 🚏	Bus Station, Bus Stop		Police Station
			🏰	Chateau		Post Office
●		Point of Interest		Church, Cathedral		Ruins
				Cinema		Shopping Centre
■		Place to Stay		Embassy or Consulate		or Department Store
▲		Camp Site	⚓	Fountain		Synagogue
		Caravan Park	⊕	Hospital or Clinic		Swimming Pool
		Hut or Chalet	ⓘ	Information		Theatre
				Internet Café		Transport
▼		Place to Eat	Ⓜ	Metro Station		Vineyard
		Place to Drink	ⓒ	Mosque		Zoo

Note: not all symbols displayed above appear in this book

LONELY PLANET OFFICES

Australia
Locked Bag 1, Footscray, Victoria 3011
☎ 03 9689 4666 fax 03 9689 6833
email: talk2us@lonelyplanet.com.au

USA
150 Linden St, Oakland, CA 94607
☎ 510 893 8555 TOLL FREE: 800 275 8555
fax 510 893 8572
email: info@lonelyplanet.com

UK
10a Spring Place, London NW5 3BH
☎ 020 7428 4800 fax 020 7428 4828
email: go@lonelyplanet.co.uk

France
1 rue du Dahomey, 75011 Paris
☎ 01 55 25 33 00 fax 01 55 25 33 01
email: bip@lonelyplanet.fr
www.lonelyplanet.fr

World Wide Web: www.lonelyplanet.com *or* AOL keyword: lp
Lonely Planet Images: lpi@lonelyplanet.com.au